Contents

Section 3   *Glasgow*

Section 4 *Regional Hotels & Restaurants*

Section 5 *Particular Places to Eat and Stay in Scotland*

Section 6 *Good Food & Drink*

Introduction

As I write, I've just completed another marathon journey around Scotland. A recent slogan described Scotland as the 'best small country in the world'. I can confirm that it's not so small (consider its jagged, island-studded outline), but also that in many respects the word 'best' is not inappropriate.

Since the last edition, we have a new government and perhaps a new optimism and I'm writing this after Scotland beat France at the fitba' but from my own determined investigations, I feel it's true to say that Scotland is very much on the up. Everywhere hotels, restaurants and bars are better, the restaurant culture of Edinburgh and Glasgow continues to flourish and some places like Skye and Inverness have improved dramatically. In these latter cases, this may partly be due to the emergence of the Highlands as a region both diverse and dynamic rather than just wild and pretty. The activity sector of tourism has proliferated hugely and from Fort William ('the UK Outdoor Capital') to a new festival, The Outsider, which I had a hand in, there is a new awareness that it is cool to be outdoors and that Scotland is a rich, natural playground.

For new readers of this book, please understand that *Scotland the Best* is not a book about all the options – it only registers and recommends the best of what there is in its various categories. There is no mention of the mediocre even if it's all there is. This principle applies to natural features as well as to areas of human endeavour that are of interest to visitors and tourists. This range of interests continues to grow and in this edition there are new sections on farm shops and spas and some rearrangements to make the book easier to use. It is chunkier which Collins think will be better and they're probably right, but let me know if you agree. Once again, I'd also be grateful for any feedback about places that you've found through the book or that you think I've neglected. Every new place suggested will be considered. With every edition, I like to think I get closer to the truth, closer to the perfect picture of how Scotland is at present.

All of the good things this book other than natural landscapes are remarkable because people have made them so. The Scots have always been enterprising (see the list of inventions and discoveries on page 26) and in our new world of easy-to-reach competing destinations we have to continue to stand out. Some people are true innovators and their example is an encouragement and inspiration to all of us. When I look back over the 15 years I've been doing *Scotland the Best*, I'm reminded of how much Scotland has changed for the better in a short time. A handful of people from the early 1990s still remain in my thoughts as 'pioneers' and it's they I have identified in a new section at the beginning of the book. In a world where there is a rising tide that has nothing to do with climate change, the tide of suffocating sameness, the endeavours of individuals like them (and in Scotland here and now there is no shortage of supply) will be our best hope of survival. They will bring élan, passion and integrity to the excellent ingredients we start with (of which we have an increasing awareness). Follow this book; I'll be honoured to help you find them.

Pete Irvine
Edinburgh
December 2007

How To Use This Book

There are three ways to find things in this book:
1. There's an index at the back.
2. The book can be used by category, e.g. you can look up the best restaurants in the Borders or the best scenic routes in the whole of Scotland. Each entry has an item number in the outside margin. These are in numerical order and allow easy cross-referencing.
3. You can start with the maps and see how individual items are located, how they are grouped together and how much there is that's worth seeing or doing in any particular area. Then just look up the item numbers. If you are travelling around Scotland, I would urge you to use the maps and this method of finding the best of what an area or town has to offer.

The maps correspond to the recognisable regions of Scotland. There's also an overall map to show how the regions fit together. The map section is in the centre of the book.

All items have a code which gives (1) the specific item number; (2) the map on which it can be found; and (3) the map co-ordinates. For space reasons, items in Glasgow and Edinburgh are not marked on Maps 1 and 2, although they do have co-ordinates in the margin to give you a rough idea of the location. City maps are readily available from any tourist office or newsagent.

A typical entry is shown below, identifying the various elements that make it up:

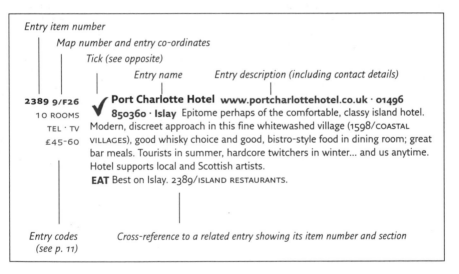

A Note On Categories

Edinburgh and Glasgow, the destinations of most visitors and the nearest cities to more than half of the population, are covered in the substantial Sections 2 and 3. You will probably need a city map to get around, although Maps 1 and 2 should give you the rough layout.

For the purposes of maps, and particularly in Section 4 (Regional Hotels & Restaurants), I have used a combination of the subdivision of Scotland based on the current standard political regions and on the historical ones, eg Argyll, Clyde Valley. Section 4 is meant to give a comprehensive and concise guide to the best of the major Scottish towns in each area. Some recommended hotels and restaurants will be amongst the best in the region (or even amongst the best in Scotland) and have been selected because they are the best there is in the town or the immediate area.

From Sections 5 to 12, the categories are based on activities, interests and geography and are Scotland-wide. Section 13 covers the islands, with a page-by-page guide to the larger ones.

There are some categories like Bed and Breakfasts, Fishing Beats, Antique Shops that haven't been included because at TGP (time of going to press) they are impracticable to assess (there are too many of them, are too small, etc). However, if there are categories that you would like to see in future editions, please let us know (see p. 448).

Ticks For The Best There Is

Although everything listed in the book is notable and remarkable in some way, there are places that are outstanding even in this superlative company. Instead of marking them with a rosette or a star, they have been 'awarded' a tick.

 Amongst the very best in Scotland

 Amongst the best (of its type) in the UK

 A particular commendation for Andrew Fairlie and Martin Wishart, acknowledged as two of the top chefs in Scotland and the UK

 Amongst the best (of its type) in the world, or simply unique

Listings generally are not in an order of merit although if there is one outstanding item it will always be at the top of the page and this obviously includes anything which has been given a tick. Hotels and restaurants are also grouped according to price and this is why a cross-marked place may appear further down the page (ticks also indicate exceptional value for money).

The Codes

1. The Item Code
At the left-hand margin of every item is a code which will enable you to find it on a map. Thus **2389 9/F26** should be read as follows: **2389** is the item number, listed in simple consecutive order; **9** identifies the particular map at the back of the book; **F26** is the map co-ordinate, to help pinpoint the item's location on the map grid. A co-ordinate such as **xA5** indicates that the item can be reached by leaving the map at grid reference **A5**.

2. The Accommodation Code
Beside each recommended accommodation or property is a series of codes as follows:

16 ROOMS	**NO KIDS**
MAR-DEC	**NO PETS**
TEL · TV	**£45-60**
NO C/CARDS	**ECO**
GAY FRIENDLY	**HS/NTS**

ROOMS indicates the number of bedrooms in total. No differentiation is made as to the type of room. Most hotels will offer twin rooms as singles or put extra beds in doubles if required.
MAR-DEC shows when the accommodation is open. No dates means it is open all year.
TEL · TV refers to the facilities: **TEL** means there are direct-dial phones in the bedrooms while

TV means there are TVs in the bedrooms.

NO PETS indicates that the hotel does not generally accept pets.

NO C/CARDS means the establishment does not accept credit cards.

NO KIDS does not necessarily mean that children are not able to accompany their parents, only that special provisions/rates are not usually made. Check by phone. In all other cases, children are welcome and special provisions/rates may be available.

£45-60 indicates the price band of the accommodation, based on per person per night. They are worked out by halving the published average rate for a twin room in high season and should be used only to give an impression of cost. They are based on 2007 prices. Add between £2 to £5 per year, though the band should stay the same unless the hotel undergoes improvements.

ECO denotes a place that takes their 'green' credentials seriously, with environmental measures in place (e.g. energy-saving policies, green purchasing, organic food, etc).

GAY FRIENDLY denotes a place that has no issue with gay clients and their partners.

HS or **NTS** denotes a place in the care of Historic Scotland or the National Trust for Scotland.

3. The Dining Codes

The price code marked against eateries refers to the price of an average dinner per person with a starter, a main course and dessert. It doesn't include wine, coffee or extras. Prices are based on 2007 rates. Where a hotel is notable also for its restaurant, this is identified by **EAT** on a separate line below the main accommodation description, with details following.

LO means last orders at the kitchen. Some close earlier if they are quiet and go later on request.

10pm/10.30pm means usually 10pm Mon-Fri, 10.30pm at weekends. It is very common, especially for city restaurants, to open later at weekends, particularly in Edinburgh during the Festival (Aug).

4. The Walk Code

Beside each of the many walks in the book is a series of codes as follows:

3-10KM   BIKES/ XBIKES/ MTBIKES

CIRC/ XCIRC   1-A-1

3-10KM means the walk(s) described may vary in length between the distances shown.

CIRC means the walk can be circular, while **XCIRC** shows the walk is not circular and you must return more or less the way you came.

BIKES indicates the walk has a path which is suitable for ordinary bikes. **XBIKES** means the walk is not suitable for, or does not permit, cycling. **MTBIKES** means the track is suitable for mountain or all-terrain bikes.

The **1-A-1** Code:

First number (**1**, **2** or **3**) indicates how easy the walk is.

1 the walk is easy.

2 medium difficulty, eg standard hillwalking, not dangerous nor requiring special knowledge or equipment.

3 difficult: care and preparation and a map are needed.

The letters (**A**, **B** or **C**) indicate how easy it is to find the path.

A the route is easy to find. The way is either marked or otherwise obvious.

B the route is not very obvious, but you'll get there.

C you will need a map and preparation or a guide.

The last number (**1**, **2** or **3**) indicates what to wear on your feet.

1 ordinary outdoor shoes, including trainers, are probably okay unless the ground is very wet.

2 you will need walking boots.

3 you will need serious walking or hiking boots.

Apart from designated walks, the 1-A-1 code is employed wherever there is more than a short stroll required to get to somewhere, eg a waterfall or a monument.

Section 1

Wha's Like Us?

Famously Big Attractions

Among the 'top 10' (paid admission) and the 'top 10' (free) visitor attractions, these are the ones really worth seeing. Find them under their item numbers.

Edinburgh Castle; Holyrood Palace; Edinburgh Zoo; The National Gallery; Our Dynamic Earth 414/417/416/423/422/MAIN ATTRACTIONS.
The People's Palace, Glasgow; The Burrell Collection; Kelvingrove 739/737/739/MAIN ATTRACTIONS.
The Museum of Transport; The Glasgow Botanic Gardens; The Gallery of Modern Art 743/744/745/OTHER ATTRACTIONS.
The Edinburgh Botanics 427/OTHER ATTRACTIONS.
Culzean Castle; Stirling Castle; Castle of Mey 1850/1847/1852/BEST CASTLES.
Mount Stuart; Manderston 911/912/COUNTRY HOUSES.
Skara Brae; The Callanish Stones 1888/1890/PREHISTORIC SITES.
Rosslyn Chapel 1941/CHURCHES

OTHER UNMISSABLES ARE:

1 9/L25 ✓✓✓ **Loch Lomond** Approach via Stirling and A811 to Drymen or from Glasgow, the A82 Dumbarton road to Balloch. Britain's largest inland waterway and a traditional playground, especially for Glaswegians; jet-skis, show-off boats. **Lomond Shores** at Balloch is the new, heavily retail gateway to the loch and the **Loch Lomond National Park** which covers a vast area. Orientate and shop here.

The west bank between Balloch and Tarbert is most developed: marinas, cruises, ferry to Inchmurrin Island. Luss is tweeville, like a movie set (it was used in the Scottish TV soap, *High Road*) but has an OK tearoom (1484/TEAROOMS). The road is more picturesque beyond Tarbert to Ardlui; see 1357/BLOODY GOOD PUBS for the non-tourist/real Scots experience of the Drover's Inn at Inverarnan.

The east bank is more natural, wooded; good lochside and hill walks (2048/MUNROS). The road is winding but picturesque beyond Balmaha towards Ben Lomond. Hire a wee rowboat at Balmaha to Inchcailloch Island: lovely woodland walks (2094/WALKS).

2 7/G19 ✓✓✓ **The Cuillins Skye** This hugely impressive east range in the south of Skye, often shrouded in cloud or rain, is the romantic heartland of the Islands and was 'sold' in 2003 to a combination of public agencies so... it's ours now! The Red Cuillins are smoother and nearer the Portree-Broadford road; the Black Cuillins gather behind and are best approached from Glen Brittle (2065/SERIOUS WALKS; 1687/WATERFALLS). This classic, untameable mountain scenery has attracted walkers, climbers and artists for centuries. It still claims lives regularly. For best views apart from Glen Brittle, see 1717/SCENIC ROUTES; 1736/VIEWS. Vast range of walks and scrambles (see also 1752/PICNICS).

3 7/M18
7/L18
7/L19 ✓✓✓ **Loch Ness** Most visits start from Inverness at the north end via the River Ness. Fort Augustus is at the other end, 56km to the south. Loch Ness is part of the still-navigable Caledonian Canal linking the east and west coast at Fort William. Many small boats line the shores of the River Ness; one of the best ways to see the loch is on a cruise from Inverness (Jacobite Cruises 01463 233999 1-6 hours, 6 options), Drumnadrochit or Fort Augustus. Most tourist traffic uses the main A82 north bank road converging on Drumnadrochit where the Loch Ness Monster industry gobbles up your money. If you must, the 'official' Loch Ness Monster Exhibition is the one to choose. On the A82 you can't miss Urquhart Castle (1885/RUINS). But the two best things about

Loch Ness are: the south road (B862) from Fort Augustus back to Inverness (1722/SCENIC ROUTES; 1696/WATERFALLS); and the detour from Drumnadrochit to Cannich to Glen Affric (20-30km) (1671/GLENS; 2072/GLEN & RIVER WALKS; 1683/WATERFALLS).

4 10/N25   ✓ ✓ **Falkirk Wheel** 08700 500 208 · **Falkirk** Tamfourhill, half-way between Edinburgh and Glasgow, signed from the M9 and M80 and locally. The splendid and deliberately dramatic massive boat-lift at the convergence of the (Millennium-funded) reinstated Union and Forth & Clyde canals – the world's first coast-to-coast ship canal (to wander or plooter along). The 35-metre lift is impressive to watch and great to go on. Boats leave the Visitor Centre every 30 minutes for the 45-minute journey. There are now 3 reasons to visit Falkirk (42/EVENTS, 1635/PARKS).

Favourite Scottish Journeys

5 **Wemyss Bay-Rothesay Ferry** www.calmac.co.uk · 01475 650100 The glass-roofed station at Wemyss Bay, the railhead from Glasgow (60km by road on the A78), is redolent of an age-old terminus. The frequent (CalMac) ferry has all the Scottish traits and sausage rolls you can handle, and Rothesay (with its period seaside mansions) appears out of blood-smeared sunsets and rain-sodden mornings alike, a gentle watercolour from summer holidays past. Visit the (Victorian) toilet when you get there and Mount Stuart (1911/HOUSES). Both are superb.

6 **Loch Etive Cruises** 01866 822430 From Taynuilt (Oban 20km) through the long narrow waters of one of Scotland's most atmospheric lochs, a 3-hour journey in a small cruiser with indoor and outdoor seating. The pier is 2km from main Taynuilt crossroads on the A85. Easter-mid Oct. Leaves 12-2pm (not Sat). Booking is not essential. Also **Loch Shiel Cruises** (01687 470322). From near Glenfinnan House Hotel (1321/SCOTTISH HOTELS) on the Road to the Isles, A830. A 1-2-stop cruise on glorious Loch Shiel. Various trips are available.

7 **Glenelg-Kylerhea** www.skyeferry.co.uk · 01599 522273 The shorter of the 2 remaining ferry journeys to Skye, and definitely the best way to get there if you're not pushed for time. The drive to Glenelg from the A87 is spectacular (1711/SCENIC ROUTES) and so is this 5-minute crossing of the deep Narrows of Kylerhea. Apr-Oct (frequent) 9am-6pm (7pm in summer) and Sun in summer (9am-6pm). There's an otter-watch hide at Kylerhea.

8 **Corran Ferry** 01855 841243 Runs from Ardgour on A861 to Nether Lochaber on the A82 across the narrows of Loch Linnhe. A convenient 5-minute crossing which can save time to points south of Mallaig and takes you to the wildernesses of Moidart and Ardnamurchan. A charming and fondly regarded journey in its own right. Runs continuously till 8.50pm in summer, 7.50pm in winter. Later at weekends.

9 **The Maid of the Forth Cruise to Inchcolm Island** 0131 331 4857 The wee boat (though they say it holds 225 people) which leaves every day at different times (phone for details) from Hawes Pier in South Queensferry (15km Central Edinburgh via A90) opposite the Hawes Inn, just under the famous railway bridge (415/MAIN ATTRACTIONS) and from Newhaven Harbour in town. 45-minute trips under the bridge and on to Inchcolm, an attractive island with walks and an impressive ruined abbey. Much birdlife and also many seals to be seen. 1 hour 30 minutes ashore. Tickets at pier. Mar-Oct.

10   **The Waverley** 0845 130 4647 See the Clyde, see the world! Report: 752/OTHER
      GLASGOW ATTRACTIONS.

11   **The West Highland Line** 08457 484950 One of the most picturesque railway
      journeys in Europe and quite the best way to get to Skye from the south. Travel to
      Fort William from Glasgow, then relax and watch the stunning scenery, the Bonnie
      Prince Charlie country (MARY, CHARLIE & BOB, p. 340) and much that is close to a
      railwayman's heart go past the window. Viaducts (including the Harry Potter one)
      and tunnels over loch and down dale. It's also possible to make the same journey
      (from Fort William to Mallaig and/or return) by steam train from Jun to mid Oct
      (details 01524 737751). There's a museum in the restored station at Glenfinnan
      with a tearoom and bunk accommodation. Trains for Mallaig leave from Glasgow
      Queen St, 3 times a day and take about 5 hours. The Fort William-Mallaig steam
      train gets very busy.

12   **From Inverness** 08457 484950 Two less-celebrated but mesmerising rail
      journeys start from Inverness. The journey to Kyle of Lochalsh no longer has an
      observation car in the summer months, so get a window seat and take an atlas;
      the last section through Glen Carron and around the coast at Loch Carron is
      especially fine. There are 3 trains a day and it takes 2 hours 30 minutes. Inverness
      to Wick is a 3 hour 50 minute journey. The section skirting the east coast from
      Lairg-Helmsdale is full of drama, followed by the transfixing monotony of the Flow
      Country. 3 trains a day in summer.

13   **The Plane to Barra** 0870 8509850 Most of the island plane journeys pass
      over many smaller islands (eg Glasgow-Tiree, Glasgow-Stornoway, Wick-Orkney)
      and are fascinating on a clear day, but BA's daily flight from Glasgow to Barra is
      doubly special because the island's airport is on Cockleshell Beach in the north of
      the island (11 km from Castlebay) after a splendid approach. The 12-seater Otter
      leaves and lands on the beach according to the tide.

The Best Scottish Film Locations

The author would like to thank Ginny Atkinson, Managing Director of the Edinburgh International Film Festival, for help with this section – ie she wrote most of it!

ISLANDS & BEACHES

14 5/C20   **Barra** *Whisky Galore* directed by Scot Sandy McKendrick (who went to Hollywood and became famous for *The Sweet Smell of Success*) was filmed on Barra. Imagine you are hiding the golden nectar from the Excise men by hanging out in the Politician (the bar named after the boat that ran aground) on Eriskay.

15 7/H20   **The Sands of Morar** The beach features in Bill Forsyth's *Local Hero* (1666/BEACHES). But the famous phone box isn't exactly round the corner. It's actually in Pennan on the Moray Coast, one of several lovely wee villages (1651/BEACHES).

16 10/R23   **St Andrews West Sands** Run along this great beach (1620/BEACHES) to Vangelis' *Chariots Of Fire* music on your iPod and take in the town's estimable qualities. You can go to the movies at the ancient New Picture House in North St (2357/CINEMAS).

17 10/R25   **Gullane Bents** The douce town of Gullane. Brigitte Bardot graced these sandy shores in *Two Weeks In September* (many Septembers ago).

CASTLES & MANSIONS

18 10/Q27   **Floors Castle Kelso** The gothic mansion that was the home that Tarzan (Christopher Lambert) returned to in *Greystoke – The Legend Of Tarzan* (directed by Hugh Hudson). (1918/COUNTRY HOUSES)

19 10/P25   **Blackness & Dunottar Castles** **Stonehaven** Both were used as the home of
10/S20   the Danish prince in Zeffirelli's *Hamlet*. Dunottar is on a clifftop sweeping drama- tically out into the North Sea (1870/RUINS). Eat at the Tolbooth, Stonehaven (1417/ SEAFOOD RESTAURANTS) after exploring the prison cells. Dunottar also features in Lewis Grassic Gibbon's classic Scots novel *Sunset Song* (4004/LITERARY PLACES).

THE GREAT OUTDOORS

21 9/J21   **Glencoe** There's no alternative for scale nor for conveying the passion for Scotland that Scots hero William Wallace had for his country, so Mel Gibson was to be found here once of a morning, reportedly in awe of the place. Parts of *Braveheart* were shot in several locations around here (1710/SCENIC ROUTES).

22 9/K22   **Rannoch Moor** The classic misty moor which was the end of the line for the city boys from *Trainspotting*. The fabulous Moor Of Rannoch Hotel waits for you too (1281/GET-AWAY HOTELS).

23 9/J20   **Glenfinnan** Loch Shiel's dark beauty lent atmosphere to the *Highlander* franchise, originally starring Christopher Lambert and Sean Connery. Glencoe, Glen Nevis, Morar and Skye also featured.

24 9/J20   **The Train from Fort William to Mallaig, the Viaduct at Glenfinnan** Memorable locations for the *Harry Potter* movies. Glen Nevis and the landscape around the Cluanie Inn (1269/INNS) were also used (11/JOURNEYS).

25 **Edinburgh** *Trainspotting* again. The film did win an award for best use of a location. The opening sequence with the zesty Ewan McGregor in the mad dash along Princes St, is one to re-enact at a more leisurely pace taking in a few retail outlets (well at least 2am).

26 **Edinburgh** *Hallam Foe*. The film that opened the 2007 International Film Festival and starred the energetic, not to say agile Jamie Bell as well as the city itself which was in practically every frame.

27 **Edinburgh** Dame Maggie Smith encapsulated *The Prime Of Miss Jean Brodie* as her crème-de-la-crème girruls were edified in their walks about the city, most memorably down The Vennel from Heriot's School to the Grassmarket.

28 **Edinburgh** The Royal Mile was closed for the first time that wasn't a royal visit, to create the bustling period market scene in *Jude* where Thomas Hardy's characters, played by Christopher Eccleston and Kate Winslet, met.

29 **Glasgow** Doubling as Victorian-era New York in *The House of Mirth*, the City Chambers' magnificent marbled halls and stairs were spectacular scene-setters.

This Year's Favourite Edinburgh & Glasgow Restaurants

The top 10 restaurants we like to go to in each city, not in order.

EDINBURGH TOP 10
Martin Wishart 0131 553 3557 Best Fine-Dining Restaurants, p. 38
The Atrium 0131 228 8882 Best Fine-Dining Restaurants, p. 38
The Wee Restaurant 01383 616263 Best Fife Restaurants, p. 168
First Coast 0131 313 4404 Best Bistros, p. 41
Urban Angel 0131 225 6215 Best Bistros, p. 41
Home 0131 667 7010 Best Bistros, p. 41
Café Marlayne 0131 226 2230 Best French Restaurants, p. 45
Bella Mbriana 0131 558 9581 Trusty Tratts, p. 48
Kalpna 0131 667 9890 Best Vegetarian Restaurants, p. 52
Dusit 0131 220 6846 Best Thai Restaurants, p. 57

GLASGOW TOP 10
The Ubiquitous Chip 0141 334 5007 Best Fine-Dining Restaurants, p. 98
Stravaigin 0141 334 2665 Best Fine-Dining Restaurants, p. 98
Fifi and Ally 0141 226 2286 Best Bistros, p. 101
City Merchant 0141 553 1577 Best Scottish Restaurants, p. 106
Baby Grand 0141 248 4942 Best Bistros (Late Night), p. 102
Café Gandolfi 0141 552 6813 Best Tearooms (upstairs and down), p. 115
Konaki 0141 342 4010 Best Greek Restaurants, p. 112
The Dhabba 0141 553 1249 Best Indian Restaurants, p. 109
Battlefield Restaurant 0141 636 6955 Trusty Tratts, p. 105
Gandolfi Fish 0141 552 9475 **Gamba** 0141 572 0899 **Two Fat Ladies** 0141 847 0088 Best Seafood Restaurants, p. 113 – I can never decide which!

Great Ways To Get Around

By Seaplane 01436 675030 · **Loch Lomond Seaplanes** See Scotland from the air, landing on land and water in the remoter parts that other transport can't reach. Most routes are West Coast but can be customised. Other excursions start from Culag Lochside guesthouse at Luss on the A82 and there is a service (2/3 times daily) from the Glasgow Science Centre to Oban (£149 return at TGP). Other trips start from £110 pp at TGP (30-minute flight). 9 adults maximum. Operates Mar-Oct.

By VW Campervan www.scoobycampers.com · **Scoobycampers** Edinburgh-based company offers VW microbuses and campervans on a self-drive rental basis to see Scotland at a gentle pace and save on accommodation. All vehicles are the classic version, converted with contemporary comforts. Microbuses take 6 people comfortably, but you can't really sleep overnight (hire the company's camping equipment). Campervans take 4 – best suited to 2 adults/2 kids. Vehicles have CD radios/DVD players and satellite navigation systems. They look really cool and you'll find that everyone's delighted to see you. Weekends from £220; weeks from £450 at TGP.

By Classic Car www.caledonianclassics.co.uk · 01259 742476 · **Caledonian Classic Car Rental** Choose a fabulous motor and take off round the by-roads, experiencing that old forgotten joy of motoring. Packages are customised, but there's unlimited mileage and free delivery/collection locally for hire of 2 days or more. Short trips come with a complimentary picnic hamper. Cars include Jaguar E-type, Porche 911, MGB Roadster, Jensen Healey Sprites, Morgan 4/4, Triumph TR6 and Beetle Convertible. Prices from £140 per day/£699 per week at TGP. They have their own 4-star B&B in Dollar.

By Motorbike www.scotlandbybike.com · **Scotlandbybike** Biking your way around Scotland offers a freedom often absent from driving today. Scotlandbybike organises a range of tours and packages that combine accommodation, insurance and the hire of BMW F-, R- and K-series bikes – or just bring along your own. There's even tuition if you want to improve your bike-riding skills *en route*. Tours are from 3-10 days and start from £220 per person at TGP.

By Kayak www.seafreedomkayak.co.uk · 01631 710173 · **Seafreedom Kayaks** Great way to see parts of Scotland from the sea is by kayak. Of course you can bring your own but for instruction, guidance and finding spectacular routes you couldn't do better than first finding Seafreedom Kayaks at Connel. The coastline here offers all kinds of sea and loch possibilities including Loch Etive and the island of Seil. Tony Hammoch and his wife Olga can also offer accommodation at their B&B situated on the A85 overlooking the Falls of Connel, and Olga does evening meals about 4 times a week. Just about anyone can do this after basic training; Tony keeps his groups small.

By Traditional Fishing Boat www.themajesticline.co.uk · 0131 623 5012 · **The Majestic Line** Unique, all-inclusive holidays on one of two traditional wooden 85-foot fishing boats which have been sensitively converted to a high standard. The Majestic Line operate various itineraries including 6-night cruises leaving Dunoon and taking in Bute and Arran or depart Oban for Mull and Iona. 6 ensuite double cabins. This is cruising, nay, coasting from a different perspective. Operates May-Sep.

The Best Events

Most of these events have websites. Go Google.

30 JAN **Up Helly Aa** 01595 693434 · **Lerwick** Traditionally on the 24th day after Christmas, but now always the last Tue in Jan. A mid-winter fire festival based on Viking lore where 'the Guizers' haul a galley through the streets of Lerwick and burn it in the park; and the night goes on.

31 JAN **Celtic Connections** 0141 353 8000 · **Glasgow** A huge festival of Celtic music from round the world held in the Royal Concert Hall and other city venues over 3 weeks. Concerts, ceilidhs, workshops.

32 12 JAN **The Auld Scots New Year** **Inverness** Identified (well... by me, actually) as a good night for a hooley and therefore the launch of Highland 2007; there are indications that this may become an annual celebration of Highland culture.

33 25 JAN **Burns Night** The National Bard celebrated with supper. No single major event (but see below).

34 MAR **Borders Potato Day** 08700 505152 · **Galashiels** Curious, but for some hundreds of people a vital event that celebrates the enduring appeal of the tattie or spud. 250 varieties on sale here (for growing). Go early to scoop the specials. Run by Borders Organic Growers (BOG).

35 APR **Glasgow Art Fair** 0141 552 6027 · **Glasgow** Britain's most significant commercial art fair outside London held in mid-Apr in tented pavilions in George Sq with selected galleries from around Scotland and the UK.

36 MID-APR **Glasgow International** **Glasgow** New festival presenting contemporary visual art in main venues and unusual or found space through out the city centre celebrating Glasgow's significance as a source of important contemporary artists. Biennial from '08.

37 APR **Melrose Sevens** 0870 608 0404 · **Melrose** This Border town is completely taken over by tournament in their small is beautiful rugby ground. 7-a-side teams from all over including overseas. It's just a good place to go, fanatical or not.

38 APR **Fife Point-To-Point** 01333 360229 · **Leven** Major 'society', ie county set, get-together at Balcormo Mains Farm. Sort of Scottish equivalent of Henley with horses organised by Fife Fox and Hounds. Range Rovers, hampers, Hermès and what's left of the Tories in Scotland.

39 APR **Glen Affric Duathlon** A bike ride/run over challenging but 'manageable' terrain (though 40 miles total) in gorgeous Glen Affric. It is, as they say, a 'blast'.

40 MAY **Paps of Jura Hill Race** 01496 820243 · **Jura** The amazing hill race up and down the 3 Paps (total of 7 hills altogether) on this large remote island (2359/MAGICAL ISLANDS). About 150 runners take part on the 16-mile challenge from the distillery in Craighouse, the village. Winner does it in 3 hours! (Info from the hotel.)

41 MAY **Burns and a' That** 01292 678100 · **Ayr & Ayrshire** Festival based on what he stands for rather than his work, mainly in Ayr and Alloway. Programme focuses on contemporary music and theatre. Not what it used to be.

42
MAY
Big in Falkirk 0141 552 6027 · Falkirk Held mainly in Callander Park outside town centre so a delightful, almost rural setting for 'Scotland's International Street Arts Festival'. Street theatre usually including one big finale show with fireworks. Hugely popular.

43
MAY-JUL
Common Ridings 0870 608 0404 · Border Towns The Border town festivals. Similar formats over different weeks with 'ride-outs' (on horseback to outlying villages, etc), 'shows', dances and games, culminating on the Fri and Sat. Total local involvement. Hawick is first, then Selkirk, Peebles/Melrose, Gala, Jedburgh, Kelso and Lauder at the end of Jul.

44
MAY
RockNess Dores Open-air nedfest in beautiful setting looking over Loch Ness at the tiny village of Dores which is besieged for the weekend. Fat Boy Slim started this.

45
JUN &
EARLY AUG
Flower Shows Edinburgh · 0131 333 0969 · & Ayr Many Scottish towns hold flower shows, mainly in autumn, but the big spring show at Gardening Scotland at the Royal Highland Centre (Ingliston) is well worth a look. Meanwhile the annual Ayr show in Aug is huge! Check local tourist information for details.

46
JUN
Skye Music Festival 07092 037963 · Broadford, Skye 2-day music fest in south of Skye in a big top on the airfield. No view of the Cuillins but a mountain of music. Home of Mylo.

47
JUN
Royal Highland Show 0131 335 6200 · Ingliston Showground, Edinburgh The premier agricultural show (over 4 days) in Scotland and for the farming world, the event of the year. Animals, machinery, food, crafts, shopping. 150,000 attend.

48
JUN
The Outsider 0131 561 3380 · Rothiemurchus New midsummer music fest with a difference: the audience are cool as well as considerate. On- and offsite activity programme with 10,000 opportunities to enjoy one of the UK's most stunning natural settings. Does that sound like an ad? You bet ya! But there's nothing like it... anywhere else.

49
LATE JUN
Scottish Traditional Boat Festival 01261 842951 · Portsoy Perfect little festival in perfect little Moray coast town over a weekend in late Jun/early Jul. Old boats in old and new harbours, open-air ceilidhs plus a great atmosphere.

50
LATE JUN
Edinburgh International Film Festival 0131 228 4051 Various screens and other 'location' in Edinburgh city centre. One of the world's oldest film festivals, in August with the other fests until '08 when it boldly moves to late Jun. All set to flourish! 10 days of film and movie matters to discover.

51
LATE JUN
St Magnus Festival 01856 871445 · Kirkwall, Orkney Midsummer celebration of the arts has attracted big names over the years. More highbrow than hoi polloi; the cathedral figures. The days are very long.

52
END JUN
Mendelssohn on Mull 01688 812377 Classical music festival in various halls and venues around the island that celebrates the connection between the composer and this rocky far-flung part of the world. Nice idea, and a great time to be here (see 2428/MULL).

53
JUL
Scottish Game Conservancy Fair 01620 850577 · Perth Held in the rural and historical setting of Scone Palace, a major Perthshire day out and gathering for the hunting, shooting, fishing and of course, shopping brigade.

54
JUL
T in the Park Balado Airfield near Kinross Scotland's highly successful pop festival with all that is current in Britpop and beyond. The T stands for Tennents, the sponsors who are much in evidence. Not as lifestyle-affirming as Glastonbury, but among the best festivals in the UK.

55
MID-JUL
Hebridean Celtic Festival 01851 621234 · Stornoway Folk-rock format festival under canvas on faraway Lewis. Celebrated 10th year in '05 with Van Morrison, Proclaimers '07. Good music and craic.

56
MID-JUL
The Great Kindrochit Quadrathlon 01567 820409 · Loch Tay The toughest one-day sporting event – swim 1.6km across loch, run 24km (including 7 Munros), canoe 11km and cycle 54km. Then slice a melon with a sword. Jings!

57
END JUL
Wickerman Festival 01738 449430 · near Gatehouse Of Fleet New annual music fest for the South West in fields on the A755 between Gatehouse and Kirkcudbright. Under wide skies on a cool coast. They burn a huge effigy at midnight on the Sat. Quite crusty.

58
EARLY AUG
Black Isle Show Muir of Ord Notable agricultural show and general country-side gathering for the Northeast Highlands. Big family day out.

59
AUG
Art Week 01333 312168 · Pittenweem Remarkable local event where the whole village of Pittenweem in Fife becomes a gallery. Over 70 venues showing work including public building and people's houses. The quality is not strained. Other events include fireworks.

60
EARLY AUG
Traquair Fair 01896 830323 · near Innerleithen In the grounds of Traquair House (1913/COUNTRY HOUSES), a mini Glastonbury with music, comedy and crafts. A respite from the Festival up the road in Edinburgh.

61
AUG
Belladrum 'Tartan Heart' Festival near Kiltarlity Off A862 Beauly road west of Inverness. Good-looking 2-day music fest with a loyal local following in terraced grounds. A family affair. Can't do better than that, Joe.

62
AUG
Edinburgh International Festival 0131 473 2000 · Edinburgh The 3-week 'biggest arts festival in the world' with **Military Tattoo** and major opera/music/drama. The **Bank of Scotland Fireworks** are on the final Sat. It incorporates **The Festival Fringe** with hundreds of events every night and **Fringe Sunday** on the second weekend. Also the **Jazz Festival** and (mainly for delegates on a bit of a jolly) the TV festival. Edinburgh in Aug is the best place to be in the world if you like people. See 496/ESSENTIAL EDINBURGH CULTURE.

63
AUG
Edinburgh International Book Festival 0131 228 5444 · Edinburgh A tented village in Charlotte Sq Gardens. Same time as the above but deserving of a separate entry as it is so uniquely good. See 496/ESSENTIAL EDINBURGH CULTURE.

64
AUG
The World Pipe Band Championships 0141 221 5414 · Glasgow Unbelievable numbers (3,000-4,000) of pipers from all over the world competing and seriously doing their thing on Glasgow Green.

65
AUG
Cowal Highland Gathering 01369 703206 · Dunoon One of many Highland games but this, along with Luss and Loch Lomond Games and Inverness in Jul, and Braemar (below) are the main events in the calendar that extends from May to Sep. Expect 'heavy events' (very big lads only), dancing, pipe bands, field and track events and much drinking and chat.

66
EARLY
SEP
Braemar Gathering Braemar Another of many Highland games (Aboyne early Aug, Ballater mid Aug on Deeside alone) up north but this is where the royals gather and probably local laird Billy Connolly and Hollywood A-list. Go ogle.

67
SEP
Blas Highlands Across the Highlands in a variety of venues. A rapidly expanding celebration of traditional and Gaelic music with an eclectic line up. It's a long week.

68
SEP
Leuchars Air Show 01334 839000 · near St Andrews Major airshow held over one day in RAF airfield with flying displays, exhibitions, classic cars etc.

69
SEP
Mountain Bike World Cup 01397 703781 · Fort William Held at Nevis Range 5K run, around the ski gondola. Awesome course with international competitors over 2 days. Evening events in town. Date varies (actually in Jun '08).

70
SEP
The Ben Nevis Race Fort William The race over 100 years old up Britain's highest mountain and back. The record is 1 hour 25 minutes which seems amazing. 500 runners though curiously little national, even local interest. Starts 2pm at Claggan Park off Glen Nevis roundabout.

71
SEP
The Pedal for Scotland Glasgow-to-Edinburgh Bike Ride Fun, charity fund-raiser annual bike event. From George Sq to Meadowbank with a pasta party at the halfway point.

72
MID-
SEP
Merchant City Festival 0141 552 6027 · Glasgow Extended weekend of diverse 'cultural' activities that reflect the commerce and concerns of this increasingly vibrant quarter of Glasgow east of George Sq. A festival on the up.

73
EARLY
OCT
Tiree Wave Classic 01879 220399 · Isle of Tiree Windsurfing heaven of the faraway island (2365/MAGICAL ISLANDS) where beaches offer difficult wind conditions and islanders offer warm hospitality.

74
OCT
Tour of Mull Rally 01688 302182 · Isle of Mull The highlight of the national rally calendar is this raging around Mull weekend. Though drivers enter from all over the world, the overall winner has often been a local man (well plenty time for practice). There's usually a waiting list for accommodation, but the camping is OK and locals put you up.

75
NOV
St Andrews Night Not such a big deal, but dinners etc and cultural ID. It is thought that Mr Salmond will make more of this.

76
31
DEC
Stonehaven Hogmanay Stonehaven Celebrated since 1910, a traditional fire festival that probably wouldn't get started nowadays for 'health and safety' reasons. 40 fireballers throw the fireballs around in the streets before processing to the harbour and heaving them in. We watch. Arrive early.

77
DEC-JAN
Edinburgh's Hogmanay 0131 557 3990 · Edinburgh Everywhere gets booked up but call the tourist information centre for accommodation. One of the world's major winter events. Launched with a **Torchlight Procession** through the city centre. A full, largely populist programme. **Night Afore International** on the 30th celebrates culture of another place (Catalonia '05, Canada '06, the Highlands '07). Main event is the **Street Party** on 31st; you need a wristband. Huge, good-natured crowd. You'll be amazed. It's the Scots at their best! See 496/ESSENTIAL EDINBURGH CULTURE.

The Scottish Pioneers

As I discovered, most things in what is loosely called 'the hospitality industry' in Scotland are getting better and better and compared to the rest of the world I'd say we are punching well above our weight. But it wasn't always like this. As in all areas of endeavour, it's particular people who lead the way, making the leaps forward that others follow. These entrepreneurs and innovators are essential to any cultural development and Scotland has been fortunate to engender and inspire these special people. For this edition of the book, I thought it would be interesting to identify some of them (though some are well known already) and recognise the part they have played in making life in Scotland better for ourselves and for visitors. I'm not talking here of the people who long ago invented Botanic Gardens or fish and chips or Chinese takeaways or who made a fortune from nightclubs. I'm celebrating those people who made a particular step forward for the first time and (in most cases) are still doing it.

Gunn Eriksson & Fred Brown In 1976 Fred Brown and Gunn Eriksson opened a hotel which though now closed, epitomises the whole idea of 'getting away from it all'. The Altnaharrie Inn was situated on the south shore of Loch Broom from Ullapool. It was either a long walk from Dundonnell or a boat across to their own quay. Although Gunn trained as an artist, she stepped into the kitchen six years later when the chef didn't turn up and the rest is culinary history. For 22 years she was the doyenne of Scottish and UK cookery. Way before her time and taking inspiration from the landscape (using hawthorn, nettles, flowers and other wild things in her recipes), she raised the game to a point where Altnaharrie was one of the few restaurants in Britain before or since that got two Michelin stars. Even now after years of superstar chefing and a media fixation with food there is still only one two-star Michelin restaurant in Scotland. Gunn and Fred gave up Altnaharrie in 2002. It is no longer a hotel.

Ken McCulloch Ken McCulloch started off as a trainee with British Transport Hotels in 1964. In 1969 he saw the gap and opened a wine bar in Glasgow. But it wasn't until 1986 that Ken did something truly and magically original – he combined three townhouses on the edge of Glasgow's West End and opened One Devonshire Gardens. In a world now which is full of boutique hotels, all credit should be given to Ken for creating the first. Now Hotel Du Vin (498/GLASGOW Hotels), it went from success to success, gathering every accolade going and attracting stars from Pavarotti to U2. Not satisfied with creating the definitive 1980s individual hotel, Ken (with partners) started the Malmaison chain in 1984 which once again sent the hotel industry into a spin. The chain, now sold on, continues to set the standard and in many cities is the single best hotel. With the proceeds from the sale of Malmaison and in addition to the hotel he built in Monaco, The Columbus (the first hotel anywhere with fingerprint ID as the door key), Ken and his partners launched the Dakota chain three years ago and two of the first have risen like black monoliths beside the motorways of central Scotland (130/HOTELS OUTSIDE EDINBURGH; 530/HOTELS OUTSIDE GLASGOW). Ken has said 'most of the things I have done would have failed a feasibility study'. He is a true innovator.

The Hendersons James McLaren Henderson ('Mac') celebrated his 100th birthday at Hendersons on Hanover Street Edinburgh in May '07. Some of his family of 7 children and 14 grandchildren continue to run a restaurant which was the first of its type in Britain or anywhere and pre-dated the vegetarian and organic revolution by decades. James and his wife Janet opened the first shop on the corner of Hanover Street and Thistle Street in 1962 to sell produce from their farm in East Lothian – in effect one of the first farm shops. The restaurant followed when the basement became available in 1963 and the bakery in Canonmills in 1964. Much of the produce on the menu at Hendersons is the same now as it was then. It has remained at the forefront of healthy eating for 40 years.

Valvona & Crolla The V&C story is long and inspirational and fairly well-known and I won't go into it all here. But as recorded in Mary Contini's evocative book, *Dear Francesca*, Alfonso Crolla left his village of Fontitune in the Abruzzi Mountains in the late 1890s and via Rome, Genoa and London ended up in Edinburgh opening an ice-cream parlour in Easter Road. It is not for this intrepid journey alone that the dynasty of V&C should be celebrated, since many Italians found their way around the world, but because the succeeding generations (and now they are on their fourth) have, with energy and enterprise and old-fashioned hard work, created a business which has hugely enhanced the city of Edinburgh and continues to do so today. Their world-famous deli (339/DELIS) and the restaurants that have followed it are all listed in this book.

Luca's Like the Crollas and others above, Luca Scappaticcio and his wife Anastasia arrived from Casino in the late 1800s and he became a pastry chef at the Balmoral Hotel. Luca learned to make ice cream from the Swiss sous chef and by 1908 had saved enough money to open a shop in Musselburgh which remains today (1519/ICE CREAM). It was called Luca's for simplicity and simplicity is what has informed all their subsequent products. Although there was an explosion of ice-cream makers from Italy in the early 20th century (there were 89 in Glasgow in 1903 and 336 in 1905), Luca's has endured and remains a superlative product.

The Allens Once not long ago there were only two or three hotels in Scotland (apart from the big railway hotels) that were 'destinations'. One of these opened by Betty and Eric Allen in 1978 and though a very long way from anywhere, became the epitome of the perfect country-house hotel and restaurant. Airds at Port Appin did not have huge grounds, swimming pools or room service but became Michelin's favourite hotel in Scotland, the first to be taken up by Relais and Chateaux, and received the highest score ever in the *Good Food Guide*. Betty and Eric with no airs or graces whatever continued with their modest ambition to run somewhere both special and homely until 2002. Now with son Graeme they run Kinloch House near Blairgowrie (1207/COUNTRY-HOUSE HOTELS) which is of course brilliant. But the world has changed, Airds is great again under different owners and there are many other country-house hotels in Scotland and the UK. But once they were 'the one'.

La Potinière, Gullane La Potinière in Gullane, an almost legendary location, a tiny country-cosy French restaurant in the main street of an East Lothian village was the first truly destination restaurant in Scotland. With a famously non-compromising menu and a locked-door policy for latecomers, La Potinière soon became known for the fact that it was booked a year ahead. The restaurant was taken over by subsequently by David and Hilary Brown and it was they at the beginning of Britain's foody fixation years who really put it on the map. With Hilary in the kitchen and David out front bearing a wine list as long as your arm and a no-choice menu which (with careful monitoring) was never repeated in any part for any guest, it became a restaurant with a worldwide reputation, that was a privilege to eat in. Once again La Potinière continues with new owners and as it happens, I am going there tonight. Now, in a world full of fabulous restaurants all competing with one another, it remains superb. But you don't have to book so far in advance.

Peter MacMillan Youth hostelling began in Germany in 1910 and took off with the YHA in the UK in the 1930s. Hostels provided cheap accommodation for hikers and cyclists. For decades and through the 1960s, they proliferated, continuing with their written and unwritten codes of practice. You helped with the chores, you left by 10am, there was a curfew and you couldn't arrive by car. Now that's all changed and it's mainly because in the 1980s, there was suddenly an alternative – the independent hostel. Peter MacMillan was quick to see the opportunity and opened Backpackers in Edinburgh. His chain of hostels (three in Edinburgh and many throughout Scotland) continue to provide the kind of sociable, cool, cheap accommodation that today's backpacking travellers take for granted. The growth of independent hostels (there are now 24 in Edinburgh, a tribute to Peter's initiative, and only 4 in Glasgow) is more evident in Scotland than probably anywhere else in the world.

And not forgetting **Ronnie Clydesdale** and the **Ubiquitous Chip** (537/GLASGOW FINE-DINING RESTAURANTS). Over 35 years at the front.

A few more things the Scots pioneered...

Scotland's population has never been much over 5 million and yet we discovered, invented or manufactured for the first time the following quite important things.

The decimal point	The hypodermic syringe
Logarithms	Finger-printing
The Bank of England	The kaleidoscope
The overdraft	Anaesthesia
Cannabis (the active principle)	Antiseptics
Documentary films	Golf clubs
Colour photographs	The 18-hole golf course
Encyclopaedia Britannica	Tennis courts
Postcards	The bowling green
The gas mask	Writing paper
The theory of combustion	The thermometer
The advertising film	The gravitating compass
The bus	The threshing machine
The steam engine	Insulin
The locomotive	Penicillin
The fax machine	Interferon
The photocopier	The pneumatic tyre
Video	The pedal bicycle
The telephone	The modern road surface
Television	Geology
Radar	Artificial ice
Helium	Morphine
Neon	Ante-natal clinics
The telegraph	Bovril
Street lighting	Marmalade
The lawnmower	The fountain pen
Kinetic energy	The Mackintosh
Electric light	Gardenias
The alpha chip	Dolly, the cloned sheep
The Thermos flask	*Auld Lang Syne*

Section 2

Edinburgh

The Best Hotels

78 1/XE5
22 ROOMS
TEL · TV
NO KIDS
£85+

✓ ✓ ✓ **Prestonfield House www.prestonfield.com · 0131 668 3346 · off Priestfield Road** 3km south of city centre. OK, it's partly because I've had so many excellent evenings at Prestonfield escaping city streets in summer, warmed and welcomed in winter or maybe because the last 2 book launches for *StB* were so graced by James Thomson's hospitality, but no – Prestonfield gets 3 ticks because there's simply nothing like it anywhere – else in the world. The Heilan' cattle in the 14-acre grounds tell you this isn't your average urban bed for the night. A romantic, almost other-worldly 17th-century building with period features still intact. In 2003 it was taken over by James Thomson of The Tower (142/BEST RESTAURANTS) and The Witchery (143/BEST RESTAURANTS), and he has turned this bastion of Edinburgh sensibilities into Scotland's most sumptuous hotel. The architecture and the detail is exceptional and romantic. All rooms are highly individualistic with hand-picked antiques and artefacts. Welcome bottle of champagne. Prestonfield probably hosts more awards dinners and accommodates more celebrity guests than anywhere else in town. Is itself in *Tatler*'s top 101 hotels in the world and was AA Hotel of the Year 2006. In summer the nightly Scottish cabaret (in the stable block) is hugely popular. House restaurant Rhubarb is a remarkable 'experience' (144/BEST RESTAURANTS) Top Rooms: 5/6/16/17.

79 1/D3
168 ROOMS
20 SUITES
TEL · TV
£85+

✓ ✓ **The Balmoral www.thebalmoralhotel.com · 0131 556 2414 · Princes Street** At east end above Waverley Station. Capital landmark with its clock always 2 minutes fast (except at Hogmanay); so you can't miss it and you don't miss your train. The old pile dear to Sir Rocco Forte's heart. Expensive for a mere tourist but if you can't afford to stay there's always afternoon tea in the piano-tinkling Palm Court. Few hotels anywhere are so much in the heart of things. Good business centre; fine sports facilities; luxurious and distinctive rooms have ethereal views of the city, though some don't and are not worth the money (so, check). Main restaurant, Number One Princes Street (146/BEST RESTAURANTS), is tops and less formal brasserie, Hadrian's (good power breakfast venue). Even the non-pretentious bar, NB, works (occasionally has music and open till 1am). Top Rooms: the 3 'Royal' suites: Presidential, Balmoral and Glamis.

80 1/A4
261 ROOMS
TEL · TV
NO PETS
£85+

✓ **The Caledonian Hilton www.hilton.co.uk/caledonian · 0131 222 8888 · Princes Street** Edinburgh institution at the West End of Princes St: former station hotel built in 1903. Upgrading under the Hilton group continues to reinforce 5-star status of Edinburgh's other landmark hotel. Good business hotel with all facilities you'd expect (though not in all rooms). 'Living Well' spa with not large pool. Endearing lack of uniformity in the rooms. Executive rooms on fifth floor (and deluxe rooms elsewhere) have great views. Capital kind of place in every respect. Main restaurant, The Pompadour, for fine and très formal dining in ornate and elegant setting does lack the glamour and gourmet cred of days gone by but Brasserie on ground floor is perfectly serviceable. Cally Bar (or Chisholms) a famous rendezvous with great whisky selection. Top Rooms: The 'Sean (Connery) Suite'.

81 1/A4
260 ROOMS
TEL · TV
£85+

✓ **The Sheraton Grand www.starwoodhotels.com/sheraton/grand edinburgh · 0131 229 9131 · Festival Square** On Lothian Rd and Conference Centre, this city-centre business hotel won no prizes for architecture when it opened late 1980s, but now both Festival Sq and the newly emerged Conference Sq behind one part of the shiny new financial district and Edinburgh looks like a real city at last. This is a reliable stopover at the heart of it with excellent service. Larger rooms and castle views carry premiums, but make big difference. Terrace restaurant adequate. 'The Grill' is the fine dining room; fine as a business hotel restaurant though little local trade and often empty. Menu features steaks with Australian wagyu and US Prime Angus beef. Santini behind the hotel also excellent (195/BEST ITALIAN). The superlative feature of the Sheraton is the health club 'One', routinely identified as one of the best spas in the UK, with great half-outdoor pool. Top Rooms: the 2 'Diplomatic Suites'.

82 1/XA3
41 ROOMS
TEL · TV
NO PETS
£85+

✓ **Channings** www.channings.com · 0131 315 2226 · **South Learmonth Gardens** Parallel to Queensferry Rd after Dean Bridge. Tasteful alternative to big-chain hospitality. 5 period townhouses joined to form a quietly elegant West End hotel. Efficient and individual service including 24-hour room service. Great views from top-floor rooms. Top Rooms: The Shackleton Suites - 5 on the top floor with great views and fabulous bathrooms. The polar explorer once lived here and pictures of his expedition adorn the walls. Restaurant under chef Karen Mackay at TGP with pleasant bar and garden terrace. A discerning and discreet corner of the West End.

83 1/F2
94 ROOMS
13 SUITES
TEL · TV
NO PETS
£85+

Royal Terrace www.primahotels.co.uk/royal-terrace.html · 0131 557 3222 · **18 Royal Terrace** Discreet multi-townhouse hotel on elegant terrace backing on to Calton Hill. Capacious though meagre pool among other sports facilities. Multi-level terraced garden out back, deceptively large number of rooms and townhouse décor a tad on the Baroque side make this fabulous for some, merely a good business bet for others. Bar/restaurant not so notable among the natives but we could love the terrace in summer. Top Rooms: Aberlour Suite.

84 1/D4
238 ROOMS
TEL · TV
ECO
£85+

Radisson SAS www.edinburgh.radissonsas.com · 0131 557 9797 · **80 High Street** Modern but sympathetic building on the Royal Mile, handy for everything and typical Radisson contemporary smart feel. Good facilities but some say service lacking. Thin walls, not great views. Leisure facilities including small pool. 'Itchycoo' bar/brasserie and less appealing restaurant downstairs. Adjacent parking handy in a hotel so central.

85 1/B3
197 ROOMS
TEL · TV
£85+

The George www.edinburghgeorgehotel.co.uk · 0131 225 1251 · **George Street** Between Hanover St and St Andrew Sq. Refurbished by Principal Hotel Group with a whole new block on the way '08. Robert Adam-designed and dating back to the late 18th century. Good views to Fife from the top 3 floors. Pricey, but you pay for the location and the Georgian niceties (and extra for the views). Busy on-street bar and impressive brasserie restaurant Tempus. Good Festival and Hogmanay hotel close to the heart of things (taken over by luvvies during TV Festival). George has shrugged off its staid, traditional image fitting in to George St's more progressive and opportunistic present.

Individual & Boutique Hotels

86 1/C2
33 ROOMS
TEL · TV
NO PETS
£85+

✓ ✓ **Tigerlily** 0131 225 5005 · **125 George Street** Edinburgh's newest designtastic hotel on style boulevard by Montpellier Group who have indigo (yard) (175/BISTROS) and Ricks nearby which also has (much cheaper) rooms (101/INDIVIDUAL HOTELS). This surprisingly large hotel sits atop the never-other-than-rammed Tigerlily bar and restaurant, the new place to go '07. Rooms fairly fab from '07 design guide with metal and pale wood and glass and full of surface. Not cheap for this, the most fashion-conscious lodging in town. Top Rooms: The Georgian Suites.

87 1/D3
69 ROOMS
TEL · TV
NO PETS
£85+

✓ ✓ The Scotsman www.thescotsmanhotel.co.uk · 0131 556 5565 ·
North Bridge Deluxe boutique hotel in landmark building (the old offices of *The Scotsman* newspaper group) converted into chic, highly individual accommodation with every modern facility: internet, flat-screen TV, privacy locker in all rooms. Labyrinthine lay-out (stairs and firedoors everywhere) and slow lifts apart, this is the convenient cool hotel in town. Nice art, intimate dining in Vermillion (149/BEST RESTAURANTS) and buzzy brasserie (160/BISTROS). Excellent leisure facilities – Escape – the low-lit, steel pool is great for grown-ups. Top Rooms: Penthouse and Director's suites.

88 1/C1
18 ROOMS
3 SUITES
TEL · TV
NO PETS
NO KIDS
£85+

✓ ✓ The Howard www.thehoward.com · 0131 315 2220 · **34 Great King Street** In the heart of the Georgian New Town, 3 townhouses in splendid street imbued with quiet elegance though only 5 minutes from Princes Street. No bar but restful drawing room and 15 spacious individual rooms, sympatico with architecture and recently refurbished. 3 new en suites (Top Rooms) downstairs have own entrances for discreet liaisons or just convenience and own drawing room for entertaining. 24-hour room service. Athol restaurant for breakfast or dinner (haven't been) and delightful afternoon tea. No leisure facilities. A very Edinburgh accommodation.

89 1/XA3
50 ROOMS
TEL · TV
ECO
NO PETS
NO KIDS
GAY FRIENDLY
£85+

✓ ✓ The Bonham www.thebonham.com · 0131 226 6050 ·
35 Drumsheugh Gardens Discreet townhouse in quiet West End crescent. Cosmopolitan service and ambience a stroll from Princes St. Much favoured by visiting celebs and writers at the Book Festival. Owned by same people as the Howard and Channings (82/BEST HOTELS). Rooms stylish and individual (with some bold colour schemes). Great views outback over New Town on floors 2 and up. Elegant dining in calm, spacious restaurant (especially the end table by back window). Chef Michel Bouyer forges a foody Auld Alliance of top Scottish ingredients and French flair. No-nonsense, simple 4/5 choices described in plain English. Popular 'boozy snoozy' lunch at weekends: 4 people, 2 bottles of wine for £65 (at TGP). Nice wine list. No bar.

90 1/XE1
100 ROOMS
TEL · TV
£60-85

✓ The Malmaison www.malmaison-edinburgh.com · 0131 468 5000 ·
Tower Place, Leith At the dock gates. Award-winning, praise-laden designer chain hotel with lavish yet homely rooms. All facilities that we who were once smart, young, modern people expect eg CD, DVD players in each chambre (borrow product from reception). Top Rooms have harbour views and 4-poster beds. Brasserie and café-bar have stylish ambience too. Pity about the flats out front, but Leith still onwards and upwards. (In an off-plan and off-yer-heid way if you paid what they asked for a boxy flat with a glint of the sea and a purposeless balcony.) Rant over. Enjoy the Malmaison.

91 1/B5
138 ROOMS
TEL · TV
£60-85+

✓ The Point www.point-hotel.co.uk · 0131 221 5555 · **34 Bread Street** This used to be a Co-operative department store. Space and colour combinations manage to look simultaneously rich and minimal; some castle views. Top Rooms, the suites come with side-lit Jacuzzis. Once mentioned as one of the great designery hotels in the world and on the cover of *Hotel Design*. Café-bar Monboddo and restaurant have modern and spacious, mid-Euro feel. Good places to meet Edinburgers though food and service can be less to the point. Conference Centre adjacent with great penthouse often used for cool Edinburgh launches and parties. (Try to get up there for a unique view of the city: 459/VIEWS.)

92 1/B3
18 ROOMS
TEL · TV
NO PETS
NO KIDS
£45-60

✓ **Le Monde** www.lemondehotel.co.uk · 0131 270 3900 · 16 George Street New in 2006, well-defined boutique hotel on Edinburgh's emerging designer dressed-up street. Part of megabar/restaurant all themed on the world on our doorstep. Highly individual rooms are named after cities and designed accordingly: Havana, Rome, New York, even Dublin but no Glasgow. Serious attention to detail and very rock 'n' roll. All a tad OTT (the bar not the coolest in town) but the theme does work and beds/bathrooms/facilities are excellent.

93 1/E2
65 ROOMS
TEL · TV
NO PETS
£85+

✓ **The Glasshouse** www.e-travelguide.info/glasshouse · 0131 525 8200 · 2 Greenside Place Between Playhouse Theatre and the Vue. First of new urban chain, this 'boutique' hotel is in many ways more like a very upmarket travel lodge or motel. It's built above the multiplex (rooms on 2 floors) and the restaurants in the mall below. Main feature is extensive lawned garden on roof around which about half the rooms look out – with patios (non-private) including their standard 'deluxe doubles'. No restaurant (breakfast in room or 'the Observatory'), honesty bar. The Mall itself is a big disappointment; the restaurants within are all High Street staples, but guests can use Virgin Active health facilities and spa (including 25m pool – 466/EDINBURGH SPORTS) for 12 quid a plunge. Interesting concept not least because of the upmarket and the downmarket juxtapositions.

94 1/XA3
29 ROOMS
TEL · TV
NO PETS
£85+

✓ **Edinburgh Residence** www.theedinburghresidence.com · 0131 226 3380 · 7 Rothesay Terrace Another townhouse affair but on extravagant scale. Several Georgian townhouses have been joined into an elegant apartment hotel by the Townhouse Group who own the Howard and the Bonham (above). No restaurant, but the Bonham do breakfasts and 24-hour room service, so a discreet and distinctive stopover in 3 different levels of suite. Big bathrooms, views of Dean Village. Drawing room if you're feeling lonely in this quiet West End retreat but nightlife and shops a stroll away. Top Rooms: The Townhouse suites (they have 2 bathrooms).

95 1/A3
30 ROOMS
TEL · TV
NO PETS
NO KIDS
£45-60

✓ **The Hudson Hotel** 0131 247 7000 · 9-11 Hope Street Near corner of Charlotte Sq. Unashamedly paying homage to North America or more specifically NYC, this '06 addition to the city's boutique portfolio has captured the urbanity without the humanity and there is no NY lot to be seen. So, cold rather than merely cool, it does have style uniformity throughout. Not as exp as others with often good walk-in rates. Café-bar on street level, also a little cool and dark for its own good, has never attracted the crowds of nearby George St.

96 1/C4
173 ROOMS
TEL · TV
ECO
NO PETS
£85+

✓ **Apex City Hotel** www.apexhotels.co.uk/hotels/edinburgh-city · 0131 243 3456 · Apex International · 0131 300 3456 Both in the middle of the Grassmarket, the picturesque but rowdy Saturday night city centre. Modern, soi-disant – but close to castle, club life and other bits of essential Edinburgh. More cool to roam from than in, though. Restaurants called Aqua and the International Metro on street level are decent and you can usually get a table in the otherwise busy Grassmarket. Heights restaurant on 6th floor of International has great view of the Castle but you can't sit on the terrace. Some castle views (4th-floor rooms at International have balconies). Shared pool and facilities are minimal. Apex City came number 2 in the UK for 'Green Tourism' activity in 2007. There's a cheaper, more travel-lodgy Apex just beyond the West End (111/ECONOMY HOTELS).

97 1/C2
30 APTS
TEL · TV
NO PETS
NO KIDS
£45-60

✓ **Royal Garden Apartments** www.royal-garden.co.uk · 0131 625 1234 ·
York Buildings, Queen Street Opposite National Portrait Gallery
(428/OTHER ATTRACTIONS) near Playhouse Theatre and funky Broughton St. Self-
catering, very well turned-out apartments with coffee shop on ground floor and
access to private gardens and surprisingly to the superior leisure facilities at the
distant Scotsman Hotel (above) though you wouldn't want to walk there in your
dressing gown. Great views especially top floor. Nightly let available (3 days'
minimum at peak periods).

98 1/E4
78 ROOMS
TEL · TV
NO PETS
£45-60

✓ **10 Hill Place** 0131 662 2080 Address as title on surprising and secret
square on South Side near University only 100m from busy Nicolson St.
Unlikely and surprising departure for the Royal College of Surgeons who occupy
the imposing neoclassical building complex which fronts onto Nicolson St, using
their building as sets to construct a new lecture hall and this unfussy, utilitarian,
very modern hotel. Masculine, clean elegance in uniform design. Far superior to
any mere bedbox, a comfy room for the night without the frills. Café-bar.

99 1/E4

Edinburgh First 0131 662 2000 This the phone number which goes through to
the **Kenneth Mackenzie Hotel** on Richmond Pl, one of the properties
administered by 'Edinburgh First' for the University. Large variety of campus
accommodation on South Side near Commonwealth Pool. The hotel with 36 very
contemporary and reasonably priced rooms is available all year round. Other
student-hall-type accommodation only in vacation period.

100 1/D2

Home House 0131 523 1523 · **12 Picardy Place** Decidedly boutique hotel but
only available to members (and guests) of exclusive/expensive Home House, the
London club – this their northern outpost. 5 rooms only. Restaurant has increasing
reputation at TGP.

101 1/B2
10 ROOMS
TEL · TV
NO PETS
NO KIDS
£60-85

Rick's www.ricksedinburgh.co.uk · 0131 622 7800 · **55 Frederick Street**
Very city centre hotel and bar/restaurant in downtown location a stone's throw
from George St. By same people who have indigo (yard) (175/GASTROPUBS) and
nearby Opal Lounge (399/COOL BARS) so the bar is full-on especially late.
Restaurant (177/GASTROPUBS) has (loud) contemporary dining. Rooms upstairs can
be quiet. Modern, urban feel eg DVD players as standard. Same rate single or twin.
Don't let the rooms above the bar thing put you off. Get as high as you can.

102 1/XD5
12 ROOMS
TEL · TV
NO PETS
NO KIDS
£38-45

Borough www.boroughhotel.com · 0131 668 2255 · **72 Causewayside** Very
urban and self-consciously hip hotel in conversion of former snooker hall/
warehouse 200m south of the Meadows. Notable designer Ben Kelly (of the legendary Hacienda) somehow failed to warm this place up or excite. Stark look and
cold lighting. Rooms small and furnishings not great, but this is still a hip hotel to
hang out in. They call it 'reassuringly individual'. Bar and restaurant are South Side
rendezvous. Food LO 9pm, bar 1am (DJs on Fri).

103 1/E2
53 ROOMS
TEL · TV
NO PETS
£60-85

Parliament House www.parliamenthouse-hotel.co.uk · 0131 478 4000 ·
15 Calton Hill Good central location, only 200m from east end of Princes Street
and adjacent to Calton Hill (457/BEST VIEWS), although tucked away. Small bar in
residents lounge and restaurant for breakfast, even meals – but OK townhouse-
style décor, funky lift. About half the rooms have views – you know where to go.

Most Excellent Lodgings

104 1/C4
2 + 6 APTS
TEL · TV
NO PETS
NO KIDS
GAY FRIENDLY
£85+

✓ ✓ **Inner Sanctum** and the **Old Rectory** at the **Witchery** www.the-witchery.com · 0131 225 5613 · **Castlehill** 2 highly individual rooms and an apartment above the Witchery Restaurant (143/BEST RESTAURANTS) at the top of the Royal Mile together with 5 sumptuous apartments across the street that put a whole new look into the Old Town. A stone's throw from the castle, few accommodations anywhere are as emphatically *mise en place* as this. Probably the most exceptional and atmospheric in town – designed by owner James Thomson and Mark Rowley – fairly camp/theatrical, OTT and very sexy. Breakfast and everything else you need en suite including champagne. Go with somebody good.

105 1/XE5
8 ROOMS
TEL · TV
NO PETS
GAY FRIENDLY
£38-45

Southside www.southsideguesthouse.co.uk · 0131 668 4422 · **8 Newington Road** On main street in s side with many hotels/guesthouses stretching halfway to Dalkeith, a surprisingly civilised haven now in new hands. Attention to decor and detail and excellent breakfast. Nice prints, rugs, books and DVDs. Some traffic noise, but upstairs rooms double-glazed. Parking nearby.

106 1/XE1
5 ROOMS · TV
NO PETS
GAY FRIENDLY
£38-45

Ardmor House www.ardmorhouse.com · 0131 554 4944 · **74 Pilrig Street** Off Leith Walk with lots of other B&Bs but this the top spot. Individual, contemporary and relaxed – we are talking about the proprietors Colin and Robin who have a gorgeous wee dog, Lola. They've also got 2 lovely New Town apartments for short lets. Gay and non-gay friendly alike.

107 1/A1
8 ROOMS
TEL · TV
NO PETS
GAY FRIENDLY
£38-45

Six St Mary's Place www.sixmarysplace.co.uk · 0131 332 8965 Vegetarian-friendly, award-winning guesthouse on main street of Stockbridge (St Mary's Pl, part of Raeburn Pl) and busy main road out of town for Forth Road Bridge and north, this is a tastefully converted Georgian townhouse. Informal, friendly, well-cared-for accommodation popular with academics and people we like. Vegetarian breakfast in conservatory overlooking garden.

108 1/C2
3 ROOMS
TEL · TV
NO PETS
NO KIDS
£45-60

24 Northumberland Street www.ingrams.co.uk · 0131 556 8140 A definitive New Town B&B. Georgian townhouse in mid-New Town (owner a notable antique dealer). Only 3 rooms so often booked; they can sleep 7. Has become a Wolsey Lodge but no dinner is served (there are many great restaurants nearby).

109 1/XA1
3 ROOMS
+ FLAT
TEL · TV
NO PETS
NO KIDS
£38-45

7 Danube Street 0131 332 2755 In elegant crescent in New Town, Stockbridge area near the Water of Leith. Very New Town experience, rooms below stairs, breakfast in drawing room; staircase winds upwards forever. Fiona Mitchell-Rose an assiduous host with Staffordshires George and Doris in attendance. Lovely flowers. Only 3 rooms but self-contained flat nearby. Many restaurants in the hood.

The Best Economy Hotels

Hotels/B&Bs below are included on grounds of price, convenience or just because we like them for some idiosyncratic reason.

110 1/D4
99 ROOMS
TEL · TV
£30-45

✓ **Ibis** www.ibishotel.com · 0131 240 7000 · **Hunter Square** First in Scotland of the Euro budget chain (one other in Glasgow, 542/TRAVEL LODGES). Dead central behind the Tron so good for Hogmanay (or not). Serviceable and efficient. For tourists doing the sights, this is best bed box for location. Rates vary through year.

111 1/XA4
234 ROOMS
TEL · TV
NO PETS
£60-85

Apex European www.apexhotels.co.uk/hotels/edinburgh-european · 0131 474 3456 · **90 Haymarket Terrace** The western, more bedbox version of the Apex triumvirate. Apex City the grooviest (96/BOUTIQUE HOTELS) and the other, Apex International, which is adjacent in the Grassmarket. The European is the cheaper option. (Location! Location!) In top 5 of Green Tourism Hotels (UK) in '07.

112 1/E2
160 ROOMS
TEL · TV
NO PETS
£45-60

Holiday Inn Express www.hieedinburgh.co.uk · 0131 558 2300/0800 434040 · **16 Picardy Place** Not unpleasant conversion of several New Town houses in exceptionally convenient location opposite the Playhouse Theatre. Rooms all same standard (twin or double). Bar, no restaurant but area awash with options. This is a very clever Holiday Inn. There are 3 others in town.

113 1/C5
180 ROOMS
TEL · TV
NO PETS
£45-60

Novotel Edinburgh Centre www.novotel.com · 0131 656 3500 · **80 Lauriston Place** New build near Tollcross and University. No charm but functional and reasonably contemporary. Small pool, bar and contemporary-like brasserie. Good beds and facilities. But Premier Travel inn adjacent is half the price (see below).

114 1/C4
44 ROOMS
TEL · TV
NO PETS
£38-45

Grassmarket Hotel www.festival-inns.co.uk/hotels_grassmarket.htm · 0131 220 2299 · **94-96 Grassmarket** Basic and boisterously located accommodation next to Biddy Mulligan's which is open till 1am, but levels 4/5 at the back are best. The Grassmarket is fairly full-on, so good for party-animal business types on a budget – stags rut here.

115 1/D4
42 ROOMS
TEL · TV
NO KIDS
£38-45

Tailors Hall www.festival-inns.co.uk · 0131 622 6800 · **Cowgate** If you don't mind the racket (or want to be part of it), this is a clubby/young thing kind of hotel in the heart of the throbbing Cowgate area and above the hugely popular 3 Sisters pub. 4 bars to choose from (till 1am), 24-hour licence for residents. Can do 4 in a room. Rooms not above the huge courtyard are best.

116 1/E4
193 ROOMS
TEL · TV
NO PETS
£30-38

Travel Lodge www.travelodge.co.uk · 0131 557 6281/08700 850 950 · **33 St Mary's Street** Edinburgh central version of national (often roadside) chain. All usual, formulaic facilities but inexpensive and near Royal Mile (Holyrood end) and Cowgate for late-night action.

117 1/C5
1/XA4
1/XE1
£30-38

Premier Travel Inn Chain www.premiertravelinn.co.uk 7 (and counting) in Edinburgh Area. All much of a less-ness. Most central is newest at 82 Lauriston Place 0870 990 6610 near University. 1 Morrison Link 0870 238 3319 is near Haymarket Station. The one in Newhaven/Leith (taxi/bus) 08701 977 093 is near bars and restaurants of Leith (1km) and Next Generation health club (helpfully not available to guests). Less than 50% rooms have 'sea' views. All other inns are sub-urban.

The Best Hostels

Edinburgh does good hostel with many independents (young and Hoochy, open 24 hours) and handy university halls of residence to let outside term time. With all the independent hostels, it's best to turn up around 11/11.30am if you haven't booked. The SYHA is the Scottish Youth Hostels Association. 01786 891400.

118 1/XE1
71 ROOMS
24 HOURS

✓ ✓ **SY Edinburgh Central** www.syha.org.uk · **0131 524 2090** · **9 Haddington Place** Central it is in a good part of town though perhaps unobvious to casual visitors, ie it's not in the Old Town area. Haddington Pl is part of Leith Walk (corner of Annandale St) near theatres/bars/restaurants and gay quarter and on way to Leith. Converted from office block with café, internet and every hostel facility. Clean, efficient; rooms from singles to family 4-7 beds.

119 1/E4
630 ROOMS
24 HOURS

✓ **Smartcity Hostels** 0870 892 3000 · **50 Blackfriars Street** Building is enormous so also opens on to Cowgate. £10 million made this place as hotel-like as you get without completely losing the hostel ethnicity. Self-service restaurant, extensive bar, facilities including self-catering kitchens and hordes of staying-up/out-late people. Massive number of rooms (630) round interior courtyard, varying from 2-12 occupancy. Good location and quite smart really.

120 1/C4
1/D4
24 HOURS
£30 OR LESS

✓ **Royal Mile Backpackers** www.royalmilebackpackers.com · 0131 557 6120 · **105 High Street** On the Royal Mile, near the Cowgate with its late-night bars. Ideal central cheap 24-hour crash-out dormitory accommodation with all the facilities for itinerant youth seeking a capital experience. The same company (who also run Mac backpackers tours) have the original hostel, **The High Street Hostel**, 8 Blackfriars St (0131 557 3984), and the **Castle Rock**, 15 Johnston Terrace (0131 225 9666) in the old Council Environmental Health HQ. Is huge (190 beds in various dorms; 6 'private' rooms book up fast) and some great views across the Grassmarket or to the castle which is just over there. Same folk (Mr Backpacker himself, Peter Macmillan) also have places in Fort William, Inverness, Oban, Pitlochry and Skye.

121 1/XA3
£30 OR LESS

✓ **Globetrotter Inn** www.globetrotterinn.com · **0131 336 1030** · **Marine Drive, Cramond** First venture of ambitious hostel chain, on the Cramond foreshore. Former hotel in great if off-centre setting. Huge no of bunks (400), excellent facilities (spa, gym, internet, kitchen and shop). Only drawback is distance from downtown (half hour); last bus 11.20pm and hostel runs own hourly service (till 11pm). Lawns and trees and riverside view do compensate.

122 1/D3
29 ROOMS
NO PETS
£30 OR LESS

✓ **St Christopher Inn** www.st-christophers.co.uk · **0207 407 1856** · **9-13 Market Street** Couldn't be handier for the station or city centre. This (with sister place in London and other Euro cultural cities) a hostel rather than hotel with bunk rooms though there are single and double rooms. Price depends on no sharing. Belushi's café-bar on ground floor open till 1am. A very central option, better than most other hostels (facilities are ensuite) but not cheap (£48 a twin). Provides linen. Internet access.

123 1/XA3
1/D3
£30 OR LESS

✓ **Belford Hostel** www.edinburghhostels.com/belford.htm · **0131 225 6209** · **Douglas Gardens** Near Gallery of Modern Art (great café, 286/BEST TEAROOMS) and quaint Dean Village but still fairly central. Bizarre concept – 98 beds in partitioned-off (un-soundproofed) 'rooms' of 6-10 in a converted church. 7 'private' rooms. Top-bunk berth gets you a view of the vaulted wooden ceiling way above. Nice stained glass. Games room, bar, MTV. Sister establishment **Edinburgh Backpackers Hostel**, 65 Cockburn St (0131 220 2200), is closer to action.

124 1/A3
£30 OR LESS
✓ **Caledonian Backpackers** www.caledonianbackpackers.net ·
0131 226 2939 · 3 Queensferry Street The city's biggest (accommodation for 300+) with a great backpacker (live music sometimes), kitchen. Doubles, triples and quads. Good all-round Euro atmosphere.

125 1/A3
£30 OR LESS
Princes Street Backpackers East www.edinburghbackpackers.com ·
0131 556 6894 · 5 West Register Street Behind Burger King at east end of Princes St. Very central for cheap accommodation. 4 doubles, 100 beds in all. Basic and attracts the usual international crowd. Near Waverley and airport bus stops.

126 1/XA3
£30 OR LESS
Eurolodge 0131 220 5141. **25 Palmerston Place** New backpacker B&B (no self-catering) in West End townhouse with immense staircase. Lofty rooms packed with bunks and subdivided. New at TGP. Various room configurations (4 doubles, 2 even ensuite, 6/8/10/20).

127 1/XB3
£30 OR LESS
Argyle Backpackers Hotel www.sol.co.uk/a/argyle · 0131 667 9991 ·
14 Argyle Place In Marchmont area of up-market student flats. Quiet area though Argyle Pl the most happening street. 2 km to centre across 'The Meadows' (not advised for women at night). Some kind of garden. Some singles and doubles.

The Best Hotels Outside Town

128 10/R25
✓✓ **Greywalls** www.greywalls.co.uk · 01620 842144 · **Gullane** On coast 36km east of Edinburgh off A198 just beyond golfers' paradise of Gullane. Unquestionably the most chic retreat near the city. Full report 910/LOTHIANS.

129 10/P25
16 ROOMS
TEL · TV
NO PETS
£85+
✓✓ **Champany Inn** www.champany.com · 01506 834532 · **near Linlithgow** On A904, 3km Linlithgow on road to Forth Road Bridge and South Queensferry. Exemplary restaurant with rooms some overlooking garden. Legendary steaks and seafood; ambience and service. Breakfast in cosy dining kitchen excellent with nice bacon. Extraordinary wine list with dinner. But veggies best not to venture here.
EAT Superb. 272/BURGERS & STEAKS.

130 10/P27
16 ROOMS
TEL · TV
NO PETS
£85+
✓✓ **Dakota** www.dakotahotels.co.uk · 0870 423 4293 · **South Queensferry** Two ticks for a very different kind of hotel from the above. Pioneer in emerging chain by the people who brought us the Malmaisons and before that, 1 Devonshire Gardens (now Hotel du Vin; 498/GLASGOW HOTELS). A bold concept from design statement of the black metropolis-type block to the locations – in this case a car park serving the mini mall of Tesco etc on the edge of South Queensferry but on main carriageway north from Edinburgh near the tolls for the Forth Road Bridge. As a businesslike bedblock it's superb, a designer (Amanda Rosa) world away from anonymous others of the ilk. No frills but far from basic. Amanda also does Gleneagles. This is the stripped-down version but rooms are calm and whisper 'understated chic'. Restaurant 'The Grill' a destination in itself (guests should book when they make a room reservation). Ken does it again! See also 530/HOTELS OUTSIDE GLASGOW.
EAT Brasserie-type daily-changing menu in setting reminiscent of a Malmaison. Spotlights, dark woods, brick and slats everywhere. Seafood, including 3 varieties of oyster. Diners come from Edinburgh.

131 10/P25
47 ROOMS
TEL · TV
NO PETS
£85+

✔ **Norton House** nortonhouse@handpicked.co.uk · **0131 333 1275** · **Ingliston** Off A8 very close to airport, 10km west of city centre. Victorian country house in 55 acres of greenery surprisingly woody and pastoral so close to city. Highly regarded 'Hand-Picked' Hotel group. 'Executive' rooms have country-side views. Labyrinthine layout with good conference/function facilities. Brasserie and small internal restaurant. Good contemporary (the bedrooms) and traditional (public rooms) mix. Some rooms quite swish.

132 10/Q26
10 ROOMS
MAR-DEC
TEL
£85+

✔ **Borthwick Castle** www.borthwickcastle.com · **0870 118 1664** · **North Middleton** On B6367, 3km off the A7, 18km bypass, 26km southeast of centre. So this is a real Border castle. Walls 30m high, this magnificent tower house knocks you off your horse with its authenticity – Mary Queen of Scots was blockaded here once and at night you expect to see her swishing up the (narrow, unavoidable) spiral stairs. 8 rooms in castle, 2 in gatehouse and the (very) grand banqueting hall is impressive but you came for the decor not, I fear, the dinner.

133 10/P25
12 ROOMS
TEL · TV
NO PETS
£45-60

✔ **Orocco Pier** www.oroccopier.co.uk · **0131 331 1298** · **Main Street, South Queensferry** A decent restaurant and boutique hotel, in tourist-thronged and Tesco-tainted South Q (which was never going to be Sausalito, but the charming Main Street hasn't nearly approached its potential and the modern stuff and schemes at the road bridge approach are appalling except of course the Dakota; see above). Best to come from Edinburgh on first turnoff from dual car-riageway. Formerly Queensferry Arms, substantial makeover has created a cool bistro and rooms with some (5) great views of 'the Bridge' (415/MAIN ATTRACTIONS) with further expansion '08 giving 14 new rooms. LO for food 10pm.

134 10/Q26
36 ROOMS
TEL · TV
£85+

Dalhousie Castle www.dalhousiecastle.co.uk · **01875 820153** · **Bonnyrigg** Just off B704 2km from the A7, 15km from bypass and 23km south of centre. It looks fantastic in its setting and some bits date way back to the 13th century; a tad ersatz inside though ideal for weddings. (Previous guests include Edward I, Cromwell, Queen Victoria, some rock stars.) Multi-chambered Dungeon restaurant has 2AA rosettes. 'Aqueous Spa' but no pool.

135 10/P25
71 ROOMS
TEL · TV
NO PETS
£85+

Houstoun House www.houstounhouse.co.uk · **01506 853831** · **Uphall** On A899 at end of Broxburn/Uphall Main St, 8km from roundabout at the start of the M8 Edinburgh-Glasgow motorway. Airport 10km, 18km west of centre. Bits of this tower house date to the 16th century, in sharp contrast to shiny leisure facilities (including nice pool) which attracts local patronage. 4-posters in some rooms, blazing fires and 2 restaurants (main has 3 dining areas and 2 AA rosettes), all in extensive (20 acres) greenery. Only quite posh hotel in barren hinterland of West Lothian. Stuffed with farmers during Royal Highland Show week.

136 10/P25
215 ROOMS
TEL · TV
NO PETS
£85+

Marriott Dalmahoy www.marriottdalmahoy.co.uk · **0131 333 1845** · **Kirknewton** On A71 (Kilmarnock road) on edge of town – bypass 5km, 15km west of centre, airport 6km. Georgian house with distinctive rooms and big modern annexe (6 turret suites best). Two internationally rated courses make this a golfing mecca. Plenty of other sports facilities to while away the hours or improve your handicaps generally include pool, tennis and 'Long Weekend' brasserie and more formal 'Pentland Restaurant'. Good corporate choice.

Open Arms Dirleton Report: 912/LOTHIANS.

Tweedale Arms Gifford Report: 917/LOTHIANS.

The Best Fine-Dining Restaurants

137 1/XE1
£32+

✓ ✓+ **Martin Wishart** www.martin-wishart.co.uk · 0131 553 3557 · **54 The Shore** Discreet waterside frontage for Edinburgh's most notable foody experience and the standard by which other fine-dining menus in Edinburgh and Glasgow can be judged. Room designed on simple lines; uncompli-cated menu and wine list (but no cheap plonk). 2-Michelin-star chef Martin and a clutch of awards raise expectation, but preparation, cooking and presentation are demonstrably a cut above the rest. Martin just has that touch that we don't have, that brings a smile as well as saliva to the lips when the plate appears. Great vegetarian menu. Unobtrusive service. No nonsense, only the best meal in town. *Good Food Guide* Scottish Restaurant of the Year '06. MW gets one of 2 ticks plus in this book – in the UK frontrunners. Lunch Tue-Fri, Dinner Tue-Sat. LO 9.30pm

138 1/B4
£32+

✓ ✓ **The Atrium** www.atriumrestaurant.co.uk · 0131 228 8882 · **Cambridge Street** Foyer of the Traverse Theatre (491/CULTURE), Lothian Rd. Longest-standing on this page, Andrew and Lisa Radford's effortlessly stylish restaurant is still the best non-fussy or -fussed-over food in town. Michelin Bib Gourmand chef Neil Forbes has a confident and magic touch but is generally underrated I say: food, wine, service always excel and a mellow ambience that gently accommodates both business and romance. A la carte, menu du jour and a tasting menu to choose from. Often easier to get a table here than the more glam foody locations. After all these years I'd still rate the Atrium as Edinburgh's all-round best bet for food to love. Lunch Mon-Fri. Dinner LO 10pm. Closed Sun.

139 10/R25
£32+

✓ ✓ **La Potinière, Gullane** www.la-potiniere.co.uk · 01620 843214 Not in town, but worth the 45-minute drive to this douce golfing village on East Lothian coast. This restaurant has a remarkable pedigree (once the best restaurant in southern Scotland; see Pioneers, p. 24), re-opened 2003 by Keith Marley and Mary Runciman and now La Pot is right up there again. The single small room is not big on atmosphere or smart decor; it's the food that matters. Simple 2-choice menu and short, exemplary wine list. Flair and integrity with market and seasonal best ingredients and quietly efficient presentation. 4 courses with amuse bouche and pre-dessert for £38 (at TGP) is great fine-dining value. Wed-Sun, lunch & dinner.

140 1/B4
£32+

✓ **Abstract** 0131 229 1222 · **33 Castle Terrace** Near Usher Hall and Traverse Theatre. Rare event of a notable Scottish restaurant moving to, rather than from Edinburgh. Abstract was the upmarket but hapless place in Inverness that Gordon Ramsay thought too condescending and fussy for the locals. With owner Barry Lawson's determination, Abstract continues in the north and this shiny, smart cousin opened to very good reviews early '07. Chef Loic Lefebvre left shortly after but most of the team remains and this is now established as an impressive foodie destination. A la carte and tasting menus. Lunch & LO 9.30pm. Closed Sun.

141 1/XE1
£32+

✓ **The Kitchin** www.thekitchin.com · 0131 555 1755 · **78 Commercial Quay, Leith** In the row of restaurants facing the Scottish Government offices. Shock, horror! Only one tick for Edinburgh's most lauded new restaurant in years. Tom Kitchin's slickly run and presented restaurant got everyone's attention including Michelin when it opened '06. Maybe expectation has been built too high, in which case glad to oblige, but I can't see how it's so mind-blowingly better than others of this ilk. But it is very good: ingredients are top, cooking first class and service taken seriously but friendly. And relatively good value. It just isn't orgasmic... enough. Lunch & dinner. LO 9pm. Closed Mon.

142 1/D4
£32+

✓ **The Tower** www.tower-restaurant.co.uk · 0131 225 3003 · **Chambers Street** At George IV Bridge above the Museum of Scotland. Restaurant supremo James Thomson's celebrated and celebrity-strewn restaurant atop the distinctive 'tower' on the corner of the sandstone museum building (benefits from the much-admired grand design and detail of Gordon Benson's architectural vision). It feels that it could be anywhere, except you're looking over Edinburgh rooftops and the castle skyline (in summer, the terrace is top). Great private dining room in the tower itself. Kitchens far below in Prehistoric Scotland, but food everything one would expect – Scottish slant on modern British. The steaks are great. Best to book. Lunch & dinner LO 11pm. 7 days.

143 1/C4
£32+

✓ **The Witchery** www.thewitchery.com · 0131 225 5613 · **Castlehill** At the top of the Royal Mile where the tourists come, many will be unaware that this is one of the city's best restaurants and certainly its most stylishly atmospheric. 2 salons, the upper more 'witchery'; in the 'secret garden' downstairs, a converted school playground, James Thomson has created a more spacious ambience for the (same) elegant Scottish menu. Locals on a treat, many regulars and visiting celebs pack this place out (although they do turn round the tables), so must book. The new Witchery Apartments encapsulate this remarkable ambience (104/LODGINGS). The wine list is exceptional. Lunch and dinner. LO a very civilised 11.30pm. See 307/LATE-NIGHT RESTAURANTS.

144 1/XE5
£32+

✓ **Rhubarb @ Prestonfield** www.prestonfield.com · 0131 668 3346 The restaurant of fabulous Prestonfield (78/HOTELS) and 1, 2, 3 in a row of great restaurants for James Thomson (see above). And as above it's the whole dining experience rather than Michelin-minded menus that drives their success. Rhubarb the most gorgeously decadent; the public rooms adjacent for before and après are *sans pareil*, especially the upstairs drawing rooms. An evening of rich romance awaits. The Rhubarb desserts leave a silky aftertaste.

145 1/B3
£32+

✓ **Oloroso** www.oloroso.co.uk · 0131 226 7614 · **33 Castle Street** Unassuming entrance and lift to this rooftop restaurant renowned for its terrace with views of the castle, the New Town and Fife. Bar snacks are a great deal – can't go wrong with 'curry of the day'. Chef/prop Tony Singh excels especially with the meatier dishes and in the main dining room light and spacious and spilling on to the terrace, steaks are rightly popular though there are many imaginative dishes with food and fish. After a few years now this is still a fashionable, foody room at the top. Excellent cocktail bar. Lunch & dinner LO 10pm. 7 days. Bar till 1am.

146 1/D3
£32+

✓ **Number One Princes Street** www.thebalmoralhotel.com · 0131 556 2414 Address with a certain ring for the principal restaurant of the Balmoral Hotel (79/BEST HOTELS) entered through lobby or off street. Opulent subterranean salons have ample space around the tables, but the lighting and lacquering do little to cosify the ritziness (and like many hotel restaurants it's often not busy or buzzy – this is good to remember when other top restaurants may be full). Michelin starred since 2003, Jeff Bland is executive chef, Craig Sandle on the pans; creation and presentation rarely fail to please. Attentive service. **Hadrian's Brasserie,** a pastel lounge at street level (grills and light choices among the mains), complements well. Closed Sat/Sun lunch. LO 9.45pm.

147 1/C2
£32+

✓ **Fisher's In The City** www.fishersbistros.co.uk · 0131 225 5109 · **58 Thistle Street** Uptown version of one of Leith's longest best eateries (222/SEAFOOD); this place works on all its levels (we're talking mezzanine). Fisher fan staples ('favourites') all here – the fishcakes, the soup and the blackboard specials, excellent wine list combined with great service. Some vegetarian and meat (steaks a special). Open all day (reduced menu late afternoon). Signature Dish: fishcakes of course, and soup! 7 days. LO 10.30pm.

148 1/D2
£22-32+
✓ **Forth Floor, Harvey Nichols** www.harveynichols.com · 0131 524 8350 · **St Andrews Square** On the fourth floor (through deli and furnishings and HN souvenirs) and you see the Forth from the balcony (superb outside dining on rare summer days, though somewhat in a row). Store and restaurant for ladies who lunch and the chic supper still Ab Fab crowd; the food and service reliably spot-on. You can partake of cheaper brasserie or more expensive (but similar) Modern British comfort-food menus either side of the glass partition – dearer dining gets the view. Not as Ab Fab as once was but close enough. Lunch 7 days, dinner Tue-Sat LO 10.30pm

149 1/D3
£32+
Vermillion www.thescotsmanhotel.co.uk · 0131 622 2814 · **North Bridge** The fine dining room of the urbane Scotsman Hotel (87/INDIVIDUAL HOTELS), deep in the baronial bowels of the building on North Bridge. Informal and intimate; no natural light so best for dinner à deux or a special night out. Somebody said it feels like being in a Jack Vettriano painting. Ghastly thought! Innovative if self-conscious foody menu. Check for (classic) movie evenings combining dinner and the screening room. Dinner only. LO 9.45pm. Wed-Sun.

150 1/B3
£32+
Circus Wine Bar & Grill www.circuswinebarandgrill.co.uk · 0131 226 6743 · **58 North Castle Street** On the site of a longstanding Edinburgh institution – Cosmo's, now with a complete overhaul and change of focus but still formal, very grown-up and somewhat stolid. Great service enhances the sombre surroundings. Good Scottish beef dominates the menu with other Scottish-sourced meats and their accompaniments. Food tends towards rich as do the clientele. Spiffy desserts. Lunch Mon-Fri. Dinner LO 9.30pm. Closed Sun.

151 1/XE1
£32+
Plumed Horse 0131 554 5556 · **50 Henderson Street** In a backstreet location between Great Junction St and the Shore, this '07 opening was always going to be tough for Michelin-starred chef Tony Borthwick who moved here from faraway Dumfriesshire. Critics panned it at first, then a few came round. There's no doubt he's still an inspired chef, but somehow the surroundings dampen the appetite (my friend said they felt like a B&B in the Dalkeith Rd). Nevertheless this restaurant is excellent value for the fine standard of cooking. A foodies' choice. Lunch & LO 9pm. Tue-Sat.

✓✓ **Champany's** 01506 834532 · **near Linlithgow** 22km from town. Report: 272/BURGERS & STEAKS.

✓✓ **The Wee Restaurant** 01383 616263 · **North Queensferry** Just over the Forth Road Bridge, 20km from town. Report: 943/FIFE RESTAURANTS.

✓✓ **The Dakota** 0870 423 4293 · **South Queensferry** The restaurant of the Dakotas, superior roadhouse hotel. Report: 130/HOTELS OUTSIDE TOWN.

✓ **Roti** 0131 221 9998 · **73 Morrison Street** They say 'not an Indian restaurant' but, well... it is. By Tony Singh who presides over Oloroso (above). And probably the best in town. Report: 250/BEST INDIAN.

✓ **Dusit** 0131 220 6846 · **49 Thistle Street** Indisputably top in a townful of Thais. Report: 261/BEST THAI.

The Best Bistros & Brasseries

152 1/XE1
£22-32
✓ ✓ **Skippers** www.skippers.co.uk · 0131 554 1018 · **1a Dock Place** In a corner of Leith off Commercial Road by the docks. Look for Waterfront (173/GASTROPUBS) and bear left into adjacent cul-de-sac. The pioneer restaurant in Leith before it was a restaurant quarter. Considered the best bistro in town by loyal clientele. Very fishy (1 vegan, 1 meat dish), very quayside intimate and friendly. Menu changes daily. Excellent apt wine list. Lunch & dinner 7 days, LO 10pm.

153 1/XA4
£15-22
✓ **First Coast** www.first-coast.co.uk · 0131 313 4404 · **99 Dalry Road** Named after a place in the far north where brothers Hector and Alan McRae used to go their holidays, this is a very grown-up and urban restaurant for 2 Highland lads. Food here is superb value and full of integrity. They wanted to make it irresistible and impossible not to come back and they did! Straight-talking menu with no bamboozling choices. A wee triumph! Mon-Sat Lunch & LO 10.30pm.

154 1/C2
£15-22
ECO
✓ **Urban Angel** www.urban-angel.co.uk · 0131 225 6215 · **121 Hanover Street** In a basement near Queen St (a long time ago the legendary Laigh, one of Edinburgh's original coffee shops). Contemporary, relaxed, great value and pressing all the integrity buttons. Organic where sensible and free trade (lots). Food wholesome British but with a light touch. Takeaway counter and great Sun brunch rendezvous (318/SUNDAY BREAKFAST). Award-winning, informal, immensely popular so best to book for supper. 7 days lunch & dinner. LO 10pm (Sun 5pm).

155 1/XE5
£15-22
✓ **Home Bistro** 0131 667 7010 · **41 West Nicolson Street** Comfort food heaven in tiny and, yes, homely bistro on South Side near University. Rowland Thomson and Richard Logan's formula of simple, reassuring modern and traditional British grub. Home-made everything. Beginning to win the recognition it deserves; you may have to book. Great value and precious simplicity. Lunch Mon-Fri, dinner Tue-Sat.

156 1/B4
£15-22
✓ **blue bar café** www.bluescotland.co.uk · 0131 221 1222 · **Cambridge Street** Upstairs in Traverse Theatre building. From the makers of The Atrium (138/BEST RESTAURANTS), a lighter, more informal menu. Went from blue to brown in 2007 but remains cool and fresh. Still the best drop-in diner in town; especially convenient for West End entertainments. The menu changes every 6 weeks and is mix 'n' match with 'light blue' snackier options. Sound levels high; people do talk. 12noon-3pm, 6pm-10.30pm daily. Bar to midnight (1am Sat). Closed Sun.

157 1/XB5
£15-22
✓ **The Apartment** 0131 228 6456 · **7 Barclay Place** The first of Malcolm Innes's hugely popular contemporary eating-out experiences (see Outsider, below, and more doubtless, to come), now a Bruntsfield food fixture. Big helpings of chunky, healthy food, famously good salads. Refurbished '07, the art cooler and more minimal than ever. 7 days dinner; LO 11pm. Lunch Sat/Sun only. Best to book.

158 1/D4
£15-22
✓ **The Outsider** 0131 226 3131 · **15 George IV Bridge** The downtown dining room of the Apartment (above). Malcolm Innes, the notoriously rude owner, once again created a sexy, contemporary and inexpensive restaurant which is always full. Minimalist design with surprising view of the castle. Innovative contrasts in the menu. Big helpings. We love it, Malcolm! 7 days, lunch & LO 10.30pm.

159 1/D4
£15-22
✓ **Herbe Bistro** 0131 226 3269 · **44 George IV Bridge** The restaurant is in basement where many come a cropper but Herbe's just works! Nothing is remarkable but people love this place and invariably return. Spacious, calm interior. Food contemporary, spot-on and excellent value. Lunch & LO 9.45pm. Closed Sun.

160 1/D3
£22-32
✓ **North Bridge** www.thescotsmanhotel.co.uk · 0131 622 2900 · **20 North Bridge** The brasserie of the Scotsman Hotel (87/INDIVIDUAL HOTELS) with separate entrance directly on to main road. Formerly the foyer and public counter of the *Scotsman* newspaper converted into excellent bar/brasserie. Surrounding balcony reached by rather intrusive metal staircase, but overall very sympathetic ambience for exemplary brasserie-type menu with seasonal variations; emphasis on North British, ie Scottish, ingredients. Toilets are a find when you find them. 7 days, all day LO 10pm/10.30pm. Bar midnight.

161 1/XB5
1/C4
£15-22
✓ **Howie's** www.howies.uk.com · 0131 221 1777 · **208 Bruntsfield Place** On the way to Morningside; also at 10 Victoria Street (0131 225 1721). One of the best in this street of many bistros. Both flagship outposts in Howie's urban village chain which serve the locals, but are worth coming across the city for. Unpretentious, inexpensive, contemporary Scottish food. Great value lunches. Also:

162 1/D3
1/A3
£15-22
✓ **Howie's Waterloo** www.howies.uk.com · 0131 556 5766 · **29 Waterloo Place** 200m from Princes St in a beautiful lofty room; and **Howie's West End** 1 Alva Street (0131 225 9594). Like both the above, Howie has taken over locations that haven't worked for others. His good value, contemporary food with some flair and no-fuss formula will doubtless prevail. All open 7 days. Great value lunch and dinner. Can BYOB; £3 corkage. Monthly changing menu in Alva St. LO 9.45pm.

163 1/XB5
£22-32
✓ **Sweet Melinda's** www.sweetmelindas.com · 0131 229 7953 · **11 Roseneath Street** In deepest Marchmont, a single not large room with nice pics on street, catering very much for the neighbourhood clientele but famous across the city. Mainly fish (from estimable Eddie's across the road), but 1 meat and 1 vegetarian. Home-made bread; everything made from scratch. Great touches, good wines and fizz. Lunch & LO 10pm. Not Mon lunch; closed Sun.

164 10/P26
£22-32
✓ **Shapes** 0131 453 2666 · **Bankhead Avenue, Sighthill** On edge of city in highly unlikely setting of an industrial estate. But this is home to Shapes furniture and auctioneers; this 100-capacity restaurant was formerly a work's canteen. Now it's more like a top showroom: the floor is Italian marble, there's darkwood and gilt and opulence wherever you look. Food's not bad either in an extensive menu and the wine list is a revelation. All down to le patron: Mr Ally Black. Mon-Fri 9am-5pm. Dinner Fri/Sat – 'Members only'.

165 1/XE5
£15-22
Blonde www.blonderestaurant.com · 0131 668 2917 · **75 St Leonard's Street** Tucked away in the South Side, you have to be good to survive here. This certainly has: a neighbourhood restaurant relaxed, inexpensive and simply good. Handily near Queens Hall and Pleasance (in Fringe time). Pale wood, spartan ie blonde rooms and easy-eat food with quaffable wine (several house wines under £12). Andy Macgregor still chefs like Jamie O. Lunch (not Mon) & LO 10pm. 7 days.

166 1/A1
£15-22
Stockbridge Restaurant 0131 226 6766 · **54 St Stephen Street** Oddly I never had this restaurant in *StB* when my new friend Juliette established it a few years ago but she set it up well and (apparently) it's hardly changed. One of the New Town's reliable bistros, with carefully sourced ingredients served in generous portions of classic Modern British dishes. Intimate, so good à deux. Often 'offers', eg BYOB on Wed (£2 corkage). Lunch Wed-Fri, dinner Tue-Sun. Lo 9.30pm.

167 1/B2
ECO
Iglu 0131 476 5333 · **2b Jamaica Street** Tiny upstairs bistro of Iglu, the New Town bar (410/COOL BARS). Organic approach to ingredients. Scottish/local and quite meaty menu. Nice accompaniments include sourdough bread. You fit in tight. Book at weekends. Lunch Fri-Sun, dinner 7 days. LO 10pm, bar 1am.

Gastropubs

It's a ghastly word, but coined with reference to places like The Eagle or The Well in London's East End, the Gastropub at least conveys the nature of those food destinations which are more pub than restaurant or café-bar. The implication is that you can drink without eating. Many of these Edinburgh examples are indeed exemplary and were here long before the word was invented.

168 1/XB5
£15-22
✓✓ **The Canny Man** 0131 447 1484 · **237 Morningside Road** Aka The Volunteer Arms on the A702 via Tollcross, 7km from centre. Idiosyncratic renowned eaterie with a certain hauteur and a true, original 'gastropub'. Carries a complement of malts as long as your arm and a serious wine list. Excellent smorrebrod lunches (12noon-3pm) and evens 6.30-9.30pm. Salads and desserts with Luca's ice-cream (and alcohol). No loonies or undesirables are welcome nor mobile phones, cameras or backpackers. A grumpy but civilised pub; a labyrinth of good dining and taste. Till 11pm Sun-Thu, 1am Fri, 12midnight Sat. 374/REAL-ALE PUBS.

169 1/XB5
£15-22
✓✓ **The New Bell** www.thenewbell.com · 0131 668 2868 · **233 Causewayside** Way down Causewayside in the South Side, the New Bell is upstairs from the Old Bell; you may walk through the pub to find it. And it is a find! Woody, warm pubby atmosphere, nice rugs etc. Richard and Michelle Heller have got the room and the Modern British menu just right. Food and very decent vino well-priced for the quality and the smart delivery. Excellent steaks and puds. Sun lunch. Dinner only Tue-Sun. LO 10.30pm.

170 1/XE1
£22-32
✓ **The Shore** www.theshore.biz · 0131 553 5080 · **3 The Shore, Leith** Long established as a 'gastropub'; an *StB* favourite. Bar (often with live light folk or jazz) where you can eat from the same menu as the dining room/ restaurant. Real fire and large windows looking out to the quayside – strewn with bods on warm summer nights. Food, listed on a blackboard, changes daily but is consistently good. Lots of fish, some meat, some vegetarian. 7 days lunch & LO 10pm, bar till 12.

171 1/XE1
£15-22
✓ **King's Wark** 0131 554 9260 · **36 The Shore** On the corner of Bernard St. Woody, candlelit, comfortable – a classic gastropub, ie the emphasis on food. Bar and bistro dining room. Pub-food classics and more adventurous even menu. Though traditional and dark rather than pale, light and modern, this has long been one of the best bets in Leith. Scottish slant on the menu, with excellent fish including beer batter and chips. Lunch & LO 10pm. Bar open to 11pm, 12midnight Fri-Sat.

172 1/XA5
£15-22
✓ **Caley Sample Room** www.thecaleysampleroom.co.uk · **58 Angle Park Terrace** The CSR sells all the expected Caledonian real ales from nearby brewery and a couple of guests besides. But '07 taken over by the people who have the Cambridge Bar (below) and Wannaburger (276/BURGERS) so the food offering has entered a different league – great burgers and steaks but full menu with daily specials. Nice, woody ambience in summer but more individual than an All Bar One. Loadsa wine by the glass. Out-of-the-way location but worth the visit. 7 days LO 9pm, 10pm Fri/Sat. Bar much later.

173 1/XE1
£22-32
✓ **The Waterfront** www.waterfrontwinebar.co.uk · 0131 554 7427 · **1c Dock Place** Long-established wine bar in this foody corner of the waterfront now joined (and spilling out at the quayside) to Skippers (152/BISTROS). The conservatory overlooks the backwater dock. It's *the* place to head in summer, but the warren of rooms is cosy in winter. Food has wavered a bit over the years but

very good under Skippers especially for fish and puds and of course, wine (20 to choose, by the glass). Site, setting and great friendly service are mostly what you come for. 7 days, Lunch & LO 9.30/10pm. Bar 12midnight.

174 1/B3 ✓ **Cambridge Bar** www.thecambridgebar.co.uk · 0131 226 2120 ·
£15-22 **20 Young Street** On the west extension of Thistle St. Discreet doorway to Edinburgh institution. Sporty in a rugger kind of way and most recently notable for its gastroburgers, thought by many to be the best in town. Huge in size and huge choice including vegetarian (bean burgers); Mackies estimable ice-cream to follow. Sadly only a handful of tables but same folk (and same menu) have Wannaburger (276/BURGERS). Food 12noon-8.45pm. Bar 11pm/12midnight & 1am Fri/Sat.

175 1/A3 **indigo (yard)** www.indigoyardedinburgh.co.uk · 0131 220 5603 ·
£15-22 **7 Charlotte Lane** Food in bar area and in restaurant upstairs in converted and glazed-over yard behind the West End. Enormously popular, always buzzing and noisy later (you may not hear your wine pop nor your coin drop in the condom machine). Earlier therefore better for food. Contemporary comfort food better than café-bar standard. 7 days from 9am. Food all day LO 10pm. Bar till 1am (406/COOL BARS). Small terrace opposite looks like it should belong to Pizza Express.

176 1/XB5 **Montpeliers** www.montpeliersedinburgh.co.uk · 0131 229 3115 ·
£15-22 **159 Bruntsfield Place** They call it 'Montpelliers of Bruntsfield' and it is almost an institution now south of the Meadows. Same ownership as above and similar buzz and noise levels, but more accent on food. From breakfast menu to late supper, they've thought of everything. All the contemporary faves. Gets very busy. 7 days 9am-10pm. LO 10pm. Bar till 1am.

177 1/B2 **Rick's** www.ricksedinburgh.co.uk · 0131 622 7800 · **55a Frederick Street**
£22-32 Basement bar/restaurant of Rick's Hotel (101/INDIVIDUAL HOTELS) by same people as indigo (yard), Montpeliers (above), Opal Lounge and Tigerlily (86/INDIVIDUAL HOTELS). Drinking is the main activity here but they do have a well thought-out café-bar-type menu. Later on probably too noisy to enjoy food, so choose time and table carefully. Up-for-it crowd enjoy champagne, cocktails and shouting. 7 days all day. LO 10pm (11pm weekends). Bar 1am. Also open for breakfast from 7am.

178 1/D3 **The Doric** www.thedoric.co.uk · 0131 225 1084 · **15 Market Street** A classic
£22-32 howff opposite the Fruitmarket Gallery and the back entrance to Waverley Station. Upstairs boho bistro. Only locals know that this is quintessential Edinburgh and though the food is neither remarkable nor cheap, we must still climb those creaking stairs from time to time for a civilised supper and a very excellent bottle of vino. Simpler bar menu upstairs and down. Changing hands at TGP. 7 days (not Sun in winter), lunch & LO 10pm. Bar 12midnight/1am.

OUTSIDE TOWN

179 10/R26 **Garvald Inn** 01620 830311 · **Garvald** About 35km east of city via A1 to
£15-22 Haddington then B6369 to Gifford and follow signs. Old pub in charming village – all just as you want it to be. Taken over as best pub food in the country with the demise of The Drover's and The Waterside. Reliable, gastropub grub. Same menu in bar and dining room. Alfresco terrace. Lunch & dinner. Closed Mon.

The Best French Restaurants

180 1/D3
£22-32
✓ **La Garrigue** www.lagarrigue.co.uk · 0131 557 3032 · 31 Jeffrey Street
Airy yet intimate restaurant near Royal Mile. Chef/prop Jean Michel Ganffre brings the south of France to your plate. Simple food with flair and unusual touches. Veggies may flounder between the langoustines and les lapins but meat eaters and gourmet diners say *Vive La France*. Mon-Sat lunch & LO 10pm

181 1/B2
£15-22
✓ **Café Marlayne** 0131 226 2230 · 76 Thistle Street The third in the triumvirate of excellent and authentic French eateries within 100m of another (Café St-Honoré, La P'tite Folie; both below), this is a wee gem (we do mean wee). Personal, intimate and very very French. Food generally fab (though not great for veggies). Isla Fraser's in the kitchen. This really is like a place you find in rural France on your hols. We love that key lime pie. Lunch & LO 10pm.

182 1/D4
£15-22
✓ **(The New) Café Marlayne** 0131 225 3838 · Old Fishmarket Close Off 190 High St just below the cathedral. Newer, smarter Café Marlayne with same formula and authentic, homely French cooking (Isla's brother Jeff on the stove). Slim outside terrace in summer. Good value. Lunch & LO 10pm. Closed Sun/Mon.

183 1/B2
£32+
✓ **Café Saint-Honoré** www.icscotland.co.uk/café-sthonore · 0131 226 2211 · 34 Thistle Street Lane Between Frederick and Hanover Sts. Suits aplenty, New Town regulars and occasional lunching ladies part of a big following for this shiny bistro-cum-restaurant which oozes and even smells like Paris. Go on a rainy day when it feels especially warm and sweet and comforting. Lunch Mon-Fri, LO 10pm. Veggies phone ahead.

184 1/C4
1/A3
£15-22
✓ **Petit Paris** www.petitparis-restaurant.co.uk · 0131 226 2442 · 40 Grassmarket & corner of Queensferry & Alva Streets · 0131 226 1890 On busy north side of street below castle, teeming on weekend nights – get an outside table and watch: this could be Montmartre apart from the general inebriation and bad behaviour. Good atmosphere and value with très typical menu. BYOB (not weekends). 7 days lunch and LO late. Newer West End branch upstairs, slightly less ambient but still 'le respect de la tradition Française'. Closed Sun/Mon in winter. Both of these places may need to be booked ahead.

185 1/XE1
£15-22
✓ **Daniel's** www.daniels-bistro.co.uk · 0131 553 5933 · 88 Commercial Quay Versatile, hard-working (open all day) café, takeaway and bistro. Main eaterie is housed in conservatory at back of old bonded warehouse off Dock Pl in Leith's 'restaurant row'. Clean lines, modern look and very popular. Offers contemporary French menu from breakfast to brasserie staples with Alsace and external influences that pack us in especially for tarte flambé and casseroles (207/PIZZAS). Also tables by the water 7 days, 10am-10pm.

186 1/XD1
£32+
Duck's at Le Marche Noir www.ducks.co.uk · 0131 558 1608 · 2-4 Eyre Place Malcolm Duck's bistro at the lower end of the very residential New Town is still one of the most reliable French meals in town. Not the most fun night out you'll have on this page, but has a loyal if conservative clientele. A great value wine list le patron clearly enjoys. Dinner 7 days, lunch Tue-Fri. LO 10/10.30pm (earlier Sun).

187 **1/XB5**
£15-22

Jacques **0131 229 6080 · 8 Gillespie Place, Bruntsfield** Endearing French staff and atmosphere. Hard-working eaterie close to the King's Theatre. Innovative variations on the classics. Deals through evening mean eating here is great value. Excellent affordable French wine list. Great steak frites, especially the frites, and crepes. Lunch (not Sun) LO 11pm.

188 **1/C4**
1/E4
£15-22

Maison Bleue **www.grassmarket.net/featured/maison_bleue.htm ·** **0131 226 1900 · 36 Victoria Street** Cosy, very Edinburgh café-bistro with a similar convivial ambiance. French and North African mezze approach, building a meal from smallish dishes they call bouchées. 7 days lunch & LO 10pm/11pm weekends.

189 **1/B2**
1/A3
£15-22

La P'tite Folie **www.laptitefolie.co.uk · 0131 225 7983 · 61 Frederick Street & Randolph Place** Best word for it: unpretentious. Mismatched furniture, inexpensive French *plat du jour*. Relaxed dining in single New Town room or the Tudoresque 'maison' in West End cul de sac. Cheap lunch. 7 days. LO 10pm (10.45pm weekends). Closed Sun lunch & all day Sun in West End.

 Restaurant Martin Wishart **54 The Shore** Report: 137/BEST RESTAURANTS.

The Best Italian Restaurants

190 1/XA4
£15-22
✓ **La Bruschetta** www.labruschetta.co.uk · 0131 467 7464 · **13 Clifton Terrace** Extension of Shandwick Pl opposite Haymarket Station. Giovanni Cariello's Italian kitchen and tiny dining room in the West End. A modest restorante with impeccable pedigree and a big following – so must book. The space does not cramp their style nor the excellent service. Lunch & LO 10.30pm. Closed Sun/Mon.

191 1/E1
£22-32
✓ **Valvona & Crolla** www.valvonacrolla.co.uk · 0131 556 6066 · **19 Elm Row** An Alexander McCall Smith kind of café at the back of the legendary deli, and with all the flair and attention to detail that you would expect. First-class ingredients, produce shipped in from Italy (fresh veg from Milan markets) and great Italian domestic cooking. One of the best and healthiest breakfasts in town, fabuloso lunch and afternoon tea. Can BYOB from shop (£6 corkage). Mon-Sat 8am-5pm, Sun 10.30am-4.30pm.

192 1/B3
£15-22
✓ **Centrotre** www.centotre.com · 0131 225 1550 · **103 George Street** Fabulous conversion of lofty, pillared Georgian room towards west end of the street by former Valvona & Crolla stalwarts Victor and Carina Contini into the most stylish Italian joint in town. Passion for food and good service always evident: ubiquitous (though they've now got **Zanzero** below, to deal with too) and never letting it slip. Bar and central pizza oven, unexpected combos in a straightforward menu. 8am till LO 10pm (10.30pm Fri/Sat), 11am-5pm Sun. Bar open later.

193 1/A1
£15-22
✓ **Zanzero** 0131 220 0333 · **15 North West Circus Place** On main road leading from the centre (Frederick and Howe Sts) to Stockbridge, the ubiquitous and unceasing V&C family (see above) have done it again. This contemporary bright and buzzy café/restaurant complements Centrotre and owners Victor and Carina somehow juggle themselves, their family and these two very different menus and rooms and not shred like spaghetti. Healthy, sexy variations on the pasta/pizza theme and lemons everywhere (the spag, the salad, the walls). Can't fail, whatever the upstairs neighbours say. 7 days 8am-11pm.

194 1/D2
£15-22
✓ **Vin Caffe** www.valvonacrolla.co.uk · 0131 557 0088 · **Multrees Walk** In the still not-quite arcadia behind Harvey Nix. Pedigrees don't come better than this, the downtown smart eaterie of the Valvona & Crolla dynasty (see above) so high expectations accompanied its opening in 2004. Café counter downstairs, restaurant above. Interesting pastas, pizzas and other lovely creations. It's always busy downstairs for authentic espresso and fast snacks and up, which can be quite star-studded (we ate with Nigella, Sean goes too), is home to some epic nights. A dolce vita kind of place. 7 days 8am-11pm (12midnight Fri/Sat), Sun 11-6pm.

195 1/A4
£15-32
Santini www.santini-restaurant.com · 0131 221 7788 · **Conference Square** Back of the Sheraton (of which it's a part, below excellent health club). Business-like Italian restaurant and bistro created by Mr Santini himself brought the same clean lines and stylish eating-out experience to London and Milan though now run by the hotel. Waiters and ingredients very Italia. Restaurant dining through the back doesn't work so well, but the bistro on square itself is smart and casual with some staples in a lighter menu. Lunch & dinner LO 10.30pm. Closed Sun.

196 1/XE1
£15-22
La Favorita www.la-favorita.com · 0131 554 2430 · **325 Leith Walk** Down from Vittoria (198/TRATTS) from which this much-heralded offshoot came. The pitch here is gourmet pasta and wood-fired pizza, 'the best in Scotland'. The jury's still out but many swear it's true. Otherwise good Italian cooking and friendly service in contemporary/retro room with windows on the Walk. 7 days 12noon-11pm.

The Trusty Tratts

198 1/E1
1/D4
£15-22

✓✓ **Vittoria www.vittoriarestaurant.com · 0131 556 6171 · Brunswick Street** On the corner of Leith Walk and new in 2007, uptown branch at **19 George IV Bridge** (0131 225 1740). For over 30 years Tony Crolla provided one of the best, least pretentious Scottish-Italian café-restaurants in town. New branch equally full-on, packed out as soon as it opened. Full Italian menu. Outside tables on interesting corner always packed when the sun's out. Pizzeria/ristorante further down the Walk (La Favorita 196/ITALIAN RESTAURANTS). 7 days. 10am-11pm.

199 1/D1
£15-22

✓✓ **Bella Mbriana 0131 558 9581 · 7 East London Street** On the roundabout at the bottom of Broughton St. Chef-proprietor Rosario Sartore left La Partenhope (below) in '06 and to high expectation opened this trattoria/ restorante in the more fashionable East Village in summer '07. Some teething/ventilation problems aside, this homage to Naples with Rosario visibly in charge in the kitchen, was an immediate must-go. Still settling in at TGP, but great Italian food with a southern twist. Nice downstairs bar where you may well wait. Big turn around, but best to book. 7 days 10am-11pm.

200 1/XA4
£15-22

✓ **La Partenhope 0131 347 8880 · 96 Dalry Road** A corner and cucina of Naples halfway up Dalry Rd (about 200m from Haymarket) where the Sartore family created the hottest tratt in town. Chef Paolo Tersigni presides in the kitchen, with daily specials from market produce. Menu as long as the Amalfi coast but fish specials are tops. Even the most basic aglio y olio shows how it should be done. This place can fill up fast so book. 7 days. Lunch Tue-Sat, dinner LO 10.45pm.

201 1/A3
£15-22

✓ **Bar Roma www.bar-roma.co.uk · 0131 226 2977 · 39 Queensferry Street** One of Edinburgh's long-standing fave Italians, revamped so it almost looks like a Pizza Express from the outside. Inside it's massive and always bustling (this includes the menu) with Italian rudeboy waiters as the floor show. We love it! 7 days, all day. LO 11.30pm (later weekends).

202 1/D2
1/XE1
£15-22

✓ **Giuliano's www.giulianos.co.uk · 0131 556 6590 · 18 Union Place** Top of Leith Walk near the main roundabout, opposite Playhouse Theatre. Giuli's has a new Al Fresco restaurant down the street after the takeaway counter but it's the original that's usually heaving with happy punters! It's just pasta and pizza but in a no-nonsense menu that appeals. The food is great, the wine list has some superb moments, the din is loud. Lunch and LO 2am daily – Giuli's is always late 'n' live. **Giuliano's On The Shore** (0131 554 5272) on the corner of the bridge in Leith Central has recently had a makeover but it's the same, reliable tratt menu. Especially good for kids (279/KID-FRIENDLY). Also 7 days, LO 10.30/11pm.

203 1/C2
£15-22

La Lanterna 0131 226 3090 · 83 Hanover Street One of several tratts sub street level in this block, all family-owned. But this gets our vote. For 20 years the Zaino family have produced a straight-down-the-line Italian menu from their open kitchen at the back of their no-frills restaurant. 80% of customers are regulars and wouldn't go anywhere else. Well chosen wines. Lunch & LO 10pm. Closed Sun.

The Best Pizza

204 1/XE1
£15-22
La Favorita www.la-favorita.com · 0131 554 2430 · **325 Leith Walk** They say it's 'the best' and many agree, but Tony – they just ain't thin and crispy enough for me... yet! Report: 196/ITALIAN RESTAURANTS.

205 1/B1
£15 OR LESS
L'Alba D'Oro/Anima 0131 558 2918 · **11 Henderson Row** The takeaway pizza section of the estimable fish 'n' chip shop L'Alba D'Oro next door. Definitely a slice above the rest. 3 sizes (including individual 7") and infinite toppings to go. Not thin but crispy/crunchy. Also pasta, great wine to go, olive oils, Luca's ice cream and fresh OJ. This is no ordinary takeaway (see 334/TAKEAWAY)! 7 days lunch & LO 11pm.

206 1/C4
1/XB5
£15-22
Mamma's www.mammaspizza.co.uk · 0131 225 6464 · **30 Grassmarket & Bruntsfield Road** · 0131 229 7008 Brash, American style. Some alternatives to pizza, eg nachos, but you come to mix 'n' match – haggis, calamari and BBQ sauce and 40 other toppings piled deep and so cheap for a filling meal though not perhaps what it once was. 7 days till 11pm/12midnight.

207 1/XE1
£15-22
Daniel's Bistro www.daniels-bistro.co.uk · 0131 553 5933 · **88 Commercial Street** On 'restaurant row' in Leith. Great for the Tarte Flambé – very like a thin thin pizza made from milk-bread dough topped with onions, crème fraîche and lardons – an Alsace and house speciality. There are other thin pizzas too (185/FRENCH RESTAURANTS). 7 days 10am-10pm.

208 1/E1
£15-22
Jolly's 0131 556 1588 · **9 Elm Row** On the part of Leith Walk near Valvona & Crolla 339/DELIS). Long-established tratt/ristorante well known locally for their thinner-than-usual wood-fired pizza and Vito the waiter. Over 40 varieties. Good family spot. Also takeaway. 7 days. Lunch & LO 10.30pm. Closed Sun lunch.

209 1/XF2
£15-22
Caprice 2 Go 0131 665 2991 · **198 High Street, Musselburgh** The number is for their takeaway joint round the corner which delivers to this eastern suburb of the city and other nearby East Lothian towns. The adjacent restaurant serves the same wood-fired pizza and the usual Italian fare. Ask them to crisp it but pizza here still lighter than most. 7 days LO 10/10.30pm.

The Best Mediterranean Food

210 1/C2
£15-22

✓ **Nargile** www.nargile.co.uk · 0131 225 5755 · **73 Hanover Street** Not so much Mediterranean, most definitely Turkish. This is where to go to mess with the meze. Huge choice of all East of the Med fares from houmous to shashlik with lots for veggies and some fish choice. Tables cramped but this is a night out with the mate(s) kind of place. Buzbag as expected and fair selection of other Turkish and non-Turkish wines. Lunch; LO 10.30pm (11pm Fri/Sat). Closed Sun.

211 1/D1
£15 OR LESS

✓ **Santorini** 0131 557 2012 · **32 Broughton Street** Cheap, charming, authentic – what more could you ask from the only proper Greek restaurant in town. Start with 'mezedes' – small portions to share, then on to moussaka, stews, souvlakis. Some sticky puds. Tue-Sun, 12noon-10.30pm.

212 1/A1
£15-22

✓ **Rafael's** 0131 332 1469 · **2 Deanhaugh Street** Secret subterranean Spanish restaurant in corner of Stockbridge by the bridge. Daily menu as it comes from Rafael Torrubia's tiny kitchen. Simple operation with honest and often sublime homemade food; great fish. A bit of a let down for veggies but great puds. Lunch Thu-Sat; dinner Tue-Sat. LO 9.45pm.

213 1/D3
£22-32

Igg's 0131 557 8184 · **15 Jeffrey Street** Since 1989 this has been a corner of Spain in Scotland near the Royal Mile. Though recently this southern sun may have dimmed, it remains a grown-up restaurant for business or affairs or both. Warm south reflected in the excellent wine list, but food from well-sourced Scottish ingredients more cosmopolitan than merely Med. Some tapas but see Barioja below. Good biz lunch spot. Lunch & LO 10.30pm. Closed Sun.

214 1/XE1
£15-22

Dominico 0131 467 7266 · **30 Sandport Street** Leith's little secret, this tiny restaurant with a loyal following has better food and is better value than most in this quarter. Great pastas and especially fresh fish (big portions). 7 days. Lunch, dinner Mon-Sat LO 10/10.15pm.

216 1/D3
£15-22

Barioja 0131 557 3622 · **19 Jeffrey Street** Next to Igg's (see above), the tapas bar in the basement. Small tables and not much room to move upstairs; more space, less ambience down. Fairly authentic tapas menu – pan con tomate, gambas pil-pil, patatas bravas, but no sideboard or counter full as in San Sebastian; Spanish waiters and vino. 11am-11pm. Closed Sun.

217 1/D1
£15-22

Café Mediterraneo 0131 557 6900 · **73 Broughton Street** Discreet frontage to small, bright rooms on busy Broughton Street. Brazilian owner Davi Bersi keeps it fairly Mediterraneo (though no pasta) with a mean espresso. This café/bistro/restaurant serves many purposes from gorging to grazing. 8am-4pm. Closed Sun.

218 1/D5
£15-22

Phenecia 0131 662 4493 · **55-57 West Nicolson Street** On corner near university. North African Mohammed Sfina's unfussy North African/Spanish eatery with couscous, lots of grilled meats and wide vegetarian choice. A culinary odyssey through the warm south and one of the most eclectic menus in town. Possible to eat very cheaply at lunch time. Goodly portions, though looking perhaps a bit tired these days. Lunch Mon-Sat & LO 10.30pm. They have the Château Musar.

219 1/E4
£15 OR LESS

Empires 0131 466 0100 · **24 St Mary's Street** Cosy, charming, chaotic, this tiny up-and-down restaurant is always an experience – for many: pure Turkish delight. Full of ceramics, rugs and all kinds of people. Usual and unusual meze; great coffee. Good for vegetarians. Service a bit mad but great atmosphere. 7 days 12noon-10pm. Winter closed Mon. BYOB.

220 1/XE5
£15 OR LESS
Hanedan **0131 667 4242** · **42 West Preston Street** Small, friendly, South Side neighbourhood Turkish restaurant. Chef-owner Gursel Bahar a considerate and enthusiastic host. Hot and cold meze to share and shish/kofte/musakka (sic) menu. Short pud and wine lists complement well. Lunch & LO 10pm. Closed Mon.

Café Truva On the Water of Leith, not Med. Report: 305/CAFFS.

The Best Seafood Restaurants

221 1/XE1 ✓ ✓ **Skippers** **www.skippers.co.uk** · **0131 554 1018** · **1a Dock Place, Leith** Bistro with truly maritime atmosphere; mainly seafood (one vegetarian, one meat). Best to book. Many would argue Skippers *is* still the best place to eat seafood in this town. Small, many-chambered with conservatory and outside waterside possibilities. Full report: 152/BEST BISTROS.

222 1/C2
£22-32 ✓ ✓ **Fishers In The City** **www.fishersbistros.co.uk** · **0131 225 5109** · **58 Thistle Street** Separate entry to sister restaurant (below). Bigger and buzzier: people go for uptown meal out kinda thing as well as the seafood. Report: 147/BEST RESTAURANTS.

223 1/XE1
£22-32 ✓ ✓ **Fishers** **www.fishersbistros.co.uk** · **0131 554 5666** · **Corner of The Shore & Tower Street, Leith** Original location, definitely the bistro-best. At the foot of an 18th-century tower opposite Malmaison Hotel and right on the quay (though no boats come by). Seafood cooking with flair and commitment in boat-like surroundings where traditional Scots dishes get an imaginative twist. Hugely popular, some stools around bar and tables outside in summer (can be a windy corner). Often, all are packed. Cheeseboard has some great Brits if you have room for a third course. 7 days. 12noon-10pm.

224 1/D4
£22-32 ✓ ✓ **Creelers** **www.creelers.co.uk** · **0131 220 4447** · **3 Hunter Square** This corner of Arran in the city behind the Tron Church is a short cast from the Royal Mile (tables alfresco in summer). Nice wine list. West Coast out of Campbeltown, and supplies from their own boat and Arran (eg hand-dived) scallops, where they have another restaurant (2425/ARRAN). Chef Martin Collins increasingly confident in the kitchen: those fish served pure, simple and fine. Lunch & LO 10.30/11pm.

225 1/B3
£15-22 ✓ **The Mussel Inn** **www.mussel-inn.com** · **0131 225 5979** · **61 Rose Street** Popular, populist. In the heart of the city centre where parking ain't easy, a great little seafood bistro specialising in mussels and scallops (kings and queens) which the proprietors rear/find themselves. Also catch of the day, some non-fish options and home-made puds. Mon-Thu offer of half kilo of mussels, chips or salad and a drink for £6.95. This formula could travel but the owners have wisely decided not to travel far – they're also in Glasgow (638/SEAFOOD RESTAURANTS). Lunch & dinner. LO 10pm.

226 1/XE1
£22-32 ✓ **The Loch Fyne Restaurant** **www.lochfyne.com** · **0131 559 3900** · **Newhaven** Large seafood emporium in excellent location on Newhaven Harbour where once Harry Ramsden sold, then got, his chips. Latest in UK chain, this at least a little nearer to the original and its oysters (1425/SEAFOOD RESTAURANTS). Great room and very on the waterfront, but not cheap mes amis and a little patchy on delivery. Stick to fish and crisp white wine and you'll be well... fyne. 7 days lunch & LO 10pm (Sun 9pm).

The Best Fish 'n' Chips

227 1/B1
£15 OR LESS
✓ **L'Alba D'Oro Henderson Row** Near corner with Dundas St. Large selection of deep-fried goodies, including many vegetarian savouries. It's a lot more than your usual fry-up – as several plaques on the wall attest (including *StB!*) and the pasta/pizza counter Anima next door is a real winner (205/PIZZAS, 334/TAKEAWAY). Great wine selection, olive oils, Luca's ice cream. Open till 11pm (12midnight weekends); pizza 10pm (11pm weekends).

228 1/D1
£15 OR LESS
✓ **The Rapido 77 Broughton Street** Fine chips. My local so I must be loyal. Popular with late-nighters stumbling back down the hill to the New Town, and the flotsam of the Pink Triangle. Open till 1.30am (3.30am Fri-Sat).

229 1/E2
£15 OR LESS
✓ **The Deep Sea Leith Walk** Opposite Playhouse Theatre. Open late and often has queues but these are quickly dispatched. The haddock has to be 'of a certain size' and is famously fresh (the same supplier for donkeys', perhaps dolphins' years). Traditional menu. Still one of the best fish suppers with which to feed a hangover. Open till 2am (-ish) (3am Fri-Sat).

230 1/D2
£15 OR LESS
Caffe Piccante Broughton Street Takeaway and café with tables on the black 'n' white tiles. Near the Playhouse Theatre, this is the clubbers' chippy with unhealthy lads purveying delicious unhealthy food to the nighthawks, owls and budgerigars. (It's also Irvine Welsh's 'favourite'.) Menu includes deep-fried Mars and chips (you'd need to be well out of it). Open till 2am (3am weekends).

Ye Old Peacock Inn Newhaven Road Report: 281/KID-FRIENDLY
King's Wark 36 The Shore Report: 171/GASTROPUBS.

The Best Vegetarian Restaurants

231 1/E5
£15-22
✓ ✓ **David Bann's www.davidbann.com · 0131 556 5888 · St Mary's Street** Bottom of the street off Royal Mile – a bit off the beaten track, but always a busy restaurant and not only with non-meaters. In fact this is one of the best restaurants in the city: mood lighting, non-moody staff and no dodgy stodge. A creative take on round-the-world dishes. Light meal selection; lovely tartlets and 'parcels'. Vegetarian and vegan and suitably 'organic'. 7 days, lunch & LO 10pm (later weekends)

232 1/E5
£15-22
✓ ✓ **Kalpna www.kalpnarestaurant.com · 0131 667 9890 · 2-3 St Patrick Square** They say 'you do not have to eat meat to be strong and wise' and are they of course right. Maxim taken seriously in this long-established Indian restaurant on the South Side – for 25 years, one of the best vegetarian menus in the UK. Thali gives a good overview. Lovely, light and long may it prevail. Lunch Mon-Sat, dinner Mon-Sat, LO 10.30pm. Report: 251/INDIAN RESTAURANTS.

233 1/E5
£15 OR LESS
✓ **Susie's Diner 0131 667 8729 · 51-53 West Nicolson Street** Cosy, neighbourhood (the university) self-service diner. Nice people behind and in front of the counter. Mexican and Middle-Eastern dishes. Lotsa choice menu includes excellent coffee. Licensed, also BYOB. 9am-9pm. Closed 8pm Sun/Mon.

234 1/C2
£15 OR LESS

✔ **Henderson's** www.hendersonsofedinburgh.co.uk · **0131 225 2131** ·
94 Hanover Street Edinburgh's original and trail-blazing basement
vegetarian self-serve café-cum-wine bar. Canteen seating to the left, candles and
live piano or guitar downstairs to the right. Pine interior is retro-perfect. Happy
wee wine list and organic real ales. Good cheese and some of those mains and
puds will go on forever. 7.30am–10.45pm. Hot food till 10pm. Closed Sun (open
during the Festival). Also has the Farm Shop upstairs with a deli and takeaway and
the more bar-like **Henderson's Bistro** round the corner in Thistle St. Note:
Henderson's (organic) oatcakes are *the* best.

235 1/E5
£15-22

✔ **Ann Purna** 0131 662 1807 · **45 St Patrick Square** Excellent vegetarian
restaurant near Edinburgh University with genuine Gujarati cuisine. Good
atmosphere – old customers are greeted like friends by Mr and Mrs Pandya. Indian
beer, some suitable wines. Lunch Mon-Fri, dinner 7 days, LO 10.30pm. Report:
253/INDIAN RESTAURANTS.

236 1/XE5
£15 OR LESS

✔ **Engine Shed Café** www.engineshed.org.uk · **0131 662 0040** ·
19 St Leonard's Lane Hidden away off St Leonard's St, this is a lunch-
oriented vegetarian café where much of the work is done by adults with learning
difficulties on training placements, so worth supporting. Simple, decent food and
great bread – baked on premises, for sale separately and found all over town. Nice
stopping-off point after a tramp over Arthur's Seat. 10.30am-3pm. Closed Sun.

237 1/D4
£15-22

Black Bo's 0131 557 6136 · **57 Blackfriars Street** Long-established proper
vegetarian restaurant, ie waiter service, foody approach to the food with some
unpredictable often inspired vegetarian ideas and combos. Lots of nuts in the mix.
Intimate and woody, laid-back set-up. Adjacent bar has been cool for years – lots
of nutters in this mix too. Dinner only. LO 9.30/10.30pm. Closed Sun. Bar 1am.

238 1/A3

Cornerstone Café 0131 229 0212 · **Princes Street at Lothian Road**
Underneath St John's Church at the corner. Very central and PC self-service coffee
shop in church vaults. Home-baking and hot dishes at lunchtime. Some seats
outside in summer (in graveyard!) and market stalls during the Festival. One World
Shop adjacent is full of Third World-type crafts and very good for presents. A
respite from the fast-food frenzy of Princes St. Open 9.30am-5pm (later in
Festival). Closed Sun.

239 1/D5
£15 OR LESS

The Forest www.theforest.org.uk · **0131 220 4538** · **3 Bristo Place** Gimme
Shelter campus eaterie. On one hand hippy-dippy and downright dirty; on the
other, refreshingly non-designery retro-sixties chic. Junk furniture, cool notice-
board and people strewn around the room. Decent veggie global menu: food till
10pm. Performance most nights. 7 days, 12noon-late.

240 1/XE1

✔ ✔+ **Restaurant Martin Wishart** 0131 553 3557 · **54 The Shore** Not
remotely a vegetarian restaurant, but does have a special vegetarian
menu. Food, ingredients and presentation are taken seriously here, so this is
where to go for *the* best vegetarian food in Scotland. Report: 137/BEST
RESTAURANTS.

The Best Scottish Restaurants

241 1/D3
£22-32
✓ **Off The Wall** www.off-the-wall.co.uk · 0131 558 1497 · **105 High Street** Not so much off the wall, but in the wall – a doorway off the tartan-and-tat Royal Mile and stairs up to this calm first-floor room. A discreet restaurant often missed by the tourists but not by locals in the know. Short, simple menu with Scottish stalwarts (quality salmon, venison, beef, etc) all nicely concocted with contemporary ingredients and twist: the underrated accomplishments of chef David Anderson. Tue-Sat, lunch & LO 10pm. Closed Sun/Mon.

242 1/D3
£22-32
✓ **Dubh Prais** www.dubhpraisrestaurant.com · 0131 557 5732 · **123b High Street** As above, slap bang (but downstairs) on the Royal Mile opposite the Radisson. Only 9 tables and a miniature galley kitchen from which proprietor/chef James McWilliams and his team produce a remarkably reliable and easy-to-read à la carte menu and specials from sound and sometimes surprising Scottish ingredients. Haggis is panfried, smoked haddock comes with Ayrshire bacon. Athol Brose is as good as it gets. Very regular clientele and lucked-out tourists in this outpost of culinary integrity on the High St. Closed Sun/Mon. Lunch & LO 10.30pm. Pronounced 'Du Prash'.

243 1/C4
£22-32
✓ **The Grain Store** www.grainstore-restaurant.co.uk · 0131 225 7635 · **30 Victoria Street** Long-established reliable repas in interesting street near Royal Mile. Regulars and discriminating tourists climb the stairs for the excellent-value grazing lunch menu or innovative à la carte at night. A laid-back first-floor eaterie in a welcoming stone-walled labyrinth. Good for groups. Perhaps more 'Mod Brit' than simply 'Scottish'. Same set up and same chef have been here al-most 20 years. Ambitious ingredients include roe deer, woodcock along with your usual oysters. They work damned hard! 7 days lunch & LO 10pm (11pm Fri/Sat).

244 1/D1
£22-32
Haldane's www.haldanesrestaurant.com · 0131 556 8407 · **39 Albany Street** Fine dining near Broughton St and probably the best proper meal in the area. Scottish by nature rather than hype. Everything done in a country-house style, though menu unpretentious and room far from sumptuous. We go for the excellent menu of chef Steven Falconer. Lunch & LO 9.30pm. Closed Sun/Mon.

245 1/B4
1/C1
1/E4
£22-32
Stac Polly www.stacpolly.com · 0131 229 5405 · **8a Grindlay Street** Opposite Lyceum Theatre. Dark wood and tartan interior is quietly smart; service, too. Scottish beef, salmon, game well sourced. Haggis filo parcels a house fave. Cheeses come from Iain Mellis. There are others below-stairs at **29-33 Dublin Street** (0131 556 2231) and at **38 St Mary's Street** near the Royal Mile (0131 557 5754). Similar menus and good wine lists. Lunch Mon-Fri. Dinner 7 days LO 10pm.

246 1/B2
1/XA4
£15-22
A Room In The Town www.a.roomin.co.uk/thetown · 0131 225 8204 · **18 Howe Street** Corner of Jamaica St. The room is in the New Town for these lads (Peter Knight and John Tindal) originally from the Highlands and reflects something of that legendary hospitality. So good value, friendly service; you can BYOB (a mere £2 corkage). Mainly Scottish menu with twists. Expect haggis, game, salmon. Their wicked banoffee pie however is as it comes. R in T is routinely packed attesting to its popularity. Best to book. Same folk have **A Room In The West End** (226 1036) in William St with an upstairs bar **Teuchters** (Scottish word for northern, rural folk with no manners – these guys love to be outsiders) and the restaurant downstairs. Similar menu. 7 days lunch & LO 10pm.

✓ **The Witchery** 0131 225 5613 Top restaurant that really couldn't be anywhere else but Scotland. Report: 143/BEST RESTAURANTS.

The Best Mexican Restaurants

247 1/D3
£15-22
✓ **Viva Mexico** www.viva-mexico.co.uk · 0131 226 5145 · **Anchor Close, Cockburn Street** Since 1984 the pre-eminent Mexican bistro in town. Judy Gonzalez's menu still throws in something innovative now and again (chilli lemon cod, prawn with tamarind), although all the expected dishes are here, genuine originals and famously good calamares and fajitas. Lots of seafood. Reliable venue for those times when nothing else fits the mood but sour cream, fajitas and limey lager; nice atmosphere downstairs. Lunch (not Sun) & LO 10.30pm (Sun 10pm).

248 1/F3
£15-22
Pancho Villa's www.panchosvilla.co.uk · 0131 557 4416 · **240 Canongate** A reliable exponent of what we've come to regard as Mexican cooking with nosh of the 'chilada, 'ajita, 'ichanga school. Contemporary décor, decent edibles, happy place for parties and Royal Mile strollers. Lunch Mon-Sat (Fri/Sat 12noon onwards) & dinner 7 days.

The Best Japanese Restaurants

249 1/E5
£15-22
✓ **Bonsai** www.bonsaibarbistro.co.uk · 0131 668 3847 · **4 West Richmond Street** On discreet street on South Side, a Jap café/bistro (good to graze) where Andrew and Noriko Ramage show a deft hand in the kitchen. Freshly made sushi/yakitori and teppanyaki. No conveyor belt in sight, just superb value in neighbourhood café setting. Teriyaki steaks, salads and crème brûlée – actually, great crème brûlée (and banana tempura)! 7 days 12noon-10pm (not Sun lunch). Can BYOB (£5).

The Best Indian Restaurants

250 1/B3
£22-32
✓✓ **Roti** www.roti.uk.com · 0131 221 9998 · **73 Morrison Street** Near Conference Centre, in a corner by Scottish Widows building. Roti moved here '07 from an even more discreet Rose St Lane location, a tiny space where decor didn't matter too much to this larger contemporary space where it does and is slightly lacking. Food though is a different matter under chef/owner Tony Singh who also has Oloroso (145/BEST RESTAURANTS) and man on the stoves, Segal. They say this is 'not an Indian restaurant' but their magic combos of flavours and lots of lightness makes for an ethnic cuisine at its best. Tue-Sat, dinner only LO 11pm.

251 1/E5
£15-22
✓✓ **Kalpna** www.kalpnarestaurant.com · 0131 667 9890 · **St Patrick Square** The original Edinburgh Indian veggie restaurant and still the business. Lighter, fluffier and not as attritional as so many tandooris. Some unique dishes. Gujarati menu. Report: 232/VEGETARIAN RESTAURANTS.

252 1/C4
£15-22
✓ **Khushi's** www.khushis.com · 0131 220 0057 · **9 Victoria Street** An Edinburgh institution for 50 years, having moved from a modest café location to a smarter site near the University and now to this grand room upstairs in Victoria St. Chandeliers dominate the dark, 2-tier interior, rich sauces the food. Having come full circle from basic to Bollywood just like India has, this is an authentic-meal-out kind of place. No alcohol. BYOB (no corkage). 7 days noon-11pm (Sun till 10pm).

253 1/E5
£15-22
✓ **Ann Purna** 0131 662 1807 · **45 St Patrick Square** Friendly and family-run Gujarati veggie restaurant with seriously value-for-money business lunch and lovely harmonious food at all times. Report: 235/VEGETARIAN RESTAURANTS.

254 1/D5
£15 OR LESS

✓ **Kebab Mahal** www.kebab-mahal.co.uk · 0131 667 5214 · **7 Nicolson Square** Near Edinburgh University and Festival Theatre. Great vegetable biryani and delicious lassi for under a fiver? Hence high cult status. Late-night Indo-Pakistani halal café that attracts Asian families as well as students and others who know. Kebabs, curries and excellent sweets. One of Edinburgh's most cosmopolitan restaurants. 7 days 12noon-12midnight (2am Fri/Sat). Prayers on Fri (1-2pm). No-alcohol zone.

255 1/E4
1/XE1
£15-22

Suruchi www.suruchi.co.uk · 0131 556 6583 · **14a Nicolson Street** · **Suruchi Too** 0131 554 3268 · **121 Constitution Street, Leith** The original is upstairs opposite Festival Theatre. Indian menu written touchingly in Scots dialect (with tatties, and nan 'het fae the tandoor'). Unfussy if somewhat worn décor and food with light touch attracts students/academics from nearby university as well as theatregoers. Loads for veggies. Better-than-average wines. In Leith, the food is better: you can usually get a table in the airport-like lounge. Both Suruchis used to be routinely praised but changed hands since the last edition and have lost some zing. Lunch (not Sun) & LO 11.30pm daily.

256 1/D5
£15-22

Namaste 0131 225 2000 · **17 Forest Road** Another Indian restaurant on the up, having moved 2007 from small, intimate premises round the corner (near the University) to this much larger though less characterful setting. Weird chairs much loved by Indian/Chinese restaurateurs do little to cheer it up. But the food with its Nepalese influence is to be recommended. Certainly this curry house stands out from the many others in the area. 7 days. LO 11pm.

257 1/XA4
£15-22

The Khukuri www.thekhukuri.co.uk · 0131 228 2085 · **8 West Maitland Street** The western extension of Princes St and Shandwick Pl before Haymarket Station. This unassuming Nepalese restaurant is a quiet secret. Costumed, endlessly polite Nepali waiters. Chef Dharam Maharjan routinely wins awards and brings the herbs himself from the mountains of Nepal (sic). Despite massive menu and mellow atmosphere, meat-eaters (lamb and chicken only) will be happiest here (there are prawns). 7 days lunch & LO 11pm (closed Sun lunch).

258 1/XE1
£15-22

The Raj on the Shore www.rajontheshore.com · 0131 553 3980 · **89 Henderson Street** On south corner of The Shore, Leith. Nice location for the irrepressible Tommy Miah's airy Indian/Bangladeshi restaurant here a long time now, but still bustling and still changing. Occasional events add to the jollity; jars of things available to buy and take home, also recipe books. Tables best on the raised front area. Totally Raj, in the non-Irvine Welsh sense (in-joke for Edinburgh readers). Lunch and LO 11.15/11.45pm, 7 days.

259 1/XA4
£15-22

Indian Cavalry Club www.indiancavalryclub.co.uk · 0131 228 3282 · **22 Coates Crescent** Off the main Glasgow road 250m from Princes St. Formerly across the road, the bargain business lunch has always attracted the suits and there's a loyal following at night. Now it's bigger, less retro and with a pakora bar doing snacks till late. Good buzz here and food always pukka. An unlikely carry-out place, but they do, and it's one of the best in town. Lunch and LO including pakora bar till 10.45pm.

260 1/D2
£15-22

Zest 0131 556 5028 · **115 North St Andrew Street** Close to St Andrew Square and Harvey Nix. Light, modern Indian café by the same people who have Eastern Spices (333/TAKEAWAYS). Lighter take on traditional menu. Owner Ashdaar Ali always there to care. 7 days lunch, LO 11pm.

The Best Thai Restaurants

261 1/C2
£22-32
✓✓ **Dusit** www.dusit.co.uk · 0131 220 6846 · **49 Thistle Street** In the continuing proliferation of Thai restaurants in Edinburgh, this one gets the gold orchid. Elegant interior (back from street), excellent service and food good in any language that just happens to be exquisite Thai cuisine. Tantalising combinations: strong signature dishes. Decent wine list. Still the tops. Lunch & LO 10.30pm. Closed Sun.

262 1/XB5
£15-22
✓ **Thai Lemongrass** 0131 229 2225 · **40 Bruntsfield Place** Smart but intimate, not too tiddlythai eatery by the people who have the estimable Jasmine (266/BEST CHINESE). Nice, solid, woody ambience, charming waitresses (Thai and Chinese) and food that's well good enough for euro/Thai afficionados; but popular and rightly so (book weekends). Can BYOB (£6 corkage) though has good wine list. Lunch (Fri-Sun), dinner 7 days LO 11pm.

263 1/XB5
£15-22
✓ **ThaisanUK** www.thaisan.com · 0131 228 8855 · **21 Argyle Place** Your classic tucked-away 'wee gem' on residential street in student and mortgaged-to-the-hilt Marchmont. Madame Ae offers healthy, fresh and authentic Thai food and other Asian specials. This place is tiny though there are now a few tables downstairs as well as up; best book. BYOB (no wine list). 7 days dinner only. LO 10.30pm.

264 1/B2
£15-22
Ruan Siam 0131 226 3675 · **48 Howe Street** On corner of Stockbridge area on the site of the first proper Thai to arrive in Edinburgh a long time ago now. This Ruan, part of a small Edinburgh chain, is the best. Subterranean but elegant enough, the menu is long with interesting combos; hard to choose, though desserts are very limited. Lunch & LO 10.30pm. 7 days (no Sun lunch).

265 1/E1
£15-22
Phuket Pavilion 0131 556 4323 · **8 Union Street** Near Playhouse Theatre and Vu cinemaplex. When other restaurants in this busy area are full, you can often get a table at this roomy, unpretentious Thai place that never lets you down. Bit of a local secret, just the right touch of holy basil and the rest. 7 days. LO 10.30pm.

The Best Chinese Restaurants

266 1/B4
£22-32
✓ **Jasmine** 0131 229 5757 · **32 Grindlay Street** Opposite Lyceum Theatre. Very Chinesey restaurant with big local following. Pre-post-theatre menus and good service to match. Seafood a speciality (Cantonese style). BYOB (though expensive corkage). Often may need to book or queue in tiny doorway. Some memorable dishes await. Mon-Fri lunch. Dinner 7 days LO 11pm.

267 1/B1
£22-32
✓ **Kweilin** www.kweilin.co.uk · 0131 557 1875 · **19 Dundas Street** The here-forever (almost 25 years) New Town choice with imaginative Cantonese cooking (and other regions); very good seafood and genuine dim sum in pleasant but somewhat uninspired setting. Excellent wine list. No kids allowed in the evening – somewhere for grown-ups to eat their quail and very good seafood in peace. You may have to book. LO 10.45pm (11.30pm Fri/Sat). Closed Mon.

268 1/A5
£15-22
✓ **Rainbow Arch** www.rainbowarch.org.uk · 0131 221 1288 · **8 Morrison Street** Unprepossessing but those who know go here and it's certainly the best real food choice adjacent Lothian Rd. Authentic menu, especially dim sum (dedicated chef). This is... well, proper Chinese cuisine. Open very late. 7 days noon-3am (Thu closes at 12midnight).

269 1/XB1   **Loon Fung** 0131 556 1781 · **2 Warriston Place, Canonmills** Upstairs (and
£15-22   down for private parties) for over 30 years the famous lemon chicken and crispy
duck have been signature dishes of this very traditional neighbourhood restaurant
though the speciality here is Cantonese food. Now there's also crispy monkfish in
honey. Good dim sum. Mon-Thu 12noon-11.30/12midnight, weekends from 2pm.

270 1/XE1   **Joanna's Cuisine** 0131 554 5833 · **42 Dalmeny Street** Still called the
£22-32   'Dalmeny St place', it's run by the delightful and decorative eponymous Joanna.
Tiny dining room on ground floor of tenement off Leith Walk, nevertheless
produces a menu of 200 Peking dishes. Home-made stocks rather than MSG and
other touches like specially imported teas make this a place people swear by, so
book. Dinner only. LO 10.30pm (11.30 weekends). Closed Mon.

271 1/B2   **Wok & Wine** www.wokandwine.com · 0131 225 2382 · **57a Frederick
Street** Next to Ricks. Find this discreet basement restaurant refreshed a couple of
years back. It's one of the best contemporary eastern restaurants in town, using all
the right supplies for meat and fish and other carefully sourced ingredients. Wok
bites allow a tapas approach but this is a proper eating-out experience, not a drop-
in as the name may suggest. Edinburgh's chilled-out Chinese. 7 days 5.30pm-
11pm.

The Best Burgers & Steaks

272 10/P25
£22-32
✓✓ **Champany's** www.champany.com · 01506 834532 On A904, Linlithgow to South Queensferry road (3km Linlithgow), but near M9 at junction 3. Accolade-laden restaurant (and 'Chop and Ale House') different from others below because it's out of town (and out of some pockets). Both surf 'n' turf with live lobsters on premises. Famously good Aberdeen Angus beef. Good service, huge helpings (Americans may feel at home). Top wine list. Chop House 7 days, from noon onwards at weekends; lunch and LO 10pm. Restaurant lunch (not Sat) and LO 10pm. Closed Sun. Hotel rooms adjacent (129/HOTELS OUTSIDE TOWN). For many Champany's has a dream menu; it's no sweet dream for veggies.

273 1/A1
£15-22
✓ **Bell's Diner** 0131 225 8116 · 7 St Stephen Street, Stockbridge Edinburgh's small, but celebrated burger joint, the antithesis of the posh nosh. Nothing has changed in 30 years except the annual paint job and (with an unusually low turnover) the gorgeous staff. Some people go to Bell's *every* week in life and why? For perfect burgers, steaks, shakes and coincidentally, the best veggie (nut) burger in town. There's nothing else to say, Bill! Sun-Fri 6-10.30pm, Sat 12noon-10.30pm.

274 1/D3
1/A1
£15-22
✓ **Buffalo Grill** www.buffalogrill.co.uk · 0131 667 7427 · 12-14 Chapel Street & 0131 332 3846 · 1 Raeburn Place, Stockbridge Opposite Appleton Tower on the University campus. 25 years in burgerland, this diner trades on its reputation for steaks and such-like (Scotch beef natch) but there are some Mexican and Southern US variants eg jambalaya and some concessions to veggies. Both great spots for easy-going nights out with chums and not large so book and BYOB (corkage only £1). Lunch Mon-Fri, LO 10.15pm (Sun 10pm).

275 1/D1
1/XE1
£15-22
Smoke Stack www.smokestack.org.uk · 0131 556 6032 · 53-55 Broughton Street From the makers of The Basement (353/UNIQUE EDINBURGH PUBS) came something equally groovy across the road – a burgundy and blue diner rather than an orange and blue bar. Modish décor complements laid-back approach. Loads of burgers (Scottish beef or vegetarian), seared salmon, blackened tuna, corn on the cob from a corn; all jollied along by a great staff. Lunch Mon-Sat, dinner 7 days, LO 10.30pm.
The Leith offshoot of the **Stack** at 19 Shore Place (0131 476 6776) has an expanded menu in a back-courtyard-warehouse kind of a room. Open 7 days, lunch and LO 10.30pm (closed Sun lunch).

276 1/D4
1/A3
£15-22
Wannaburger www.wannaburger.com · 0131 225 8770 · 217 High Street & 7 Queensferry Street · 0131 220 0036 The first is bang in the middle of the Royal Mile below the Cathedral; the second a large West End window-watching room. Emphatically (gastro) burger joint with no starters and limited desserts (though Mackie's ice cream and 'chilli chocolate cake'). Towering burgers in huge variety (also vegetarian) and top toppings. Same people (and similar menu) have the Cambridge Bar (174/GASTROPUBS). 7 days all day, LO 9.30pm.

Kid-Friendly Places

277 1/XB5
£15-22

✓ **Luca's** www.s-luca.co.uk · 0131 446 0233 · **16 Morningside Road** The ice cream kings (1519/ICE CREAM) from Musselburgh opened this modern ice creamerie and café where kids with dads will enjoy their spag and their sundae. Big cups of capp. Crowded if not claustrophobic upstairs especially on weekends. Excellent for daytime snacks, family evening meals and gorgeous ice-cream at all times. BYOB. 9am-9.30pm. 7 days.

278 1/XF2
£15 OR LESS

✓ **Reds** 0131 669 5558 · **254 High Street, Portobello** In main street, a much-welcomed, purposefully kid-friendly café. A camera projects the rear playing/climbing area to a plasma screen in front. Regulation rather than inspired kids' food though all freshly and conscientiously prepared. Reopens as local bistro on weekend nights. 10am-4.30pm, weekends till 3.30pm then 5.30-10pm.

279 1/XE1
£15-22

✓ **Giuliano's on the Shore** www.giulianos.co.uk · 0131 554 5272 · **1 Commercial Street** By the bridge, the Leith version of 'Giuli's' (202/TRUSTY TRATTS) has all the traditional Italian trappings especially through the back (with a more contemporary feeling front-end; same food throughout), with cheerful pizza/pasta and waiters. Kids love it. For grown-ups nice antipasto, fish specials and a decent wine list. Always a birthday party happening at weekends. Luca's ice-cream (see above). 12noon-10.30/11pm. 7 days.

280 1/C4
£15-22

Café Hub www.thehub-edinburgh.com · 0131 473 2067 · **Castlehill** Top of Royal Mile so tourist central. Roomy restaurant for adults that caters in a superior way for kids. This café is within the International Festival Centre, so busy busy in Aug. Outside terrace a child-friendly zone (387/DRINKING OUTDOORS). Dinner only at weekends. Topping desserts. 7 days Sun-Thu 11am-5pm, Fri/Sat 11am-10pm.

281 1/XB1
£15 OR LESS

Ye Olde Peacock Inn 0131 552 8707 · **Newhaven Road** Near the harbour. One of Edinburgh's unsung all-round family eateries for years – you can take gran as well as the bairns. The fish here really is fresh, the menu is more adventurous than you'd think with lots that wee kids and we kids like. High tea is a treat. Pud list is a classic Scottish dietary disaster, but irresistible. Lunch & LO 9.45pm. Bar till 11pm. 7 days.

282 1/E1

Vittoria www.vittoriarestaurant.com · 0131 556 6171 · **Corner of Brunswick Street & Leith Walk** Excellent Italian all-rounder that can seat 200 people including outside on pavement people-watching corner. Report: 198/TRUSTY TRATTS.

OUTSIDE TOWN

283 10/Q26
£15-22

Cramond Brig www.cramondbrig.com · 0131 339 4350 · **Cramond** At the River Almond as you hit Edinburgh on the dual carriageway from the Forth Road Bridge. This inn has always put effort into attracting families, and although there's no longer a kids' play area on the premises, there is one by the old brig itself, a pony field and a walk by the river. Food better after recent refurbishment. Half portions available throughout the menu. Lunch & LO 9pm, 7 days. Weekends noon onwards.

284 10/R25
£15-22

Goblin Ha' www.goblinha.com · 01620 810244 · **Gifford** 35km from town in neat East Lothian village. One of two hotels, this has the pub grub cornered. Lunch and supper (6-9pm, 9.30pm Fri-Sat). The garden which gets very busy in summer is nice for kids.

285 10/P25
£15-22
Bridge Inn www.bridgeinn.com · 0131 333 1320· **Ratho** 16km west of centre via A71, turning right opposite Dalmahoy Golf Club. Large choice of comforting food in canalside setting. Has won various awards, including for its kids' menu. Restaurant, traditional and basic bar food and canal cruises with nosh. Pop Inn 12noon-9pm daily. Children not after 8pm. Restaurant lunch daily and LO 9pm Mon-Sat. Bar till 11pm, 12midnight Fri-Sat.

The Best Tearooms & Coffee Shops

286 1/XA3
✓ **Gallery (Of Modern Art) Café** www.nationalgalleries.org · **Belford Road** Unbeatable on a fine day when you can sit out on the patio by the grass, with sculptures around, have some wine and a plate of Scottish cheese and oatcakes. Hot dishes are good – always 2 soups, meat/fish/vegetarian dish. Coffee and cake whenever. Originally conceived by Helen Ruthven (see below), it remains to be seen what remains to be seen but food seems to have the edge over the Portrait Gallery. Art upstairs may provoke; this is always sound. 7 days 10am-4.30pm (428/OTHER ATTRACTIONS). Lunch dishes usually gone by 2.30pm. **Café Newton** at the Dean Gallery (430/OTHER ATTRACTIONS) across the road and the gardens from GOMA (above) is a smaller, more interior café by the same people. Soup, sandwiches and 2 hot lunch dishes. Coffee from mega machine. Same hours as GOMA.

287 1/C2
✓ **Queen Street Café** **Queen Street** In the National Portrait Gallery (428/OTHER ATTRACTIONS), between Hanover and St Andrew's Square. And through the arched window... a civil slice of old Edinburgh gentility. For years. under Helen Ruthven this galley café served seriously good light meals (same as at GOMA, above), tasteful sandwiches, coffee and excellent cake – best scones in town, exquisite salads, 2 daily soups and 2 hot mains. Now bought over and in the Heritage portfolio, the touch is unmistakeably gone but for the moment the food and ambiance are still reminiscent of a consummate Edinburgh hostess. Self service though you rarely wait long. Mon-Sat 10am-4.30pm, Sun 11am-4.30pm.

288 1/D3
✓ **Fruitmarket Café** www.fruitmarket.co.uk · 0131 226 1843 · **45 Market Street** Attached to the Fruitmarket Gallery, a cool spacious place for coffee, pastries or a light lunch. Big salads, home cookin', creative ciabattas and 2 daily specials. Some imaginative and surprising combos. Mhairi and Roy do great coffee and still work damned hard (1548/FARM SHOPS). Bookshop to browse with Andy Miller's lovely shelves, big windows to look out; good mix of tourists, Edinburgh faithfuls, art seekers and people like me in a meeting. Mon-Sat 11.30am-4pm, Sun from 12noon. Open till 5.30pm (Sun 4.30pm) for coffee and cakes.

289 1/C2
✓ **G&T (Glass & Thompson)** 0131 557 0909 · **2 Dundas Street** Patrician New Town coffee shop and deli with contemporary food and attitude. Nothing much changed since the last edition: well, it is a near-perfect formula for its time and place. Many 'ladies who latte', a phrase coined by Alexander McCall Smith whom you'd expect to see with a notepad in a corner seat. Great *antipasti*, salads, sandwiches to go; and very fine cakes that you won't find anywhere else (cake doyenne Sue Lawrence uses their recipes). 8am-5.45pm, Sun 10.30am-4.15pm. See 329/TAKEAWAYS.

290 1/B5
Made In France 0131 221 1184 · **5 Lochrin Place** In a side street in Tollcross behind the Cameo, a soupçon of France. Amanda and Graham Evans-Nash are obviously Francophiles and their café's packed with delicious tid-bits and freshly baked baguettes, croissants and tarts. Mon-Fri 10am-5pm, Sat 10am-4pm.

291 1/XB1   **Circle Coffee Shop** 0131 624 4666 · **Canonmills** Near the clock. Deli/take-away counter and lovely café in the back. Very quiet New Town. Salads, soups, ciabattas and bagels. Nice place to read the papers or rendezvous. 7 days 8.30am-5.30pm, open to 9.30pm Fri/Sat in summer. Sun 9am-4.30pm.

292 1/XD5   **Toast** 0131 446 9873 · **146-148 Marchmont Road** Converted bank in the heart of student flat land, taken over by half of the Sweet Melinda's team (140/BISTROS) – it's just up the road. Haven't hung out at this place, being far from my stamping ground, but it gets a good reputation. Reports please. 7 days 10am-9.30pm.

293 1/D4   **Black Medicine Coffee Shop** 0131 622 7209 · **2 Nicolson Street** Corner of Drummond St. Funky American-style coffee shop on busy South Side corner opposite Festival Theatre and University Old Quad. Good place to take your book from Blackwells; get a window seat! Good smell. Big bagels, cookies and fab smoothies. 7 days 8am-6pm, Sun 10am-6pm. Also at 108 Marchmont Rd in student land. 7 days 8am-5pm (till 6pm weekends). Sun 10am-6pm.

294 1/F3   **Clarinda's** 0131 557 1888 · **69 Canongate** Near the bottom of the Royal Mile near the Palace and Parliament building. Small but despite frilly touches, has total tearoom integrity. With hot dishes and snacks that may seem more of a sit-down stop on the tourist trail but has some of the best home-baking in town (especially the apple pie). Very reasonable prices; run by good Edinburgh folk who work that tiny kitchen. Takeaways possible. 7 days 8.30am-4.45pm (from 9.30am Sun).

295 1/D4   **The Elephant House** www.elephant-house.co.uk · 0131 220 5355 ·
    1/D5   **21 George IV Bridge** Near libraries and Edinburgh University, a rather self-conscious but elephantine and well-run coffee shop with light snacks and big choice. J.K. Rowling (2009/LITERARY PLACES) once sat here: they say 'the birthplace of Harry Potter'. Counter during day, waitress service evens. Cakes/pastries are bought in but can be taken out. View of graveyard and castle to dream away student life in Edinburgh. 7 days 9am-10pm (7pm in winter). Same people have **Elephants & Bagels** at Nicolson Square. Soup 'n' a bagel takeaway and sit-in. 7 days 8.30am-6pm (weekends 9.30am-5pm).

296 1/XB1   **Botanic Gardens Cafeteria** www.rbge.org.uk By 'the House' (where there are regular exhibitions) within the gardens (427/OTHER ATTRACTIONS). For café only, enter by Arboretum Place. Disappointing catering-style food though some improvement of late. The outside tables and view of the city is why we come. And the squirrels. 10am-5pm.

297 1/C3   **Police Box Coffee Bars** 0131 228 5001 Kiosks not caffs! Rose Street (behind
    1/XB5   Jenners), Morningside Park, Hope Park Crescent (east of Meadows), top of Middle
    1/D5   Meadow Walk (opposite Forrest Road) and outside John Lewis' department store
    1/D2   and St Andrew's Cathedral. Caffeine kiosks in former police boxes. Similar fare to Starbucks and Costas but these are home-grown and have, in their way, reclaimed the streets. Hours vary but early-late. Great coffee to go.

The Best Caffs

Also see Best Takeaway Places, p. 66.

298 1/D4 ✓ **Spoon** 0131 556 6922 · **15 Blackfriars Street** Off the Royal Mile opposite High Street Hostel (120/BEST HOSTELS). Richard and Moira's friendly, off-high street, almost neighbourhood but modern, even minimalist café. Counters service for snacks and imaginative hot dishes using selected ingredients and more TLC than usual. Big bowls of soup, nice coffee. 9am-5pm, Sat from 10am. Closed Sun.

299 1/E1 ✓ **Café Renroc** 0131 556 0432 · **91 Montgomery Street** Ambitious owners Billy and Jane Ross quickly established this café as a destination and rendez-vous in '06 and expanded downstairs at TGP. Breakfasts, ciabattas, stromboli, nice coffee. Treatment/massage rooms in the basement – nice idea. 7 days 8am-9pm.

300 1/D1 ✓ **Blue Moon Café** www.bluemooncafe.co.uk · 0131 557 0911 · **1 Barony Street** Longest-established gay café in Scotland (1177/GAY EDINBURGH). Straight-friendly and a good place to hang out from breakfast to late. All-day breakfast. Female staff efficient, boys more spacey. Nachos-and-burgers kind of menu. Free condoms in the gents for the impecunious or impatient. 7 days 11am-11pm. Food all day till 10pm, bar till 11pm. **Deep Blue** bar downstairs is open later.

301 1/XB5 ✓ **Luca's** www.s-luca.co.uk · 0131 446 0233 · **16 Morningside Road** In town version of legendary ice cream parlour in Musselburgh (1519/ICE CREAM). Ice cream and snacks downstairs, more family food parlour up. Cheap and cheerful. Great for kids. 7 days. Report: 262/KIDS.

302 1/A1 ✓ **Spiro** 0131 226 7533 · **37 St Stephen Street** Italian shoe shop below (sic) and small, authentic Italian coffee shop above. Few tables but you can take away. This '06 arrival in Edinburgh's old hippy street freshened things up. Paninis, piadines, cakes and the best espresso make it worth footling down this stamping ground of the sixties again. 7 days. Mon-Sat 8.45am-5.30pm, Sun 10am-5.30pm.

303 1/D5 **Monster Mash** www.monstermashcafe.co.uk · 0131 225 7069 · **4 Forrest**
1/C2 **Road** Near the University and a roomier version at **47 Thistle Street** (0131 225 5782). Comfort-food café capitalising on the mash comeback with big sausages (Crombies) and gravy; shepherd's pie, steak pie, etc. Puds similarly retro. Vegetarian options. Nice idea, slightly lost in delivery. 7 days 8am-10pm (Sat 9am, Sun 10am).

304 1/D4 **Always Sunday** www.alwayssunday.co.uk · 0131 622 0667 · **170 High Street** A café on the Royal Mile unusually that's trying and at least reflects contemporary tastes. Deli-style counter offering 'healthy' breakfasts through lunch to afternoon 'treats'. Home baking. 7 days 8am-6pm (Sat/Sun from 9am).

305 1/XE1 **Café Truva** www.cafetruva.com · 0131 554 5502 **77** · **The Shore, Leith** Cute Turkish café strong coffee of course and other Turkish delights, but mainly a snacky (ciabattas, paninis, couple of hot dishes like moussaka and fresh salads) and sit-around bolthole in Leith. And on the waterfront. 7 days 9am-6.30pm.

306 1/XE1 **Diner 7** 0131 553 0624 · **7 Commercial Street** Along from the bridge at the shore in Leith. Sliver of local diner/restaurant on a busy road. Burger/steaks and more adventurous dishes like fig and feta tart and pork and prawn curry all at cheapo prices make this a popular, casual and local diner. 10am-10.30pm, 7 days.

Kebab Mahal 7 Nicolson Square Report: 254/INDIAN.

The Best Late-Night Restaurants

307 1/C4
£22-32

✓ **The Witchery** www.thewitchery.com · 0131 225 5613 · **Castlehill** Top of Royal Mile near the Castle. Not open very late, but does take bookings up till 11.30pm, that crucial half hour beyond 11 that allows you to eat after the movies. Special after-theatre menu from 10.30pm has 2 courses for £12.95, a very good deal from one of the best restaurants in town (143/BEST RESTAURANTS). 7 days, lunch and **LO 11.30pm.**

308 1/E2
£15-22

✓ **Giuliano's** www.giulianos.co.uk · 0131 556 6590 · **18 Union Place** Leith Walk opposite Playhouse. Buzzing Italian tratt day and night. Report 202/TRUSTY TRATTS. **Handily open till 2am (2.30am weekends).**

309 1/B3
£15-22

✓ **Living Room** www.thelivingroom.co.uk · 0131 226 0880 · **113 George Street** Best of many for eats on 'stylish' George St and open later than similar others especially at weekends. Like everywhere else on George St it's part of a chain. Full-on bar at front like Candy Bar downstairs; surprisingly large dining area at back. Modern British menu with food better than you'd expect. Very noisy and music too loud at weekends, but service excellent. This ain't a bad 'product'. **7 days LO 11pm, 12midnight weekends.**

310 1/A5
£15-22

✓ **Rainbow Arch** www.rainbowarch.org.uk · 0131 221 1288 · **8 Morrison Street 7 days 12noon-3am.** Authentic Chinese food of high standard. Report: 268/CHINESE.

311 1/D5
£22-32

Favorit www.favouritedinburgh.co.uk · 0131 220 6880 · **20 Teviot Place** New York diner-type café/restaurant – salads, pasta, wraps, Ben and Jerry's from dawn till almost dawn (319/SUNDAY BREAKFAST). Food not so favourite these days but a useful nightowl/nighthawk spot. **7 days till 2.30am.**

312 1/A3
£15-22

Bar Roma www.bar-roma.co.uk · 0131 226 2977 · **39a Queensferry Street** Near west end of Princes Street. Buzzing day and night. An Edinburgh institution even better after revamp. All the old standbys snappily served and lots of late night Italian jive. Best wine list you'll find in West End after midnight. (See 201/TRUSTY TRATTS). **12noon-12midnight Sun-Thu; 12.45am Fri-Sat.**

313 1/D5
£15-22

Negociants 0131 225 6313 · **45 Lothian Street** Near the University, a long-established all-day and late-night hangout. Chairs outside in summer. Food of the 'popular' variety ain't the strongest point but it is available late. Good mix of people. DJs downstairs. **Till 12midnight & 2am Fri-Sat.**

314 1/C4
£15-22

Mamma's www.mammaspizza.co.uk · 0131 225 6464 · **30 Grassmarket** Open **till 11pm always & 12midnight** if you're lucky. Report: 206/PIZZAS.

Good Places For Sunday Breakfast

315 1/D3 ✓ **Hadrian's** www.thebalmoralhotel.com · 0131 557 5000 · **2 North Bridge** At the corner and brasseries restaurant of Balmoral (79/HOTELS). Good daily (power) brunch place, but also Sun. **From 7am (Sun 7.30am)**. Not cheap, but light (or lavish) and laid-back.

316 1/D3 ✓ **The Breakfast Room @ The Scotsman Hotel** 0131 556 5565 · www.thescotsmanhotel.co.uk · **20 North Bridge** Breakfast in Edinburgh's top boutique hotel (87/HOTELS). Many references to the morning paper this hotel replaces in the building, and this morning's is there to read. Interior room (adjacent Vermillion – 149/BEST RESTAURANTS), but an excellent, leisurely start to the day for guests and non-guests alike. **From 7-10.30am, 8-11.30am weekends.**

317 1/B2 ✓ **Ricks** www.ricksedinburgh.co.uk · 0131 622 7800 · **55a Frederick Street** The cool café-bar (407/COOL BARS) with rooms (101/INDIVIDUAL HOTELS) opens early and late, but an excellent spot for laid-back or power breakfast brunch 7 days, including unusually early start on Suns. Eclectic, contemporary menu. **Open 7 days from 8am.**

318 1/C2 ✓ **Urban Angel** www.urban-angel.co.uk · 0131 225 6215 · **121 Hanover Street** Convivial, contemporary breakfast from good sausages to honey and waffles. Potato scones natch! Full of bright people that can still remember their Sat night. **Open 10am.**

319 1/B5 **Favorit** www.favouritedinburgh.co.uk · 0131 221 1800 · **30 Leven Street** The all-people all-rounder. **Open 7 days from 8am**. Report: 311/LATE-NIGHT RESTAURANTS.

320 1/D4 **City Café** www.thecitycafe.co.uk · **Blair Street** It's been here so long, it's easy to take for granted... but for that 'BIG' breakfast (carnivore or veggie), few places in the city beat the content or American diner atmosphere. Not open exactly early as most of clientele have been up very late. **From 11am.**

321 1/XE1 **King's Wark** 0131 554 9260 · **36 The Shore** On busy corner for traffic, but calm and comforting inside. Dining room or bar. No early start (**11am**), but a civilised brunch on the waterfront.

322 1/D4 **Black Medicine Coffee Shop** 0131 622 7209 · **2 Nicolson Street** Great atmosphere American-style coffee with bagels/muffins type start to Sundays. 293/COFFEE SHOPS. **From 10am.**

323 1/D4 **Elephant House** www.elephant-house.co.uk · 0131 220 5355 · **21 George IV Bridge** Another (this time extensive) coffee-house near the University that's open early for caffeine and sustenance. 295/COFFEE SHOPS. **From 9am.**

324 1/D1 **The Broughton Street Breakfast** There's lots of choice in the main street of
1/D2 Edinburgh's East Village. From the top down: **Mather's** the no-compromise drinking den does a traditional fry-up from **12.30pm**, as does **The Outhouse** down the lane but with veggie variants and until 4pm. **Baroque** kicks in from **10am** with similar nosh (slightly more expensive). **The Basement** also does Tex-Mex brex from **12.30pm** and regulars attest to its ability to hit the spot. Further down on corner with people-watching windows is **The Barony** with breakfast and papers from **12.30-3.30pm** (great live music Sun late afternoon); and last but not least:

325 1/D1   **The Olive Branch** www.theolivebranchscotland.co.uk · **0131 557 8589** · **Corner of Broughton Street & Broughton Place** Big windows, outside tables. Med menu and breakfast fry-ups. This place is routinely packed. **From 10.30am.**

326 1/A3   **indigo (yard)** www.indigoyardedinburgh.co.uk · **0131 220 5603** · **7 Charlotte Lane** Another fashionable spot (same organisation as Rick's above) and probably best brunch bet in West End. Details: 406/COOL BARS. **From 8.30am.**

The Globe 23 Henderson Row   332/TAKEAWAY (below).

The Best Takeaway Places

327 1/B2   ✓ **Appetite** www.appetitedirect.com · 0131 225 3711. **42 Howe Street** Formerly (the legendary) Rowlands, this son-of follows the same formula. Great home-made food for takeaway, parties or just for your own supper/picnic etc. Nearest thing in Edinburgh to a traiteur. Daily soups/curry/quiche/pizza and specials. Good vegetarian and salads. Best in the Stockbridge quarter and just possibly the best in town. Mon-Fri 8.30am-4pm.

328 1/B1   ✓ **Anima** 0131 558 2918 · **11 Henderson Row** Adjacent and part of L'Alba D'Oro (227/FISH & CHIPS). Smart, busy Italian hot 'n' cold takeaway. 'Italian soul food' includes great pizza, freshly prepared pastas, ciabatta, etc. Excellent wine selection, some desserts. An excellent expansion from chips, our soul food – to theirs. 7 days. Lunch & LO 10pm (11pm weekends). Closed Sun lunch.

329 1/C2   ✓ **G&T (Glass & Thompson)** 0131 557 0909 · **2 Dundas Street** Deli and coffee shop on main street in New Town, but also takeaway sandwiches/rolls in infinite formats using their drool-making selection of quality ingredients (breads, cheeses, salamis, etc). Very fine cakes. Take away to office, gardens or dinner party. Excellent sit-in area and small terrace for whiling away Edinburgh days. Mon-Sat 8am-5.45pm, Sun 10.30am-4.15pm. Report: 289/BEST TEAROOMS.

330 1/XF1   **The Manna House** 0131 652 2349 · **22 Easter Road** Unlikely spot for a relatively genuine French patisserie. Cakes to drool over. some tables with quiche/ salad/sandwich menu. Bakery through back. 8am-7pm (Sat 6pm). Closed Sun.

331 1/XE1   **Embo** 0131 652 3880 · **29 Haddington Place** Half way down Leith Walk and one of the reasons for going that far. Mike and Erin's neighbourhood hangout and takeaway way better than the rest. Bespoke sandwiches, wraps, etc. Excellent coffee and smoothies. 'Panino Bar' and a couple of tables outside the door. Nice baking. This place is good to know. Mon-Fri 8am-4pm, from 9am on Sat. Closed Sun.

332 1/D1
1/B1
1/XE1
1/C2   **The Globe** www.broughtonstreet.co.uk/theglobe.htm · **0131 558 3837** · **42 Broughton Street** A bright spot on the corner in the middle of the East Village. Open all day till 3/4pm for sandwiches/rolls and toasted focaccia. Big window for people-watching. Branches at 23 Henderson Row and Bernard Street, Leith (another busy shop on the corner) and most recently Thistle Street near Hanover Street. Henderson Row branch the best for real breakfast and newspaper reading and is open on Sun.

333 1/XB1   **Eastern Spices** 0131 558 3609 · **2 Canonmills** Bridge by the clock. Long on the grapevine, this place is simply better than most – phone in your order or turn up and wait. Also home delivery 2-mile radius. Full Indian menu from pakora to pasanda and meals for one. 5-11.30pm. 7 days.

334 1/B1 **L'Alba D'Oro** 0131 557 2580 · **5-11 Henderson Row** Excellent pizza, pasta, wine as well as fish 'n' chips. A very superior chippy and pizza joint. Report: 205/PIZZAS.

335 1/XE5 **Juice Monkeys** **www.juicemonkeys.com** · **0131 667 4450** · **Clerk Street** In University area heading south. Small internet/newspaper-reading/lecture-note-revising café with good fresh takeaway soups, juices and sandwiches. Open early. 7 days 8am-8pm (Sun 9am-8pm). Nice breakfasts.

336 1/C4 **Hula** **103 West Bow** Juice bar with sit-in and takeaway at the bottom of Victoria Street. Usual squeezings with bagels and other snacks. New '07 on the smoothie bandwagon, but fresh look and the wheatgrass grows. 7 days 8am-8pm (from 10am weekends).

337 1/XB4 **Jaspers** 0131 229 8944 · **Grove Street** Bottom of the street, round corner of Morrison Street near Haymarket. Small, simple café/takeaway with home-made quiches/tartlets as well as soups/sandwiches etc. They do a nice omelette. 7.30am-3pm (Sat 8.30am). Closed Sun.

338 1/XB5 **Ndebele** **www.ndebele.co.uk** · **0131 221 1141** · **59 Home Street, Tollcross** Near the Kings Theatre. Ndebele are a South African people and although there are ingredients from elsewhere in Africa, this takeaway deli (and formerly café) celebrates all things SA. Soups come with cornbread. 7 days 9.15am-6pm, Sun 12noon-5pm.

The Best Delis

339 1/E1 ✓✓✓ **Valvona & Crolla** www.valvonacrolla.com · **19 Elm Row** Near top of Leith Walk. Since 1934, an Edinburgh institution, the shop you show visitors. Full of smells, genial, knowledgeable staff and a floor-to-ceiling range of cheese (Ital/Scot, etc.), meats, oils, wines and more. Fresh veg trucked in from Milan markets, on-premises bakery, great café/bar (191/ITALIAN RESTAURANTS). Also demos, tastings, Fringe venue. Valvona's an Edinburgh landmark and a national treasure; and see p. 24, PIONEERS. 8am-6.30pm (Sun 11am-5pm).

340 1/C4 ✓✓ **I.J. Mellis** **Victoria Street & Bruntsfield** Started out as the cheese
1/XB5 guy, now more of a very select deli for food that's good and 'slow'. Coffees, hams, sausages, olives and seasonal stuff like apples and mushrooms (branches vary), so smells mingle. Irresistible! Branches also in Glasgow (690/GLASGOW DELIS) and St Andrews (1530/REALLY GOOD DELIS). 7 days though times vary. See also 1556/CHEESES.

341 1/C2 ✓ **Glass & Thompson** **2 Dundas Street** Exemplary and contemporary New Town provisioner. Selective choice of Mediterranean-style goodies to eat or take away and bread/pâtisserie; also those all-important New Town dinner-party essentials. Report: 289/TEAROOMS.

342 1/A1 ✓ **Herbie** **1 North West Circus Place (& 66 Raeburn Place)** · **7 William**
1/XA1 **Street (takeaway)** Notable originally mainly for cheese and other cold-
1/XA3 counter irresistibles (1557/CHEESES). Herbie's has expanded notably here on the main road to Stockbridge with a takeaway and coffee shop and loads of well selected and sourced munchies. 7 days till 6pm. Closed Sun.

343 1/D1 ✓ **Broughton Delicatessen** **7 Barony Street** Near corner with Broughton Street. 2 doors away from main street but busy through growing reputation ('07). Some tables by window and through back. Mainly coffee shop but selection of good products. Baking, pasta, Adamson's oatcakes. 9am-6pm (Sat 5pm). Closed Sun.

344 1/XA1 ✓ **The Store** 0131 315 0030 · **13 Comely Bank Road** At the end of main street in Stockbridge. Beautifully presented deli selling produce from the home farm (1546/DELIS) and all good things besides. Ready meals, homegrown fruits. Perfect for a Stockbridge dinner party. 7 days. Times vary but open till 7.30pm Mon-Thu.

345 1/B2 **Homegrown Whole Foods** **36 Howe Street** Small, ethical food shop in New Town with organic meats, seasonal produce, free trade and right-on coffees plus some environmentally friendly home supplies. A worthy local shop. 10am-7pm (Sat till 5.30pm). Closed Sun.

346 1/XB5 **Lupe Pintos** **24 Leven Street** Unusual Latin deli (ie Mexican, Central American, Spanish). Where to go for chorizo, manchego and 20 kinds of tequila. Takeaway including home-made burritos and the usual Tex-Mex. Every kind of chili and great Riojas. Also in Glasgow (693/GLASGOW DELIS). 10am-6pm. Closed Sun.

Unique Edinburgh Pubs

347 1/XE1 ✔ ✔ **Port o' Leith www.lumison.co.uk/~portoleith · 58 Constitution Street** The legendary Leith bar on the busy road to what used to be the docks. The incorrigible and incorruptible Mary Moriarty still puts up the odd sailor but it's mainly the rest of us from the sea of life who frequent this unchanging neighbourhood pub full of warmth, chat, good music and all the things we left behind. DJs (great life-affirming music) Fri/Sat night. Truly a port in the storm. Go find it. Till 12.45am.

348 1/XB5 ✔ **Bennet's Leven Street** By King's Theatre. Just stand at the back and watch light stream through the stained glass on a sunny day as it always did. Same era as Café Royal and similar ambience, mirrors and tiles. Decent food at lunch and early even (385/PUB FOOD). Till 12.30am Mon-Fri, 1am Sat, 11pm Sun.

349 1/XE1 ✔ **The Pond** 0131 467 3815 · **2 Bath Road, Leith** Cool Edinburgh bar off Seafield Road on the edge of dead dockland. They don't make 'em as under-stated or laid-back as this anymore. Funky fishtanks and al fresco bit out the back. Till 1am. (408/COOL BARS).

350 1/D5 ✔ **Sandy Bells** 0131 225 2751 · **Forrest Road** Near the University and Greyfriars Kirk and seems like it's been there as long. Mainly known as a folky/traditional music haven (live 7 nights), it reeks (and we do mean reeks) of atmosphere. Should be given a dispensation from the smoking ban. Long may it... 7 days till 1am (Sun 11pm).

351 1/D2 ✔ **Café Royal Princes Street** Behind Burger King at the east end of the street, one of Edinburgh's longest-celebrated pubs. Unrelated to the London version, though there is a similar Victorian/Baroque elegance. Through the partition is the Oyster Bar (good atmosphere rather than food). Central counter and often standing room only. Open to 11pm (later at weekends).

352 1/D1 **Barony Bar www.broughtonstreet.co.uk/barony.htm · 81 Broughton Street** Real-ale venue with a mixed clientele and good vibe. Belgian and guest beers. Newspapers to browse over a Sun afternoon breakfast or a (big) lunchtime pie. Bert's band on Sun aft/evens one of the best pub nights in town. Till 12midnight Mon-Thu, 12.30am Fri-Sat, 11pm Sun.

353 1/D1 **The Basement www.thebasement.org.uk · 109 Broughton Street** Much-imitated, still crucial, this is a chunky, happening sort of, er, basement with perennially popular Mex-style food during the day served by laaarvely staff in Hawaiian shirts. At night, the punters are well up for it – late, loud and still alive. Till 1am daily.

354 1/B2 **Kay's Bar 39 Jamaica Street** The New Town – including Jamaica Street – sometimes gives the impression that it's populated by people who were around in the late 18th century. It's an Edinburgh thing (mainly male). They care for the beer (375/REAL-ALE PUBS) and do nice grub at lunchtime. Until 11.45pm (11pm Sun).

355 1/A3 **Mather's 1 Queensferry Street** Edinburgh's West End has a complement of 'smart' bars that cater for people with tight haircuts and tight agendas. The alternative is here – a stand-up space for old-fashioned pubbery, slack coiffure and idle talk (367/'UNSPOILT' PUBS). Wimmin rarely venture. Till 12midnight Mon-Thu, 1am Fri-Sat, 11pm Sun.

356 1/XE1   **Robbie's Leith Walk** On the corner with Iona Street. Some bars on Leith Walk are downright scary and there are many new, fluffier ones of late but Robbie's stays real. Good range of beer, TV will have the football on (or not). Magi mix of Trainspotters, locals and the odd dodgy character. (365/'UNSPOILT' PUBS). Till 12midnight Mon-Sat, 11pm Sun.

357 1/D4   **City Café www.thecitycafe.co.uk · 0131 220 0127 · 19 Blair Street** Seems ancient, but almost 20 years on, the retro Americana chic has aged gracefully. Pool tables, all-day food, decent coffee. A hip Edinburgh bar that has stood the test of mind-altering time. Music downstairs weekends courtesy of guest DJs (320/SUNDAY BREAKFAST). 11am-1am daily.

358 1/D4   **Three Sisters www.festival-ends.co.uk · Cowgate** Of many booming bars in the Cowgate, we still select this one – one of Edinburgh's busiest. Nothing very special but good conversion of old warehouse and better than your average super bar (with vast courtyard – usually rammed). 3 DJs at weekends. Also has rooms. 7 days, 11am-1am.

359 1/C2   **The Dome www.thedomeedinburgh.com · 0131 624 8624 · 14 George Street** Edinburgh's first megabar but not a chain. Former bank and grandiose in the way that only a converted temple to Mammon could be. Main part sits 15m under elegant domed roof with island bar and raised platform at back for determined diners. Staff impeccable; you come for the surroundings more than the victuals perhaps. Recent reports on the food ain't good but there is a snack menu for casual diners away from roped-off posh nosh area. Adjacent real-ale Art Deco bar Frazers is separate, more intimate, better for a blether. 'Garden' patio bar at back (in good weather) – enter via Rose Street. Final bit, downstairs: Why Not? – a nightclub for over-25s still lookin' for lurv (Fri/Sat). Main bar Sun-Thu till 11.30pm, Fri-Sat till 1am.

360 1/D3   **The Doric www.thedoric.co.uk · 0131 225 1084 · 15 Market Street** More a bistro/restaurant than a mere pub, but the smaller room by the bar is Edinburgh in a nutshell (178/GASTROPUBS). The window tables upstairs looking over the town offer one of the defining views of the city. New ownership '08.

The Best Old 'Unspoilt' Pubs

Of course it's not necessarily the case that when a pub's done up, it's spoiled, or that all old pubs are worth preserving, but some have resisted change and that's part of their appeal. Money and effort are often spent to 'oldify' bars and contrive an atmosphere. The following places don't have to try.

361 1/XA4   ✓ **The Diggers 1 Angle Park Terrace** (Officially the Athletic Arms.) Jambo pub *par excellence*, stowed with the Tynecastle faithful before and after games. Still keeps a great pint of McEwan's 80/-, allegedly the best in Edinburgh. The food is basic ie pies. Till 11pm/12midnight Mon-Sat, 11pm Sun.

362 1/D4   ✓ **The Royal Oak www.royal-oak-folk.com · Infirmary Street** Tiny upstairs and not much bigger down. During the day, pensioners sip their pints (couple of real ales) while the cellar opens till 2am. Has surprisingly survived the smoking ban. Mainly known as a folk-music stronghold, they definitely don't make 'em like this any more. Gold carat pubness.

363 1/XA4 ✓ **Roseburn Bar 1 Roseburn Terrace** On main Glasgow road out west from Haymarket and one of the nearest pubs to Murrayfield Stadium. Wood and grandeur and red leather, bonny wee snug, fine pint of McEwan's and wall-to-wall rugby of course. Heaving before internationals. Till 11pm (midnight weekends).

364 1/C2 ✓ **Clark's 142 Dundas Street** A couple of snug snugs, red leather, brewery mirrors and decidedly no frills. Good McEwan's – just the place to pop in if you're tooling downhill from town to Canonmills. A local you might learn to love. Till 11pm (11.30pm Thu-Sat).

365 1/XE1 **Robbie's Leith Walk** On the corner of Iona St. Real ales and new lagers in a neighbourhood howff that tolerates everyone from the wifie in her raincoat to multi-pierced yoof of indeterminate gender. More rough than smooth of course, but with the footy on the box, a pint and a packet of Hula Hoops – this is a bar to save or savour life. Till 12midnight Mon-Sat, 11pm Sun. Report: 356/UNIQUE EDINBURGH PUBS.

366 1/B3 **Oxford Bar www.oxfordbar.com · 8 Young Street** Downhill from George Street. No time machine needed – just step in the door to see an Edinburgh that hasn't changed since yon times. Careful what you say; this is an off-duty cop shop possibly including Inspector Rebus (and Ian Rankin fans from far and wide). Some real ales but they're as beside the point as the pies and the hastily constructed sandwich rolls. Till 1am (midnight Sun).

367 1/A3 **Mather's 1 Queensferry Street** Not only a reasonable real-ale pub but almost **1/D2** worth visiting just to look at the ornate fixtures and fittings – frieze and bar especially. Unreconstructed in every sense. Pies all day. Till 12midnight Mon-Thu, 1am Fri-Sat, 11pm Sun. Report: 355/UNIQUE PUBS. There's another, unrelated, **Mather's** in Broughton Street which is managing to keep its head in the city's grooviest thoroughfare by remaining pub-like and unpretentious. Football telly.

The Best Real-Ale Pubs

368 1/C1 ✓ **The Cumberland Bar www.thecumberlandbar.co.uk · Cumberland Street** Corner of Dundonald St. After work this New Town bar attracts its share of suits, but later the locals (and recently droves of ya students) claim it. CAMRA (Campaign for Real Ale) supporters seek it out too. Average of 8 real ales on tap. Nicely appointed, decent pub lunches, unexpected beer garden (393/DRINK OUTDOORS). 7 days till 1am.

369 1/C4 ✓ **The Bow Bar www.bowbar.com · 80 West Bow** Halfway down Victoria St. They know how to treat drink in this excellent wee bar. Huge selection ales and whiskies – no cocktails! One of the few places in the Grassmarket area an over 25-year-old might not feel out of place. Bliss. Till 11.30pm Mon-Sat, 11pm Sun.

370 1/B5 ✓ **Cloisters 26 Brougham Street, Tollcross** This is a drinker's paradise: 9 real ales on tap, 70 whiskies with 35ml measures and 9 wines by the glass in this simple and unfussy bar with its wooden floors and laid-back approach. Same owners as the Bow Bar (above). Good pub grub till 8pm (not Mon or Fri), bar closes 12midnight (12.30am Fri-Sat).

371 1/D2 ✓ **The Guildford Arms www.guildfordarms.com · 1 West Register Street** Behind Burger King at east end of Princes St on same block as the Café Royal (351/UNIQUE PUBS). Forever in the same family. Lofty, ornate Victorian hostelry with loadsa good ales, typically 7 Scottish, 3 English (and 16 wines by the glass). There are some you won't find anywhere else in the city. Pub grub available on 'gallery' floor as well as bar. Mingin' carpet by the way! Sun-Wed till 11pm, Thu-Sat till 12midnight.

372 1/B5 ✓ **Blue Blazer 2 Spittal Street** Opposite Point Hotel (91/INDIVIDUAL HOTELS). No frills, no pretensions, just wooden fixtures and fittings, pies and toasties in this fine howff that carries a huge range of real ales. Regularly a CAMRA pub of the year with 8 ales on tap. More soul than any of its competitors nearby even after recent refurbishment. 7 days till 1am.

373 1/XA4 **Bert's 29 William Street** Rare ales as well as house IPA and 80/-, suits as well
1/A1 as casual crowd in this *faux* Edwardian bar. Decent pies for carnivores or veggies alike all day, with other pub-grub lunch till 9pm. A good place to escape from office neurosis. Good range guest ales. Till 11pm Sun-Thu, 12midnight Fri-Sat. More local but similar **Bert's** (with pies) at 2 Raeburn Place, Stockbridge.

374 1/XB5 **The Canny Man 237 Morningside Road** Officially known as the Volunteer Arms, but everybody calls it the Canny Man. Good smorrebrod at lunch time and evenings (168/GASTROPUBS), a wide range of real ales and myriad malts. Casual visitors may feel that management have an attitude (problem) – there's a list of dos and don'ts on the door – but this family fiefdom has been here forever.

375 1/B2 **Kay's Bar 39 Jamaica Street** Off India Street in the New Town. Go on an afternoon when gentlemen of a certain age talk politics, history and rugby over pints of real ale. The Poirot-moustached barman patiently serves. All red and black and vaguely distinguished bar with a tiny snug – The Library. Comfort food simmers in the window (lunch only). Till 12midnight (11pm Sun). (354/UNIQUE PUBS)

376 1/XB1 **Starbank Inn www.starbankinn.co.uk · 64 Laverockbank Road, Newhaven** On the seafront road west of Newhaven harbour. Handful of different ales on offer. Great place to sit with pint in hand and watch the sun sink over the Forth. The food is fine (383/PUB FOOD). Bar till 11pm Sun-Wed, 12midnight Thu-Sat.

377 1/D1 **Cask & Barrel www.broughtonstreet.co.uk/cask&.htm · 115 Broughton Street** Wall-to-wall distressed wood, great selection of real ales and a mixed crowd at the foot of groovy Broughton St. 'Cept here they prefer a good pint and the football. Till 12.30am Sun-Wed, 1am Thu-Sat.

378 1/C4 **Black Bull Grassmarket** Below the Castle (north side). Vast woody cavern of a pub with ales, ok food and big-screen sports. Deuchars, Caledonian 80/- and 5 guests. Daily till 1am.

Pubs With Good Food

Also see Gastropubs, p. 43. These below are not so high-falutin' foodwise, but nevertheless are worth going to for food as well as drink.

379 1/XE1 ✓ **The Compass** 0131 554 1979 · **44 Queen Charlotte Street** Corner of Constitution St opposite Leith Police Station. This 'Bar & Grill' is a popular Leith haunt, maybe missed by uptown grazers. Stone and woody look with mix-match furniture; food better and more ambitious than you might first think. Staples and some Scottish cheeses. Taken over by Kings Wark '07 (171/GASTROPUBS). Bar kicks in later. 7 days, lunch & LO 9pm.

380 1/XE5 ✓ **Sheep's Heid** www.sheepheid.co.uk · 0131 656 6951 · **Causeway, Duddingston** 18th-century inn 6km from centre behind Arthur's Seat and reached most easily through the Queen's Park. OK grub including alfresco dining when possible and comfy upstairs room at weekends. Village and nearby wildfowl loch should be strolled around if you have time. Great atmosphere; food improving. Lunch & 6.30-8pm, LO 7.45pm. Bar till 11pm/12midnight. Book weekends.

381 1/XA4 ✓ **Caley Sample Room** www.thecaleysampleroom.co.uk · **58 Angle Park Terrace** The CSR purveys all the Caledonian ales from the nearby brewery and a couple of guests besides. But in '07 taken over by the people who have the Cambridge Bar (174/GASTROPUBS) so food has entered a different league. Great burgers and steaks but full menu and specials. Nice woody ambiance. Out-of-the-way location but go find. 7 days, lunch & LO 9pm (10pm Fri/Sat). Bar later.

382 1/D3 **Ecco Vino** www.eccovinoedinburgh.com · 0131 225 1441 · **19 Cockburn Street** Discreet frontage in street strewn with pierced youth. A narrow room where wines are supped. Med menu from tiny gantry kitchen with imaginative soups, spags and tarts. Nice antipasto. How do they do it? Food 12noon-10pm, bar till 12midnight, 1am Fri/Sat.

383 1/XB1 **Starbank Inn** www.starbankinn.co.uk · 0131 552 4141 · **64 Laverockbank Road** The seafront road in Newhaven. Long-established family pub with real ales (348/REAL ALE PUBS) and excellent value food, with big helpings. Great seafood salad as well as mince 'n' tatties on special. 7 days lunch and dinner LO 9pm (Sun all day menu). Bar 11pm, 12midnight weekends.

384 1/XB1 **Old Chain Pier** www.oldchainpier.co.uk · 0131 552 1233 · **1 Trinity Crescent** On the Forth just west of Newhaven Harbour. Right on the waterfront near Starbank (above), both near Ocean Terminal. Well-kept real ale, great bar snacks and decent-value bar meals with specials on blackboard. Main attraction is over-the-sea location and sun going down over Fife. LO food 9pm. Bar 11pm, 12midnight Thu-Sat. Wed is 'Ladies' Night'.

385 1/XB5 **Bennet's** 0131 229 5143 · **8 Leven Street** Next to the King's Theatre. An Edinburgh standby, listed for several reasons (348/UNIQUE PUBS), not least its honest-to-goodness (and cheap) pub lunch. À la carte (stovies, steak pie, etc.) and daily specials under the enormous mirrors. Lunch & till 8.30pm (not Sun).

386 1/C3 **The Abbotsford** www.theabbotsford.com · 0131 225 5276 · **3 Rose Street** A doughty remnant of Rose St drinking days of yore, and still the best pub lunch near Princes St. Fancier than it used to be but still grills and bread-and-butter pudding. Huge portions. Restaurant upstairs serves food in evening too – LO 9.45pm. Bar till 11pm. Closed Sun.

The Best Places To Drink Outdoors

387 1/C4   **The (Café) Hub** www.thehub-edinburgh.com · 0131 473 2067 · **Castlehill**
The café-bar of the International Festival Centre much improved for food with and
a great enclosed terrace for people-watching. Brollies and heaters extend the
possibilities.

388 1/XE1   **The Shore** www.theshore.biz · 0131 553 5080 · **3 The Shore, Leith** Excellent
place to eat (170/GASTROPUBS), some tables just outside the door, but it's fine to
wander over to the dock on the other side of the street and sit with your legs over
the edge. Do try not to fall in. From 11am daily.

389 1/XE1   **The Waterfront** www.waterfrontwinebar.co.uk · 0131 554 7427 · **1C Dock
Place** Another very good Leith eaterie (173/GASTROPUBS) but with waterside
tables and adjacent pontoon for those who fancy a float. Great wine list: 20 by the
glass. From 12noon Mon-Sat, 12.30pm Sun.

390 1/XF2   **The Dalriada** 0131 454 4500   Edinburgh's 'beachfront' bar on the Promenade
at Portobello (Joppa end, approach from main road/Portobello High St via
Brunstane Rd North). Hotel bar reminiscent of Oz with tables in the garden overlooking the strand (454/BEACHES). Food at lunchtime only. Music most nights.

391 1/D5   **Pear Tree** www.thepeartreehouse.co.uk · 0131 667 7533 · **38 West
Nicholson Street**   Adjacent to parts of Edinburgh University so real student style
with big beer garden – serried ranks of tables and refectory-style food. Good malt
list. From noon Mon-Sat, 12.30pm Sun. Round the corner on main drag, the oppor-
tunistically named **Human Be-In** spills out onto the wide pavement.

392 1/D2   **The Outhouse** 0131 557 6668 · **12a Broughton Street Lane**   Large enclosed
patio out back, home to summer Sun afternoon barbecues. No view except of
other people. Report: 404/COOL BARS.

393 1/B1   **The Cumberland Bar** 0131 558 3134 · **Cumberland Street**   Some tables by
the door slightly raised above street level but more space in the beer garden
below. Packed on summer evenings. Report: 368/REAL ALE.

394 1/E4   **The Pleasance** www.pleasance.co.uk · **The Pleasance**   Open during the
Festival only, this is one of the major Fringe venues, and has a large open courtyard. If you're here, you're on the Fringe, so to speak.

395 1/A5   **Cargo** 0131 659 7880 · **129 Fountainbridge**   At the so-called 'Edinburgh Quay'.
Lofty emporium pub with over-ambitious menu, mainly distinguished by outdoor
seating (in ranks of tables) on the basin of the Caledonian Canal – a surprising
waterside spot in the city centre.

396 1/D2   **The Street** 0131 556 4272 · **Corner of Picardy Place & Broughton Street**
Great people-watching potential on busy corner. See 405/COOL BARS.

General locations: **Greenside Place** (**Theatre Royal** and **Café Habana**), bars in
The Grassmarket, and **Negociants** and **Assembly** on **Lothian Street**. All make
a stab at pavement café culture when the sun's out.

Cool Bars

Depends what you mean by 'cool', of course. On this page there's the ultra-contemporary, style bar ethos of Tigerlily/Opal Lounge/indigo yard/Rick's and the funkier, not-trying-so-hard ambiance of 99 Hanover/Villager/Outhouse/Pond etc. It may depend on whether you care about looks, or feels.

397 1/B4 ✓ ✓ **Dragonfly www.dragonflycocktailbar.com · 0131 228 4543 · West Port** On the western extension of the Grassmarket. Discreet frontage but you enter a more beautiful, more stylish world where alcohol is treated like food in a fine-dining restaurant and cocktails are king. Lofty room with mezzanine. Tapas-type menu (12noon-9pm). Not too many distractions from the aesthetic. 7 days till 1am.

398 1/C2 ✓ **Tigerlily 0131 225 5005 · 125 George Street** Some will revel in it, others go 'yuck' to this style-blinding bar/restaurant/hotel. Opened '06 in the middle of all the other style bars on George St and immediately became 'it'. Every design feature of the times with great attention to detail. A destination for the smart and ambitious and those with nice hair and teeth. 7 days till 1am.

399 1/B3 ✓ **Opal Lounge www.opallounge.co.uk · 0131 226 2275 · 51a George Street** Basement in Edinburgh's fashion mile for ambitious 'lifestyle' project from the indigo (yard) stable (see below). Sunken and sexy lounges including dancefloor and restaurant (fusion menu though not what they do best). Great staff know how to serve cocktails. Big door presence. Wills with St Andrews mates was once a regular. Admission and queue after 10pm. Open till 3am 7 days (food till 10pm).

400 1/C3 ✓ **99 Hanover Street 0131 225 8200** Address as is. Unlikely location perhaps but through the curtain into a civilised, draped and candlelit world with cool clientele and excellent music (live Tue/Sat). It rocks. Till 1am.

401 1/C2 ✓ **Bramble 0131 226 6343 · Queen Street at Hanover Street** Discreet, hidden-away corner basement but cool as whatever (is cool these days), especially for cocktails. Discerning drinkers' haven so great gins, voddies, whiskies, etc. Nice Gen X (and Y and Z) people in the mix. Evenings only; till 1am.

402 1/D4 ✓ **The Jazz Bar 0131 220 4298 · Chambers Street** Down long stairs to the basement, this is not an obvious 'cool' bar unless you like good music and then it's very cool. No 'live band' tokenism here. Great ambiance, interesting people. Mostly free but occasional name -band nights. An Edinburgh treasure chest. 7 days 5pm-3am (2am Mon). Go groove!

403 1/D4 **Villager www.villager-e.com · 0131 226 2781 · 50 George IV Bridge** Near University and National Library a funked-up, laid-back place to hang out. DJs (Fri/Sat), reasonable pub food till 9.30 but mainly the right faces in a photo from the early days of the 21st century. Bar till 1am.

404 1/D2 **The Outhouse 0131 557 6668 · 12a Broughton Street Lane** Happily mixed and unobtrusive modern bar off Broughton Street 'in the lane' off the Pink Triangle. Modish food 12noon-7pm (4pm weekends) for self-conscious business diners and a regular (every other week) Sun barbecue on the patio (not the greatest of views). Till 1am.

405 1/D2 **The Street** 0131 556 4272 · **2 Picardy Place** Corner glass box at the top of Broughton Street at central crossroads in the Pink Triangle; so gay friendly. Great people-watching spot (outside tables) and pre-club venue. DJs weekends. Madame (Trendy) Wendy and gals in charge. 7 days till 1am.

406 1/A3 **indigo (yard)** www.indigoyardedinburgh.co.uk · 0131 220 5603 · **7 Charlotte Lane** Tucked away off Queensferry St in the West End, this long-established spacious nineties-thing café-bar offers exposed brickwork, balcony tables, booths and babes in blue of both genders serving good food and drink. More Med than Mex cuisine with flexible menu, but possibly too loud later on for serious dining (175/GASTROPUBS). Bar till 1am daily. Same people have **Rick's** (below), **Opal Lounge** and, of course, **Tigerlily** (above).

407 1/B2 **Rick's** www.ricksedinburgh.co.uk · 0131 622 7800 · **55a Frederick Street** New Town variant of the above. Another café-bar-restaurant but this time also with rooms (101/INDIVIDUAL HOTELS). Same problem with the eating experience here as the others viz too much noise from the bar, though probably best on this page. Bar service good and they know how to make cocktails. Rocks from 10 onwards (till 1am). Also good for breakfast.

408 1/XE1 **The Pond** **Bath Road & Salamander Street, Leith** Turn right at foot of Constitution St past the warehouses. This anti-style bar is a million miles from George St (and hard to find). Originally from the people who had clubs like Soft, Edinburgh Beige Cricket Team and the fanzine, *Shavers Weekly*, The Pond is where you'll find the people who don't want to be cool; they want to watch fish.

409 1/XE1 **Boda Bar** www.bodabar.com · **Corner of Leith Walk & Lorne Street**
1/B1 Swedish import unlikely but very welcome on the Walk. Boda a small village in north of Sweden, and this has village feel. Friendly staff. Well-chosen fare including snax (moose sausages anyone?). Sister bar **Sofi's** in Henderson St is similarly laid-back: the atmosphere is just right. 7 days 1am (Sun 12midnight).

410 1/B2 **Iglu** www.theiglu.com · **Jamaica Street** Off Howe St in the New Town. Surprisingly cool bar in conservative territory. Handily open late. Small upstairs garret with nice fish tank. Well regarded bistro upstairs (167/BISTROS). Very Edinburgh, kind of lovely! 4pm-1am (Fri/Sat from 12noon).

411 1/E4 **Brass Monkey** 0131 556 1961 · **14 Drummond Street** Light-touch conversion of former legendary pub with younger/studenty crowd than glory days. Backroom Bedouin boudoir full of cushions to lounge and big screen (movies at 3pm every day) – can hire for private functions. 7 days. LO 12.45am.

412 1/D4 **City Café** www.thecitycafe.co.uk · 0131 220 0127 · **19 Blair Street** A true original that went from *the* hippest, to nowhere, and now back again with cool night people. Buzzing at the weekend, downstairs the DJs play all kinds depending on the night. Pool tables never stop. 11am-1am daily. Then Sun: 320/SUNDAY BREAKFAST.

413 1/B5 **The Cameo Bar** 0131 228 2800 · **Tollcross** Enter round the corner on Lochrin Pl. This is the bar of the Cameo Cinema but is a cool drop-in bar in its own right. With coffee and cakes and soup and chat about the movie of life. 7 days till 12midnight.

The Main Attractions

414 1/B4
HS
ADMISSION

✓ ✓ ✓ **Edinburgh Castle** www.historic-scotland.gov.uk · 0131 225 9846 Go to Princes St and look up. Extremely busy all year round and yet the city's must-see main attraction does not disappoint. St Margaret's 12th-century chapel is simple and beautiful, the rolling history lesson that leads up to the display of Scotland's crown jewels is fascinating; the Stone of Destiny is a big deal to the Scots (though others may not see why). And, ultimately, the Scottish National War Memorial is one of the most genuinely affecting places in the country – a simple, dignified testament to shared pain and loss. The Esplanade is a major concert venue just before the Tattoo in Jul. The International Tattoo is the 'major event' of the Festival in August. Last ticket 45 minutes before closing. Apr-Oct 9.30am-6pm, Nov-Mar 9.30am-5pm.

415 10/P25

✓ ✓ ✓ **The Forth Bridge** www.forthbridges.org.uk · **South Queensferry** 20km west of Edinburgh via A90. First turning for South Queensferry from dual carriageway; don't confuse with signs for road bridge. Or train from Waverley to Dalmeny, and walk 1km. Knocking on now and showing its age (and true to legend takes forever to paint), the bridge was 100 in 1990. But still ... Can't see too many private finance initiative wallahs rushing in to do anything of similar scope these days. And who would have the vision? An international symbol of Scotland, it should be seen, but go to the north side, South Queensferry's very crowded and sadly, very tacky these days (shame on Tesco for spoiling the view from the road bridge approach and well done the Dakota for dramatising it; 130/HOTELS OUTSIDE TOWN). There is also a good hotel restaurant in South Queensferry (133/HOTELS OUTSIDE TOWN) with views of the bridge.

416 1/XA4
ADMISSION
ECO

✓ ✓ ✓ **Edinburgh Zoo** www.edinburghzoo.org.uk · 0131 334 9171 · **Corstorphine Road** 4km west of Princes St; buses from Princes St Gardens side. Whatever you think of zoos (see *Life of Pi*, the 2003 Booker prize winner), this one is highly respected and its serious zoology is still fun for kids (organised activities in Jul/Aug). The penguins waddle out at 2.15pm daily over summer months, and the sad, accusing eyes of the wolves connect with onlookers in a profoundly disconcerting manner. Opening late 2007 is the new enclosure for rainbow lorikeets and look out for the chimps on the Budongo Trail which opens Easter 2008. But there are many animals here to love and cherish. Open all year round 7 days, 9am-6pm Apr-Sep, 9am-4.30pm Nov-Feb, 9am-5pm Mar & Oct. (1776/KIDS)

417 1/XF3
HS
ADMISSION

✓ ✓ **Palace of Holyroodhouse** www.royal.gov.uk · 0131 556 5100 At the foot of the Royal Mile, the Queen's North Brit timeshare – she's here for a wee while late Jun/early Jul every year. Large parts of the palace are dull (Duke of Hamilton's loo, Queen's wardrobes) and only a dozen or so rooms are open, most dating from the 17th century but a couple from the earlier 16th-century bit. Lovely cornices abound. Anomalous Stuart features, adjacent 12th-century abbey ruins quite interesting. Apr-Oct: 9.30am-5pm (last ticket), daily. Nov-Mar: 9.30am-3.45pm (last ticket) daily. Also...
The Queen's Gallery 0131 556 5100 Relatively recent addition to the foot of the Royal Mile (opposite the Parliament building) with separate entrance and ticket from Holyroodhouse. By architect Ben Tindall (who also did the Hub at the top of the Royal Mile – this is better). Beautiful, contemporary setting for changing exhibits from Royal Collection every 6 months which include art, ceramics, tapestries, etc. Shop stuffed with monarchist mementoes. 7 days 9.30am-6pm (closed 4.30pm in winter).

418 1/C4 ✓ ✓ **The Royal Mile** www.edinburgh-royalmile.com The High Street,
1/D4   the medieval main thoroughfare of the capital following the trail from
1/D3 the volcanic crag of Castle Rock and connecting the 2 landmarks above. Heaving
1/E3 during the Festival but if on a winter's night you chance by with a frost settling on
1/F3 the cobbles and there's no one around, it's magical. Always interesting with its
wynds and closes (Dunbar's Close, Whitehorse Close, the secret garden opposite
Huntly House), but lots of tacky tartan shops too. Central block closed to traffic
during Festival Fringe to create best street performance space in UK. See it on a
walking tour – there are several especially at night (ghost/ghouls/witches, etc.).
Mercat Tours (0131 225 5445), Witchery (0131 225 6745) and City of the Dead (0131
225 9044) are pretty good.
Mary King's Close is part of a medieval street actually under the Royal Mile.
Tours daily 10am-9pm (last tour), till 4pm Nov-Mar. Enter through Warriston's
Close near City Chambers. **Scottish Poetry Library** is in Crichton's Close on right
between St Mary's Street and the Parliament. Great collections, lovely contempla-
tive space. Endorses Edinburgh's status as City of Literature. Mon-Fri 11am-6pm,
Sat 1-5pm. Closed Sun.

419 1/F3 ✓ ✓ **The Scottish Parliament** www.scottish.parliament.uk · **Royal**
ADMISSION   **Mile** · 0131 348 5200 Adjacent Holyrood (above) and Our Dynamic
Earth (below). Designed by Catalan architect Enric Morales who died long before it
opened, this building has been mired in controversy since first First Minister
Donald Dewar laid the first stone. Opened finally after huge cost overruns in 2004,
it is loved and hated in equal measure but should not be missed. Guided tours and
ticketed access to the Debating Chamber. Unquestionably the finest modern building in the city (in my view and others – it won the 2005 Stirling Prize, the UK's premier architectural award).

420 1/D4 ✓ ✓ **Royal Museum** www.nms.ac.uk · 0131 247 4422 · **Chambers**
FREE   **Street** From the skeletons to archaeological artefacts, stuffed animal
habitats to all that we have done. Humankind and its interests encapsulated (and
displayed) here. Building designed by Captain Francis Fowkes, Royal Engineers, and
completed in 1888. Impressive galleried atrium (with coffee shop) often hosts
dinners and parties. Closing in May 2008 for 4-year renovations. 7 days 10am-
5pm.

421 1/D4 ✓ ✓ **Museum of Scotland** www.nms.ac.uk · 0131 247 4422 · **Chambers**
FREE   **Street** The story of Scotland from geological beginnings to Kirsty Wark's
Saab Convertible, all housed in a marvellous, honey-sandstone building by Gordon
Benson and Alan Forsyth. Opened in Dec '98. World-class space with resonant
treasures like St Filian's Crozier and the Monymusk Reliquary, said to contain bits
of St Columba. Early peoples to famous recent ones. 7 days 10am-5pm. Tue open
till 8pm. **Tower Restaurant** (own entrance) is on the top floor (142/BEST
RESTAURANTS).

422 1/F3 ✓ ✓ **Our Dynamic Earth** www.dynamicearth.co.uk · 0131 550 7800 ·
ADMISSION   **Holyrood Road** Edinburgh's Millennium Dome, an interactive
museum/visitor attraction, made with Millennium money and a huge success
when it opened summer '99 though a little less dynamic than it was. Now within
the orbit and campus of the Parliament building. Salisbury Crags rise above. Vast
restaurant, and outside an amphitheatre. Apr-Oct 10am-6pm daily. Nov-Mar:
10am-5pm Wed-Sun. Last admission 1 hour 10 minutes before closing.

423 1/C3
FREE

✓ ✓ **National Gallery Of Scotland** www.nationalgalleries.org · 0131 624 6200 · **The Mound** Neoclassical buildings housing a superb collection of Old Masters in a series of hushed salons. Many are world famous, but you don't emerge goggle-eyed as you do from the National in London – more quietly elevated. Many blockbuster exhibitions in the pipeline. The building in front, the **Royal Scottish Academy**, reopened in Aug '03 after a lengthy refurbishment. Daily 10am-5pm, Thu 7pm. Extended hours during Festival.

424 1/XE1
ADMISSION

✓ ✓ **Royal Yacht Britannia** www.royalyachtbritannia.co.uk · 0131 555 5566 · **Ocean Drive, Leith** In the docks, enter by Commercial St at end of Great Junction St. Berthed outside Conran's shopping mall, the Ocean Terminal. Done with ruling the waves, the royal yacht has found a permanent home as a tourist attraction (and prestigious corporate night out). Close up, the Art Deco lines are surprisingly attractive, while the interior was one of the sets for our best-ever soap opera. Apr-Oct 9.30am-4.30pm; Jan-Mar & Oct-Dec 10am-3.30pm. Booking advised in Aug.

425 1/XE5

✓ **Royal Commonwealth Pool** www.edinburghleisure.co.uk/list · 0131 667 7211 · **Dalkeith Road** Hugely successful pool complex which includes a 50m main pool, a gym, sauna/ steam room/suntan suites, children's pool and play area, crèche and a jungle of flumes. Goes like a fair, morning to night. Some people find the water overtreated and over noisy, but Edinburgh has many good pools to choose from; this is the one that young folk prefer. Some lane swimming. Mon-Fri 6am-9.30pm (closed 9-10am Wed), Sat-Sun 10am-9pm. Sat-Sun 10am-4.30pm.

426 10/Q26
ADMISSION

✓ ✓ ✓ **Rosslyn Chapel, Roslin** www.rosslynchapel.org.uk · 0131 440 2159 The ancient chapel 12km south of city, made famous recently by the world bestseller, *The Da Vinci Code*. Apr-Oct Mon-Sat, 9.30am-6pm. Oct-Mar Sun only, 12noon-4.45pm. Report: 1941/CHURCHES.

The Other Attractions

427 1/XB1
ADMISSION
FOR
GLASSHOUSES;
OTHERWISE
FREE

✓ ✓ ✓ **Royal Botanic Garden** www.rgbe.org.uk · 0131 552 7171 · **Inverleith Row** 3km Princes Street. Enter from Inverleith Row or Arboretum Place. 70 acres of ornamental gardens, trees and walkways; a joy in every season. Tropical plant houses, landscaped rock and heath garden and space just to wander. Chinese Garden coming on nicely, precocious squirrels everywhere. The 'Botanics' have talks, guided tours, events (info 0131 248 2968). They also look after other important outstanding gardens in Scotland. Gallery with occasional exhibitions and café with outdoor terrace for serene afternoon teas (296/BEST TEA-ROOMS). Total integrity and the natural high. Houses the National Biodiversity Interpretation Centre. Open 7 days Nov-Feb 10am-4pm, Mar & Oct 10-6pm, Apr-Sep 10am-7pm.

428 1/C2
FREE

✓ ✓ **Scottish National Portrait Gallery** www.nationalgalleries.org · 0131 624 6200 · **1 Queen Street** Sir Robert Rowand Anderson's fabulous and custom-built neo-Gothic pile holds paintings and photos of the good, great and merely famous. Alex Ferguson hangs out next to Queen Mum and Nasmyth's familiar Burns pic is here. Good venue for photo exhibitions, beautiful atrium with star-flecked ceiling and frieze of (mainly) men in Scottish history from a Stone-Age chief to Carlyle. Splendid. Great café (287/BEST TEAROOMS). Get there soon as the whole gallery closes at the end of 2008 for major renovations lasting at least 18 months. Mon-Sat 10am-5pm, 7pm on Thu.

429 1/XA3
FREE

✓ **Scottish National Gallery of Modern Art** www.nationalgalleries.org · **0131 624 6200** · **Belford Road** Between Queensferry Rd and Dean Village (nice to walk through). Best to start from Palmerston Pl and keep left or see below (Dean Gallery). Former school with permanent collection from Impressionism to Hockney and the Scottish painters alongside. An intimate space where you can fall in love (with paintings or each other). Important temporary exhibitions. Excellent café (286/BEST TEAROOMS). Charles Jencks art in the landscape piece outside is stunning. Mon-Sat 10am-5pm, 7pm on Thu. Extended hours during Festival.

430 1/XA3
FREE

Dean Gallery www.nationalgalleries.org · **0131 624 6200** · **Belford Road** Across (busy) road from GOMA. Relatively new addition to Edinburgh art and life – sexy, intimate spaces, communal coffee shop, gardens to wander. Superb 20th-century collection; many surreal moments. Great way to approach both galleries is by Water of Leith Walkway (435/WALKS IN THE CITY). Mon-Sat 10am-5pm, Thu 7pm.

431 1/E3
FREE

Museum of Childhood www.museumofchildhood.org.uk · **0131 529 4142** · **42 High Street** Local-authority-run shrine to the dreamstuff of tender days where you'll find everything from tin soldiers to Lady Penelope on video. Full of adults saying, 'I had one of them!' Child-size mannequins in upper gallery can be very spooky if you're up there alone. Mon-Sat 10am-5pm. Jul & Aug Sun 12noon-5pm. Report: 1776/KIDS.

432 1/D4
FREE

St Giles' Cathedral www.stgilescathedral.org.uk · **0131 225 9442** · **Royal Mile** Not a cathedral really, although it was once – the High Kirk of Edinburgh, Church of Scotland central and heart of the city since the 9th century. The building is mainly medieval with Norman fragments, all encased in a Georgian exterior. Lorimer's oddly ornate and chapel and the 'big new organ' are impressive. Simple, austere design and bronze of John Knox set the tone historically. Holy Communion daily and other regular services. Atmospheric coffee shop in the crypt. Mon-Fri 9am-7pm (till 5pm in winter), Sat 9am-5pm, Sun 1-5pm.

433 1/A3
NATIONAL
TRUST FOR
SCOTLAND

The Georgian House www.nts.org.uk · **0131 225 2160** · **7 Charlotte Square** Built in the 1790s, this town house is full of period furniture and fittings. Not many rooms, but the dining room and kitchen are drop-dead gorgeous – you want to eat and cook there. Delightful ladies from the National Trust for Scotland answer your queries. Apr-Oct 10am-5pm (1 Jul-31 August 10am-7pm), Mar & Nov 11am-3pm. Closed Dec-Feb.

434 10/P25
ADMISSION

Lauriston Castle www.cac.org.uk · **0131 336 2060** · **Cramond Road South** 9km west of centre by A90, turn right for Cramond. Elegant architecture and gracious living. Largely Jacobean tower house set in tranquil grounds overlooking the Forth. The liveability of the house and preoccupations of the Reid family make you wish you could poke around but exquisite decorative pieces and furniture mean it's guided tours only. Continue to Cramond for the air (437/WALKS IN THE CITY). Apr-Oct 11.20am, 12.20pm, 2.20pm, 3.20pm, 4.20pm. Closed Fri. Nov-Mar 2.20pm & 3.20pm weekends only.

Arthur's Seat Report: 436/WALKS IN THE CITY.
The Pentlands Report: 439/WALKS OUTSIDE THE CITY.
The Scott Monument/Calton Hill Report: 460/457/BEST VIEWS.
Newhailes House Report: 1914/COUNTRY HOUSES.
Dr Neil's (Secret) Garden Report: 1597/GARDENS.

The Best Walks In The City

See p. 12 for walk codes.

435 1/XA2
1/A2
1/A1
1/XA1
1–15KM
XCIRC
BIKES
1-A-1

✓ ✓ **Water Of Leith** www.waterofleith.org.uk The indefatigable wee river that runs from the Pentlands through the city and into the docks at Leith can be walked for most of its length. The longest section from Balerno 12km outside the city, through Colinton Dell to the Tickled Trout pub car park on Lanark Road (4km from city centre). The 'Dell' itself is a popular glen walk (1–2km). All in all a superb urban walk. The Water of Leith visitor centre opposite the Tickled Trout is worth a look. (0131 455 7367). Open 7 days 10am-4pm all year round.
START (A) A70 to Currie, Juniper Green, Balerno; park by High School. (B) Dean Village to Stockbridge: enter through a marked gate opposite Menzies Belford Hotel on Belford Road (combine with a visit to the art galleries) (429/430/ATTRACTIONS). (C) Warriston, through the spooky old graveyard, to The Shore in Leith (plenty of pubs to repair to). Enter by going to the end of the cul-de-sac at Warriston Crescent in Canonmills; climb up the bank and turn left. Most of the Walkway (A, B and C) is cinder track and good cycling.

436 1/XF3
1–8KM
CIRC
MTBIKES
(RESTRICTED
ACCESS)
2-B-2

✓ ✓ **Arthur's Seat** Of many walks, a good circular one taking in the wilder bits, the lochs and great views (458/BEST VIEWS) starts from St Margaret's Loch at the far end of the park from Holyrood Palace. Leaving the car park, skirt the loch and head for the ruined chapel. After 250m in a dry valley, the buttress of the main summit rears above you on the right. Keeping it to the right, ascend over a saddle joining the main route from Dunsapie Loch which appears below on the left. Crow Hill is the other peak crowned by a triangular cairn – both can be slippery when wet. From Arthur's Seat head for and traverse the long steep incline of Salisbury Crags. Paths parallel to the edge lead back to the chapel. Just cross the road by the Palace and head up. No mountain bikes. For info on the Ranger service and special events through the year, call 0131 652 8150.
PARK There are car parks beside the loch and in front of the palace (paths start here too, across the road).
START Enter park at palace at foot of the High Street. Cross main road or follow for 1km; the loch is on the right.

437 1/XA1
1/3/8KM
XCIRC
BIKES
1-A-1

Cramond This is the charming village (though not the suburb) on the Forth at the mouth of the Almond with a variety of great walks. (A) To the right along the 'prom'; the traditional seaside stroll. (B) Across the causeway at low tide to Cramond Island (1km). Best to follow the tide out; this allows 4 hours (tides are posted). People have been known to stay the night in summer, but this is discouraged. (C) Enter estate by the East Craigie gate to west of Cramond Brig Hotel (at TGP the tiny passenger boat which used to cross the mouth of the Almond, has stopped running) then follow coastal path to Dalmeny House which is open to the public in the afternoons (Jul & Aug, Sun-Tue); or walk all the way to South Queensferry (8km). (D) Past the boathouse and up the River Almond Heritage Trail which goes eventually to the Cramond Brig Hotel on the A90 and thence to the old airport (3-8km). Though it goes through suburbs and seems to be on the flight path of the London shuttle, the Almond is a real river with a charm and ecosystem of its own. **The Cramond Gallery Bistro** (0131 312 6555) on the riverside is not a bad wee bistro – its great cakes await your return. 7 days. **Cramond Inn** is another great place to recharge.
START Leave centre by Queensferry Road (A90), then right following signs for Cramond. Cramond Road North leads to Cramond Glebe Road; go to end.
PARK Large car park off Cramond Glebe Road to right. Walk 100m to sea.

438 1/XA4
1-7KM
CIRC
XBIKES
1-A-1

Corstorphine Hill www.corstorphinehill.ukf.net West of centre, a knobbly hilly area of birch, beech and oak, criss-crossed by trails. A perfect place for the contemplation of life's little mysteries and mistakes. Or walking the dog. It has a radio mast, a ruined tower, a boundary with the wild plains of Africa (at the zoo) and a vast redundant nuclear shelter that nobody's supposed to know about. See how many you can spot. If it had a tearoom in an old pavilion, it would be perfect. **START** Leave centre by Queensferry Road and 8km out turn left at lights, signed Clermiston. The hill is on your left for the next 2km.
PARK Park where safe, on or near this road (Clermiston Road).

Easy Walks Outside The City

439 10/P26
1-20KM
CAN BE CIRC
MTBIKES
2-B-2

✓ **The Pentlands** www.edinburgh.gov.uk/phrp · 01968 677879 or 0131 445 3383 (Pentland Hills Regional Park) A serious range of hills rising to almost 600m, remote in parts and offering some fine walking. There are many paths up the various tops and round the lochs and reservoirs. (A) A good start in town is made by going off the bypass at Colinton, follow signs for Colinton Village, then the left fork up Woodhall Road. Second left up Bonaly Road (signed Bonaly Scout Camp). Drive/walk as far as you can (2km) and park by the gate leading to the hill proper where there is a map showing routes. The path to Glencorse is one of the classic Pentland walks. (B) Most walks start from signposted gateways on the A702 Biggar Road. There are starts at Boghall (5km after Hillend ski slope); on the long straight stretch before Silverburn (a 10km path to Balerno); from Habbie's Howe about 18km from town; and from the village of Carlops, 22km from town. (C) The most popular start is probably from the visitor centre behind the Flotterstone Inn, also on the A702, 14km from town (decent pub lunch and 6-10pm, all day weekends); trailboard and ranger service. The remoter tops around Loganlea Reservoir are worth the extra mile.

440 10/Q25
1-4KM
CAN BE CIRC
XBIKES
1-A-1

Hermitage of Braid www.fohb.org Strictly speaking, still in town, but a real sense of being in a country glen and from the windy tops of the Braid Hills there are some marvellous views back over the city. Main track along the burn is easy to follow and you eventually come to Hermitage House info centre; any paths ascending to the right take you to the ridge of Blackford Hill. In winter, there's a great sledging place over the first bridge up to the left and across the main road. **START** Blackford Glen Road. Go south on Mayfield to main T-junction with Liberton Road, turn right (signed Penicuik) then hard right.

441 10/Q26
1-8KM
XCIRC
BIKES
1-A-1

Roslin Glen www.midlothian.gov.uk Spiritual, historical, enchanting, now very famous with the chapel (1941/CHURCHES), a ruined castle and woodland walks along the River Esk.
START A701 from Mayfield or Newington (or bypass, turnoff Penicuik, A702 then fork left on A703 to Roslin). Some parking at chapel (1881/CHURCHES), 500m from corner of Main Street/Manse Road, or follow B7003 to Rosewell (also marked Rosslynlee Hospital) and 1km from village the main car park is to the left.

442 10/P25
2-8KM
XCIRC
BIKES
1-A-1

Almondell www.westlothian.gov.uk · 01506 882254 A country park to west of city (18km) near (and one of the best things about) Livingston. A deep, peaceful woody cleft with easy paths and riverine meadows. Fine for kids, lovers and dog walkers. Visitor centre with teashop. Trails marked. Apr-Oct 9am-5pm. Nov-Mar 11am-4pm. Closed 12.30-1am daily. .
START Best approach from Edinburgh by A71 via Sighthill. After Wilkieston, turn right for Camps (B7015) then follow signs. Or A89 to Broxburn past start of M8. Follow signs from Broxburn.

443 10/N25
2–8KM
CIRC
MTBIKES
1-A-1

Beecraigs and Cockleroy Hill www.beecraigs.com Another country park south of Linlithgow with trails and clearings in mixed woods, a deer farm and a fishing loch. Great adventure playground for kids. Best is the climb and extra-ordinary view from Cockleroy Hill, far better than you'd expect for the effort – from Ben Lomond to the Bass Rock; and the gunge of Grangemouth in the sky to the east. 01506 844516 for opening times which vary on a 9am-4.30pm theme.
START M90 to Linlithgow (26km), through town and left on Preston Rd. Go on 4km, park is signed, but for hill you don't need to take the left turn. The hill, and nearest car park to it, are on the right.

444 10/Q26
7KM
XCIRC
XBIKES
1-B-2

Borthwick and Crichton Castles www.borthwickcastle.com Takes in 2 impressive castles, the first a posh hotel (113/HOTELS OUTSIDE TOWN) and the other an imposing ruin on a ridge overlooking the Tyne. A walk through dramatic Border Country steeped in lore. From Borthwick follow the old railway line. From Crichton, start behind ruined chapel. In summer the vegetation can be high and may defeat you.
START From Borthwick: A7 south for 16km, past Gorebridge, left at North Middleton; signed. From Crichton: A68 almost to Pathhead, signed then 3km past church. Park and walk 250m.

Woodland Walks Near Edinburgh

445 10/P27
ADMISSION

✓ **Dawyck Gardens** www.rbge.org.uk · **01721 760254** · **Near Stobo** 10km west of Peebles on B712 Moffat road. Outstation of the Edinburgh Botanics. Tree planting here goes back 300 years. Sloping grounds around the Scrape Burn which trickles into the Tweed. Landscaped woody pathways for meditative walks. Famous for shrubs, fungi and blue Himalayan poppies. New visitor centre opening in February 2008. Apr-Sep 10am-6pm, Mar & Oct 10am-5pm, Nov & Feb 10am-4pm. 7 days. Closed Dec-Jan. Major upgrading of facilities at TGP.

446 10/Q25
ADMISSION

✓ **Dalkeith Country Park** www.dalkeithcountrypark.com · **Dalkeith** 15km SE by A68. The wooded policies of Dalkeith House; enter at end of Main Street. Along the river banks and under these stately deciduous trees, carpets of bluebells, daffs and snowdrops, primroses and wild garlic according to season. Most extensive preserved ancient oak forest in southern Scotland. Excellent adventure playground. Rangers 654 1666. Open 7 days 10am-5.30pm through summer.

447 10/R26

✓ **The Yester Estate** Gifford With the decease of opera impresario Minotti, the large estate surrounding his house has become at last more approachable and there are some beautiful woodland walks in these grounds. Hard to find (and I won't tell you how) is the legendary Goblin Ha', the bad-fairy place (the hotel in the village takes its name; 1404/GASTROPUBS). Can walk in from The Avenue in the village or better: 3km along the B6365 road, foot of steep tree-lined hill, on bend. Park by house and go through marked gate. 3km through to village, it's 2km to Goblin Ha' itself.

448 10/R26

Humbie Woods 25km SE by A68 turnoff at Fala. Follow signs for church. Most open woods (beech) beyond car park. The churchyard is as reassuring a place to be buried as you could wish for; if you're set on cremation, come here and think of earth. Follow path from churchyard wall past cottage.

449 10/R25

Smeaton Nursery & Gardens www.eastlothian.gov.uk · **01620 860501** · **East Linton** 2km from village on North Berwick road (signed Smeaton). Up a drive in an old estate is this walled garden going back to the early 19th century. An additional pleasure is the Lake Walk halfway down the drive through a small gate in the woods. A 1km stroll round a secret finger lake in magnificent woodland. Garden Centre hours Mon-Sat 9.30am-4.30pm, Sun from 10.30am; phone for winter hours. Tearoom 10.30am-4pm Wed-Sun. (2304/GARDEN CENTRES) Lake walk 10am-dusk.

450 10/R25   **Woodhall Dean** www.swt.org.uk · **Near Dunbar** From Spott roundabout on A1 by Dunbar, go to spotless Spott village then follow old road sign for Woodhall and Elmscleugh (take left halfway down main road through village, uphill then 3km. After another old road sign to Innerwick, it's 200m. You'll see a red gash in the hillside before 'The Ford'). Damp walk to ancient oak woodland. Not many people!

451 10/Q26   **Vogrie Country Park** www.midlothian.gov.uk · **Near Gorebridge** 25km south by A7 then B6372 6km from Gorebridge. Small country park well organised for 'recreational pursuits'. 9-hole golf course, tearoom and country ranger staff. 01875 821990 for events and opening times. Busy on Sun, but otherwise a corral of countryside on the very edge of town.

452 10/Q27   **Cardrona Forest/Glentress** www.7stanes.gov.uk · **Near Peebles** 40km south to Peebles, 8km east on B7062 and similar distance on A72. Cardrona on same road as Kailzie Garden. Tearoom (Apr-Oct). Forestry Commission woodlands so mostly regimented firs, but Scots pine and deciduous trees up the burn. Glentress (on A72 to Innerleithen) has become a major destination for mountain bikers, but great track also to walk. Consult at **The Hub** (01721 721736) by car park (1464/GREAT CAFÉS). See 2103/CYCLING.

The Best Beaches

453 10/R25   ✓**Seacliff** The best: least crowded/littered; perfect for picnics, beachcombing and gazing into rock pools. Harbour good for swimming. 50km from Edinburgh, off the A198 out of North Berwick, 3km after Tantallon Castle (1883/RUINS). At a bend in the road and a farm (Auldhame) is an unsigned road off to the left. 2km on there's a barrier, costing £2 (2 x £1 coins) for cars. Car park 1km then walk. From A1, take East Linton turnoff, go through Whitekirk towards North Berwick, then same. Seacliff: if Edinburgh had its own beach, this would be it!

454 10/Q25   **Portobello** Edinburgh's town beach, 8km from centre by London Rd. When sunny – chips, lager, bad ice cream and hordes of people like Bondi, minus the surf. When miserable – soulful dog walkers and the echo of summers past. Arcades, mini-funfair, long prom and pool (454/SPORTS FACILITIES). But with more summers like 2007, the comeback is on hold. **Dalriada** pub is great for a seaside drink and food; lunch and LO 9pm.

455 10/R25   **Yellowcraigs** Nearest decent beach (35km). A1 or bypass, then A198 coast road. Left outside Dirleton for 2km, park and walk 100m across links to fairly clean strand and sea. Gets busy, but big enough to share. Hardly anyone swims, but you can. Many a barbie has braved the indifferent breeze, but on summer evenings, the sea slips ashore like liquid gold. See also 1779/KIDS PLACES. Scenic. **Gullane Bents**, a sweep of beach, is nearby and reached from village main street. Connects westwards with **Aberlady Reserve**.

456 10/R25   **Silver Sands** Aberdour Over Forth Bridge on edge of charming Fife village (1645/COASTAL VILLAGES). Can go by train from Edinburgh. Café and cliff walk.

The Best Views of the City

457 1/E2 ✓ ✓ **Calton Hill** Great view of the city easily gained by walking up from east end of Princes Street by Waterloo Place, to the end of the buildings and then up stairs on the left. The City Observatory and the Greek-style folly lend an elegant backdrop to a panorama (unfolding as you walk round) where the view up Princes St and the sweep of the Forth estuary are particularly fine. At night, the city twinkles. Popular cruising area for gays – take care if you do.

458 1/XF3 ✓ ✓ **Arthur's Seat** East of city centre. Best approach through Holyrood Park from foot of Canongate by Holyrood Palace. The igneous core of an extinct volcano with the precipitous sill of Salisbury Crags presiding over the city and offering fine views for the fit. Top is 251m; on a clear day you can see 100km. Surprisingly wild considering proximity to city. Report: 436/WALKS IN THE CITY.

459 1/B5 **Penthouse of the Point Hotel** www.point-hotel.co.uk · 0131 221 5555 · **34 Bread Street** Unknown spot but the small penthouse function space of the cool, design-driven Point Hotel (91/INDIVIDUAL HOTELS) offers a unique perspective of the city. They allow you up if there's nothing booked in. This room is where a group first met to 'rebrand' the city in a campaign where Edinburgh is now Edinburgh Inspiring Capital. This view is where the 'inspiration' came from.

460 1/C3
ADMISSION **Scott Monument** www.cac.org.uk · 0131 529 4068 · **Princes Street** Design inspiration for Thunderbird 3. This 1844 Gothic memorial to one of Scotland's best-kent literary sons rises 61.5m above the main drag and provides scope for the vertiginous to come to terms with their affliction. 287 steps mean it's no cakewalk; narrow stairwells weed out claustrophobics too. Those who make it to the top are rewarded with fine views. Underneath, a statue of the mournful Sir Walter gazes across at Jenners. Apr-Sep Mon-Sat 9am-6pm, Sun 10am-6pm; Oct-Mar, Mon-Sat 9am-3pm, Sun 10am-3pm. Last entry 30 minutes before closing.

461 1/C4
ADMISSION **Camera Obscura** www.camera-obscura.co.uk · 0131 226 3709 · **Castlehill, Royal Mile** At very top of street near castle entrance, a tourist attraction that, surprisingly, has been there for over a century. You ascend through a shop, photography exhibitions and interactive gallery to the viewing area where a continuous stream of small groups are shown the effect of the giant revolving periscope thingie. All Edinburgh life is visible – amazing how much fun can be had from a pin-hole camera with a focal length of 8.6m. Apr-Oct 9.30am-6pm. Nov-Mar 10am-5pm. 7 days.

462 10/R25
BOTH 1-A-1 **North Berwick Law** www.eastlothian.gov.uk The conical volcanic hill, a beacon in the East Lothian landscape easily reached from downtown North Berwick. **Traprain Law** nearby is higher, tends to be frequented by rock-climbers, but has major prehistoric hill fort citadel of the Goddodin and a definite aura. Both are good family climbs.

The Pentlands/Hermitage Report: 439/440/WALKS OUTSIDE CITY.
Edinburgh Castle Ramparts Report: 414 ATTRACTIONS.

The Best Sports Facilities

SWIMMING AND INDOOR SPORTS CENTRES

463 1/XE5 ✓ ✓ **Royal Commonwealth Pool** www.edinburghleisure.co.uk/list ·
1/XB5   0131 667 7211 · **Dalkeith Road** (425/MAIN ATTRACTIONS). The biggest,
1/XE1 but Edinburgh has many others. Recommended are **Warrender** (0131 447 0052),
1/XA1 Thirlestane Road 500m beyond the Meadows south of centre; **Leith Victoria**
(0131 555 4728), in Junction Pl off the main street in Leith complete with crèche
facilities; **Glenogle** (0131 343 6376) in Stockbridge, the New Town choice, very
friendly. All these pools are old and tiled, 25 yards long, seldom crowded and
excellent for lane swimming – at certain times. Also all have Pulse centres and fitness classes. Different sessions, phone to check.

464 1/A4 ✓ ✓ **One Spa** www.starwoodhotels.com/sheraton/grandedinburgh ·
0131 229 9131 · **Sheraton Grand Hotel** (81/BEST HOTELS) Actually a
separate 4-storey building behind hotel, offering the 'height' of luxury with usual
pool and a highly unusual outdoor one dangling over Conference Sq; spa and gym.
Exotic hydrotherapy, whole-body mud encasement and treatments for anything
and everything. Emphasis on pampering rather than sport. Treat yourself to a day
or half-day ticket (1335/BEST SPAS).

465 1/D3 ✓ **Escape** www.thescotsmanhotel.co.uk · 0131 556 5565 · **Scotsman
Hotel** Enter through Scotsman Hotel (87/INDIVIDUAL HOTELS) or from Market
St. Metallic, modern health club with all facilities and excellent service. Low-lit
pool, floor of machinery. Sexy, almost cruisy. Best to look good *before* you get here!
Some day membership available.

466 1/E2 ✓ **Virgin Active** 0131 550 1650 · **Greenside Place** Part of the 'Omnicentre'
with its mediocre multiplex and predictable restaurants. But VA, as elsewhere
UK, has upmarket aspirations if High Street realisation. This place very clean,
corporate and well – cruisy. 25-lane pool, usual machinery. Many courses, classes
and the attentions of a lithe young trainer. Day membership available.

467 1/XF2 **Portobello** www.swimportobello.com · 0131 669 6888 · **Portobello
Esplanade** (454/BEACHES) Similar to other civic pools above. Refurbished,
excellent Turkish baths still there, ladies-only, gents-only and mixed days. Phone
for details.

468 1/XE1 **Ainslie Park** www.edinburghleisure.co.uk/list-73 · 0131 551 2400 · **Pilton
Drive** Off Ferry Rd, north of centre, 5km from Princes St. Has serious keep-fit side
but all the usual spa, sauna, steam too. Mon-Thu 7.30am-10pm, Fri 7.30am-9pm,
Sat & Sun 8am-5.30pm. No day membership.

469 1/XB1 **Next Generation** www.nextgenerationclubs.co.uk · 0131 554 5000 ·
Newhaven Harbour Very much part of the regeneration of the waterfront, this
sportsarama complex in the David Lloyd stable (in fact son of, hence naff name).
Courts, gym, 2 pools including one outdoor overlooking Forth (only in non-wet
weather). Assorted summer courses for children. Not cheap, but not as expensive
as some in town. 7 days till 11.30pm. Day memberships.

470 1/XF1 **Meadowbank** www.edinburghleisure.co.uk/list-87 · 0131 661 5351 ·
London Road Well-worn city athletics stadium; major refurbishment may be on
the way. Squash and badminton courts (book), Pulse centre, weights room, 13m
indoor climbing wall, all-weather football/hockey pitches, velodrome. No pool.

471 1/E4 **University Gym** www.sport.ed.ac.uk · 0131 650 2585 · **The Pleasance**
No-nonsense complex, relatively cheap. The best in town for weights (all the right
machinery) and circuit training. Squash, badminton, indoor tennis, etc. Membership required (can be short-term) but not during the quiet vacation periods. For a
reasonable fee, the Fitness and Sports Injury Centre (FASIC) is an excellent
alternative to the 'take 2 aspirin and go away' school of GP. Few fake suntans or
lardarses here.

472 1/XA3 **Drumsheugh Baths Club** www.drumsheughbaths.com · 0131 225 2200 ·
5 Belford Road Private swimming club in elegant building above Dean Village
that's more exclusive than most. Gorgeous Victorian pool with rings and trapeze
over the water, sauna, multigym and bistro. Frequented by the quality. Go as a
guest.

473 1/D3 **Balmoral Spa, Balmoral Hotel** www.thebalmoralhotel.com · 0131 556
2414 Health club for residents (79/BEST HOTELS), members and visitors (half-day
tickets). Pool, sauna, steam, gym.

GOLF COURSES

*There are several municipal courses (see phone book under City of Edinburgh Council)
and nearby, especially down the coast, some famous names not open to non-members.*

474 1/XE5 **Braid Hills** www.edinburghleisure.co.uk/list-4 · 0131 447 6666 Braid Hills
approach. 2 18-hole courses (no. 2 summer only). Thought to be the best in town.
Never boring; exhilarating views. Booking usually not essential, except evenings
and weekends. Women welcome (and that ain't true everywhere round here).

 Gullane No. 1 01620 842255 The best of 3 courses in pretty village.
Report: 2132/GREAT GOLF COURSES.

 Glen Golf Club (aka North Berwick East) 01620 892726 36 km
from Edinburgh, worth the drive. Report: 2133/GREAT GOLF COURSES.

Musselburgh 0131 665 5438 Original home of golf. Report: 2134/GREAT GOLF
COURSES.
Gifford 01620 810591 Off the beaten track. Report: 2161/GOOD GOLF.

OTHER ACTIVITIES
475 10/P25 **Climbing: The Edinburgh International Climbing Arena**
www.adventurescotland.com · 0131 333 6333 · **Platt Hill, Ratho**
Follow signs from the M8, M9 and A71. Opened late 2003 after a long climb!
Ambitious and exciting facility designed to appeal to Joe Public and elite athletes
alike. Activities include abseils, team-building games, the Arial Assault, a state-of-
the-art adventure sports gym, spa, sauna and steamroom, softplay area for kids
under 9, not to mention the **National Rock Climbing Centre** – the best climbing
arena in the world in the roofed-off quarry. There's a café, 220-seater theatre,
corporate facilities and retail sector (including the excellent Tiso). 9am-10pm Mon-
Fri; 10am-7pm Sat/Sun. Best to book by phone. Also:

476 1/XD1 **Alien Rock** www.alienrock.co.uk · 0131 552 7211 · **Pier Place, Newhaven**
Indoor rock climbing in Old St Andrew's Church, a converted kirk. Laid-back
atmosphere, bouldering room and interesting 12m walls of various gnarliness to
scoot up. Daily; phone for sessions. Have a pint after in **The Starbank** or **The Old
Chain Pier** nearby (383/384/PUB FOOD).

477 10/P25 ✓ **Skiing: Midlothian Ski Centre (Hillend)** www.midlothian.gov.uk ·
0131 445 4433 Artificial slopes at on A702, 10km south of centre. Excellent facility with various runs. The matting can be bloody rough when you fall and the chairlift is a bit of a dread for beginners, but once you can ski here, Vale is all yours. Tuition available. Open 9.30am-9pm (7pm Sun in summer). Snowboarders welcome but Whistler it ain't.

478 1/XE5 **Tennis** www.edinburghleisure.co.uk Many private clubs though only the **Grange** (0131 332 2148) has lawn tennis and you won't get on there easily. There are places you can slip on (best not to talk about that), but the municipal centres (Edinburgh residents/longer-stay visitors should get a Leisure Access card from any Edinburgh leisure centre allowing advance reservation) are: **The Meadows** (northeast corner by University Library). Just turn up. Many courts; **Saughton** (0131 444 0422). Stevenson Dr. 8km west of city centre. 2 astroturf courts and one other. Also used for football and hockey, so phone to book; **Craiglockhart** (0131 444 1969). Colinton Road. 8km southwest of centre via Morningside and Colinton Road. 6 indoor courts, 7 outdoor and a 'centre court'. Best to check/book by phone. Other separate sports facilities include squash, badminton and gym (0131 443 0101). Centre open Mon-Thu 9am-11pm, Fri 10am-11 pm, Sat-Sun 9am-10.30pm.

479 1/XA4 **Football: World of Football** 0131 443 0404 Part of the 'Newmarket Leisure Village' complex at the Corn Exchange, off Chesser Avenue. Newest of its type. 8 covered pitches. Can be booked between 9am-10pm daily.

480 1/XE5 **Pony-trekking: Lasswade Riding School** www.phicelandics.co.uk · **0131 663 7676** Lasswade exit from city bypass then A768, right to Loanhead 1km and left to end of Kevock Rd. Full hacking and trekking facilities and courses for all standards and ages.

481 1/XA4 **Ice-Skating: Murrayfield Ice Rink** www.murrayfieldicerinkltd.co.uk ·
   1/C3 **0131 337 6933** Riversdale Crescent, just off main Glasgow Road near zoo. Cheap, cheerful and chilly. It has been here forever and feels like a great 1950s B movie ... go round! Sessions daily from 2.30pm. Also ...
Winter Wonderland Princes Street Gardens Big open-air ice rink in the gardens below the Scott Monument (460/EDINBURGH VIEWS). Open late Nov-early Jan. 7 days. Mass fun!

The Best Small Galleries

482 1/XF2 ✓✓ **Ingleby Gallery** www.inglebygallery.com · 0131 556 4441 · **6 Calton Terrace** Important chic gallery in a private house backing onto Calton Hill. Shows work by significant UK artists, eg Callum Innes and Alison Watt.

483 1/D3 ✓✓ **The Fruitmarket Gallery** www.fruitmarket.co.uk · 0131 225 2383 · **Market Street** Opposite City Art Centre. Around for a while but very much on a roll these days, a smaller, warehousey space for contemporary work, retrospectives, installations; this is the space to watch. Excellent bookshop. Always interesting. Café (288/BEST TEAROOMS) highly recommended for meeting and eating and watching the (art) world go by.

484 1/E1 ✓✓ **doggerfisher** www.doggerfisher.com · 0131 558 7110 · **11 Gayfield Square** Susanna Beaumont's vital gallery in a converted garage in heart of the East Village. Limited wall space but always challenging new work. Weekend viewing. She does the Venice Biennale and good openings in old Edinburgh.

485 1/C2 ✓ **Open Eye Gallery** www.openeyegallery.co.uk · 0131 557 1020 & **i2** 0131 558 9872 · **both at 34 Abercromby Place.** Excellent 2 galleries in residential part of New Town. Always worth checking out for accessible contemporary painting and ceramics. Almost too accessible (take a cheque book) – Tom Wilson will know what you want (and probably sell it to you).

486 1/E1 ✓ **The Printmakers' Workshop & Gallery** 0131 557 2479 · **23 Union Street** · www.edinburgh-printmakers.co.uk Off Leith Walk near London Rd roundabout. Workshops that you can look over. Exhibitions of work by contemporary printmakers and shop where prints from many of the notable names in Scotland are on sale at reasonable prices. Bit of a treasure.

487 1/D3 **The Collective Gallery** www.collectivegallery.net · 0131 220 1260 · **22 Cockburn Street** Installations of Scottish and other young contemporary trailblazers. Members' work won't break the bank.

488 1/C2 **The Scottish Gallery** www.scottish-gallery.co.uk · 0131 558 1200 · **16 Dundas Street** Guy Peploe's influential New Town gallery. Where to go to buy something painted, sculpted, thrown or crafted by up-and-comers or established names – everything from affordable jewellery to original Joan Eardleys. Or just look.

489 1/D3 **Photography** Edinburgh has 2 significant contemporary photo-art venues:
1/C4 **Stills** www.stills.org · 0131 622 6200 · **23 Cockburn Street** with a café; and **Portfolio** www.portfoliocatalogue.com · 0131 220 1911 · **43 Candlemaker Row** is a small 2-floor space in what used to be the city's left-wing bookshop.

Essential Culture

UNIQUE VENUES

For the current programmes of the places recommended below and all other venues, consult The List *magazine, on sale at most newsagents.*

490 1/B4 **The Traverse** www.traverse.co.uk · 0131 228 1404 · **Cambridge Street** Small but influential, dedicated to new work (though mainly touring companies) in modern Euro, very architectural 2-theatre premises behind Lyceum and Usher Hall. Often sweeps the Fringe First awards board during the Festival. Good rendezvous café-bar upstairs (156/BEST BISTROS) plus excellent adjacent restaurant (140/BEST RESTAURANTS).

491 1/C4 **Dance Base** www.dancebase.co.uk · 0131 225 5525 · **14-16 Grassmarket**
Scotland's award-winning national centre for dance, in a purpose-built location in the heart of the Grassmarket which it's planned will be a major new events/ market arena for the city. Classes and workshops all year round but check *The List* for dance performance in its larger studio. State of the art building, worth a visit on its own.

492 1/B5 **The Cameo** www.picturehouses.co.uk · 0131 228 4141 · **Home Street, Tollcross** 3 screens showing important new films and cult classics. Some late movies at weekends. Good snug bar. 413/COOL BARS.

493 1/A4 **Filmhouse** www.filmhousecinema.com · 0131 228 2688 · **Lothian Road**
Opposite Usher Hall. 3 screens with everything from first-run art-house movies to subtitled obscurities and retrospectives. Home of the annual Film Festival; café-bar (till 11.30pm Sun-Thu, 12.30am Fri-Sat) is a haven from the excesses of Lothian Road. Open to non-cinephiles.

494 1/XE5 **The Queen's Hall** www.thequeenshall.net · 0131 668 2019 · **Clerk Street**
Converted church with good atmosphere and very varied programme. Your best bet if you want to go somewhere for decent music. Café-bar and art exhibitions. Diverse (choral, jazz, art pop). Good atmosphere.

495 1/D4 **The Festival Theatre** www.eft.co.uk · 0131 529 6000 · **Nicolson Street**
Edinburgh's showcase theatre re-created from the old Empire with a huge glass frontage of bars and a stage and screen dock large enough to accommodate the world's major companies. Eclectic programme all year round.

THE FESTIVALS

496 ✓ ✓ ✓ Edinburgh invented arts festivals (more than 50 years ago) and now can truly be called a Festival City. Most of the festivals listed below are world leaders. Unless otherwise stated, they are in Aug.
Edinburgh International Festival www.eif.co.uk · 0131 473 2000
Edinburgh Festival Fringe www.edfringe.com · 0131 226 0026
Edinburgh International Book Festival www.edbookfest.co.uk · 0131 228 5444
Edinburgh Military Tattoo www.edintattoo.co.uk · 08707 5551188
Edinburgh International Jazz & Blues Festival 0131 467 5200 · www.edinburghjazzfestival.co.uk
Edinburgh International Film Festival www.edfilmfest.org.uk · 0131 229 2550 Moving from Aug to late Jun in '08.
Edinburgh International Science Festival www.sciencefestival.co.uk · 0131 220 1882 1-2 weeks Apr.
Scottish International Children's Festival www.imginate.org.uk · 0131 225 8050 1 week end May/beginning Jun.
Edinburgh Mela www.edinburgh-mela.co.uk · 0131 557 1400 2 days end Aug/early Sep.
Edinburgh's Christmas www.edinburghschristmas.com · 0131 557 3900 4 weeks. End Nov-Christmas Eve. Mainly centred in East Princes St Gardens with UK's biggest ice rink.
Edinburgh's Hogmanay www.edinburghshogmanay.org · 0131 557 3990 4 days, end of Dec-1 Jan.

Section 3

Glasgow

GLASGOW MAP CODES:
WE = WEST END
SS = SOUTH SIDE

The Best Hotels

498 WE ✓✓ **Hotel du Vin** www.onedevonshiregardens.com · 0141 339 2001 ·
49 ROOMS **1 Devonshire Gardens, off Great Western Road (A82)** Glasgow's
TEL · TV landmark smart hotel (and arguably the first 'boutique hotel' in the UK), now
£85+ absorbed into the small but beautiful Hotel/Bistro du Vin chain. Other recent
change for old customers (many rich/famous who wouldn't stay anywhere else) is
that having acquired the one remaining townhouse, the hotel now occupies the
whole prestigious block. It means you don't have to go out and round for breakfast – a charming but inconvenient quirk of old. Now the five townhouses are
integrated into an elegant and sumptuous and yes, boutique hotel. Rooms are
large, as are beds, bathrooms, drapes, etc. Great bar (especially late) with malt list
and as you'd expect, well chosen wines. Outside terrace and excellent informal
restaurant (538/BEST RESTAURANTS). And it's still the best in town.

499 2/C3 ✓✓ **Radisson SAS** www.glasgow.radissonsas.com · 0141 204 3333 ·
247 ROOMS **301 Argyle Street** Bold, brash relative newcomer in emerging West end
TEL · TV of Argyle St. Frontage makes major modernist statement, lifts the coolest in town.
NO PETS Leaning to minimalist, but rooms have all you need. 2 restaurants: **Tapaell'Ya**
ECO (627/SPANISH RESTAURANTS) more fun than Collage. Top Rooms: The 'Apartment'
£85+ on the 6th (top) floor and corner suites on floors below. Fitness facilities c/o LA
Leisure Club in basement includes a pool. No parking.

500 2/B2 ✓ **The Malmaison** www.malmaison-glasgow.com · 0141 572 1000 ·
74 ROOMS **278 West George Street** Sister hotel of the one in Edinburgh and
TEL · TV elsewhere and originally from the same stable and same team as One Devonshire
NO PETS (see Hotel du Vin above). This 'chain' of good design hotels has all the must-have
£60-85 features – well-proportioned rooms (though small), with CDs, cable, etc. – though
the location just off West End affords no great views. However this is reliable,
stylish and discreet. Contemporary French menu sits well in the woody clubbiness
of The Brasserie (589/FRENCH RESTAURANTS).

501 2/C2 ✓ **Abode Glasgow** www.abodehotels.co.uk/glasgow · 0141 572 6000 ·
63 ROOMS **129 Bath Street** Smart, contemporary townhouse hotel, formerly The
TEL · TV Arthouse, with wide, tiled stairwell and funky lift to 3 floors of individual rooms (so
NO PETS size, views and noise levels vary a lot). Fab gold embossed wallpaper in the hall-
£45-60 ways, notable stained glass and nice pictures. Grill downstairs has Modern British
dishes and bar ('Vibe Bar') where vibe can be somewhat lacking. The restaurant,
Michael Caines@Abode is a welcome mouthful (544/BEST RESTAURANTS). Top
Rooms: 129 and 204/5/6 (the Velvet Suites).

502 2/D2 ✓ **Langs** www.langshotels.co.uk · 0141 333 1500 · **Port Dundas Place**
100 ROOMS Near the Concert Hall. Good-looking modern high-rise hotel with designs –
TEL · TV from lofty atrium/bar to penthouse suites on 5th floor – millennium-period decor
NO PETS wearing well. Glass tiles in internal bathroom wall and sunken beds (though very
£85+ comfy) won't suit everybody. Satellite TV/DVD and Playstations in all rooms. Oshi
restaurant on ground floor with oriental pretension (nice plates) and spa (no pool,
but treatments). Modern Scottish though cosmopolitan cooking at Aurora on the
mezzanine floor. Excellent service; Langs tries very hard to please. Provided you
get a room you like, they will. Top Rooms: Duplexes on first floor. Innovative late-
checkout facility on Sun.

503 2/D3 ✓ **The Millennium Hotel** www.millenniumhotels.com · 0141 332 6711 ·
117 ROOMS **50 George Square** Situated on the square which is the municipal heart of

TEL · TV the city and next to Queen St Station (trains to Edinburgh and points north), Glasgow
£85+ will be going on all about you and there's a conservatory terrace, serving breakfast
and afternoon tea, from which to watch. Bedrooms vary. No parking or leisure facilities. Can be busy brasserie.

504 2/B3
319 ROOMS
TEL · TV
£85+

✓ **Glasgow Hilton** www.hilton.co.uk/glasgow · 0141 204 5555 ·
1 William Street Approach from the M8 slip road or from city centre via
Waterloo St. It has a forbidding Fritz Lang/Metropolis appearance and entrance via
underground car park is grim. But hotel is one of the best in town with good service and appointments. Japanese people made especially welcome. Huge atrium.
20 floors with top 3 'executive'. Views from here to north are stunning. Leisure
facilities include pool. Cameron's, the hotel's main restaurant, is present and correct, and the most highly Michelin-rated restaurant in town (though we don't
agree). Minsky's bistro and Raffles bar are not so special. La Primavera is an excellent Italian restaurant so all in all does offer the best hotel food in town.

505 2/XA4
164 ROOMS
TEL · TV
NO PETS
NO KIDS
£60-85

✓ **City Inn** www.cityinn.com/glasgow · 0141 240 1002 · **Finnieston Quay**
Modern block by the big crane near the SECC makes most of its Clydeside
location with deck and views; rooms here are a cut above the usual though not
large. Uniformity is at least thought out. City Café on ground floor takes itself seriously as a restaurant. Part of small UK chain, price and particularity elevate from
the economy travel lodge to the designer, though not quite boutique hotel. The
river's the thing.

506 2/D2
64 ROOMS
TEL · TV
NO PETS
£60-85

Carlton George www.carltonhotels.co.uk/george · 0141 353 6373 ·
44 West George Street By Queen St Station and George Sq, this is a smart and
discreet central option and apart from parking (a hike to car park behind the station) a decent bet in the city centre for the business traveller. It's more 'fun' than
that though, with a huge Irish bar, the bafflingly popular Waxy O'Connor's downstairs and an airy 7th-floor restaurant, **Windows**, up top. Residents' lounge and
drinks in room all on the house. Good service and the usual comforts.

507 2/B3
300 ROOMS
TEL · TV
£85+

Glasgow Marriott www.marriott.com · 0141 226 5577 · **500 Argyle Street**
Modern and functional business hotel on 12 floors near M8. Rooms do seem small.
Parking is a test for the nerves. Nevertheless, there's a calm, helpful attitude from
the staff inside; for further de-stressing you can hypnotise yourself by watching
the soundless traffic on the Kingston Bridge outside; or there's a pool to lap and
separate gym. Mediterraneo restaurant ain't bad (ain't good).

508 2/C1
300 ROOMS
TEL · TV
£38-85+

Thistle Hotel www.thistlehotels.com · 0141 332 3311 · **Cambridge Street
near Holiday Inn** Part of the UK chain and here in all its concrete-block
anonymity. For years. Included here because room rates vary hugely and if the
hotel isn't busy you can get a room that's inexpensive – so negotiate. (It is big, so
good chance.) Usual facilities. Token pool.

509 2/XA4
283 ROOMS
TEL · TV
£85+

Crown Plaza www.qmh-hotels.com · 0870 448 1691 · **Congress Road**
Beside the SECC, on the Clyde, this towering, glass monument to the 1980s feels
like it's in a constant state of 'siege readiness'. Science Centre and Tower gleam
and twinkle on the opposite bank and the new BBC HQ; there's a footbridge
across. Some good river views from the 16 floors. The Marine Restaurant in the
lobby has a good reputation and ring-side seating for river-gazing. Somewhat
removed from city centre (about 3km, you wouldn't want to walk), it's especially
handy for SECC and Armadillo goings-on.

Individual & Boutique Hotels

510 2/E3
22 ROOMS
TEL · TV
NO PETS
£45-60

✓ **The Brunswick Hotel** www.brunswickhotel.co.uk · 0141 552 0001 · **104-108 Brunswick Street** Very contemporary, minimalist hotel almost epitomises Merchant City style emerging way back in the 1990s but standing up well to time and taste. Bright and cheerful rooms economically designed to make use of sometimes very tight space. Bold colours. Good base for nocturnal forays into pub- and clubland. Restaurant till 8pm, breakfast pleasant, especially on Sun. The excellent penthouse suite is often used for parties. No parking.

511 2/D1
8 ROOMS
TEL · TV
NO PETS
£45-60

✓ **The Pipers' Tryst Hotel** www.thepipingcentre.co.uk · 0141 353 5551 · **McPhater Street** Visible from dual carriageway near the *Herald* HQ at Cowcaddens, but hard to get to the street in a car. Hotel upstairs from café-bar of the adjacent piping centre and whole complex a beautiful conversion of an old church and manse. Centre has courses, conferences and a museum, so staying here is to get close to Highland culture. Small restaurant.

512 WE
10 ROOMS
TEL · TV
NO PETS
£38-45

✓ **The Town House** www.thetownhouseglasgow.com · 0141 357 0862 · **4 Hughenden Terrace** Quiet street off Great Western Rd via Hyndland Rd, overlooking rugby and cricket grounds. Same area as Hotel du Vin (498/HOTELS) for a fraction of the price. Spacious rooms faithfully restored – even if you don't happen to live in a well-appointed townhouse on a gracious terrace yourself, you'll feel at home. Smallish bathrooms and only one (room 2) has bath. Close to the West End. Don't confuse with the Townhouse Hotel, Royal Cres.

513 2/E4
99 ROOMS
TEL · TV
NO PETS
£38-45

✓ **The Fraser Suites** www.fraserhospitality.com · 0141 553 4289 · **1-19 Albion Street** Not exactly a hotel, these are serviced apartments with kitchen facilities but has the ambiance and front-desk service of a hotel (24 hour) and a breakfast suite. Rooms (mostly) surprisingly large. Range from 'studios' to 1/2 bedroom apartments. Usually do 1-night stays.

514 2/F5
6 APTS
TV
NO PETS
£38-45

✓ **Number 52 Charlotte Street** www.52charlottestreet.co.uk · 0845 230 5252 Serviced apartments in superb conversion of the one remaining Georgian town house in historic (now decimated) street between the Barrows Market and Glasgow Green. Tobacco Merchant's house by Robert Adam refurbishment by NTS. Very good rates for bedroom/lounge/kitchen; everything but breakfast. Usually by the week but shorter lets possible; units sleep 1-5.

515 2/C2
103 ROOMS
TEL · TV
£45-60

✓ **Marks Hotel** 0141 353 0800 · **110 Bath Street** In the downtown section of Bath St but near the style bars and designer restaurants, a bed block with more taste and character than most. Recently reinvented (it was Bewley's) with big wallpaper and big price hike. Brasserie not reviewed at TGP.

516 2/B2
5 ROOMS
TEL · TV
NO PETS
NO KIDS
£45-60

St Jude's www.saintjudes.com · 0141 352 0220 · **190 Bath Street** Glasgow's first small boutique hotel (started off as a northern Groucho Club. Refurbishment at TGP. Originally very designery restaurant now replaced by faux French café Français which gets mixed reviews. All rooms upstairs (no lift) retain 'original' ie 1990s design features. Bar still cool; now has live music Fri and Sat. A stylee stopover.

517 2/E3
4 RMS · TEL
TV · NO KIDS
£38-45

Rab Ha's www.rabhas.com · 0141 572 0400 · **83 Hutcheson Street** Rooms above a pub in the urban heart of the Merchant City. Pub goes like a fair with good food and friendly folk so noisy late night and seems permanently surrounded by building works. Cheap 'n' cheerful though not a long-stay choice.

518 2/XF3
8 ROOMS
TEL · TV
£38-45

Cathedral House www.cathedralhousehotel.com · 0141 552 3519 ·
Cathedral Square Opposite Glasgow Cathedral Rooms above the bar, their main appeal being outlook to the edifice north of the Cathedral and the Necropolis beyond (1963/GRAVEYARDS). Functional and friendly. A walk to Merchant City.

519 2/F3
6 ROOMS
TEL
NO PETS
NO KIDS
£38-45

Babbity Bowster 0141 552 5055 · **16-18 Blackfriars Street** This late 18th-century town house was pivotal in the redevelopment of the Merchant City and famous for its bar (715/REAL-ALE PUBS, 594/SCOTTISH RESTAURANTS) and beer garden, Schottische restaurant upstairs and rooms above with basic facilities. Bathrooms ensuite. No TV but nice books. A very Glasgow hostelry so popular that though I've tried many times I still can't get in there on a Saturday night (so that I can also try Sunday breakfast). I do know it's still fine.

520 WE

Kirklee Hotel www.kirkleehotel.co.uk · 0141 334 5555 · **11 Kensington Gate** In a city curiously short of appealing and individual guesthouses here at least is one to recommend – a tidy Edwardian house and most notably a tidy garden in a leafy suburb near Botanics and Byres Rd. Lots of pics.

521 WE
32 UNITS
TEL · TV
£38-45

The White House www.whitehouse-apartments.com · 0141 339 9375 ·
12 Cleveden Crescent Not a hotel, but self-catering apartments near Botanics. A friendly hame from hame in this civilised crescent and a sensible alternative, especially if there are a few of you or you are staying a week. Some quiet mews out back.

522 2/B1
56 ROOMS
TEL · TV
£38 OR LESS

The Victorian House www.victorianhouse.co.uk · 0141 332 0129 ·
212 Renfrew Street Behind Sauchiehall St and adjacent School of Art (793/MACKINTOSH). One of several city-centre 'commercial' hotels in this street but probably the best appointed and tries harder than the rest. Basic facilities. Pleasant front garden. Surprisingly large behind the facade.

Travel Lodges

523 2/E2
2/B2
239/279
ROOMS
TEL · TV
NO PETS
£30-38

Premier Travel Inns www.premiertravelinn.co.uk Of 16 in Glasgow area, most convenient probably east on corner of Merchant City at **187 George Street** (0870 238 3320) and West at **10 Elmbank Gardens** (0870 990 6312) above Charing Cross Station. Latter once an office block, now a vast city-centre budget hotel, with no frills and no pretence, but a very adequate room for the night. Functionality, anonymity and urban melancholy may suit the lonesome traveller or the family/mates packed into a room. George St in area of many restaurants, Charing Cross opposite the excellent Baby Grand and it's open late (565/BISTROS). Under £55 per room at TGP.

524 2/B2
139/141
ROOMS
TEL · TV
£45 OR LESS

Novotel www.novotel.com · 0141 222 2775 · **181 Pitt Street** Branch of the French bedbox empire in quiet corner near the west end of Sauchiehall St. Nothing much to distinguish, but brasserie/restaurant is bright enough and Novotel beds are very good. Small bathrooms. The 2- as opposed to the 3-star **Ibis** (0141 225 6000) is adjacent. If it's merely a bed for the night you want, it's much cheaper and hard to see what difference a star makes. They're both pretty soulless but parent chain Accor due more accord than UK rivals.

525 2/D2
113/119 ROOMS
TEL · TV
NO PETS
£38-85

Holiday Inn, City Centre www.higlasgow.com · 0141 352 8300 · 161 West Nile Street Another block off the old block. In the city centre near Concert Hall. Gym, but no pool; restaurant but not great shakes. Holiday Inn Express adjacent is better value (25% less). Room rates vary depending on occupancy. There's a lot of shopping goes on around you.

526 2/D5
128 ROOMS

Express by Holiday Inn www.hiexpressglasgow.co.uk · 0141 548 5000 · Corner of Stockwell & Clyde Streets (But only 5 rooms on the river with small windows.) Functional bedbox that's not a bad deal. All you do is sleep here. Near Merchant City so plenty of restaurants, nightlife and other distractions and curiously midway between 2 of Glasgow's oldest, funkiest bars, The Scotia and Victoria (701/700/PUBS). Another Express adjacent Holiday Inn (City Centre) but this one best.

The Best Hostels

The SYHA is the Scottish Youth Hostel Association, of which you have to be a member (or a member of an affiliated organisation from another country) to stay in their many hostels round Scotland. Phone 01786 451181 for details, or contact any YHA hostel.

527 2/XA1
150 BEDS

✓ **SY Hostel** www.syha.org.uk · 0870 004 1119 · 8 Park Terrace Quiet, elegant terrace in posh West End near the University and Kelvingrove Park. This building was converted in 1992 from the Beacons Hotel, which was where rock 'n' roll bands used to stay in the 1980s. Now the bedrooms are converted into dorms for 4-6 (some larger) and the public rooms are common rooms with TV, games, etc. You must be a member of the YHA. See above.

528 2/F2
70 BEDS

Murray Hall, Strathclyde University www.strath.ac.uk · 0141 553 4148 · Cathedral Street Modern but not sterile block of single rooms on edge of main campus and facing towards Cathedral. Part of large complex (also some student flats to rent by the week) with bar/shop/laundrette. Quite central, close to Merchant City bars. Vacations only. There's also Chancellors Hall adjacent, 218 rooms, same deal same no.

529 2/C4
365 BEDS

Euro Hostel Glasgow www.euro-hostels.co.uk · 0141 222 2828 · 318 Clyde Street A very central independent hostel block at the bottom of Union/Renfield St and almost overlooking the river. Mix of single, twin or dorm accommodation, but all ensuite and clean. Breakfast included in price. Kitchen and laundry. Games and TV room. The ground-floor bar, Osmosis, is open to the public. They have hostels also in Edinburgh and Newcastle. Not as cheap as some but very well appointed. Open all year.

Note: Both Strathclyde and Glasgow Universities have several other halls of residence available for short-term accommodation in the summer months. Phone: Glasgow 0141 330 4116/2318 or Strathclyde 0141 553 4148 (central booking).

The Best Hotels Outside Town

530 10/M26
92 ROOMS
TEL · TV
NO PETS
£38-45

✓ ✓ **Dakota** www.dakotahotels.co.uk · 0870 220 8281 · EuroCentral 24km from centre on the M8. Like the South Queensferry version (130/ HOTELS OUTSIDE EDINBURGH) this is a chip off the new (black granite, smoked glass) block and similarly situated overlooking the highway in this spot of regenerating Lanarkshire. Behind the severe exterior is a design-driven roadhouse that is a paean to travel and elegantly rises to meet the requirements of modern travellers. Another hotel hit for the McCulloch/Rosa team. **EAT** The Grill is superb – really!

531 9/L25
53 ROOMS
TEL · TV
NO PETS
£60-85

✓ ✓ **Mar Hall** www.marhall.com · 0141 812 9999 · Earl of Mar Estate, Bishopton M8 junction 28A/29, A726 then A8 into Bishopton. 5-star luxury 10 minutes to airport and 25 minutes to central Glasgow. £15M conversion of imposing, *très elegant* baronial house with grand, slightly gloomy public spaces including the hall and rooms that vary (some huge) but all with 5-star niceties. Spa/leisure club adjacent with 15m pool. Great restaurant under Jim Kerr (fusion Scottish) though it'll cost you! The new rock 'n' roll stopover for the city.

532 9/L25
96 + 35
(NEW) ROOMS
TEL · TV
NO PETS
£60-85

✓ **De Vere Cameron House Hotel** www.devere.co.uk · 01389 755565 · Loch Lomond A82 via West End or Erskine Bridge and M8. 45km from centre. Highly regarded mansion-house hotel complex with excellent leisure facilities in 100 acres open grounds on loch's bonny banks. Sports include 9-hole golf (and 10km Loch Lomond course; 2147/GOLF), good pool, tennis and a busy marina for sailing, windsurfing, etc. Redecoration in progress at TGP, giving it the new dark/ sombre/masculine look that is so 2006/8. Let's hope you don't feel depressed. New block of rooms on the way '08. The restaurant 'Lomonds' less formal than it was. Many famous names have holed up here; it's a short helicopter hop to town.

533 9/L24
47 ROOMS
TEL · TV
£38-45

✓ **The Lodge On Loch Lomond** www.lochlomondlodge.co.uk · 01436 860201 Edge of Luss on A82 north from Balloch; 40 minutes to Glasgow's West End. In a linear arrangement that makes the most of a great lochside setting. This hotel, ignored by most of the posher guides, punches well above its weight. Wood-lined rooms overlook the bonny banks with balconies and saunas, though Luss is not everybody's cup of tea (or sausage roll). Colquhoun's restaurant has the view and the terrace and is surprisingly good; book at weekends. Rooms in Munro Lodge, back from lochside, are more corporate. Spa and nice pool. Many weddings; some conferences. You can't fail to notice Bill Clinton among the many pictures.

534 10/L25
12 ROOMS
TEL · TV
£38-45

The Black Bull Hotel www.blackbullhotel.com · 01360 550215 · 2 The Square, Killearn A81 towards Aberfoyle, take the right fork after Strathblane, and the hotel is at the top end of the village next to the church. Urban values, design and comforts in this restaurant with rooms in pleasant situation. Clubby casual bistro and bar meals and finer-dining conservatory restaurant.

535 10/M26
35 ROOMS
TEL · TV
£30 OR LESS

Eglinton Arms Hotel www.eglintonarms.co.uk · 01355 302631 · Eaglesham Sprawling inn in a charming conservation village, a quiet contrast to downtown Glasgow but a surprisingly close 10km to south city boundary. A different green world and gurgling brook besides. Very decent and locally popular bar/ restaurant – Simpson's – and refurbished rooms for less than budget-hotel rates.

536 9/L25
6 ROOMS
FEB-NOV
TEL · TV
£38-45

Kirkton House www.kirktonhouse.co.uk · 01389 841951 · Cardross A814, past Helensburgh to Cardross village then north up Darleith Rd. Kirkton House is 1km on right. 18th-century Scottish farmhouse/guesthouse round a courtyard that combines rustic charm with modern cons (the flatscreen TV). Near Loch Lomond (12km).

The Best Fine-Dining Restaurants

537 WE
£22-32+
✓ ✓ **Ubiquitous Chip** www.ubiquitouschip.co.uk · 0141 334 5007 · **12 Ashton Lane** A cornerstone of culinary Glasgow and still superb: even Gault Millau agrees. 2-storey, covered courtyard draped with vines, off a bar-strewn cobbled lane in the heart of the West End, heaped with accolades over 35 years in residence: a pioneer restaurant since 1971 but still acutely 'now'. The main bit is still one of the most atmospheric of rooms and Ian Brown's menu is exemplary – the best of Scottish seafood, game and beef and fine, original cooking. An outstanding wine list. Chip upstairs has a different, lighter brasserie menu. Signature dish: Dishes with list of ingredients, Scottish provenance noted (they were the first to do this, now everyone does). They make everything sound... well, scrumptious. And it is! Not at all overpriced for this foodie experience and the brasserie has 3 courses for £25 (TGP). Daily lunch and 6.30-11pm.

538 WE
£22-32
✓ ✓ **Bistro du Vin** 0141 339 2001 · **1 Devonshire Gardens off Great Western Road** Glasgow's oldest boutique hotel (471/BEST HOTELS) has, since it opened, had one of the city's classiest fine-dining rooms. Was once a home to Gordon Ramsay's Amaryllis and is now a part of the Hotel and Bistro du Vin chain. The dining rooms in house 5 in this elegant row are now confidently established as a less formal restaurant which Joanna Blythman described as 'a masterpiece'. Posh London club-like setting and a great chef Paul Tamburrini restore Devonshire Gardens as a must-eat destination in the West End. 7 days lunch and dinner (closed Sun lunch). LO 9.30/10pm.

539 2/C2
£22-32
✓ **Le Chardon D'Or** www.brianmaule.com · 0141 248 3801 · **176 West Regent Street** Brian Maule's (formerly head chef at the Roux brothers' famed Le Gavroche) Golden Thistle in French with contemporary spin on Auld Alliance as far as the food's concerned – impeccable ingredients, French influence in preparation. Delightfully simple menu, tranquil room. A temple to culinary excellence. Excellent, well-priced wine list especially French. Good halves choice. Signature dish: food that is what it says on the menu. Lunch Mon-Fri, LO 9.30pm. Closed Sun.

540 WE
£15-32
✓ **Stravaigin** www.stravaigin.5pm.co.uk · 0141 334 2665 · **28-30 Gibson Street** One of Glasgow's most dependable restaurants and yet a reliably good, constantly changing, innovative and consciously eclectic menu from award-winning chef Colin Clydesdale. Mixes cuisines, especially Asian and Pacific Rim. 'Think global, eat local'. Excellent, affordable food without the foodie formalities and open later than most. The bar on street level has probably the best bar food in town, similarly eclectic and accomplished. Can be cramped but nowt cramps the style. Signature dishes: ever-changing with precise long list of ingredients too long to mention here. 7 days 11am-11pm; bar till 12midnight (yes, even the opening hours are easy to take). Also **Stravaigin 2**; 0141 334 7165 (see 546/BISTROS).

541 2/C2
£22-32
Rococo 0141 221 5004 · **202 West George Street** Corner of Wellington St and just along from Bouzy Rouge to which it is related (548/BISTROS). But this is the upmarket, fine-dining and impeccable-service version. Basement but light and relaxing. Excellent contemporary menu has the lot in the mix. Nice private dining area and courtyard outside for post-prandial chat and coffee. Chef Mark Tamburrini. Excellent wine list; look no further than the French! Great pre-theatre menu (till 6.30pm). 7 days. Lunch & LO 10pm.

542 2/D3
£32+
Rogano www.roganoglasgow.com · 0141 248 4055 · 11 Exchange Place
Between Buchanan and Queen Streets An institution in Glasgow since the 1930s. Décor replicating a Cunard ship, the *Queen Mary*, is the major attraction. Long since in private hands and recently changed again. Though the restaurant is spacious and perennially fashionable, there's a sense of trading on fading glory, especially downstairs in 'Café Rogano', the cheaper, shabbier alternative (to be refurbished at TGP). Outdoor 'terrace'. Restaurant: lunch and 6.30pm-10.30pm. Café Rogano: 12noon-11pm (Sun until 10pm). Upstairs for seafood especially oysters, you may even venture the lobster thermidor; some glamour still lingers.

543 WE
£22-32
La Parmigiana www.laparmigiana.co.uk · 0141 334 0686 · 447 Great Western Road 'Simply the best' Italian for many a discriminating Glaswegian of the old school (convenient location near Kelvin Bridge – usually parking nearby), the favourite place to eat posh pasta and vitello but that's just for starters. Main courses elaborate with Italian take on local provision. Lunch (good deal 'pre-theatre' menu). LO 10.30pm. Closed Sun. Signature dish: lobster ravioli, carpaccio with rocket and parmesan. Report: 573/ITALIAN RESTAURANTS.

544 2/C2
£22-32
Michael Caines @ Abode www.michaelcaines.com · 0141 221 6789 · 129 Bath Street Ground-floor fine-dining restaurant of boutique hotel Abode (501/HOTELS) in the midst of restaurant-packed Bath St. This a cut above the rest. The eponymous Caines is also in Canterbury and Exeter, though like other celebrity chefs he's rarely rattling the pans. Here Martin Donnelly confidently in charge of Modern British menu using sound Scottish ingredients; it goes from strength to strength. Classy room with glass-walled wine cellar. Lunch; LO 10pm. Closed Sun.

✓ ✓ **Gandolfi Fish** 0141 552 9475 Report: 635/SEAFOOD.

✓ ✓ **Gamba** 0141 572 0899 Report: 630/SEAFOOD.

Amber Regent Report: 614/FAR-EASTERN.

The Best Bistros & Brasseries

See also Best Scottish Restaurants, p. 106.

545 WE
£15-22

✓ **No. Sixteen** www.number16.co.uk · 0141 339 2544 · **16 Byres Road** Mags and Ronnie's tiny restaurant on 2 postage stamp floors at the bottom end of Byres Road now established as hugely popular West End haunt – so you probably have to book and squeeze in. Winning combo is good bistro food, no fuss and good value. This applies also at their new place, Louis' Grill (see below). Sublime puds. 7 days. Lunch and LO 9.45pm, Sun 9.15pm.

546 WE
£15-22

✓ **Stravaigin 2** www.stravaigin.5pm.co.uk · 0141 334 7165 · **8 Ruthven Lane** Just off Byres Road through vennel opposite underground station. Off-shoot of **Stravaigin** (540/BEST RESTAURANTS), one of Glasgow's finest. Similar eclectic often inspirational but lighter menu somewhere between the upstairs bar and downstairs finer dining of the mothership. Smallish rooms (upper brighter) and couple of tables in lane; book weekends. Famously good burgers (come in many meats). Signature dish: deep fried jeely piece with Carnation Milk ice cream. 7 days all day from 11am/12noon to 11pm.

547 2/C2
£22-32

✓ **Manna** www.mannarestaurant.co.uk · 0141 332 6678 · **104 Bath Street** A bistro in a basement among many (in Bath St) but as many Glaswegians know, food, service and wine list here are spot-on. Chef David Clunas's contemporary Scottish menu in Michelin and AA. A perennial fave. Apart from the chef, this review hasn't changed in 3 editions of *StB* even though in 2006 a makeover, new chef and name change appeared (this used to be Papingo). Menu changes seasonally but it and the whole experience here is reassuringly and reliably good. Lunch & LO 10/10.30pm. Closed Sun lunch.

548 2/C2
£15-22

✓ **Bouzy Rouge** www.bouzyrouge.co.uk · 0141 221 8804 · **111 West Regent Street** Key restaurant in the Bouzy Rouge chain, made by the enterprising Brown family and one of the few chains we heartily endorse (it's now restricted to Glasgow only). An excellent bistro for eclectic, affordable contemporary food and wine. Good vegetarian choice. 7 days, lunch and LO 9.30pm (10.30pm weekends). 'Express' lunch and suppers. Also:

549 2/D3
£22-32

Bouzy Rouge Seafood & Grill www.bouzyrouge.co.uk · 0141 333 9725 · **71 Renfield Street** Different emphasis but similar menu. Focussing both surf 'n' turf on good Scottish-sourced ingredients (Aberdeen Angus steaks, Loch Fyne oysters). Beautiful, atmospheric room. Service varies. 7 days, lunch and LO 10pm.

550 WE
£22-32

✓ **An Lochan** 0141 338 6606 · **340 Crow Road** West End borders (can approach via Hyndland Rd – Clarence Drive to bottom then right onto Crow Rd) but not so far to go for authentic, mainly seafood bistro that's been winning awards since it opened '04 when it was called the Café Royale. Name change is to fit the new corporate brand which includes their hotel in Perthshire (953/PERTH HOTELS): the same family run the estimable An Lochan in Tighnabruaich (815/BEST ARGYLL). Many fishy ingredients come from the west (sourcing noted on menu). Clair McKie on the stoves. Lunch Tue-Sun; dinner Tue-Sat. Closed Mon.

551 WE
£15-22

✓ **Fanny Trollopes** www.fannytrollopes.co.uk · 0141 564 6464 · **1066 Argyle Street** Discreet presence on this unlovely boulevard and a narrow room, but Fanny's was a winner when it opened a few years back and since reopening after some fixing and furbishment, it's more of a dining destination than ever. Lunch & LO 9pm. Can BYOB. Closed Sun/Mon.

552 2/C3
£15-22
✓ **Fifi and Ally** www.fifiandally.com 0141 226 2286 · 80 Wellington **Street** Following the success of their luncheon and tearoom in Princes Sq (647/TEAROOMS), a much larger, more ambitious deli and restaurant opened in late '07 here on the edge of the financial district. Dark interior which twinkles at night. Delicious food and delicious wine. A big room to fill but if the food keeps up at the level it started, this place is guaranteed to please. Lunch & LO 10pm. Closed Sun.

553 2/C2
£22-32
✓ **48 West Regent St** www.48bistro.co.uk · 0141 331 0303 · **Same address** Another venture of the Bouzy Rouge family (see above) and another smart though more discreet rendezvous. In a basement (like most of their establishments) but makes the most of dark, urban interior. Food 'cheap but chic' is very good value. All the sophisticated staples are here. Feels like a New York or London theatre restaurant (say, Joe Allan). They do good cocktails. 7 days 12noon-10pm.

554 WE
£22-32/
£15-22
✓ **Lux/Stazione** www.luxstazione.com · 0141 576 7576 · 1057 Great **Western Road** Near Gartnavel Hospital which for non-Glaswegians means a long way along Great Western Rd from the Botanic corner. (Lux pays for taxis up to 20 miles on Thursdays). Two distinct offerings here: an informal Italian bar/bistro and the more formal white-linen, proper restaurant of **Lux** (upstairs) in former station. Both have relaxed ambience. Outside tables in summer. Lux quite highly rated by some (Michelin 3 forks) and more relaxed than other city centre Modern British-Med eateries. Both restaurants are routinely packed despite their location - says it all, really. 7 days, lunch and 5-11pm. Lux dinner only. Closed Sun.

555 SS
£15-22
✓ **The Urban Grill** www.urbangrill.co.uk · 0141 649 2745 · 61 Kilmarnock **Road** Main road south on the South Side. Not as urban as one might hope (last orders 9.45pm during the week and not much stretch) but brasserie-like layout and atmosphere. Fish bias to menu. 7 days. Weekend LO 10.15pm. Bar later.

556 2/D3
£22-32
✓ **The Urban Brasserie** www.urbanbrasserie.co.uk · 0141 248 5636 · **23 St Vincent Place** More downtown/urban and more brasserie-like; all as one might expect. Outside terrace good for people-watching. Clubby atmosphere in different seating areas. Both owned by estimable Alan Tomkins and executive chef Derek Marshall (of Gambas, so good for fish). LO 10pm & 10.30pm Fri/Sat.

557 SS
£15-22
✓ **Dine** 0141 621 1903 · 205 Fenwick Road New in '07 and has somewhat eclipsed the Ivy (see below) which is only 6 doors down but which is suggested by *The List Eating Out Guide* to be 'beyond the pale' (geographically). The reason Dine escapes the 'hard-to-get-to' reputation is because it's new, sparse and modish, but really it's another great neighbourhood restaurant far away on the South Side. Lunch & LO 9/9.30pm. Closed Mon.

558 WE
✓ **Louis' Grill** 0141 339 7195 · 18 Gibson Street As of days of Glasgow yore, Gibson Street is becoming a foodie destination again. Stravaigin here forever but this is a new venture for the No. Sixteen team (545/BISTROS - see above). More casual, less foodie-fantastic than the older sister but grills and salads and staff are all friendly/properly made. It definitely works. 7 days. 10am-9.45pm.

559 2/D3
✓ **The Restaurant Bar & Grill** 0141 225 5630 · The Glass House, **Springfield Court** Off Queen St or through Princes Square. Combining the Conran concept restaurants Etain and Zinc into one extensive restaurant, bar, grill as it says on the tin. A similar though perhaps superior version of the Mod Britpop menus springing up everywhere but with hints from all over (mezze, tagine, green curry). Tables on balcony and large light room through the back. Competent rather than special. Open 7 days 10am-10.30pm. From 12noon on Sun. Bar later.

559A 2/E3 ✓ **Guy's Restaurant & Bar** www.guysrestaurant.co.uk · 0141 552 1114 · **24 Candleriggs** This intimate and busy Merchant City restaurant serves 'real food' which is why it's so popular. The eponymous Guy serves everything from Scottish staples like mince 'n' tatties and prawn cocktail to sushi and olive-oil ice cream. Everything home made. Wines vary from good house to Crystal Rosé at £600 a bottle. Piano Fri/Sat, jazz Thu. And he's some Guy. 7 days 12noon-10pm (11.30pm Fri/Sat). A good-to-know late choice.

560 2/C2 **Red Onion** www.red-onion.co.uk · 0141 221 6000 · **247 West Campbell**
£15-22 **Street** Chef to the stars and TV and tabloid-watchers, John Quigley confidently in command here of a good-value, eclectic menu featuring all the things we like. Informal, accessible, easy to drop in. It buzzes and I wish I could give John a tick or two. 7 days 9am-10 (10.30) pm; from 12noon Sat/Sun.

561 SS **The Giffnock Ivy** 0141 620 1003 · **219 Fenwick Road, Giffnock** Set in
£15-22 Glasgow's South Side and not London's West End, the joke may be lost but Kate and Naomi could graze here, too. Big local reputation and at weekends it may be just as difficult to get a table. Great bistro atmosphere in small, busy room; modest menu with blackboard specials. Very Scottish. 7 days, lunch & LO 9.30pm.

562 WE **Òran Mór; The Brasserie** www.oran-mor.co.uk · 0141 357 6226 · **731 Great**
£22-32 **Western Road** Down the side of this converted church/drink emporium at the end of Byres Rd. A one-stop celebration of the parts of Scottish culture that go well with a drink, includes food (572/GASTROPUBS), music, comedy, clubbing it and plays at lunchtime. The Brasserie is the upmarket-dining bit. Nice room (becomes a cocktail bar later at weekends) away from the hustle and hubbub of the rest. Scottish fare with French bits. Lunch Wed-Sat; dinner Mon-Sat.

563 WE **The Sisters** www.thesisters.co.uk · 0141 434 1179 · **1a Ashwood Gardens,**
£15-22 **off Crow Road, Jordanhill** Out of the way and a little out of the ordinary, a great Scottish eaterie run by sisters Pauline and Jacqueline O'Donnell. Great atmosphere, home cooking from fine ingredients. Loyal clientele. A bit of a find. If you've never been beyond the bright lights of Byres Rd, out of townies phone for directions. Tue-Sun lunch and dinner. LO 9.30pm.

564 WE **Sisters Kelvingrove** www.thesisters.co.uk · 0141 564 1157 · **36 Kelvingrove**
£15-22 **Street** From the same sisters as above and previously the terminally hip Air Organic, this opened '06 with the same approach, some Scottish-sourced ingredients and virtually the same menu. Perhaps a smarter crowd still appreciate the good value, decidedly non-haute cuisine.

565 2/A2 **Baby Grand** www.babygrandglasgow.com · 0141 248 4942 · **3-7 Elmbank**
£15 OR LESS **Gardens** Inviting haven among high-rise office blocks opposite hotel (496/TRAVEL LODGES); a downtown-USA location. (Go behind the King's Theatre down Elmbank St, right at gas station and look for the hotel.) Narrow room with bar stools and banquettes, often with background music from resident mad pianist. Char-grilled fish, steak and specials or you can graze. Best late meal in town. Daily 8am-11.45 (1am on weekends). Report: 669/LATE RESTAURANTS.

✓ ✓ **City Merchant** Long established Merchant City restaurant still has the edge over many newcomers. Report: 590/SCOTTISH RESTAURANTS.
✓ **Firebird** Recently more bistrotastic than only pizza, for which it's renowned, but report: 585/BEST PIZZA.
✓ **Café Gandolfi** Last but right up there with the best. Report: 644/BEST TEAROOMS.

Gastropubs

567 WE ✓✓ **Stravaigin** www.stravaigin.5pm.co.uk · 28-30 Gibson Street Excellent pub food upstairs from one of the best restaurants in town. Doors open on to sunny Gibson St and mezzanine above. Crowded maybe, but inspirational grub and no fuss. These must be the busiest, most exercised waiters in town. Nice wines to go with. 7 days all day & LO 10pm. Report: 540/BEST RESTAURANTS.

568 2/E4 ✓✓ **Bar Gandolfi** www.cafegandolfi.com · 0141 552 6813 · 64 Albion Street Above Café Gandolfi (644/TEAROOMS). Bar Gandolfi and Stravaigin still head up this section where Glasgow and gastropub don't quite go together. A foody pub with no pretence, just great comfort food in a light, airy upstairs garret, served all day till 10pm. Bar later. Good veggie choice. Great rendezvous spot. 7 days 9am-11.30pm (Sun from 12noon).

569 2/D3 ✓ **Sloans** 0141 221 8886 · Argyle Arcade, Argyle Street In the jewellery arcade that runs between Argyle and Buchanan Sts, one of Glasgow's most original, still-stylish eating parlours on 2 floors. Both offer authentic, early-20th century decor in wood and tiles and stained glass with an atmosphere that retro style bars can only dream of. Upstairs Crystal restaurant with beautiful snug (private use) open for dinner at weekends. Downstairs an all-day pub and dining room with gastropub fare and daily specials. Food still finding its way at TGP. On the top floor there's a ballroom; guided tours and private hires are available. Let's hope in Billy Macananay's hands it survives Glasgow's vagaries of fashion. Bar 7 days 12noon-10pm.

570 WE ✓ **Liquid Ship** www.stravaigin.com/liquid.htm · 0141 331 1901 · 171 Great Western Road From the makers of Stravaigin (above), a venture on the highway to the west. Eclectic menu as you'd expect from the Clydesdale camp – from Spain to the Ukraine and lots of Stravaigin touches. Food 10am-10pm then tapas menu till 11pm/12midnight. Bar 11pm but 12midnight on frequent quiz/live-music nights. 7 days.

571 WE **McPhabbs** www.mcphabbs.com · 0141 221 0770 · 22 Sandyford Place West of Sauchiehall St, other side of the M8. Long-standing great Glasgow pub with loyal following. Tables in front 'garden' and on back decks. Standard home-made pub-grub menu and great specials. Food till 9pm. Bar 11/12midnight. A West End secret.

572 WE **Òran Mór** www.oran-mor.co.uk · 0141 357 6200 · 731 Corner of Byres and Great Western Roads Converted church and reverence due for the scale of ambition here and the unflagging commitment, a paean to all things 'Scottish contemporary'. Every cloister and chapel has been turned into an albeit designery den for drinking in and the din can be heaven or hell, depending on your proclivity. However 'The Conservatory' to one side has a very passable gastropub-style menu and 'The Brasserie' (562/BISTROS) takes its grub quite seriously. Expect contemporary versions of Scottish traditional cooking here. Lunch & LO 10pm.

✓ **The Goat** Report: 729/COOL BARS.

✓ **Babbity Bowsters** Report: 594/SCOTTISH RESTAURANTS.

The Best Italian Restaurants

573 WE
£22-32

✓ **La Parmigiana** www.laparmigiana.co.uk · 0141 334 0686 · **447 Great Western Road** Sophisticated ristorante that blends traditional service and contemporary Italian cuisine into a seamless performance. Carefully chosen dishes and wine list; solicitous service. Milano rather than Napoli. Expect to find Italians (who consider this to be one of the city's great restaurants – 543/BEST RESTAURANTS). Mon-Sat lunch and 6-10.30pm. Closed Sun.

574 2/C2
2/D2
£15-32

✓ **Fratelli Sarti** www.sarti.co.uk · 0141 248 2228 · **133 Wellington Street & 0141 204 0440 (best number for bookings) 121 Bath Street** Glasgow's famed *emporio d'Italia* combining a deli/wine shop in Wellington St, wine shop in Bath St and bistro in each. Great bustling atmosphere. Eating upstairs in deli has more atmosphere. Both may have queues at lunchtime. Good pizza, specials change every day, *dolci* and *gelati* in super-calorific abundance. 7 days 8am-10/11pm (Sun from noon) (587/PIZZA). The Sarti restaurant at 43 Renfield St (corner of West George St; 0141 572 7000) is for finer Italian dining in elegant room with exceptional marble tiling and wine list. Same menu as others, but more ristorante specials. 7 days lunch and LO 10pm, 10.30/11pm.

575 10/N27
£22-32

✓ **La Vigna, Lanark** www.lavigna.co.uk · 01555 664320 · **40 Wellgate** Not Glasgow, but downtown Lanark 40km away – worth the drive for the authentic ristorante, family-run for 20 years. 7 days, lunch & LO 10pm (Sun dinner only).

576 2/D3
£22-32

L'Ariosto www.lariosto.com · 0141 221 0971 · **92 Mitchell Street** Old-style ristorante set in an indoor courtyard near Buchanan St. Full-blown Tuscan fare with flair and after 40 years still some passion; obliging staff. Notable for using only the right ingredients including wild mushrooms and many meats (veal, venison, etc). Dinner-dancing: this is old-style but real style. Great wine list with good house. A full night's entertainment. Tue-Sat. Lunch & LO 11pm. Closed Sun lunch.

577 2/XA5
£22-32

La Fiorentina/Little Tuscany www.la-fiorentina.com · 0141 420 1585 · **2 Paisley Road West** Not far from river and motorway over Kingston Bridge, but approach from Eglinton St (A77 Kilmarnock Rd). It's at the Y-junction with Govan Rd. Fiorentina has absorbed traditional tratt Little Tuscany from next door. Fabulous, old-style room and service, always busy. Usually seafood specials; lighter Tuscan menu. As Italian as you want it to be, enormous menu and wine list. Great mayo. Mon-Sat lunch & LO 10.30pm. Closed Sun.

578 2/B1
WE
£15-22

Paperino's www.paperinosglasgow.com · 0141 332 3800 · **283 Sauchiehall Street & 0141 334 3811 · 227 Byres Road** Ordinary-looking though smart restaurant is better than the rest; down to the Giovanazzi brothers who also own La Parmigiana (see above) and The Big Blue (724/PUB FOOD). Perfect pasta and good service. The newer Byres Rd version is vast and often packed. Attests to the endless attraction of straightforward Italian food done well. 7 days. LO 10.50/11.30pm. Weekend 8.30am-11pm.

The Trusty Tratts

Old-style family-run restaurants (real Italians) with familiar pasta/pizza staples and the rest. There are many of these in Glasgow as elsewhere; these are the best.

579 2/D2
£15-22

✓ **Ristorante Caprese 0141 332 3070 · 217 Buchanan Street** Basement café near the Concert Hall. Glaswegians (and footballers) love this place judging by the wall-to-wall gallery of happy, smiling punters. Our fave too! Checked tablecloths and crooning in the background create the authentic 'mamma mia' atmosphere. Friendly service, totally reliable pasta 'n' pizza joint, usually busy. Everything made for you; ask about specials. The antidote to Est Est Est! LO 10/11pm. Closed Sun. Book at weekends. Caprese may be moving in '08; check by phone.

580 SS
£15-22

✓ **Battlefield Rest www.battlefieldrest.co.uk · 0141 636 6955 · 55 Battlefield Road** On South Side near Victoria Park and opposite Infirmary in landmark pavilion building, former tram station. Family-run with great pasta list and home-made puds and lovely thin bread. Small but light, this place unquestionably still one of the best places to eat on the South Side. 7 days 10am-10pm. Closed Sun.

581 9/L25
£15-22

✓ **La Scarpetta www.lascarpetta.co.uk · 01389 758247 · Balloch Road near the bridge, Balloch** Not perhaps many reasons to linger in Balloch – the busy lochside (Lomond) here is not one of them, but this family-run restaurant once a fave of writer A.L. Kennedy (she ain't easy to please). Great service; integrity Italia when visiting Lomond shores (1/BIG ATTRACTIONS). 7 days LO 10pm.

582 SS
£15-22

✓ **Roma Mia www.romamia.co.uk · 0141 423 6694 · 164 Darnley Road** Near the Tramway on the South Side and the best option pre-/post-theatre. Family-friendly tratt, members of 'Ciao Italia' (denoting a 'real' Italian restaurant). Out of the way, but this is a backstreet of Rome, not just Glasgow. Closed Sun lunch & Mon. LO 10.30pm.

583 SS
£15-22

✓ **Bella Napoli 0141 632 4222 · 83 Kilmarnock Road** Another family tratt on the main road of the South Side, this one a' things to a'body (meaning universal appeal). Big hams in the cold counter may amuse the kids. Bright presence on the street, goes on forever inside. Closed Mon/Tue lunch. LO 10.30pm.

584 SS
£15 OR LESS

Buongiorno 0141 649 1029 · 1012 Pollokshaws Road near Shawlands Cross Ronaldo follows parents' footsteps and recipe book. Pasta/pizza straight-up. Some home-made desserts. Conveniently there are 3 good tratts within 100m of each other near these corners: **Di Maggio's**, the **Brooklyn** (657/CAFÉS) and Buongiorno. All are often full, so it's good to have the choice. Takeaway menu. 7 days, lunch & LO 10/11pm.

The Big Blue Report: 586/PIZZA.
Di Maggio's Report: 664/KIDS.

The Best Pizza

585 WE
£15-22
✔ **Firebird** www.firebirdglasgow.com · 0141 334 0594 · **1321 Argyle Street** Big-windowed, spacious bistro at the far west end of Argyle St. Mixed modern menu but notable for wood-smoked dishes, of which their light, imaginative pizzas are excellent. Firebird is a perennially popular hangout, a key Glasgow spot and incidentally, a better pizza is hard to find in this town. 12noon-10/10.30pm (bar midnight/1am).

586 WE
£15-22
✔ **Big Blue** 0141 357 1038 · **445 Great Western Road** On corner of Kelvinbridge and with terrace overlooking the river. Bar and restaurant together so noise can obliterate meal and conversation later on. Lots of other dishes and morsels including spot-on pasta, but the big thin pizzas here are good and that's a well-known fact. 7 days lunch & LO 9.45pm (weekends 10.30pm).

587 2/C2
2/D2
£15-22
Fratelli Sarti www.sarti.co.uk · 0141 248 2228 · **133 Wellington Street, 121 Bath Street & 404 Sauchiehall Street** Excellent, thin-crust pie, buffalo mozzarella and freshly made *pomodoro*. 7 days, hours vary. It's the ingredients that count here, the pizza dough still on the chunky side. Full report: 574/ITALIAN RESTAURANTS.

The Best French Restaurants

588 2/C2
✔ **Le Chardon D'Or** www.brianmaule.com · 0141 248 3801 · **176 West Regent Street** Superlative French-style restaurant. Report: 539/BEST RESTAURANTS.

589 2/B2
£22-32
✔ **Malmaison** www.malmaison-glasgow.com · 0141 221 6401 · **278 West George Street** The brasserie in the basement of the hotel (500/BEST HOTELS) with the same setup as Edinburgh and elsewhere and a very similar menu – based on the classic Parisian brasseries like La Coupole. Excellent brasserie ambience in meticulously designed woody salon. Seating layout and busy waiters mean lots of buzz; also private dining rooms and the adjacent Champagne Bar which serves lite bites (oysters, burgers, eggs Benedict) throughout the day. Chef Donald McInnes sources sound Scottish ingredients for their 'homegrown' menu. 7 days, lunch & LO 10.30pm.

The Best Scottish Restaurants

Restaurants where there is a conscious effort to offer traditional or contemporary Scottish dishes and/or using sourced Scottish seafood/beef/lamb etc.

590 2/E3
£22-32
✔✔ **City Merchant** www.glasgowmerchantcity.net · 0141 553 1577 · **97 Candleriggs** Predating (here nigh on 20 years) and still one of the first restaurants in the Merchant City. The Matteo family's love affair with Scotland has an enduring appeal. 'Seafood, game, steaks' focussing on quality Scottish produce with Italian flair. Lovely oysters; top espresso (with perfect tablet) to finish. Daily and à la carte menus in warm bistro atmosphere. Good biz restaurant or intimate rendezvous. Lunch & dinner LO 10.30pm. Closed Sun.

591 WE
£15-22
✔ **Roastit Bubbly Jocks** 0141 339 3355 · **450 Dumbarton Road** Far up in the West End but many beat their way to this Partick dining room where Mo Abdulla has expanded his cosy wee empire (see Fanny Trollope's 551/BISTROS) but

kept it cosy and excellent value. Not so much 'Scottish' as Scottish-sourced (ingredients) and -presented (ambience). And things we Scots like including mince 'n' tatties and other meaty dishes your mammy made (and pavlova). Lunch & dinner. LO 10pm. Can BYOB.

592 2/C2
£15-22
✓ **Arisaig** www.arisaigrestaurant.co.uk · 0141 204 5399 · 140 St Vincent Street A stylish, airy, smartly presented Scottish bistro inspired by the area where Arisaig village lies on the Road to the Isles (1724/SCENIC ROUTES). Well-sourced ingredients, menu splits 'Sea and Land', combos here you simply don't find anywhere else. Good vegetarian choice. Big portions. Nice prints on the walls. More claim to be presenting contemporary Scotland food, ingredients and culture than others that have clambered on the bandwagon. Thought-out wine list. 7 days, lunch & LO 9.30/10.30pm.

593 WE
£15-22
✓ **Blas** 0141 357 4328 · 1397 Argyle Street (Opposite Kelvingrove Museum; 736/ATTRACTIONS.) A smart, modern café/restaurant with decidedly Scottish slant which means down-to-earth dishes and very good value: stovies to haggis (millefeuille, my goodness!). Sound ingredients: black pud from Stornoway, cheese from Ayrshire, ice cream is Mackies, decor by Timorous Beasties. Proprietor Willie Knox has pulled another one out of the hat - or 'bunnett', as we might say around here. 7 days 10am-10pm.

594 2/F3
✓ **Babbity Bowster** 16 Blackfriars Street Already listed as a pub for real ale and as a hotel (there are rooms upstairs), the food is mentioned mainly for its Scottishness (haggis and stovies) and all-day availability. It's also pleasant to eat outside on the patio/garden in summer. There is a restaurant upstairs called **Schottische** (dinner only Tue-Sat) where I have never ventured. Also breakfast served from 8am (Sun 10am). Report: 715/REAL-ALE PUBS, 519/INDIVIDUAL HOTELS.

595 2/D3
✓ **The Horseshoe** 17 Drury Street A classic pub to be recommended for all kinds of reasons. But lunch is a particularly good deal with 3 courses for £3.45, and old favourites on the menu like mushy peas, macaroni cheese, jelly and fruit. Lunch 12noon-2.30pm. Upstairs open all afternoon, then high tea till 7.45pm (not Sun) (not quite the same atmosphere, but pure Glasgow). All Glasgow characters and what they still love best to eat, are here. Pub open daily till 12midnight. Report: 695/UNIQUE GLASGOW PUBS.

596 2/D3
£22-32
78 St Vincent www.78stvincent.com · 0141 221 7710 · 78 St Vincent Street Based on century-old Le Chartier restaurant in Paris (on railway carriages in fact), this restaurant has more of a brasserie atmosphere than many who aspire though food more calculated than casual. Impressive split-level room with a high ceiling and a big mural by Glasgow artist Donald McLeod. Stylish cuisine balancing the tried and tested with some originality. They say 'Scottish with a continental twist'. Slightly formal with an atmosphere of discreet efficiency. Not bad wines. Lunch (not Sun) and LO 10/10.30pm.

597 WE
£15-22
The Bothy 0141 334 4040 · 11 Ruthven Lane Part of Stefan King's G1 Group's takeover of the West End, this tucked-away site has housed several restaurants of note. This latest reflects current return to roots, ie simpler, more comfort food from the gastrification of café-bar menus and the glorification of chefs. Contemporary-retro design and menu confidently conceived and presented. All Scottish fares and notable ingredients present and correct. A pleasant ambiance; doesn't seem contrived (even if it was). 7 days 12noon-10pm.

Òran Mór 572/GASTROPUBS, 697/UNIQUE PUBS.

The Best Indian Restaurants

598 2/E3
£15-22
✓ ✓ **Dakhin www.dakhin.com · 0141 553 2585 · 89 Candleriggs** Upstairs and out of sight but a must-find for lovers of Indian food. Same owners as The Dhabba (below) but menu is a subcontinent away (ie south as opposed to north India). Lighter, saucier with coconut, ginger and chilli and selection of light-as-a-feather dosas make essential different to the tandoori/tikka-driven menus of most other restaurants on this page. Signature dish: the must-have paper dosa. 7 days. Lunch & LO 10/10.30pm.

599 2/XA1
£15-22
✓ ✓ **Mother India 0141 221 1663 · 28 Westminster Terrace** Famously good Glasgow restaurant for Indian home-cooking now in a 3-floor laid-back but stylish set up where the food rarely lets you down. Most recent addition: the basement has a different, more oven-baked menu (or you can order from upstairs). Many faves and specialities by people who know how to work the flavours and textures. House wine and Kingfisher beer but for £1.25 corkage you can BYOB. You have to book. Take-away too. Lots of vegetarian choice. Very relaxed atmosphere. 7 days, lunch (not Sun-Tue) & LO 10.30/11pm.

600 WE
£15 OR LESS
✓ **Mother India Café 0141 339 9145 · 1355 Argyle Street** (Opposite Kelvingrove Museum; 705/ATTRACTIONS.) Rudely healthy progeny of Mother (above) and cousins to Wee Currys (below); a distinctive twist here ensures another packed house at all times. Menu made up of 40 thali or tapas-like dishes (4/5 for a party of 2), so just as we always did, we get tastes of each other's choices – only it's cheaper! Fastidious waiters (do turn round the tables). Miraculous tiny kitchen. Lunch & LO 10/10.30pm.

601 2/C1
WE
£15 OR LESS
✓ **The Wee Curry Shop 0141 353 0777 · 7 Buccleuch Street near Concert Hall & Ashton Lane (above Jinty McGinty's), 0141 357 5280** Tiny outposts of Mother India above, 2 neighbourhood home-style cooking curry shops, just as they say. Cheap, always cheerful. Stripped-down menu in small, if not micro rooms. Buccleuch St – 6 tables. House red and white and Kingfisher but can BYOB (wine only; £1.50, £2.50 West End). Lunch & LO 10.30pm. Closed Sun lunch. LO 10.30pm. No credit cards.

602 WE
£15-22
✓ **Balbirs 0141 439 7711 · 7 Church Street** At the bottom end of Byres Rd at Dumbarton Rd, the grandee Glasgow proprietor, Balbir Singh Sumal presides in a cavernous but routinely packed restaurant with both regular and innovative dishes from the Subcontinent that Glasgow has taken to its heart and stomach. Closed lunch. LO 10.30/11pm.

603 2/XA2
£15-22
Shish Mahal www.shishmahal.co.uk · 0141 339 8256 · 68 Park Road First-generation Indian restaurant that still, after 'only 42 years', remains one of Glasgow's faves. Modernised some years back but not compromised. Still feels like it's been here forever. Menu of epic size. Many different influences in the cooking, and total commitment to the Glasgow curry. 7 days. Till 11pm/12midnight.

604 WE
£15-22
Ashoka Ashton Lane www.harlequinrestaurants.com · 0141 357 5904 · 19 Ashton Lane & Ashoka West End · 0141 339 0936 · 1284 Argyle Street Part of the Harlequin Restaurants chain, they have always been good, simple and dependable places to go for curry but have kept up with the times. Argyle St is *the* original. Nothing surprising about the menus, just sound Punjabi via Glasgow fare. Good takeaway service (0800 195 3 195). Lunch & LO 11.30pm (not Sun lunch Ashton Lane; West End evenings only at weekends). Open till 12midnight (West End even later).

605 2/E4
£15-22
The Dhabba www.thedhabba.com · 0141 553 1249 · **44 Candleriggs** Mid-Merchant City curry house which presented itself as ground-breaking when it opened in 2003. It is at least modern and enthusiastic. North Indian cuisine in big-window diner. Complemented by sister restaurant Dakhin (above) and often busy, the Dhabba is a well-informed Merchant City choice. 7 days 12noon-10.30pm.

606 WE
£15-22
Mrs Majhu's 0141 339 1339 · **41 Byres Road** A tiny Indian bistro-caff in a place near the bottom of Byres Rd that has seen many cuisines. The eponymous missus presides over a gantry kitchen and a few tables down and up perpetuating her love affair with India, and ours. Refreshingly short menu; real chefs. 7 days. 12noon-11pm.

607 2/A2
£15-22
The Ashoka www.thebestashoka.com · 0141 221 1761 · **108 Elderslie Street** Confusingly, no relation to the Ashokas above. Designery interior but that old pink pakora sauce still runs through the veins. Only the basement on corner with Berkeley St open when we called. Persian and Indian influences. Meticulous service. 7 days. Lunch & LO 12midnight.

608 SS
£15-22
Ali Shan www.alishantandoori.co.uk · 0141 632 5294 · **250 Battlefield Road** Haven't tried but South Siders and many from further afield swear by this Indo-Pak restaurant that's especially good for veggie and other diets. It's been here for 20 years and hasn't changed much but honesty and integrity are very much in their mix of spices. 7 days, lunch Thu/Fri only, LO 11pm (12midnight weekends).

The Best Far-Eastern Restaurants

THAI

609 2/D2
£22-32
✓ **Thai Lemongrass** 0141 331 1315 · **24 Renfrew Street** Noticing perhaps that Glasgow has far fewer good Thai restaurants than Edinburgh, TL has opened up here, near the Concert Hall and opposite Cineworld and become quite possibly the best in town. Contemporary while still cosy. It seems set to give old Thai Fountain (below) a run for its baht. Good service and presentation of all the new Thai faves. 7 days lunch & LO 11.30pm.

610 2/A1
£22-32
Thai Fountain www.thai-fountain.com · 0141 332 2599 · **2 Woodside Crescent, Charing Cross** Same ownership as Amber Regent (see below), this was for a long time Glasgow's best Asian restaurant; now there are many contenders. Genuinely Thai and not at all Chinese. Innovative dishes with great diversity of flavours and textures, so sharing several is best. Of course you will eat too much. Room very interior and rather dated now. 7 days. LO 11/11.30pm. Signature dish: weeping tiger beef.

611 WE
£22-32
Thai Siam www.thaisiamglasgow.com · 0141 229 1191 · **1191 Argyle Street (West End)** Traditional homely (if dimly lit) atmosphere but fashionable clientele who swear it has the prawniest crackers and greenest curry in town. All-Thai st↗ in kitchen and up front maintain authenticity. What it lacks in style up front i↗ made up for in the kitchen. There's another Thai Siam now in Paisley. Lunc↗ 11pm. Closed Sun lunch.

CHINESE

612 2/XA1
£15 OR LESS
✓ **Asia Style** 0141 332 8828 · **185 St George's Road, Charin↗** Discreet, authentic and exceptionally good value, this make↗ late-night rendezvous though you'd have to love Chinese food↗

banter to match. Traditional Chinese without MSG loading. Malaysian dishes. Wine comes red or white. 7 days, dinner only LO 2.30am.

613 2/D1
£22-32
✓ **Dragon-i** www.dragon-i.co.uk · 0141 332 7728 · **311 Hope Street** Refreshingly contemporary Chinese-Far East fusion restaurant opposite Theatre Royal. Thai/Malaysia and rice/noodle/pak choi dishes with sound non-MSG, often Scottish ingredients. Proper puds. Chilled-out room and creative Chinese cuisine at last. Lunch Mon-Fri, dinner 7 days LO 12midnight (11pm Suns).

614 2/C2
£22-32
✓ **Amber Regent** www.amberregent.com · 0141 331 1655 · **50 West Regent Street** Elegant Cantonese restaurant that prides itself on courteous service and the quality of its cuisine, especially seafood. The menu is traditional, the atmosphere too. Has very interior feel. Creditable wine list, quite romantic at night and a good business lunch spot. Only Glasgow Chinese restaurant in AA and Michelin. Lunch, LO 10.30pm weekends 11/11.30pm. Closed Sat lunch & Sun.

615 2/C2
£22-32
✓ **Peking Inn** 0141 332 8971 · **191 Hope Street** Smart, urban kind of Chinese restaurant on busy corner (with West Regent St) but light, relaxing room. Famous for its spicy, Szechuan specials as well as Beijing cuisine via Hong Kong; and nights on town. Perennially popular. Lunch (not Sun), LO 10.30/11.30pm.

616 2/C1
£15-22
✓ **China Town** 0141 353 0037 · **42 New City Road** Just off centre but near Cowcaddens, under the M8. Here you're in Hong Kong (almost). Endless food for lunch (especially Sun) or dinner. Divine dim sum. If you love Chinese food, you must come here. 7 days, 12noon-11.30pm.

617 2/B1
£22-32
✓ **The New Loon Fung** 0141 332 1240 · **417 Sauchiehall Street** 'New' since '06 makeover but still after 35 years possibly Glasgow's most 'respected' Cantonese, the place where the local Chinese community meet for lunch on a Sun/Mon/Tue. Pace is fast and friendly while the food is fresh and authentic. Great dim sum. Everybody on chopsticks. 2 of the 3 menus are in Chinese only. 7 days, 12noon-11/11.30pm.

618 2/C4
£22-32
Ho Wong www.ho-wong.com · 0141 221 3550 · **82 York Street, between Clyde & Argyle Streets** Unlikely location for discreet, urbane Pekinese/Cantonese restaurant which relies on its reputation and makes few compromises. Calm, quite chic room with mainly up-market clientele; roomful of suits at lunch and champagne list. Notable for seafood and duck. Lunch (not Sun) & LO 11/11.30pm.

619 WE
£15-22
Chow 0141 334 9818 · **98 Byres Road** Away from other Chinese restaurants clustered downtown, this is the contemporary, smarter and buzzy West End version. Broad menu includes speciality Singapore noodles and Szechuan dishes. Good vegetarian choice. Can be a tight squeeze down or up. Takeaway and delivery. 7 days lunch & dinner (Sun from 4.30pm). LO 11.30pm.

620 2/B1
£15 OR LESS
Glasgow Noodle Bar 0141 333 1883 · **482 Sauchiehall Street** Authentic, Chinese-style noodle bar, 100m from Charing Cross. Along with **Canton Express** opposite at 407 Sauchiehall St (0141 332 0145), two fast food joints with genuine, made on the spot – in the wok – food late into the AM. Both shabby. Noodle Bar is the smartest, Express down to earth, especially if you go to the toilets; but groovy in a West End way. 7 days, 12noon-4am. 672/LATE-NIGHT RESTAURANTS.

JAPANESE

621 2/D2 **Wagamama** www.wagamama.com · 0141 229 1468 · **97 West George**
£15-22 **Street** Wagamama brand and formula came to Scotland though on an unprepossessing site in mid-town. If you like Asian food that's good for you and fast, you'll be a fan of their unique formula: big canteen tables, 'healthy' Japanese-based food made to order and brought when ready. Seems to work universally but the novelty does wear off. 7 days 12noon-11pm (Sun 12.30-10pm).

622 2/D3 **Ichiban** www.ichiban.co.uk · 0141 204 4200 · **50 Queen Street &**
WE **184 Dumbarton Road, Partick** Noodle bar based loosely on the Wagamama
£15-22 formula. Fundamental food, egalitarian presentation, some technology. Ramen, udon, soba noodle dishes; also chow meins, tempuras and other Japanese snacks. Long tables, eat-as-it-comes 'methodology'. Light, calm, hip. Lunch and LO 10pm (weekends 10.30pm), Sun 1-10pm. The Partick Ichiban which is near Byres Road is possibly better of the 2; certainly the healthiest caff in the quarter.

FUSION

623 2/E3 **Café Mao** www.cafemao.com · 0141 564 5161 · **Corner of Brunswick &**
£15-22 **Wilson Streets, Merchant City** Bright, hip east-Asian restaurant on Merchant City corner. Indonesian, Malaysian, Korean dishes prep with varying degrees of flair and flava. Good service, right-on wine list. Asian beers and smoothies. Nice rice. Open all day. 7 days. Lunch 12-5pm, LO 10/11pm (Sun 1pm-10pm).

624 2/XA4 **Yen** www.yenrotunda.com · 0141 847 0110 · **28 Tunnel Street** In the
£15-32 Rotunda building near the SECC so often busy with pre- or après-concert audiences. Upstairs café has Cantonese/Japanese/ Thai noodle vibe, ground floor has more expensive, more full-on teppanyaki restaurant with 8-course menus you sit and watch being prepared on the searing hobs (must book). You might yearn for a better exchange rate. 7 days, lunch & LO 10.30pm (closed Sun lunch).

625 2/D2 **Oshi** www.oshi.5pm.co.uk · 0141 333 5702 · **Port Dundas Place** The ground
£15-22 floor restaurant of Langs Hotel (502/BEST HOTELS) with adjacent spa sees itself as an 'urban retreat'. It is a very nice space, ambient and urban. This reflected in menu where Euro meets Asia on almost equal split. 7 days 12noon-10pm.

▌ Other Ethnic Restaurants

SPANISH

626 WE **Café Andaluz** www.cafeandaluz.com · 0141 339 1111 · **2 Cresswell Lane, off**
2/D3 **Byres Road & St Vincent Place** ·0141 222 2255 The original is a basement on
£15 OR LESS corner of Cresswell (the less heaving) lane where folks gather of an evening. Nice atmosphere encased in ceramica with wide choice tapas and mains (including vegetarian). Owned by Di Maggio (Italian) chain. St Vincent Pl busy like Spain but through location rather than authenticity. 7 days LO 10.30/11pm.

627 2/C3 **Tapaell'ya at the Radisson Hotel** www.tapaellya.com · 0141 225 2047 ·
£15-22 **Robertson Street at Argyle Street** The walk-in restaurant of the audacious Radisson (499/BEST HOTELS) is not often busy so who knows if this formula will remain, but the paellas, tapas and great Spanish wine selection are refreshingly particular in a Fusion-infused world. Mon-Fri 12noon-10.30pm, Sat 6-10.30pm, Sun 11am-3pm.

628 ss **Tinto Tapas Bar** 0141 636 6838 · 138 Battlefield Road On the South Side near the Victoria Infirmary. Sliver of a restaurant serving tapas and specials all day with good inexpensive wine selection. 7 days 10am-11pm.

MEXICAN

629 2/E4 **Pancho Villa's** www.panchovillas.co.uk · 0141 552 7737 · 26 Bell Street
£15-22 Bright, colourful restaurant lives up to crowded cantina expectations. Menu in Spanish/ingredients in English. No burritos ('an American invention'). Plenty of veggie choices but you really have to try the *albondigas en salsa* (that's spicy meatballs). Mon-Sat lunch & 6-11pm, Sun 6-10.30pm.

630 2/D5 **Salsa** www.salsa.5pm.co.uk · 0141 420 6328 · 63 Carlton Place On the
£15-22 south bank of the river at end of Glasgow Bridge (pedestrian), an unlikely location perhaps since bright, spicy salsa lurks in a basement here. Bar with relatively small restaurant section but some of the best Mexican staples and lovely, imaginative mains in town. Some big tables, good for parties! This place deserves to do well – cross that bridge when you come to it! Lunch & LO 9.30/10pm (bar later).

GREEK

631 2/XA1 ✓ **Konaki** www.konakitaverna.com · 0141 342 4010 · 920 Sauchiehall
£15 OR LESS **Street** West of M8 opposite Kelvin Park Lorne Hotel. A significant makeover since the last edition of *StB* so Konaki, the famously real Greek restaurant in Glasgow now looks as good as it tastes. Down-to-earth Greek grub (including pastas) with proper ingredients eg oregano from the home village in Crete. Deli in front, surprisingly big room through the back. Cheap treats.7 days, lunch & dinner (not Sun lunch). LO 11pm.

MIDDLE EASTERN

632 WE **Bay Tree Café** 0141 334 5898 · 403 Great Western Road Near Kelvinbridge.
£15 OR LESS For years a veggie haven now serving lamb and chicken dishes (kept separate in the kitchen) extending Turkish, Lebanese and North African range. Diverse menu from homous (sic) to those sweet sweet desserts with many a casserole in between. Simple caff; great value. 7 days 9.30am-10pm (9pm-Sun).

633 2/B2 **Al-Zagros** 0141 332 5300 · 192 Pitt Street Near Sauchiehall St with an off-mainstreet and off-mainstream menu though the mainly barbecued lamb and chicken dishes are not unfamiliar. Interesting variants on Middle Eastern cuisine with some vegetarian choice. Small, contemporary room. Lunch & LO 10pm/11pm. Closed Sun lunch.

NORTH AFRICAN

634 2/XA2 **Mzouda** 0141 221 3910 · 141 Elderslie Street Excellent recent addition to ethnic eateries, named after a faraway village in the Atlas. Mix of Catalan and Moroccan 'country' cuisine. Menu somewhere between Berber and Basque is a refreshing change. Signature dish: Djas Harissa is... hot. Lunch & LO 10/11pm.

The Best Seafood & Fish

635 2/E4
£22-32
✓ ✓ **Gandolfi Fish** www.cafegandolfi.com · 0141 552 9475 · **84 Albion Street** Once there was Café Gandolfi (644/TEAROOMS), then Bar Gandolfi (568/GASTROPUBS) and once there were only a couple of fish restaurants in all of Glasgow. Now see what happened. This the latest (2007) has a good location, a stylish look (nice paintings by Lewis artist Moira Maclean), good proprietorship (Seumas MacInnes) and a direct link to the West Coast and Hebridean fishing grounds, especially Barra (where Seumas is from) and fish supplier Jonathan Boyd. It's bound to catch on! 7 days. Lunch & LO 10.30pm.

636 2/C2
£22-32
✓ ✓ **Gamba** www.gamba.co.uk · 0141 572 0899 · **225a West George Street** In basement at corner of West Campbell St, a seafood bistro which happens to be one of the best restaurants in the city. Fashionable clientele enjoy uncluttered setting and snappy service, as well as excellent fresh fish unfussily presented à la mode. Chef Derek Marshall assured and eclectic. Exemplary wine list. Unlike many, open on Mon (closed Sun). Lunch & LO 10.30pm but may serve later so check.

637 WE
2/C2
£22-32
✓ ✓ **Two Fat Ladies** www.twofatladies.5pm.co.uk · 0141 339 1944 · **88 Dumbarton Road & 118 Blythswood Square** · 0141 847 0088 The landmark West End restaurant expanded downtown. Everything is selectively sourced and both tiny kitchens produce delicious dishes with a light touch. Splendid puds. Similar if not the same menus. 7 days (not Sun lunch in West End).

638 2/C2
£15-22
✓ **Mussel Inn** www.mussel-inn.com · 0141 572 1405 · **157 Hope Street** Downtown location for light, bright bistro (big windows) where seafood is serious, but fun. Mussels, scallops, oysters and vegetarian option, but mussels in variant concoctions and kilo pots are the thing. As in Edinburgh (225/SEAFOOD), this formula is sound and the owners, Messrs Johansson, Spiers and Watford, are to be commended for keeping it real and for giving excellent value. 7 days. Lunch & LO 10pm (not Sun lunch).

639 2/E3
Grand Fish and Chips 0141 552 4017 · **17 John Street** Merchant City location between Cochrane and Ingram Sts near George Sq. Latest attempt to make this site work (it does when the weather's good with tables spread across the pedestrian street) in the versatile hands of Mr Billy Macanany. It's simple fish (battered, breaded or clay-oven roasted) and chips (with sides). Still looking for the perfect (beef dripping used) chip at TGP. Not a bad idea this time. We'll hope it's not a fish out of water. 7 days. 12noon-10pm.

An Lochan Report: 550/BISTROS.

Rogano Report: 542/BEST RESTAURANTS.

The Best Vegetarian Restaurants

640 WE
£15 OR LESS

✓ **Grassroots Café** www.grassrootsorganic.com · 0141 333 0534 ·
97 St George's Road This is the caff offshoot of Grassroots (the deli) round the corner at 48 Woodlands Road (687/DELIS): serving proper vegetarian and vegan food. Nutritious, worthy – all this, but round the world dishes as vegetarian food should be and some simply splendid salads. Calming as well as healthy despite proximity of M8. 7 days. BYO possible. 10am-8.45pm (9.45pm weekends).

641 2/E4
£15 OR LESS

✓ **Mono** 0141 553 2400 · **Kings Court** In odd no-man's land between Merchant City and East End behind Parnie St, a cool hangout in a forlorn mall. PC in a 'people's collective' kind of way; the antithesis of Glasgow's manufactured style. Great space with art, music, occasional performance and interesting if utilitarian vegetarian food served with few frills by friendly staff. Organic ales/wines. 7 days 12noon-10pm (bar midnight).

642 2/E4

The 13th Note www.13thnote.co.uk · 0141 553 1638 · **50-60 King Street** Old-style veggie hangout – a good attitude/good vibes café-bar with live music downstairs. Menu unexceptional but honest, from vegeburgers to Indian and Greek dishes. All suitable for vegans. Organic booze on offer, but also normal Glasgow bevvy. 7 days, 12noon-12midnight. Food LO 10pm.

643 WE
SS

Tchai-Ovna www.tchaiovna.com · 0141 357 4524 · **Otago Lane &** **169 Deanston Drive** · 0141 649 7258 Old-style vegetarian caffs for modern people; both teashops boast best boho credentials. Report: 651/TEAROOMS.

Restaurants serving particularly good vegetarian food but not exclusively vegetarian:

The Ubiquitous Chip Report: 537/BEST RESTAURANTS.

Baby Grand, **Arisaig** and **Tron Café-Bar**. Reports: 565/BEST BISTROS, 592/BEST SCOTTISH RESTAURANTS, 688a/KID-FRIENDLY PLACES.

Bay Tree Café Report: 632/OTHER ETHNIC.

Mother India, **Dakhin** Report: 599/598/INDIAN RESTAURANTS.

Café Gandolfi Report: 644/TEAROOMS.

The Best Tearooms & Coffee Shops

644 2/E4 ✓ ✓ **Café Gandolfi** www.cafegandolfi.com · 0141 552 6813 · **64 Albion Street, Merchant City** For over 20 years Seumas MacInnes's definitive and landmark meeting/eating place – bistro menu, but casual ambience of a tearoom or coffee shop. Bohemian, Europe-somewhere atmosphere. Stained glass and heavy, over-sized wooden furniture create a unique ambience that has stood the fashionability test. The food is light and imaginative and served all day. You may have to queue. 7 days, 9am-11.30pm, Sun from 12noon (677/SUNDAY BREAKFAST). The more recent Bar upstairs (568/GASTROPUBS) has added a new room and a new dimension.

645 WE 2/E3 ✓ **Tinderbox** 0141 339 3108 · **189 Byres Road & 14 Ingram Street** ·0141 552 6907 Stylish, shiny, state-of-the-art neighbourhood coffee shops. Stuff for kids, stuff to buy. Snacks and Elektra, the good-looking coffee machine. Great people-watching potential inside and out. Better sandwiches and cakey things than others of this ilk. Daily soups and porridge for breakfast. Tinderbox has made that huge leap to London and can be found in Upper St, Islington. 7 days, 7.15am-11pm (Sun from 7.45am).

646 WE ✓ **Kember & Jones** www.kemberandjones.co.uk · 0141 337 3851 · **134 Byres Road** They call it a 'Fine Food Emporium' and it is, though some would say 'at a price'. A deli with well-sourced nibbles and the stuff of the good life especially cheese and olives. Tables outside and on the mezzanine. Great sandwiches and the best tartes and tortes in town. Home baking to a high standard - how they do it all from that small kitchen is a triumph of cookery. The new star on the Byres Road in the early noughties. 7 days, 9am-10pm (till 6 Sat/Sun and from 10am Sun).

647 2/D3 2/C3 ✓ **Fifi and Ally** www.fifiandally.com · 0141 229 0386 · **Princes Square & 80 Wellington Street** · 0141 226 2286 More a lifestyle experience than a mere tearoom but this they do so uniquely well. Both have gift shop as part of mix and newer Wellington St unit has a deli and a restaurant/bar (552/BISTROS). Both good for hot snacks, sandwiches and cakes, especially meringues. Many ladies lunch! Afternoon tea 2-5pm. Hours vary but both closed Sun. Princes Square branch closed in evenings.

648 2/C2 **Where The Monkey Sleeps** www.monkeysleeps.com · 0141 226 3406 · **182 West Regent Street** Adjacent Compass Gallery and in basement below Chardon D'Or (539/BEST RESTAURANTS), its commercial and spiritual opposite. Exhibition space ie hanging as well as hanging out. Coffee, soups and picmix sandwiches. Art students and what they turn into (especially bike couriers). 7 days. 7am-5pm. (6pm Sat). Closed Sun.

649 WE **North Star** 0141 946 5365 · **108 Queen Margaret Drive** Portuguese-cum-Iberian deli-cum-neighbourhood caff. Minimalist approach to design and product range; very laid-back in cramped surroundings. All home-made except bread. Daily specials on the tiles. Can BYOB. 7 days Mon-Sat. 8am-7/8pm. Sun 11am-5pm.

650 2/D1 **Café Hula** www.cafehula.co.uk · 0141 353 1660 · **321 Hope Street** Central, some say overlooked café opposite Theatre Royal by people who have North Star (above). Simple, imaginative menu with home-made appeal; good vegetarian choice. Anti-style, mix 'n' match – a boho atmosphere rare in this town. Famous brownies. 7 days 8.30am-10pm, Sun 11am-6pm.

651 WE Tchai-ovna www.tchaiovna.com · 0141 357 4524 · 42 Otago Lane & 161
SS Deanston Drive, Shawlands A 'house of tea' hidden away off Otago St on the
banks of the Kelvin with verandah and garden terrace. A decidedly boho tearoom
which could be Eastern Europe, North Africa or Kathmandu. 70 kinds of tea, soup,
organic sandwiches and cakes. Impromptu performances likely. A real find but
suits and le chic not comfortable here. Newer, more arabesque branch on South
Side. All-veggie menu is stickier and spicier than the West End variant. 7 days
11am-11pm.

652 2/E3 Berits & Brown 0141 552 6980 · 6 Wilson Street First Glasgow branch of
developing deli/coffee shop chain. A tad formulaic but a welcome addition to this
part of town where there is coffee - lounging as well as grazing to do - anything
but cooking! Choice tid-bits. 8am-10pm (till 11pm Sat) Sun 9am-9pm.

653 2/B1 CCA Café 0141 332 7959 · 350 Sauchiehall Street The atrium café of this city
art centre, spectacularly refurbished 2002. It's like eating in a covered street.
Stylish/contemporary of course – the room and the menu. Good rendezvous.
Always people concocting and creating or just conspiring. Though now 'run by the
cooncil', a real chef in the kitchen (at TGP) does care about what comes over the
counter. 11am-7.30pm (9pm weekends). Closed Sun.

654 SS Art Lover's Café www.houseforanartlover.co.uk · 0141 353 4779 ·
10 Dumbreck Road, Bellahouston Park On the ground floor of House for an
Art Lover, a building based on drawings left by Mackintosh (801/MACKINTOSH).
Bright room, crisp presentation and a counterpoint to wrought iron, purply, swirly
Mockintosh cáffs elsewhere. This is unfussy and elegant. Garden views. Soup 'n'
sandwiches and à la carte; a serious lunch spot. 7 days 10am-4pm.

The Best Caffs

655 WE ✓✓ **University Café 87 Byres Road** 'People have been coming here for generations to sit at the "kneesy" tables and share the salt and vinegar. Run by the Verecchia family who administer advice, sympathy and pie, beans and chips with equal aplomb.' These astute words of the late Graeme Kelling describing a real Glasgow gem, still stand 4 editions later. 6 booths only; it resists all change. BYOB. Daily till 10pm (weekends till 10.30pm). Closed Tue. Takeaway open later.

656 2/XF3 ✓ **Coia's Café 473 Duke Street** 'Since 1928, supplying this East End high street with ice cream, great deal breakfasts and the kind of comforting lunch (they might call it dinner) café-bar places just cannot do,' is what I wrote last edition and what does it do? It has a complete makeover and turns into something that looks suspiciously like a café-bar or café diner/deli. Probably no bad thing and still packed despite expansion. Traditional grub and ice cream along with the olive-oil niceties. Sit-in or takeaway. 7 days. 7.30am-9pm (LO 7.30pm); Sun from 10am.

657 SS ✓ **Brooklyn Café 0141 632 3427 · 21 Minard Road** Whatever fancy café-bar Stefan King throws up on the South Side, this caff off Pollokshaws Rd, here over 70 years, will probably outlive the lot of them. More tratt perhaps than caff with pasta/pizza, 3 risottos, 6 salads, excellent puds and great ice-cream. Recent refurbishment but still and forever the real thing! 7 days 9am-8pm (weekends 10pm). Sun from 10am.

658 2/XC1 ✓ **Café D'Jaconelli 570 Maryhill Road** Near Queen's Cross Church (794/MACKINTOSH). Neighbourhood caff with toasties, macaroni cheese and award-winning ice cream to go that's been here for ever. This is the disappearing Glasgow, but used often as a film location (*Trainspotting*, *Carla's Song*). These are the real banquettes, though only 5. The fish 'n' chips next door is under different management. 7 days, 10am-5pm, counter 10pm.

659 2/C2 **Bradfords 245 Sauchiehall Street** Since 1924 the coffee shop/restaurant upstairs from the flagship shop of this local and estimable bakery chain. Familiar wifie waitresses, the macaroni cheese is close to mum's and the cakes and pies from downstairs represent Scottish bakery at its figure-building best. The best strawberry tarts. Mon-Sat 9am-5.30pm.

660 WE **Kebabish 0141 334 1100 · 23 Gibson Street** A take and take away on the old kebab theme, the cheap 'n' cheerful in gastrofying Gibson St. Upfront you see everything being grilled, stirfried and sorted; tables at the back. Like a bus-station caff on a backpacker trail, we could all happily relive our gap years here. Curries include fish and vegetarian and unusual specials. Lassis and fresh juice. All cheap as chapatis (no chips here!). 7 days till 12midnight, 1am weekends.

661 WE **Jack McPhee's www.jackmcphee.com · 285 Byres Road** 'Jack McPhee Fresh from the Sea' it says above the door of this traditional though traded-up fish 'n' chip shop caff still frying up among the olive groves of Byres Rd. Chips pale like the punters; surprisingly good bolognese and mixed platters are the thing, but a US-style Scottish breakfast (hash browns *and* potato scones) must be considered. No bad coffee. 7 days 9am-10pm.

662 2/E4 **Trans-Europe Café 0141 552 7999 · 25 Parnie Street** Easygoing caff in the emerging gallery quarter off the east end of Argyle St has buzzed along since it opened in '06. Light food especially bespoke sandwiches during the day; becomes bistrofied at night (Thu-Sat only). Friendly vibe. 10am-5pm (weekends till 11pm).

Kid-Friendly Places

663 WE ✓ **Rio Café** 0141 334 9909 · **27 Hyndland Street, Partick** At last a kid-friendly caff that's cool, cool for parents that is with decent food and service for both. Here there's also live bands, DJs, the 'spoken word' jazz on Thursdays, and sweeties. An all-round neighbourhood place to go by new guys on the block, Willy Knox & Co. 7 days 9am-7.30pm (bar 11pm/12midnight).

664 WE
SS
2/D3 **Di Maggio's** www.dimaggios.co.uk · 0141 334 8560 · **61 Ruthven Lane off Byres Road & 1038 Pollokshaws Road** · 0141 632 4194 & **21 Royal Exchange Square** · 0141 248 2111 'Our family serving your family' they say and they do. Bustling, friendly pizza joints with good Italian attitude to bairns. There's a choice to defy the most finicky kid. High chairs, special menu. Handy outdoor section in Exchange Sq is best for runaround kids. 7 days.

665 SS **Tramway Café** 0141 422 2023 · **25 Albert Drive** Caff at the back of Tramway arts venue on the South Side. Venue itself cavernous, contemporary with continuously changing programme always worth visiting. Caff well run with great grub and facing on to 'The Secret Garden' (1612/GARDENS). Play area and healthy options; nice for kids. 10am-8pm, Sun 12noon-6pm. Closed Mon.

666 SS **Brooklyn Café** 0141 632 3427 · **21 Minard Road** The unassuming, long-established caff on the South Side (off Pollokshaws Road) where families are very welcome for the carbo and the cones and the jars of sweeties on the shelf. Report: 627/CAFFS.

667 SS
2/B1 **Art Lover's Café & The CCA Café** www.houseforanartlover.co.uk · 0141 353 4779 · **Dumbreck Road & 350 Sauchiehall Street** · 0141 332 7959 2 informal, light cafés with space for kids and parents not to feel confined. Reports: 654/653/COFFEE SHOPS.

668 2/D3 **Princes Square** **Buchanan Street** Glasgow's smart downtown mall on 4 floors has many eateries with outside tables and suitable kids' choices. Basement has mosaic area that kids like and **Il Pavone**, good family Italian fare.

668A 2/E4 **Tron Café** 0141 552 8587 · **63 Trongate** The Child-friendly Bar of the Year 2003. Special family section.

Bella Napoli Family-run and run for families: a tratt with the standard Italian fare we've all loved ever since we could get spaghetti in our mouths. Report: 583/TRUSTY TRATTS.

Sorry there aren't more.

The Best Late-Night Restaurants

669 2/A2 ✓ **Baby Grand** www.babygrandglasgow.com · 0141 248 4942 · **Elmbank Gardens** It's not easy to find by Charing Cross Station and Premier Lodge skyscraper hotel behind King's Theatre, but persevere – this is a decent bar/diner at any time of day (565/BISTROS), but comes into its own after 10pm when just about everywhere that's decent is closing. Chargrilled food and grazing contemporary menu. Piano player; night-time people. **Daily till 12midnight, Fri/Sat 1am.**

670 2/XA1 ✓ **Asia Style** 0141 332 8828 · **185 St George's Road** Simple, authentic Chinese and Malaysian café/canteen with familiar sweet 'n' sour, curry and satays and 4 kinds of noodle but exotic specials and 5 kinds of 'porridge'. Only open evenings. **7 days 5pm-3am** (may close 2am if quiet).

671 2/C4 **Spice Garden** www.spicegarden.com · 0141 492 4422 · **11 Clyde Place** Just across the river, under the Glasgow Bridge where trains rumble over, a restaurant that's long been a late-night destination. Now most definitely Indian, it's for the late and last curry craving of the day. Pleasantly light, food surprisingly good. BYOB till 12midnight. Free 2-mile-radius taxi service. **7 days 6pm-4am, Sun till 1am.**

672 2/B1 **Glasgow Noodle Bar** 0141 333 1883 · **482 Sauchiehall Street** Better of the 2 stripped-down noodle bars opposite each other in Sauchiehall St. Authentic, fast, no-frills Chinese (ticket service and eezee-kleen tables). The noodle is 'king'; but cooking *is* taken seriously. 620/FAR-EASTERN RESTAURANTS. **7 days, 12noon-4am.**

673 WE **The Salon** www.socialeating.co.uk · 0141 576 1700 · **17 Vinicombe Street** Used to be Gong; all ripped out and start again. Mentioned here because on Fri and Sat they have a 'supper club' where you can keep drinking with light meals till **2am.**

674 WE **Stravaigin & Stravaigin 2** www.stravaigin.5pm.co.uk · 0141 334 2665 · **Gibson Street & 334 7165 Ruthven Lane off Byres Road** Worth remembering that both these excellent restaurants (540/RESTAURANTS and 546/BISTROS) serve food **to 11pm.** Well, it is later than most in 'cosmopolitan' Glasgow.

✓ **Guy's Restaurant & Bar** 559A/BISTROS. **11.30pm Fri/Sat.**

Ashoka West End & Ashoka Ashton Lane 604/INDIAN RESTAURANTS. **12.30am/1am weekends.**

Good Places For Sunday Breakfast

675 WE ✓ **Tinderbox** 0141 339 3108 · **corner of Byres & Highburgh Roads & corner of Ingram & Montrose Streets** Great café/diner open early to late. Probably the earliest decent breakfast for out-all-nighters. Porridge and muesli. Weekdays from 7.15am. 645/COFFEE SHOPS. Weekends **from 7.45am.**

676 2/F3 ✓ **Babbity Bowster** 0141 552 5055 · **16 Blackfriars Street** The seminal Merchant City bar/hotel recommended for many things (594/SCOTTISH RESTAURANTS, 722/DRINKING OUTDOORS), but worth remembering as one of the best and earliest spots for Sun breakfast. **From 10am.**

677 2/E4 ✓ **Café Gandolfi** www.cafegandolfi.com · 0141 552 6813 · **64 Albion Street** Atmospheric room, with daylight filtering through stained glass and comforting, oversized wooden furniture. This is pleasant start to Sun, that day of rest and more shopping made even better with baked eggs, a pot of tea and the papers. 644/BEST TEAROOMS. Bar upstairs has all-day menu. **Both from 12noon.**

678 2/XF3 ✓**Coia's Café** **473 Duke Street** They've been doing breakfast here for over 75 years. Refurbished and still damned good. The full-fry monty lasts all day (vegetarian too). Papers provided. East End choice. 656/BEST CAFFS. **From 10am.**

679 WE ✓**Stravaigin** **www.stravaigin.5pm.co.uk · 0141 334 2665 · 28 Gibson Street** Same care and flair given to breakfast menu as the rest (540/BEST RESTAURANTS). Cramped maybe, but reflects appetite for Sun breakfast from home-made granola to French toast, Ramsay's Ayrshire bacon, even a steak sandwich. Served till 5pm. **From 11am.**

680 2/A1 **Grassroots Café** **www.grassrootsorganic.com · 97 St George's Road** An especially calm, healthy Sun thing (640/VEGETARIAN RESTAURANTS). **From 10am.**

The Best Takeaway Places

681 WE ✓✓**Heart Buchanan** **www.heartbuchanan.co.uk · 0141 334 7626 · 380 Byres Road** Deli and takeaway with tables; adjacent 'saucier' joins the 'traiteur': Fiona Buchanan endorses the French idea that excellent food can be pre-prepared to take home. Certainly an extraordinary daily changing menu is produced in the kitchens downstairs according to a published menu of the week. Lots of other selected goodies to go. Fiona puts her 'heart' into this place. Every urban neighbourhood should have a Heart and Buchanan but who but a foodaholic would give food this time and attention? 7 days 8.30am-9.30pm. Sun 10am-6pm.

682 WE ✓✓**Delizique** **www.delizique.co.uk · 0141 339 2000 · 70 Hyndland Street** Down from Cottiers and two doors up from their original corner, a still-larger emporium serving the luvvies, loaded and long-term denizens of Hyndland and beyond. More old-fashioned provisioner than spanking new deli. Fruit/veg outside, cheese counter; the unusual alongside dinner-party essentials. Gorgeous food to go includes salads, tarts and scrumptious cakes. 7 days 8am-8pm (Sun from 9am).

683 WE ✓**Roots and Fruits** **0141 339 3077 · Great Western Road** A row of wholefood provisioner shops near Kelvinbridge, famously where to go for fruit and veg in the West End. Now has 'traiteur' section and a couple of chairs by one of the windows, but the delicious home-made food and bakery is mainly to take home. 7 days. 8.30/9am-6.30pm (7pm Thu/Fri).

684 2/E3 ✓**Fresh** **0141 552 5532 · 51 Cochrane Street** At last a takeaway with integrity in the Merchant City, at George Sq. Hearty (and lite) healthy soups and famously good juices. Sandwiches made up or ready-to-go. Much vegetarian. All dolphin-friendly. 7 days 9am-5pm (Sun from 11am).

685 **The Cheese Bar & Deli** Not so much a takeaway as a café/restaurant cum deli. 692/DELIS.

686 2/A1 **Grassroots** **www.grassrootsorganic.com · 0141 353 3278 · 20 Woodlands Road, Charing Cross** Food to go, but mainly big organic deli. Vegetarian ready meals, bespoke sandwiches. 7 days 8am-6/7pm, Sat 9-6pm, Sun 11-5pm.

Philadelphia Fish & Chicken Bar The West End standby! 1442/FISH 'N' CHIPS.

The Best Delis

687 2/XA1 ✓ ✓ **Grassroots Organic** **48 Woodlands Road** First-class vegetarian food and provisions store, everything chemically unaltered and environmentally friendly. Great breads and sandwiches for lunch and the best organic fruit/veg range in town. Vegetarian restaurant round the corner (640/GLASGOW VEGETARIAN). 7 days 8am-8pm (Sat 9am-6pm, Sun 11am-5pm).

688 WE ✓ ✓ **Delizique** **70 Hyndland Street** Excellent neighbourhood deli for the affluent Hyndlanders and others who roam and graze round here. Great prepared meals (in-house chef) and hand-picked goodies including oils, hams, flowers and Mellis cheeses. 7 days 9am-8pm. 682/TAKEAWAY.

689 WE ✓ ✓ **Heart Buchanan** **380 Byres Road** Great deli and first-rate takeaway. Report: 681/TAKEAWAY.

690 WE ✓ ✓ **I.J. Mellis** **Great Western Road** Started out as the cheese guy, now more of a very select deli for food that's good and 'slow'. Coffees, hams, sausages, olives and seasonal stuff like apples and mushrooms (branches vary), so smells mingle. Irresistible! Branches also in Edinburgh (340/EDINBURGH DELIS) and St Andrews (1530/REALLY GOOD DELIS). 7 days though times vary. See also 1556/CHEESES.

691 2/XF3 **Garlic** **793 Shettleston Road** **0141 763 0399** A foody oasis in the unfashionable East End. A great Italian wine range (including organic) and beer, and a superb choice of home-made and fresh foods with an imaginative, ever-changing take-home range. Giovanna is passionate about good food and personally souces items from Italy. Have a coffee as you peruse. Tue-Sat 8.30am-5.30pm. Times are approximate; they're there cooking before and after. Giovanna works hard! Set to expand to Gibson St at Park Rd in the West End as **Eusebi's** in early '08.

692 WE **The Cheese Bar & Deli** **61 Otago Street** Middle of residential street near Gibson St with its many restaurants. This also a restaurant/coffeeshop and upfront a purveyor of cheeses and wines. Extension of the burgeoning food empire of Messrs Tomkins and McInanay, it'll be interesting to see how this slightly off-the-map 'unit' fares. 11am-9pm (till 10pm weekends).

693 WE
2/E4 **Lupe Pintos** **313 Great Western Road** Unusual Latin deli (ie Mexican, Central American, Spanish). Where to go for chorizo, manchego and 20 kinds of tequila. Takeaway including home-made burritos and the usual Tex-Mex. Every kind of chili and great Riojas. Also in Edinburgh (346/EDINBURGH DELIS). 10am-6pm. Closed Sun.

694 WE **Peckham's** **Glasgow, Lenzie, Newton Mearns & Edinburgh** Scotland's most prolific deli chain, but each shop individually run. Hyndland (43 Clarence Dr) and Merchant City (61 Glassford St) are the best of them. Expensive but always serviceable and loads of choice from staples to wines and cheeses, and a good range of up-market nibbles.

Unique Glasgow Pubs

695 2/D3 ✓ ✓ **The Horseshoe 17 Drury Street** A mighty pub since the 19th century in the small street between West Nile and Renfield Sts near Central Station. Early example of this style of pub, dubbed 'gin palaces'. Island rather than horseshoe bar ('the longest in the UK'), impressive selection of alcohols and an upstairs lounge where they serve lunch and high tea. The food is amazing value (595/SCOTTISH RESTAURANTS). All kinds of folk. Daily till 12midnight.

696 WE ✓ **Òran Mór www.oran-mor.co.uk · Corner of Byres & Great Western Roads** Huge and hugely popular pub emporium in converted church on prominent West End corner, the still-evolving vision of Colin Beattie. Drinking on all levels (and outside) but also good pub food (572/GASTROPUBS) and separate brasserie (562/BISTROS). Big entertainment programme from DJs to comedy and 'A Play and a Pint'. They thought of everything. 7 days till 12midnight.

697 2/XA1 ✓ **The Halt Bar 160 Woodlands Road** Edwardian pub largely unspoiled, unchanged though paint job wouldn't go amiss. Original counter and snug intact. Always great atmosphere – live music and DJs Wed-Sun, football on the telly. Open mic nights. Open till 11pm/12midnight.

698 2/E1 ✓ **Corinthian www.g1group.co.uk · 191 Ingram Street** Mega makeover of impressive listed building to form cavernous bar/restaurant, 2 comfy lounge/cocktail bars and a restaurant serving 'traditional Scottish food' (though tapenade soufflé alongside broth and haggis). Near George Sq and Gallery of Modern Art. Awesome ceiling in main room transformed into the 'Lite Bar' – better than megabars elsewhere. 7 days, till 12midnight. (Piano bar Thu-Sun).

699 2/E4 ✓ **Arta www.arta.co.uk · Old Cheesemarket, Walls Street, Merchant City** Near and same ownership as Corinthian (above) and similar scale of vision completely realised. This massive OTT bar/restaurant/club somewhere between old Madrid and new Barcelona could probably only happen in Glasgow. 'Mediterranean' menu upstairs but also burgers (till 11pm) and down the full-on Glasgow drinking, dressing-up and chatting-up experience. Enter those chambers into a dream or just possibly a nightmare. Wed-Sun from 5pm-1am (Thu/Fri/Sat till 3am). It's a long way for a fag.

700 2/D5 ✓ **Victoria Bar 157 Bridgegate** 'The Vicky' is in the 'Briggait', one of Glasgow's oldest streets, near the Victoria Bridge over the Clyde. Once a pub for the fishmarket and open odd hours, now it's a howff for all those who like an atmosphere that's old, friendly and uncontrived. Ales. Mon-Sat till 12midnight, Sun 11pm.

701 2/D5 ✓ **Scotia Bar 112 Stockwell Street** Near the Victoria (above), late-1920s Tudor-style pub with a low-beamed ceiling and intimate, woody 'snug'. Long the haunt of folk musicians, writers and raconteurs. Music and poetry sessions, folk and blues Wed-Sun. Open till 12midnight.

702 2/D5 ✓ **Clutha Vaults 167 Stockwell Street** This and the pubs above are part of the same family of traditional Glasgow pubs. The Clutha (ancient name for the Clyde) has a Victorian-style interior and an even longer history. Known for live music (Wed-Sun). Mon-Sat till 12midnight, Sun till 11pm.

703 2/D3 **Bar 10 10 Mitchell Lane** Off Buchanan St opposite the Lighthouse and near the Tunnel, this was one of the original 'cool' and pre-club bars before the Glasgow style-bar explosion. Dating now but remarkably resilient to fashionista trends, the Ben Kelly interior still looks good though there was a proposed refurbishment at TGP. Food till 8pm (4.30pm Fri/Sat). Regular DJs at weekends. 732/COOL BARS.

704 WE **Lismore** **206 Dumbarton Road** Lismore/Lios mor named after the long island off Oban. Great neighbourhood (Partick) bar that welcomes all sorts. Gives good atmosphere, succour and malts. Occasional music. Daily till 12midnight.

705 2/XA2 **Ben Nevis** **www.geocities.com/bennevisbar · Argyle Street** Owned by same people as Lismore and Òran Mór (above) but run by others. An excellent makeover in contemporary but not faux-Scottish style. Small and pubby, the Deuchars is spot-on and great malt list. Live music Thu/Sun.

The Best Old 'Unspoilt' Pubs

The following places don't have to pretend to be old. Open till 11pm/midnight.

Horseshoe **17 Drury Street** 695/UNIQUE PUBS.
Halt Bar **160 Woodlands Road** 696/UNIQUE PUBS.
Victoria Bar **157 Bridgegate** 700/UNIQUE PUBS.
Scotia Bar **112 Stockwell Street** 701/UNIQUE PUBS.
Clutha Vaults **167 Stockwell Street** 702/UNIQUE PUBS.

706 2/B2 ✓ **The Griffin (& The Griffiny & The Griffinette)** **266 Bath Street** Corner of Elmbank St near King's Theatre. Built in 1903 to anticipate the completion of the theatre and offer the patrons a pre-show pie and a pint. Stand at the Edwardian Bar like generations of Glaswegians. Main bar still retains 'snug' with a posh, etched-glass partition; booths have been added but the atmosphere is still 'Old Glasgow'. Food till 6.30pm. Closed Sun. Amazingly cheap lunches in the bar (723/PUB FOOD).

707 2/E3 **Steps** **66 Glassford Street** Tiny pub and barely noticed but has the indelible marks of better by-gone days. In no way celebrated like Rogano (542/FINE-DINING), but also refers to the *Queen Mary* with stained glass and great panelling. Very typical, friendly Glasgow. Often with free snacks on the house. A real find.

708 SS **M.J. Heraghty** **708 Pollokshaws Road** More than a touch of the Irish here and easily more authentic than recent imports. A local with loyal regulars who'll make you welcome; old pub practices still hold in this howff in the sowff. Ladies' loos introduced in 1996! Sun-Thu till 11pm, Fri-Sat till 12midnight.

709 2/XA5 **Brechin's** **803 Govan Road** Near junction with Paisley Road West and M8 overpass. Established in 1798 and, as they say, always in the same family. A former shipyard pub which is close in heart and soul to Rangers FC. It's behind the statue of shipbuilder Sir William Pearce (which, covered in sooty grime, was known as the 'Black Man') and there's a feline 'rat-catcher' on the roof (making it a listed building). Unaffected neighbourhood atmosphere, some flute-playing. 7 days till 11pm, Fri/Sat 12midnight.

710 2/XA5 **The Old Toll Bar** **1 Paisley Road West** Opposite the site of the original Parkhouse Toll, where monies were collected for use of the 'turnpikes' between Glasgow and Greenock. Opened in 1874, the original interior is still intact; the *fin de siècle* painted glass and magnificent old gantry preserved under order. A 'palace pub' classic. Real ale and some single malts. 7 days till 11pm.

711 2/XF4   **Baird's Bar** and **The District** 2 bars from opposite sides of the great divide.
    2/XA5   **Baird's** in the Gallowgate adjacent Barrowlands is a Catholic stronghold green to
the gills where, on days when Celtic play at home up the road in Parkhead, you'd
have to be in by 11am to get a drink. **The District,** 252 Paisley Road West, Govan,
near Ibrox Park, is where Rangers supporters gather and rule in their own blue
heaven. Both pubs give an extraordinary insight into what makes the Glasgow
time-bomb tick. Provided you aren't wearing the wrong colours (or say something
daft), you'll be very welcome in either.

The Best Real-Ale Pubs

*Pubs on other pages may purvey real ale; the following take it seriously. All open 7
days till 11pm (midnight weekends) unless stated.*

712 2/A2   ✓ **Bon Accord www.thebonaccord.freeserve.co.uk · 153 North Street**
On a slip road of the motorway swathe near the Mitchell Library. One of the
first real-ale pubs in Glasgow. Good selection of malts and up to 12 beers; always
Theakstons, Deuchars and IPA plus many guest ales on hand pump. Food at
lunchtime and till 7.45pm. Light, easy-going atmosphere here, but they do take
their ale seriously; there's even a 'tour' of the cellars if you want it. Mon-Sat till
12midnight, Sun till 11pm.

713 WE   **Tennent's 191 Byres Road** Near the always-red traffic lights at University Ave,
a big, booming watering-hole of a place where you're never far away from the
horseshoe bar and its dozen excellent hand-pumped ales, including up to 3 or 4
guests. 'Tennent's is an institution' – some regulars do appear to live here. Basic
bar meals including 'the steak pie' till 9pm.

714 WE   **The State 148 Holland Street off Sauchiehall Street at West End** No com-
promising old-style pub: all wood and old pictures. 8 guest ales. No fancy extras.
Will probably outlive the many makeovers around here. Some music. 7 days till
12midnight.

715 2/F3   **Babbity Bowster 16 Blackfriars Street** In a pedestrianised part of the
Merchant City and just off the High St, a highly successful pub/restaurant/hotel
(519/INDIVIDUAL HOTELS); but the pub comes first. Caledonian, Deuchars, IPA and
well-chosen guests. Many malts and cask cider. Food all day (594/SCOTTISH
RESTAURANTS), occasional folk music, outside patio (722/DRINK OUTDOORS).

716 2/E4   **Blackfriars www.blackfriarsonline.co.uk · 36 Bell Street, Merchant City**
Mixed crowd in this a' thing to a' body kind of pub (food till 8pm, then bites, also
comedy and jazz programme). Ind Coope, Burton guest beers, bottled and draught
Euro beers.

717 2/D3   **The Horseshoe 17 Drury Street** Great for lots of reasons (695/UNIQUE GLAS-
GOW PUBS), not the least of which is its range of beers: Caledonian, Greenmantle,
Maclays and Bass on hand pump.

718 2/D5   **Victoria Bar 157 Bridgegate** Another pub mentioned before (700/UNIQUE
GLASGOW PUBS) where IPA, Maclays and others can be drunk in a dark woody
atmosphere enlivened by traditional music (Tue and Fri-Sun).

Places To Drink Outdoors

719 WE **Lock 27 www.lock27.com · 1100 Crow Road** At the very north end of Crow Rd beyond Anniesland, an unusual boozer for Glasgow: a canalside pub on a lock of the Forth & Clyde Canal (755/WALKS IN THE CITY), a (very wee) touch English, where of a summer's day you can sit outside. Excellent bar food, always busy.

720 WE **Cottier's www.thecottier.com · 0141 357 5825 · 93 Hyndland Street** First on the left after the swing park on Highburgh Road (going west) and the converted church is on your right, around the corner. Heart of West End location. Think: a cold beer on a hot day sitting in the leafy shade of a churchyard. Some barbeques – it's a Hyndland kind of life!

721 WE **Cul de Sac, Bar Brel & Jinty McGinty www.barbrelrestaurant.com · Ashton Lane** As soon as the sun comes out, so do the punters. With the **Cul De Sac** and **Bar Brel** at one end and **Jinty McGinty's** at the other, benches suddenly appear and the whole lane becomes a cobbled, alfresco pub. The nearest Glasgow gets to Euro or even Dublin drinking. Brel has a grassy bit outback.

722 2/F4 **Babbity Bowster 0141 552 5055 · 16 Blackfriars Street** Unique in the Merchant City for several reasons (715/REAL-ALE PUBS, 594/SCOTTISH RESTAURANTS), but in summer certainly for its napkin of garden in an area bereft of greenery. Though enclosed by surrounding Streets, it's a concrete oasis. Feels like Soho, Soho NYC? Naw, feels like Glasgow! Always good craic.

Big Blue Outside terrace overlooks the murky Kelvin. 586/PIZZA.
The Goat Not the cleanest air but clear views from this corner all the way into town. 729/COOL BARS.

Pubs With Good Food

See also Gastropubs, p. 103.

723 2/B1 ✓ **The Griffin 266 Bath Street** On corner of Elmbank St across from King's Theatre. The Griffin rooms have always been there on that corner and your basic pie/chips/beans *and a pint* will not be bettered at this price: meals for less than £3 at TGP. Other staples available and a more elaborate menu in the lounge or the Griffinette next door. Food: 12noon-2.30pm and evenings till 6.30pm (not Sun). Pub till 12midnight. 706/'UNSPOILT' PUBS.

724 WE **The Big Blue 445 Great Western Road** A modern bar/bistro in a great uptown location literally on the (river) Kelvinside. Drinking may drown the eating later on, but till mid/late-evening there's excellent Italian pasta/pizza pub grub. LO 10/10.30pm. Bar 12midnight.

725 2/E4 **Blackfriars www.blackfriarsonline.co.uk · 36 Bell Street** Great Glasgow pub for all-round ambience, provision of real ale and music, and food available all day (meals till 8pm, then 'bites') (but drinkers are loud after 9pm). Regular comedy venue downstairs. 716/REAL-ALE PUBS.

726 WE **Brel www.barbrelrestaurant.com · Ashton Lane** Always busy bar in often teeming West End lane so 'Belgian'/Belgo menu can take (literally) the back seat. Still, pots of moules/frites help the many euro brews go down. Lunch and food till 10.30pm, bar 12midnight. 721/OUTSIDE DRINKING.

727 10/M26 **White Cart Inn, Busby** 0141 644 2711 South of city 20km via M77 or Albert Bridge via Gorbals to Carmunnock. Traditional inn serving food on huge scale in many-roomed bar. Pub grub (Chef and Brewer) rather than gastro standard but hits the spot. Good fish; Sunday roasts. Efficient service. 7 days. Lunch & LO 9.30pm.

Bon Accord Report: 712/REAL-ALE PUBS.
Strata Report: 733/COOL BARS.

Cool Bars

728 2/C3 ✓ **Arches** www.thearches.co.uk · 0901 022 0300 (box office) · **253 Argyle Street** The boho bar/café of the essential Arches Theatre, the club and experimental theatre space refurbished with millennium money. Design by Timorous/Taller (see Strata below), this is an obvious pre-club pre-theatre space, but works at any time. Food and DJs and lots going on. Even if you're only in Glasgow for the weekend, you should come here for the vibe.

729 WE ✓ **The Goat** www.thegoat.co.uk · 0141 357 7373 · **1287 Argyle Street** Up west near Kelvingrove Gallery a comfortable, friendly sitting room pub (with mezzanine and upstairs snug) known for its excellent food. Big windows and pavement terrace look down Argyle St; a great corner for people gazing and a Glasgow affirming experience. 7 days. Food 12noon-9pm, bar 12midnight.

730 2/E4 ✓ **The Brunswick Hotel Bar** www.brunswickhotel.co.uk · 0141 552 0001 · **104 Brunswick Street** This small Merchant City hotel and its ground-level bar/restaurant has stood the style test of times and 15 years on is still a cool hangout for a mixed crowd, especially at Sunday brunch and all over the weekend.

731 WE **The Belle** **617 Great Western Road** Laid-back West End pub. Good selection of wines and beers including Krusovice light and dark on draft. Great coffee, daytime light snacks, mixed crowd. Open fire. Occasional light music. It's a long road (Great Western Rd) but this will be up your street. 7 days. LO 11.45pm.

732 2/D3 **Bar 10** 0141 221 8353 · **10 Mitchell Lane** Halfway up Buchanan St pedestrian precinct on the left in the narrow lane that also houses the Lighthouse design centre. There's an NYC look about this joint that is so loved by its habitués, they still pack it at weekends over 10 years after it arrived. Ben Kelly design has worn well though faces a refreshment at TGP. Food, DJs and pre-club preparations. 7 days till midnight. 703/UNIQUE PUBS.

733 2/D3 **Strata** www.strataglasgow.com · 0141 221 1888 · **45 Queen Street** Nothing hugely obvious to distinguish this from a clutch of others, but somehow it works. By Timorous Beasties and One Food Taller (ubiquitous Glasgow design team), the room is not intrusive and food better than most. Food till 10pm, bar 12midnight.

734 2/E3 **Polo Lounge** 0141 553 1221 · **84 Wilson Street** Urbane, stylish bar/disco by the ubiquitous (though rarely seen) Stefan King. Unmistakably gay in the heart of the quarter (not him, it). Clubbable rather than clubby crowd (until later) arranged on the comfortable, now rather shabby (ok, call it lived-in) furniture; at weekends you go downstairs to disco. Mellow Sundays; papers, jazz. 1186/GAY GLASGOW.

735 2/E3 **Bar 91** 0141 552 5211 · **91 Candleriggs** A better bar among many of this ilk hereabouts, food also is well-considered and put together, though it stops at 6pm to make way for pre-club ministrations (and till 12midnight).

The Main Attractions

736 WE
FREE

✓ ✓ **Kelvingrove Art Gallery and Museum** 0141 287 2699 ·
**www.glasgowmuseums.com · Argyle Street (west end by
Kelvingrove Park)** Huge Victorian sandstone edifice with awesome atrium. On
the ground floor is a natural history/ Scottish history museum. The upper salons
contain the city's superb British and European art collection. Reopened '06 after
major refurbishment and reconfiguring of the exhibits and at TGP almost 3 million
people had been through the doors: this is a prodigious success. Endless interest
and people-friendly presentations. See the world from a Glasgow point of view! (Go
through 'Glasgow Stones' to get to 'Ancient Egypt'.) And it's all free, folks! 7 days.
10am-5pm (Fri/Sun from 11am).

737 SS
FREE/
ADMISSION
NTS

✓ ✓ **The Burrell Collection, Pollok Park & Pollok House** 0141 287
2550 · **www.nts.org.uk** South of the river via A77 Kilmarnock Rd (over
Jamaica St Bridge) about 5km, following signs from Pollokshaws Rd. Set in rural
parkland, this award-winning modern gallery was built to house the eclectic acqui-
sitions of Sir William Burrell. Showing a preference for medieval works, among the
8500 items the magpie magnate donated to the city in 1944 are artefacts from the
Roman empire to Rodin. The building itself integrates old doorways and whole
rooms reconstructed from Hutton Castle. Self-serve café and restaurant on the
ground floor (Mon-Thu, Sat 10am-5pm, Fri and Sun 11am-5pm). **Pollok House**
(0141 616 6410) and gardens further into the park (with works by Goya, El Greco
and William Blake) is worth a detour and has, below stairs, the better tearooms
and gardens to the river. Both open 7 days. 10am-5pm. 725/WALKS IN THE CITY.

738 2/XF3
FREE

✓ **Glasgow Cathedral & Provand's Lordship** 0141 552 6891/553 2557 ·
www.glasgowcathedral.org.uk · Castle Street Across the road from one
another they represent what remains of the oldest part of the city, which (as can
be seen in the People's Palace, see below) was, in the early 18th century, merely a
ribbon of streets from here to the river. The present Cathedral, though established
by St Mungo in AD 543, dates from the 12th century and is a fine example of the
very real, if gloomy, Gothic. The house, built in 1471, is a museum which strives to
convey a sense of medieval life. Watch you don't get run over when you re-emerge
into the 21st century and try to cross the street. In the background, the Necropolis
piled on the hill invites inspection and offers a viewpoint and the full Gothic perspective (though best not to go alone). Open 7 days. Times vary slightly.

739 2/XF5
FREE

✓ **The People's Palace** **www.glasgowmuseums.com · 0141 271 2951**
Approach via the Tron and London Road, then turn right into Glasgow Green.
This has long been a folk museum *par excellence* wherein, since 1898, the history,
folklore and artefacts of a proud city have been gathered, cherished and displayed.
But this is much more than a mere museum; it is the heart and soul of the city
and together with the Winter Gardens adjacent, shouldn't be missed, to know
what Glasgow's about. Tearoom in the Tropics, among the palms and ferns of the
Winter Gardens. Opening times as most other museums: Mon-Thu, Sat 10am-
5pm, Fri & Sun 11am-5pm.

740 2/XA5
ADMISSION

✓ **Glasgow Science Centre** **www.glasgowsciencecentre.org · 0871 540
1000** On south side of Clyde opposite SECC, Glasgow's newest attraction
built with Millennium dosh. Approach via new bridge or walk from SECC complex
by Bell's Bridge. Impressive titanium-clad mall, Imax cinema and 127m-high
tower. 4 floors of interactive exhibitions, planetarium and theatre. Separate tickets
or combos. Book slot for tower (closed on windy days). 7 days. 10am-6pm.

741 2/XF3
FREE
St Mungo Museum of Religious Life & Art www.glasgowmuseums.com ·
0141 553 2557 · **Castle Street** Part of the lovely and not-cherished-enough
cathedral precinct (see above), this houses art and artefacts representing the
world's 6 major religions arranged tactfully in an attractive stone building with a
Zen garden in the courtyard. The assemblage seems like a good and worthwhile
vision not quite realised, but in a city where sectarianism is still an issue and a
problem, this is a telling and informative display. 7 days 10am-5pm (Fri/Sun from
11am)

742 WE
FREE
Hunterian Museum & Art Gallery www.hunterian.gla.ac.uk · 0141 330
4221/5431 · **University Avenue** On one side of the street, Scotland's oldest
museum with geological, archaeological and social history displayed in a venerable
building. The **University Chapel** and the cloisters should not be missed. Across
the street, a modern block holds part of Glasgow's exceptional civic collection –
Rembrandt to the Colourists and the Glasgow Boys, as well as one of the most
complete collections of any artist's work and personal effects to be found anywhere, viz that of Whistler. Fascinating stuff, even if you're not a fan. There's also a
print gallery and the superb **Mackintosh House** (795/MACKINTOSH). Mon-Sat
9.30am-5pm. Closed Sun.

The Other Attractions

743 WE
FREE
✓✓ **Museum of Transport** www.glasgowmuseums.com ·
0141 287 2720 · **off Argyle Street behind the Kelvin Hall** May not
seem your ticket to ride, but this is one of Scotland's most fascinating museums.
Has something for everybody, especially kids. The reconstruction of a cobbled
Glasgow street c.1938 is an inspired evocation. There are trains, trams and unique
collections of cars, motorbikes and bicycles. And model ships in the Clyde room, in
remembrance of a mighty river. Make a donation and the Mini splits in two. Mon-
Thu, Sat 10am-5pm, Fri & Sun 11am-5pm.

744 WE
✓✓ **Botanic Gardens & Kibble Palace** www.glasgow.gov.uk · 0141
334 2422 · **Great Western Road** Smallish park close to River Kelvin
with riverside walks (754/WALKS IN THE CITY), and pretty much the 'dear green
place'. Kibble Palace (built 1873; major renovation 2006) is the distinctive domed
glasshouse with statues set among lush ferns and shrubbery from around the
(mostly temperate) world. 'Killer Plant House' especially popular. Main range
arranged through smell and colour and seasonality. A wonderful place to muse and
wander. Perish the thought of the nightclub the G1 group wanted to open in the
corner at TGP. Gardens open till dusk; palace 10am-4.45pm (4.15pm in winter).

745 2/D3
FREE
✓✓ **Gallery Of Modern Art** www.glasgowmuseums.com · 0141 229
1996 · **Queen Street** Central, controversial and housed in former
Stirling's Library, Glasgow's big visual arts attraction opened in a hail of art-world
bickering in 1996. Main point is: does it reflect Glasgow's eminence as a provenance of cutting edge or conceptual work (all those Turner and Becks Prize nomi-
nees and winners?). Murmurs stilled of late by more representative exhibitions.
Leaving aside the quibbling, it should definitely be on your Glasgow hit list. Smart
café up top. Mon-Wed, Sat 10am-5pm, Thu 10am-8pm, Fri & Sun 11am-5pm.

746 2/F4
✓ **The Barrows East End** (Pronounced 'Barras') The sprawling street and
indoor market area around the Gallowgate. Even a dozen years ago when I
first wrote this book, the Barras was pure dead brilliant, a real slab of Glasgow life.
Its glory days are over but, as with all great markets, it's full of character and

characters and it's still possible to find bargains and collectibles. Everything from clairvoyants to the latest scam. Sat & Sun only 10am-5pm.

747 2/B1
NTS
ADMISSION
The Tenement House www.nts.org.uk · 0141 333 0183 · 145 Buccleuch **Street** Near Charing Cross but can approach from near the end of Sauchiehall St and over the hill. Typical 'respectable' Glasgow tenement, kept under a bell-jar since Our Agnes moved out in 1965. She lived there with her mother since 1911 and wasn't one for new-fangled things. It's a touch claustrophobic when busy and is distinctly voyeuristic, but, well... your house would be interesting, too, in 50 years if the clock were stopped. Daily, Mar-Oct 1-5pm. Reception on ground floor.

748 2/E4
ADMISSION
Sharmanka Kinetic Gallery & Theatre www.sharmanka.com · 0141 552 **7080 · 64 Osborne Street** Off King Street in the Merchant City. A small and intimate experience cf most others on this page, but an extraordinary one. The gallery/theatre of Russian emigré Eduard Bersindsky shows his meticulous and amazing mechanical sculptures. Performances Thu 7pm, Sun 3pm & 7pm. Other times by arrangement.

749 SS
NTS
Greenbank Gardens www.nts.org.uk · 0141 616 5126 10km southwest of centre via Kilmarnock Road, Eastwood Toll, Clarkston Toll and Mearns Road, then signposted (3km). A spacious oasis in the suburbs; formal gardens and 'working' walled garden, parterre and woodland walks around elegant Georgian house. Very Scottish. Gardens open all year 9.30am-dusk, shop/tearoom Apr-Oct 11am-5pm, Nov-Mar Sat & Sun 2-4pm.

750 2/E3
FREE
City Chambers www.glasgow.gov.uk · 0141 287 4018 · George Square The hugely impressive building along the whole east side of Glasgow's municipal central square. This is a wonderfully over-the-top monument to the days when Glasgow was the second city of the empire. Guided tours Mon-Fri 10.30am-2.30pm (subject to availability).

751 9/L25
ADMISSION
Finlaystone Country Estate www.finlaystone.co.uk · 01475 540505 · **30km west of city centre via M8/A8** Signed off dual carriageway just before Port Glasgow. Delightful gardens and woods around mansion house with many pottering places and longer trails (and ranger service). Estate open all year round 10.30am-5pm. Visitor centre and the Celtic Tree tearoom. Open Apr-late Sep 11am-5pm (visitor centre also open winter weekends). Spectacular bluebells in May, colour therapy in autumn.

752 2/C4
ADMISSION
The Pride o' the Clyde www.clydewaterbusservices.co.uk · 07711 250969 Amsterdam-style water-bus ferrying passengers between Glasgow (board at Broomielaw, Jamaica Bridge) and Braehead Shopping and Leisure Centre (board at Maritime Heritage Centre). A 35-minute journey includes commentary on the sights and history of the Clyde. Refreshments available. Operates all year. 5/6 sailings a day. Also, while we're on the water...

753 2/A4
ADMISSION
The Waverley 0845 130 4647 'The World's Last Sea-going Paddle Steamer' which plied the Clyde in the glorious 'Doon the Water' days is fresh from its £7M lottery-funded refit. definitely the way to see the West Coast. Sailings from Glasgow's Anderson Quay (by Kingston Bridge) to Rothesay, Kyles of Bute, Arran. Other days leaves from Ayr or Greenock, many destinations. Call for complex timetable.

Paisley Abbey Report: 1976/ABBEYS.
Bothwell Castle, Uddingston Report: 1876/RUINS.

The Best Walks In The City

See p. 12 for walk codes.

754 WE
2-13+KM
XCIRC
BIKES
1-A-1

Kelvin Walkway **www.northkelvin.net** A path along the banks of Glasgow's other river, the Kelvin, which enters the Clyde unobtrusively at Yorkhill but first meanders through some of the most interesting parts and parks of the northwest city. Walk starts at Kelvingrove Park through the University and Hillhead district under Kelvin Bridge and on to the celebrated Botanic Gardens (744/OTHER ATTRAC-TIONS). The trail then goes north, under the Forth and Clyde Canal (*see below*) to the Arcadian fields of Dawsholm Park (5km), Killermont (posh golf course) and Kirkintilloch (13km from start). Since the river and the canal shadow each other for much of their routes, it's possible, with a map, to go out by one waterway and return by the other (e.g. start at Great Western Road, return Maryhill Road). **START** Usual start at the Eildon St (off Woodlands Road) gate of Kelvingrove Park or Kelvin Bridge. Street parking only.

755 2/XC1
ANY KM
XCIRC
BIKES
1-A-1

Forth & Clyde Canal Towpath The canal, opened in 1790, reopened 2002 as the Millennium Link and once a major short cut for fishing boats and trade between Europe and America, provides a fascinating look round the back of the city from a pathway that stretches on a spur from Port Dundas just north of the M8 to the main canal at the end of Lochburn Road off Maryhill Road and then east all the way to Kirkintilloch and Falkirk (Falkirk Wheel: 01324 619888; 4/BIG ATTRAC-TIONS), and west through Maryhill and Drumchapel to Bowling and the Clyde (60km). Good option is go as far as Croy and take very regular train service back. Much of the route is through the forsaken or redeveloped industrial heart of the city, past waste ground, warehouses and high flats, but there are open stretches and curious corners and, by Bishopbriggs, it's a rural waterway. More info from British Waterways (0141 332 6936).
START (1) Top of Firhill Road (great view of city from Ruchill Park, 100m further on – 766/BEST VIEWS). (2) Lochburn Road (see above) at the confluence from which to go east or west to the Clyde. (3) Top of Crow Road, Anniesland where there is a canalside pub, **Lock 27** (719/DRINK OUTDOORS), with tables outside, real ale and food (12noon-evening). (4) Bishopbriggs Sports Centre, Balmuildy Road. From here it is 6km to Maryhill and 1km in other direction to the 'country churchyard' of Cadder or 3km to Kirkintilloch. All starts have some parking.

756 SS

Pollok Country Park **www.glasgow.gov.uk** The park that (apart from the area around the gallery and the house – 737/MAIN ATTRACTIONS) most feels like a real country park. Numerous trails through woods and meadows. The leisurely guided walks with the park rangers can be educative and more fun than you would think (0141 632 9299 for details). Burrell Collection and Pollok House and Gardens are obvious highlights. There's a good restaurant and an 'old-fashioned' tearoom in the basement of the latter serving excellent range of hot, home-made dishes, soups, salads, sandwiches as well as usual cakes and tasties. Open 7 days 10am-4.30pm (0141 616 6410). Enter by Haggs Road or by Haggs Castle Golf Course. By car you are directed to the entry road off Pollokshaws Rd and then to the car park in front of the Burrell. Train to Shawlands or Pollokshaws West from Glasgow Central Station.

757 10/L25
5-20KM
CAN BE CIRC
BIKES
1-A-2

Mugdock Country Park www.mcp.ndo.co.uk · **0141 956 6100** Not perhaps within the city, but one of the nearest and easiest escapes. Park which includes Mugdock Woods (SSSI) and 2 castles is northwest of Milngavie. Regular train from Queen St Station takes 20 minutes, then follow route of the West Highland Way for 4km across Drumclog Moor to south edge of the park. In summer, shuttlebus will meet the trains at Milngavie Station and take you right into park. By car to Milngavie by A81 park is 5km north. Well signed. 5 car parks; the main one includes Craigend Visitor Centre (9am-9pm), Stables Tearoom (10am-5pm daily), discovery room and theatre. Many trails marked out and further afield rambles. This is a godsend between Glasgow and the Highland hills.

Cathkin Braes South edge of city with views. Report: 764/BEST VIEWS.

Easy Walks Outside The City

See p. 12 for walk codes.

758 10/M25
10+KM
CAN BE CIRC
MTBIKES
2-B-2

Campsie Fells www.eastdunbarton.gov.uk Range of hills 25km north of city best reached via Kirkintilloch or Cumbernauld/Kilsyth. Encompasses area that includes the Kilsyth Hills, Fintry Hills and Carron Valley between. (1) Good approach from A803, Kilsyth main street up the Tak-me-Doon (*sic*) road. Park by the golf club and follow path by the burn. It's possible to take in the two hills to left as well as Tomtain (453m), the most easterly of the tops, in a good afternoon; views to the east. (2) Drive on to the junction (9km) of the B818 road to Fintry and go left, following Carron Valley reservoir to the far corner where there is a forestry road to the left. Park here and follow track to ascend Meikle Bin (570m) to the right, the highest peak in the central Campsies. (3) The bonny village of Fintry is a good start/base for the Fintry Hills and Earl's Seat (578m). (4) Campsie Glen – a sliver of glen in the hills. approach via Clachan of Campsie on A81 (decent tearoom) or from viewpoint high on the hill on B822 from Lennoxtown-Fintry. This is the easy Campsie introduction.

759 10/L26
2-10KM
CAN BE CIRC
MTBIKES
1-A-2

Gleniffer Braes **Paisley** Ridge to the south of Paisley (15km from Glasgow) has been a favourite walking-place for centuries. M8 or Paisley Road west to town centre then: (1) south via B774/B775 (Causeyside St then Neilston Rd) and sharp right after 3km to Glenfield Rd. For (1) go 2km after last houses, winding up ridge and park/start at Robertson Park (signed). Here there are superb views and walks marked to east and west. (2) 500m along Glenfield Rd is a car park/ranger centre (0141 884 3794). Walk up through gardens and formal parkland and then west along marked paths and trails. Eventually, after 5km, this route joins (1).

760 9/K25
15/16KM
CIRC
MTBIKES
1-B-2

Greenock Cut 45km west of Glasgow. Can approach via Port Glasgow but simplest route is from A78 road to Largs. Travelling south from Greenock take first left after IBM, brown-signed Loch Thom/Cornalees. Lochside 5km up winding road. Park at Cornalees Bridge Centre (01475 521458). Walk left along lochside road to Overton (5km) then path is signed. The Cut, an aqueduct built in 1827 to supply water to Greenock and its 31 mills, is now an ancient monument. Great views from the mast along the Cut though it is a detour. Another route to the right from Cornalees leads through a glen of birch, rowan and oak to the Kelly Cut. Both trails described on board at the car park.

761 9/K25 **Clyde Muirshiel** **www.clydemuirshiel.co.uk** General name for vast area of 'Inverclyde' west of city, including Greenock Cut (see above), Lochwinnoch, Castle Semple Country Park and Lunderston Bay, a stretch of coastline near the Cloch Lighthouse on the A770 south of Gourock for littoral amblings. Best wildish bit is around Muirshiel Centre itself, Muirshiel Country Park (01475 521129), with trails, a waterfall and Windy Hill (350m). Nothing arduous, but a breath of air. The hen harrier hunts here. From M8 junction 29, take A737 Lochwinnoch, then B786 to top of Calder Glen Road. Follow brown signs.

762 10/L25
5KM
CIRC
XBIKES
NO DOGS
1-A-1

The Whangie On A809 north from Bearsden about 8km after last roundabout and 2km after the Carbeth Inn, is the car park for the Queen's View (765/BEST VIEWS). Once you get to the summit of Auchineden Hill, take the path that drops down to the W (a half-right-angle) and look for crags on your right. This is the 'back door' of The Whangie. Carry on and you'll suddenly find yourself in a deep cleft in the rock face with sheer walls rising over 10m on either side. The Whangie is more than 100m long and at one point the walls narrow to less than 1m. Local mythology has it that The Whangie was made by the Devil, who lashed his tail in anticipation of a witchy rendezvous somewhere in the north, and carved a slice through the rock, where the path now goes.

763 10/M26
2-7KM
CIRC
BIKES
1-A-2

Chatelhérault **www.southlanarkshire.gov.uk** · **near Hamilton** Junction 6 off M74, well signposted into Hamilton, follow road into centre, then bear left away from main road where it's signed for A723. The gates to the 'château' are about 3km outside town. A drive leads to the William Adam-designed hunting lodge of the Dukes of Hamilton, set amid ornamental gardens with a notable parterre and extensive grounds. Tracks along the deep, wooded glen of the Avon (ruins of Cadzow Castle) lead to distant glades. Good walks and ranger service (01698 426213). House open Mon-Thu 10am-4.30pm (Sun 12-4.30pm); walks at all times.

The Best Views Of The City & Beyond

764 SS **Cathkin Braes, Queen Mary's Seat** **www.glasgow.gov.uk** The southern ridge of the city on the B759 from Carmunnock to Cambuslang, about 12km from centre. Go south of river by Albert Bridge to Aikenhead Road which continues south as Carmunnock Road. Follow to Carmunnock, a delightfully rural village, and pick up the Cathkin Road. 2km along on the right is the Cathkin Braes Golf Club and 100m further on the left is the park. Marvellous views to north of the Campsies, Kilpatrick Hills, Ben Lomond and as far as Ben Ledi. Walks on the Braes on both sides of the road.

765 10/L25
1-A-1

Queen's View **www.savequeensview.co.uk** · **Auchineden** Not so much a view of the city, more a perspective on Glasgow's Highland hinterland, this short walk and sweeping vista to the north has been a Glaswegian pilgrimage for generations. On A809 north from Bearsden about 8km after last roundabout and 2km after the Carbeth Inn, a very decent pub to repair to. Busy car park attests to popularity. The walk, along path cut into ridgeside, takes 40-50 minute to cairn, from which you can see The Cobbler (2025/HILLS), that other Glasgow's favourite, Ben Ledi and sometimes as far as Ben Chonzie 50km away. The fine views of Loch Lomond are what Queen Victoria came for. Further on is The Whangie (762/EASY WALKS).

766 2/XC1   **Ruchill Park www.glasgow.gov.uk** An unlikely but splendid panorama from this overlooked but well-kept park to the north of the city near the infamous Possilpark housing estate. Go to top of Firhill Road (past Partick Thistle football ground) over Forth and Clyde Canal (755/WALKS IN THE CITY) off Garscube Road where it becomes Maryhill Road. Best view is from around the flagpole; the whole city among its surrounding hills, from the Campsies to Gleniffer and Cathkin Braes (see above), becomes clear.

767 10/M25   **Bar Hill www.barhill.org.uk · Twechar near Kirkintilloch** 22km north of city, 1-A-2   taking A803 Kirkintilloch turnoff from M8, then the 'low' road to Kilsyth, the B8023, bearing left at the 'black-and-white Bridge'. Next to Twechar Quarry Inn, a path is signed for Bar Hill and the Antonine Wall. Steepish climb for 2km, ignore strange dome of grass. Over to left in copse of trees are the remains of one of the forts on the wall which was built across Scotland in the 2nd century AD. Ground plan explained on a board. This is a special place with strong history vibes and airy views over the plain to the city which came a long time after.

768 10/M26   **Blackhill near Lesmahagow** 28km south of city. Another marvellous outlook, 1-A-2   but in the opposite direction from above. Take junction 10/11 on M74, then off the B7078 signed Lanark, take the B7018. 4km along past Clarkston Farm, head uphill for 1km and park by Water Board mound. Walk uphill through fields to right for about 1km. Unprepossessing hill that unexpectedly reveals a vast vista of most of east-central Scotland.

769 10/L26   **Paisley Abbey www.paisleyabbey.org.uk · 0141 889 7654 · Paisley** M8 to Paisley; frequent trains from Central Station. Abbey Mon-Sat 10am-3.30pm. Every so often on Abbey 'open days', the tower of this amazing edifice can be climbed. The tower (restored 1926) is 50m high and from the top there's a grand view of the Clyde. This is a rare experience, but phone the tourist information centre (0141 889 0711) or abbey itself (mornings) for details; could be your lucky day. 1976/GREAT ABBEYS.

770 9/K25   **Lyle Hill Gourock** Via M8 west to Greenock, then round the coast to relatively genteel old resort of Gourock where the 'Free French' worked in the yards during the war. A monument has been erected to their memory on the top of Lyle Hill above the town, from where you get one of the most dramatic views of the great crossroads of the Clyde (Holy Loch, Gare Loch and Loch Long). Best vantage-point is further along the road on other side by trig point. Follow British Rail station signs, then Lyle Hill. There's another great view of the Clyde further down the water at **Haylie, Largs**, the hill 3km from town reached via the A760 road to Kilbirnie and Paisley. The island of Cumbrae lies in the sound and the sunset.

Campsie Fells & Gleniffer Braes Reports: 758/759/WALKS OUTSIDE THE CITY.

The Best Of The Sports Facilities

PUBLIC SWIMMING & INDOOR SPORTS CENTRES

771 2/XF3 **Whitehill Pool** www.glasgow.gov.uk · 0141 551 9969 · **Onslow Drive** East End, parallel to Duke St at Meadowpark St. Mon-Fri 7.45am-9pm, Sat/Sun 8.30am-2pm. 25m pool with sauna/multigym.

772 2/XB1 **North Woodside Leisure Centre** www.glasgow.gov.uk · 0141 332 8102 · **Braid Square** Not far from St George's Cross near Charing Cross at the bottom of Great Western Rd. In a rebuilt area; follow AA signs. Modern pool (25m) and sauna/steam/sun centre plus the usual fitness suite and classes. Mon 10.15am-8pm, Tue 10.15am-9pm, Wed & Thu 8am-9pm, Fri 7.30am-9pm; Sat/Sun 9am-4pm.

773 ss **Pollok Leisure Centre** www.glasgow.gov.uk · 0141 881 3313 · **Cowglen Road** Not a do-your-lengths kind of a pool - more a family water outing. Plus fitness suite and classes. Mon-Fri 10am-9pm, Sat/Sun 10am-4pm.

774 9/L25 **Gourock Bathing Pool** 01475 631561 On the road south, an open-air heated pool on the Clyde. Great prospect for summers like they used to be. May-Sept. 2199/SWIMMING POOLS.

775 WE **Kelvin Hall International Sports Arena** www.glasgow.gov.uk · 0141 357 2525 · **Argyle Street** By Kelvingrove Museum (736/MAIN ATTRACTIONS). Major venue for international indoor sports competitions, but open otherwise for weights/ badminton/tennis/athletics/climbing classes. Book hour-long sessions. No squash. Mon-Sun 9am, Wed 10am, all to 10.30pm (6.30pm Sat).

776 WE **Scotstoun Leisure Centre** www.glasgow.gov.uk · 0141 959 4000 · **Danes Drive** Huge state-of-the-art sports multiplex. 10 lane pool, indoor halls and out-door pitches. Mon, Wed, Fri 7.30am-10pm, Tue 9am-10pm, Thu 10am-10pm, Sat 9am-5pm, Sun 9am-9pm. 2194/LEISURE CENTRES.

777 2/XF4 **Tollcross Park Leisure Centre** www.glasgow.gov.uk · 0141 763 2345 · **Wellshot Road** Another biggie. 10-lane pool, indoor halls, split-level fitness suite. Mon-Fri 7am (Thu 10am)-10pm, Sat 9am-5pm, Sun 9am-9pm.

778 2/XC1 **Allander Sports Complex** 0141 942 2233 · **Milngavie Road, Bearsden** 16km north of centre via Maryhill Road. Best by car. Squash (2 courts), sports halls, snooker, badminton, swimming pool, fitness suite. Mon-Fri 7.30am-11pm, Sat 9am-9pm, Sun 9am-10pm.

779 ss **Bellahouston Leisure Centre** www.glasgow.gov.uk · 0141 427 9090 · **Bellahouston Drive** Modern (2001), multi-purpose sport/leisure centre. Mon-Fri 6.30am-10.30pm (Tue 9am-10pm), Sat 10am-6pm, Sun 9am-10pm.

780 9/L25 **Greenock Waterfront Leisure Complex** 01475 797979 Pool with flumes, etc. Gym looks on to the river; there's an ice rink.

GOLF COURSES

Glasgow has a vast number of parks and golf courses. The following clubs are the best open to non-members.

781 SS   **Cathkin Braes** www.cathkinbraesgolfclub.co.uk · **0141 634 0650** · **Cathkin Road** Southeast from the centre via Aikenhead Rd/Carmunnock Rd to Carmunnock village, then 3km. Best by car. Civilised hilltop course on the south edge of the city. Non-members Mon-Fri (though probably not Fri am).

782 SS   **Haggs Castle** www.haggscastlegolfclub.com · **0141 427 0480** · **Dumbreck Road** Near junction 22 of the M8; go straight on to clubhouse at first roundabout. Part of the grounds of Pollok Park; a convenient course, perhaps overplayed. Non-members Mon-Fri. (Handicap certificate required.)

783 SS   **Pollok Golf Club** www.pollokgolf.com · **0141 632 1080** · **Barrhead Road** On the other side of White Cart Water and Pollok House and rather more up-market. Well-wooded parkland course, flat and well kept but not cheap. Women may play but call for specific timeslots!

784 2/XA5   **Gleddoch** www.gleddochhouse.com · **01475 540704** · **Langbank** Excellent 18-hole course adjacent and part of Gleddoch House Hotel. Restricted play.

TENNIS

785 WE SS   Public courts (Apr-Sep), membership not required:
Kelvingrove Park 4 courts, **Queen's Park** 5 courts, **Victoria Park** 6 courts www.glasgow.gov.uk Mon-Fri 12noon-9pm, Sat 12noon-7pm, Sun 12noon-8pm.

The Best Small Galleries

Apart from those listed previously (Main Attractions, Other Attractions), the following galleries are always worth looking into. The Glasgow Gallery Guide, free from any of them, lists all the current exhibitions.

786 2/E4 ✓✓ **Glasgow Print Studio** www.gpsart.co.uk · 0141 552 0704 · **25 & 48 King Street** Influential and accessible upstairs gallery with print work on view and for sale from many of Scotland's leading and rising artists. Closed Sun and Mon. Print Shop over the road at 48.

787 2/E4 ✓✓ **Transmission Gallery** www.transmissiongallery.org · **45 King Street** Cutting edge and often off-the-wall work from contemporary Scottish and international artists. Reflects Glasgow's increasing importance as a hot spot of conceptual art. Stuff you might disagree with. Closed Sun and Mon. Both Transmission and the Print Studio are in temporary locations on King St while a new art centre is being refurbished.

788 2/C4 ✓✓ **The Modern Institute** www.themoderninstitute.com · 0141 248 3711 · **73 Robertson Street** Not really a gallery – more a concept. International reputation for cutting-edge art ideas and occasional events. By appointment. MI shows at London's pre-eminent, highly selective Frieze Art Fair: not many Scottish galleries do.

789 2/D3 ✓✓ **The Glasgow Art Fair** www.glasgowartfair.com · **George Square** Held every year in tented pavilions in mid April. Some of the galleries on this page and many more are represented; selective but essential and good fun. 2283/WHERE TO BUY ART.

790 2/C2 ✓ **Compass Gallery** www.compassgallery.co.uk · 0141 221 6370 · **178 West Regent Street** Glasgow's oldest established commercial contemporary art gallery. Their 'New Generation' exhibition in Jul-Aug shows work from new graduates of the art colleges and has heralded many a career. Combine with the other Gerber gallery (see below). Closed Sun.

791 2/C2 ✓ **Cyril Gerber Fine Art** www.gerberfineart.co.uk · 0141 221 3095 · **148 West Regent Street** British paintings and especially the Scottish Colourists and 'name' contemporaries. Gerber and the Compass (see above) have Christmas exhibitions where small, accessible paintings can be bought for reasonable prices. Closed Sun.

792 2/XF3 **Sorcha Dallas** www.sorchadallas.com · 07812 605745· **5 St Margaret's Place** Deep in the East End the secret salon of La Dallas where interesting new artists first come into the light. Phone first. Sorcha also usually does Frieze (see MI above).

Sharmanka Kinetic Gallery Report: 748/OTHER ATTRACTIONS.

The Mackintosh Trail

The great Scottish architect and designer Charles Rennie Mackintosh (1868–1928) had an extraordinary influence on contemporary design.

793 2/B1 ✓ ✓ ✓ **Glasgow School of Art** www.gsa.ac.uk · 0141 353 4526 · **167 Renfrew Street** Mackintosh's supreme architectural triumph. It's enough almost to admire it from the street (and maybe best, since this is very much a working college) but there are guided tours at 11am and 2pm (Sat 10.30am, 11.30am, and many more in summer) of the sombre yet light interior, the halls and library. You might wonder if the building itself could be partly responsible for its remarkable output of acclaimed artists. Temporary exhibitions in the Mackintosh Gallery. The Tenement House (747/OTHER ATTRACTIONS) is nearby.

794 2/XC1
ADMISSION ✓ ✓ **Queen's Cross Church** www.queenscrosschurch.org.uk · 0141 946 6600 · **870 Garscube Road at Maryhill Road** Built 1896-99. Calm and simple, the antithesis of Victorian Gothic. If all churches had been built like this, we'd go more often. The HQ of the Charles Rennie Mackintosh Society which was founded in 1973. Mar-Oct Mon-Fri 10am-5pm, Sun 2-5pm. Nov-Feb Mon-Fri 10am-5pm.

795 WE
ADMISSION ✓ ✓ **The Mackintosh House** www.hunterian.gla.ac.uk · 0141 330 5431 · **University Avenue** Opposite and part of the Hunterian Museum (742/MAIN ATTRACTIONS) within the University campus. The Master's house has been transplanted and methodically reconstructed from the next street (they say even the light is the same). If you've ever wondered what the fuss is about, go and see how innovative and complete an artist, designer and architect he was, in this inspiring yet habitable set of rooms. Mon-Sat 9.30am-5pm. Closed Sun.

796 2/XA5
FREE ✓ ✓ **Scotland Street School Museum** www.glasgowmuseums.com · 0141 287 0500 · **225 Scotland Street** Opposite Shields Road underground station; best approach by car from Eglinton St (A77 Kilmarnock Road over Jamaica St Bridge). Entire school (from 1906) preserved (and recently renovated) as museum of education through Victorian/ Edwardian and wartimes. Original, exquisite Mackintosh features, especially tiling, and powerfully redolent of happy school days. This is a uniquely evocative time capsule. Café and temporary exhibitions. Mon-Thu, Sat 10am-5pm, Fri & Sun 11am-5pm.

797 2/D3
ADMISSION ✓ **The Lighthouse** www.thelighthouse.co.uk · 0141 221 6362 · **Mitchell Lane off Buchanan Street** Glasgow's legacy from its year as UK City of Architecture and Design. Changing exhibitions in Mackintosh's 1893–5 building for the *Glasgow Herald* newspaper. Also houses a shop with cool design stuff, a café-bar and an interpretation centre on the great architect with fantastic rooftop views from the corner tower. Mon-Sat 10.30am-5pm (Tue 11am), Sun 12noon-5pm.

798 9/K25
NTS
ADMISSION ✓ **The Hill House** www.nts.org.uk · 01436 673900 · **Upper Colquhoun Street, Helensburgh** Take Sinclair St off Princes St (at Romanesque tower and Tourist Information Centre) and go 2km uphill, taking left into Kennedy Dr and follow signs. A complete house incorporating Mackintosh's typical total unity of design, built for publisher Walter Blackie in 1902-4. Much to marvel over and wish that everybody else would go away and you could stay there for the night. There's even a library full of books to keep you occupied. Tearoom; gardens. Apr-Oct 1.30-5.30pm. Helensburgh is 45km northwest of city centre via Dumbarton (A82) and A814 up the north Clyde coast.

799 2/C2
2/D2
The Willow Tea Rooms www.willowtearooms.co.uk · 0141 332 0521 ·
Sauchiehall Street & Buchanan Street A café he designed (or what's left of it);
where to go for a break on the trail.

800 2/XF2
FREE
Martyrs' Public School www.glasgowmuseums.com · 0141 553 2557 ·
Parson Street Latest renovation and public access to another spectacular
Mackintosh building. Check those roof trusses. Mon-Sun 2-4pm, by appointment.

801 ss
ADMISSION
House For An Art Lover www.houseforanartlover.co.uk · 0141 353 4770 ·
10 Dumbreck Road, Bellahouston Park Take the M8 west then the M77; turn
right onto Dumbreck Road and it's on your left. These rooms were designed, nearly
a century ago, specifically, it would seem, for willowy women to come and go,
-talking of Michelangelo. Detail is the essence of Mackintosh, and there's plenty
here, but the overall effect is of space and light and a complete absence of clutter.
Design shop and Café (654/BEST TEAROOMS) on the ground floor. Phone for opening times.

Essential Culture

UNIQUE VENUES

802 2/XF4
✓ ✓ ✓ **Barrowland Ballroom** www.glasgow-barrowland.com · 0141
552 4601 · **Gallowgate** When its lights are on, you can't miss it.
The Barrowland is world-famous and for many bands one of their favourite gigs.
It's tacky and a bit run-down, but distinctly venerable; and with its high stage and
sprung dance floor, perfect for rock 'n' roll. The Glasgow audience is 'the best in
the world'.

803 2/XD5
✓ ✓ **The Citizens' Theatre** www.citz.co.uk · 0141 429 0022 · **Gorbals
Street** Fabulous main auditorium and 2 small studios. Drama at its very
best. Though not all that it once was, it's still one of Britain's most influential
theatres, especially for design. Refurbished with lottery funds. Love the theatre?
Love this theatre!

804 ss
✓ ✓ **The Tramway** www.tramway.org · 0141 422 2023 · **25 Albert Drive**
South Side studio, theatre and vast performance and exhibition space.
Dynamic and influential with a varied, innovative programme from all over the
world. New home of Scottish Ballet. Secret Garden behind (1612/GARDENS). Worth
a visit.

805 2/B1
✓ **CCA** www.cca-glasgow.com · 0141 332 7521 · **Centre for Contemporary
Arts, 350 Sauchiehall Street** Major refurbishment of central arts-lab complex for all kinds of performance and visual arts presentation. Impressive
atrium/courtyard houses cool café/restaurant called Tempus. Watch press for CCA
programme.

806 2/B1
✓ **ABC** www.abcglasgow.com · 0141 332 2232 · **Sauchiehall Street**
Purposeful conversion of old ABC film centre in middle of Sauchiehall St into
large-capacity live-music venue with intimate ambience, clubrooms downstairs
and light bar overlooking street. See *The List* for programme.

807 2/C4
✓ **The Arches** www.thearches.co.uk · 0870 240 7528 · **253 Argyle Street**
Experimental and vital theatre on a budget in the railway arches under Central
Station. Director Andy Arnold's gong must surely be in the post! Opening times
vary. Weekend clubs among the best. Bar/café cool place to hang and even talk.

808 2/E4 **Tron Theatre** www.tron.co.uk · 0141 552 4267 · 63 Trongate Contemporary Scottish theatre and other interesting performance, especially music. Great café-bar with food before and *après* (668a/KID-FRIENDLY PLACES).

809 2/C1 **Glasgow Film Theatre** www.gft.org.uk · 0141 332 6535 · Rose Street Known affectionately as the GFT, has café/bar and 2 screens for essential art-house flicks. Quentin Tarantino was there on a visit when I wrote this.

810 2/B2 **King Tut's Wah Wah Hut** www.kingtuts.co.uk · 0141 221 5279 · 272 St Vincent Street Every bit as good as its namesake in Alphabet City used to be; the room for interesting new bands, make-or-break atmosphere and cramped. Bands on the club circuit play to a damp and appreciative crowd. See flyers and *The List* for details.

FESTIVALS

Celtic Connections www.celticconnections.com · 0141 353 8000 3 weeks in Jan. Festival with attitude and atmosphere.

Glasgow International www.glasgowinternational.org · 0141 552 6027 Biennial contemporary visual arts in selected venues celebrating Glasgow's pre-eminence in producing significant new artists. In 2008/10/12 etc.

Glasgow Art Fair www.glasgowartfair.com · 0141 552 6027 4 days in Apr. 2283/WHERE TO BUY ART.

West End Festival www.westendfestival.co.uk · 0141 341 0844 2 weeks in Jun. Neighbourhood and arts festival that includes parade in Byres Road and a lot of drinking.

Glasgow International Jazz Festival www.jazzfest.co.uk · 0141 552 3552 1 week in Jul. Scotland's most credible jazz (in its widest sense) programme over different venues.

Merchant City Festival www.merchantcityfestival.com · 0141 552 6027 A weekend in mid Sep in quarter to east of George Sq. A great new festival waiting to spill out of its quarter.

Glasgay www.glasgay.co.uk Mid Nov. Modest but eclectic programme for gays and straight people alike over several days and venues.

Hogmanay www.hogmanay.net · 0141 552 6027 31 Dec. Not on the same scale as Edinburgh. Usually a stage in George Sq (ticketed).

Section 4

Regional Hotels & Restaurants

The Best Hotels & Restaurants In Argyll

✓ ✓ **Isle Of Eriska** 01631 720371 20km north of Oban. 1203/COUNTRY-HOUSE HOTELS.

✓ ✓ **Ardanaiseig** 01866 833333 · **Loch Awe** 1208/COUNTRY-HOUSE HOTELS.

811 9/J22
12 ROOMS
TEL · TV
NO PETS
£85+/
£45-60

✓ ✓ **Airds Hotel** www.airds-hotel.com · **01631 730236** · **Port Appin** 32km north of Oban 4km off A828. For a long time one of the foremost hostelries in the north and a legendary gourmet experience (see the Allens, p. 24, PIONEERS). Shaun and Jenny McKivragan have continued this tradition and with recent and extensive refurbishing brought Airds firmly to the forefront of the 'civilised escape in a hectic world' market. 'Contemporary cosy' might describe bedrooms and both lounges (and conservatory). Dining is the culmination of a hard day on the croquet lawn or just gazing over the bay. Gentle service and confident cuisine naturel from considerate chef Paul Burns who's cooked through the transition from old-style elegance to new-style elegance and will, for example, take guests mushrooming in the autumn to find their dinner. 3 lovely suites, one with patio. Go on, treat yourself. Port Appin is one of Scotland's most charming places. Lismore passenger ferry 2km away (2371/MAGIC ISLANDS).

£32+
EAT Always (and forever?) one of the best meals you will find in the North.

812 9/H24
22 ROOMS
TEL · TV
£45-60

✓ ✓ **Crinan Hotel** www.crinanhotel.com · **01546 830261** · **Crinan** 8km off A816. On coast, 60km south of Oban (Lochgilphead 12km) at head of the Crinan Canal which joins Loch Fyne with the sea. Outside on the quay is the boat which has landed those massive prawns, sweet clams and other creatures with legs or valves, which are cooked very simply and brought on heaped tureens to your table. Stunning views overlooking canal basin (especially from the Galley bar 6.30-8.30) and from other rooms, the Sound of Jura. This hotel has long housed one of the great seafood restaurants in the UK. Nick Ryan presides; his wife's (the notable artist, Frances Macdonald) pictures of these shorelines and those of son, Ross, are hung around you and for sale.

£32+/ £15
EAT Choice of 'Westward' dining room or pub grub in bar.

813 9/J22
7 ROOMS
FEB-NOV
TV
NO PETS
£38-45

✓ ✓ **Dun Na Mara** www.dunamara.com · **01631 720233** · **Benderloch** Off A828 Oban-Fort William road, 12km north of Oban. Contemporary conversion of seaside mansion in stunning setting, beach below and a perfect vista from all front (3) bedrooms, breakfast room and lounge. A dream guesthouse done in immaculate (mainly white) taste retaining beautiful original features. Former architects are now your unobtrusive hosts. In December/January they go quietly off on their hols and gaze at a bluer sea.

814 9/J26
3 ROOMS
+ 3 SELF-
CATERING
TV
NO KIDS
NO PETS
£60-85

✓ **Balmory Hall** www.balmoryhall.com · **01700 500669** · **Ascog, Isle of Bute** 6km Rothesay towards Mount Stuart (1911/COUNTRY HOUSES). Grand but liveable and lived-in big hoose up road 150m from 30mph sign. A country-house hotel with guesthouse intimacy. Deer on the lawn. 3 excellent self-catering apartments all in the house and a sweet little lodge at the foot of the drive. Famously good breakfast then eat at the Smiddy (1397/GASTROPUBS) 7km or The Pier at Craigmore on the way back to Rothesay (edge of town) which does great home cooking (01700 502867). Balmory is *the* top stay on the island.

815 9/J25
11 RMS · TEL
TV · NO KIDS
£45-60

✓ **An Lochan** 01700 811239 · **Tighnabruaich** Roger and Bea McKie with daughters Louise and Claire in the kitchen have continued to transform this seaside mansion into one of the best hotels in the west of Scotland. AA and others agree. Lovely rooms, many looking over to Bute, comfy furnishings and a plethora of pictures. Bea leads great out-front service and Roger and the girls toil in the kitchen. Doon the Water was never as good as this. Same stripped-down menu throughout, though Shinty Bar adjacent (1200/GAY) even more minimalist.

£15-32 **EAT** Same menu in various dining area including conservatory with the great view. Few words, eg 'Pigeon/Feta/Watermelon £6'; but great food.

816 9/J24 ✓**George Hotel www.thegeorgehotel.co.uk · 01499 302111 · Inveraray**
15 ROOMS   Main street of interesting town on Loch Fyne with credible attractions.
TEL · TV   Ancient inn (1770) still in the capable and friendly hands of the Clark family with
£38-45   real atmosphere in bar. Rooms refurbished tastefully in a Highland-chic kind of
£15 OR LESS   way. Open fire, great grub in extensive bar. Exceptionally good value.
EAT Gastropub grub in multichambered stone wood setting. Good ales, wines and eclectic menu.

817 9/H23 ✓**Lerags House www.leragshouse.com · 01631 563381 · near Oban**
6 ROOMS   7km south of Oban. 4km from A816, a very particular guesthouse unobtru-
FEB-NOV   sively brilliant (even the signage off the road is low-key). Mansion in deep country
TV · NO KIDS   with contemporary feel and style. Lovely gardens in almost estuarine setting to sit
NO PETS   before dinner. Charlie and Bella Miller from Australia do good rooms and excellent
£45-60   food. Fixed menu; neat wine list including selected Oz wines. A cool and calming place.

818 9/J23 ✓**Roineabhal www.roineabhal.com · 01866 833207 · Kilchrenan**
3 ROOMS   Another hotel near Kilchrenan (Ardanaiseig, above and Taychreggan, below)
TV   which is deep in the Loch Awe interior (10km the A85 road to Oban, near
£38-45   Taynuilt). Roger and Maria Soep call this a Highland country house (pronounced 'Ron-ay-val') and it is, though, not a country house hotel. More like a gorgeous guesthouse. Intimate (you eat round the same table) but all in excellent taste and especially the food. You don't have to have dinner but you should (can BYOB).

819 9/J23 **Taychreggan www.taychregganhotel.co.uk · 01866 833211 · Kilchrenan**
19 ROOMS   Signed off A85 just before Taynuilt, 30km from Oban and nestling on a bluff by
TEL · TV   Loch Awe in imposing countryside. Quay for the old ferry to Portsonachan is
£85+   nearby with boats available. With a spruce refurbishment and new rooms, rowan tree at the door and water lapping at garden's edge, this hostelry has always been on our radar, but alas we haven't stayed for a while. Do tell!

820 9/J25 **Kilfinan Hotel www.kilfinanhotel.com · 01700 821201 · Kilfinan** 13km
11 ROOMS   from Tighnabruaich on B8000. A much-loved inn on the beautiful single-track
TEL · TV   road that skirts Loch Fyne. The Wyatts have taken over this classic, quiet getaway
£45-60   inn (quiet as the graveyard adjacent) with long-standing manager Madalon. Building back the good reputation this hostelry always had for food. For a not-too-expensive retreat on a quiet peninsula, this is still a good bet and a nice place to bring kids.

821 9/J24 **Loch Fyne Hotel www.crerarhotels.com · 01499 302148 · Inveraray**
74 ROOMS   Another ok hotel (though not aimed at individuals) in this charming town. On
TEL · TV   main A83 towards Lochgilphead overlooking loch. Part of the Crerar Group, the
£38-45   remains of British Trust Hotels; this one of their best. Pleasing and simple design makeover with a touch of tartan. Pool and facilities. They do take coach parties.

822 9/H25 **Stonefield Castle Hotel www.stonefieldhotels.com · 01880 820836 ·**
33 ROOMS   **Tarbert (Argyll)** Just outside town on the A83, a castle which evokes the 1970s
TEL · TV   more than preceding centuries. Splendid luxuriant gardens leading down to Loch
£45-60   Fyne. Rhodies in spring, hydrangeas in summer. Dining room with baronial splen-

dour and staggering views. Friendly, flexible staff; overall, it seems quintessentially Scottish and ok, especially for families though the style police would have words about those clashing carpets. Most deals include dinner too.

823 9/H25
8 ROOMS
FEB-DEC
TV
£30-38

West Loch Hotel www.westlochhotel.co.uk · 01880 820283 · **Tarbert (Argyll)** Picturesque 1710 former coaching inn on the cusp of Kintyre, just outside of Tarbert on A83. Within easy reach of ferries to Islay, Gigha and Arran. Lovely views of loch over road, nice staff, relaxed atmosphere, ok food in conservatory restaurant. You can feel at home here; forgive the Jack Vettrianos! (1261/INNS)

824 9/H25
10 ROOMS
TEL · TV
£30-38

Columba Hotel www.columbahotel.com · 01880 820808 · **Tarbert** Long-established hotel on the waterfront in this perfect Argyll town. Bar very popular with yachties and locals. Major refurbishment of rooms in hand at TGP (to be completed '08).

825 9/H23
12 ROOMS
MAR-NOV
TV
£38-45

Glenburnie Hotel www.glenburnie.co.uk · 01631 562089 · **Oban** Corran Esplanade. In the middle of a broad sweep of hotels overlooking the bay, this is the best! Graeme Strachan's a natural innkeeper so everything in his seaside mansion is welcoming and easy on the eye. Great detail. Home-made muesli; happy plants; nice furnishings. No dinner but he'll tell you exactly where to go.

Kames Hotel 01700 811489by · **Tighnabruaich** Report: 1270/SEASIDE INNS.

RESTAURANTS

826 9/J24
£15-22

✓ **Inver Cottage** www.invercottage.co.uk · 01369 860537 · **Strathlachlan, Loch Fyne** South of Strachur on B8000, the scenic south road by Loch Fyne, a cottage bar/bistro overlooking loch and ruins of Castle Lachlan. Home baking and cooking at its best. Comfort food and surroundings. Lovely walk to the ruins (40 minutes return) before or after. A real find! Apr-Oct. All-day menus till 5pm. Dinner Thu-Sun (7 days Jul/Aug). LO 9pm.

827 9/K25
£22-32

✓ **Chatters** www.chattersdunoon.co.uk · 01369 706402 · **58 John Street, Dunoon** Rosie Macinnes' long-established and most excellent restaurant in town is, by itself, a good reason for getting the ferry to Dunoon; however, the Cowal peninsula awaits your explorations (and Younger Gardens 1585/GARDENS). Bar menu and à la carte, a small garden for drinks or lunch on a good day and a garden room pre and post dinner when not. All delightful. Wed-Sat only, lunch and dinner.

828 9/H23
£15-22

✓ **The Seafood Temple** 01631 560000 · **Gallanach Road, Oban** On the south coast road out of town and adjacent Oban Sailing Club in a converted temple-like building. Stylish, simple conversion with conversation-numbing views over the lawn and out to sea, and Oban over there. John Ogden's quirky approach but simple, good, fresh-as-fresh seafood (possibly the cheapest oysters and lobsters in the land), 4 quaffable reds/whites, Mackie's ice cream – instantly a top spot in '07. Must book at weekends. Closed Tue/Wed.

829 9/G25

✓ **Kilberry Inn** 01880 770223 · **near Tarbert** Report: 1393/GASTROPUBS.

830 9/G25
£22-32

Pascal 01880 820263 · **Castle Street, Tarbert** Round the corner from The Corner House on quayside. The bistro venture of one Pascal Thezé, your inimitable host and chef. Extensive menu with many fish dishes. Apr-Oct, 6.30-9.30pm.

If you're in Oban...

WHERE TO STAY

✓✓ **Dun Na Mara** 01631 720233 · **Benderloch** A guesthouse off main A828 Oban-Fort William road at Benderloch 12km n of Oban. Gorgeous setting with beach adjacent for fab contemporary conversion of seaside mansion. No ordinary B&B by the sea. Report: 813/BEST ARGYLL.

11 ROOMS
TEL · TV
£60-85

✓ **Manor House** 01631 562087 · **Gallanach Road** On south coast road out of town towards Kerrera ferry, overlooking bay. Quiet elegance in contemporary style, and a restaurant that serves (in an intimate dining room) probably the most 'fine-dining' dinner in town. Bedrooms small but probably the cosiest (the competition ain't great). More delightful than deluxe. Nice bar. In summer dinner is part of the deal.

✓ **Glenburnie Hotel** www.glenburnie.co.uk · 01631 562089 · **Corran Esplanade** Run by the inimitable Graeme Strachan. From tea and shortbread on arrival and the bowl of good-looking apples, it's clear this is a superior bed for the night. See 825/ARGYLL HOTELS.

59 ROOMS
TEL · TV
£60-85

Caledonian Hotel www.obancaledonian.com · 01855 821582 Lashings of money were spent on this refurbished seafront hotel. Can't beat the captain's rooms – comfort and urban facilities. Restaurant and café. But being in the centre of things, the port and the people, the Cally can be noisy and just a tad too on the street for some tastes.

13 ROOMS
DEC-OCT
TEL · TV
£45-60

The Kimberley 01631 571115 · **Dalriach Road** Above the town centre (2 minutes from the main street). Solid Victorian mansion converted quite tastefully by Austrian folk, then new owners '07. Nice public rooms including restaurant and with contemporary bedrooms and bathrooms it's a cut above the rest and may improve further.

11 ROOMS
MAR-NOV
TV
£30-38

Barriemore Hotel www.barriemore-hotel.co.uk · 01631 566356 · **Corran Esplanade** The last in the long sweep of hotels to north of centre and better than most, a reputation established years ago – some changes of owners later it's still a nice guesthouse with great views.

S.Y. Hostel 01631 562025 · **Esplanade** Good location on the front.

WHERE TO EAT

✓ **The Seafood Temple** 01631 566000 · **Gallanach Road** Report: 828/BEST ARGYLL.

£22-32

✓ **Coast** 01631 569901 · **104 George Street** Middle of the main street on corner of John St. Richard (in the kitchen) and Nicola (out front) Fowler have created the best (non-seafood) restaurant in Oban. Modern British menu by a pedigree chef in contemporary, laid-back room. Excellent value for this quality and no fuss. Menu changes seasonally. Awards attest to enduring appeal. Open all year. 7 days lunch & LO 9.30pm.(Closed Sun in winter.)

£22-32

✓ **Ee-Usk** www.eeusk.com · 01631 565666 & **Piazza** 01631 563628 · **North Pier** You can't miss these 2 adjacent identical contemporary steel and glass houses on the corner of the bay, both the ambitious creation and abiding passion of the Macleod family. Macleod père runs a tight ship at Ee-Usk, a bright, modern seafood café with great views. Wild halibut though frozen haddock/cod, hand-cut chips; all home-made starters and puds. Piazza run by Macleod fils purveys standard though good standard Italian fare. Both address perfectly what people want here. 7 days lunch & LO 9.30pm.

£22-32 ✓ **The Waterfront At The Pier** www.waterfrontoban.co.uk · 01631 563110 In the port, by the station in the midst of all that coming and going, the place that's serious about seafood. 'From pier to pan' is about right. Blackboard menu and monkfish à la carte. Locals fill this airy upstairs diner with mainly tourists in the large café/bar on the ground floor (a seafood, ie fish 'n' chips bar meal menu, though not at all bad). You are on the waterfront. Open lunch and LO 9pm-ish. All year.

£32+ ✓ **The Manor House** (see above). The best hotel dining room in town. Creative sauces on fresh seafood and other good things from long-established chef team, Patrick and Sean. Booking essential.

Oban Chocolate Coffeeshop 01631 566099 · **Corran Esplanade** Recent arrival on the front in Oban and the place to go for coffee, cake and of course chocolate. The chocs are made on the premises. You can have the hot variety. Comfy seating. Tue-Sat, closed 5.30pm. Closed Jan.

£22-32 **Café 41** 01631 564117 · **41 Combie Street** Before the big church on the Campbeltown road out of town. Informal, always-busy bistro/caff where chef Vilas Roberts produces a quality no-fuss menu from a tiny kitchen. Regulars swear by the place. BYOB. Dinner only LO 8.45pm (9.30pm Fri/Sat). Closed Mon/Tue.

£15-22 **Julie's Coffee House** 01631 565952 · **33 Stafford Street** Opposite Oban Whisky Visitor Centre. Only 10 tables, so fills up. Nice approach to food (snacky, with home baking) and customers. Best coffee shop in town. Tue-Sun 10am-5pm.

£15-22 **The Studio** 01631 562030 · **Craigard Road** Off main street at Balmoral Hotel and up the hill to find this here forever, candle-lit restaurant; a local fave. Way beyond time for a makeover but who needs it? Surprising menu. Often have to book. Apr-Oct, 5-10pm.

The Kitchen Garden www.kitchengardenoban.co.uk · 01631 566332 · **14 George Street** Deli-café that's often busy and you may have to queue to go upstairs to the small gallery caff. Not a bad cup of coffee and a sandwich (other food varies). Great whisky selection and a plethora of cheese. 7 days 9am-5pm; open later Thu-Sat in summer. (Sun from 10.30am).

Tourist Office 01631 563122 · **Argyll Square** Open all year.

The Best Hotels & Restaurants In Ayrshire & The Clyde Valley

832 9/K28
221 ROOMS
TEL · TV
£85+

✓✓ **The Westin Turnberry Resort** www.turnberry.co.uk · 01655 331000 · Turnberry Not just a hotel on the Ayrshire coast, more a way of life centred on golf. Looks over the 2 courses which are difficult to get on unless you're a guest (2129/GREAT GOLF COURSES). All that should be expected of a world-class hotel except, perhaps, the buzz; but plenty of golf reminiscing and time moving slowly. The spa complex adjacent has state-of-the-art 'treatments', even exercise – with deals for day visitors and nice pool. Colin Montgomerie 'Golf Academy' takes all sorts. Brasserie here (The Terrace) has excellent 'light' and 'Espresso' all-day menus; main dining room looks over the courses to Ailsa Craig beyond – dinner only but closed Sun/Mon. Lovely lodges down the hill.

£22-32+
EAT The Terrace is the light place to eat; pastas, risottos, etc. Main restaurant has 2 AA rosettes. Fine dining in grand style.

833 9/J29

✓✓ **Glenapp Castle** www.glenappcastle.com · 01465 831212 Discreet and immensely distinguished. A jewel in the Scottish crown here in deepest South Ayrshire. Report: 1202/SUPERLATIVE COUNTRY-HOUSE HOTELS.

834 9/K28
3 SUITES
+ COTTAGES
APR-OCT
TEL · TV
NO PETS
£85+

✓ **Culzean Castle** www.culzeanexperience.org · 01655 760615 · near Maybole 18km south of Ayr (coast road most pleasant), this is accommodation in the suites of Culzean, the house itself (1850/CASTLES) so a bed for the night rarely comes as posh as this (includes the famous Eisenhower suite). Rates are expensive, but include afternoon tea. Dinner (including wine) is available. The cliff-top setting, the gardens and the vast grounds are superb. Programme of events throughout year.

835 9/K26

✓ **Lochgreen House** www.costley-hotels.co.uk · 01292 313343 · Troon Top hotel of the Bill Costley group which is so preeminent in this neck of the woods, Lochgreen (adjacent to Royal Troon Golf Course) the most full-on upmarket – a newer extension gives 38 rooms. The **Brig o' Doon** at Alloway is the romance-and-Rabbie Burns hotel (01292 442466), now with a self-catering house, **Doonbrae**, opposite (1352/HOUSE PARTIES) in gorgeous gardens, while **Highgrove** (01292 312511), a bit more intimate, is just outside Troon. All operate at a very acceptable standard. These Costleys also have the Ellisland Hotel in Ayr (847/AYR) and a good roadside inn, the **Cochrane** at Gatehead, (1400/GASTROPUBS).

£32+
EAT Lochgreen: The top restaurant with a real Costley in the kitchen. 3 AA Rosettes.

836 9/K27
5 ROOMS
TEL · TV
NO PETS
£45-60
£15-22

✓ **The Alloway Inn** 01292 442336 · Ayr North Park on the Alloway Rd, almost feels like the country. Cosy, well-appointed rooms with bathrooms relatively lavish. Now part of the Costley empire (see above), this more a posh country pub with rooms. Rammed with happy Ayrshire eaters at weekends. Can walk to douce wee Alloway, the heart of the Burns industry.
EAT Gastro pub grub – the Costley comfort food menu.

837 10/L27
4 ROOMS
TEL · TV
£38-45

✓ **The Sorn Inn** www.sorninn.com · 01290 551305 · 35 Main Street, Sorn 8km east of Mauchline on the B743 off the A76. Traditional inn in rural setting and pleasant village in deepest Ayrshire. The Grant family have established a big reputation for food (Gastropub of the Year 2005 with many other recognitions including Michelin) and there are 4 delightful and great-value rooms. DVD etc.
EAT People travel from miles around to eat here. Restaurant and pub meals. See 1381/GASTROPUBS.

838 9/L28
6+1 ROOMS
TEL · TV
NO KIDS/PETS
£85+

Enterkine House www.enterkine.com · 01292 521608 · **near Annbank**
10km from Ayr in beautiful grounds. Self-consciously upmarket with pleasant
though not-so-modern public rooms. Paul Moffat presides over conservatory
restaurant with good local reputation. A piano is sometimes played. The 'Bothy'
under the trees in the garden is a recent addition: a quirky, 'romantic' hideaway.

839 9/K27
30 ROOMS
TEL · TV
NO PETS
£60-85

Piersland Hotel www.piersland.co.uk · 01292 314747 · **Craig End Road,
Troon** Opposite Portland Golf Course which is next to Royal Troon (2050/GREAT
GOLF). Mansion house of some character and ambience much favoured for
weddings. Wood-panelling, open fires, lovely gardens only a 'drive' away from the
courses (no preferential booking on Royal, but Portland usually possible) and lots
of great golf nearby. Refurbished rooms best. 2 restaurants: one 'traditional', one
'contemporary', though not much to choose between them.

840 9/L27
50 ROOMS
TEL · TV
£38-45

The Park Hotel www.theparkhotel.uk.com · 01563 545999 · **Kilmarnock**
Rugby Park ie adjacent Kilmarnock's football stadium. Contemporary business and
family hotel better than chains of travelodge ilk. Good café/restaurant. Sports
facilities at the ground opposite. Weddings and dinner-dances.

841 9/K28
10 ROOMS
TEL · TV
£38-45
£22-32

Wilding's Hotel & Restaurant 01655 331401 · **Maidens** Maidens is a
coastal village in South Ayrshire, south of Maybole and lovely Culzean (1791/
CASTLES), so a good base. Run by Brian Sage, restaurateur, this is perhaps more a
restaurant with rooms. Many overlook serene harbour; being refurbished '07/08..
EAT May be a drive for dinner, but a beautiful spot and excellent gastropub-style
menu in 2 large, buzzing dining rooms. Food LO 9pm. They come from all over the
county (and Turnberry) so book weekends.

842 9/L25
70 ROOMS
TEL · TV
£45-60

Gleddoch House www.gleddochhouse.com · 01475 540711 · **Langbank
near Greenock** 35km from Glasgow by fast road – M8/A8 turnoff marked
Langbank/Houston after junction 31, follow Langbank then signs. Set in extensive
grounds (including 18-hole golf course), with commanding view of Clyde by
Dumbarton Rock. Leisure club adjacent with a 15km pool. Once one of the great
Clyde Coast hotels, has gone downmarket since the fire and rebuild in '05. So, not
what it was but nice for the golf and the view.

✓ ✓ **Mar Hall** 0141 812 9999 · **Bishopton** The other great house overlooking the Clyde. A top choice. 531/HOTELS OUTSIDE GLASGOW.

RESTAURANTS

843 9/K26
£22-32

✓ ✓ **Braidwoods** www.braidwoods.co.uk · 01294 833544 · **near Dalry**
Simplest approach is from recently completed section of A78 north of
Irvine; take B714 for Dalry. Cottage restaurant discreetly signed 5km on left. Once
you find Keith and Nicola's place, you'll be glad you made the effort. Michelin star,
3 AA rosettes, impeccable, light food and best meal in the shire. Wed/Sun lunch
(not Sun lunch in summer) and Tue-Sat dinner.

844 10/N27
£22-32

✓ **Ristorante La Vigna** www.lavigna.co.uk · 01555 664320 · **40
Wellgate, Lanark** Here almost 25 years yet this famously good Italian
restaurant in a back street in Lanark is unexpected, and quite a find if you're lost
in the Lanarkshire badlands. Superb Italian wine-list. This is not a tratt! Lunch
Mon-Sat, dinner 7 days.

✓ **MacCallums** 01292 319339 · **Troon** Report: 1420/SEAFOOD.

845 10/M26
£15-22

Restaurants in Strathaven 2 good eating places in and about this Lanarkshire village (pronounced *Stray*-ven) south of East Kilbride and west of Lanark and the Clyde Valley.
Steayban www.steayban.com · 01357 523400 A gastropub in Glassford, 2km from Strathaven, it serves excellent suppers (Wed-Sat) and Sun lunch.
Trattoria Da Mario 01357 522604 A fine Italian tratt comparable with any in the city. Lunch Tue-Sat, dinner Tue-Sun. Closed Mon.

Fins 01475 568989 · Fairlie near Largs 8 km south of Largs on A78. Excellent seafood bistro. Report: 1427/SEAFOOD RESTAURANTS.

GASTROPUB GRUB IN AYRSHIRE
There are several estimable establishments to choose from, all routinely packed with happy Ayrshire eaters who travel to treat and treat themselves, especially at weekends.

✓ **The Sorn Inn 01290 551305** 837/AYRSHIRE HOTELS.

✓ **The Alloway Inn 01292 313343** Report: 836/AYRSHIRE HOTELS.

846 9/L27

The Wheatsheaf www.wheatsymington.co.uk · 01563 830307 · Symington near Ayr & Prestwick Off main A77 (2km), just north of main Prestwick roundabout. Roadside and village inn tucked away off main road with big local reputation for wholesome pub grub. Their steak pie is famous. No fuss, great service. 10am-10pm. 7 days. 1387/GASTROPUBS.

The Cochrane 01563 570122 Report: 1400/GASTROPUBS.
Carrick Lodge Hotel 01292 262846 Report: 847/AYR.

If you're in Ayr...

847 9/K27 **WHERE TO STAY**

38 ROOMS
TEL · TV
£60-85

✓ **Lochgreen House 01292 313343 · Monktonhall Road, Troon** 12km north on way in from Ayr. White seaside mansion near famous golf courses of Troon (2130/GREAT GOLF COURSES). Elegant setting; some tacky touches, but spacious from grounds to bedrooms. Flagship hotel of Costley family (see below and all over Ayrshire). 835/AYRSHIRE HOTELS.

5 ROOMS
TEL · TV
£60-85

✓ **The Alloway Inn 01292 442336** 3km from centre on road to Alloway. Small but very well-appointed establishment, more a superior restaurant with rooms. Especially good bathrooms. Quietly absorbed into Costley empire '07; some refreshing of bedrooms and characteristic upping of gastropub menu: now goes like a fair. Must book weekends. 836/AYRSHIRE HOTELS.

15 ROOMS
TEL · TV
£38-45

✓ **Savoy Park 01292 266112 · 16 Racecourse Road** Period mansion run by the Hendersons for over 40 years. Very Scottish, very Ayrshire. Lovely garden for summer breakfast. 1322/SCOTTISH HOTELS.

44 ROOMS
TEL · TV
£45-60

Fairfield House www.fairfieldhotel.co.uk · 01292 267461 · Fairfield Road 1km centre on the front. For years the 'best' hotel in town. 'Deluxe' facilities include pool/sauna/steam, conservatory brasserie 'Martins' and breakfast and refurbished dining room. Only 3 rooms have sea view.

49 ROOMS TEL · TV £60-85	**Western House Hotel 08700 555510 · Craigie Road** Adjacent and very much part of Ayr Racecourse. Close to the first major roundabout into Ayr on A77 from north. Former jockey dorm and big hoose, now Ayr's most contemporary bed for the night. 10 rooms in old mansion, the rest in 2 adjacent blocks. Lacking a little in charm but efficiently run and reliable.
9 ROOMS TEL · TV £60-85	**The Ellisland 01292 260111 · 19 Racecourse Road** On road towards Alloway of many hotels (see Savoy Park, above). Another makeover by the Costley group who have Lochgreen (above) and Brig o' Doon (below). Rooms vary but mostly large and well appointed. Decent restaurant with the Costley touch: irresistible comfort food.
118 ROOMS TEL · TV £38-45	**Ramada Jarvis www.ramadajarvis.co.uk · 01292 269331 · Dablair Road** Centrally situated, best bedbox in town with facilities including tiny pool. Rooms recently refurbished, heating fixed and the windows open at last. Café Mezzaluna opposite (see below) for more charming meals.
6 ROOMS NO C/ CARDS NO PETS £30 OR LESS	**The Richmond www.richmond-guest-house.co.uk · 01292 265153 · 38 Park Circus** Best of bunch in a sedate terrace near the centre, though haven't stayed recently.

Piersland Troon 01292 314747 12km north of Ayr. 839/AYRSHIRE HOTELS.

Enterkine House 01292 521608 · Annbank 12km Ayr town centre across ring road. Country house comforts. 838/AYRSHIRE HOTELS.

The Sorn Inn 01290 551305 · near Mauchline 25km east. Top gourmet pub with rooms. 837/AYRSHIRE HOTELS.

WHERE TO EAT

✓ ✓ **MacCallum's of Troon Oyster Bar** The douce part of the coast beyond Prestwick, this faraway dock on the bay has both the best restaurant hereabouts and also the best fish 'n' chip takeaway. Report: 1420/SEAFOOD RESTAURANTS.

Fouters 01292 261391 · 2 Academy Street Long-established favourite Ayr restaurant changed hands again at TGP. Reports please.

The Tudor Restaurant 8 Beresford Street Superb caff. They don't make 'em like this any more! Till 8pm. Report: 1444/TEAROOMS.

The Alloway Inn 01292 442336 Restaurant of hotel above 836/AYRSHIRE RESTAURANTS. The best just outside town with comfortable pub-grub menu. Hugely popular at weekends. LO 9/9.30pm.

The Hunny Pot 01292 263239 · 37 Beresford Terrace Wholemeal-slanted, kid-friendly, GM-free café – some home baking and light meals. Mon-Sat 9am-9pm, Sun 10.30am-8pm. Less stuck on this than I was.

Carrick Lodge Hotel www.carricklodgehotel.co.uk · 01292 262846 · 46 Carrick Road On main road out of town in Alloway direction. At TGP probably the most popular dining rooms in town. A la carte menu of wholesome pub food following in Ayrshire's Costley footsteps (proprietors Jim and Tracey Murdoch used to serve the Costley empire; see above). They pack 'em in; book Fri/Sat. Lunch & 5.30-9pm.

Mezzaluna 01292 288598 · Dablair Road Opposite Ramada Jarvis. Contemporary bistro with wide-ranging à la carte and specials. Good value, so popular. Ok pasta. 7 days LO 9.30/10.30pm. Sun 4-9pm.

Harvey's 01292 261026 · 1A Alloway Place Near Wellington Sq. Pleasant Mod-Brit café/bistro. Nothing remotely offensive, but not much to say either. 7 days. Lunch & LO 9.30pm.

Cecchini's www.cecchinis.com · 01292 317171 · 72 Fort Street & 39 Portland Street, Troon Excellent Italian and Mediterranean restaurant run by the estimable Cecchini family. Mon-Sat, lunch & LO 10pm.

£15-22 **Scott's www.scotss-troon.com · 01292 315315 · Troon** Harbour road within the Marina about 2km downtown Troon. Serving as a caff for the sailors and the less serious water-bound folk around here, a stylish, contemporary bar/restaurant upstairs and overlooking the surprisingly packed marina. Same people have Elliots in Prestwick. Food ok, great views and very well thought-out watering hole on the water. 7 days. All day LO 10/11pm.

£15-22 **The Rupee Room 01292 283002 · Wellington Square** Ordinary-looking restaurant on the square serving the denizens of Ayr so they do fish 'n' chips but rather good Indian food that's exactly what you want. 7 days. Lunch & LO 11pm.

✓✓ **Mancini's Ayr** Ice cream and a' that. Report: 1520/ICE CREAM.

✓✓ **The Wee Hurrie Ayr** The best fish 'n' chips. See MacCallum (above) and report: 1438/FISH 'N' CHIPS.

Tourist Office 01292 290300 Open all year.

848 11/J30
9 ROOMS
TEL · TV
£85+

✓ ✓ **Knockinaam Lodge** www.knockinaamlodge.com · 01776 810471 · **Portpatrick** Tucked away on dream cove, historic country house full of fresh flowers, great food, sea air and informal, but very good service. Sian and David Ibbotson (2 kids, 3 black labs) balance a family home and a top-class get-away-from-it-all hotel. Some new suites may be on the way. 1205/COUNTRY-HOUSE HOTELS.

£32+

EAT Best meal in the South from outstanding and long-standing chef, Tony Pierce. Fixed menu – lots of unexpected treats. Michelin Star is right.

849 11/J30
9 ROOMS
TEL · TV
£60-85

✓ **Corsewall Lighthouse Hotel** www.lighthousehotel.co.uk · 01776 853220 · **Stranraer** A718 to Kirkcolm 3km, B738 to Corsewall 6km (follow signs). Wild location on cliff top. Cosily furnished clever but cramped (or snug) conversion. Best to go with someone you like. The adjacent fully functioning lighthouse (since 1817) makes for surreal evenings. 3 suites are actually outside the lighthouse (and 2 further away added '08) – all have the sea and sky views. Small dining room. Food fine (and it's a long way to the chipper).

850 11/N30
7 ROOMS
NO KIDS
TEL · TV
£45-60

✓ **Cavens** www.cavens.com · 01387 880234 · **Kirkbean** 20km south Dumfries via A710, Cavens on edge and signed from Kirkbean. This elegant mansion (once home to tobacco baron Sir Richard Oswald) in 6 landscaped acres has been converted by Angus and Jane Fordyce into a homely, informal haven of peace and quiet – great base for touring the South West. Lots of public space so you can even get away from each other. Simple, good cooking using locally sourced ingredients. The Loch Arthur granola for breakfast is *the* best. Internet cubby hole a contemporary concession, all else a more classic modernity. Inexpensive to take over the whole lot. 1358/HOUSE PARTIES.

851 11/M30
10 ROOMS
FEB-DEC
TEL · TV
£45-60

✓ **The Ship Inn** 01557 814217 · **Gatehouse of Fleet** Main street of delightful village with good forest walking all round. Recent refurbishment to a high contemporary standard: light oak everywhere, plasma screens, nice bathrooms – simple and elegant to make this the best stay around. Great pub/bistro food by the guy who put the Masonic on the map. 858/SOUTHWEST RESTAURANTS.

852 11/K30
17 ROOMS
FEB-DEC
TEL · TV
£85+

Kirroughtree Hotel www.kirroughtreehouse.co.uk · 01671 402141 · **Newton Stewart** On A712. Built 1719, Rabbie Burns was once here. Extensive country house refurbished with heavy drapes and plush atmosphere. Original panelled hall and stairs, some spacious rooms the epitome of country-house living; nice grounds. Food here gets 3 AA rosettes: Ralph Mueller's menu may be your main reason for coming. Closed mid Jan to mid Feb.

853 11/N31
20 ROOMS
FEB-NOV
TEL · TV
£60-85

Balcary Bay www.balcary-bay-hotel.co.uk · 01556 640311 · **Auchencairn** 20km south of Castle Douglas and Dalbeattie. Off A711 at end of shore road and as close to the water as you can get without getting wet. Ideal for walking and bird watching. Kitchen continues a strong commitment to local produce. A well-run hideaway and romantic break!

854 11/N30
17 ROOMS
TEL · TV
£38-45

Clonyard House www.clonyardhotel.co.uk · 01556 630372 · **Colvend** On Solway Coast road near Rockcliffe and Kippford (1643/COASTAL VILLAGES; 2120/COASTAL WALKS) but not on sea. Later extension to house provides (11 of the) bedrooms adjacent to patio garden with own private access and... aviary! Friendly family; decent pub grub. Refurbishment and more TLC wouldn't go amiss.

855 11/M31   **Good Spots in Kirkcudbright** Pronounced 'cur-*coo*-bree'; a gem of a town. On a street filled with posh B&Bs, the **Gladstone House 01557 331734 · High Street · www.kirkcubright.co.uk** stands out . Only 3 (lovely attic) rooms so book well ahead.

Selkirk Arms www.selkirkarmshotels.co.uk · 01557 330402 · High Street Much more your 'proper hotel' (a Best Western). Standard facilities and under ambitious new ownership '07 so refurbished rooms and much improved pub and restaurant food likely. 16 of the best medium-expensive rooms in this most interesting of southwest towns.

856 11/N30
5 ROOMS
+COTTAGES
TV · KIDS
£30-38

Anchor 01556 620205 · Kippford Seaside hotel in cute village 3km off main A710. Basic accommodation but great pub atmosphere and extensive food operation in and out; seafood menu (local lobster, pints of prawns). On the shore.

Cally Palace 01557 814341 Report: 1222/KID-FRIENDLY HOTELS.
Aston Hotel 01387 272410 Report: 866/DUMFRIES.

RESTAURANTS

857 11/N29
£22-32

✓ **The Linen Room www.linenroom.com · 01387 255689 · 53 St Michael Street, Dumfries** Direction Caerlaverock. Russell Robertson has stuck it out in this town not known for its culinary excellence and continues to strive and succeed. Easily the most considered and only fine dining around. Great sourcing and real, imaginative cooking. Great wine-list! Go on, Dumfries, treat yourself and support this guy! Lunch & dinner Tue-Sat.

858 11/M30
£15-22

The Masonic Arms www.themasonic-arms.co.uk · 01557 814335 · Gatehouse Of Fleet Put on the map as *the* place to eat by others, new owners (small pub chain) will hopefully keep clientele. 3 separate rooms and atmosphere (pub/conservatory – in summer/contemporary room) but same menu featuring local produce especially fish and beef. Good vegetarian choices and special kids' menu. Apr-Oct 12noon-2pm, 6-9pm. Nov-Mar: closed Mon-Tue.

859 11/P28
£22-32

Lime Tree Restaurant www.limetree-restaurant.co.uk · 01683 221654 · High Street, Moffat Recommended by many food critics, this ambitious venture has become a destination restaurant in this historic spa town. Mat and Artemis Seddon aim to serve good food at sensible prices. Most agree that they do! Tue-Sat 6.30-8.30pm, Sun 12.30-2.30pm.

860 11/J30
£15-22

Campbells www.campbellsrestaurant.co.uk · 01776 810314 · Portpatrick For many this is the best in town and is often packed. Unpretentious fishy fare (some pork/lamb/beef/duck/chicken dishes ie something for everyone). The Campbells have a boat, so crab and lobster a good, fresh bet. Lunch & LO 9.30pm. Closed Mon.

861 11/J30
£15-22

The Crown www.crownportpatrick.com · 01776 810261 · Portpatrick The other (harbourside) hotel/pub restaurant with better than your average pub-grub. Goes like a fair in summer. Lounge and conservatory and outside. AA Seafood Pub of the Year '05. 7 days. LO 10pm. Competition next door from the **Waterfront** (01776 810800). The Crown is the better pub for food.

862 11/M30
£15-22
Carlo's 01556 503977 · 211 King Street, Castle Douglas Curiously, Castle Douglas is Scotland's food town even though there are virtually no good restaurants. Carlo's is your nearest best option. Bustling tratt atmosphere and offering. It is said that Carlo's is the best Italian food in the South. Open Tue-Sat 6-9pm.

863 11/N29
£15-22
Hullabaloo www.hullabaloorestaurant.co.uk · 01387 259679 · Dumfries At the Robert Burns Centre and hard to approach by car: it's opposite the tourist information centre, so best walk over the bridge to the west side of the river. The Centre also houses the local art-house cinema. Wraps, steaks, burgers and superior soup; oh and sandwiches. Closing time varies according to movie times, but usually 11am-8.30pm. Closed Sun/Mon dinner.

864 11/N29
£15-32
Marchills 01387 268728 · Dumfries In suburbs north of centre. Off A701 (off A75 at Bloomfield roundabout) so not easy to find, but worth seeking for bistro menu in the town's most contemporary setting. Lofty room has 'fine dining' option upstairs but it's bistro/brasserie (informal and less expensive) that scores. Presses all the right food buttons. Lunch, LO 10pm. Closed Sun/Mon.

865 11/M31
£15-22
Kirkpatrick's 01557 330888 · Kirkcudbright Scottish restaurant opened in 2002 and highly regarded by locals despite unprepossessing frontage (upstairs and round corner from Main St). Dinner is where Tom Kirkpatrick shows his stuff. Open 7 days lunch & LO 9pm. Closed Jan.

If you're in Dumfries...

866 11/N29

WHERE TO STAY

There's nowhere to recommend in Dumfries. The following are the best bests.

Cavens 01387 880234 · Kirkbean 20km from Dumfries by A710. Report: 850/SOUTHWEST HOTELS.

7 ROOMS
TEL · TV
£45-60
Aston Hotel 01387 272410 · Bankend Road Newish hotel in 'The Crichton Estate' (signposted throughout town centre), a curious 100-acre suburb of listed sandstone buildings now including a conference centre. Contemporary-furnished hotel with 'Brasserie'. A little far to walk to town but best bet for modern facilities and decent food.

10 ROOMS
TEL · TV
£38-45
Trigony House Hotel www.trigonyhotel.co.uk · 01848 331211 · Closeburn Comfortable manor house just off A76 18km north of Dumfries. Restaurant does lunch and dinner. Nice gardens. Rooms vary.

7/4 ROOMS
TV
£30-38
Criffel Inn www.criffelinn.com · 01387 850305 · New Abbey & **Abbey Arms 01387 850489 · New Abbey** 12 km south of Dumfries A710. 2 decent old-style pubs on either side of the green in this lovely wee village where Sweetheart Abbey is the main attraction (1979/ABBEYS). Criffel best for food and rooms. Locals seem to patronise the bar in both.

WHERE TO EAT

✓ **The Linen Room www.linenroom.com · 01387 255689 · 53 St Michael Street** Only fine dining in the area. Report: 857/SOUTHWEST RESTAURANTS.

Marchills 01387 268728 Curiously located in faraway suburbs. 864/SOUTHWEST RESTAURANTS.

£15-22 **Hullabaloo** www.hullabaloorestaurant.co.uk · **01387 259679 · Robert Burns Centre** 863/SOUTHWEST RESTAURANTS.

£15-22 **The Brasserie @ The Aston** 01387 272410 On edge of town near the University and Infirmary; follow signs for The Crichton (866/DUMFRIES). Pleasant room with bar. Contemporary menu. 7 days. Lunch & LO 9.30pm.

2 stalwart Italians and a new one:

£15-22 **Pizzeria Il Fiume** 01387 265154 · **Dock Park** · www.pizzeriailfiume.co.uk Near St Michael's Bridge, underneath Riverside pub. Usual Italian menu but great pizzas and the best for cosy tratt atmosphere. 5.30-10pm daily.

£15-22 **Bruno's** 01387 255757 · **3 Balmoral Road** Off Annan Rd. Well-established Italian eaterie beside **Balmoral** chippy (1448/FISH & CHIPS). They are not related. 6-10pm, closed Tue.

£15-22 **Casa Mia** www.casamiadumfries.co.uk · **01387 269619 · 53 Nunholm Road** Direction Edinburgh. Newer version of the 2 above. Hugely popular. 7 days. Lunch & LO 9pm.

The Best Hotels & Restaurants In Central Scotland

867 10/M24
14 ROOMS
TEL · TV
£85+

✓✓ **The Roman Camp** www.romancamphotel.co.uk · 01877 330003 · **Callander** Nothing much changes in this exemplary hotel; freshening up here and there – oh and new bathrooms. But this hotel remains a unique and absolute gem. Behind the main street (at east or Stirling end), away from the tourist throng and with extensive gardens on the River Teith; another, more elegant world. Roman ruins nearby, but the house was built for the Dukes of Perth and has been a hotel since the war. Rooms low-ceilinged and snug; period furnishings; some rooms small, many magnificent. In the old building corridors do creak. Delightful drawing room and conservatory. Oval dining room very sympatico. Private chapel should a prayer come on and, of course, many weddings. Rods for fishing – the river swishes past the lawn.

£32+ **EAT** Dining room effortlessly the best food in town and country with a great chef – Ian McNaught.

868 10/L23
13 ROOMS
TEL · TV
£45-60

✓✓ **Monachyle Mhor** www.monachylemhor.com · 01877 384622 · **near Balquhidder** Along the ribbon of road that skirts Loch Voil 7 km beyond the village (which is 4km) from the A84 Callander-Crianlarich road. Relatively remote (1276/GET-AWAY HOTELS) and splendid location for this informal farmhouse hotel with great food, fabulous sexy, contemporary rooms and altogether good vibes.

£22-32 **EAT** It's a long way to go for dinner, but currently some of the best dining in Scotland to be had here. Tom Lewis and a great team on the stoves.

869 10/M24
14 ROOMS
(8 SUITES)
TEL · TV
£85+

✓✓ **Cromlix House** www.cromlixhouse.com · 01786 822125 · **Dunblane** 3km from A9 and 4km from town on B8033; follow signs for Perth, then Kinbuck. A leisurely drive through old estate with splendid mature woodlands to this spacious country mansion both sumptuous and homely. Some redecoration '07 but best to leave well alone. No leisure facilities but unnecessary with woods to walk and 3000 acres of meadows and fishing lochs. House Loch is serenity itself. Private chapel.

£32+ **EAT** Chef Steven MacCallum, great conservatory and cosy dining rooms.

870 10/M24
4 ROOMS · TV
NO PETS
£38-45
£15-32

✓ **The Inn at Kippen** www.theinnatkippen.co.uk · 01786 871010 · **Kippen** Middle of village on road in from Loch Lomond direction. Thoroughly good village-inn experience with some style. Real chef, real nice people. Rooms are good value and only 4, so book well ahead.

EAT Restaurant, 'middle section' and bar: choose where to sit but same menu. Often full so once again, book. LO 8.30pm (9.30pm weekends).

871 10/M23
5 ROOMS
TEL · TV
£45-60

✓ **Creagan House** www.creaganhouse.co.uk · 01877 384638 · **Strathyre** End of the village on main A84 for Crianlarich (as above). Gordon & Cherry Gunn's Creagan House is the place to eat in Rob Roy and Callander country (one of only 4 Michelin Bib Gourmand restaurants in Scotland and the only one with accommodation). They have 5 inexpensive rooms, small but home from home. You eat in a pleasant baronial dining room. There are many hills to walk and forest trails that start in the garden (2027/HILLS). Closed Feb.

EAT Gordon's been in that kitchen creatively cooking for 21 years. From '08 they're going to take Wed and Thu off. Who could blame him?

872 10/M24
16 ROOMS
TEL · TV
£45-60

✓ **Lake Hotel** www.lake-hotel.com · 01877 385258 · **Port Of Menteith** A very lake-side hotel on the Lake of Menteith in the purple heart of the Trossachs. Good centre for touring and walking. The Inchmahome ferry leaves from nearby (1989/MARY, CHARLIE AND BOB). 5 rooms overlook lake (and are more expensive, but worth the extra). Conservatory restaurant for sunset supper or lazy lunch; also bar area/menu. Only 5 bedrooms have the view but for clean air and/or dirty weekend, this is a romantic spot.
EAT Different menus to choose from but all stylish and well done; has varied, now better.

873 10/N24
10 ROOMS
TEL · TV
NO PETS
£45-60

✓ **Queens Hotel** www.queenshotelscotland.com · 01786 833268 · **Bridge of Allan** Main street of pleasant town (good shops and restaurants). Surprisingly and self-consciously 'stylish' and modern with cool interiors and art (though main picture odd choice). Groovy restaurant (Jekyll's) and bars. Outside terrace. All-day brasserie menu and evening menu in Jekyll's.

874 10/M25
12 ROOMS
TV
£45-60

Black Bull www.blackbullhotel.com · 01360 550215 · **Killearn** In this good-looking village, 30 minutes north of Glasgow between Loch Lomond (Drymen) and the Campsies, a good conversion of an old inn and a testament to the good taste of the (previous) owners. Bar and bistro with same menu. Rooms simple and decent value (534/HOTELS OUTSIDE GLASGOW). In Killearn check also **The Old Mill** (1398/GASTROPUBS).

875 10/M24
210 ROOMS
TEL · TV
£60-85

Dunblane Hydro www.dunblanehydrohotel.com · 01786 822551 · **Dunblane** One of the huge hydro hotels left over from the last health boom, being refurbished by recent new owners – Scottish-based management company on behalf of international Starwood Group. Nice views for some and a long walk down corridors for most. Leisure facilities include pool. Something of a days-gone-by feel – it is likely to remain a dinner-dance and wedded world.

876 9/K23
12+16
ROOMS
£30 OR LESS

Inverarnan Hotel/The Drover's Inn and Lodge (aka The Stagger Inn) www.thedroversinn.co.uk · 01301 704234 · **Inverarnan** North of Ardlui on Loch Lomond and 12km south of Crianlarich on the A82. Much the same as it was when it began in 1705; bare floors, open fires and heavy drinking (1357/BLOODY GOOD PUBS). Highland hoolies here much recommended. Bar staff wearing kilts look like they mean it. Rooms not Gleneagles but highly individual and recent refurbishment mean full of surprises (5 have jacuzzis). A wild place in the wilderness. Expect atmosphere not service. They also own the Drover's Lodge (aka the Stagger Inn) across the road (01301 704274). 16 en suite rooms – the rooms more standard here with 4-posters. Neither places have phones, only a couple have TV and mobiles probably don't work. Hey, you're away!

877 10/M24
6 ROOMS
MAR-NOV
TV · NO PETS
£30-38

Arden House www.ardenhouse.org.uk · 01877 330235 Bracklinn Rd off Main St at Stirling end and uphill. Superior B&B in elegant mansion. This one used to be featured in that seminal Sunday night series, *Dr Finlay's Casebook* and is still redolent of Tannochbrae.

✓ ✓ **Mar Hall** 0141 312 9999 · **Bishopton** Opulent country house on big scale near Glasgow and airport. Report: 531/HOTELS OUTSIDE GLASGOW.
✓ **Cameron House** 01389 755565 · **Loch Lomond** Report: 532/OUTSIDE TOWN HOTELS.
✓ **Lodge on Loch Lomond** 01436 860201 · **Loch Lomond** Report: 533/OUTSIDE TOWN HOTELS.

RESTAURANTS

878 10/L25
£22-32

✓ **Brown's 01360 661466 · Drymen** '06 arrival to dreamy little Drymen and at last the destination restaurant it deserves. Civilised dining in large, light room. Modern British menu; local sourcing. Lunch & dinner LO 9pm. Closed Tue.

879 10/N25
£15 OR LESS/
£32+

✓ **Glenskirlie House & Castle www.glenskirliehouse.com · 01324 840201 · Banknock** On A803 Kilsyth-Bonnybridge road, junction 4 off M80 Glasgow-Stirling. The Macaloney family have one of Central Scotland's foodie destinations in this many-roomed mansion in an unlikely spot (though near the motorway – 2km – and Falkirk/Stirling). Victorian house and new 'castle' offer fine dining and more informal bar menu respectively. House for lunch and dinner (not Mon), castle evenings only (not Wed). Mod Brit menu with Scottish ingredients.

880 10/N24
£15 OR LESS

✓ **The Allan Water Café www.bridgeofallan.com · Bridge of Allan ·** Caff that's been here for ever at end of the main street in Bridge of Allan now has big brassy, glassy extension and it occupies the whole block. Original features and clientele still remain in the old bit. It's all down to fish 'n' chips and the family ice cream (Bechelli's). 1462/CAFÉS. 7 days, 8am-8.30pm.

881 10/M24
£15 OR LESS

Atrium 01877 331611 · Main Street, Callander Above CCW (Caledonian) outdoor shop. Unprepossessing approach through shop and upstairs to light, spacious mezzanine self-service restaurant probably best easy-eat choice in stopover town. Home-made comfort food. Daytime only (till 5pm).

882 10/M24
£15-22

Ciro's 01877 331070 · Main Street, Callander Not half bad Italian tratt/restaurant adding at last to Callander's foodie offering to the tourists who throng through. Ciro and Nikki Cirillo speak the language of the classic Italian diet we love: pasta/pizza/scaloppina. Closed Wed. Lunch Thu-Sun, dinner LO 9.30pm..

If you're in Stirling...

883 10/N24
96 ROOMS
TEL · TV
£45-85

WHERE TO STAY

Paramount Stirling Highland www.paramount-hotels.co.uk · 01786 475444 Reasonably sympathetic conversion of former school (with modern accommodation block) in the historic section of town on road up to castle. Serviceable businessy hotel in prime location; light 17m pool. Scholars restaurant ok. None of this is particularly good value for what you get.

33/11 ROOMS
TEL · TV
£38-85

Royal Hotel www.royal-stirling.co.uk · 01786 832284 · Bridge of Allan Middle of main street of the civilised suburb/adjacent town where the money is. Stately mansion with good service and ok restaurant. Also 100m along same street, the **Royal Lodge** (01786 834166). Both a better-than-average billet.

9 ROOMS
TEL · TV
£45-60

Park Lodge www.parklodge.net · 01786 474862 · 32 Park Terrace Off main King's Park Rd, 500m from centre. Posh-ish hotel in Victorian/Georgian town (they say 'country') house near the park and golf course. Objets and lawns. French chef/prop.

4 ROOMS
TEL · TV
£38-45

Portcullis Hotel www.theportculishotel.com · 01786 472290 · Castle Wynd Jim and Lynne Walker's pub with rooms, no more than a cannonball's throw from the castle and one of the best locations in town. Pub and pub food (hearty, very popular, may be noisy); upstairs only 4 rooms, but 3 have brilliant views of Castle, graveyard, town and plain. Food till 8pm.

76 ROOMS	**Stirling Management Centre** www.smc.stir.ac.uk · **01786 451666** Not a hotel, but as good as. Fully serviced rooms on university campus (7km from centre in Bridge of Allan which has a good choice of restaurants). Excellent leisure facilities nearby. No atmosphere but a business-like option.
TEL · TV	
NO PETS	
£38-45	

Queen's Hotel 01786 833268 · **Bridge of Allan** 5km Stirling centre but Bridge of Allan is the best place to be. Report: 873/CENTRAL HOTELS.

S.Y. Hostel 01786 473442 On road up to castle in recently renovated jail is this new-style hostel, though still very SYH (1229/HOSTELS). **Willy Wallace Hostel**, 77 Murray Pl at Friars St (01786 446773) is more funky. Upstairs in busy centre with caffs and pubs nearby. Unimposing entrance but bunkrooms for 48.

WHERE TO EAT

£15 OR LESS ✓ **L'Angevine** 52 **Spittal Street** · 01786 446124 On road up to Castle. Named after a gastronomically renowned region of France, this a very sound Scottish/French alliance. Expect choucroute and croustillant with your haggis and neeps. Upstairs and down. Lunch & dinner LO 9pm. Closed Mon/Tue.

£15-32 **The Tolbooth** www.stirling.gov.uk/tolbooth · 01786 274010 · **Jail Wynd** Between 2 streets leading to Castle (250m). Stirling's bright, perhaps attractively tarnished arts centre and auditorium has a café-bar (11am-late) and restaurant (6-9.30pm). Italian-Scottish 'fusion' called Sala d'Oro.

£15 OR LESS **Corrieri's** 01786 472089 On road to Bridge of Allan at Causewayhead. For 70 years this excellent café/restaurant near busy corner below the Wallace Monument serving pasta/pizza and ice-cream as it should be. A genuine family caff. 7 days, LO 9.30pm. Closed Tue.

£22-32 **Hermann's** www.hermanns.co.uk · 01786 450632 · **Mar Place** House on road up to (and very close to) Castle. Hermann Aschaber's (with Scottish wife, Kay) corner of Austria where schnitzels and strudels figure along with Scottish fare. 2 floor, ambient well run rooms. Conservatory best. Upstairs when busy. LO 9.30pm.

£15-22 **The East India Company** 01786 471330 · **7 Viewfield Place** Years on it still proclaims to be the best Indian in town (*Glasgow Herald* 1975) though a bit shabby now. Good atmosphere in woody basement room. Open 7 days till 11pm.

£15 OR LESS **Italia Nostra** 01786 473208 · **25 Baker Street** Great name. The tratt to try. Busy atmosphere; decent wine list, pastas. 7 days 10.30pm (12midnight weekends).

£15-22 **Birds & Bees** www.thebirdsandthebees-stirling.com · 01786 473663 Between Stirling and Bridge of Allan at Causewayhead. Towards Stirling, first on right (Easter Cornton Rd): a great pub and grub worth finding. A roadhouse which is the Scottish *pétanque* (*boules*) centre. Good for kids. 7 days. LO 9.15/10pm.

£15 OR LESS **Allan Water Café** www.bridgeofallan.com · **Bridge of Allan** 8km up the road in Bridge of Allan main street near bridge itself. Great café, the best fish 'n' chips 'n' ice cream. Nostalgia no longer, now it's just massive. See 1463/CAFÉS.

£15-22 **Clive Ramsay's** www.cliveramsay.com · **Bridge of Allan** Great deli and café/restaurant in Bridge of Allan main st. Latter no longer run by Ramsay's, borders on conventional caff with snack and graze menu. LO 8/9pm.

Tourist Office 01786 479901 Open all year.

The Best Hotels & Restaurants In The Borders

884 10/S27
22 ROOMS
TEL · TV
£60-85

✓ **Roxburghe Hotel** www.roxburghe.net · 01573 450331 · near Kelso
The consummate country-house hotel in the Borders. Owned by the Duke and Duchess of Roxburghe, who have a personal input. Rooms distinctive, all light with garden views. Once – no twice, a crow fell down my chimney. This is very good luck! Reliable wine list and Keith Short's safe hands in the kitchen. The 18-hole golf course has major appeal – it's challenging and championship standard and in a beautiful riverside setting. Non-residents can play (2148/GREAT GOLF). 'Health and Beauty Suite' for golf widows. Compared with other country-house hotels, the Roxburghe is good value. Personal, not overbearing service.

£32+
EAT Where to go for fine dining and wining in the east Borders. Chef Keith Short. Also Fairways Brasserie overlooking golf course open weekends. Excellent private dining in plantful conservatory.

885 10/Q27
13 ROOMS
TEL · TV
£85+

✓ **Cringletie House** www.cringletie.com · 01721 730233 · Peebles
Country house 5km from town just off A703 Edinburgh road (35km). Late 19th-century Scottish baronial house in 28 acres. Recent new owners making many improvements. Comfortable and civilised with an imperturbable air of calm. Restful garden view from every room. Top disabled facilities including a lift! Conservatory does light lunches and nice aft tea (reservations only). Walled garden. Tennis.

£32+
EAT Gracious dining (overlooking) conservatory and garden from which those salad leaves may have come.

886 10/P27
5 ROOMS
MAR-DEC
TV
£38-45

✓ **Skirling House** www.skirlinghouse.com · 01899 860274 · Skirling On A72. 3km from Biggar as you come into Skirling village. In an Arts and Crafts house (by Ramsay Traquair, son of Phoebe), Bob and Isobel Hunter have created the definitive rural guesthouse. All aspiring couples go see! From the toiletries (Arran Aromatics) to the white doves in the doocot and the hens from which your breakfast eggs come, it's just perfect. Bob cooks, Isobel waits (and then goes to work). Breakfast a model of its kind; didn't have dinner but food has a very good reputation.

887 10/R27
20 ROOMS
TEL · TV
£45-60

✓ **Burts** www.burtshotel.co.uk · 01896 822285 · Melrose In Market Sq/main street; some (double-glazed) rooms overlook. Busy bars, especially for food. The dining room is *where to eat* in this part of the Borders. Traditional, but comfortably modernised small town hotel, though some rooms also feel small. Convenient location. Good service (2002/ABBEYS; 2044/HILL WALKS; 1602/GARDENS). Where to stay for the Sevens, but try getting in!

£32+
EAT Bar serves top gastropub food (an AA Pub of the Year); more refined dining room has 2 AA rosettes. Both in a class of their own hereabouts.

888 10/R27
11 ROOMS
TEL · TV
£60-85

✓ **The Townhouse** www.thetownhousemelrose.co.uk · 01896 822645 · Melrose Burts (above) has now spawned a more fashion-conscious little sister across the street. Charming, contemporary and almost boutiqueish with a coherent, elegant look by Michael Vee Decor (from down the street) and nothing too over the top. Dining room and busy brasserie confidently positioned between Burts' fine dining and its bar. The Hendersons (père et fils) here and over the road. They have this town down to a 'T'.

889 10/S27
4 ROOMS
TV
NO PETS
£38-45

✓ **Edenwater House** www.edenwaterhouse.co.uk · 01573 224070 · **Ednam near Kelso** Find Ednam on Kelso–Swinton road B6461, 4 km. Discreet manse-type house beside old kirk and graveyard overlooking the said Eden Water, the lovely garden and tranquil green countryside. You have the run of the home of Jeff and Jacqui Kelly and Jacqui's superb cooking. Good wines, good life and a gorgeous garden.

890 10/R26
8+2 ROOMS
MAR-JAN
TEL · TV
£38-45

✓ **Black Bull** 01578 722208 · **Lauder** Main street near the clock of strip of town on A68 that leads to the real Border Country. Eminent especially for its food (1383/GASTROPUBS), it also has 8 (and 2 family) very pleasant rooms above the many-chambered pub. All in very good taste.

891 10/R26
10 ROOMS
TEL · TV
£38-60

Lodge At Carfraemill www.carfraemill.co.uk · 01578 750750 · **near Lauder** On A68 roundabout 8km north of Lauder. Old coaching type lodging. This sure beats a motel! Old-style cooking, a good stop on the road for grub ('Jo's Kitchen' LO 9pm, all-day menu Sat/Sun) and a gateway to the Borders. Nice for kids.

892 10/R27
38 ROOMS
TEL · TV · ECO
£60-85

Dryburgh Abbey Hotel www.dryburgh.co.uk · 01835 822261 · **near St Boswells** Secluded, elegant 19th-century house in abbey (1978/ABBEYS) grounds banking River Tweed. Peaceful and beautiful location; good though small swimming pool. Not big on atmosphere despite surroundings, and rather average dining. But lovely riverside walks. And the abbey: pure romance by moonlight.

893 10/Q27
17 ROOMS
TEL · TV
£60-85

Philipburn www.philipburnhousehotel.co.uk · 01750 720747 · **Selkirk** 1km from town centre on A707 Peebles Rd. Excellent hotel for families, walkers, weekend away from it all. Selkirk is a good Borders base. Restaurant and bar-bistro and rare outdoor pool (with 2 family rooms overlooking). Comfy rooms, some luxurious. Best vegetarian food for miles around here.

894 10/S27
32 ROOMS
TEL · TV
£38-45

Ednam House www.ednamhouse.com · 01573 224168 · **Kelso** Just off town square overlooking River Tweed; majestic Georgian mansion with very old original features including some of the guests! Dated in a comfy way; quietly getting on with the main business of fishing, rugger and dozing off in an old armchair. The restaurant's river view is, however, the main attraction (this is one of *the* great garden rooms). Only half the bedrooms have view. *The* place to stay when fishing these parts.

895 10/R27
5 ROOMS
TV
NO C/ CARDS
£38-45

Clint Lodge www.clintlodge.co.uk · 01835 822027 · **St Boswells** On B6356 (1719/SCENIC ROUTES) between Dryburgh Abbey (1978/ABBEYS) and Smailholm Tower (1940/MONUMENTS). Small country guesthouse in great border country with tranquil views from rooms. Very good home cooking and service from Bill and Heather Walker with a splendid Border breakfast.

896 10/R27
3 ROOMS
TEL
£30-38

Fauhope www.melrose.bordernet.co.uk · 01896 823184 · **Melrose** Borders house in sylvan setting overlooking Tweed. Only 3 rooms but run by Sheila Robson who also has Marmions (see below), so worth a stopover. Highly awarded.

897 10/R28
4 RMS · TEL
MAR-OCT
NO C/ CARDS
£30 OR LESS

Hundalee House www.accommodation-scotland.org · 01835 863011 · **Jedburgh** 1km south of Jedburgh off A68. Lovely 1700 manor house in 10-acre garden. Brilliant value, great base, views of Cheviot hills. Near the famously old Capon Tree.

898 **10/R28** **Allerton House** www.allertonhouse.co.uk · 01835 869633 · Jedburgh Up
6 ROOMS · TV the road by the swimming baths. Pleasant small mansion guesthouse in gardens
NO PETS but no great views. Contemporary facilities including good disabled. Best in town.
£38-45

S.Y. Hostels Very good in this area. Report: 1235a/HOSTELS.

Glentress Hotel near Peebles Report: 1221 THAT WELCOME KIDS.
Wheatsheaf Swinton Report: 1387/GASTROPUBS.
Traquair Arms Innerleithen Report: 1257/ROADSIDE INNS.
Gordon Inn Yarrow Valley Report: 1275/ROADSIDE INNS.

RESTAURANTS

899 **10/R27** ✓**Marmion's** www.marmionsbrasserie.co.uk · 01896 822245 ·
£15-22 **Buccleuch Street, Melrose** Near the abbey. Local fave bistro, now going a
long time under same owners though different (new) management. Still as good
food-wise and holding its own as the bistro in the Borders' food capital. Lunch
and dinner LO 9pm. Closed Sun.

900 **10/R27** ✓**Chapters** www.melrose.bordernet.co.uk · 01896 823217 · Gattonside
£22-32 **near Melrose** Over the River Tweed (you could walk by footbridge as quick
as going round by car). Kevin and Nicki Winsland's surprising bistro – a bit of a
find. Huge choice from à la carte and specials. Tue–Sat dinner only.

✓**Burts & Townhouse Melrose · Cringletie Peebles** (see above) Burts
for best dining hereabouts (including gastropub and brasserie at the
Townhouse), Cringletie for country treat (Cringletie is near Peebles). Reports:
887/885/BORDERS HOTELS.

901 **10/R27** **King's Arms** www.melrose.bordernet.co.uk · 01896 822143 · High Street,
Melrose Excellent bar food in 17th-century coaching inn. The locals' choice (not
gastropub standard nor cost, like Burts). LO 9pm (10pm Sat).

902 **10/R27** **The Hoebridge Inn** www.thehoebridgeinn.co.uk · 01896 823082 ·
£15-22 **Gattonside near Melrose** At Earlston end of village, signed to right. Long
reputation through changing managements for superior and imaginative pub food
with flair. Book for weekend.

903 **10/R27** **Monte Cassino** www.melrose.bordernet.co.uk · 01896 820082 · Melrose
£15-22 Great setting, occupying old station building just up from main square. Cheerful,
non-pretentious and locally popular Italian with pasta/pizza staples and the odd
ok special. LO 9pm. Closed Mon.

904 **10/Q27** **Sunflower Restaurant** www.thesunflower.net · 01721 722420 ·
£15-22 **Bridgegate, Peebles** Off Main St at Veitches corner. Long-standing spot for
restaurant, a local fave. Integrity and design in café menu during day and nice for
kids. Thu/Fri/Sat for dinner 7-9 pm. Closed Suns.

905 **10/Q27** **Lazel's** 01721 730233 · **Peebles** Restaurant in the bowels of the Hydro
£15-22 (1220/FAMILY HOTELS), but real chef so good for healthy lunch if passing through.
Modern makeover and menu, but well below stairs. 12noon-4pm.

906 10/T26   **Giacopazzi's & Oblo's** 01890 752527 · **Eyemouth** Great fish 'n' chips and
    £15-22   ice-cream plus new upstairs bistro near harbour of this fishy and friendly town.
         Report: 1446/FISH 'N' CHIPS.

907 10/R28   **Brydons** 01450 372672 · **16 High Street, Hawick** Once Brydons were bakers,
    £15-22   now they have this oddly funky family caff-cum-restaurant. Home cooking, good
         folk – this is a totally Hawick experience. 8am-4.30pm. Closed Sun (1466/CAFÉS).

908 10/R28   **The Nightjar** 01835 862552 · **Jedburgh** Corner of Abbey Close and Canongate
         100m up from Square. Small evening restaurant with local reputation.
         Thai/Scottish props so usually a green curry on menu and Thai nights every last
         Tue of month. Evenings only.

909 10/R28   **Damascus Drum Café & Books** 0786 7530709 · **2 Silver Street, Hawick**
  £15 OR LESS   near tourist information centre. Surprisingly contemporary, laid-back second-hand
         bookshop and caff in this cultural backwater. Comfy seats. Home-made soups,
         quiche and bagels (1409/VEGETARIAN RESTAURANTS). Mon-Sat 10am-5pm.

         Auld Crosskeys Inn **Denholm** Report: 1389/GASTROPUBS.
         The Craw Inn **Auchencrow** Report: 1258/ROADSIDE INNS.

The Best Hotels & Restaurants In The Lothians

See Section 2 for Edinburgh Hotels & Restaurants just outside the city.

910 10/R25
23 ROOMS
MAR-DEC
TEL · TV
NO KIDS
£85+

✓✓ **Greywalls www.greywalls.co.uk · 01620 842144 · Gullane** On the coast, 36km east of Edinburgh off A198 just beyond Gullane towards North Berwick. Overlooks Muirfield, the championship course (no right of access but some 'golf packages' available) and near Gullane's 3 courses and North Berwick's 2 (2132/2133/GREAT GOLF). No grey walls here but warm sandstone and light, summery public rooms in this Lutyens-designed manor with gardens attributed to Gertrude Jekyll. It's the look that makes it special and the roses are legendary. To wander the garden or sit at the front overlooking Muirfield to the sea in the late summer light is as good as an after-dinner digestif can get. Lovely dining room; indeed all the public rooms are homely and full of nice books and things. A brilliant summer house hotel – it seems a pity to waste it on golfers!

£32+
EAT Fine and subtle dining in elegant room adjacent the course; chef David Williams, a confident player, has 3 AA rosettes. Wine list has depth and character. Cheese is superb.

911 10/P25
16 ROOMS
TEL · TV
NO KIDS
NO PETS
£85+
£15-32+

✓✓ **Champany Inn www.champany.com · 01506 834532 · near Linlithgow** Excellent restaurant with rooms near M9 junction 3 (Edinburgh-Stirling), 30 minutes from Edinburgh city centre, 15 minutes from the airport. Convenient high standard hotel adjacent to nationally famous restaurant (129/HOTELS OUTSIDE EDINBURGH) especially if you love your meat well-hung and properly presented. Superlative wine-list, especially South African vintages.
EAT As much mentioned, the best meal in West Lothian.

912 10/R25
12 ROOMS
TEL · TV
£45-85

✓ **Open Arms www.openarmshotel.com · 01620 850241 · Dirleton** Dirleton is 4km from Gullane towards North Berwick. Comfortable, cosy and countrified hotel in tiny village opposite ancient ruins. If this were in France it would be a 'Hotel du Charme'. Location means it's a golfers' haven and special packages are available. Nice public rooms with much lounging space. 'Deveaus' Restaurant LO 9pm.

913 10/R25
83 ROOMS
TEL · TV
£60-85

✓ **Marine Hotel www.marinehotel-edinburgh.co.uk · 01620 892406 · North Berwick** The old seaside hotel of North Berwick underwent a long and extensive re-fit and re-emerged as a Spa Conference Centre. Done in the sombre/elegant, corporate style à la mode with lots of public space and everywhere (except the leisure area) the great views of the Links and the sea. Dining fine though not exactly Fine; excellent pool and other 'vital' facilities. Some rooms have telescopes as well as the fluffy towels.

914 10/Q25
26 ROOMS
TEL · TV
£45-60

Kilspindie House www.kilspindie.co.uk · 01875 870682 · Aberlady Old-style village inn taken over by Edinburgh restauranteur of repute, Malcolm Duck. Rooms adequate and recently upgraded but hotel excels not surprisingly in the food department. Bar and proper dining. Excellent wine list.
EAT Ducks Restaurant and Bar with à la carte and plats du jour. The new gastropub dining on the coast – well sourced, all home made.

915 10/R25
12 ROOMS
TEL · TV
£30-38

The Rocks www.experiencetherocks.co.uk · 01368 862287 · Dunbar At the east (ie Edinburgh) and John Muir Park end of Dunbar with great views across to the rocky harbour area, a made-over hotel with big local reputation for food. Rooms vary – you would want 'the view'. Big beds, all the mod cons.
EAT They do come from far and wide (phone for directions). Big food operation

downstairs. Seafood and the rest in bar and 'Piano Room'. They have the inexplicable touch. Book weekends.

916 10/R25
13 ROOMS
TEL · TV
NO PETS
£45-60

Nether Abbey www.netherabbey.co.uk · 01620 892802 · **20 Dirleton Avenue, North Berwick** On way in on 'Coastal Trail' from Gullane. Long-established family 'seaside' hotel with recent makeover including major bar/restaurant operation – the Fly-Half Bar and Grill (well- and locally sourced dishes). Busy downstairs, comfy up.

917 10/R26
18 ROOMS
TEL · TV
£38-45

Tweedale Arms www.tweedalearmshotel.co.uk · 01620 810240 · **Gifford** One of two inns in this heart of East Lothian village 9km from the A1 at Haddington, within easy reach of Edinburgh. Set among rich farming country, Gifford is conservative and couthy. Some bedrooms small, but public rooms pleasant and comfy in a country way. Has been here forever, like some of the guests.

✓✓ **The Dakota** 0870 423 4293 · **South Queensferry** Report: 130/HOTELS OUTSIDE EDINBURGH.

✓ **Orocco Pier** 0131 331 1298 · **South Queensferry** Report: 133/HOTELS OUTSIDE EDINBURGH.

Houstoun House 01506 853831 · **Uphall** Report: 135/HOTELS OUTSIDE EDINBURGH.

RESTAURANTS

918 10/R25

✓✓ **La Potinière** www.la-potiniere.co.uk · 01620 843214 · **Gullane** On the main st of East Lothian golfing mecca, a once-legendary restaurant with new owners restoring its reputation. A top meal on this coast. Report: 139/EDINBURGH RESTAURANTS.

919 10/N25
£15-22

✓ **Livingston's** www.livingstons-restaurant.co.uk · 01506 846565 · **Linlithgow** Through arch at east end of High St opposite PO. Cottage conversion with conservatory and garden – a quiet bistro with imaginative modern Franco-Scottish cuisine. 2 AA rosettes. Polite and formal; easily the best in town; but see below. Straightforward menu; good vegetarian. Tue-Sat, lunch and dinner. Closed Jan.

920 10/P25
£15-22

✓ **The Boathouse** 0131 331 5429 · **South Queensferry** Enter through their deli on main street or down steps to terrace overlooking shingly beach and excellent views of the Bridge (415/MAIN ATTRACTIONS). South Q picking up these days and this all-purpose deli/wine bar/bistro/restaurant fills (literally) a big gap. Nothing too fancy but nice food in a lucky location. Times vary but you can eat 7 days till 9pm. Deli closed on Wed.

921 10/R25
£15-22

✓ **The Osteria** 01620 890589 · **High Street, North Berwick** The legendary Italian chef from Edinburgh, called just simply Cosmo, having long left the eponymous restaurant in the city (and others that followed), set up quietly here in North Berwick at the age of 75. Old-fashioned values in menu and service; some great Italian wines. Closed Sun and Mon lunch. LO 10pm.

922 10/N25
£15-32

Marynka www.marynka.com · 01506 840123 · **Linlithgow** Couple of doors down from 4 Marys pub (1373/REAL ALE PUBS), not far from Livingston's (see above), so not bad choice in old Linlithgow. This is a stylish, bright, modern town restaurant with bistro-light lunches and more serious dinners. Small New World wine list and Iain Mellis cheese. Tue-Sat 12noon-2pm, 6-9.30pm. Fourth Sat of the month has a 'Farmer's Market Lunch'. Nice idea.

923 10/R25 **Bonar's** 01620 822100 · **Haddington** Douglas Bonar's smart East Lothian
£32+/ dining room and adjacent brasserie Poldrates in the old mill on the road out to
£22-32 Gifford. Accomplished and polite in an East Lothian way but reliable,
unpretentious food that is much liked. Well-priced and thought-out wine list.
Wed-Sun, lunch and dinner.

924 10/R25 **Creel** www.creelrestaurant.co.uk · 01368 863279 · **Lamer Street, Dunbar**
£15-32 Scotsman Logan Thorburn went out in the world and learned to be a good chef.
He returned to this discreet corner of old Dunbar near the harbour, working to
surpass previous good reputations for quality bistro food and ambiance. Not overly
seafood biased. Thu-Mon lunch and dinner LO 9pm or later.

925 10/R25 **The Old Clubhouse** www.oldclubhouse.com · 01620 842008 · **East Links**
£15-22 **Road, Gullane** Behind main street, on corner of Green. Large woody clubhouse;
a bar/bistro serving food (of the burgers/pasta/nachos variety) all day till 9.45pm.
Great busy atmosphere. Surprising wine selection.

926 10/Q25 **Restaurant 102** 01356 653535 · **102 New Street, Musselburgh** 2 gals run
£15-22 this contemporary room in this suburb with a strong local identity but not much
to do at nights. Now there's this. 12noon-8.45pm (later Fri/Sat). 7 days.

927 10/R25 **The Waterside** 01620 825674 · **1-5 Waterside, Haddington** On the river,
£15-22 opposite side of the pedestrianised old bridge from St Mary's (1958/CHURCHES).
This was the pioneer bistro in these parts, now perhaps a shadow of its gastropub
heyday but the riverside location is still classic. Daily lunch/supper, LO 10pm (Sun
9pm).

928 10/R25 **Drover's Inn** www.thedroversinn.co.uk · 01620 860298 · **Bridge Street,**
£15-32 **East Linton** Middle of neat village just off A1. Pub with good atmosphere; once a
real foodie destination, still listed for old times' sake but like the Waterside above,
they're just not cookin' up a storm any longer. Beer garden out back. Lunch and
dinner all areas, LO 8.45pm. Pub till 11pm, 1am weekends.

The Best Hotels & Restaurants In Fife

929 10/R23
144 ROOMS
TEL · TV
£85+

✓✓ **Old Course** www.oldcoursehotel.co.uk · 01334 474371 · **St Andrews** This world-famous hotel is the one you come to first on the A91 from north or west. Unlike many deluxe UK hotels, this has a lightness and accessibility – surrounded by greens and full of golfers coming and going. Designed by NY architects with Americans in mind. Most rooms overlook the famous course and sea (immaculate and tastefully done with no facility or expense spared), as do the Sands Brasserie and less informal Road Hole Grill up top. Bar here also for lingering views. Truly great for golf, but anyone could unwind here, towelled in luxury. Excellent Kohler (the hotel's US owners) 'water spa' with 20m pool, great tub etc and some top treatments (1336/BEST SPAS). Old Course adjacent but the hotel has its own course, Dukes, 5km away.

£32+/
£22-32

EAT Road Hole Grill for spectacular dinner especially in late light summer and superb whisky selection for a late dram. Sands on ground floor for lighter and later food. Both excellent.

930 10/Q24
30 ROOMS
TEL · TV
£85+

✓ **Balbirnie House** www.balbirnie.co.uk · 01592 610066 · **Markinch** Signed from the road system around Glenrothes (3km) in surprisingly sylvan setting of Balbirnie Country Park. One of the most sociable and comfortable country-house hotels in the land, with high standards in service and décor that's easy to be at home with. Library Bar leads on to tranquil garden. Orangery restaurant has 2 AA rosettes with chef Ian Macdonald and good wine list. No leisure facilities. Nice wedding/honeymoon destination. Good golf in the park.

£32+

EAT An elegant hotel for lunch and dinner in Orangery or downstairs bistro.

931 10/R23
24 ROOMS
+ 2 LODGES
TEL · TV · ECO
£60-85

✓ **Rufflets** www.rufflets.co.uk · 01334 472594 · **St Andrews** 4km from centre via Argyle St opposite West Port along Strathkinness Low Rd past university buildings and playing fields. Calm, elegant feel to this country-house hotel on edge of town. The celebrated gardens are a joy. Garden restaurant fine dining with 2 AA rosettes. Cosy rooms with half on garden. New conference/wedding suite on the way at TGP but a separate building so serenity should remain intact (except for photo calls on the lawns).

932 10/R23
209 ROOMS
+ 2 LODGES
TEL · TV
£60-85

✓ **Fairmont St Andrews (aka St Andrews Bay)** 01334 837000 · **near St Andrews** 8km east on A917 to Crail overlooking eponymous bay. Modern edifice in rolling greens. Soulless perhaps but every facility a golfing family could need. Brasserie-type restaurant in immense atrium. Fine dining in 'Esperanto' up top – Mediterranean menu (closed Mon/Tue).

933 10/R23
8 ROOMS
TV · NO KIDS
£38-45

✓ **Old Station** www.theoldstation.co.uk · 01334 880505 · **near St Andrews** On B9131 (Anstruther road) off A917 from St Andrews. Individualist makeover of old station with contemporary look by previous owners. Design features remain in boutique-style rooms. Colin and Fiona Wiseman (of milk dynasty) welcome you to their home. Conservatory dining room, comfy lounge with log fire. 2 'suites' in a railway carriage in the garden! B&B only.

934 10/R24
2 FLATS
+2 COTTAGES
£38-45

Cambo Estate www.camboestate.com · 01333 450313 · **near Crail** 2km east of Crail on A917. Huge country pile in glorious gardens on the coastal road between St Andrews and Crail. Only 2 flats (and 2 cottages), but this is self catering in the grand if quirky manner. A real period piece and not expensive. Grounds are always superb; great walks and Kingsbarns golf and beach adjacent (2141/GREAT GOLF). Rattle around, pretend you're house guests and be grateful you don't have to pay the bills.

935 10/P25   **29 Bruce Street**   www.29brucestreet.co.uk · **01383 840041** · **Dunfermline**
17 ROOMS   Very central (and adjacent main car park) conversion of townhouse into Italian
TEL · TV   restaurant (Ristorante Alberto) and contemporary boutique-style rooms. Bar/club
NO PETS   adjacent. Well targeted to urban traveller, though what they're doing in
£38-45   Dunfermline... and not so far off the motorway.

936 10/R24   **The Ship Inn**   www.ship-elie.com · **01333 330246** · **Elie**   6 basic rooms in
5 ROOMS   Rock View adjacent pub notable for food and good life (1395/GASTROPUBS) close to
TV   beach in an excellent neuk of Fife. Summer only.
£38-45

937 10/P25   **Woodside Hotel**   www.thewoodsidehotel.co.uk · **01383 860328** · **Aberdour**
20 ROOMS   Refurbished inn in main street of pleasant village with prize-winning rail station,
TEL · TV   castle and church (1950/CHURCHES), coastal walk and nearby beach. This is where
£38-45   to come from Edinburgh (by train, of course) with your bit on the side.

938 10/R23   **Inn on North Street**   www.theinnonnorthstreet.com · **01334 474664** · **127**
13 ROOMS   **North Street, St Andrews**   Corner of Murray park where there are numerous
TEL · TV   guesthouse options. This a hipper, younger alternative to the stalwart, elegant but
£45-60   expensive offerings above. Lizard bar in basement, the Oakrooms on street level is
quite civilised café-bar. Comfy, contemporary rooms best for students and their
mates, rather than their parents (perhaps!).

939 10/R23   **Greyfriars**   01334 474906 · **129 North Street, St Andrews**   And immediately
20 RMS · TEL   adjacent to the Inn (above), a sports-type bar with rooms above with a very similar
TV · NO KIDS   offering. 20 contemporary rooms including a golfers' suite for 4. Mods and cons.
NO PETS
£45-60

2 Good Guesthouses in St Andrews:
18 Queens Terrace 01334 478849   Highly individual, boho, homely and
5 Pilmour Place 01334 478665   Contemporary and stylish near Old Course.
Reports: 949/ST ANDREWS.

RESTAURANTS

940 10/Q24   ✓ ✓ **The Peat Inn**   www.thepeatinn.co.uk · **01334 840206** · **near**
£32+   **Cupar & St Andrews**   Legendary restaurant (with rooms) at eponymous crossroads of Fife. Once the domain of the 'boss', one David Wilson, taken
over and transformed by Geoffrey and Katherine Smeddle into (once again, and
it's so much harder now) one of the top dining-out experiences in the country. It
is very much in the country so you might want to stay in one of the 8 refurbished
rooms. Conducive, cottagey suite of dining rooms for elegant combos of sourced
ingredients: flair without fuss. Sensible Irish and Scottish cheeseboard; superb
wine list. Lunch & LO 9pm Tue-Sat.

941 10/R24   ✓ ✓ **The Cellar**   01333 310378 · **Anstruther**   This classic bistro serves
£22-32   some of the best fish you'll eat in Scotland or anywhere. Off courtyard
behind Fisheries Museum in this busy East Neuk town (1644/COASTAL VILLAGES) –
you'd never think this was a restaurant from the entrance but inside is a
welcoming oasis of epicurean delight. Peter Jukes sources only the best produce
and he does mean *the best*. Even the crabs want to crawl in here. One meat dish,
excellent complementary wine list. Pure, simple food and great atmosphere.
Wed–Sun lunch, 6.30-9.30pm 7 days. Times may change but let's hope the Cellar
goes on for almost ever. 1415/SEAFOOD RESTAURANTS.

942 10/Q23 ✓ **Ostler's Close** www.ostlersclose.co.uk · 01334 655574 · **Temperance**
£22-32 **Close, Cupar** Down a close off the main street, Amanda and Jimmy Graham
run a bistro/restaurant that has been on the gastronomic map (for over 20 years).
Intimate, cottagey rooms. Amanda out front also does puds, Jimmy a star in the
kitchen. Often organic, big on mushrooms and other wild things, lots of fish
choice. Amanda gave me a row because I haven't eaten here for years – fair
enough! Though they put Cupar on the map, there ain't many other reasons for
going there for the evening. But trust me, I know this is a reliable wee gem with a
progressive and innovative approach to food – it probably deserves an extra twirl
on the tick. Sat lunch & Tue-Sun 7-9.30pm. Must book.

943 10/P25 ✓ **The Wee Restaurant** www.theweerestaurant.co.uk · 01383 616263 ·
£22-32 **Main Street, North Queensferry** Just over the Road Bridge from
Edinburgh and in the shadow of the Rail Bridge (415/MAIN ATTRACTIONS). Wee, it is:
a few tables up a few stairs from the street. But chef Craig Wood (assisted by his
missus) is seriously making his mark here. No-fuss menu with a bit of everything
delivered to your table as one of the most accomplished and downright satisfying
meals you'll have had in a while. This is no flash in the pan. Lunch Tue-Sun,
dinner Tue-Sat.

944 10/R23 ✓ **The Seafood Restaurants** www.theseafoodrestaurant.com · 01334
£15-22 **479475 · St Andrews & 01333 730327 · St Monans** Both excellent,
unpretentious restaurants by the Butler family in perfect, if very different, settings.
Reports: 1418/1419/SEAFOOD RESTAURANTS.

945 10/R24 ✓ **Sangster's** www.sangsters.co.uk · 01333 331001 · **Main Street, Elie** A
£22-32 favourite town. Bruce Sangster has impressive form and all in evidence here.
AA Restaurant of the Year '06-07 and many other accolades. Only a few tables so
must book for dinner. Welcome, stripped-down menu with impeccable
ingredients. Simple, divine food and excellent value at this level. Lunch Wed-Fri &
Sun. Dinner Tue-Sat.

946 10/Q24 **Old Rectory** www.theoldrectoryinn.com· 01592 651211 · **Dysart** 2km east
£22-32 of Kirkcaldy (5km centre); still worth the drive from town or anywhere west Fife.
Loyal regulars wouldn't go anywhere else but this 18th-century inn with 3
separate dining areas. Chef Gordon Pirrie has been here almost 20 years which
must be some kind of a record. Lunch: same menu throughout; dinner has supper
menu in the bar area and à la carte in the dining room. The OR features in few
other guide books because they don't need any further attention. Tue-Sun lunch
and dinner (not Sun eve).

947 10/Q24 **Fish 'n' Chips In Fife: Valente's Kirkcaldy, The Anstruther Fish Bar**,
£15 OR LESS **The Pittenweem Fish & Chip Bar** 3 great fish 'n' chip shops with queues
every day. Famously good, that's why! 1451/1455/FISH & CHIPS.

948 10/R24 **Wok & Spice** 01333 730888 · **St Monans** On main A917 road turning past St
£15 OR LESS Monans. Not a caff but a takeaway. Sizzling woks, proper rice, a taste of real
Malaysian food (please don't have the chips). This would work in anywhere but
when in Fife, order here (they deliver between Largo and Crail). 7 days 4.30pm till
whenever.

The Grange Inn St Andrews Report: 1385/GASTROPUBS.
The Ship Inn Elie Report: 1395/GASTROPUBS.

If you're in St Andrews...

The fact is that many of the best places to stay and eat in Fife are in St Andrews. Those that are 'best' in a wider Scottish context are cross-referenced and reported elsewhere. Those that are 'best' in a St Andrews-only context, ie worth trying if you're there, are described here.

949 10/R23 ## WHERE TO STAY

✓ ✓ **Old Course Hotel** 01334 474371 Report: 929/FIFE HOTELS.

✓ **Rufflets** 01334 472594 Report: 931/FIFE HOTELS.

✓ **Fairmont (St Andrews Bay)** 01334 837000 Report: 932/FIFE HOTELS.

✓ **Old Station** 01334 880505 Report: 933/FIFE HOTELS.

Inn on North Street 01334 474664 Report: 938/FIFE HOTELS.
Greyfriars 01334 474906 Report: 939/FIFE HOTELS.

78 ROOMS
TEL · TV
£45-60

Rusacks www.rusacks-hotel.co.uk · 01334 474321 Long-standing golfy hotel near all courses and overlooking the 18th of the Old. Nice sun-lounge and breakfast overlooking the greens. Jack Nicklaus looms large. Reliable and quite classy for a Macdonald Hotel.

22 ROOMS
TEL · TV
NO PETS
£60-85

Albany Hotel 01334 477737 **56 North Street** Townhouse hotel with surprising number of rooms and beautiful back garden. 50% of rooms overlook and are individually (though not in a boutique sense) done; 3 have outside decks and there's a suite with a patio. Bar and basement restaurant, 'The Garden'. A very St Andrews kind of a hostelry.

4 ROOMS
NO KIDS
NO PETS
£38-45

2 Good Guest Houses: 18 Queens Terrace www.18queensterrace.com · 01334 478849. Address as is. Family home run by the enthusiastic Jill Hardie. Her lounge, gardens, very individual bedrooms and lovely breakfast are yours. You'll become friends (or not).

6 ROOMS
TV · NO PETS
£45-60

5 Pilmour Place www.5pilmourplace.com · 01334 478665 Address as is. Adjacent 18th green of Old Course. Contemporary-style guesthouse with lounge.

WHERE TO EAT

£32+
✓ ✓ **The Peat Inn** 01334 840 206 15km southwest. 940/FIFE RESTAURANTS.

✓ **The Seafood Restaurant** 01334 479475 Top seafood, top view. 1418/SEAFOOD RESTAURANTS.

£15-22
✓ **Grange Inn** 01334 472670 4km east off Anstruther road A917. Very popular country pub in several rooms with local reputation. 1395/GASTROPUBS.

£22-32
The Vine Leaf 01334 477497 · **131 South Street** Inauspicious entrance belies civilised St Andrews' long-established 'top' restaurant with eclectic menu that covers all bases, including good vegetarian options and good wines. Morag and Ian Hamilton know how to look after you and what you like especially for pud. Tue-Sat dinner only.

£15-22 **The Doll's House www.dolls-house.co.uk · 01334 477422 · Church Square**
Very central café/restaurant that caters well for kids (and teenagers). Eclectic
range, smiley people and tables outside in summer. Same people have **The Grill
House**; and more recently:

£15-22 **The Glasshouse 01334 473673 · 80 North Street** Contemporary building
with few tables downstairs and few more up. Bright, buzzy surroundings of metal
and glass. Mainly Italian (pasta and thin stone-oven pizza and specials). 7 days
11am-10pm.

£15-22 **Howie's 01334 478479 · North Street** Adjacent New Picture House (the
cinema). Branch of the tried and tested Edinburgh bistro that knows all the things
we currently like, from Buccleuch beef to banoffi pie and changes menu monthly
(well not the banoffi pie). 7 days lunch & LO 9.30pm.

£15-22 **Le Rustique 01334 475380 · 5 College Street** Down side street near tourist
information centre, reasonably 'French restaurant' run by French people, with
freshly baked bread and decent French wine list. Casual dining. 7 days 11am-
10pm.

**Nahm-Jim 01334 474000 · Crails Lane & L'Orient 01334 470000 ·
62 Market Street** 2 newish ethnic restaurants which at TGP we haven't tried
but are being recommended. Nahm-Jim apparently has excellent Thai food.
Reports please.

£22-32 **Balaka Bangladeshi Restaurant www.balaka.com · 01334 474825 ·
3 Alexandra Place** One of those 'Best Curry in Scotland' winners. But certainly
as good as many in Edinburgh or Glasgow. Celebrated herb and spice garden out
back which supplies other restaurants in St Andrews. Handily open later than
most (7 days, 1am).

£15 OR LESS **North Point North Street** Top of the street. Great little caff (daytime only).
Soups, salads, home-made stuff. 8.30am-4.30pm (opens 10am on Sun).

Janetta's 31 South Street Known for ice-cream (1522/ICE CREAM), but popular
caff. Open 7 days till 5/5.30pm.

The Best Hotels & Restaurants In Perthshire & Tayside

950 10/M22
20 ROOMS
TEL · NO KIDS
NO PETS
£85+
MED-EXP

✓✓ **Ardeonaig** www.ardeonaighotel.co.uk · 01567 820400 · **South Shore, Loch Tay** This lochside inn ain't easy to get to (midway Killin and Kenmore on bumpy road) but that's what it's about (1277/GET-AWAY HOTELS). A real stylish haven when you get there. Great views of loch and ben (Lawyers), no TV but books and excellent food and service. Though only here and refurbished 4 years back, the Grottgens are onwards and upwards: remodel and more rooms on the way '08.

£32+
EAT Pete Grottgens: hot chef, hot kitchen. Great service out front from hot, mainly South African waiting staff. South African flair, Ecosse ingredients. Don't expect cheap 'n' cheerful pub grub.

951 10/P22
42 ROOMS
TEL · TV
£85+

✓ **Ballathie House** www.ballathiehousehotel.com · 01250 883268 · **near Perth** A true country-house hotel on the Tay that you fall in love with, especially if you hunt/shoot/fish/lounge around. Good dining, great fishing; good for the weekend away. Riverside rooms are removed and uniform but you taste the Tay. Also cheaper, motel-like 'Sportsman's Lodge' adjacent main house. Love the approach: red squirrels, copper beeches, golden corn.

£32+
EAT Award-winning chef Johnny Greer. Great local produce especially beef/lamb.

952 10/Q22
6 ROOMS
TEL · TV
£60-85

✓ **Castleton House** www.castletonglamis.co.uk · 01307 840340 · **Eassie near Glamis** 13km west of Forfar, 25km north of Dundee. Approach from Glamis, 5km southwest on A94. Unlikely, perhaps unprepossessing location for a delightful, very civilised country-house hotel meticulously run by the Websters and their excellent, mainly local staff. Castleton House piles up accolades and has had 3 AA rosettes for food for a while now under chef Andrew Wilkie. Best Angus option by far. Our First Minister and his missus often dine here.

£22-32
EAT Pleasing conservatory restaurant. All foodie formalities observed.

953 10/N24
12 ROOMS
+2 ADJACENT
TEL · TV
£38-45

✓ **An Lochan** 01259 781252 · **Tormaukin near Auchterarder** 12km south of Auchterarder and Gleneagles via A823 or via A91 east of Stirling and the charmingly called Yetts o' Muckhart. The old Tormaukin inn taken over and considerably polished up by the intrepid Mackay family venturing far from their base in Tignabruaich (815/ARGYLL HOTELS) and their largely seafood restaurant in Glasgow (550/BISTROS) – both rebranded with the 'An Lochan' name. So here now an almost boutique hotel in the heart of the glen (Glen Devon) and a restaurant that demonstrates their uncompromising and simple approach to gastronomy (under chef Gary Noble). Rooms pleasant and unpretentious. All easy on the eye/stomach/even the wallet. Go find!

954 10/M23
16 ROOMS
TEL · TV
NO PETS
£45-60

✓ **Royal Hotel** www.royalhotel.co.uk · 01764 679200 · **Comrie** Central square of cosy town, a sympathetic and stylish if traditional small-town hotel. Excellent restaurant with good light and superb pub out back with ale and atmosphere. Nice rugs and pictures. A pleasing bit of style in the county bit of the country. Delightful restaurant and bar meals. Great value.

955 10/N21
13 ROOMS
TEL · TV
NO KIDS
NO PETS
£38-45

✓ **Craigatin House** www.craigatinhouse.co.uk · 01796 472478 · **Pitlochry** The house built 1820s is now a stylish guesthouse on road north out of Pitlochry. Aspiring perhaps to be part of the cool/hip hotels network, this is a contemporary first for the area. More guesthouse than hotel, this place is excellent value and a real find. Rooms have simple good taste with great bathrooms. Breakfast in conservatory – you may have whisky in your porridge!

956 10/P21
17 ROOMS
TEL · TV
£38-45

✓ **Dalmunzie House** www.dalmunzie.com · 01250 885224 · **Spittal o'**
Glenshee 3 km from Perth-Braemar road close to Glenshee ski slopes and good base for Royal Deeside without Deeside prices. 9 hole golf-course for fun. Everything improving here under new(ish) owners. Hills all around offer a truly peaceful outlook and something to do. Fire to come home to.

957 10/Q22
17 ROOMS
TEL · TV
£38-45

✓ **Lands of Loyal** 01828 633151 · **Alyth** Been here forever and in the same private hands for 17 years but somehow missed by me (and every other guide book) till my spies insisted I check it out. This Victorian mansion on the Loyal Hill with fantastic views from the south-facing rooms and the rambling terraced garden, has a real presence and extraordinary interior. Same chefs also for 17 years and nice dining rooms (3) with open fires (2). An all-round great hotel experience.

958 10/P22
96 ROOMS
TEL · TV
£85+

✓ **(Hilton) Dunkeld House** www.hilton.co.uk/dunkeld · 01350 727771 · **Dunkeld** Former home of Duke of Atholl, a very large impressive country house on the banks of the Tay in beautiful grounds (some time-share) outside Dunkeld. Leisure complex with good pool etc and many other activities laid on eg quad bikes, clay pigeons. Very decent menu. Fine for kids. Pleasant walks. Not cheap but often good deals available. Rooms in old house best. Many weddings.

959 10/N22
11 ROOMS
TEL · TV
£45-60

✓ **Fortingall House** 01887 830367 · **near Aberfeldy** Historical roadhouse hotel near gorgeous Glen Lyon, refurbished to high boutique-style standard. It is near the famous 'Oldest Tree in Europe'. Part of the local estate with their own decor and produce. Decent dining and wine list from House of Menzies nearby (2250/SHOPPING).

960 10/P23
34 ROOMS
TEL · TV
£45-60

Huntingtower Hotel www.huntingtowerhotel.co.uk · 01738 583771 · **near Perth** Crieff road (1km off A85, 3km west of ring route A9 signed). Elegant, modernised mansionhouse outside town. Good gardens with spectacular copper beech and other trees. Subdued, panelled restaurant with decent menu (especially lunch) and wine list. Businesslike service.

961 10/N21
20 ROOMS
TEL · TV
NO PETS
£45-60

Pine Trees Hotel www.pinetreeshotel.co.uk · 01796 472121 · **Pitlochry** A safe haven in visitor-ville – it's above the town and above all that (there are many mansions here). Take Larchwood Rd off west end of main street. Woody gardens, woody interior. Scots owners, with taste (nice rugs).

962 10/N21
13 ROOMS
TEL · TV
£45-60

East Haugh House www.easthaugh.co.uk · 01796 473121 · **near Pitlochry** On south approach to Pitlochry from A9, a mansion house built 18th century; part of the Atholl estate. Family run and notable for hunting/shooting and especially fishing hols and for very decent food in dining room or bar. Nice rooms especially up top, romantic with it (8 rooms have 4-posters).

963 10/N21
10 ROOMS
MAR-DEC
TEL · TV
£60-85

Killiecrankie Hotel www.killiecrankiehotel.co.uk · 01796 473220 · **Killiecrankie** 5km north of Pitlochry off A9 on B8079 signed Killiecrankie. This inn has been difficult for me to assess fairly: it's in many other guides though I haven't been able to stay or eat here for ages. But I know the Waters keep a good thing going. It is popular for meals in the bar or conservatory and the dining room and has a notable wine list. So, I recommend it on the basis of other reviews and my readers' comments. More reports please (and I will come by).

964 10/M22
40 ROOMS
TEL · TV
£38-45

Kenmore Hotel www.kenmorehotel.com · 01887 830205 · **Kenmore**
Ancient coaching inn (16th century) in quaint conservation village. Excellent
prospect for golfing with preferential rates at the adjacent Taymouth Castle
(2160/GOLF IN GREAT PLACES) and fishing. On the river (Tay) itself with terrace and
restaurant overlooking it. Layout bitty, food so-so but real fires (and Robert Burns
was definitely here).

965 10/Q21
10 ROOMS
TEL · TV
NO PETS
£38-45

Glen Clova Hotel www.clova.com · 01575 550350 Near end of Glen Clova,
one of the great Angus Glens (1676/GLENS), on B955 25km north of Kirriemuir. A
walk/climb/country retreat hotel; very comfy. Superb walking nearby. Often full.
Also bunkhouse accommodation behind. This place a very civilised Scottish inn in
the hills and great value. The lovely Claire is everywhere. 2 rooms take pets. 2 new
luxury lodges out back.

966 10/N23
10 ROOMS
TEL · TV
£60-85+

Cairn Lodge www.cairnlodge.co.uk · 01764 622634 · **Ochil Road,
Auchterarder** On way into village from M9 south or Gleneagles). Privately owned
mansion-house hotel overshadowed by Gleneagles up the road; this small but
perfectly formed by comparison. Personal touches and a strong local reputation.
Capercaillie Restaurant and bar.

967 10/M21
28 ROOMS
TEL · TV
£38-45

Dunalastair Hotel www.dunalastair.co.uk · 01882 632323 · **Kinloch
Rannoch** Dominates one side of cute Victorian village square on this road
(B8019) that stabs into the wild heart of Scotland. 30km Pitlochry on A9 (station
for Edinburgh train) and 30km Rannoch station further up (station for Glasgow
train). Schiehallion overlooks and must be climbed (2049/MUNROS); many other
easy hikes. Welcoming Highland lodge that can point you in the direction of many
outdoor activities. Newer rooms on tartan edge and pics need a radical rethink,
but on the whole pleasant hotel with good bar for locals.

968 10/N23
8 RMS · TEL
TV · NO PETS
£60-85

Coll Earn House www.collearnhousehotel.co.uk · 01764 663553 ·
Auchterarder Signposted from main street. Extravagant Victorian mansion with
exceptional stained glass. Comfy rooms, huge beds. Pleasant garden.

✓✓✓ **Gleneagles** 01764 662231 Report: 1201/COUNTRY-HOUSE HOTELS.

✓✓ **Kinloch House** 01250 884237 · **Blairgowrie** 5km west of
Blairgowrie on A923 to Dunkeld. Quintessential Perthshire comfort and
joy. Report: 1207/COUNTRY-HOUSE HOTELS.

✓✓ **Kinnaird House** 01796 482440 Report: 1204/COUNTRY-HOUSE
HOTELS.

✓✓ **Crieff Hydro** 01764 655555 Superb for many reasons, especially kids.
Quintessentially Scottish. Report: 1210/KIDS.

✓✓ **The Bield at Blackruthven** 01738 583238 Report: 1326/RETREATS.

✓✓ **The Barley Bree** Muthill · 01764 681451 Report: 1252/ROADSIDE
INNS.

✓ **The Inn on the Tay** Grandtully · 01887 840760 Report: 1256/ROADSIDE
INNS.

RESTAURANTS

969 10/N24
£32+

✓✓+ **Andrew Fairlie at Gleneagles** www.gleneagles.com · 01764
694267 The 'other' fine-dining restaurant apart from main dining
room in this deluxe resort hotel (1201/COUNTRY-HOUSE HOTELS) and comfortably
the best meal to be had in this and many other counties. Mr Fairlie comes with a

big reputation, Michelin star and good PR. Understated opulence in interior room and confident French food of a very superior nature. Andrew, who stares from the wall while generally keeping to the kitchen, continues to remind us that Scotland is becoming as good a country to eat out in as any. Mon-Sat dinner only. LO 10pm.

970 10/P23 ✓✓ **Deans @ Let's Eat** www.letseatperth.co.uk · 01738 643377 · £22-32 **Kinnoull Street, Perth** Long Perth's premier eaterie, taken over by highly estimable chef Willie Deans in '06 so reputation remains intact. Excellent contemporary cuisine. Good value for this quality. Tue-Sat lunch & LO 9.30pm.

971 10/Q22 ✓✓ **Lochside Lodge** www.lochsidelodge.com · 01575 560340 · £22-32 **Bridgend of Lintrathen** 9km from Alyth towards Glenisla on B954 past Reekie Linn (1693/WATERFALLS), or via Kirriemuir. Deep in watery countryside. Converted stone steading near loch; great setting, decent accommodation (6 rooms) and notable especially for food. Joint proprietor/chef Graham Riley is a 'Master Chef of Great Britain' and it shows. The best meal you'll get for a long country mile. Fine ingredients that look great on the plate. Lunch/dinner LO 9pm. Closed Sun evening & Mon.

972 10/P23 ✓ **63 Tay Street** www.63taystreet.co.uk · 01738 441451 · **Perth** On the £22-32 new riverside road and walk. Set up in the early noughties by chef Jeremy Wares, 63 quickly became the other place to eat in Perth. Now the province of another chef, Graeme Pallister from Parklands. Not tried at TGP. Reports, please. Tue–Sat lunch, LO 9pm.

973 10/R22 ✓ **Gordon's** www.gordonsrestaurant.co.uk · 01241 830364 · **Inverkeilor** £22-32 Halfway between Arbroath and Montrose on the main street. A restaurant with rooms (3) which has won loadsa accolades for Gordon, now son Gary in the kitchen. It's been here for more than 20 years! Splendid people doing good Franco-Scot cooking. What it lacks in atmosphere more than made up for by what's on the plate. Owners now have a restaurant in Blairgowrie. Lunch Tue-Fri & Sun; dinner Tue-Sat LO 8.45pm. Advisable to book.

974 10/P23 ✓ **Apron Stage** 01738 8288885 · **King Street, Stanley** 3km from A9 just £15-22 north of Perth. Tiny local but magic bistro in the main street of sleepy village. It was chef Shona Drysdale who along with Tony Heath established Let's Eat (above) – this is where Shona came for a quieter life. Only 4 tables, limited choices, dinner only Wed-Sat. Simple!

975 10/R22 ✓ **The But 'n' Ben** 01241 877223 · **Auchmithie** 2km off A92 north from £15-22 Arbroath, 8km to town or 4km by cliff-top walk. Village on cliff top where ravine leads to small cove and quay. Adjacent cottages are now a cosy restaurant. Menus vary but all very Scottish and informal, emphasising fresh fish/seafood. Brilliant value: 30 years on Margaret Horn still provides a Scottish experience for her ain folk and others (hub out front, son Angus in the kitchen): an amazing output. Lunch & 6-9.30pm. Closed Tue. High teas Sun 4pm & 5.30pm (2 sittings).

976 10/R22 **Taste** 01241 878104 · **59 Ladybridge Street, Arbroath** Off the harbour. I've £15-22 been told, this is a great new place to eat (in a part of the world that needs one). Still haven't eaten but the menu looks good. So reports, please.

977 10/P22 **Cargills** 01250 876735 · **Blairgowrie** Cosy wine bar ambience, busy à la carte £15-22 menu and blackboard. Serviceable, reliable. Unprepossessing frontage, but on river side. Mon-Sat lunch & dinner until 10pm, Sun 12.30-9pm. Closed Tue. Cargills used to be the only place in Blairgowrie but '07 a new lunch place opened slap-bang next door: **The Antiquary** (01250 873232). Run by the people who have the estimable Lochside Lodge (see above), this should give Cargills a good run for the money. 7 days till 4.30pm (4pm Sun).

978 10/N21 **Old Armoury** www.theoldarmouryrestaurant.com · **01796 474281** ·
£15-32 **Pitlochry** On road from main street that winds down to Salmon Ladder. Old Black Watch armoury gives spacious, light ambience and nice terrace/tea garden. Best food in town and all things to all people: morning coffee, lunches, outdoor tables, afternoon tea, 2 evening menus (LO 8.30pm). Mar-Oct; winter hours vary.

979 10/N21 **The Loft** www.theloftrestaurant.co.uk · **01796 481377** · **Blair Atholl** Off
£15-22 the A9, in village turn left at Bridge of Tilt Hotel. Odd location (corner of a caravan park) and totally unprepossessing entrance for this solidly reputable restaurant which has 2 AA rosettes. Hearty bistro food with a good combo of new and traditional touches in lofty setting. Lunch & LO 9pm. Closed Mon.

980 10/N23 **The Bank** www.thebankrestaurant.co.uk · **01764 656575** · **32 High**
£22-32 **Street, Crieff** Middle of the High St near the town clock. A real meal out in cosy Crieff in a former bank. Chef/proprietor Bill McGuigan's modern Scottish cooking. Sparse atmosphere, great food; or so everybody tells me. I came by twice in '07 to sample but the bank was closed – once I travelled 40 miles. You'd phone first, wouldn't you? And enjoy the best meal in town. Lunch & dinner Tue-Sat.

981 10/P22 **Darjeeling** 01350 727427 · **Main Street, Dunkeld** Perfectly good local Indian
£15-22 restaurant along clean, contemporary lines. A welcome variation to beef and banoffee pie in these parts. 7 days, lunch & LO 10.30pm.

982 10/N21 **Port-na-Craig** www.portnacraig.com · **01796 472777** · **Pitlochry** Just by
the Pitlochry Theatre, cottage-style bistro in a 17th-century inn. Informal and friendly with a Mod-Euro menu. Especially handy pre/post theatre.

983 10/M23 **Deil's Cauldron** www.deilscauldron.co.uk · **01764 670352** · **Comrie** 27
£15-22 Dundas St on bend of A85 main road through town and road to Glen Lednock. Cottage restaurant with quietly effective menu includes staples like haggis and neeps or tiger prawns and eclectic tapas early evenings. Seriously good wine list; cosy ambiance. Loyal clientele keep this a Perthshire secret. Lunch Tue-Sun, dinner Tue-Sat.

If you're in Perth...

984 10/P23 **WHERE TO STAY**

34 ROOMS **Huntingtower Hotel** www.huntingtowerhotel.co.uk · **01738 583771** Crieff
TEL · TV road (1km off A85, 3km west of ring route A9 signed). Elegant, modernised
£45-60 mansion house outside town. Good gardens. Subdued, panelled restaurant with decent menu (especially lunch) and wine list. Business-like service.

14 ROOMS **Parklands** www.theparklandshotel.com · **01738 622451** · **2 St Leonards**
TEL · TV **Bank** Near station overlooking expansive green parkland of North Inch.
£60-85 Reasonable town mansion hotel on the up. 2 restaurants with reputation for food (though sometimes only the bistro is open) under chef Graeme Pallister.

39 ROOMS
TEL · TV
£45-60

Royal George www.theroyalgeorgehotel.co.uk · 01738 624455 · **Tay Street** By the Perth Bridge over the Tay to the A93 to Blairgowrie, near Dundee road and motorway system. Bridge is illuminated at night. Georgian proportions and nostalgic niceties eg dainty bright flowers in the garden, twinkly chandeliers; feels comfortably replete, like an old-style town hotel after a wedding. Big on high tea, especially Sun. Mums, farmers and visiting clergy seem happy here.

WHERE TO EAT

✓ ✓ **Deans @ Let's Eat** 01738 643377 970/PERTHSHIRE RESTAURANTS.

✓ **63 Tay Street** 01738 441451 972/PERTHSHIRE RESTAURANTS.

£15-22

✓ **Deli-cious** **46 Methven Street** Small, cheery take-away and sit-in coffee shop. Some hot dishes. Great sandwiches. 7.30am–evening, Sun 11am-7pm.

£22-32

Café Tabou 01738 446698 · **4 St John's Place** Central corner of pedestrianised square; from outside and in, it feels like an unassuming caff de la place in out-of-city France. French staff, French wine and a reasonable pass at French country food. A piano may be played. 7 days lunch & LO 9.30pm.

£15-22

Keracher's www.kerachers-restaurant.co.uk · 01738 449777 · **Corner of South & Scott Streets** Upstairs diner run by notable local seafood supplier. Great fish/seafood of course, but menu 50% meat. Excellent ingredients and service. Dinner only Tue-Sat.

£15-22

Duncans in Perth 01738 626016 · **33 George Street** Bistro-style diner/ dining: a local favourite in a long-established site. Lunch & dinner. Closed Sun.

£15-22

The Bothy 01738 449792 · **33 Kinnoull Street** Recent creation by Glasgow's expansive GI group, this a version of their 'Bothy' in Glasgow's West End. Capitalising on rediscovery of Scottish roots in cuisine, this will appeal to Perth residents and passing tourists alike, especially with high design value evident: Hielan' coo chic. Food till 10pm bar 11.30pm.

£15-22

Krungthai 01738 633090 · **161 South Street** Authentic fare offered by proper Thai chefs has earned good local reputation. Open late daily, lunch Tue-Sat only.

£15-22

Paco's www.pacos.co.uk · 01738 622290 · **Mill Street** Mega family restaurant. Still the happy burger 'n' pasta 'n' Mex restaurant in Mill St (behind M&S) and a newer takeaway. Also St John's Place by the city hall and church (daily until 7pm, 5pm Sun). LO in restaurant 11pm.

£15-22

Breizh 01738 444427 · **28 High Street** Breizh, the Breton name for Brittany, is a buzzy and inexpensive addition to informal eating out in Perth. Galettes galore, salads, grillades; some home-made puds. Good fun place. 7 days lunch & LO 9pm.

£15-22

Marcello's **143 South Street** Pizza pasta pit stop (eek... and kebabs). Takeaway only. Noon-11pm (midnight Fri/Sat). Guys not so good looking as they used to be. Many takeaways now on South St but Marcello is the real thing.

£15-22

Holdgate's Fish Teas **South Street** A classic for over 100 years!

Tourist Office **Lower City Mills** · 01738 636103 Open all year.

The Best Hotels & Restaurants In The North East

Excludes the city of Aberdeen (except Marcliffe); for Aberdeen see p. 197–201. Speyside listings on p. 181.

985 8/S19
42 ROOMS
TEL · TV
£85+

✓✓ **Marcliffe of Pitfodels** www.marcliffe.com · **01224 861000** · **North Deeside Road** En route to Royal Deeside 5km from Union St. On the edge of town, a successful mix of the intimate and the spacious, the old (mansion house) and the new (1993 refurbishment). Personally run by the Spence family, the sort of hoteliers whom no detail or guest's face escapes. Pics on the piano of Stuart Spence with the famous and political attest to this hotel's enduring primacy. 2 excellent restaurants, breakfast in refurbished light conservatory. Nice courtyard and terrace overlooking gardens. Hugely popular spa facilities but no pool. Honeymoon suites are fab and there are more than a few weddings but this understated hotel caters for all sorts not least the great and good of Aberdeen. Unquestionably one of the best all-round hotels in Scotland.

986 8/Q20
18 ROOMS
FEB-DEC
TEL · TV
£85+

£32+

✓✓ **Darroch Learg** www.darrochlearg.co.uk · **01339 755443** · **Ballater** On main A93 at edge of town. The Franks maintain high standards at this Deeside mansion especially for food. With a relaxed ambience and an excellent dining room, it is the best in this hotel-studded town and on Deeside. They've had three AA rosettes longer than anyone else in Scotland and chef David Mutter has been there since '95 – a long time in chef world. Informal, comfortable with attentive and considerate staff. Some great views of grounds (8 rooms at the front) and Grampian hills. No bar, but civilised drinks before and *après*. Good base for touring. They also run the Station Restaurant in Ballater itself which caters for all kinds of folks in a stunning period room, part of the station which Queen Victoria made famous (she's still there on the platform – honest!) **EAT** Conservatory dining room and one of best restaurants in the North East; chef David Mutter continues to impress. Great wine list. Nice garden view, fab food.

987 8/R20
20 ROOMS
+ SELF-
CATERING
TEL · TV
£85+

✓✓ **Raemoir House** www.raemoir.com · **01330 824884** · **Banchory** 5km north from town via A980 off main street. Mansion in the country just off the Deeside conveyor belt; quirky, romantic – it has something which sets it apart. Old-fashioned, very individual comfy rooms given contemporary details. Flowers everywhere, candles at night. Stable annex and self-catering apartments. Extensive grounds (helicopter pad). New chef '07 and new owners David and Verity Webster who also have Castleton (952/PERTHSHIRE HOTELS). dinner a treat and lots of public space to slouch about in. Event programme includes theatre on the lawn and recitals. Girls from Banchory, light from God. Bliss!

988 8/R19
27 ROOMS
TEL · TV
£85+

✓ **Pittodrie House** www.macdonaldhotels.co.uk · **01467 681444** · **Pitcaple** Large 'family' mansion house on estate in one of the best bits of Aberdeenshire with Bennachie above. 40km Aberdeen but 'only 30 minutes from airport' via A96. Follow signs off B9002. Lots of activities available on the estate, croquet lawn, billiards, many comfortable rooms. Exquisite walled garden 500m from house. A Macdonald hotel (and possibly their best) with very individual rooms in old house and a new extension out back. Nice pictures, great whisky bar. Many weddings!

989 8/T19
27 ROOMS
TEL · TV
NO PETS
£38-45

£22-32

✓ **Udny Arms** www.udny.co.uk · 01358 789444 · **Newburgh** A975 off A92. Village pub with great food and character formerly run by the Craig family, took a dip as a Swallow hotel but on the up again under Oxford Hotels. Major refurbishment and kitchen under Chris Robertson returning to former glory. Reports please. A favourite spot of Alex, our leader. Golf course Cruden Bay (2137/GREAT GOLF) 16km north and walks beside Ythan estuary (1838/WILDLIFE). **EAT** Good grub in bar or dining room. Good ambience. Lunch; LO 9.30pm. This was where Sticky Toffee Pudding was launched on an unsuspecting and highly susceptible Scottish public – the rest is culinary history.

990 8/Q20
45 ROOMS
TEL · TV
NO PETS
£85+

Hilton Craigendarroch www.hilton.co.uk/craigendarroch · 013397 55858 · **Ballater** On the Braemar road (A93). Part of a country-club/time-share operation with elegant dining, good leisure facilities and discreet resort-in-the-woods feel. 2 restaurants: an informal one by the pool (like a leisure-centre caff) and the self-conscious Oaks. Jacket and tie if you please. Lodges can be available on short lets, a good idea for a group holiday or weekend.

991 8/S18
14 ROOMS
(5 IN LODGE)
TEL · TV
£85+

Meldrum House www.meldrumhousegolf.co.uk · 01651 872294 · **Oldmeldrum** 1km from village, 30km north of Aberdeen via A947 Banff road. Immediately impressive and solid establishment – Scottish baronial style. Set amid new 18-hole golf course (private membership, but guests can use) landscaped and managed to high standard (great practice range). Rooms large with atmosphere and nice furnishing – many original antiques and chosen pictures. New lodge added bed space. This hotel could be truly great but has somehow never regained the glory it had 2 decades ago. Always feels a bit unloved. Many weddings.

992 8/S18
3 ROOMS
TEL · TV
£30-38

The Red Garth www.redgarth.com · 01651 872353 · **Oldmeldrum** Oddly enough there is a hotel in Oldmeldrum that really has its act together (4 Star Tourist Board, Meldrum House only 3), a third of the price of the above. This inn (signed from main road system) only has 3 rooms but it's great value; bar meals on the premises. Nice flowers.

993 8/R17
21 ROOMS
TEL · TV
£38-45

Seafield Hotel 01542 840791 · **Cullen** On the main Brae; an activity-oriented hotel with lots to do on nearby Seafield estate (hunt, shoot, fish). Single rooms can be a bit pokey but there's a comfortable lounge with a fair range of malts. Restaurant not recommended. New owners '07 for this enduring and family hotel.

994 8/R18
18 ROOMS
TEL · TV
NO PETS
£45-60

Castle Hotel www.castlehotel.uk.com · 01466 792696 · **Huntly** Behind the spooky, eyeless ruin of Huntly Castle; approach from town through castle entrance and then over River Deveron up impressive drive. Former dowager house of the Dukes of Gordon, family-run and not bad value for the grandeur/setting – tourists and business travellers keep it busy.

995 8/T18
106 ROOMS
TEL · TV
£45-60

Waterside Inn www.swallow-hotels.com/hotels/waterside-inn · 01779 471121 · **Peterhead** Edge of town on A952 to Fraserburgh on tidal River Ugie. Standard, well-run modern hotel, recommended for its service and convenience and because it's the best option around. Good for kids (1226/KIDS).

996 8/Q20
6 ROOMS
TEL · TV
NO PETS
£38-45

The Auld Kirk 01339 755762 · **Ballater** On Braemar road heading out of town. It is indeed an auld kirk with 6 rooms being refurbished at TGP and a growing reputation for dinner. Peter Gradon and Tony Fuell creating a great-value stopover in Deeside where there are few bargains to be had.

997 8/T17
3 ROOMS
TV
£30-38

Lonmay Old Manse 01346 532227 · **Lonmay near Fraserburgh** Off B9033 between St Combs and Crimond, south of Fraserburgh. Not much to recommend around here but this early-19th-century manse has a growing reputation. Haven't tried, so reports please. There is a remarkable Elvis Presley connection!

998 8/R19
12 ROOMS
TEL · TV
£30-38

£15-22

Grant Arms www.grantarmshotel.com · 01467 651226 · **Monymusk** The village inn on a remarkable small square, a good centre for walking, close to the 'Castle Trail' (1864/CASTLES; 1921/COUNTRY HOUSES) and with fishing rights on the Don. Rooms in hotel and 6 'chalets' around a courtyard (old stables) but the food, especially in the bar, is why folk find the GA.
EAT Best pub food for miles, and dining. Daily lunch, 6.30-9pm.

RESTAURANTS

✓ ✓ **Tolbooth** 01569 762287 · **Stonehaven** Excellent location on Stonehaven Harbour gives great lobster. 1471/SEAFOOD RESTAURANTS.

✓ **Lairhillock Inn** www.lairhillock.co.uk · 01569 730001 · **near Stonehaven** 15km south of Aberdeen off A92. Excellent country pub and restaurant, good for kids. Report: 1098/ABERDEEN RESTAURANTS; 1392/GASTROPUBS.

999 8/S20
£22-32

✓ **The (Art Deco) Carron Restaurant** www.carron-restaurant.co.uk · 01569 760460 · **20 Carron Street, Stonehaven** Off main street near the square. They use 'art deco' in the title, but you couldn't miss the reference in this fantastic period piece faithfully restored and embellished. Run by Robert Cleaver who has the Tolbooth (1417/SEAFOOD RESTAURANTS), this is one of the top dining-out experiences in the North East. Closed Sun/Mon.

1000
8/S20
£15-22

✓ **Milton Restaurant** www.themilton.co.uk · 01330 844566 On main A93 Royal Deeside road 4km east of Banchory opposite the entrance to Crathes (1587/GARDENS; 1922/COUNTRY HOUSES). Roadside and surprisingly contemporary restaurant in old steading adjacent craft village of varying quality (not related). Light and exceedingly pleasant space. All-day menu from brunch to dinner so they cater for everything (and rather well). Restaurant of the Year (a local award) '07. Likely to do more weddings in the future. Tue-Sat LO 9pm, Sun and Mon lunch/tea till 7pm. A contemporary corner of Deeside.

1001
8/T18
£15-22

✓ **Eat On The Green** www.eatonthegreen.co.uk · 01651 842337 · **Udny Green near Ellon** Former pub now restaurant on green of cute village in deepest Aberdeenshire. Craig Wilson (formerly cheffing at Cromlix and Ballathie) is the estimable chef/proprietor. The room and menu are all simply done and it's always agreeably busy. So best to book. Wed-Sun lunch, LO 9pm.

1002
8/Q20

The Green Inn www.green-inn.com · 01339 755701 · **Victoria Road, Ballater** Small frontage, surprisingly opens out at back. Long-established restaurant in this town has good reputation again under the O'Halloran family with son Chris in the kitchen. 2 inexpensive rooms upstairs. Dinner only Mon-Sat 7-9pm.

1003
8/R20
£15-22

White Cottage www.whitecottage.eu · 01398 885757 · **near Aboyne** On the main A93 outside Aboyne from Aberdeen. John Inches's (formerly of the long-estimable Faradays at Cults) roadside white cottage (conservatory attached) serving Modern British menu to loyal locals and travellers. Thu-Sat dinner only & Sun lunch. LO 8.30pm.

1004 **The Candlestick-Maker** www.thecandlestick-maker.com · 01339 886060 ·
8/R20 **Aboyne** Just off A93 in Deeside, middle of Aboyne by the PO and overlooking the
£15-22 green. Haven't tried but Bevan and Jacqui Griffiths work hard at their (everything)
homemade menu in an unfussy room... on the green... in Aboyne. Reports please.
Lunch & dinner LO 9pm. Closed Mon.

1005 **The County Hotel** www.thecountyhotel.com · 01261 815353 · **Banff**
8/R17 Francophile dining options in dear sleepy Banff. Bistro and bar downstairs
£15 OR LESS/ (lunches and bar suppers Mon-Sat); posh evening meals upstairs (daily 7-9pm,
£32+ booking advisable). Quite a find (there's a letter from Alex Salmond saying how
much he liked it). There's a beer garden with an apple tree.

The Black-Faced Sheep **Aboyne** Report: 1473/TEAROOMS.
The Creel Inn **Catterline** Report: 1386/GASTROPUBS.
The Raemoir Garden Centre Report: 2299/GARDEN CENTRES.
The Falls of Feugh **Banchory** Report: 1474/TEAROOMS.

The Best Hotels & Restaurants In Speyside

1006
8/P18
11 ROOMS
MAR-JAN
TEL · TV
£45-60

✓ ✓ **Minmore House** www.minmorehousehotel.com · 01807 590378 · **Glenlivet** Adjacent Glenlivet Distillery (1568/WHISKY TOURS) so signed from all over, but on the B9008 off the A95 between Keith and Grantown. The former home of the distillery founder now Lynne and Victor Jansson's comfortable, not overly dressed-up country-house hotel with an excellent reputation for food. This extends from their sumptuous dram-driven dinners to top breakfast and an afternoon tea, which is a local event in its own right. Rooms look down the glen; lovely suites. Full of personal touches. This is a very Speyside experience.

£22-32
EAT A long way for dinner, non-residents make do with tea: a fine ritual.

1007
8/Q18
25 ROOMS
TEL · TV
NO PETS
£60-85

✓ **Craigellachie Hotel** www.craigellachie.com · 01340 881204 · **Craigellachie** The quintessential Speyside hotel, off A941 Elgin to Perth and Aberdeen road by the bridge over Spey. Especially good for fishing, but well placed for walking (Speyside Way runs along bottom of garden; see 2062/LONG WALKS) and distillery visits (1569/WHISKY). Informal; some fab rooms. The food is well regarded and the Quaich bar could keep a whisky lover amused for years. Simply one of the best places in Scotland for a dram.

1008
8/Q18
5 ROOMS
TEL · TV
£45-60

✓ **The Mash Tun** 01340 881771 · **8 Broomfield Square, Aberlour** Off the main street, behind the church by lovely river meadow park. A restaurant/pub with rooms above (all named after whiskies). They call themselves a whisky bar and this is a very Malt Trail destination that's boutique standard and informal and better value than most.
EAT Unpretentious gastropub-style food. Great whisky choice.

1009
8/N19
8 ROOMS
TEL · TV
£60-85

Muckrach Lodge 01479 851257 · **Dulnain Bridge by Grantown on Spey** Off Carrbridge road out of Dulnain Bridge which is off A95 Aviemore-Grantown road. Mansionhouse presiding over bucolic demesne to the river. Long established as a country-house hotel but taken over '07 by Andy Picheta and Rebecca Ferrand who have ambitions to freshen it up big time. Work in progress at time of last visit. Nice bar leading on to deck terrace, and conservatory restaurant which I'm sure will improve. Could become a big National Park asset. Reports please.

1010 8/P17
23 ROOMS
TEL · TV
NO PETS
£60-85

The Mansion House www.mansionhousehotel.co.uk · 01343 548811 · **Elgin** Sits discreetly under the monument to the last Duke of Gordon and near the big Tesco store. Comfortable and elegant town house in a comfortable and gentle town with leisure facilities, including small pool/gym and drop-in (very small) bistro. Nice dining room.

1011 8/P18
9 ROOMS
TEL · TV
£38-45

Delnashaugh Inn www.delnashaugh.co.uk · 01807 500255 · **Ballindalloch** Road-side and Speyside (actually the Avon, pronounced 'Arn') inn, comfy, unpretentious. On bend of A95 between Craigellachie and Grantown near confluence of main roads and rivers. Much ado about fishing, and golf. New owners '08.

1012
8/P18
11 ROOMS
TEL · TV
£45-60

Archiestown Hotel www.archiestownhotel.co.uk · 01340 810218 · **Archiestown** Main street of small village in heart of Speyside near Cardhu Distillery (1571/WHISKY). A village inn/hotel with comfortable rooms and celebrated food in bistro setting (LO 8.30pm). Fishers and people who don't mind high-minded hosts with attitude. Here I met Speyside's snootiest wifie who made me feel like shit on her shoe. I got over it. Locals stay away but others do recommend.
EAT It's not a gastropub and they don't want to call it a bistro (even though it's

writ large on the side of the hotel) so let's just call it a room where you can eat well.

1013 8/Q18 **Tannochbrae** www.tannochbrae.co.uk · 01340 820541 · **22 Fife Street,**
6 ROOMS **Dufftown** Twee by name (older readers will remember *Dr Finlay's Casebook*) and
TV twee by nature (from Scotty-dog doorstops to Jack Vettriano) guesthouse in
NO PETS Speyside centre. Conscientiously run accommodation and à la carte restaurant
£30-38 and a good dram selection. This place, though tartantastic, is the genuine article.

£15 OR LESS For the complete over-indulgent dose you might want to experience the world-
famous, award-winning **Glenfiddich Restaurant** near the town clock. Enough to
send a modern Scot gibbering into his Irn Bru cocktail, others may be in their
unreconstructed heaven. The food is ghastly but this is as camp as the Black
Watch on manoeuvres. 7 days (LO 9pm, winter hours vary).

RESTAURANTS
1014 **La Faisanderie** www.dufftown.co.uk/faisanderie-la.htm · 01340 821273 ·
8/Q18 **Dufftown** The Whisky Trail with Eric Obry's French twist. A small Franco-Scots
£15-22 affair, corner of The Square and Balvenie St, near the tourist information centre. A
welcome departure for these parts – and well known as *the place* to eat. Lunch &
dinner daily LO 9pm (except closed all day Tue & Wed lunch).

The Best Hotels & Restaurants In The Highlands

See also Inverness, p. 205–08; Skye, p. 404 and 408; Outer Hebrides, p. 416–18.

1015
9/K21
17 ROOMS
TV
£85+

✓✓ **Inverlochy Castle** www.inverlochycastlehotel.com · 01397 702177 · **Fort William** 5km from town on A82 Inverness road, Scotland's flagship Highland hotel filled with sumptuous furnishings, elegant decor and occasional film stars, luminaries and royalty. Not surprisingly, little has changed here since the last edition. As you sit in the atrium after dinner marvelling at the ceiling and stylish people swish up and down the staircase, you know this is no ordinary country-house hotel. And it has all you expect of a 'castle'; the epitome of grandeur and service. Huge comfortable bedrooms, acres of rhododendrons, trout in the lake, tennis and a lovely terrace. The big Ben is over there. **EAT** Not a drop-in dining room, but non-residents can book. Long-serving chef Matthew Gray makes this a destination in its own right (3 AA rosettes).

1016
7/H16
7 ROOMS
MAR-DEC
TEL · TV
NO KIDS
NO PETS
£85+

✓✓ **Pool House Hotel** www.poolhousehotel.com · 01445 781272 · **Poolewe** Formerly owned by Osgood MacKenzie who founded the gardens up the road (1586/GARDENS). The Harrisons have transformed with immaculate style and sheer determination this Highland home into one of the must-do stopovers in the land. Only 7 but fabulously themed suites, including new 'Indian' suite with amazing bed and also the Boathouse overlooking the river mouth and out to the bay. Huge bathrooms. Great dining with chef John Moir; bar has great malt collection. Simultaneously special and personable. Fab new ornamental and kitchen gardens. Surely a new destination hotel for Scotland.

1017
8/N17
9 ROOMS
(2 SUITES)
TEL · TV
£85+

✓✓ **The Boath House** www.boath-house.com · 01667 454896 · **Auldearn** Signed from the main A96 3km east of Nairn. A small country-house hotel in a classic and immaculately restored mansion – Don and Wendy Matheson's family home; well chosen pics (for sale). Add chef Charlie Lockley (3 AA) and you're in for a memorable stay. Sometimes you think: getting it right in the hotel biz can't be that difficult. Don and Wendy started from scratch. You budding hoteliers – come here, see what they've done in 10 years and still at it: Don was himself converting and building 2 new suites when I was there '07. Delightful grounds with walled garden in restoration (and beautiful Brodie nearby; 1849/CASTLES) and a lake. **EAT** Mr Lockley: intuitive, obliging, unassuming, great judgement. 'Local ingredients' a matter of course including the kitchen garden.

1018
6/J14
7 ROOMS
MAR-DEC
TEL · TV
NO KIDS
NO PETS
£85+
£22-32

✓✓ **The Albannach** 01571 844407 · **Lochinver** 2km up road to Baddidarach as you come into Lochinver on the A837 at the bridge. Lesley and Colin have created a unique and comfortable haven in their 18th-century house. The suite adjacent used to be a byre and looks over 'the croft' with Stac Polly peeping over. The two new rooms upstairs are very contemporary, cool and calm to be in. One, 'The Penthouse', has its own terrace. Dining room now extended so more non-residents can dine: Lesley's 5-course innovative set menu uses impeccable ingredients and includes Colin's perfect puds. Suilven over there from a relatively midge-free terrace. **EAT** When in far-flung Assynt, you must eat at the Albannach.

✓✓ **Ballachulish House** www.ballachulishhouse.com · 01855 811266 · **Ballachulish** On A828 Fort William/Glencoe-Oban road just south of bridge. Brilliant dining in historic house with 9-hole golf course overlooking loch. Report: 1318/SCOTTISH HOTELS.

1019
7/M18
30 ROOMS
TEL · TV
£85+

Glenmoriston Townhouse www.glenmoristontownhouse.com ·
01463 223777 · **20 Nessbank, Inverness** Along riverside opposite
Eden Court Theatre. No expense spared in the conversion of this long-reputed
hotel (and the one next door) into a chic boutique and very urban hotel in the
ascendant city of Inverness. Rooms split 50/50 between main hotel and adjacent
annex. All the latter refurbished to urban-chic standard; old building more traditional. Some rooms overlook the river. 'Piano' bar, top restaurant 'Abstract' and
bistro/brasserie 'Contrast'. Definitely the most *au courant* stay in the North.
EAT Room could be Edinburgh/NY/London. Great staff (mainly French), excellent
wine lists and malts.

1020
7/M18
28 ROOMS
TEL · TV
£85+

Culloden House www.cullodenhouse.co.uk · 01463 790461 ·
Inverness 5km east of town near A9, follow signs for Culloden village,
not the battlefield. Hugely impressive, Georgian mansion and lawn a big green
duvet on edge of suburbia and, of course, history. Old-style, deluxe hotel near
town and airport. Lovely big bedrooms overlooking the policies. Some fab garden
suites, and elegant dining in beautifully restored room under chef Michael
Simpson. Refurbishment in progress will add 8 new suites and a splendid pool in
'08.

1021
7/M20
8 ROOMS
FEB-DEC
TEL · TV
NO PETS
£60-85

The Cross www.thecross.co.uk · 01540 661166 · **Kingussie** Off main
street at traffic lights, 200m uphill then left into glen. Tasteful hotel and
superb restaurant in converted tweed mill by river which gurgles outside most
windows. Comfy rooms, CDs; don't let the midges in! David and Katie Young,
considerate hosts, will help you get the most from the National Park area.
EAT To stay, you're expected to eat; you'd be mad not to. Open to non-
residents for what is after all these years still the best restaurant in the
region. 2 choices each course. Fixed price including all the tastery bits a steal at
£43. Fabulous wine list! Closed most Sun/Mon.

1022
7/L17
4 ROOMS
TEL · TV
NO KIDS
£60-85

£22-32

Dower House www.thedowerhouse.co.uk · 01463 870090 · **near
Muir Of Ord** On A862 between Beauly and Dingwall, 18km northwest of
Inverness and 2km north of village. Charming, personal place; you are a house
guest so best to fit in. Cottagey-style nay, stylish small country house, with comfy
public rooms. Also self-catering cottage but not adjacent. Robyn (in the kitchen)
and Mena Aitchison are consummate hosts and here a long time. Stay longer!
EAT Robyn Aitchison's cooking: simple, sophisticated. Fixed menu. Friendly
exchanges – you might end up in the kitchen.

1023
7/M18
11 ROOMS
+2 COTTAGES
TEL · TV · ECO
£60-85

Dunain Park www.dunainparkhotel.co.uk · 01463 230512 · **Inverness**
6km southwest of town on A82 Fort William road. Mansion-house just off
the road, a lived-in, civilised and old-style alternative to hotels in town for those
on business or pleasure. Some good deals out of season. Gorgeous gardens; real
countryside beyond. Notable restaurant in various cosy dining rooms with sound
Scottish menu, though the famous creamy puds have gone. Excellent wine and
malt list. Nice people who care, and enviro-friendly garden.

1024
7/N16
6 ROOMS
+3 COTTAGES
TEL · TV
NO PETS
£60-85

Glenmorangie House at Cadboll www.theglenmorangiehouse.com ·
01862 871671 · **near Fearn** South of Tain 10km east of A9. Old mansion in
open grounds overlooking the sea. Owned, like the distillery, by Louis Vuitton
Moët Hennessy so expect some luxury (though everything is understated). No
leisure facilities but no shortage of distraction around. Return to comfy rooms,
open fires and communal, house-party atmosphere. Fixed dinner round one table,
honesty bar, great service.

1025
6/J15
13 ROOMS
APR-OCT
TEL · NO KIDS
£60-85
£22-32

✓ **The Summer Isles Hotel** www.summerisleshotel.co.uk · 01854 622282 · **Achiltibuie** 40km from Ullapool with views over the isles; Stac Polly and Suilven are close by to climb. For sale at TGP so may change, but for over 20 years Mark and Gerry Irvine's famous for dining romantic retreat enduring and endearing. Adjacent pub offers similar quality food at half the price (1384/GASTROPUBS). 2 great suites and a fab crofter's cottage on the hill. **EAT** Formal dining: don't be late! Fixed (truly individual) menu, trolleys of puds and cheese: the big moment. Sunsets. Bar is great value.

✓ **The Torridon** www.lochtorridonhotel.com · 01445 791242 · **Loch Torridon near Kinlochewe** At the end of Glen Torridon in immense scenery. Highland Lodge atmosphere, big hills to climb. Now with adjacent **Torridon Inn** (inexpensive, with bar and bistro). Report: 1278/GET-AWAY HOTELS.

1026
6/N15
22 ROOMS
TEL · TV
£60-85

✓ **Royal Marine Hotel** www.royalmarinehotel.co.uk · 01408 621252 · **Golf Road, Brora** Turn-of-the-century mansionhouse by Robert Lorimer overlooking the harbour below and self-catering apartment block newly built overlooking the golf course. Ambition to be on par with great golf hotels elsewhere. Contemporary public rooms. Bedrooms vary. Spa has good pool. Restaurant in dining room and bar have the same menu though this may change.

1027
6/P12
14 ROOMS
TEL · TV
£45-60

✓ **Forss House Hotel** www.forsshousehotel.co.uk · 01847 861201 · **near Thurso** 8km west on A836. Richard's (of Ackergill Tower, 1267/HOUSE PARTIES) welcoming mansionhouse set in 20 woodland acres by the sea is the best quality hotel for miles. Popular restaurant (you should book), nearly 300 malts in the bar, comfortable spacious rooms and 6 additional rooms in the grounds too. Breakfast in the conservatory then walks, old mill and waterfall. Good fishing.

1028 9/J21
15 ROOMS
TEL · TV
NO KIDS
£60-85

✓ **Lodge On The Loch** www.lodgeontheloch.com · 01855 821237 · **Onich** The best hotel in this strip south of Fort William (16km) back in private ownership at TGP. Notable relaxed ambience, furnishings etc. Beautiful, contemporary bedrooms, many overlook loch. Open all year but Nov-Feb weekdays only. Most deals include (very good) dinner.

1029
9/J22
10 ROOMS
TEL · TV
£60-85

✓ **Holly Tree** www.hollytreehotel.co.uk · 01631 740292 · **Kentallen** On A828 Fort William (Ballachulish)–Oban rd, 8km south of Ballachulish Bridge. On road and sea and once the railway; formerly a station. A recently much improved hotel, redecorated to a high standard with fab views from bedrooms and dining room. Superb location for surf 'n' turf restaurant. Nice for kids. New pool and the jetty to the sea outside. 1219/KIDS HOTELS.

1030
7/M18
16 ROOMS
TEL · TV
£60-85

Bunchrew House www.bunchrew-inverness.co.uk · 01463 234917 · **near Inverness** On A862 Beauly rd only 5km from Inverness yet completely removed from town; on the wooded shore of the Beauly Firth. Almost completely positioned as a wedding hotel, but there may be midweek stay possible. It's an atmospheric place.

1031
7/L17
18 ROOMS
TEL · TV
£45-60

Coul House Contin www.coulhousehotel.com · 01997 421487 · **near Strathpeffer** Comfortable country-house hotel on the edge of the wilds with some elegant public rooms, particularly the refurbished octagonal dining room. Well-kept lawns. An accessible, not-too-posh country-house retreat. Traditional music on Fri in summer. Varied menu: à la carte and specials. Good vegetarian choice. Well-priced wines.

1032
7/N17
44 ROOMS
TEL · TV
£45-60

Golf View www.golfviewhotelnairn.co.uk · 01667 452301 · **Nairn** Seafront on Inverness side of town. Not so much golf, more beach view but near the famous course (2138/GREAT GOLF). Well appointed, refurbished rooms with conservatory restaurant and leisure facilities including good pool for kids. Management changes at TGP.

1033
9/J21
27 ROOMS
TEL · TV
£45-60

Onich Hotel www.onich-fortwilliam.co.uk · 01855 821214 · **Onich by Fort William** As above 16km south on main A82, one of many roadside and in this case, lochside hotels which are more attractive than those in Fort William. Onich is good value with excellent public space; some bedrooms overlook Loch Linnhe. Busy bars, grassy terrace and nice garden.

1034
6/N16

Royal Golf www.royaldornoch.com · 01862 810283 · **Dornoch** Sits on golf course near small town square. New ownership under Peter de Savery and complete overhaul at TGP. Savery created Skibo (now The Carnegie Club; 1239/GET-AWAY HOTELS) so expect top-notch guests (Madonna got married in Dornoch) among many golfers.

✓✓ **Ackergill Tower** 01955 603556 · **near Wick** Report: 1343/HOUSE PARTIES.

✓✓ **House Over-By** 01470 571258 · **Skye** Report: 2373/SKYE HOTELS.

✓ **Eilean Iarmain** 01470 833332 · **Skye** Report: 2375/SKYE HOTELS.

✓ **Kinloch Lodge** 01470 833333 · **Skye** Report: 2374/SKYE HOTELS.

✓ **Scarista House** 01859 550238 · **South Harris** Report: 2391/ISLAND HOTELS.

RESTAURANTS

✓✓ **Three Chimneys** www.threechimneys.co.uk · **Skye** · 01470 511258 Report: 2398/SKYE RESTAURANTS.

1035 6/N16
£22-32

✓ **2 Quail Restaurant** www.2quail.com · 01862 811811 · **Castle Street, Dornoch** Unassuming townhouse on road into centre conceals best restaurant northeast of Inverness. Tiny rooms (lounge and library/dining room). 4 tables so book! 4-course fixed menu; personally selected and much-loved wine list: lovely wines! The Carrs do everything to make you feel comfortable. Rooms above (1040/LESS EXPENSIVE HOTELS). Dinner only Tue-Sat. Must book.

1036 8/P18
£22-32

✓ **The Glass House** www.theglasshouse-grantown.co.uk · 01479 872980 · **Grant Road, Grantown On Spey** Parallel to Main St. Welcome dining destination by proprietor/chef Stephen Robertson with loyal local clientele. Built with conservatory, the light is nice. Aviemore environs has a good restaurant at last. No-nonsense Mod Brit menu. Closed Sun evening & Mon/Tue lunch.

Best Restaurants In Inverness see pp. 206–08, especially:
Abstract At Glenmoriston Hotel 01463 223777 · **Ness Bank**
Rocpool 01463 717274 · **Ness Walk** Corner of main bridge.
Café One 01463 226200 · **Castle Street**

Good Less Expensive Hotels In The Highlands

1037
6/K15
11 ROOMS
+ BUNKS
TEL
£60-85

✓✓ **The Ceilidh Place** www.ceilidhplace.com · 01854 612103 · **Ullapool** Jean Urquhart's oasis of hospitality, craic and culture in the Highlands. What started out in the 1970s as a coffee/exhibition shop in a boat shed, has spread along this row of cottages now comprising a restaurant, bookshop, café/bar (and performance) area, and bedrooms upstairs. In winter food is served in front of the roaring fire in the Parlour Bar. Bunkhouse across the road offers cheaper accommodation: stay 'luxuriously rough'. Live music and events throughout the year, or you can simply sit in the lounge upstairs with honesty bar or on the terrace overlooking Ullapool. We come back!

£22-32

EAT Restaurant and coffee shop/bistro 8am-LO 9pm. Folk say food can vary but nowhere else in these Highlands has the atmosphere or the integrity.

1038 5/M20
5 ROOMS
+ FLAT
GAY FRIENDLY
TV
£45-60

✓ **Coig na Shee** www.coignashee.co.uk · 01540 670109 · **Newtonmore** Road out of Newtonmore (which is just off the A9) for Fort William. Mansion house with light, contemporary feel and furnishings. Near where they filmed *Monarch of the Glen* and some of the principals stayed here (one of them wrote to me about this 'stunning' guesthouse). B&B only. Friendly new proprietors from last edition. Once you've been you become one of theirs! Exceptional value.

1039
8/N19
32 ROOMS
TEL · TV
£38-45

✓ **Boat Hotel** www.boathotel.co.uk · 01479 831258 · **Boat of Garten** Centre of village overlooking the steam train line and golf course (2153/GOOD GOLF). Great old-style (Victorian/1920s) hotel in rolling refurbishment at TGP (big difference in old and new rooms) and good restaurant, The Capercaillie, which has 2 AA rosettes. Bar the locals use and hotel bar with good bar meals. Pub at the side is a very different local world.

1040 6/N16
3 RMS · TEL
TV · NO KIDS
NO PETS
£38-45

✓ **2 Quail** www.2quail.com · 01862 811811 · **Castle Street, Dornoch** As you arrive from south. Rooms above restaurant (1035/HIGHLAND RESTAURANTS), only 3 but every bit as much detail and elegance as the food below. The Carrs run a tight but small, elegant ship.
EAT Report: 1035/BEST RESTAURANTS.

1041
9/J20
13 ROOMS
MAR-NOV
£38-85

✓ **Glenfinnan House Hotel** www.glenfinnanhouse.com · 01397 722235 · **Glenfinnan** Victorian mansion with lawns down to Loch Shiel and the Glenfinnan Monument over the water. No shortbread-tin twee or tartan carpet here; instead a warm welcome from the MacFarlanes and managers the Gibsons (everything just gets better here). Refurbished bar has not lost its great atmosphere. A cruise on this stunning loch (01687 470322) or row boat at the foot of the lawn! Great for kids. More rooms '08. 1321/SCOTTISH HOTELS.

1042
7/L19
30 ROOMS
TEL · TV
£45-60

✓ **Lovat Arms** 0845 450 1100 · **Fort Augustus** On edge of town, the road south to Fort William. Refurbished by the Rose-Bristow family who brought us Torridon (1278/GET-AWAY HOTELS), into a contemporary, comfortable roadside hotel, unquestionably the best option hereabouts. Bar meals, private dining and a light breakfast room. One bedroom set aside for dog owners.

1043
9/K20
4 ROOMS
MAR-OCT
TV · NO PETS
£30-38

✓ **Corriechoille Lodge** www.corriechoille.com · 01397 712002 · **by Spean Bridge** 4 (riverside) km out of Spean Bridge on the small road by the station. Justin and Lucy Swabey's hideaway house facing the mountains. Beautiful corner of the country with spectacular views towards the Grey Corries and Aonach Mor. Lovely dinner, cosy rooms. 2 turf-roofed self-catering chalets over by. Great walks begin here. Also 1286/GET-AWAY HOTELS.

1044 9/K21 ✓ **Lime Tree Studios** 01397 701806 · **Achintore Road, Fort William** At
9 ROOMS the roundabout as you come from the south. Regional and local art gallery
£45-60 with rooms above and good restaurant – fills all the gaps in Fort William. Simple,
contemporary, convivial atmosphere. Cool spot! Some excellent exhibitions.

1045 6/P15 ✓ **Bridge Hotel** 01431 821100 · **Dunrobin Street, Helmsdale** End of the
19 ROOMS main street and along from the Mirage (1270/INEXPENSIVE HIGHLAND RESTAU-
TEL · TV RANTS). Recent refurbishment has transformed this edifice into a comfortable,
£38-45 contemporary take on a Highland shooting lodge without being twee. Flagstones
throughout and antlertastic (there are more deer here than in your average glen
and in museum-like diversity). Spacious public rooms and cosy bar (though locals
mainly stay away). Lorraine Dunnett your capable host. Great value.

1046 9/K20 ✓ **Old Pines** www.oldpines.co.uk · 01397 712324 · **near Spean Bridge**
8 ROOMS 3km Spean Bridge via B8004 for Garlochy at Commando Monument. Open-
TEL · TV plan pine cabin with log fires, neat bedrooms and a huge polytunnel (where bits of
NO PETS your dinner come from). A very comfy, unpretentious hotel with great food; excel-
£38-45 lent for kids.

✓ **Mackays** www.visitmackays.com · 01971 511202 · **Durness** An unlikely
restaurant with rooms in the North. Report: 1284/GET AWAY HOTELS.

1047 7/K20 **Glengarry Castle** www.glengarry.net · 01809 501254 · **Invergarry** A
26 ROOMS family-run hotel in the Highlands for almost 50 years, in the charge of the
MAR-NOV younger MacCallums. Rhodies, honeysuckle as you walk to the loch. Magnificent
TEL · TV trees and a ruined castle in the grounds the stronghold of the Macdonells: you
£45-60 may remember the famous portrait by Raeburn – the epitome of the fashionable
Highland chief. Romantic in every way. Big rooms.

1048 7/H18 **The Plockton Inn** www.plocktoninn.com · 01599 544222 · **Plockton** Neat
14 ROOMS village inn and seafood restaurant in neat little seaside village (1636/COASTAL
TEL · TV VILLAGES). Some good cask ale in bar. Simple, quiet tasteful rooms. Bar and bistro,
£38-45 mainly seafood. Tables on terrace in summer, back garden for kids. 7 rooms in
hotel and 7 more in contemporary annex over the street.

1049 7/H18 **The Plockton Hotel** www.plocktonhotel.com · 01599 544274 · **Plockton.**
15 ROOMS Another Plockton hotel to recommend, this by the water's edge. Busier, buzzier;
TEL · TV pub and pub meals seem always packed. Maybe noisy weekends (1262/INNS).
£45-60 Rooms nice (4 in separate cottage).

1050 7/N19 **Cairngorm Hotel** 01479 810233 · **Aviemore** On main street in Aviemore
31 ROOMS where the Macdonald Hotel Resort holds sway. Not exceptional in any way but a
TEL · TV rather pleasant place to base as we did '07 for the Outsider Festival (48/EVENTS).
£38-45 Station-type hotel so rooms vary. Friendly folk. Food so-so, bar full-on with live
music most nights. We were happy here.

1051 7/J17 **Old Mill Highland Lodge** www.oldmillhighlandlodge.co.uk · 01445
6 ROOMS 760271 · **Loch Maree** On A832 15km north of Kinlochewe, the road that follows
MAR-OCT · TEL Loch Maree. Across road from loch in woody, as they say, Highland situation. The
TV · NO KIDS Byrne family house/guesthouse; 3 rooms in newer section are more uniform. Deal
NO PETS includes dinner which comes highly recommended by readers. Many pine martens
NO C/ CARDS come to the kitchen.
£30-38

1052 6/N16
24 ROOMS
TEL · TV
£45-85+

Dornoch Castle Hotel 01862 810216 · Dornoch Main street of delightful northern town with nice beaches, great golf and a cathedral made famous by the new Madonna (rather than the original). Very castle-like, up-and-down building where rooms vary hugely (as do prices: £50-£250 at TGP). Garden Restaurant (ground floor and yes, on the garden) gathering accolades in '07. Joanna Blythman gave it 8.5 out of 10 though methinks this was very generous. Some atmosphere.

1053 6/M13
19 ROOMS
APR-OCT
TEL · TV
£45-60

Tongue Hotel www.tonguehotel.co.uk · 01847 611206 · Tongue One of 2 hotels in Tongue at the centre of the North Coast where Ben Loyal presides. This the most presentable though a little more expensive. Nicely turned-out rooms. Same menu bar and dining room. Very Highland. Other hotel, the Ben Loyal: front rooms best.

1054 7/H17
11 ROOMS
APR-OCT
£60-85

Tigh-an-Eilean 01520 755251 · Shieldaig Lovely freshly furnished hotel on waterfront overlook Scots Pine island on loch. The Fields run a pleasant house – the locale has that serene otherness. Chris is a folk-buff so possibly music in the adjacent pub. Dinner or seafood supper in bar. The view remains fab, like a Colin Baxter postcard.

1055 7/M17
9 ROOMS
TV
£38-45

The Anderson www.theanderson.co.uk · 01381 620236 · Fortrose Main street of town in the middle of the Black Isle. Restaurant, bar and reasonable rooms in very individual hotel notable for an extraordinary whisky collection. **EAT** Along with the whisky and the speciality beers, the pub-grub food here is a cut above the usual. Joanna Blythman raved; so do locals. Best book.

1056 7/L18
28 ROOMS
TEL · TV
£38-45

Lovat Arms www.lovatarms.com · 01463 782313 · Beauly Best hotel of many in main street of market town 20km from Inverness. Relaxed, welcoming family-run hotel with good bar meals and comfy public rooms. Much tartan upstairs. Locals also recommend the Priory for bar meals.

1057 7/K18
8 ROOMS
TEL · TV
£38-45

Tomich Hotel www.tomichhotel.co.uk · 01456 415399 · Tomich near Drumnadrochit The inn of a quiet conservation village, part of an old estate on the edge of Guisachan Forest. Near fantastic Plodda Falls (1683/WATERFALLS) and Glen Affric (1671/GLENS). Rooms pleasant and cosy. Use of pool nearby in farm steading (9am-9pm); especially good for fishing holidays. 25km drive from Drumnadrochit by A831. Nice bar, though fewer locals these days.

FIVE GREAT HIGHLAND B&Bs

1058 7/G19
3 ROOMS
£30-38

✓ **Tigh An Dochais 01471 820022 · Broadford, Skye** Signed and on the road coming into Broadford from the south (the bridge and ferries). Stunning contemporary building by award-winning architects Dualchas, this long, light house makes the most of its location. Bedrooms open out to and practically merge with the beach. Breakfast in upstairs lounge; bread home made, etc. A superb introduction to Skye.

1059 6/J16
3 ROOMS
MAR-OCT
TV · NO KIDS
NO C/ CARDS
£45-60

The Old Smiddy www.oldsmiddyguesthouse.co.uk · 01445 731696 · Laide This book doesn't feature many B&Bs, but readers' letters sent us here and elsewhere on this page. Landlady Julie Clements keeps the place on the map (Gruinard Bay, Wester Ross on the A832). She's a fine cook and does serious dinners (book then BYOB) including non-residents'.

1060 6/K15
3 ROOMS
TV
NO C/CARDS
£38-45

Tanglewood House www.tanglewoodhouse.co.uk · 01854 612059 · **Ullapool** Just outside town on A835 south overlook Loch Broom. Family guesthouse very personally run by Anne Holloway who reckons she serves the best dinner to be had in Ullapool. It is available to non-residents. BYOB. Dining and all rooms have great view.

1061 6/K13
3 ROOMS
NO KIDS
NO PETS
£30-38

Scourie Guest House 01971 502396 · **Scourie** I must admit I haven't been to this guesthouse on the far northwest corner north of Lochinver, but people say it's a good 'un and the owners (the Stephens) apparently have been avid followers of *StB* since the first edition. Hence I must conclude that this guesthouse and coffee shop will be worth trying. Reports please.

1062 6/K15
3 ROOMS
£45-60

Braemore Square 01854 655357 · **near Loch Broom & Ullapool** On the main A835 Inverness-Ullapool road about 20km south of Ullapool close to Corrieshalloch Gorge (1690/WATERFALLS). Extensive B&B and self-catering operation in rambling, superbly renovated house around the said square. 2 lounges and conservatory for guests; and kitchen. Excellent breakfast includes own eggs, home-made bread, kippers or the full monty. Ed and Wendy Hughes have excelled themselves here. Aspiring landladies go look!

Good Inexpensive Restaurants In The Highlands

1063 9/H22
£22-32

✓**Whitehouse** www.thewhitehouserestaurant.co.uk · 01967 421777 · **Lochaline, Ardnamurchan** Sits above the ferry port as the boats come in from Mull, a restaurant adjacent the village shop with all the right/best principles: local produce, organic, simple and slow cooking means you may wait but apart from the ferry, where are you going, anyway? Ingredients from Mull and Lochaber – the bay, the woods and the hedgerow. Quiet days in Ardnamurchan then dinner here. Perfect! Apr-Dec. 11.30am-afternoon tea-dinner LO 9.30pm. Closed Mon.

1064 7/H18
£15-22

✓**The Potting Shed** 01520 744440 · **Applecross** In north Applecross along the strand at the back of a gorgeous walled garden. 6 years in restoration after 50 years of neglect – you enter via a pergola of roses (in summer). A destination coffee shop/restaurant like the Inn (1285/GET-AWAY HOTELS) putting Applecross on the map. Everything home made and often from the garden. Full menu lunch and dinner and excellent cakes.

1065 8/P17
£15-22

✓**The Bakehouse** 01309 691826 · **Findhorn** Follow the one-way system round end-of-the-road village and you can't miss it. Same people who have the Phoenix Stores in the Findhorn Community (1532/DELIS, 1325/RETREATS), this is a brilliant new coffee shop/restaurant where you eat ethically and really well. Home made/home grown/organic naturally and part of the slow-food movement so all individually prepared. A new destination in the North. 7 days. 10am-9pm. Closes 6pm Sun/Mon.

1066 7/H18
£15-22

✓**Plockton Shores** 01599 544263 · **Plockton** Recently arrived on the foreshore of lovely little Plockton, an all-purpose eaterie with fine home cooking making the most of location and hinterland (for ingredients). Breakfast, lunch and dinner (LO 9pm). Decent vegetarian choice.

1067 5/M17
£15-22

✓**Sutor Creek** www.sutorcreek.co.uk · 01381 600855 · **21 Bank Street, Cromarty** Near the seafront. From an idea of local worthy and man of the peoples' TV, Don Coutts, an end-of-the-road diner that's there when you need it most (in lovely little Cromarty – 1639/COASTAL VILLAGES). Wood-fired oven turning out great crispy pizza and more; many specials. Great craic. Wed-Sun. LO 9/10pm.

1068 7/H18
£22-32

✓ **The Seafood Restaurant** www.theseafoodrestaurant.com · 01599 534813 · **Kyle of Lochalsh** Great atmospheric bistro near (and still an actual station platform) the busy port, off the road to Skye and with that bridge in the distance. Seafood from Kyle/Mallaig/Skye ie very local, and vegetarian selection. Closed for '07 season. Expected to open '08. Phone to book and check hours.

1069 7/H18
£15-22

✓ **The Seafood Restaurant** www.theseafoodrestaurant.com · 01599 544423 · **Plockton** Same folk as above and once again on the platform of a working railway station. No droopy sandwiches here, just good home cooking. Snacks in the day then blackboard specials and evening menu later. 10am-9.30pm in summer. Weekends only in winter. Brilliant faraway-bistro atmosphere. Take the trail or the train! (Also 1636/COASTAL VILLAGES).

1070 6/P15
£15-22

✓ **La Mirage** www.lamirage.org · 01431 821615 · **Dunrobin Street, Helmsdale** Near the Bridge Hotel. A bright little gem in the Sutherland straths and a homage to Barbara Cartland, the romantic novelist, who once lived near in this wee village by the sea. Snacks of every kind all day; with life-size photos of the once-proprietor Nancy Sinclair and various celebs gracing the walls. Now owned by the Wakefields but Nancy's family still in the kitchen and out front. Great fish and chips. All year 11am-9pm.

1071 9/K20

✓ **Russell's @ Smiddy House** www.smiddyhouse.co.uk · 01397 712335 · **Spean Bridge** Near junction of A82 for Skye on A86 for Laggan, a guesthouse more a restaurant with rooms. Good, unpretentious fare all home made. Hugely popular so best to book. A tick overdue here as readers attest. Afternoon tea in light lounge with great choice of teas and tier of tea things; looks nice. 7 days in summer, lunch & LO 9.30pm. Wed-Sun winter.

1072 6/K14
£15-22

✓ **Kylesku Hotel** www.kyleskuhotel.co.uk · 01971 502231 · **near Kylestrome** On A894; tucked down beside Loch Glencoul where the boat leaves to see Britain's 'highest waterfall' (1688/WATERFALLS). Small quayside pub/hotel (8 rooms) serving great seafood in seafood setting with mighty Quinag behind (2023/HILLS). 12noon-9pm all year (see also 1394/GASTROPUBS).

1073 5/N19
£15-22

The Einich www.rothiemurchus.net/einich.html · 01479 812334 · **Coylumbridge** Discreetly lodged in the Rothiemurchus visitor centre on the A951 Cairngorm road 5km Aviemore. Nice old room doing daytime snacks and specials and dinner weekends. Best choice in the Coylumbridge ski zone. 7 days 9.30am-5pm, dinner Wed-Sat LO 9pm.

1074 7/N19
£15 OR LESS

The Boathouse www.kincraig.com · 01540 651394 · **Kincraig** 2km from village towards Feshiebridge along Loch Insh. Part of Loch Insh Water sports (2213/WATER SPORTS), a balcony restaurant overlook beach and loch. Fine setting and ambiance, friendly young staff (but they come and go). Some vegetarian. Salmon from the loch; you're in competition with the ospreys. Bar menu and home baking till 6pm; supper till 9pm, bar 11pm. Apr-Oct. Check winter hours.

1075 6/L15
£15-22

Carron Restaurant www.carron-restaurant.co.uk · 01520 722488 · **Strathcarron** On A890 road round Loch Carron (joins A87 Kyle of Lochalsh road) just south of Strathcarron. Peter and Michelle Teago's roadside diner and grill a destination in these parts. Local seafood, good reputation for steaks, home-made bread, puds etc. All-day menu. Apr-Nov, 10.30am-9pm. Closed Sun.

1076 **7/N17** **The Classroom** www.visitnairn.com · 01667 455999 · **Cawdor Street, Nairn** At top end of main shopping street – ask directions. Ambitious, stylish makeover in this conservative, golfy town. Contemporary bar/ restaurant menu. Lunch & LO 9.30pm. Nice room. 7 days.
Nearby at 10 High St a new bistro '07, **The Kist** (01667 459412), has a good reputation, and next door the **Victoria Tearoom** offers the Nairn ladies somewhere to take cake.

1077 **6/J14** **Riverside Bistro** www.piesbypost.co.uk · 01571 844356 · **Lochinver** On
£22-32 way into town on A837. Self-serve during day; vast array of Ian Stewart's home-made pies and calorific cakes. The banoffi pie is truly wicked. You can eat in or take away. Conservatories out front and back. Bistro on riverside serves very popular meals at night; using local seafood, venison, vegetarian – something for everyone including, apparently, Michael Winner (though don't let that put you off). Food 10am-8pm although bistro menu kicks in evening, LO 8.30pm.
The **Caberfeidh** pub (01571 844391) next door has new owners and their pub grub, all home made and locally sourced, offers a new Lochinver alternative.

1078 **7/M16** **The Oystercatcher** www.the-oystercatcher.co.uk · 01862 871560 ·
£15 OR LESS **Portmahomack** On promontory of the Dornoch Firth (Tain 15km) this hidden seaside village (the only East Coast village that faces west) could bring back childhood memories. Restaurant (more a caff during the day – they switch rooms) is a destination in itself. The wine list and malt choice are truly extraordinary. Food is inventive, multi-ingredient, somewhat rich, but always interesting. Michael Winner was here too! Café dining, lunch & dinner 6.15pm (LO 9.30pm). Closed Nov-Feb & Mon/Tue. Dinner: best book.

1079 **6/K15** **The Arch Inn** 01854 612836 · **West Shore Street, Ullapool** West from ferry
£15-22 terminal. Pub by the water, mentioned mainly because it's hard to find anywhere in Ullapool. Dinner only Tue-Sat. LO 9pm.

1080 **6/H16** **Blueprint Café** www.blueprintgairloch.com · 01445 712397 · **Gairloch**
£15-22 Main part of strung-out village opposite Mountain Restaurant (daytime only, see 1414/VEGETARIAN). Contemporary café/restaurant with mixed menu including ok pizza, pasta and specials. 'Café' LO 4pm, evening menu LO 8.45pm. Closed Mon. Takeaway chip shop next door is separate.

1081 **6/M15** **Falls of Shin Visitor Centre** www.fallsofshin.co.uk Self-serve café/
restaurant in visitor centre and shop across road from Falls of Shin on the Achany Glen road 8km south of Lairg (1697/WATERFALLS). Excellent home-made food better than it probably has to be in an unlikely emporium of Harrods (Mohammed al Fayed's Highland estate is here). Somebody in that kitchen cooks like your mum. 9.30am-6pm; winter 10am-5pm. Food LO 4.30pm.

1082 **7/M16** **Carnegie Lodge** 01862 894039 · **Tain** At 'top' of the town signed from A9 (ring road). It's a Tain thing, but the Wynes sold Morangie House and moved over here, quickly building the reputation they had for food (inexpensive). Motel-type rooms on edge of town and easy dining. bed value.

Good Inexpensive Restaurants In Inverness: see p. 206–08, especially:
La Tortilla Asesina **Castle Street** 1169/INVERNESS RESTAURANTS.
River Café **Bank Street** 1166/INVERNESS RESTAURANTS.
Castle Restaurant **Castle Street** The legendary caff. 1458/CAFÉS.
Girvans Top-quality caff. 1459/CAFÉS.

Other Inexpensive Restaurants in the North
Lochbay Seafood Skye 1424/SEAFOOD RESTAURANTS.
Thai Café Stornoway 2427/OUTER HEBRIDES.
Tigh Mealros Lewis 2427/OUTER HEBRIDES.
Applecross Inn Applecross 1285/GET-AWAY HOTELS.
Glenelg Inn Glenelg 1253/INNS.
Crannog At The Waterfront Fort William 1431/SEAFOOD RESTAURANTS.

If you're in Fort William...

1083 9/K21 ## WHERE TO STAY

✓ ✓ **Inverlochy Castle** 01397 702177 5km out on A82 Inverness road. In the forefront of hotels in Scotland. Victorian elegance, classically stylish and impeccable service. 1015/HIGHLANDS HOTELS.

9 ROOMS
TEL
£30-38

✓ **Lime Tree Studios** www.limetreefortwilliam.co.uk · 01397 701806 Achintore road as you come in along the loch from south, last 'hotel' of many almost at end of main street. Effortlessly became *the* place in Fort William '07, combining regional art-gallery space with rooms above and a bar/restaurant with open kitchen and terrace. David Wilson (whose art is on the walls) and Charlotte Wright have given Fort William just what it needs; let's hope there's more to follow for the self-appointed 'Outdoor Capital of the UK'. National art exhibitions stop here – so should you.

4 ROOMS
MAR-NOV
TV · NO KIDS
NO PETS
£45-60

✓ **The Grange** www.thegrange-scotland.co.uk · 01397 705516 · Grange Road Overlooks the loch and the main road south. Joan and John Campbell have been running a top, contemporary B&B in bereft Fort William for years. Discreet, almost suburban house but great views from garden terrace and lovely rooms. They don't do dinner.

29 ROOMS
TEL · TV
£38-45

The Moorings www.moorings-fortwilliam.co.uk · 01397 772797 · Banavie 5km out on A830 Corpach/Mallaig by the Caledonian canal by 'Neptune's Staircase' (some rooms overlook). Good location, pub dining best. Serviceable enough.

20 ROOMS
NO KIDS
NO PETS
£30-38

The Underwater Centre 01397 703786 On the north Lochside near Morrisons supermarket etc. Rooms for the dive school but inexpensive and serviceable. Like a chain lodge thing without the chain. Loch views (ish!).

Lodge On The Loch 01855 821237 · Onich Quite stylish peace and quiet in Onich. Rooms to high standard. 1028/HIGHLAND HOTELS.

Onich Hotel 01855 821214 · Onich 16km south on A82. Lochside; good value. 1033/HIGHLANDS HOTELS.

S.Y. Hostel 0870 004 1120 · Glen Nevis 5km from Fort William by picturesque but busy Glen Nevis road. The Ben is above. Grade 1. Fax possible. Many other hostels in area (ask for list at tourist information centre) but especially **FW Backpackers** 01397 700711 · Alma Road.

Achintee Farm 01397 702240 On approach to Ben Nevis main route and adjacent Ben Nevis Inn (see below). Guesthouse/self catering and bunkhouse. A walkers' haven.

Camping/Caravan Site 01397 702191 · **Glen Nevis** Near hostel. Well-run site, mainly caravans (also for rent). Many facilities including restaurants.

WHERE TO EAT

✓ ✓ **Inverlochy** (as above) Compared with the rest, think Ben Nevis.

✓ **Crannog At The Waterfront aka The Seafood Restaurant**
www.oceanandoak.co.uk · 01397 705589 Finlay Finlayson's landmark restaurant on the waterfront (others may follow one day), long established as the best meal in town. Freshly caught seafood mainly (one meat/one vegetarian) in informal bistro setting. All year. 7 days. Lunch & LO 9pm.

✓ **Lime Tree Restaurant** 01397 701806 · **Cameron Square** Achintore Rd at roundabout as you arrive from south, or at the south end of the main street. Restaurant of boutiquey hotel (see above) with good atmosphere, open kitchen and terrace. 4 starters/mains/desserts. Scottish cheeses, neat wine list. It's where to go. Lunch & LO 9pm.

£22-32 **No 4** www.no4-fortwilliam.co.uk · 01397 704222 · **Cameron Square** Behind the tourist information centre. Best bet in main street area though mixed reviews. À la carte and daily specials. Lunch and LO 9.30pm.

£15-22 **Café Beag** 01397 703601 · **Glen Nevis** 5km along Glen Nevis road; past visitor centre. Alpine-looking cabin, ok atmosphere; open fires, books. Restaurant, bar and coffee stop. (Probably) till 5pm. Closed Sep-Mar.

£15-22 **Café 115** 01397 702500 Average caff in average main st. Possibly new owners at TGP but currently the best bet for home-made light meals and coffee and cake. 7 days LO 9.30pm.

Ben Nevis Inn www.ben-nevis-inn.co.uk · **Achintee** On main approach to the Ben itself. Reach across river by footbridge from visitor centre or by road on right after Inverlochy/Glen Nevis roundabout on A82 (3km). Excellent atmosphere inn in converted farm building. Good grub/ale and walking chat. LO 9pm. Weekends only in winter.

The Moorings www.moorings-fortwilliam.co.uk · 01397 772797 · **Banavie** 5km by A830 (see above). Pub best.

Tourist Office 01397 701801 · **Cameron Square, Fort William** Open all year.

If you're around Wick & Thurso...

WHERE TO STAY

22 ROOMS
TEL · TV
£38-45

✓ **Portland Arms** 01593 721721 · **Lybster** On main A9 20km south of Wick and 45km south of Thurso by A895. A coaching inn since 1851; still hospitable though recently swallowed like so many hotels in the North, by a chain, then another. Small rooms are a bit, well, small but this is a homely hotel with decent food in a choice of settings. Log fires. Feels part of the community. While in Lybster, pop down and see Waterlines (nice restoration, poignant story).

9 ROOMS
JAN-OCT
TEL · TV
£38-45

Borgie Lodge Hotel www.borgielodge.co.uk · 01641 521332 · **near Bettyhill** A836 12km east of Tongue. Secluded traditional huntin', shootin', fishin' sort of a place: 20 hill lochs and 2 rivers with salmon and trout. Shooting on the adjacent 12,000 acre estate (courtesy of the Countess of Sutherland) but bird watching, walking and just escaping for the rest of us. Family-run, and families and their pets welcome.

41 ROOMS
TEL · TV
£38-45

Pentland Hotel www.pentlandhotel.co.uk · 01847 893202 · **Princes Street, Thurso** Near centre. Not the most wonderful but the most wonderful of what's on offer. Public rooms are fine including No 23, a café-bar with Caithness flagstone floor that's a pleasure to eat and drink in. Rooms vary.

6 ROOMS
TEL · TV
NO PETS
£30 OR LESS

Quayside B&B www.quaysidewick.fsnet.co.uk · 01955 603229 · **25 Harbour Quay, Wick** Brenda Turner's great little establishment, right on the harbour across from the boats. Basic, economical and friendly – with parking and summer barbies in the back yard.

Forss House www.forsshousehotel.co.uk · 01847 861201 · **near Thurso** 8km west to Tongue off A836. Best in the North West. 1027/HIGHLAND HOTELS.

Ackergill Tower 01955 603556 · **near Wick** A rare treat. 1343/HOUSE PARTIES.

S.Y. Hostel 0870 004119 · **Canisbay** John o' Groats (7km). Wick 25km. Regular bus service. The furthest-flung youth hostel on the mainland. Thurso has **Sandra's** at 24-26 Princes Street (01847 894575). Cheap 'n' cheerful with snack bar adjacent.

WHERE TO EAT

£15-22

✓✓ **Captain's Galley** www.captainsgalley.co.uk · 01847 894999 · **Scrabster** The best on this coast. Seafood with simplicity and integrity. Report: 1416/SEAFOOD RESTAURANTS.

✓ **Forss House Hotel, Portland Arms, Borgie Lodge Hotel** All as above, Where to Stay.

£15-22

✓ **La Mirage** **Helmsdale** 60km south so a fair drive, but Viva Las Vegas! (1070/INEXPENSIVE HIGHLAND RESTAURANTS).

£15-22

The Ferry Inn www.ferryinnscrabster.co.uk · 01847 892814 · **Scrabster** 3km west of Thurso in busy port area overlooking BP and ferry terminal for Orkney. Near Captain's (above). Surf but mainly turf and all-round family fare. 7 days. Lunch & 6-9pm.

£22-32 **Bord de L'Eau** www.caithness.org · 01955 604400 · **Market Street, Wick**
By the bridge, very much on the waterside. Passably French bistro (menu in
French as well as English) where locals might go for big night out, though not a lot
of atmosphere. Lunch Tue-Sat, dinner Tue-Sun.

The Tempest Café 01847 892500 · **Thurso** On harbour adjacent Tempest Surf
shop (2235/SURF). Laid-back, surfee, kind of waiting on the wave place. Nice
home-made soup, butties, cakes etc. LO 4.30pm. Closed Mon.

Tourist Offices 01847 893155 · **Whitechapel Road, Wick** Open all year.
Riverside, Thurso Apr-Oct.

The Best Places To Stay In & Around Aberdeen

✓✓ **Marcliffe of Pitfodels** www.marcliffe.com · 01224 861000 · **North Deeside Road** (en route to Royal Deeside 5km from Union St). Aberdeen's premiere hotel: nothing else is remotely close for comfort and service (though a Malmaison coming '08). Report: 985/NORTHEAST HOTELS.

1085 8/T19
7 ROOMS
TEL · TV
NO KIDS
NO PETS
£30 OR LESS

✓ **The Globe Inn** www.travelodge.co.uk · 01224 624258 · **15 Silver Street** Rooms above the Globe pub, the civilised pub in a street off Union St (1078/ABERDEEN PUBS). Pub has good reputation for ales, food (and does live music Tue and weekends, so no early to bed). The recently created accommodation is cheap, very serviceable and purposefully good value. Since good value and individuality are hard to find in Aberdeen, this place gets booked far ahead.

1086 8/S20
40 ROOMS
TEL · TV
NO PETS
£60-85

Maryculter House Hotel www.maryculterhousehotel.com · 01224 732124 · **Maryculter** Out of town, 7km further on than Ardoe (below). Excellent setting on banks of Dee: riverside walks and an old graveyard and ruined chapel. Newer annex; rooms overlook river. Poacher's Bar is special, dining room not. Many weddings, so be prepared if over weekend. Hotel on site of 13th-century preceptory.

1087 8/S20
110 ROOMS
TEL · TV
£85+

Ardoe House www.mercure-uk.com · 0870 194 2104 · **Blairs** 12km southwest of centre on South Deeside (possible to turn off the A92 from Stonehaven and the south at the first bridge and get to the hotel avoiding the city). The Dee is nearby on other side of road from hotel. A granite chunk of Scottish Baronial with few, but more individual (they call them 'feature') rooms and an annex where most rooms are featureless but have pleasant country views. Restaurant gets 2 AA rosettes. Leisure facilities adjacent corporate but all-round, reliable biz hotel.

1088 8/T19
49 ROOMS
TEL · TV
NO PETS
£60-85+

The Carmelite 01224 589101 Aberdeen's 'design' or 'boutique' hotel (well, until the arrival of Malmaison in '08). Very central in the quarter 'below' Union St near the Port. 3 types of room, all very modern. Most have good light, including bathrooms. Suites themed. Bar and restaurant. Not as smart as they'd probably like to be (and you'd like them to be) at this price.

1089 8/T19
168 ROOMS
TEL · TV
£60-85+

The Patio Hotel www.patiohotels.com · 01224 633339 · **Beach Boulevard** Accommodation in the Beach pleasure zone, slightly apart from both the dire mall-type development and the beautiful long seafront that it dominates. Serviceable biz hotel wins no architectural plaudits from the outside, but is comfortable and contemporary in its inner courtyard. Lightsome though older bedrooms have curiously wee windows. Own pool etc. Not far to Silver Darling for dinner (1109/ABERDEEN RESTAURANTS).

1090 8/T19
77 ROOMS
TEL · TV
£85+

Thistle Caledonian Hotel www.thistlehotels.com · 01224 640233 · **Union Terrace** Victorian edifice, one of 3 Thistles in the city. Of several city centre hotels just off Union St, this always somehow seems the easiest to deal with; the most likely to be calm and efficient. Dining room and on-street bar/brasserie. Some nice suites overlooking the gardens.

1091 8/T19
50 ROOMS
TEL · TV
NO PETS
£45-85+

Simpson's Hotel www.simpsonshotel.co.uk · 01224 327777 · **59 Queen's Road** Very late 90s hotel (peach and turquoise throughout) tries hard to please. Huge bar and brasserie/restaurant adjacent is hugely popular: they say it 'evokes a Roman bath house'. 'Classic', 'Executive' rooms and suites vary in size but not decor. Some people will probably like all this; take your sunglasses. The opening of a Malmaison 2 doors down in '08 will probably take the shine off the 'glamour'.

1092 8/T19
34 ROOMS
TEL · TV
NO PETS
£38-85

Atholl Hotel www.atholl-aberdeen.com · 01224 323505 · 54 King's Gate On a busy road in west towards Hazelhead. An Aberdeen stalwart, the sort of place you sort out for your rellies and join them for dinner or a bar meal. I've never stayed, but people say this is the best among many mansions. The Atholl people say it's 'in a class of its own'.

1093 8/T19
65 ROOMS
TEL · TV
£30-38

The Brentwood Hotel www.brentwood-hotel.co.uk · 01224 595440 · 101 Crown Street In an area of many hotels and guesthouses to the south of Union St, this one's somewhat garish though flower-covered appearance belies a surprisingly commodious hostelry that is a better prospect than most. An adequate business hotel on a budget. Close to Union St and bars/restaurants. Bar meals in subterranean 'Carriages' recommended; the ale is real.

1094 8/T19
155 ROOMS
TEL · TV
NO PETS
£38-45

Express by Holiday Inn www.hieaberdeen.co.uk · 01224 623500 · Chapel Street In the middle of West End nightlife zone. The title's a mouthful – what they mean is a better than average bedbox in a central location for, say, urban weekend breakers. Contemporary and convenient. You'd eat out (there's plenty to choose from) and there's the legendary all-night bakery opposite.

1095 8/T19

Hostels SYHA www.syha.org.uk · 8 Queen's Road On an arterial road to west. Grade 1 hostel 2km from centre (plenty buses). No café. Rooms mainly for 4-6 people. You can stay out till 2am. Other hostels and self-catering flats c/o University, of which the best is the **Robert Gordon** (01224 262134). Campus in Old Aberdeen is good place to be though 2km city centre has university-halls accommodation (01224 273444). Both these vacation-times only.

The Best Places To Eat In Aberdeen

BISTROS & CAFÉ BARS

1096 8/T19
£15-22

✓ **Café 52 www.cafe52.net · 01224 590094 · 52 The Green** Not easy for a non-Aberdonian to find but close to – in fact below – east end of Union St. Go down steps by Virgin Megastore or approach via Market St. They'd say this place was 'a little bit different'. It has a boho, verging on chaotic buzz. A sliver of a cosy bistro with big outside tables and a presence in this emerging eating-out quarter. Sometimes chef/owner Steve Bothwell keeps customers (happy) and guessing with unusual dishes and combinations. Lunch more straight up: 'steak with potatoes a tenner'. Lunch & LO 10pm (bar midnight). 6pm Sun; may close Mon.

1097 8/T19
£15-22

✓ **The Foyer www.aberdeenfoyer.com · 01224 582277 · 82a Crown Street** Remarkable in that this busy, contemporary restaurant with good Modern British seasonal menu and great service is part of a local charity helping homeless and disadvantaged people. No hint of charity surfaces, but you can satisfy your conscience as well as your appetite for food and tasteful surroundings. There should be more places like this. Lunch onwards LO 10pm. Closed Sun/Mon.

1098 8/S20
£22-32/
£15-22

✓ **The Lairhillock Inn www.lairhillock.co.uk · 01569 730001** Not in the city at all, but a roadside inn at a country crossroads to the south, reached from either the road to Stonehaven or the South Deeside Rd west. Easiest is: head south on main A92, turn off at Durris then 5km. Famous for pub food (1392/GASTROPUBS) and informal atmosphere, though new owners and renewed effort '07. Restaurant adjacent, **Crynoch**, has more ambitious menu, excellent cheeseboard and malt selection. Both are worth the drive from town. Restaurant: dinner & Sun lunch. Closed Mon. LO 9pm. Inn: 7 days lunch & LO 9pm (10pm Fri/Sat).

1099 8/T19
£22-32

✓ **The Eating Room** www.eatingroom.com · 01224 212125 · **239 Great Western Road** The front end of the Clubhouse Hotel. '05 addition to smart dining in Aberdeen. Chris Wills in kitchen and Jackie Spence (of the Spences who run the Marcliffe, above) on the tables. Many folk say this is one of the best dinners in the 'toun'. Not open for lunch. Tue-Sat LO 9.30pm with early supper menu 5.30-6.30pm.Its reputation is as straight-talking as the title.

1100 8/T19
£32+

✓ **Olive Tree** www.olive-tree.co.uk · 01224 208877 · **32 Queen's Road** Off-centre but a significant part of smart dining in the Granite City. From the start Mike Reilly certainly made sure it had the look and the good management, and nothing much has changed. Fine dining bistro and **Black Olive** brasserie in conservatory annex. Tangible difference in offering – brazz very pleasant but fairly average, restaurant pretty good. Service and presentation tip-top in both. The Olive Branch adjacent is curiously more Spar than special. Mon-Sat Lunch & LO 10pm, Black Olive till 11pm & on Sun.

1101 8/T19
£15-22

✓ **The Square** www.1thesquare.com · 01224 646362 · **1 Golden Square** Enter by South Silver St off Union St near Music Hall. Well-liked restaurant in a spacious, modern room, contemporary menu, consistently good service and relaxing ambience. Same folk have **Matchams** at His Majesty's Theatre in the glass house (01224 337677); only open lunch Wed-Sat and pre-theatre at night when there's a show on. Square open: lunch & dinner LO 10/11pm. Closed Sun/Mon.

1102 8/T19
£15-22

✓ **Howie's** www.howies.uk.com · 01224 639500 · **50 Chapel Street** Follows successful formula in Edinburgh (161/162/EDINBURGH BISTROS) and elsewhere in classic/contemporary bistro style, this discreetly fronted restaurant presses all the right Aberdonian buttons (yes, including the price!). Along with The Square (above) these 2 have the best rooms in town. 7 days, lunch & LO 10pm.

1103 8/T19
£15-22

Bistro Verde 01224 586180 · **The Green** Down steps from Union St at Virgin Megastore opposite Café 52 (above). Hard to find in a car but off Market St. Unpretentious fish restaurant (one steak, one chicken dish) with blackboard daily catch. Nice place. Lunch & LO 10pm. Closed Sun/Mon.

1104 8/T19
£15 OR LESS

La Bonne Brasserie 01224 644445 · **off Union Street** Down steps at side of graveyard. Très popular and kind of French café Aberdeen-style – loadsa French fries. Pâtisserie, snacks (baguettes, etc) and specials. 7 days. LO 4pm.

1105 8/T19
£15 OR LESS

Beautiful Mountain www.thebeautifulmountain.com · 01224 645353 · **11 Belmont Street** In an area of many eateries, this unpretentious caff stands out. Takeaway and tables jammed together in 2 rooms upstairs. Great combos and ingredients – just better and probably healthier! 7 days till 5pm (Sun 4pm).

1106 8/T19

Le Café Bohème 01224 210677 · **Windmill Brae** Recent addition to this list of good restaurants. Decidedly French. Haven't tried! Tue-Sun. Lunch & LO 9pm.

1107 8/T19
£15 OR LESS

Moonfish 01224 644166 · **9 Correction Wynd** Round corner from La Bonne Brasserie (above), this funkier food-wise though flatter in atmosphere. Light food Euro-style: meze, tapas, etc. Lunch Tue-Sat, dinner Thu-Sat. Closed Sun/Mon.

1108 8/T19
£15-22

✓ **The Victoria** 01224 621381 · **Upstairs at 140 Union Street** Not a bistro or café-bar as such, more a luncheon- and tearoom, but too good not to include here. Same staircase and foyer as adjacent jewellery-and-gift emporium so an odd alliance. Great light menu, everything home-made and terribly well including the bread and the biscuits and in Jul (actually all year), a lemonade. Soup and Eve's Pudding for a song – perfect! Gillian and Gordon Harold keeping Aberdeen happy. 9am-5pm (6.30pm Thu). Closed Sun.

SEAFOOD

1109 8/T19
£32+

✓ **Silver Darling** www.silverdarling.co.uk · 01224 576229 Didier Dejean's breakthrough bistro still going strong in this perfect spot. Not so easy to find – head for Beach Esplanade, the lighthouse and harbour mouth (Pocra Quay). The light winks and boats glide past. Upstairs dining room not large (best to book) and you so want to be by the window. Different menu for lunch and dinner, depends on the catch and season. Apposite wines, wicked desserts. But wait, oh gosh... Silver Darling has lost its sheen. Maybe it was the night I was there but many others do say. So one tick gone. However, this is still the best and most dynamic location of any seafood restaurant in the land. Mon-Fri lunch, Mon-Sat dinner 7-9.30pm (but may close early).

1110 8/T19
£22-32

✓ **Atlantis at the Mariner Hotel** www.themarinerhotel.co.uk · 01224 591403 · 349 **Great Western Road** Those that know where to go in Aberdeen for excellent fish and seafood may not necessarily go to Silver Darling, but come here off centre and in a hotel but always busy. Hotel dining room atmosphere is not too evident (tables in conservatory) and the fish very good. Bar menu also available. Moderately priced wines. Lunch (not Sat) and dinner LO 9pm.

ITALIAN

1111 8/T19
£15-22

Rustico 01224 658444 · **Corner of Union Row & Summer Street** 50m from Union St. If this were French I'd say it had the *je ne sais quoi*, but it is most definitely Italian (Sicilian actually). Tony and Niko's love for Sicily evident (their brill photos on the walls) though Niko is Greek. And the food is well above the tratt average: everything home made, including the puds. As good as anywhere in Edinburgh or Glasgow. Lunch & LO 10pm. Closed Sun.

1112 8/T19
£15 OR LESS

Carmine's Pizza 01224 624145 · 32 **Union Terrace** This tiny slice of a room for *the* best pizza in town and behind, slaving over a hot stove, the eponymous, much-loved chef. Take away (to the Gardens opposite). Real authentic pasta in basic spag/tag and penne variants. Lunch & 4.45-6.45pm. Closed Sun.

EASTERN

1113 8/T19

✓ **Jewel In The Crown** www.thejewelinthecrown.com · 01224 210288 · 145 **Crown Street** Way down the street on corner with Affleck. Great North Indian food all home made and authentic. The best curry in town – always arguments about that, natch, though not from the 4 sons of Farooq Ahmed who work like a football team to make this place the top spot. Lunch & LO 11pm. 7 days.

1114 8/T19
£15-22

Saigon www.saigonrestaurantaberdeen.com · 01224 213212 · **Crown Terrace** Vietnamese obviously and long established (7+ years). Refreshing, Asian, intimate and better than the Royal Thai next door which has lost its way. Daily lunch & LO 10.30pm.

1115 8/T19

Blue Moon www.bluemoon-aberdeen.com · 01224 589977 · 11 **Holburn Street** Contemporary curry house, long thin and quite blue. Also **Blue Moon 2**, a blue replica denoted by their rude pepper motif over the road in Alford Lane. Ok curries in cool surroundings. Traditional menu including kids'. 7 days, lunch & LO 12midnight (a good though not infallible late bet in a city that tucks up early).

1116 8/T19 **Nargile** www.nargile.co.uk · 01224 636093 · **77 Skene Street** Turkish
£22-32 survivor that has made its regulars happy for over 20 years. Turkish owner, who
also spawned the **Meze Café** at 3 Rose St (great takeaway and open very late ie
3/4am, and has another **Nargile** in Edinburgh (210/BEST MEDITERRANEAN FOOD).
Doric and, of course, Polish staff, reliable meze, kebabs, swordfish etc and good
puds. Dinner only LO 11pm. Closed Sun.

The Best Pubs In Aberdeen

PUBS WITH ATMOSPHERE (& FOOD)

1117 8/T19 ✓**The Prince Of Wales** **7 St Nicholas Lane** just off Union St at George St.
An all-round great pub always mentioned in guides and one of the best
places in the city for real ale: Old Peculier, Caledonian 80/- and guest beers. Very
cheap self-service food at lunchtime. Lots of wood, flagstones, booths. Large area
but gets very crowded. 7 days, 11am-midnight (11pm Sun).

1118 8/T19 ✓**Under The Hammer** **11 North Silver Street** Basement bar along the
street from above, very intimately Aberdonian and a good place to meet
them. Slightly older and mixed crowd. Only open evenings (till midnight) and best
late on. My kind of place: a very civilised bar!

1119 8/T19 ✓**The Globe** **13 North Silver Street** Urban and urbane bar in single room –
a place to drink coffee as well as lager, but without self-conscious,
pretentious 'café-bar' atmosphere. Known for its food at lunch and 5-7.45pm (not
weekends) and for live music Tue and weekends – jazz and blues in the corner.
The Globe Inn now has rooms upstairs (1085/ABERDEEN HOTELS) so not a bad
place to base a weekend in Aberdeen.

1120 8/T19 **The Lemon Tree** www.lemontree.org · **5 West North Street** A theatre
(upstairs) and a spacious bar/restaurant on street level where there's lunchtime
food (Thu-Sun) and a mixed programme of entertainment. Phone (01224 642230)
or watch for fliers, but programme will include comedy, jazz, folk, pop and cabaret.
This is one of the best live rooms in the land.

1121 8/T19 **Ma Cameron's Inn** **Little Belmont Street** The 'oldest pub in the city' (though
the old bit is actually a small portion of the sprawling whole – but there's a good
snug). No nonsense oasis in buzzy street. **Food** from a huge menu including all
(we mean all) the pub staples: lunch and early evening. Terrace up top for
smokers and their mates.

CONTEMPORARY PUBS

1122 8/T19 **The Priory** **Belmont Street** Excellent conversion of town centre church. If
churches were like this we might go back (actually no we wouldn't).

1123 8/T19 **Paramount** **Bon Accord Street** Designer café-bar still looking good after many
years (and a refurbishment). Very popular and great place to check out the club
scene (flyers etc). Till midnight.

The Best Places To Stay In & Around Dundee

1124
10/Q23
153 ROOMS
TEL · TV
NO PETS
£38-60

✓ **The Apex** www.apexhotels.co.uk · 01382 202404 · **West Victoria Dock Road** I have perhaps been overly modest in my recommendation of the Apexs in Edinburgh (96/INDIVIDUAL HOTELS) where there is a slew of top hotels to compare (this small chain also has an Apex in London). Here in Dundee this 21st-century edifice is in a league of its own. It's really the only place to stay! Overlooking both the bridge and the new waterfront and with good detail in the very modern facilities (including the 'Yu' spa and pool; 1340/SPAS). Not cheap (for Dundee) but very good value compared to elsewhere. Metro restaurant also one of the city's reliably good eats. Rooms facing the firth and out to sea are best.
EAT Very acceptable brasserie and grazing menu overlooking the waterfront.

1125
10/Q23
128 RMS · TEL
TV · £60-85

Hilton www.hilton.co.uk/dundee · 01382 229271 On riverside adjacent Olympic Centre near Discovery Point. Serviceable, mainly business hotel with little charm but reasonable facilities. Tired now compared to Apex (above). Living Well leisure centre with ok pool. The rooms facing south have some great Tay views.

1126
10/Q23
52 RMS · TEL
TV · £45-60

The Queen's Hotel www.queenshotel-dundee.com · 01382 322515 · **160 Nethergate** Not much charm but convenient location now finding itself in the middle of 'the Cultural Quarter' (adjacent DCA, the Arts Centre). Back rooms (about 50%) overlooking distant River Tay are best.

1127
10/Q23
4 ROOMS
TV · NO KIDS
NO PETS
£38-45

Number Twenty-Five 01382 200399 · **25 South Tay Street** In the 'cultural quarter' near Dundee Rep Theatre and DCA (2337/PUBLIC GALLERIES). Dundee's 'boutique hotel'. Rooms above bar/restaurant with 'Underground' niteclub in basement (till 2.30am weekends), so an up-for-it rather than escape-from-it bed for the night. 'Continental breakfast' in room. Not expensive but rooms here, though clean and modern, seem a bit of an afterthought.

1128
10/Q23
12 ROOMS
TEL · TV
£38-45

The Shaftesbury www.shaftesbury-hotel.co.uk · 01382 669216 · **1 Hyndford Street** Just off Perth Rd (about 3km from city centre). A suburban (jute baron's) mansion converted into a comfortable hotel with neat back garden (though the kitchen pervades). All rooms different; loungeable lounge. Decent food courtesy of chef Bill Morrison in one of 2 restaurants, the 3 Olives. Chinese chefs in the other, the Royal China.

1129
10/Q23
11 ROOMS
(9 EN SUITE)
£30-38

Fisherman's Tavern www.fishermans-tavern-hotel.co.uk · 01382 775941 · **Fort Street, Broughty Ferry** Near the river/sea. 17th-century fisherman's cottage converted to a pub in 1827. Rooms above pub and next door much more recent! Excellent real ales, but also nearby Ship Inn (1135/DUNDEE RESTAURANTS) which is preferred for eats (Tavern does lunch only).

1130
10/Q23
38 ROOMS
TEL · TV
£38-45

Woodlands www.bw-woodlandshotel.co.uk · 01382 480033 · **Broughty Ferry** In the 'burbs between BF and Monifieth, signposted up Abercromby St. High-falutin' house in substantial acreage. Good disabled access. Popular out-of-town wedding venue quite complete with small swimming pool and gym.

Hostels There is no SYH in the area but in summer months university accommodation is available: details from tourist information centre (01382 527527).

The nearest really good hotel to Dundee is:
✓ **Castleton House near Glamis** 28km north. Report: 952/TAYSIDE HOTELS.

The Best Places To Eat In & Around Dundee

1131
10/Q23
£15 OR LESS

✓ **The Tasting Rooms** 01382 224188 · **5 South Ward Road** Not so easy to find for non-Dundonians (phone or ask), but very central in emerging quarter. Former jute warehouse meticulously and imaginatively transformed into deli/wine emporium with tables upstairs. Lovely light Med-style lunches, all-day menu and dinner at weekends. Some art, some music. Graeme Scott and David Walker have created an ambient foody experience that any city would want. Closed Sun/Mon.

1132
10/Q23
£15 OR LESS

✓ **Jute at Dundee Contemporary Arts** www.dca.org.uk · **01382 909246** · **Perth Road** Jute, the downstairs bar/restaurant of Dundee's acclaimed art centre, DCA, is the most convivial place in town to eat – no contest. Chef Chris Wilson offers a menu far superior to any old arts venue especially one which is all things to all people. Bar and restaurant: your rendezvous in Dundee. A good kids' menu. Book weekends. All day LO 9.30pm.

1133
10/Q23
£15-22

✓ **Bon Appétit** www.bonappetit-dundee.com · **01382 809000** · **Exchange Street** Near Commercial St corner. Owners Audrey and John Batchelor spent 16 years in France then came back to Dundee to 'make a difference'. Well, they have: in a culinary desert and without even French chefs they've created an authentic French café with food as good as any bistro de la gare you'll find in some obscure town on your hols (and that's a compliment). All the Francophile faves from bourguignon to crème brulée done just so. Excellent value. Lunch & LO 10pm. Closed Sun.

1134
10/Q23
£15-22

✓ **The Agacan** 01382 644227 · **113 Perth Road** Fabled bistro for Turkish eats and wine. OTT frontage and much art on the walls (and the furniture). Bohemian ambience and you smell the meat (veggies go meze). Turkish wines (red or white!). 5-9/10pm. Closed Mon.

1135
10/Q23
£15-22

✓ **The Ship Inn** 01382 779176 · **Broughty Ferry** On the front. Weathered by the River Tay since the 1800s, this cosy pub has sustained smugglers, fishermen and foody folk alike. Bar and upstairs restaurant; no-nonsense Scottish menu and picture windows overlook the Tay. Lunch & bar food till 7.30pm, restaurant 8.30pm (9.30pm weekends).

1136
10/Q23
£15 OR LESS

✓ **Fisher & Donaldson** www.fisheranddonaldson.com · **Whitehall Street off Nethergate** Traditional bakers the very best in Scotland (1507/BAKERS) with elevated tearoom. Snacks and all their fine fare. Mon-Sat LO 4.45pm.

1137
10/Q23
£15 OR LESS

✓ **The Parrot Café** 01382 206277 · **91 Perth Road** In an emerging café zone which seems to have submerged since last I visited, Val Ireland holds her own coz she makes her own (rye bread, cakes, scones, soups, blackboard specials) with a regular following of students and ladies who lunch and tea. No cellophaned muffins in sight. Tue-Sat 10am-5pm.

1138
10/Q23
£15-22

The Italian www.theitalian.co.uk · **01382 206444** · **36 Commercial Street** 2-floored restaurant in city centre aptly named – it is *the* Italian. Somewhere between a tratt and a restaurant with well-chosen wine list and excellent service. Look no further than this. 7 days lunch & LO 9.30pm.

1139
10/Q23
£15 OR LESS

Visocchi's 01382 779297 · **40 Gray Street, Broughty Ferry** More of a café than the original Kirriemuir branch caff (1524/ICE CREAM). After 70 years they're still making mouth-watering Italian flavoured ice creams (*amaretto, cassata* etc.) alongside home-made pasta and snacks. Till 8pm (4pm Tue, 10pm Fri/Sat). Closed Mon.

1140
10/Q23

Frasers 01382 730890 · **Broughty Ferry** Though it's been here for years, this sometime restaurant is a bit of a local secret. Dick Fraser chef/owner keeps this place almost as a hobby and only opens on Fri/Sat for set 5-course dinner: Modern Scottish dining real good and excellent wine selection. Must book.

1141
10/Q23
£15-22

Dandilly's Bistro 01382 669218 · **181 Perth Road** Small but must be welcome bistro up the Perth Rd. Pastas/pizza/crêpes with chicken and fish mains. Light room, light menu. dinner only. Closed Sun/Mon.

1142
10/Q23
£22-32

Dil Se www.dilse-restaurant.co.uk · 01382 221501 · **99-101 Perth Road** Bangladeshi restaurant; on two floors and food from all over the subcontinent but it's for curries ain't it? Related to Balaka in St Andrews, this is just a bit smarter than the competition. Lunch & dinner Sun-Thurs, open all day Fri & Sat. Until late!

1143
10/Q23
£15-22

The Glass Pavilion 01382 732738 · **Broughty Ferry** On 'The Esplanade' overlooking the Tay so you'd think it would be easy to find! Actually it's tricky and maybe easier to walk from Broughty Ferry Castle and harbour east to Monifieth, about 1.5km. Food so-so, but glass pavilion right enough, a contemporary reconstruction of an Art Deco gem. The pictures of Broughty Ferry beach and Esplanade in days gone by are a revelation (corridor by the toilets) and worth the journey alone. Nice coffee and chat, and walk further to Barnhill Rock Garden. A bracing and educative outing.

1144
10/Q23
£15-22

Taychreggan Hotel 01382 778626 · **4 Ellieslea Road, West Ferry** On main road between Dundee and Broughty Ferry signed just before the latter. Mansionhouse hotel (may be ok stopover) with big local reputation for food, especially high teas and suppers. Fairly standard fare but reliably good. Surprising malt whisky selection. Lunch, high tea (5-6pm; from 4pm on Sun) & LO 9pm.

1145 7/M18
11 ROOMS
TEL · TV
NO PETS
£85+

✓✓ **Rocpool Reserve** www.rocpool.com · 01463 240089 · **14 Culduthel Road** On town-centre side of main Ness Bridge opposite Eden Court Theatre. The very self-consciously presented boutique hotel followed Rocpool Restaurant (see below). Each room a design statement. Divided into 'Hip', 'Chic' or 'Decadent', though most are all of the above. You may feel you have to live up to the titles. 2 rooms have hot tubs on outdoor decks. Probably best to have someone to shag in these circumstances. Bar and restaurant are similarly soi-disant. This place very much at the forefront of Inverness: the brightening light in the North.

✓✓ **Glenmoriston** 01463 223777 · **Ness Bank** The smart stay and fabulous food experience lives up to expectations. 1019/HIGHLAND HOTELS.

✓✓ **Boath House** 01667 454896 · **Auldearn** Half an hour east on A96. Excellence! 1017/HIGHLAND HOTELS.

✓✓ **Culloden House** 01463 790461 5km east near (but not adjacent) to the battlefield. An outpost of elegance. 1020/HIGHLANDS HOTELS.

✓ **Dunain Park Hotel** 01463 230512 6km southwest on A82 Fort William road. 1023/HIGHLANDS HOTELS.

1146 7/M18
7 ROOMS
TEL · TV
NO KIDS
NO PETS
£45-60

✓ **The Heathmount** www.heathmounthotel.com · 01463 235877 Kingsmills, then centre (from Eastgate Mall). Fiona Newton's surprisingly groovy boutique-style hotel with popular, and at weekends buzzing, bar/restaurant. High standard of mod-con; rich boudoir decor with personal attention to detail. Famously, some rooms have TVs in the shower. Very good value at the price.

1147 7/M18
76 ROOMS
TEL · TV
£38-45

Columba Hotel 01463 231391 · **7 Ness Walk** An excellent central location overlooking the main bridge over the Ness and across the river to the castle. Was at the heart of the events that launched The Year of Highland Culture. Pleasant and friendly, contemporary feel. Rooms vary, some small; river views best. Nice bar/restaurant.

1148 7/M18
70 ROOMS
TEL · TV
£60-85

Royal Highland Hotel www.royalhighlandhotel.com · 01463 231926 · **Academy Street** Formerly the Station Hotel; continuing refurbishment under new owners. 15 new rooms to be added '08. Nice staircase. Some rather average rooms. A surreal start to the day in the very interior breakfast room. Very much in the centre of things but a little disappointing.

1149 7/M18
83 ROOMS
TEL · TV
£60-85

Marriott Hotel www.marriott.com · 01463 237166 · **Culcabock Road** In suburban area south of centre near A9. Modern, very well-appointed with pleasant garden. Best of the chain hotels. Leisure facilities include small pool

1150 7/M18
10, 7 ROOMS
TV
£38-45

The Alexander/Felstead www.thealexander.net · 01463 231151/712266/ 231634 2 hotels on Ness Bank, along the river opposite Eden Court and very central. Alexander (formerly Ardmuir) new owners and shiny (well, the floors) new makeover '05. Nice uniformity in block out back. Other rooms bigger but some contemporary look. Felstead old-style comfort. Belongings belong. Both B&B only. Many other hotels in this street. These ones are good value.

1151 7/M18 **Moyness House** www.moyness.co.uk · 01463 233836 · **6 Bruce Gardens**
7 ROOMS Accolade-gathering suburban guesthouse over bridge south of river but 10
TV minutes' walk to centre and on-street parking. Friendly family house. B&B only.
£38-45 The writer Neil Gunn used to live here!

Bunchrew House Hotel 01463 234917 4km north on the road to Beauly on firth shore. Wedding hotel sometimes free. Report: 1030/HIGHLAND HOTELS.

1152 7/M18 **3 Good Hostels: SY Hostel** www.syha.org.uk · 01463 231771 · **Victoria Drive;** Large official hostel (SYHA). More funky are the **Student Hostel**, 8 Culduthel Rd (01463 236556), and 3 doors down **Bazpackers** (01463 717663).

1153 7/M18 **Camping & Caravan Parks** Most central (2km) at **Bught Park** www.invernesscaravanpark.com · 01463 236920 Well-equipped and large-scale site on flat river meadow. Many facilities. Approach via A82 Fort William road.

The Best Places To Eat In Inverness

1154 7/M18 ✓✓ **Boath House** www.boath-house.com · 01667 454896 · **Auldearn**
£22-32 Well out of town, but worth drive. Just off A96 3km east of Nairn. 30mins from Inverness. Chef Charlie Lockely accumulating AA rosettes (watch out for 4) and reputation. A fine-dining night out. 1017/HIGHLAND HOTELS.

1155 7/M18 ✓✓ **Abstract @ The Glenmoriston** 01463 223777 · **20 Nessbank** ·
£32+ www.glenmoristontownhouse.com Along the river. The top-end restaurant in town, part of Barry Larsen's Glenmoriston Hotel (see above). Made famous or infamous by Gordon Ramsay's TV visit and assessment that the cuisine and the chef Loic Lefebvre were too haut up their arse for Inverness. Not much compromise later, it's doing very well, thank you, under chef Geoffrey Malmedy (Loic long left). Abstract opened in Edinburgh '07 with similar formula: sophisticated setting, smart service from mainly French staff, excellent Michelin-level food in à la carte or 'tasting' menus. Can eat at chef's table in the kitchen (that was a good idea Gordon, now fuck off).

1156 7/M18 ✓ **Rocpool Reserve** www.rocpool.com · 01463 240089 · **Culduthel Road**
£32+ 3 rooms and private dining overlooking town. All très moderne. Chef Davey Aspin uses good Scottish produce and presents well. Interesting wines. 7 days. Lunch & LO 10pm.

1157 7/M18 ✓ **Rocpool** www.rocpool.com · 01463 717274 · **Ness Walk** Corner of main
£15-22 bridge over river. Excellent modern diner with accent on inexpensive daytime and eclectic evening menu. For some time now the consistently good place to eat in the centre. Forerunner of the Reserve (above). 7 days. LO 9.45pm. Closed Sun lunch.

1158 7/M18 ✓ **Café One** 01463 226200 · **10 Castle Street** Near the Castle.
£22-32 Contemporary décor and cuisine in hands of good team. Menu changes monthly, carefully sourced ingredients – salmon wild all summer – reasonably priced for this standard of food and service. Express menu a good deal. Another restaurant for Inverness to be pleased about. Lunch, dinner LO 9.30pm. Closed Sun.

1159 7/M18
£15-22

✓ **Contrast** 01463 227889 · **Ness Bank** Part of the Glenmoriston Hotel, the bistro/brasserie contrasts with fine-dining Abstract adjacent (see above). Genuinely quite French, informal and light. Many outside tables overlook the river. Lunch & LO 9.30pm.

1160 7/M18
£15-22

The Mustard Seed 01463 220220 · **16 Fraser Street** Catriona Bissett's cool restaurant in spectacular riverside room attests (with Rocpool above) to Inverness's new confidence and city status. Contemporary menu, ok wine. Service inconsistent, but a restaurant that would not be out of place in any European city. 7 days 12noon-4pm, 6-10pm.

1161 7/M18
£15-22

The Kitchen on the River 01463 259119 · **15 Huntly Street** As it says, on the river. Emerging best location in emerging Inverness, this a new building almost opposite its parent, The Mustard Seed (see above) and new kid on the block '07. Working hard for both the local and the Eastern European economy, this kid knows exactly how to do its thing (though somehow Mum 'n' Dad still know best). 7 days lunch & LO 10pm.

1162 7/M18
£22-32

Peat by the Bridge 01463 701900 · **20 Bridge Street** Right enough on the corner by the main bridge over the Ness, but 3 words too many (as far as I know there are no Peats anywhere else) and does try a tad too hard to set the heather alight (with stiff competition; see above and below). Still, it's another welcome addition to Inverness foodtown. Modern British menu with accent on seafood and a brilliant view of a river that's always rushing to the sea. 7 days lunch & LO 9.45pm.

1163 7/M18
£15 OR LESS

Delices de Bretagne 01463 712422 · **6 Stephens Brae** Just up from Girvans (see below), another café/restaurant. This one brings 'a taste of France to Inverness'. Well, up to a point, monsieur! The patisserie is fine but not a patch on the real '*chose*', the crêpes on the other hand are light and welcome in the land of heavy carb. Nice coffee. 9am-5.30pm. Closed Sun.

1164 7/M18
£22-32/
£15-22

Riva & Pazzo's 01463 237377 · **4 Ness Walk** Prominent (adjacent main bridge) central Italian restaurant and (upstairs) tratt. Probably best in town. Contemporary room overlooking riverside. Decent Italian menu with clear distinction between treat and tratt (below). Riva lunch & LO 9.30pm, Pazzo's evenings only (serviceable pasta and pizza).

1165 7/M18
£22-32

Riverhouse Restaurant 01463 222033 · **Greig Street** Over the pedestrian bridge. Intimate restaurant with contemporary food from Alan Little's open kitchen. Gets busy so can feel cramped but good reputation. Lunch Tue-Sat, dinner Tue-Sun, LO 9pm.

1166 7/M18
£15-22

River Café www.rivercafeandrestaurant.co.uk · 01463 714884 · **Bank Street** On town side of river near pedestrian bridge. Small, friendly café/restaurant. Solid and unpretentious evening menu and ladies who lunch. 7 days LO 9pm.

1167 7/M18
£15-22

Shapla 01463 241919 · **2 Castle Road** On town side of main road bridge. Indian restaurant with the usual UK curry-house menu served in upstairs lounge with river views. Open late (LO 11pm). Some say **Raja (**01463 237190) downstairs in Post Office Lane (between Church St and Academy St, behind Queensgate) is the better curry. But most are agreed **The Beauly Tandoori** (01463 782221) 20km away on Beauly High St is the best Indian restaurant in the area.

168 7/M18 **Red Pepper** 01463 237111 · 74 Church Street The cooler coffee-shop by the
£15-22 people that brought us the Mustard Seed (above). Daytime caffeine hit with
bespoke sandwiches etc. 7.30am-4.30pm. Closed Sun.

1169 7/M18 **La Tortilla Asesina** www.latortillaasesina.co.uk · 01463 709809 · Top of
£15-22 **Castle Street** Near castle and hostels (see above). Reasonably authentic Spanish
restaurant serving the UK version of tapas ie 2/3 portions as a meal. All the faves
and some variants are here. 'Scotland's only' sherry bar upstairs with surprising
range. Otherwise the Rioja and all the beers are here. 7 days. LO 10pm (bar later).

✓ **Girvans Stephens Brae** Behind M&S. Fast-turnover food for all folks.
Report: 1459/CAFÉS.
✓ **Castle Restaurant Castle Street** Legendary caff of the Highlands.
Hardest-working tearoom in the North. Report: 1458/CAFÉS.

Gay Scotland the Best!

EDINBURGH
BARS & CLUBS

1172A 1/D2 ✓**GHQ 0131 550 1780 · 4 Picardy Place** New (late '07) superbar/club by Glasgow G1 in the heart of the Pink Triangle. Flexispace with dance depending on crowd. Banquettes can be booked (for watching and gossip). 7 days 5pm-3am. You don't have to be gay to be exploited, but it helps.

1170 1/D2 ✓**New Town Bar www.thenewtownbar.co.uk · 26 Dublin Street · 0131 538 7775** Basement and underground club. It became Twist for a bit but now it's back doing what it does best: a watering hole for the older crowd. Few twinks. Downstairs bar open weekend nights for more shady corners and dance action. 7 days till 12midnight/1am, weekends 2am. Mixed crowd. Food at lunchtime.

1171 1/E1 ✓**Planet Out 0131 524 0061 · Greenside Place** Traditionally the pre-club, pre-CCs hangout. Now has loyal following of bright-er, younger things. Handy for the Hill later on (the 'Gardens of Fun' for open-air liaisons). An unthreatening vibe (except for the door dykes). 7 days till 1am. Last admission 12.45am.

1172 1/E2 ✓**CC Bloom's www.ccbloomshotel.com · 0131 556 9331 · Greenside Place** Next to Playhouse. Bar up, (too small) disco down (too busy). An institution, this is where everybody eventually ends up. Or it was until the new super duper club GHQ opened (see above). Busy bar with karaoke upstairs and club below. It's well... impossibly crowded at weekends. 7 days 7pm-3am (your second-last chance! See 'The Gardens' above). Last admission 1.45am.

1173 1/E2 **Habana www.gayscotland.com/habana · 0131 558 1270 · 22 Greenside Place** Adjacent CCs above. Banging music. Young crowd. Always seems about to lead to trouble but rarely does. 7 days till 1am. Outside tables very cruisy.

1174 1/B3 **Frenchie's 0131 225 7651 · Rose Street Lane North** Near Castle St. Intimate bar quite removed from the East End Pink Triangle. Hence more intimate but no less trashy. Age before beauty so suits all. 7 days till 1am. (Sun 12midnight.)

1175 1/F2 **The Regent 0131 661 8198 · Corner of Abbeyhill** Adjacent well-known cruising area. Friendly locals, relaxed, straight friendly. Even have ales (Deuchars, Cally 80/- and guests). 7 days till 1am.

1176 1/D1 **Deep Blue Corner of Broughton & Barony Streets** Below Blue Moon Café (see below). Subterranean cocktail-type bar; cosy and blue. 7 days 6pm-1am.

OTHER PLACES

1177 1/D1 ✓**Blue Moon Café www.bluemooncafe.co.uk · Broughton & Barony Streets · 0131 556 2788** The boys and girls serve quick and chattily in this all-day café. Always busy with lively mixed (and earnest) crowd for food and drink and catching up. Exhibitions and **Out of the Blue** gay accessories shop next door in Barony St, Deep Blue below (see above). If you arrive in Edinburgh and don't know anybody, come here first. Food 7 days till 10ish; bar 11/11.30pm. (300/CAFÉS)

1178 1/D1 ✓**Sala www.salacafe.co.uk · 0131 556 5758 · 60 Broughton Street** Tapas bar and restaurant run by Spanish gels. Hence the bravas and chorizo autentico and Euro atmosphere – the kind of place you will want to fit in. Open Tue-Sun 11am-11pm.

1179 1/D1 **Claremont Bar & Restaurant** www.claremontbar.com · 0131 556 5662 · **133 East Claremont Street** Small and cheery wee local. Regular crowd and frequent fetish nights. Bulkies, bears and furries have own nights. Food 7 days till 10pm. Bar 7 days till 1am. Details from the website.

1180 1/D1 **No. 18** 0131 553 3222 · **18 Albert Place** Sauna for gentlemen (mainly older). Discreet doorway halfway down Leith Walk. Dark room. Mon–Sat 12noon–10pm. Sun 2–10pm.

1181 1/D1 **Steamworks** 0131 477 3567 · **Broughton Market** At the end of Barony St off Broughton St at the Blue Moon. Modern, Euro-style wet and dry areas. Cubies. Café. Dark room. Mixed crowd. 7 days 11am–10pm.

GUESTHOUSES

1182 1/E1
5 ROOMS
TV
£45-60
✓ **Ardmor House** www.ardmorhouse.com · 0131 554 4944 · **74 Pilrig Street** Quiet mix of contemporary and original design meet in this stylish guesthouse run by nice boys (in the media) who have a gorgeous wee dog called Lola. Family room so straight-friendly. They have apartments too.

1183 1/E1
5 ROOMS · TV
NO PETS
£38-45
Acorn Guesthouse www.purpleroofs.com · 0131 554 2187 · **70 Pilrig Street** Near Ardmor (above) and Garlands (below) and the scene (though it is a stroll). No twins. Contemporary; lesbian-owned but not gay only.

1184 1/E1
6 ROOMS
TV
£30 OR LESS
Garlands www.garlands.demon.co.uk · 0131 554 4205 · **48 Pilrig Street** The third of the 3 guesthouses on Pilrig St, Garlands predates others; more old-style here. Probably the most gay.

GLASGOW
BARS & CLUBS

1185 2/E3 ✓ **Delmonica's** 0141 552 4802 · **68 Virginia Street** Glasgow-stylish pub with long bar and open plan in quiet lane in Merchant City gay quarter. Pleasant and airy during day but busy and 'sceney' at night, especially weekends. As they say in Scots Gay – 'it's nice if your face fits'. 7 days till 12midnight.

1186 2/E3 ✓ **Polo Lounge** 0141 553 1221 · **84 Wilson Street** Long-established venue with stylish refurbished decor, period furnishings. Gents' club meets Euro-lounge. Downstairs disco (Fri-Sun) with 3am licence; otherwise till 1am (not many pubs in town serve after midnight). Report: 734/GLASGOW COOL BARS.

1187 2/C3 **Waterloo Bar** 0141 229 5891 · **306 Argyle Street** Scotland's oldest gay bar and it tells. But an unpretentious down-to-earth vibe so refreshing in its way. Old-established bar and clientele. Not really for trendy young things. You might not fancy anybody but they're a friendly old bunch. 7 days till 12midnight.

1188 2/E4 **Court Bar** 0141 552 2463 · **69 Hutcheson Street** Centre of Merchant City area. Long-going small bar that's straight till mid evening then turns into a fairy. 7 days till 12midnight.

1189 2/E4 **Bennet's** www.bennets.co.uk · 0141 552 5761 · **80 Glassford Street** In the beginning and in the end... Bennet's. Relentless, unashamed disco fun without attitude on 2 floors. Wed-Sun 11pm-3am, Tue is 'traditionally' straight night, first Fri of the month is ladies' night.

1190 2/E3 **Revolver www.revolverbar.com · 0141 553 2456 · 6a John Street** in basement opposite Italian Centre. Civilised subterranea. Great free juke box, pool, ale. Some uniform nights. Most of the men will be men. 7 days all day to 12midnight.

OTHER PLACES

1191 2/D4 **GGLC (Glasgow Gay & Lesbian Centre) 0141 221 7203 · 11 Dixon Street** In a car-park zone. Café-bar drop-in centre with newspapers, info, 'garden of reflection', art gallery and they do bargain cocktails. Good spot! Daily 11am-12midnight.

1192 2/C4 **Club Eros 0845 4562310 · 1 Bridge Street** First building on left across Jamaica St Bridge. 3-floor sauna, spa and caff. Dark room. 7 days till 10pm (Sat till 6am).

1193 2/C4 **The Lane 0141 221 1802 · 60 Robertson Street** Near Waterloo (above), other side of Argyle St, lane on right. You 'look for the green light'. Sauna and private club. You wouldn't call it upmarket, that cabin fever! 7 days, afternoons till 8/9pm.

1194 2/D4 **The Pipeworks aka The Garage 0141 552 5502 · 5 Metropole Lane** East of St Enoch Centre, near Slater Menswear, down an unlikely lane. Probably Glasgow's smartest/cleanest sauna, so younger crowd than above. 7 days 12noon-3am.

1195 2/XA1
18 ROOMS
TEL · TV
£30-38
Belhaven Hotel www.belhavenhotel.com · 0141 339 3222 · 15 Belhaven Terrace In heart of West End near Byres Rd so near restaurants/bars but a 15-minute taxi from gay scene. Gay friendly rather than gay.

ABERDEEN
Gay scene in Aberdeen still in disarray at TGP.

1196 8/T19 **Bar Indigo 01224 586949 · 20 Adelphi Lane** Off Market St. Bar and disco. Quite friendly – just as well, it's about all there is. Call for opening.

DUNDEE

1197 10/Q23 **Liberty 01382 200660 · 124 Seagate** Bar and dancefloor. Everybody knows everybody else, but not you. This may have its advantages. Wed-Sun till 2.30am. Also ...

1198 10/Q23 **Brooklyn Bar 01382 200660 · St Andrews Lane** Behind and above Liberty. Small bar, a pre-club bar on disco nights (reduced tickets available at bar). Wed-Sun till 12midnight (11pm Sun).

1199 10/Q23 **Gauger 01382 226840 · 75 Seagate** Near the above. Pub with disco Fri/Sat. Till 12midnight 7 days. Non-threatening haven in sometimes scary zone.

HOTELS ELSEWHERE

1200 9/J25
7 ROOMS
MAR-OCT
TV · NO KIDS
£45-60
An Lochan 01700 811239 · Tighnabruaich Fab hotel by the water. Not remotely gay but the **Shinty Bar** adjacent has pictures of the shinty teams over the decades all over the walls. If you're in the area, check it out (the bar food's great as well). And the local team are in there on Sat.

Section 5

Particular Places to Eat & Stay in Scotland

Superlative Country-House Hotels

1201
10/N24
271 ROOMS
TEL · TV
£85+

✓✓✓ **Gleneagles** www.gleneagles.com · 01764 662231 · **Auchterarder** Off A9 Perth-Stirling road and signposted. Scotland's truly luxurious resort hotel. For facilities on the grand scale others pale into insignificance; it is an international destination. More famously fabulous than ever since the G8 Summit '05. All sport and leisure activities you could want including shooting, riding, fishing, off-roading (even jeeps for kids), 2 pools with outdoor tub. Spa for ladies (they refurbished for '08). Oh and the world-renowned golf (3 courses). Refurbished rooms by Amanda Rosa and the new wing 'Braid House' contemporary and remote (in the 'handset to control temperature, lights, curtains and fireplace' sense). Strathearn Restaurant is a foodie heaven but expensive. New casual dining in '07 in Deseo: lighter and brighter and au courant cuisine in every sense, and there are 2 other restaurants on the estate. Andrew Fairlie's intimate dining room is considered by many to offer the best fine dining in Scotland. Report 969/PERTHSHIRE RESTAURANTS. Gleneagles could be anywhere but it is quintessentially Scottish. It has airs and graces but it's a friendly old place too. Its top suites (also by Ms Rosa) are to die for.

1202
11/J29
17 ROOMS
EASTER-OCT
TEL · TV
£85+

✓✓ **Glenapp Castle** www.glenappcastle.com · 01465 831212 · **near Ballantrae** Luxury manor south of Ballantrae. Very discreet entrance (first right turn after village – no sign; entryphone system). Home of Inchcape family for most of 20th century, opened as a hotel in first year of 21st. Run by Graham and Fay Cowan (Fay's family has other hotels in the South West). Fabulous restoration on a house that fell into disuse in the 1990s. Excellent and studied service, top-notch food (a rare in Scotland Michelin star), impeccable environment. The rooms are all individually beautiful; the suites are enormous. Quality costs but the price is inclusive of just about everything, so relax and join this effortless house party. Tennis, lovely walks in superb grounds (especially May and Sep). A southern secret though with many accolades.

1203
9/J22
16 ROOMS
7 SUITES
2 COTTAGES
FEB-DEC
TEL · TV
£85+

✓✓ **Isle Of Eriska** 01631 720371 · **Ledaig** 20km north of Oban (signed from A85 near Benderloch Castle). Hotel, spa and island! As you drive over the Victorian iron bridge onto the isle (a real island), you enter a more tranquil and gracious world. Its 300 acres are a sanctuary for wildlife; you are not the only guests. The famous badgers come almost every night to the door of the bar for their milk. Comfortable baronial house with fastidious service and facilities. Rooms named after islands very individual. Two 2-bedroom and five 1-bedroom suites in spa outbuilding more contemporary, with private terraces and hot tubs. The picturesque 9-hole golf, great 17m pool and gym excellent in summer when it opens on to the garden. Also putting, tennis and clay shooting; it's all there if you feel like action, but it's v pleasant just to stay still. Espa treatment rooms (3) and café with deck adjacent for lunch. Dining, with a Scottish flavour and impeccable local ingredients from a rich backyard and bay, has 3 AA rosettes under chef Robert MacPherson.

1204
10/N22
9 ROOMS
(8 COTTAGES)
TEL · TV
£85+

✓✓ **Kinnaird** www.kinnairdestate.com · 01796 482440 · **Dunkeld** 12km north of Dunkeld (Perth 35km) via A9 and B898 for Dalguise. In Kinnaird estate, a bucolic setting beneath woody ridge of Tay Valley, this country house envelops you with good taste and comfort. Good, unobtrusive service from friendly arrival to sad departure. You get a teddy on your bed and there's a stylish 'K' on everything. Great snooker room and drawing room warmed by open fires. Jean-Baptiste Bady prepares very fine dining in very fine dining room; jacket and tie preferred. Owner, the American-born Connie Ward, lives nearby. This was her family home and she welcomes you to somewhere you will love, but not as much as she. Mementoes and personal touches. Fine walking and fishing, especially to the millpond 45 minutes up the hill. A superb and secret spot. A bothy and log fire await. 'The Retreat' upstairs does 'treatments'. Silently beyond the grounds and river, endless traffic ploughs north and south on the A9. One day you'll have to join it again. Until then, live Kinnaird. There are individual cottages (especially recommended: 'Castle Peroch') for more privacy – 2 in the nearby courtyard.

1205
11/J30
9 ROOMS
MAR-DEC
TEL · TV
£85+

✓✓ **Knockinaam Lodge** www.knockinaamlodge.com · 01776 810471 · **Portpatrick** An ideal place to lie low; an historic Victorian house nestled on a cove. The Irish coastline is the only thing on the horizon, apart from discreet service and excellent food. Long-standing Michelin chef Tony Pierce excels with a tasting menu set to your likes and dislikes and which never disappoints. Winston Churchill was once very comfortable here, too! Superb wine (especially French) and whisky lists. 15km south of Stranraer, off A77 near Lochans. Report 814/SOUTH-WEST HOTELS.

1206
10/R25

✓✓ **Greywalls** www.greywalls.co.uk · 01620 842144 · **East Lothian** Close to Edinburgh and adjacent the rarefied world of Muirfield, but one of the most homely and aesthetically pleasing country-house hotels in the UK in an Edwardian summerhouse built by the humanist genius architect Lutyens. Fabulous gardens. Report: 910/LOTHIAN HOTELS.

1207
10/P22
18 ROOMS
TEL · TV
£85+

✓✓ **Kinloch House** 01250 884237 · **near Blairgowrie** 5km west on A923 to Dunkeld. Quintessential Perthshire comfort and joy. Beautiful mansion among the green fields and woods of Perthshire where the Allen family, formerly at Airds Hotel, Port Appin, have been much praised in this book. They've now established Kinloch as the premier hotel in this country quarter. Comfy rooms, informal but sure service, excellent food (Graeme Allen often in the kitchen) and a top wine list (especially French). Fine south-facing views. Surprising pool you may have to yourself. 3 suites. Enjoy!

1208
9/J23
16 ROOMS
FEB-DEC
TEL · TV
£85+

✓ **Ardanaiseig** www.ardanaiseig.com · 01866 833333 · **Loch Awe** 16km from Taynuilt signed from main A85 to Oban down beautiful winding road and 7km from Kilchrenan. In sheltered landscaped gardens dotted with ongoing sculpture project to complement this rambling gothic mansion's collection of selected antiques (proprietor owns antique biz in London) overlooking an enchanting loch. Peaty water on tap and all amongst great trees. Genuine 'faux' grand that works. Outside by the loch, deer wander and bats flap at dusk. Pure romance. I've said it before, but in this far corner, chef Gary Goldie deserves more credit perhaps, than he gets. There's a new suite, the 'Boatshed', with its boat and its loch and its idyllic...ness.

✓ **Ballathie House** www.ballathiehousehotel.com · 01250 883268 · **Kinclaven near Blairgowrie & Perth** Superb situation on River Tay. Handy for Perth and probably the best place to stay near the town. Full report and codes: 951/PERTHSHIRE HOTELS.

✓✓ **Cromlix House** www.cromlixhouse.com · 01786 822125 · **Dunblane** Near A9 north of Perth, 4km Dunblane. New owners autumn '05 for this quintessential country-house hotel in beautiful grounds. Report: 869/CENTRAL HOTELS.

✓✓ **Raemoir House** 01330 824884 · **Banchory** 5km north from town via A980. A gem in the North East. Historical with contemporary comforts and excellent dining. Report: 987/NORTHEAST HOTELS.

Hotels That Welcome Kids

1210
10/N23
213 ROOMS
+SELF-
CATERING
TEL · TV
£38-45

✓✓ **Crieff Hydro** www.crieffhydro.com · 01764 655555 · **Crieff**
A national institution and still a family business; your family is part of theirs. Approach via High St, turning off at Drummond Arms Hotel uphill then follow signs. Vast Victorian pile with activities for all from bowlers to babies. Still run by the Leckies from hydropathic beginnings but with continuous refurbishments, including the fabulous winter gardens moving graciously with the times (fine coffee shop: freshly squeezed OJ and big donuts). New sports hall (the Hub), café and kids' centre '07 as good as any local authority facility. Formal dining room and the Brasserie (best for food Med-style; open all day). Great tennis courts, riding school, Lagoon Pool. Tiny cinema shows family movies; nature talks, donkey rides. Kids endlessly entertained (even while you eat). Chalets in grounds are among the best in Scotland. Great for family get-togethers. Populism with probity and no preciousness: Gordon Brown would approve.

1211
9/J22
59 ROOMS
TEL · TV
£38-85

✓ **Isles Of Glencoe Hotel** www.islesofglencoe.com · 01855 811602 ·
Ballachulish Beside the A82 Crianlarich to Fort William: a modern hotel and leisure centre jutting out onto Loch Leven. Adventure playground outside and nature trails. Conservatory restaurant overlooking the water. Lochaber Watersports next door have all kind of boats from pedalos to kayaks and bikes. Hotel has pool. 2 different standards of family rooms. Snacks in the restaurant all day. Glencoe and 2 ski areas nearby.

1212
7/E15
5 ROOMS
MAR-DEC
£60-85

✓ **Scarista House** www.scaristahouse.com · 01859 550238 · **Harris**
20 minutes south of Tarbert on west coast of South Harris, just over an hour to Stornoway. Big, comfortable former manse overlooking amazing beach (1658/BEACHES); also golf course (2157/GOOD GOLF). Lots of other great countryside around. The Martins have 3 school-age kids and yours may muck in with them (including 6pm supper). Laid-back but civilised ambience.

1213
7/E14
7 ROOMS
APR-OCT
£38-45

✓ **Baile-Na-Cille** www.baillenacille.com · 01851 672242 · **Timsgarry,**
Lewis Far far into the sunset on the west of Lewis 60km Stornoway so a plane/ferry and drive to somewhere you and the kids can leave it all behind. Exquisite, vast beach, garden, tennis, games room. No TV/phone/mobile/smoking. Plenty books. The kids will never forget it.

1214
9/F23
16 & 27
ROOMS
£38-60

✓ **Argyll Hotel & St Columba Hotels** www.argyllhoteliona.co.uk &
www.stcolumba-hotel.co.uk · 01681 700334 & 01681 700304 · **Iona**
2 related hotels on this charmed and blessed little island. Holidays here are remembered forever. Both hotels fairly basic but child- and people-in-general-friendly. Unhurried, hassle-free; kids run free. Beautiful gardens. The Argyll is open Feb-Dec; St Columba Apr-Oct.

1215
9/J20
13 ROOMS
MAR-NOV
£38-45/
£60-85

✓ **Glenfinnan House** www.glenfinnanhouse.com · 01397 722235 ·
Glenfinnan Just off the 'Road to the Isles' (the A830 from Fort William to Mallaig). Very large Highland 'hoose' with so many rooms and such large gardens you can be as noisy as you like. Great intro to the Highland heartland; music, scenery and local characters. Row on the loch leaves from the foot of the lawn. Midge-eater in the garden. More rooms '08. 1041/INEXPENSIVE HIGHLAND HOTELS.

1216
10/R24
15 ROOMS
TEL · TV
£38-45

Kilconquhar Castle Estate www.kilconquharcastle.co.uk · 01333 340501 · **near Elie** On B942 near Colinburgh, 3km from Elie (that famously nice town). Mainly time-share villas (newer ones seem especially naff), but 'club rooms' and suites available in castle itself with access to all facilities including pool, tennis, golf and especially riding. 2-night minimum. Bistro and posher dining room in baronial setting (only used occasionally).

1217
10/N22
5 ROOMS
TV
£38-45

Inn on the Tay www.theinnonthetay.co.uk · 01887 840760 · **Grandtully** Road and riverside inn in small village of Aberfeldy. This stretch of river famous for its rapids so usually plenty of kayak action. Stylish refurbishment by Josie and Geoff determined to make it family-friendly. Most rooms have 3 beds but only adults pay. Nice lounge and café/bar.

1218
9/K20
8 ROOMS
NO PETS
£38-45

Old Pines www.oldpines.co.uk · 01397 712324 · **near Spean Bridge** 3km Spean Bridge via B8004 for Gairlochy at Commando Monument. A ranch-like hotel in a good spot north of Fort William. This hotel has long had a big reputation not only for food but also for welcoming kids. Newish owners the Daileys have restored this as a family-friendly destination; they have little kids too. Separate mealtimes with real food then a great dinner for the adults.

1219
9/J22
10 ROOMS
TEL · TV
£60-85

Holly Tree Hotel www.hollytreehotel.co.uk · 01631 740292 · **Kentallen** On A828 Fort William-Oban road south of Ballachulish. Long-established roadside and seaside hotel recently much improved. Many rooms have great views. Garden on the shore with pier. Former railway station with Mackintosh references (sic). Surf 'n' turf restaurant, bar and surprising swimming pool. Kids £20 each; special menu.

1220
10/Q27
128 ROOMS
TEL · TV
£38-45/
£60-85

Peebles Hydro www.peebleshydro.co.uk · 01721 720602 · **Innerleithen** Road, Peebles One of the first Victorian hydros and one of the best remaining. A complete resort for families and very nice, with a well-worn look. Huge grounds, corridors (you get lost) and floors of rooms where kids can run around. Pool and leisure facilities. Entertainment and baby-sitting services. Very traditional and refreshingly untrendy. Rooms vary. Dining room is vast and hotel-like. Lazels bistro downstairs is light, contemporary and unnecessarily good (905/BORDER RESTAU- RANTS). Many family rooms and teatime in Lazels.

1221
10/Q27
14 ROOMS
TEL · TV
£30-38

Glentress Hotel www.glentress.org.uk · 01721 720100 · **near Peebles** 3km east of Peebles on the main A72 road to Innerleithen. Roadside lodge ideally situated for families who do the outdoors especially cycling together. Adjacent Glentress Mountain Bike Centre (2183/CYCLING); hotel itself hires bikes. Restaurant has growing local reputation Family rooms. The delights of Peebles nearby.

1222
11/M30
56 ROOMS
TEL · TV
£45-60

The Cally Palace www.callypalace.co.uk · 01557 814341 · **Gatehouse of Fleet** The big all-round family and golf hotel in the South West in charming village with safe, woody walks in the grounds and beaches nearby. Leisure facilities include pool and tennis. 500 acres of forest good for cycling. There are allegedly red squirrels. 9 family rooms. Kids' tea at 5pm.

1223
9/J25
11 ROOMS
TEL · TV
£45-60

Kilfinan Hotel 01700 821201 · **Kilfinan** North of Tignabruaich on B8000 close to but not on Loch Fyne in the country heart of Cowal and Argyll. A long-estab- lished coaching inn with a good reputation for food, now in the hands of the Wyatts who have 3 kids and will welcome yours. Proper kids' menu. Wild walks nearby. Kids go free.

1224
7/N19
175 ROOMS
(INCL FAMILY)
TEL · TV
£85+

Hilton Coylumbridge www.hilton.co.uk/coylumbridge · 01479 810661 · **near Aviemore** 8km from Aviemore Centre on B970 road to ski slopes and nearest hotel to them. 2 pools of decent size, sauna, flume, etc. Plenty to do in summer and winter (1796/KIDS) and certainly where to go when it rains. Best of the often-criticised Aviemore concrete blocks, the most facilities, huge new shed with kids' play area (the 'Funhouse'), staff wandering around in animal costumes, kids' mealtimes and evening programme.

1225
9/G22
9 ROOMS
MAR-NOV
£38-45

Calgary Hotel www.calgary.co.uk · 01688 400256 · **near Dervaig, Mull** 20km south of Tobermory (and a long way from Balamory), a roadside farmhouse/bistro/gallery, ie very laid-back place. Main features are beautiful wood out back (with art in it, but an adventure land for kids) and Mull's famously fab beach adjacent. 2 great family rooms. 2393/ISLAND HOTELS.

1226
8/T18
109 ROOMS
(16 FAMILY)
TEL · TV
£45-60

Waterside Inn www.swallow-hotels.com/hotels/waterside-inn · 01779 471121 · **Peterhead** Edge of town on A952 to Fraserburgh. Modern hotel with pool etc and some activities for kids. Aden Country Park nearby (1795/KIDS). Kids' meal and playroom 7-9pm while you eat, and family rooms. Ugie and Deedee (the bears) have been a great success, but you wouldn't want to take them to bed. Adventure playground and pool. Sometimes special family weekends.

1227
10/Q27
14 ROOMS
+ 5 LODGES
TEL · TV
£45-60

Philipburn www.philipburnhousehotel.co.uk · 01750 720747 · **Selkirk** 1km town centre on Peebles Rd. Main attraction is open-air pool; 2 family rooms overlook. Also easy-eat bistro restaurant with separate kids' mealtime. Giant chess in the garden, other physical (kids' adventure playground in woods at Bowmore) and cerebral (St Mary's Loch/Grey Mare's Tail; 1691/WATERFALLS) nearby.

Stonefield Castle Hotel www.stonefieldhotels.com · 01880 820836 · **Tarbert** Outside Tarbert on A83 on slopes of Loch Fyne with wonderful views. A real castle with 60 acres of woody grounds to explore. Full report and codes: 822/ARGYLL HOTELS.

Comrie Croft 01764 670140 · **near Comrie** Hostel accommodation on a working farm. 1231/HOSTELS.

Pier House 01631 730302 · **Port Appin** Report: 1264/SEASIDE INNS.

The Best Hostels

For hostels in Edinburgh, see p. 35–36; for Glasgow, see p. 96. SYHA Info: 01786 891400. Central reservations (SYHA) 0870 155 3255. www.syha.org.uk

1228
6/L15
189 BEDS

✓ ✓ ✓ **Carbisdale Castle SYH** www.carbisdale.org · 0870 004 1109 · **Culrain near Bonar Bridge** The flagship hostel of the SYHA, an Edwardian castle in terraced gardens overlooking the Kyle of Sutherland on the edge of the Highlands. Once the home of the exiled King of Norway, it still contains original works of art (nothing of great value though the sculptures are elegant). The library, ballroom, lounges are all in use and it's only a few quid a night. Mostly shared dorms as usual but no chores. Kitchens and café. Bike hire in summer; lots scenic walks. Station (from Inverness) 1km up steep hill. Buses: Inverness/Thurso/Lairg. 75km Inverness, 330km Edinburgh. You can have the whole place (1350/HOUSE PARTIES).

1229
10/N24
126 BEDS

✓ **Stirling SYH** www.stirlinghostel.co.uk · 0870 004 1149 · **Stirling** Modern conversion in great part of town, close to castle, adjacent ancient graveyard and with fine views from some rooms. One of the new hotel-like hostels with student-hall standard and facilities. Many oldies and international tourists. Breakfast included or self-catering. Access till 2am.

1230
9/L25
160 BEDS

✓ **Loch Lomond SYH** www.syha.org.uk · 0870 004 1149 · **Alexandria** Built in 1866 by George Martin, the tobacco baron (as opposed to the other one who produced the Beatles), this is hostelling on the grand scale. Towers and turrets, galleried upper-hall, space for banqueting and a splendid view across the loch, of where you're going tomorrow. 30km Glasgow. Station (Balloch) 4km. Buses 200m. Access till 2am.

1231
10/M23

✓ **Comrie Croft** www.comriecroft.com · 01764 670140 · **near Comrie** On A85 Comrie-Crieff/Perth road 3km before Comrie. 2 self-contained buildings: the Farmhouse and the Lodge and courtyard of a working farm in beautiful countryside including a loch and a mountain. Excellent facilities including shop, games room, kitchen and lounges. Mountain bikes for hire. Eco friendly. Good for kids.

1232
7/N19

✓ **Aviemore Bunkhouse** www.aviemore-bunkhouse.com · 01479 811181 · **Aviemore** Near main road into Aviemore from south (A95) off Coylumbridge road to Cairngorm and by the river. Part of Old Inn (1391/ GASTROPUBS) so great food adjacent. Ensuite rooms for 6/8 and family rooms available. All year.

1233
6/K14

✓ **Inchnadamph Lodge** www.inch-lodge.co.uk · 01571 822218 · **Assynt** 25km north of Ullapool on A837 road to Lochinver and Sutherland. Well appointed mansion house for individuals or groups in geology-gazing, hill-walking, mountain-rearing Assynt. Kitchen, canteen (dinner not provided but self-service breakfast), DVDs. Some twin rooms.

1234
7/M20

✓ **Pottery Bunkhouse** www.potterybunkhouse.co.uk · 01528 544231 · **Laggan Bridge** On A889 east-west near Loch Laggan, 12km from A9 at Dalwhinnie. Homely bunkhouse and great home-bakes caff (1481/TEAROOMS). Lounge overlooking hills; wood stove, hot tub on deck. All year (tearoom Easter-Oct).

1235
3/R10

✓ **Bis Geos** www.bis-geos.co.uk · 01857 677420 · **Isle of Westray, Orkney** Remote and fabulous: this is how this traditionally rebuilt croft is described, because I haven't been. Sounds like perhaps 2 ticks may be due. Exceptional standard with nautical theme. Conservatory overlooks the wild ocean. Minibus from the ferry. Sleeps 12. 2 cottages.

1235A

The Borders SYH *There are some ideal wee hostels in this hill-walking tract of Scotland (where it all began). These 2 are especially good, one grand, one very small.*

Melrose 0870 004 1141 Grade 1, 90 beds, very popular. Well-appointed mansion on Meadow 250m by riverside from the Abbey.
Broadmeadows 8km from Selkirk off A708, the first hostel in Scotland (1931) is a cosy howff with a stove and a view.

1236
7/M18

Inverness Student Hostel www.scotlands-top-hostels.com · 01463 236556 · **8 Culduthel Road** Best independent hostel in town uphill from town centre (some dorms have views). Run by same folk who have the great Edinburgh one (120/HOSTELS), with similar laid-back atmosphere and camaraderie.
Bazpackers 100m downhill, similar vibe.

1237
9/L24

Rowardennan SYH www.rowardennanhotel.co.uk · 0870 004 1148 · **Loch Lomond** The hostel at the end of the road up the east (less touristy) side of Loch Lomond from Balmaha and Drymen. Large, well managed and modernised and on a water-side site. On West Highland Way and obvious base for climbing Ben Lomond (2048/MUNROS). Good all-round activity centre and lawns to the loch of your dreams. Rowardennan Hotel boozer nearby. Can do 'private' rooms.

1238
7

Hostelling In the Hebrides www.syha.org.uk Simple hostelling in the crofting communities of Lewis, Harris and the Uists. Run by a trust to maintain standards in the spirit of Highland hospitality with local crofters acting as wardens. Lewis, Harris and one each in North and South Uist. No advance bookings necessary or accepted: suggests they will always fit you in, except no Sun arrival or departure. Check local tourist information centres for details (2427/OUTER HEBRIDES). Also:

1239
5/E16

Am Bothan www.ambothan.com · 01859 520251 · **Harris** At Leverburgh in the south of South Harris, a bunkhouse handbuilt and personally run – a bright, cool building with contemporary feel. Good disabled facilities. Caff, shop nearby. 18 spaces and camping nearby. One of 8 hostels in Scotland given 5 Stars by VisitScotland. Also **Na Gearrannan** near Carloway, North Lewis. The remarkable hostel in a village of blackhouses. An idyllic spot. 2309/MUSEUMS.

1240
9/F23

Iagandorain www.langadorain.com · 01681 700781 · **Iona** Bunkhouse at north tip of island 2km from ferry on John Maclean's farm. This feels like the edge of the world looking over to Staffa and beyond; beach besides. Open all year. Sleeps 21. Iona is very special (2360/ISLANDS).

1241
9/G22

Tobermory SYH www.tobermory.co.uk · 0870 004 1151 · **Mull** Looks out to Tobermory Bay. Central, relatively high-standard hostel very busy in summer. 39 places 7 rooms (4 on front). Kitchen. Internet. Near ferry to Ardnamurchan main Oban ferry 35km away (1641/COASTAL VILLAGES). Mar-Oct.

1242
9/J26

Lochranza Youth Hostel SYH www.syha.org.uk · 0870 004 1140 · **Lochranza** On left approaching village from south – Victorian house overlooking fab bay and castle ruins. Swans dip at dawn. Full self-catering facilities. Comfortable sitting room and lots of local books. Mar-Nov.

1243
9/J21
Glencoe SYH www.glencoehostel.co.uk · 0870 004 1122 · **Glencoe** Deep in the glen itself, 3km off A82/4km by back road from Glencoe village and 33km from Fort William. Modern timber house near river; especially handy for climbers and walkers. Clachaig pub, 2km for good food and craic. (Also 1710/SCENIC ROUTES; 2011/SPOOKY PLACES; 1984/BATTLEGROUNDS; 1360/PUBS; 2170/SKIING; 2066/SERIOUS WALKS.)

1244
10/N22
National Kayak School Hostel www.glencoehostel.co.uk · 01887 820498 · **Weem near Aberfeldy** Newly made hostel and self-catering cottages in main street of tiny village near Glen Lyon and 3km from Aberfeldy. 9 rooms can sleep 40. Well appointed. Great pub and food next door – the Weem Hotel (1268/ROAD-SIDE INNS). And all the water action you can handle.

1245
7/J19
Ratagan SYH 0870 004 1147 29km from Kyle of Lochalsh, 3km Shiel Bridge (on A87). A much-loved Highland hostel on the shore of Loch Duich and well situated for walking and exploring some of Scotland's most celebrated scenery, eg 5 Sisters of Kintail/Cluanie Ridge (2069/SERIOUS WALKS), Glenelg (1711/SCENIC ROUTES; 1904/PREHISTORIC SITES), Falls of Glomach (1682/WATERFALLS). From Glenelg there's the short and dramatic crossing to Skye through the Kylerhea narrows (continuous, summer only), quite the best way to go. Mar-Oct.

1246
7/F20
Kinloch Castle www.kinlochcastle.co.uk · 01687 462037 · **Rum** The hostel on first and second floor (53 beds) in one of the most opulent castle-fantasies in the Highlands. Currently subject to grant-aid to restore to former glory, the hostel operates to allow visitors to experience the rich natural wildlife, grandeur and peace of Rum. Self-catering. For ferry details see Rum: 2363/ISLANDS.

1247
7/G17
Dun Flodigarry www.hostelflodigarry.co.uk · 01470 552212 · **near Staffin, Skye** In far north 32km from Portree beside Flodigarry Country House Hotel, which has a decent bistro but no pub, and amidst big scenery. Overlooks sea. Bunkrooms for 2-6 and 3 singles (holds up to 40) and great refectory. Open all year.

1248
7/H18
120 BEDS
Skye Backpackers Guest House 01599 534510 · **Kyleakin** Convenient guesthouse with mainly 4-bunk rooms and smallish gantry/lounge near bridge for last/first stop on what used to be an island. Open all year. There are many other independent hostels in Kyleakin and on Skye including 2 in Portree. The largest is the SYHA hostel also in Kyleakin (08701 533255).

1249
10/P21
Prosen Hotel 01575 540238 · **Glen Prosen** Glen Prosen, heart of the Angus glens. A 'green' hostel; wood-burning stove, internet. Red squirrels, apparently (I haven't visited). Sounds nice and a great spot.

1250
10/S26
Mount Coldingham Sands Youth Hostel SYH 01890 771298 · **Coldingham** Impressive position and views over North Sea, north of Berwick. Usual ascetics of hostel life (SYH) but village has some facilities. Great surfing and kayaking spot. An easy walk to the beach for the rest of us and Coldingham is a great old cove. Closed Oct-Mar.

The Best Roadside, Seaside & Countryside Inns

1251
7/F18
8 ROOMS
TEL · TV
£85+

✓✓ **The Three Chimneys** www.threechimneys.co.uk · 01470 511258 · **Colbost, Skye** 7km west of Dunvegan on B884 to Glendale. Rooms in a new build across the yard from the excellent, long-established and much-awarded Three Chimneys restaurant (2398/SKYE RESTAURANTS) called **The House Over-by**. Roadside though few cars and within sight and smell of the sea. Good standard split-level rooms with own doors to the sward. Breakfast lounge, self-service, very healthy buffet. A model of its kind in the Highlands, hence often full. And be sure to book for dinner!

1252
10/N23
5 ROOMS
TV
£38-45

✓✓ **The Barley Bree** www.barleybree.com · 01764 681451 · **Muthill near Crieff** Instant hit from summer '07: stylish, excellent value, great food, tasteful and comfortable rooms. Must be the French connection (chef Fabrice Bouteloup). Bar/restaurant open for lunch and dinner (closed Mon). Not much to do in Muthill itself but the amazing Drummond Gardens are nearby (1589/GARDENS) and there's Crieff and Comrie.

1253
7/H19
6 ROOMS +1
£38-45

✓ **Glenelg Inn** www.glenelg-inn.com · 01599 522273 · **Glenelg** At the end of that great road over the hill from Shiel Bridge on the A87 (1711/SCENIC ROUTES)...well, not quite the end because you can drive further round to ethereal Loch Hourn, but this halt is a civilised hostelry to repair to. Decent food, good drinking, snug lounge. Garden with tables and views. Charming rooms. Simon cooks Tue-Sat. Adjacent cottage (Room 7) available. From Glenelg, take the best route to Skye (7/FAVOURITE JOURNEYS).

1254
9/F23
16 ROOMS
MAR-NOV
£38-45

✓ **Argyll Hotel** www.argyllhoteliona.co.uk · 01681 700334 · **Iona** On beautiful, turquoise bay between Iona and Mull on road between ferry and abbey. Day trippers come and go, but stay! This is a charming hotel and a remarkable island. Cosy rooms (1 suite), good food (especially vegetarian) fresh from the organic garden. The real peace and quiet and that's just sitting on the bench outside – it's Colourist country and this is where they would have stayed too. Nice for kids (1214/HOTELS THAT WELCOME KIDS).

1255 9/H26
4 ROOMS
MAR-DEC
TV
£38-45

✓ **Kilberry Inn** www.kilberryinn.com · 01880 770223 · **near Tarbert, Argyll** Half-way round the Knapdale peninsula on the single-track B8024 (1726/SCENIC ROUTES), the long way to Lochgilphead. Homely roadside inn with simple, inexpensive rooms and excellent cooking (1393/GASTROPUBS). Michelin Bib Gourmand '07. A gem.

1256
10/N22
5 ROOMS
TV
£38-45

✓ **Inn on the Tay** www.theinnonthetay.co.uk · 01887 840760 · **Grandtully** Recent conversion of roadside inn that also has a commanding position on the riverbank where rapids tax all the kayakers and canoeists of Perthshire – so constant entertainment. Contemporary café/bar with good food, residents' lounge and comfortable modern bedrooms – each with 3 beds, so a good family or ménage à trois option.

✓ **The Applecross Inn** www.applecross.uk.com/inn · 01520 744262 The legendary end of the road, seaside inn on the shore opposite Applecross. Report: 1285/GET AWAY HOTELS.

✓ **The Ship Inn** www.theshipinngatehouse.co.uk · 01557 814217 ·
Gatehouse of Fleet Old inn on corner of main street of this most charming
of Galloway towns. Recent refurbishment and great grub. Report: 851/SOUTHWEST
HOTELS.

1257
10/Q27
14 ROOMS
TEL · TV
£38-45

✓ **Traquair Arms** www.traquairarmshotel.co.uk · 01896 830229 ·
Innerleithen 100m from the A72 Gala-Peebles road towards Traquair, a
popular village and country inn that caters for all kinds of folk (and, at weekends,
large numbers of them). Notable for bar meals, real ale and family facilities.
Rooms refurbished to a good standard. David and Jane Roger making a fair go of it
here. Nice garden out back. All food very home-made in what they call 'Traqs'.

1258
10/S26
3 ROOMS
£30-38

Craw Inn www.thecrawinn.co.uk · 01890 761253 · **Auchencrow near
Reston** 5 km A1 and well worth short detour into Berwickshire countryside.
Quintessential inn with cosy pub and dining room. Funky furniture, simple rooms.
Food decent, wines extraordinary. Lunch and dinner.

1259
7/F17
5 ROOMS
£30 OR LESS

The Stein Inn www.stein-inn.co.uk · 01470 592362 · **Waternish, Skye** Off
B886 the Dunvegan-Portree road, about 10km Dunvegan. In row of cottages on
waterside. The 'oldest inn on Skye' with great pub (open fire, good grub) and comfortable small rooms above. Great value in a special spot. Excellent seafood restaurant adjacent (1424/SEAFOOD RESTAURANTS) for variation.

1260 7/H18
11 ROOMS
TEL · TV
NO PETS
£38-45

Plockton Hotel www.plocktonhotel.com · 01599 544274 · **Plockton** On
shoreline of one of Scotland's most picturesque villages (1636/COASTAL VILLAGES).
Dreamy little bay. Many visitors and this pub gets busy, but food is great and
rooms upstairs are recently refurbished and not without charm. 4 of the rooms
are in cottages. Has been and no doubt will be again, a 'Pub of the Year'.

1261
9/H25
8 ROOMS
TV
£38-45

West Loch Hotel www.westlochhotel.co.uk · 01880 820283 · **Tarbert**
Beside A83 just west of Tarbert; reasonable inexpensive stopover en route to the
islands. Comfortably furnished; with some original features. Board games and
books dotted around, children welcome in relaxed, friendly atmosphere. New
owners. Good value, but roadside rooms may be noisy.

1262
7/H16
17 ROOMS
TEL · TV
£38-45

Old Inn 01445 712006 · **Gairloch** Southern approach on A832, tucked away by
river and 'old bridge'. Excellent pub for food, music (traditional and contemporary
nights Tue/Fri). Recent acquisition of hotel up the road. For the moment you'd
want to stay here. Nice, simple rooms (though the pub goes like a fair). Routinely
recommended in pub guides.

1263
9/H25
12 ROOMS
TEL · TV
£38-45

Cairnbaan Hotel www.cairnbaan.com · 01546 603668 · **Cairnbaan near
Lochgilphead** Main attraction here is the location overlooking lochs of the
Crinan Canal – nice to watch or walk (all the way to Crinan) if not messing about
on a boat yourself. Decent pub grub in or out and less successful dinner menu.
Some ales.

1264
10/M24
12 ROOMS
TEL · TV
NO PETS
£38-60

Pier House www.pierhousehotel.co.uk · 01631 730302 · **Port Appin** An
inn at the end of the road (the minor road that leads off the A828 Oban to Fort
William) and at the end of the 'pier', where the tiny passenger ferry leaves for
Lismore (2371/MAGIC ISLANDS). Bistro restaurant with decent seafood
(1435/SEAFOOD RESTAURANTS) in great setting. Comfy motel-type rooms (more
expensive overlook the sea and island) and conservatory restaurant and lounge.
Great place to take kids.

1265
10/P21
6 ROOMS
£38-45

Glenisla Hotel www.glenisla-hotel.com · 01575 582223 · **Kirkton Of Glenisla** 20km northwest of Kirriemuir via B951 at head of this secluded story-book glen. A home from home: hearty food, real ale and local colour. Fishers, stalkers, trekkers and walkers all come by. Miles from the town literally and laterally. Neat rooms look into countryside but could do with a wee makeover; convivial bar (sometimes live music).

1266
10/P22
5 ROOMS
TV
£45-60

Meikleour Hotel www.meikleour-inn.co.uk · 01250 883206 · **Meikleour** Just off the A93 Perth-Blairgowrie road (on the B984) by and behind the famously high beech hedge (a Perthshire icon). Roadside inn with quiet accommodation and food in dining room or (more atmosphere) the bar. Refurbished rooms in progress.

1267
9/K22
10 ROOMS
TEL · TV
£38-45

Bridge of Orchy Hotel www.bridgeoforchy.co.uk · 01838 400208 · **Bridge of Orchy** Unmissable on the A82 (the road to Glencoe, Fort William and Skye) 11km north of Tyndrum. Old inn extensively refurbished and run as a stopover hotel. Simple, quite stylish rooms. A la carte menu and specials in pub/conservatory. Good spot for the malt or a munch on the West Highland Way (2060/LONG WALKS). Food LO 9pm. Also 54-bed bunkhouse (very cheap).

1268
10/N22
12 ROOMS
TV
£38-45

Weem Hotel www.weemhotel.com · 01887 820381 · **Weem by Aberfeldy** A hotel with a chequered past, now heading in the right direction. Nothing too fancy going on here, just solid accommodation and a friendly local bar with decent food. Good walking nearby and on the way to magical Glen Lyon (1672/GLENS).

1269 7/J19
12 ROOMS
+BUNKHOUSE
TEL
£30-38/
£45-60

Cluanie Inn www.cluanieinn.com · 01320 340238 · **Glenmoriston** On main road to Skye 15km before Shiel Bridge, a traditional inn surrounded by the mountain summits that attract walkers and travellers – the 5 Sisters, the Ridge and the Saddle (2069/SERIOUS WALKS). Club house adjacent has some group accommodation while inn rooms can be high-spec – one with sauna, one with jacuzzi! Bar food LO 9pm. Rooms do vary. Friendly staff.

1270
9/J25
10 ROOMS
TV
£38-45

The Kames Hotel www.kames-hotel.com · 01700 811489 · **by Tighnabruaich** Frequented by passing yachtsmen who moor alongside and pop in for lunch. Good base for all things offshore; marine cruises or a nostalgic journey on a 'puffer', with a great selection of malts to warm you up before or after. Hotel recently taken over by enterprising and tasteful threesome so it all looks lovely now: calming neutral colours, simply stylish. Food LO in bar 9pm.

1271
10/P22
17 ROOMS
TV
£38-45

Bridge Of Cally Hotel www.bridgeofcallyhotel.com · 01250 886231 · **Bridge Of Cally** Wayside pub on a bend of the road between Blairgowrie and Glenshee/Braemar (the ski zone and Royal Deeside). Cosy and inexpensive between gentle Perthshire and the wilder Grampians. Rooms quiet and pleasant and good value. Restaurant and bar meals till 9pm.

1272
9/J21
23 ROOMS
TV
NO PETS
£30-38

Clachaig Inn www.clachaig.com · 01855 811252 · **Glencoe** Basic accommodation but you will sleep well, especially after walking/climbing/drinking, which is what most people are doing here. Great atmosphere both inside and out. Food available bar/lounge and dining room. 4 lodges out back. Harry Potter and film crew was once here.

1273 10/N21   **Moulin Hotel** www.moulinhotel.co.uk · 01796 472196 · **Pitlochry**
16 ROOMS   Kirkmichael Rd; at the landmark crossroads on the A924. Basic rooms above and
TEL · TV   beside notable pub for excellent pub food and especially ales – they brew their
£38-45   own out the back. (1371/REAL ALES). They have an annexe across the street.

1274   **Glenmoriston Arms Hotel** www.glenmoriston-arms-hotel.co.uk · 01320
7/L19   351206 · **Invermoriston Loch Ness** On main A82 between Inverness (45km)
8 ROOMS   and Fort Augustus (10km) at the Glen Moriston corner, and a worthwhile corner of
TEL · TV   this famous loch side to explore. Busy local bar, fishermen's tales. Bistro over-by
£38-45   (LO 8.30pm – 7 days summer, Thu-Sat in winter) tables outside in summer. Bar
meals look ok and extensive malt list – certainly a good place to drink them. Inn-
like bedrooms. New, friendly owners '07.

1275   **Gordon Inn** 01750 82222 · **Yarrow, Yarrow Valley** Old Borders coaching inn
10/Q27   at historic crossroads deep in James Hogg country (2006/LITERARY PLACES) –
5 ROOMS   there's a letter above the mantelpiece. Recent refurbishment has brought this
+BUNKHOUSE   place to a comfortable as well as cosy standard. Reasonable accommodation and
£30-38   decent meals (till 9/10pm).

✓ ✓ **Ardeonaig** 01567 820400 · **Loch Tay** On tiny lochside road, a haven
with superb dining. 1277/GET-AWAY HOTELS.

✓ **The Harbour Inn** 01496 810330 & **The Port Charlotte Hotel** 01496
850360 · **Islay** 2390/2389/ISLAND HOTELS.

✓ **An Lochan** www.royalhotel.org.uk · 01700 811239 · **Tighnabruaich**
More hotel perhaps than inn (though great pub meals), but top service and
attention to detail in glorious seaside setting. 815/ARGYLL HOTELS.

✓ **The Sorn Inn** www.sorninn.com · 01290 551305 · **Sorn, Ayrshire**
1381/GASTROPUBS.

Anchor Hotel 01556 620205 · **Kippford** 856/SOUTHWEST HOTELS/
RESTAURANTS.

The Best Restaurants With Rooms

✓ ✓ **The Sorn Inn** 01290 551305 · **Sorn** 8km east of Mauchline on the
B743, half an hour from Ayr. 837/AYRSHIRE HOTELS.

✓ ✓ **The Peat Inn** 01334 840206 · **near Cupar** At eponymous Fife crossroads. Long-established brilliant restaurant now under masterchef
Geoffrey Smeddle. 940/FIFE RESTAURANTS.

✓ ✓ **The Three Chimneys** 01470 511258 · **Colbost, Skye** State-of-the-
art dining and contemporary rooms far away in the west. Near
Dunvegan. 2398/SKYE HOTELS.

✓ ✓ **The Barley Bree** 01764 681451 · **Muthill near Crieff** French guy in
the kitchen, Scots partner on decor and design have transformed this old
pub in a sleepy village to a destination. 1252/ROADSIDE INNS.

✓ ✓ **The Cross** 01540 661166 · **Kingussie** Rooms upstairs in converted Tweed Mill. Downstairs the best restaurant and wine list in the region. 1021/HIGHLAND HOTELS.

✓ **The Alloway Inn** 01292 442336 · **Ayr** Just outside Alloway in deepest Burns country. Cosy rooms. Gastropub food. 836/AYRSHIRE HOTELS.

✓ **Lochside Lodge** 01575 560340 · **Bridgend of Lyntrathen near Alyth** 9km from Alyth towards Glenisla. Excellent food. 971/PERTH RESTAURANTS.

✓ **Mackays** 01971 511202 · **Durness** Contemporary makeover of long-established hotel in the far North West. 1284/GET-AWAY HOTELS.

✓ **The Inn At Kippen** 01786 871010 · **Kippen** Excellent bar and restaurant in centre of village just off the road from Stirling to Loch Lomond. 870/CENTRAL HOTELS.

✓ **The Mash Tun** 01340 881771 · **Aberlour** Boutique-style rooms above pub in whisky country. 1008/SPEYSIDE.

✓ **2 Quail** 01862 811811 · **Dornoch** Centre of town. Small and beautiful. 1040/HIGHLAND HOTELS.

✓ **The Inn on the Tay** 01887 840760 · **Grandtully near Aberfeldy** Another made-over inn, this on the banks of the rushing River Tay. Great for kids. 1256/ROADSIDE INNS.

✓ **Creagan House** 01877 384638 · **Strathyre** Rob Roy and Trossachs country. On the road west and to the islands. 871/CENTRAL HOTELS.

✓ **The Creel Inn** 01856 831311 · **St Margaret's Hope, Orkney** 2429/ORKNEY.

✓ **Wildings Hotel** 01655 331401 · **Maidens** Huge local reputation for food; refurbished rooms '07. 841/AYRSHIRE HOTELS.

Kilspindie House 01875 870682 · **Aberlady** Main St of East Lothian village. 914/LOTHIAN HOTELS.

The Rocks 01368 862287 · **Dunbar** At east end of town. Overlooking harbour area. 915/LOTHIAN HOTELS.

The Great Get-Away-From-It-All Hotels

1276
10/L23
13 ROOMS
TEL · TV
£38-45

✓✓ **Monachyle Mhor** www.monachylemhor.com · 01877 384622 · **near Balquhidder** Not so remote, but seems so once you've negotiated the thread of road alongs Loch Voil from Balquhidder (only 11km from the A84 Callander-Crianlarich road) and Rob Roy's now-famous grave (1971/GRAVEYARDS). Farmhouse overlooking Loch Voil from the magnificent Balquhidder Braes where the children Tom and Madeleine and Dick grew up and then turned into the first really cool boutique hotel in the Highlands. Ongoing refurbishment of rooms: contemporary, calm and sexy as hell. Some in courtyard annexe; some are cheaper. All very individual. Bar locals and visitors use. Tom on stoves cooking up some of the best food in the North. Friendly, cosy, inexpensive; a place to relax summer or winter. Tastefully done, great informal atmosphere. A very Mhor-ish experience.

1277
10/M22
20 ROOMS
TEL
£45-85+

✓✓ **Ardeonaig** www.ardeonaighotel.co.uk · 01567 820400 · **Loch Tay** On narrow, scenic south Loch Tay road midway between Kenmore and Killin. An airy inn by the water opposite Ben Lawers. South African chef/proprietor making the most of this perfectly remote location. Stylish rooms, great bar and excellent dining with top urban service standards. And friendly! See also 950/BEST TAYSIDE. Library with cool books and dreamy view of the Ben. Further improvement to the idyll '08 . Room rate includes dinner but there is nowhere else to go!

1278
7/J17
19 ROOMS
TEL · TV
NO KIDS
NO PETS
£85+

✓✓ **The Torridon** www.lochtorridonhotel.com · 01445 791242 · **Glen Torridon near Kinlochewe** Impressive former hunting lodge on lochside, surrounded by majestic mountains. A comfortable but cosy family-run baronial house with very relaxed atmosphere, now developing into an all-round Highland 'experience'. Focuses on outdoor activities like clay-pigeon shoots, mountain biking or fishing with 2 full-time guides in season. Lots of walking possibilities nearby including the Torridon big 3: Beinn Alligin (2053/MUNROS), Liathach right in front of the hotel and Beinn Eighe. This great hotel has spawned a cheaper travel lodge in the outdoors kind of option: **The Torridon Inn** in adjacent block with own bar and bistro. Excellent budget choice (12 rooms). Fantastic malts bar in the dwindling day (1576/WHISKY).

1279 9/G22
6 ROOMS
+2 COTTAGES
MAR-NOV
TV
NO PETS
£60-85

✓ **Tiroran House** www.tiroran.com · 01681 705232 · **Isle of Mull** Southwest corner on road to Iona from Craignure then B8035 round Loch na Keal. 1 hour Tobermory. Family-friendly small country house in fabulous gardens by the sea, being refurbished under conscientious owners Laurence Mackay and Katie Munro (Katie a Cordon Bleu cook). Near Iona and Ulva ferry; you won't miss Tobermory. Excellent food from sea and kitchen garden. Lovely rooms. Sea eagles fly over, otters in the bay. I missed Tiroran in '07; I did miss it.

1280
9/F23
15 ROOMS
(1 SUITE)
MAR-NOV
£38-45

✓ **Argyll Hotel** www.argyllhoteliona.co.uk · 01681 700334 · **Iona** Quintessential island hotel on the best of small islands just large enough to get away for walks and explore (2360/ISLANDS). You can hire bikes (or bring). Abbey is nearby (1974/ABBEYS). 3 lounges (1 with TV, 1 with sun) and 1 lovely suite (with wood-burning stove). Good home-grown/made food from their famous organic garden.

1281 9/L22
5 ROOMS
MID FEB-
MID NOV
£38-45

✓ **Moor of Rannoch Hotel** www.moorofrannoch.co.uk · 01882 633238 · **Rannoch Station** Beyond Pitlochry and the Trossachs and far west via Loch Tummel and Loch Rannoch (B8019 and B846) so a wonderful journey to the edge of Rannoch Moor and adjacent station so you could get the sleeper from London and be here for breakfast. 4 trains either way ea day via Glasgow. Literally the end of the road but an exceptional find in the middle of nowhere. Cosy, wood-panelled rooms, great restaurant (open to non-residents but book first). Quintessential Highland Inn. Great walking.

1282
10/Q21
10 ROOMS
TEL · TV
NO PETS
£38-45

✓ **Glen Clova Hotel** www.clova.com · 01575 550350 · **near Kirriemuir** Well, not that near Kirriemuir; 25km north to head of glen on B955 and once you're there there's nowhere else to go except up. Rooms all en-suite and surprisingly well appointed. Climbers' bar (till all hours). Superb walking hereabouts (eg Loch Brandy and the classic path to Loch Muick). A laid-back get-away though lots of families drive up on a Sun for lunch. Also has a bunkhouse (cheap) and 2 new 'luxury' lodges. Great value.

1283 11/J30
6 ROOMS
+ SUITES
TEL · TV
£60-85

✓ **Corsewall Lighthouse Hotel** www.lighthousehotel.co.uk · 01776 853220 · **near Stranraer** Only 20 minutes from Stranraer (via A718 to Kirkcolm) and follow signs, but way up on the peninsula and as it suggests a hotel made out of a working lighthouse. Romantic and offbeat, decent food too, and there are attractions nearby especially at Portpatrick 30 minutes away through the maze of quiet backroads.

1284 6/L12
7 ROOMS
APR-OCT
TV
NO PETS
£38-45

✓ **Mackays** www.visitmackays.com · 01971 511202 · **Durness** Remote from rest of Scotland (the top northwest corner where this hot spot is the only real option) but actually in centre of township. Many interesting distractions nearby (2164/GOLF, 1932/MONUMENTS, Smoo Cave, etc). Highland chic: a comfortable, contemporary restaurant with rooms. Wood and slate: the coolest retreat in the North. Great food.

1285 7/H18
8 ROOMS
£30-38

✓ **Applecross Inn** www.applecross.uk.com/inn · 01520 744262 · **Applecross** At the end of the road (the Pass of the Cattle which is often snowed up in winter, so you can really disappear) north of Kyle of Lochalsh and west of Strathcarron. After a spectacular journey, this waterside inn is a haven of hospitality. Buzzes all seasons. Rooms small (1+7 best), finally all ensuite '07. Judy Fish and a great team and a real chef look after you. Poignant visitor centre (2315/HERITAGE), walled garden, lovely walks (2122/COASTAL WALKS) and even a real pizza hut in summer (1490/COFFEE SHOPS) to keep you happy in Applecross for days.

1286 9/K20
5 ROOMS
MAR-OCT
TV · NO PETS
£30-38

✓ **Corriechoille Lodge** www.corriechoille.com · 01397 712002 · **by Spean Bridge** 3km from south Bridge via road by station. Lovely road and spectacularly situated; it's great to arrive. Justin and Lucy share their perfect retreat with you in house and 2 turf-covered chalets outs back. Report 1043/HIGHLAND HOTELS.

1287 7/N16
9 ROOMS
TEL · NO PETS
£60-85

✓ **Glenmorangie House** www.theglenmorangiehouse.com · 01862 871671 · **Cadboll by Fearn near Tain** On the little peninsula east of Tain off A9 (10km). Comfortable mansion once owned by distillery, now by LVMH. Chef has good reputation. Class not just in the glass. Report: 1024/HIGHLAND HOTELS.

1288 7/K20
10 ROOMS
£38-45

Tomdoun Hotel www.tomdoun.com · 01809 511218 · **near Invergarry** 20km from Invergarry, 9km off the A87 to Kyle of Lochalsh. A 19th-century coaching inn that replaced a much older one; off the beaten track but perfect (we do mean perfect) for fishing and walking (Loch Quoich and Knoydart, the last wilderness, have been waiting a long time for you). Superb views over Glengarry and Bonnie Prince Charlie's country. House-party atmosphere, mix-match furniture and nice dogs. Real chef with meticulously sourced seafood menu.

1289 7/H20
4 ROOMS
MAR-OCT
NO PETS
£30 OR LESS

The Pier House www.pierhousehotel.co.uk · 01687 462347 · Inverie, **Knoydart** Currently the only restaurant on this far-away peninsula, though good grub at the pub nearby (1359/BLOODY GOOD PUBS). Accessible on foot (sic) from Kinlochourn (25km) or Bruce Watt's boat from Mallaig (Mon-Fri summer; Mon, Wed, Fri winter. 01687 462320). Friendly couple offer warm hospitality in their home and surprisingly good cooking for somewhere so remote; rovers often return.

1290 7/H20
4 ROOMS
+ LODGE
APR-SEP
NO PETS
£38-45

Doune Stone Lodge www.doune-knoydart.co.uk/stlodge.html · 01687 462667 · **Knoydart** As above, on this remote peninsula and this great spot on the west tip overlooking a bay on the Sound of Sleat. They have own boats so pick you up from Mallaig and drop you round the inlets for walking. Otherwise 8km from Inverie. Rooms and lodge for 12. Own restaurant. Only lodge available in winter.

1291 7/K18
8 ROOMS
TEL · TV
£38-45

Tomich Hotel www.tomichhotel.co.uk · 01456 415399 · **near Cannich** 8km from Cannich which is 25km from Drumnadrochit. Fabulous Plodda Falls are nearby (1683/WATERFALLS). Cosy country inn in conservation village with added bonus of use of swimming pool in nearby steading. Faraway feel, surprising bar round the back where what's left of the locals do linger. Good base for outdoorsy weekend. Glen Affric across the way.

1292 7/H16
13 ROOMS
TV
£38-45

Shieldaig Lodge www.shieldaiglodge.com · 01445 741250 · **near Gairloch** South of Gairloch by A832 then out towards Redpoint on B8056, a beautiful drive. This hunting/shooting/mainly fishing hotel with a spectacular setting overlooking Loch Gairloch has old-style rooms and service which means it's comfy to be in. Decent value. Badachro Inn nearby for grub (1403/GASTROPUBS) or the Old Inn back in Gairloch (1262/ROADSIDE INNS). Big Victorian rooms at front are best.

ALSO ...

1293 6/M16
21 ROOMS
(11 LODGES)
TEL · TV
NO PETS
£85+

✓ ✓ ✓ **The Carnegie Club** www.carnegieclub.co.uk · 01862 894600 · **Skibo Castle, Dornoch** Not a hotel, they stress, but you may want to check their website and join their waiting list. Mentioned here because it is top top and it is in Scotland. Found just over Dornoch Bridge, off A9 at Clashmore. A vast estate once home to the formidable Carnegies (those halls in NYC, Dunfermline, etc.). They declared it to be 'heaven on earth' which may be your sentiment too. The sumptuous castle retains its original furnishings (silk wallpaper, panelling, etc.) and the service from your discreet 'hosts' is exemplary. Lodges in the grounds offer more privacy, with the obligatory 2 golf courses (which are solely for guests), spa, gym, pool and 'beach', all oases of relaxing indulgence – vintage Rolls Royces take you around. Many dining options. Everything here has a plus factor, including the cost. You will need to work harder.

✓ ✓ **Knockinaam Lodge** 01776 810471 · **near Portpatrick** Report: 848/SOUTH WEST HOTELS.

✓ ✓ **Glenapp Castle** 01465 831212 · **Ballantrae** Report: 1202/COUNTRY-HOUSE HOTELS.

✓ ✓ **Three Chimneys** 01470 511258 · **Skye** Report: 1251/ROADSIDE INNS, 2398/SKYE RESTAURANTS.

✓ ✓ **Ackergill Tower** 01955 603556 · **near Wick** Report: 1343/HOUSE PARTIES.

✓ **Glenelg Inn** 01599 522273 · **Glenelg** Report: 1253/ROADSIDE INNS.

✓ **Dalmunzie House** 01250 885224 · **Spittal o' Glenshee** Report: 956/PERTHSHIRE HOTELS.

Stein Inn 01470 59232 · **Skye** Report: 1259/ROADSIDE INNS.

Great Wild Camping Up North

In Scotland the Best we don't do caravans. In fact, because we spend a lot of time behind them on Highland roads, WE HATE CARAVANS, but wild camping is a different matter. Although arguably irresponsible to encourage it, it's a good and inexpensive way to experience Scotland, provided you are sensitive to the environment and respect the rights of farmers and other landowners.

1294 9/F26   **Kintra Islay** Bowmore-Port Ellen road, take Oa turn-off then follow signs 7km. Long beach one way, wild coastal walk the other. Camping (room for a few caravans) on grassy strand looking out to sea; not a formal site but facilities available.

1295 9/H21   **Lochailort** A 12km stretch south from Lochailort on the A861, along the southern shore of the sea loch itself. A flat, rocky and grassy foreshore with a splendid seascape and backed by brooding mountains. Nearby is Loch nan Uamh where Bonnie Prince Charlie landed (1996/MARY, CHARLIE & BOB). Once past the salmon farm laboratories, you're in calendar scenery; the Glenuig Inn at the southern end is the pub to repair to. No facilities except the sea.

1296 9/F22   **Mull www.isle.of.mull.com · Calgary Beach** 10km from Dervaig, where there are toilets; also south of Killiechronan on the gentle shore of Loch na Keal where there is nothing but the sky and the sea. Ben More is in the background (2054/MUNROS). Both sublime!

1297 9/K22   **Glen Etive near Ballachulish & Glencoe** One of Scotland's great unofficial camping grounds. Along the road/river side in a classic glen (1674/GLENS) guarded where it joins the pass into Glencoe by the awesome Buachaille Etive Mor. Innumerable grassy terraces and small meadows on which climbers and walkers have camped for generations, and pools to bathe in (1753/SWIMMING HOLES). The famous Kingshouse Pub is 2km from the foot of the glen for sustenance, malt whisky and comparing midge bites.

1298 7/H19   **Glenelg** Near the village of Glenelg itself which is over the amazing hill from Shiel Bridge (1711/SCENIC ROUTES). Village has great pub, the Glenelg Inn (1253/INNS) and coffee shop for sustenance and a shop. Best spots 1km from village on road to Skye ferry (1711/SCENIC ROUTES) on the strand.

1299 6/K13   **Oldshoremore near Kinlochbervie** 3km from village and supplies. Gorgeous beach (1654/BEACHES) and **Polin**, next cove. On the way to **Sandwood Bay** where the camping is legendary (but you have to carry everything 7km).

1300 6/J14   **Achmelvich near Lochinver** Signed off the fabulous Lochinver to Drumbeg road (1716/SCENIC ROUTES) or walk from village 3km via Ardroe (and a great spot to watch otters that have been there for generations). There is an official campsite adjacent horrible caravan park, but walk further north towards Stoer. The beach at Alltan na Bradhan with the ruins of the old mill is fabulous. Best sea-swimming on this coast. Directions: 1660/BEACHES.

1301 7/H18   **On the Road to Applecross** The road that winds up the mountain from the A896 that takes you to Applecross (1712/SCENIC ROUTES) is one of the most dramatic in Scotland or anywhere. At the plateau before you descend to the coast, the landscape is lunar and the views to die for. Camp here (wind permitting) with the gods. Once over and 8km downhill there's the foreshore for more leisurely camping and proper campsite with caff (see next page).

1302
5/C20

Barra www.isleofbarra.com Lots of quiet places but you may as well be next to an amazing beach – one by 'the airport' where the little Otters come and go has added interest (and mobile phone reception – unlike rest of the island) but the twin crescent beaches on **Vatersay** are probably too beautiful to miss (1663/BEACHES).

1303
5/E16

Harris West coast south of Tarbert where the boat comes in. 35km to Stornoway. Follow road and you reach some truly splendid beaches (eg Scarista 1658/BEACHES). Bring on your own private sunset.

1304
10/M22

Loch Tay South bank between Kenmore and Killin. A single-track road. Stunning views of the loch and Ben Lawyers. Very woody in places. Great variety of potential pitches. Great restaurant half-way, the Ardeonaig Hotel (expensive, but excellent; see 1277/GET-AWAY HOTELS).

Camping With The Kids

Caravan sites and camp grounds that are especially kid-friendly, with good facilities and a range of things to do (including a good pub).
Key: HIRE Caravans for rent NO HIRE No rental caravans available
X C'VAN Number of caravan pitches X TENT Number of tent pitches
FLEXIBLE They take caravans and tents according to demand.

1305
7/N19
240 TENTS
DEC-OCT
NO HIRE

✓ **Glen More Camp Site** 01479 861271 · **near Aviemore** 9km from Aviemore on the road to the ski slopes, the B970. Across the road from the Glen More Visitor Centre and adjacent to Loch Morlich Watersports Centre (2214/WATER SPORTS). Extensive grassy site on loch side with trees and views of the mountains. Loads of activities include watery ones especially the reindeer (1796/KIDS) and at the Coylumbridge Hotel (1224/HOTELS THAT WELCOME KIDS) where there' s a pool and The Fun House – a separate building full of stuff to amuse kids of all ages (soft play, mini golf, etc). Well stocked shop at site entrance.

1306
7/H18
FLEXIBLE
APR-OCT
NO HIRE

✓ **Applecross Campsite** www.applecross.uk.com/campsite · 01520 744268 First thing you come to as you approach the coast after your hair-raising drive over the *bealach*, the mountain pass. Grassy meadow in farm setting 1km sea. Usual facilities and Flower Tunnel bakery and café (1490/COFFEE SHOPS) Apr-Oct till 9pm, till 5pm Mon and Tue. A green, grassy safe haven.

1307
9/H22
80 TENTS
30 C'VAN
APR-MID OCT
NO HIRE

✓ **Shieling Holidays** www.shielingholidays.co.uk · 01680 812496 · **Craignure, Mull** 35km from Tobermory but right where the ferry comes in. Great views and a no-nonsense, thought-of-everything camp park. Self-catering 'shielings' (carpeted cottage tents with heaters and ensuite facilities) or hostel beds if you prefer. Loads to do and see, including nearby Torosay and Duart Castles (1858/1857/CASTLES); the fun and novel Mull Light Railway next door. Village inn and public swimming pool on the way.

1308
10/R26
60 TENTS
MAR-OCT
NO HIRE

Carfraemill Camping & Caravanning Site aka Lauder Camping & Caravanning Club www.campingandcaravanningclub.co.uk · 01578 750697 Just off A697 where it joins the A68 near Oxton. Small, sheltered and friendly campsite in the green countryside with trickling burn. 4 chalets for hire on site. Good gateway to the Borders (Melrose 20km). The Lodge (or Jo's Kitchen as it is also known) adjacent has great family restaurant where kids made very welcome (play area and the food they like, etc).

1309 7/H16
MANY TENTS
100 C'VAN
HIRE

Sands Holiday Centre www.highlandcaravancamping.co.uk · **01445 712152** · **Gairloch** 4km Gairloch (road to Melvaig) with views to the islands, a large park with dunes and its own sandy beach. Kids' play area but plenty to do and see in Gairloch itself – a great pub, the Old Inn, for adults (1262/ROADSIDE INNS). Well equipped shop, mountain bikes for hire; great camping in dunes plus walking, fishing, etc.

1310 8/N19
37 TENTS
HIRE

Boat Of Garten Caravan Park www.boatofgartenholidaypark.com · **01479 831652** In village itself, a medium-sized, slightly regimented site tailored to families with play area for the kids and even cots available to rent for the very wee. Cabins if the Scottish weather gets too much. Not the most rural or attractive site in the Highlands, but lots on doorstep to keep the kids happy, including brilliant ie kid-brilliant Landmark Centre (1798/KIDS) and Loch Garten ospreys (1815/BIRDS).

1311 9/H23
32 TENTS
30 C'VAN
MAR–OCT
NO HIRE

Oban Divers Caravan Park www.obandivers.co.uk · **01631 562755** · **Oban** 1.5 miles out of Oban. Quiet, clean and friendly ground with stream running through. All sorts of 'extras' such as undercover cooking area, BBQ, adventure playground. No dogs. A good base for day trips including Rare Breeds Farm and Sealife Sanctuary (1804/1803/KIDS).

1312 9/L24
135 TENTS
100 C'VAN
MAR–OCT
NO HIRE

Cashel Caravan & Campsite 01360 870234 · **Rowardennan** Forestry Commission site on the quieter shores of Loch Lomond in Queen Elizabeth Forest Park. Excellent facilities and tons to do in the surrounding area which includes Ben Lomond and plootering by the loch.

1313 9/H22
FLEXIBLE
APR–OCT
NO HIRE

Balmeanach Park 01680 300342 · **Fishnish, Mull** Farm-like camp site on main road to Tobermory 1km from Lochaline (Ardnamurchan) Ferry. Sheltered, grassy site with café serving breakfast-dinner. Friendly, central, safe.

1314 7/F18
FLEXIBLE
JAN–DEC

Sligachan 01478 650204 · **Skye** The camp site you see at the major bend in the road on the A87 going north to Portree from the bridge and the ferries. Sligachan is major hotel landmark and all its facilities include all-day bistro/Seumas' bar. Lovely site by river with many walks from here. Warden lives on site. Pitch up and check in.

1315 9/G21
FLEXIBLE
APR–OCT

Resipole Farm www.resipole.co.uk · **01967 431235** · **Loch Sunart, Ardnamurchan** Arrive via Corran Ferry (8/JOURNEYS) or from Mallaig or Fort William route via Lochailort (1725/SCENIC ROUTES). Extensive grassy landing on lochside with all mod cons including shop, dishwashers, mashing machines. Gorgeous Ardnamurchan all around you.

The Best Very Scottish Hotels

1316 6/K15
23 ROOMS
TEL
£60-85/
£30 OR LESS

✓✓ **The Ceilidh Place** www.ceilidhplace.com · 01854 612103 · **Ullapool** Off main street near port for the Hebrides. Inimitable Jean Urquhart's place which more than any other in the Highlands, encapsulates Scottish traditional culture and hospitality and interprets it in a contemporary manner. Caters for all sorts: there's an excellent hotel above (with a truly comfortable lounge – you help yourself to drinks) and a bistro/bar below with occasional live music and performance (ceilidh-style). A bunkhouse across the way with cheap and cheerful accommodation and a bookshop where you can browse through the best new Scottish literature. Scottish-ness is all here and nothing embarrassing in sight. These comments unchanged in 4 editions: that says it all.

1317 6/J14
5 ROOMS
MAR-DEC
TEL
£38-45

✓✓ **The Albannach** www.albannach.com · 01571 844407 · **Lochinver** 2km up road to Baddidarach as you come from south into Lochinver on A837, at the bridge. Lovely 18th-century house in one of Scotland's most scenic areas, Assynt, where the mountains can take your breath away even without going up them (2021/2033/ FAVOURITE HILLS). The outbuilding overlooking the croft gives extra privacy and space. Some rooms have been turned into gorgeous suites: 'the loft' and 'the penthouse' with outside cliff-enclosed terrace. You unwind in tasteful, informal surroundings. Food is the best for miles. Great walk behind house to Archemelvich beach – otters on the way. Non-residents can and should, eat.

1318 9/J22
8 ROOMS
TEL
NO PETS
£60-85+

✓✓ **Ballachulish House** www.ballachulishhouse.com · 01855 811266 · **Ballachulish** On A828 to Oban near south side of the bridge, not to be confused with the nearby Ballachulish hotel. The house is through a charming golf course; you pass the clubhouse which serves excellent light meals 12-8.30pm. Marie McLaughlin very much in charge of it all will make you very welcome and chef Darin Campbell and a strong team in the kitchen keep Ballachulish up there in the top fine-dining rooms in Scotland. Great breakfast to fuel Glencoe walking. This small country-house hotel has become a west of Scotland destination. House very Scottish and makes much more of its historical background (Appin murder, Glencoe etc) and tasteful update of 17th-century laird's lair.

1319 8/Q18
16 ROOMS
FEB-DEC
TEL · TV
£85+

✓ **Kildrummy Castle Hotel** www.kildrummycastlehotel.co.uk · 01975 571288 · **near Alford** 60km west of Aberdeen via A944, through some fine bucolic scenery and the green Don valley to this spectacular location with real Highlands aura. Well placed if you're on the 'Castle Trail', this comfortable chunk of Scottish Baronial has the redolent ruins of Kildrummy Castle on the opposite bluff and a gorgeful of gardens between. Some rooms small, but all very Scottish. Romantic in autumn when the gardens are good. Jacket and tie needed for dinner.

1320 7/H19
12 ROOMS
+4 SUITES
TEL · TV
£60-85/
£85+

✓ **Eilean Iarmain** www.eilean-iarmain.co.uk · 01471 833332 · **Skye** Sleat area on south of island, this snug Gaelic inn nestles in the bay and is the classic island hostelry. A dram in your room awaits you; from the adjacent whisky company. Bedrooms in hotel best but cottage annexe quieter. New suites in adjacent steading more expensive but nice. Food real good in dining room or pub. Mystic shore walks. Gallery with selected exhibitions and shop nearby. This hostelry is very Highland as well as very Scottish – its charm is subtle but sure. Not all mod cons are considered necessary.

1321 9/J20
13+ ROOMS
MAR-NOV
£38-60

✓ **Glenfinnan House** www.glenfinnanhouse.com · 01397 722235 ·
Glenfinnan Off the Road to the Isles (A830 Fort William to Mallaig). The
MacFarlanes owned this legendary hotel in this historic house for 30 years
(1997/MARY, CHARLIE & BOB); the Gibsons keep onwards and upwards and always
sympatico. Ongoing refurbishment retains its charm; the huge rooms remain
intimate and cosy with open fires. Impromptu sessions and ceilidhs wherever
there's a gathering in the bar. Solitude still achievable in the huge grounds, or
fishing or dreaming on Loch Shiel at foot of the lawn (row boat and a cruise boat
nearby). Day trips to Skye and small islands nearby. Quintessential!

1322 9/L28
15 ROOMS
TEL · TV
£38-45

Savoy Park www.savoypark.com · 01292 266112 · **16 Racecourse Road,**
Ayr In a street and area of many indifferent hotels this one, owned and run by
the Henderson family for over 40 years, is a real Scottish gem. Many weddings
here. Period features, lovely garden, not too much tartan, but a warm cosy lived-in
atmosphere. Round one of the fireplaces, 'blessed be God for his giftis'.

Crieff Hydro 01764 655555 · **Crieff** The quintessential Scottish family hotel.
Report: 1210/HOTELS FOR KIDS.
Stonefield Castle 01880 820836 · **Tarbert** Report: 822/ARGYLL HOTELS.

Real Retreats

1323
11/P29
✓ ✓ ✓ **Samye Ling** www.samyeling.org · 01387 373232 ·
Eskdalemuir near Lockerbie & Dumfries Bus or train to
Lockerbie/ Carlisle then bus (Mon-Sat 0870 6082608) or taxi (01576 470480). 2km
from village, community consists of an extraordinary and inspiring temple incongruous in these border parts. The complex comprises main house (with some
accommodation), dorm and guesthouse blocks many single rooms, a café (open 7
days 9am-5pm) and shop. Further up the hill, real retreats – months and years –
in annexes. Much of Samye Ling, a world centre for Tibetan Buddhism, is still
under construction under the supervision of Tibetan masters, but they offer daily
and longer stays (£15-25) and courses in all aspects of Buddhism, meditation, tai
chi, yoga, etc. Daily timetable from prayers at 6am and work period. Breakfast/
lunch and soup, etc for supper at 6pm; all vegetarian. Busy, thriving community
atmosphere; some space cases and holier-than-thous, but rewarding and unique
and thriving. This is Buddhism with no celebrity, pure and simple. See also World
Peace Centre (below).

1324
8/P17
✓ ✓ **Pluscarden** www.pluscardenabbey.org · fax: 01343 890258 ·
between Forres & Elgin Signed from the main A96 (11km from Elgin)
in a sheltered glen south-facing with a background of wooded hillside, this is the
only medieval monastery in the UK still inhabited by monks. It's a deeply calming
place. The (Benedictine) community keep walled gardens and bees. 8 services a
day in the glorious chapel (1975/ABBEYS) which visitors can attend. Retreat for
men (14 places) and women (separate, self-catering) with 2 week maximum and
no obligatory charge. Write to the Guest Master, Pluscarden Abbey, by Elgin IV30
8VA; no telephone bookings. Men eat with monks (mainly vegetarian).
Restoration/building work always in progress (of the abbey and of the spirit).

1325
8/P17
✓ ✓ **Findhorn Community** www.findhorn.org · 01309 690311 ·
Findhorn near Forres The world-famous spiritual community (now a
foundation) begun by Peter and Eileen Caddy and Dorothy Maclean in 1962, a village of mainly caravans and cabins on the way into Findhorn on the B9011. Open
as an ordinary caravan park and visitors can join the community as 'short-term
guests' eating and working on-site but probably staying at recommended B&Bs.
Full programme of courses and residential workshops in spiritual growth/dance/
healing, etc. Accommodation mainly at Cluny Hill College in Forres. Many other
aspects and facilities available in this cosmopolitan and well-organised township
which is now more of an eco village than a new-age community. Excellent shop
(1532/DELIS) and cafe – the Blue Angel (1410/VEGETARIAN).

1326
10/P23
✓ ✓ **The Bield at Blackruthven** www.bieldatblackruthven.org.uk ·
01738 583238 · Tibbermore Take Crieff road (A85) from Perth and
A9/ring road past Huntingtower then left for Tibbermore. 2km. 'Bield' an old
Scottish word for a place of refuge and shelter also means to nurture, succour,
encourage. All are possible here. A Georgian home with outbuildings containing
accommodation, lounges, meeting rooms in 30 gorgeous garden acres with a
swimming pool and a chapel (in an old carpenter's workshop) which are always
open. More like a country-house hotel but there are prayers, courses and support
if you want it. No guests on Mon, so 6 days max. Very cheap for this level of comfort. It is beautiful, peaceful and all very tasteful. Meals and self catering. Serenity!

1327
10/L24
✓ **Lendrick Lodge** www.lendricklodge.com · 01877 376263 ·
Brig o' Turk On A821 scenic road through the Trossachs, 15km from
Callander. Near road but in beautiful grounds with gurgling river. An organised

retreat and get away from it all 'yoga and healing' centre. Yoga/reiki and shamanic teaching throughout year. Individual rooms and full board if required. New 'River Retreat' in separate building overlooking the river has a pool and 2 ensuite rooms.

1328
10/L23
✓ **Dhana Kosa** **www.dhanakosa.com** · **01877 384213** · **Balquhidder** 3km village on Loch Voilside 9km from A84 Callander-Crianlarich road. Gentle Buddhist place with ongoing retreat programmes (1 week or weekends in winter). Guidance and group sessions. Meditation room. Dorms hold 3/4. Vegetarian food. Beautiful serene setting on Balquhidder Braes.

1329
9/J27
✓ **The World Peace Centre** **www.holyisland.org/peacecentre.html** · **01770 601100** · **Holy Island** Take a ferry from Lamlash on Arran (ferry 01770 600349/600998) to find yourself part of a Tibetan (albeit contemporary) mystery. Escape from the madding crowd on the mainland and compose your spirit or just refresh the parts that need it. Built by Samye Ling Abbots on this tiny Celtic refuge, the centre offers a range of activities to help purge the soul or restore the faith. Day trippers to the island welcome. Can accommodate 60 and has conference/gathering centre. Do phone ahead. Ferries very limited in winter.

1330
8/P17
✓ **Shambala** **www.shambala-retreat.org** · **01309 690690** · **Findhorn** Adjacent to the Findhorn community and across the road facing the bay, this comfortable, airy mansionhouse caters for individual or group retreats with daily meditations and some courses. Buddhist library, sauna and massage. Organic vegetarian cuisine. Not connected to Findhorn except spiritually. A very nice spot to centre on.

1331
9/K26
College of the Holy Spirit **www.argyll.anglican.org/millport.htm** · **01475 530353** · **Millport, Island of Cumbrae** Continuous ferry service from Largs (hourly in winter), then 6km bus journey to Millport. Off main street through gate in the wall, into grounds of the Cathedral of the Isles (1946/CHURCHES) and another more peaceful world. A retreat for the Episcopal Church since 1884, there are 16 comfortable rooms, all renovated 2003, some ensuite, in the college next to the church with B&B (around £33). Also half/full board. Morning and night prayer each day, Eucharist on Sun and concerts in summer. Warden available for direction and spiritual counselling. Fine library. Bike hire available on island. Phone the warden. Try the island's great café (1463/CAFÉS).

1332
10/Q25
Carberry Towers **www.carberrytower.com** · **0131 665 3135** · **Musselburgh** Sitting in extensive, well-kept grounds 3km south of Musselburgh, parts of this fine old house date back to the 15th century. Now a Christian residential and conference centre, most accommodation is in new block 50m away; student-hall standard. Courses for church workers/group weekends which visitors may some-times join. Not a quiet retreat but inexpensive for a break; high on 'renewal', low on rock 'n' roll. But they receive 'everyone'.

1333
10/R25
Nunraw Abbey **www.nunraw.org.uk** · **01620 830228** · **Garvald near Haddington** Cistercian community earning its daily bread with a working farm in the land surrounding the abbey but visitors can come and stay for a while and get their heads together in the Sancta Maria Guesthouse (a house for visitors is part of their doctrine). Payment by donation. Very Catholic monastic ambience throughout. Guesthouse is 1km from the monastery, a modern complex built to a traditional Cistercian pattern. Services in the Abbey at 8am and 8pm open to visitors.

1334
9/F25
Camas Adventure Centre www.iona.org.uk/camas · **01681 700404** · **Mull**
Part of Iona Community near to Fionnphort in south of island. Good bus service then a yomp over the moor. On a rocky coast with limited electricity, no cars, TV or noise except the waves and the gulls. Outdoor activities (eg canoeing, hill-walking). 2 dorms; share chores. Week-long stays. You'll probably have to relate but this spiritual place while invoking the simple life and the outdoor life also enjoins the life where you're not alone. May-Sep.

■ The Best Spas

All these spas offer day visits and specific treatments.

1335
10/P25
✓✓ **One Spa** www.one-spa.net · **0131 229 9131** · **The Sheraton Grand Hotel, Edinburgh** Unquestionably the best spa in the city; and on loads of national/international lists. And probably the best thing about the hotel which is very centrally situated on Festival Sq opposite the Usher Hall (81/BEST HOTELS). As well as the usual (but reasonably spacious) pool there's another one which extends outdoors dangling infinity-style over Conference Sq at the back of the hotel. Decent gym. Exotic hydrotherapy and a host of treatments. Day and half-day tickets available.

1336
10/R23
✓✓ **The Kohler Waters Spa** www.oldcoursehotel.co.uk · **01334 474371** · **The Old Course Hotel, St Andrews** In the lovely Old Course golfing resort (929/FIFE HOTELS), this beautifully designed leisure and treat-ment suite is just one of many reasons for staying. The spa was designed by the team who created the original Cow Shed at Babington House in Somerset. Owners of the hotel, the Kohler Company produces iconic kitchens and bathrooms in the US and have other luxury resorts. Here the gym looks out over the Old Course (and there's a roof-top hot tub). In the main suite the 20 metre pool, monsoon showers, saunas and crystal steam rooms are in a very calm and relaxing environment. 11 therapy rooms offer a vast range of treatments.

1337
10/P27
✓✓ **Stobo Castle** www.stobocastle.co.uk · **01721 725300** · **Stobo near Peebles** Border baronial mansion 10km south of Peebles in beautiful countryside of towering trees and trickling burns. Dawyk Botanic Gardens nearby (1595/GARDENS) and there are Japanese Water Gardens in the grounds. Mainly a hotel but day visits possible; the spa is the heart of the whole pampering experi-ence. Over 70 treatments. Not too much emphasis on exercise. Classic, standard rooms and suites; also lodge. Bespoke treatment for men and women. You do feel they know what they are doing; all medical peculiarities accounted for. Accommodation from £100 per person (sharing), £159 single 'taster days' from £99.

1338
10/N23
✓✓ **The Spa** www.gleneagles.com · **01764 662231** · **Gleneagles Hotel, Auchterarder** The leisure suites at Gleneagles have always offered (obviously) one of the best spa experiences. At TGP the spa was being completely refurbished and various relocations were under way in the complex. All will be luxuriously reinstated as this edition of *StB* becomes available. Gleneagles offers Espa body treatments and uses all their oils and unguents. Treatments vary from the usual aromatherapy and facials to hot-stone therapy and Balinese and ayurvedic applications. In superb surroundings.

1339
9/J22

✓ **The Spa** www.eriska-hotel.co.uk · 01631 720371 · **Isle of Eriska Hotel, Ledaig** The Isle of Eriska ('hotel/spa/island'), one of Scotland's most comfy country-house hotels (1203/COUNTRY-HOUSE HOTELS), is 20km north of Oban. Apart from the usual indulgences they have created (and are still developing at TGP) a lovely spa separate from the main building in the gardens overlooking the new golf course. There's a pool and gym a separate café with terrace and several treatment rooms using Espa products. Perfect tranquillity.

1340
10/Q23

Yu Spa www.apexhotels.co.uk · 01382 309309 · **Apex City Quay Hotel, Dundee** The inexpensive and accessible spa is part of the overall offering at this central business hotel, most definitely the best in the city (1124/DUNDEE HOTELS). A new build on the emerging waterfront with spa and swimming pool occupying a corner of the ground floor. Therapies combine the ethos and products from 'Elemis' in over 50 treatments for men and women. Japanese-inspired wooden hot tubs, herb infused steam room and sauna. Everything you need to do before you go out again and face Dundee.

1341
10/R25

The Spa www.macdonaldhotels.co.uk · 01620 897333 · **The Macdonald Marine Hotel, North Berwick** The spa in the newly renovated ('07) Marine Hotel which has been here forever overlooking the golf course. Salt-water hydro pool, aroma steam room, 'bio sauna', a 'cold therapy room' and a 'serenity relaxation room' all contribute to a well thought-out suite of facilities removed from the main hustle and bustle of the hotel. 'Decleor' products are offered in a wide range of treatments which includes a men's menu. All the usual beautifications and the exotica.

1342
9/L25

The Spa www.devere.co.uk · 01389 713659 · **Cameron House Hotel, Loch Lomond** The spa in the recently made over De Vere Cameron House Hotel and Golf Course on the banks of the loch. Spa inculcates the 'Kirsten Florien philoso-phy' which revolves around hydrotherapy, aromatherapy and thalassotherapy, balnotherapy and pelotherapy (whatever they are) with a host of products includ-ing the 'highly acclaimed, ageless Caviar Collection' (it says here). There's also a new skincare range called Carita. I don't know anything about these but there's a comprehensive booklet. There's a pool and a steam room and all the usual facili-ties including a 'rasul' chamber.

For The Best House Parties

Places you can rent for families or friends and have to yourselves.

1343
6/Q13
✓ ✓ **Ackergill Tower** www.ackergilltower.co.uk · 01955 603556 · **near Wick** Deluxe retreat totally geared for parties and groups (mostly corporates). 5 times a year, eg Valentines/Hogmanay, you can join their house parties. Fixed price (3-night minimum stay) all inclusive: this means fab atmosphere dinners (huge fires, candlelight) but you may not eat in the same place twice. Host of activities (there's even an 'Opera House') and outside, the wild coast. A perfect treat/retreat. Individual prices on request. You'll probably have to mingle.

1344
8/P20
✓ ✓ **Mar Lodge Estate** www.ntsholidays.com · 0131 243 9331 · **near Braemar** There are several remarkable properties including apartments in the 'big hoose' in the NTS-run, 72,000-acre estate 15km from Braemar. Classic Highland scenery superb in any season with the upper waters of the River Dee running through it. 5 apartments in main mansion and 2 other houses sleeping 8 and 10. Public rooms including library, billiard room and ballroom can be hired separately. Expensive of course but not, divided between all your mates. And live like the royals down the road.

1345
10/P24
✓ **Myres Castle** www.myrescastle.com · 01337 828350 2 km Auchtermuchty on Falkland road. Well-preserved castle/family home in stunningly beautiful gardens. High country life though at a price. 9 rooms individually refurbished to exceptional standard. Formal dining room, evocative Victorian kitchen and impressive billiard room. The perfect setting for a murder mystery shindig. Central to all Fife attractions especially Falkland and St Andrews. £295 per person per night at TGP, can take 18. Dinners up to 20.

1346
10/Q27
✓ **Glen House** 01896 830210 · **Traquair** On A709 4km from village in stunning Border scenery, the notable family home of the Tennants (Colin Tennant the man who made Mustique and host to royalty). House reeks of atmosphere and echoes of swinging parties gone by. Hire complete (including Princess Margaret's bedroom). Lots of public space (5 reception rooms, ballroom, snooker room) and grounds (5000 acres). 19 bedrooms, can sleep 36 of your best mates. £2.5K per 24 hours, £4-5K per weekend. Meals extra but you can BYOB. Live like they did!

1347
8/N17
✓ **Drynachan Lodge** www.cawdor.com · 01667 402402 · **near Nairn** This fab 19th-century hunting lodge is on the Cawdor Estate south of Nairn. The castle is signed from all over (1853/CASTLES). While there are many cottages here for let this is the big house (sleeps 20) and was personally decked out by Lady Isabella Cawdor. Like all things on the estate it's done with great taste. Fully staffed, it's like a hip shooting lodge. But it'll cost ya.

1348
7/M17
✓ **Ness Castle Lodges** www.nesscastlelodges.co.uk · 01463 229342 · **Inverness** 15 minutes from centre along the riverside, 3km from main A9. Spectacular location and appointments with excellent fishing rights on 1 mile of river. Beautifully done. Main lodge 6 double/twin and 1 single. Benula Lodge retreat sleeps 7. Food at 'The Bothy'. Kennel for dogs. Book well ahead and save!

1349
7/M17
✓ **Castle Stuart** www.castlestuart.com · 01463 790745 · **Inverness** 15 minutes city centre on airport road via A96 Aberdeen road. Authentic pile of 17th-century history; a real castle experience complete with ghost. Antique in every sense. Guided tour on arrival. More detail from website or call. Quite snobby people live here. If Kate 'n' Pete are among your houseguests, I wouldn't bother.

1350
6/L15
Carbisdale Castle www.carbisdale.org · 01549 421232 · **Culrain near Bonar Bridge** Another castle and hugely impressive but on a per head basis, very inexpensive. Carbisdale is the flagship hostel of the SYHA (1228/BEST HOSTELS for directions). From Nov-Feb you can hire the whole place so big Highland hoolies over Xmas/Hogmanay are an option. More than 150 people can be accommodated in the 32 rooms (varying from singles to 12-bed dorms). Per-night price around £1500 plus. Bring your own chef or muck in. You get the whole place to yourself. Other SYHA hostels can be hired Oct-May. Check 0870 1553255.

1352
9/K28
Doonbrae 01292 442466 · **Alloway** In heart of unspoilt village still evocative of Burns whose birthplace, gardens and Tam o' Shanter graveyard are nearby. Opposite and part of **Brig o' Doon Hotel** (853/AYRSHIRE HOTELS), much favoured for weddings. This refurbished mansion is separate and you can have it to yourself. On Doon banks in delightful gardens. Self-catering or eat at hotel. 5 suites.

1353
11/N30
Cavens www.cavens.com · 01387 880234 · **Kirkbean** Off A710, the Solway Coast road 20km south of Dumfries. Well appointed mansion in gorgeous grounds near the beach. Up to 12 accommodated with exclusive use and service. Very reasonable compared to many grand houses of this type. 850/SOUTHWEST HOTELS.

1354
9/J24
Castle Lachlan www.castlelachlan.com · 01369 860669 · **Loch Fyne** For directions see Inver Cottage, the tearoom on the estate (793/ARGYLL RESTAURANTS). Stunning setting in heart of Scotland scenery, the 18th-century ancestral home of the Clan Maclachlan. Beautiful library, snooker room – you are guests of Lisa and Ewan Maclachlan. Sleeps 13 (22 for dinner). £2-3K per week. En tout cas tennis. Sumptuous surroundings for rock stars and the rest of us.

1355
6/H16
Rua Reidh Lighthouse www.ruareidh.co.uk · 01445 771263 · **Melvaig near Gairloch** End of the road 20km from Gairloch but yes, you can have this lighthouse to yourself. Sleeps up to 24 in 8 bedrooms (£500 for 2 nights low season, £1600 7 nights New Year at TGP). Gairloch has good food/pub options but dinner available here. Plus the sea and the scenery!

1356
5/E15
Amhuinnsuidhe Castle www.amhuinnsuidhe.com · 01859 560200 · **Harris** North from Tarbert then west into the faraway strand (for directions see Lost Glen 2413/FANTASTIC ISLAND WALKS). Staffed, fab food and gothic Victorian castle/shooting and fishing lodge (the salmon arrive in a foaming mass at the river mouth). 12 bedrooms take 20 guests: mainly sporting groups but individuals can join at certain times for a mixed house party. Grand interiors and top fishing on 9 lochs and rivers. Info supplied by Vivienne Devlin who stayed there – me not!

1356A
10/R24
Cambo www.camboestate.com · 01333 450313 · **near Crail** Old, interesting mansion in beautiful grounds near St Andrews. Up to 17 rooms available. Very reasonable rates. Report: 934/FIFE HOTELS.

National Trust for Scotland *have many interesting properties they rent out for weekends or longer. 0131 243 9331 or www.nts.org.uk for details.*

The Landmark Trust *also have 18 mostly fabulous properties in Scotland including* **The Pineapple** *(1931/MONUMENTS),* **Auchenleck House** *in Ayrshire which sleeps 13 and the wonderful* **Ascog House** *or* **Meikle House** *on the Isle of Bute which sleep 9 and 10 respectively. Phone 01628 825925 to get their beautiful handbook (properties throughout the UK) or see www.landmarktrust.org.uk*

Scotland's Great Guesthouses

✓ ✓ **Balmory Hall** 01700 500669 · **Isle of Bute** In Ascog, 6km from Rothesay towards Mount Stuart. Report: 814/ARGYLL HOTELS.

✓ ✓ **Dun Na Mara** 01631 720233 · **Benderloch** Off the A828 Fort William road. 12 km north of Oban. Report: 813/ARGYLL HOTELS.

✓ ✓ **Skirling House** 01899 860274 · **near Biggar** On the A72 3km from Biggar. Report: 886/BORDERS HOTELS.

✓ **Lerags House** 01631 563381 · **near Oban** 7km south of Oban and 4 km from the main A816. Report: 817/ARGYLL HOTELS.

✓ **Edenwater House** 01733 224370 · **Ednam near Kelso** On the Kelso-Swinton Rd B6461. 4km from Kelso. Report: 889/BORDERS HOTELS.

✓ **Coig Na Shee** 01540 670109 · **Newtonmore** Just outside the village towards Fort William, just off the A9. Report: 1038/HIGHLAND HOTELS.

✓ **Roineabhal** 01866 833207 · **near Kilchrenan, Loch Awe** 10km from the A85 road to Oban near Taynuilt. Report: 818/ARGYLL HOTELS.

Clint Lodge 01899 860274 · **near St Boswells** Near Dryburgh Abbey in Scott country. Report: 895/BORDERS HOTELS.

Old Station 01334 880505 · **near St Andrews** On B9131, the Anstruther road off the A917 St Andrews-Crail (3km). Report: 933/FIFE HOTELS.

The Bield 01738 583238 · **Tibbermore near Perth** Crieff road, from Perth off the ring road. Report: 1326/RETREATS.

Craigatin House 01796 472478 · **Pitlochry** Surprisingly stylish guesthouse in this traditional tourist town. Report: 955/PERTHSHIRE HOTELS.

Tanglewood House 01854 612059 · **near Ullapool** Beautiful house overlooking Loch Broom. Bedrooms and dining have the view. Report: 1060/INEXPENSIVE HIGHLAND HOTELS.

Ptarmigan House 01688 302863 · **Tobermory, Mull** Modern house with swimming pool high above the village. Report: 2428/MULL.

Doune Stone Lodge 01687 462667 · **Knoydart** Remote but comfy house on this faraway peninsula. Will collect from Mallaig. Boat excursions and wonderful walks. Report: 1290/GET-AWAY HOTELS.

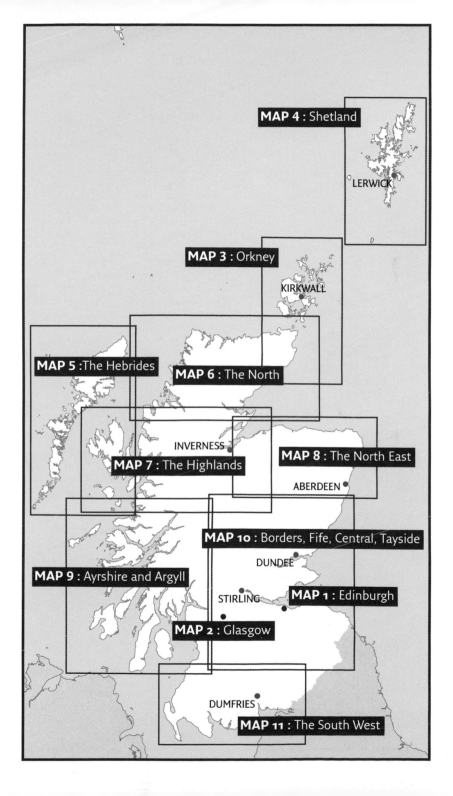

MAP 4 : Shetland

LERWICK

MAP 3 : Orkney

KIRKWALL

MAP 5 :The Hebrides

MAP 6 : The North

INVERNESS

MAP 8 : The North East

MAP 7 : The Highlands

ABERDEEN

MAP 10 : Borders, Fife, Central, Tayside

DUNDEE

MAP 9 : Ayrshire and Argyll

STIRLING

MAP 1 : Edinburgh

MAP 2 : Glasgow

DUMFRIES

MAP 11 : The South West

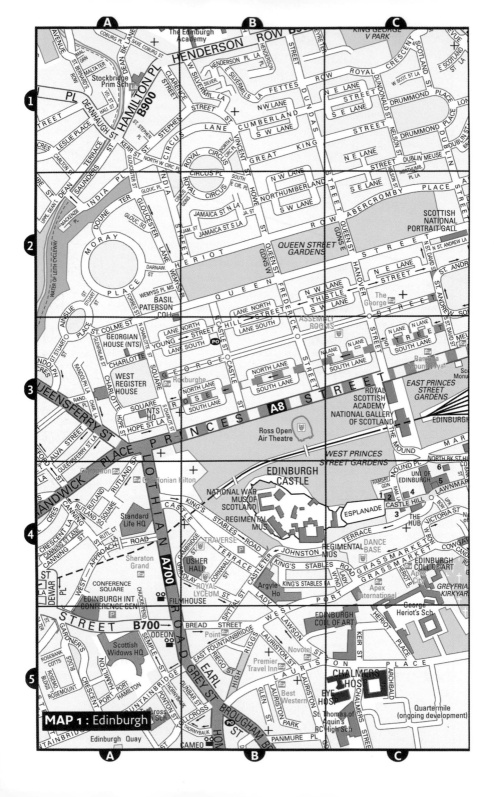

MAP 1 : Edinburgh

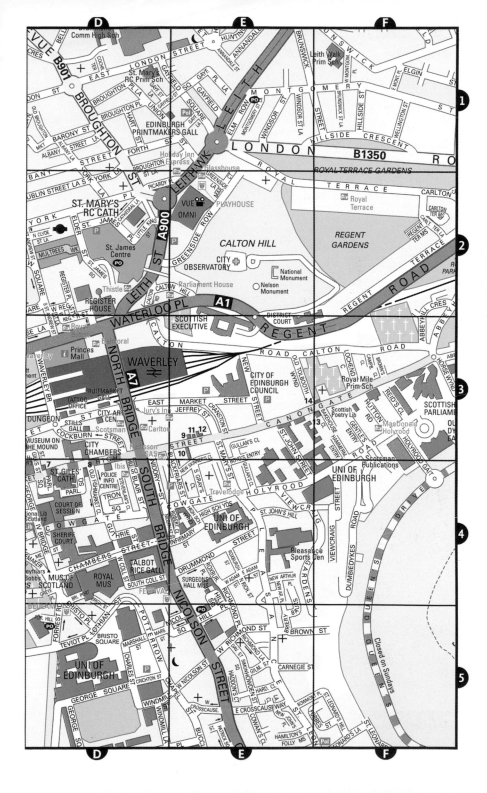

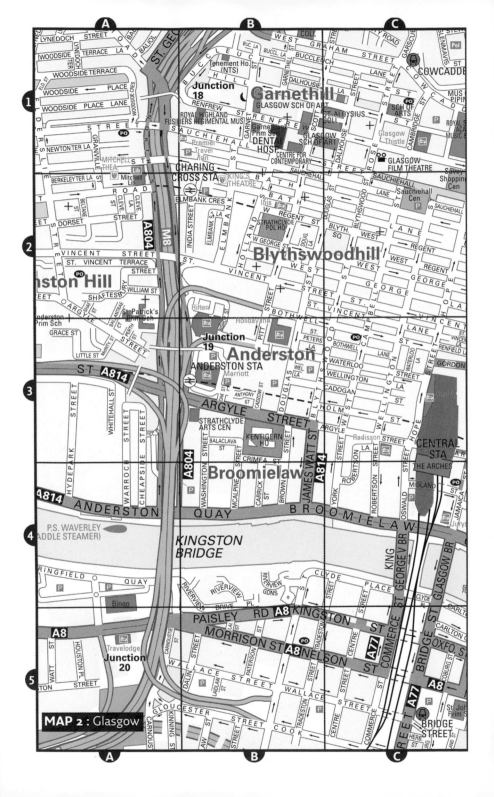
MAP 2 : Glasgow

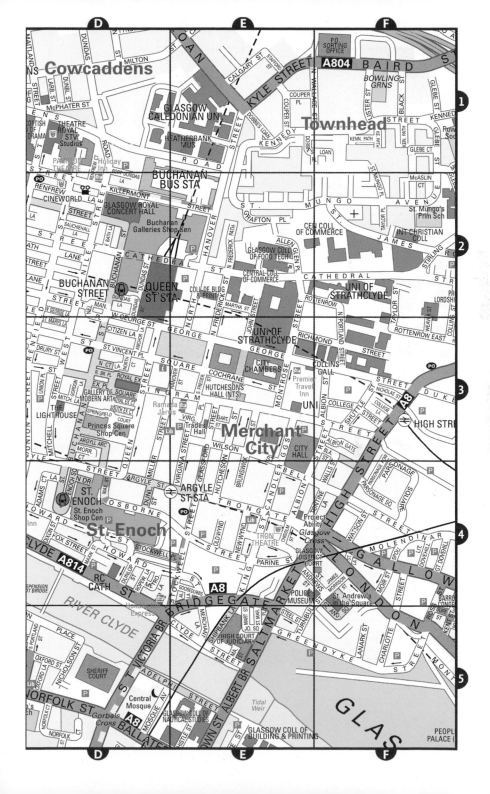

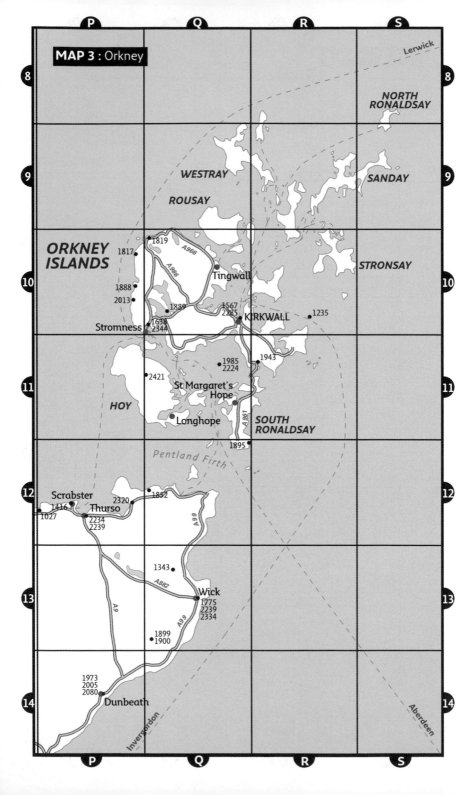

MAP 3 : Orkney

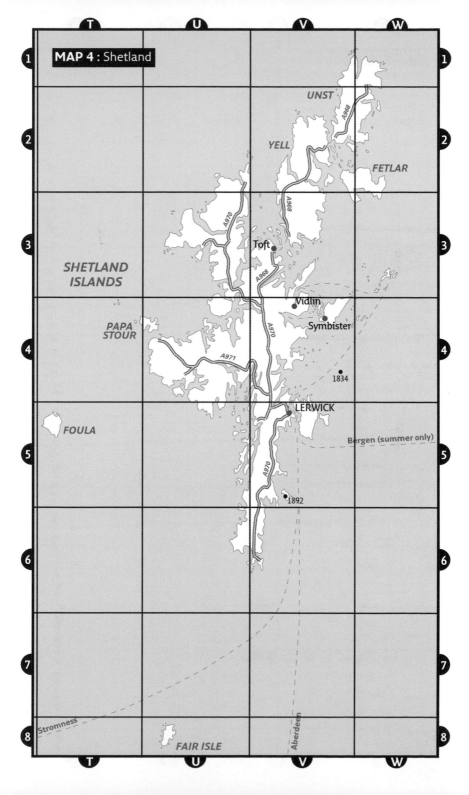

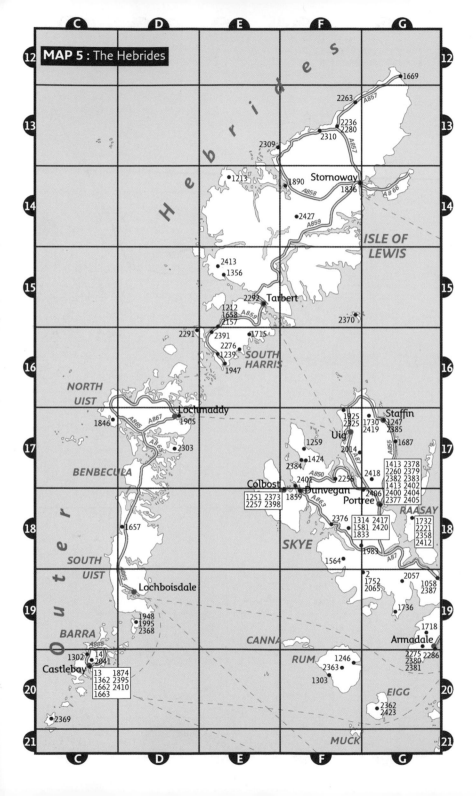

MAP 5 : The Hebrides

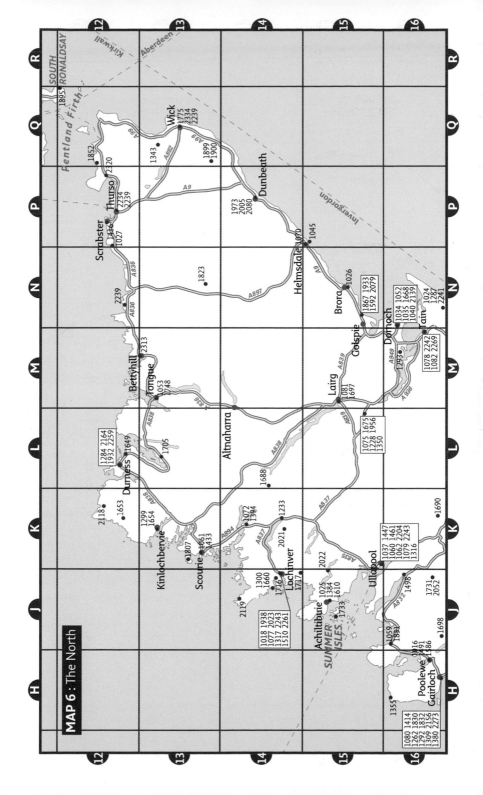

MAP 6 : The North

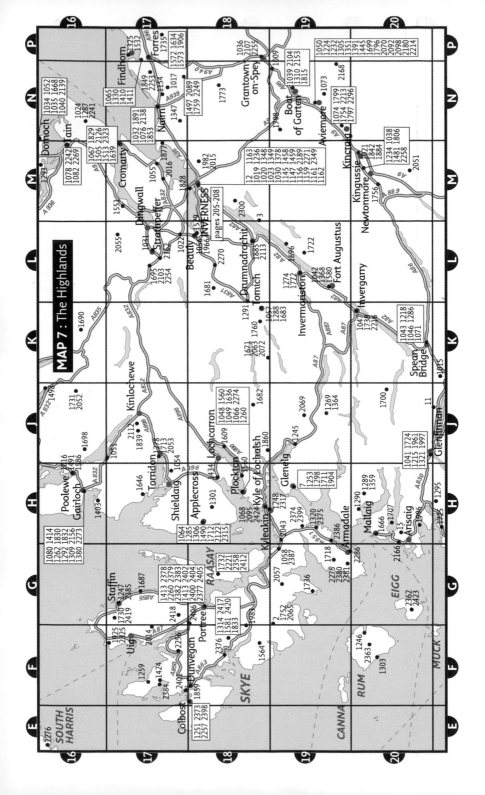

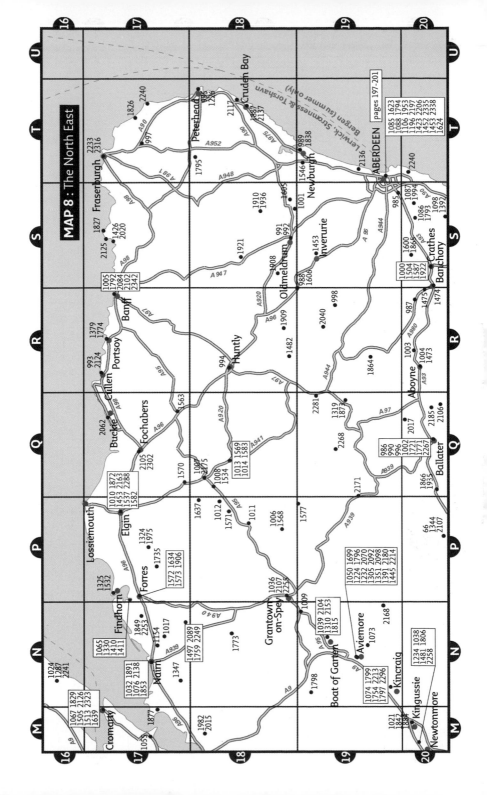

MAP 8 : The North East

pages 197-201

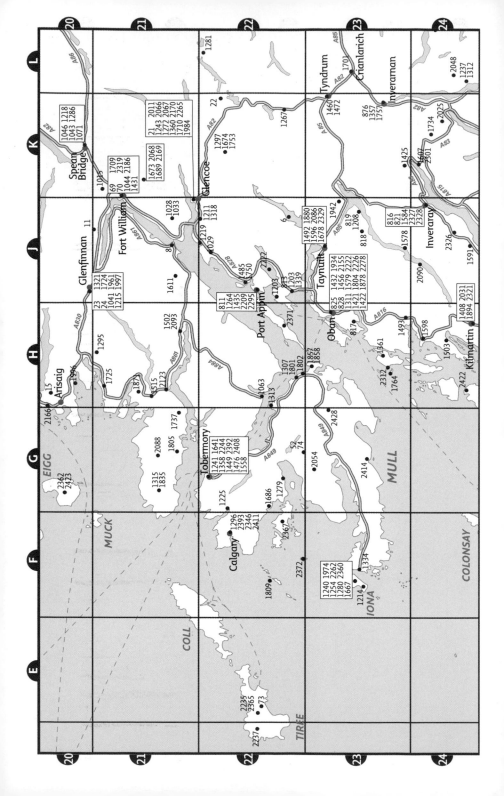

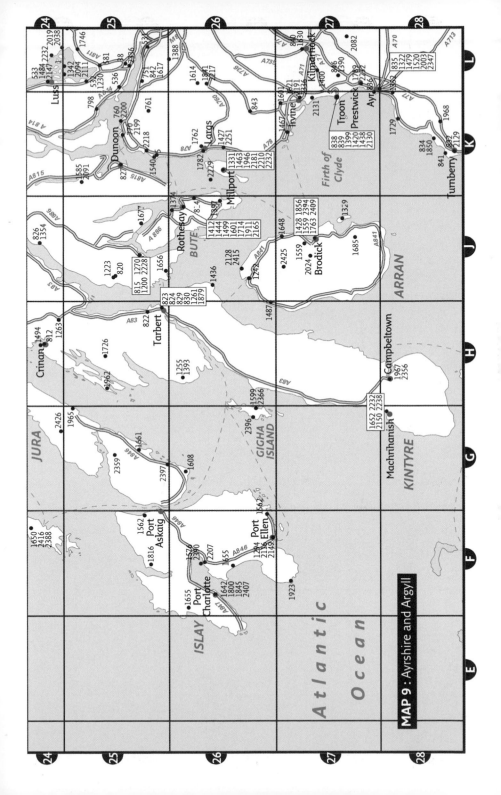

MAP 9 : Ayrshire and Argyll

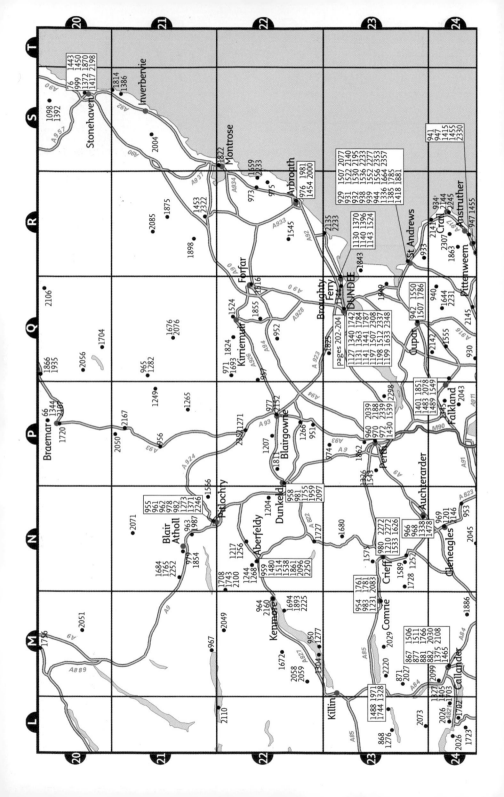

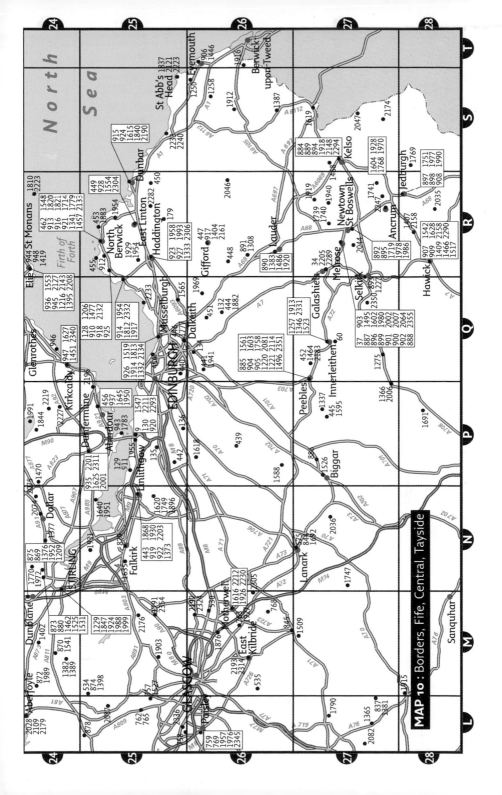

MAP 10 : Borders, Fife, Central, Tayside

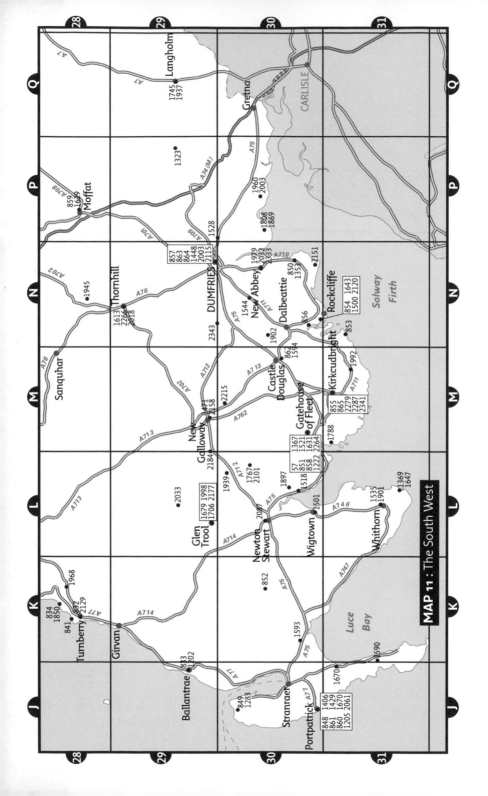

MAP 11 : The South West

Section 6

Good Food & Drink

scotland the best

Bloody Good Pubs

Pubs in Edinburgh, Glasgow and Aberdeen are listed in their own sections.

1357
9/K23

✔ ✔ **Drover's Inn** www.thedroversinn.co.uk · **Inverarnan** A famously Scottish drinking den/hotel on the edge of the Highlands just north of Ardlui at the head of Loch Lomond and 12km south of Crianlarich on the A82. Smoky, low-ceilinged rooms, open ranges, whisky in the jar, stuffed animals in the hall and kilted barmen; this is nevertheless the antithesis of the contrived Scottish tourist pub. Also see 879/HOTELS CENTRAL.

1358
9/G22

✔ ✔ **The Mishnish** www.mishnish.co.uk · **Tobermory** The family-run Mish has always been the real Tobermory. 7 days till late. Often live music from Scot traditional to DJs and indie especially Sat. Different rooms, nooks and crannies. Great pub grub, open fire. Something, as they say, for everybody.

1359
7/H20

✔ **Old Forge** www.theoldforge.co.uk · **01687 462267** · **Inverie, Knoydart** A warm haven for visitors to this remote peninsula. Suddenly you're part of the community, real ales and real characters, excellent pub grub. Lunch & LO 9pm. Stay along the road at brilliant guesthouse (1289/GET-AWAY HOTELS) or bunk along the road (info@knoydart.org).

1360
9/J21

✔ **Clachaig Inn** www.clachaig.com · **01855 811252** · **Glencoe** Deep in the glen itself down the road signed off the A82, 5km from Glencoe village. Both the pub with its wood-burning stove and the lounge are woody and welcoming. Backdoor best for muddy boots or those averse to leather-studded furniture. Real ale and real climbers and walkers. Handy for hostel 2km down road. Decent food (in bar/lounge and good, inexpensive accommodation including 4 lodges. They have beer fests – the Oct one is a biggie.

1361
9/H23

Tigh-An-Truish www.tigh-an-truish.co.uk · **01852 300242** · **Clachan, Isle of Seil** Beside the much-photographed 'Bridge over the Atlantic' which links the 'Isle' of Seil with the 'mainland'. On B884, 8km from B816 and 22km south of Oban. Country pub with 2 apartments above (with views of the bridge). A place where no one cares how daft your hair looks after a hard day's messing about on boats. Food LO 8.30pm (Mar-Oct).

1362
5/C20

Castlebay Bar www.castlebay-hotel.co.uk · **Barra** Adjacent to Castlebay Hotel. A brilliant bar. All human life is here. More Irish than all the Irish makeovers on the mainland. Occasional live music including The Vatersay Boys; conversations with strangers. New owners '07. Report: 2395/ISLAND HOTELS.

1363
10/Q23

Taybridge Bar 129 **Perth Road, Dundee** Legendary drinking place. Established in 1867: the smoke-filled gloom of a Dundee afternoon. When Peter Howson runs out of Glaswegian gnarled heads, he might come here. Women are present, but usually accompanied by their 'man' or behind the bar listening to their views on the world outside.

1364
7/J19

Cluanie Inn www.cluanieinn.com · **01320 340238** · **Loch Cluanie** On A87 at head of Loch Cluanie 15km before Shiel Bridge on the long road to Kyle of Lochalsh. A wayside inn with good pub food, a restaurant and the accommodation walkers want. Good base for climbing/ walking (especially the Five Sisters of Kintail, 2069/SERIOUS WALKS). A cosy refuge. LO 9pm for food.

1365
10/L27
Poosie Nansie's www.mauchlinevillage.co.uk · **Mauchline** Main street of this Ayrshire village where Burns lived in 1788. This pub there then, those characters still there at the bar. 4 of his children buried (yes, 4) in the churchyard opposite. A room in the pub left as was. Living heritage at its most real! Lunch & 6-8pm Fri/Sat. Otherwise just the ale.

1366
10/P27
Tibbie Shiels Inn www.tibbieshielsinn.com · **Borders** Off A708 Moffat-Selkirk road. Occupies its own particular place in Scottish culture, especially literature (2006/LITERARY PLACES) and in the Border hills southwest of Selkirk where it nestles between 2 romantic lochs. On Southern Upland Way (1691/WATERFALLS) a good place to stop and refuel (very busy on Sun).

1367
11/M30
The Murray Arms & The Masonic www.gatehouse-of-fleet.co.uk · **Gatehouse Of Fleet** 2 adjacent unrelated pubs that just fit perfectly into the life of this great wee town. The Masonic is the best for food with great atmosphere. Masonic symbols still on the walls of the upstairs rooms. Murray Arms has Burns connection. **The Ship** (851/SOUTHWEST HOTELS) on the main street is the new good-lookin' kid on the block.

1368
7/L19
Lock Inn **Fort Augustus** Busy canalside (Caledonian Canal which joins Loch Ness in the distance) pub for locals and visitors. Good grub (you should book for the upstairs restaurant) The Gilliegorm, reasonable malts. Food LO 9.30pm. Some live music. Seats on the canal in summer where boats go by.

1369
11/L31
The Steampacket Inn www.steampacketinn.com · 01988 500334 · **Isle of Whithorn** The hub of atmosphere wee village at the end of the road (1647/COASTAL VILLAGES) south. On harbour that fills and empties with the tide. Great for ales and food (brunch & LO 9pm all year).

Great Pubs For Real Ale

For pubs in Edinburgh, see p. 69-76, Glasgow p. 122-26.

1370
10/Q23
✓**Fisherman's Tavern** www.fishermans-tavern-hotel.co.uk · **Broughty Ferry** In Dundee, but not too far to go for great atmosphere and the best collection of ales in the area. In Fort St near the seafront. Regular ales and many guests. Low-ceilinged and friendly. Inexpensive accommodation adjacent (1229/DUNDEE HOTELS).

1371
10/N21
✓**Moulin Inn/Hotel** www.moulinhotel.co.uk · **Pitlochry** 4km uphill from main street on road to Bridge of Cally, an inn at a picturesque crossroads since 1695. Some rooms and big rep for pub grub, but also for cosy (smoky) bar and brewery out back from which comes 'Moulin Light', 'Ale of Atholl' and others. Live music some Sun. Food (LO 9.30pm), methinks, could be better.

1372
10/S20
✓**Marine Hotel** **Stonehaven** Popular local on great harbour front with seats outside; has undergone major improvement under new owner Robert Lindsay. 4/5 guest ales, big Belgian and wheat-beer selection and food getting better at TGP. New upstairs dining room. (Thanks for this one, Jeremy.) Open all day.

1373
10/N25
✓**The Four Marys** **Linlithgow** Main street near road up to palace so handy for a pint after schlepping around the historical attractions. Mentioned in most beer guides. 7 ales on tap including various guests. Beer festivals May and

Oct. Notable malt whisky collection and popular locally for lunches (daily) and evening meals (LO 8.45pm) weekends 12noon-food LO.

1374
9/J26
✔ **The Port Royal Port Bannatyne near Rothesay** Seafront on Kames Bay in Bute. A 'Russian' tavern with latkas and sauerkraut with your stroganoff. Some live music. 5 rooms upstairs and a great selection of ales. Brill atmosphere.

1375
10/M24
The Lade Inn Callander At Kilmahog, the western approach to the town at the beginning of road into the Trossachs – so a good place to stop. Inn known for food, also brews its own ale (Waylade, Ladeback, etc) but runs an ale shop adjacent with over 100 of Scotland's finest. Shop 12noon-9/10pm. Pub food till 8.45pm.

1376
10/J26
The Tappit Hen Dunblane By the cathedral. Good ales (usually Deuchars and 4 guests and many malts), atmosphere and live music (well, once a month). A good find in these parts.

1377
10/N24
The Woolpack Tillicoultry Via Upper Mill St (signed 'Mill Glen') from main street on your way to the Ochils. They come far and wide to this ancient pub. Bar food and a changing selection of ales which they know how to keep. Sup after stroll.

1378
7/M18
Clachnaharry Inn Inverness On A862 Inverness-Beauly road just outside Inverness overlooking firth and railway, with beer garden. Long list of regulars posted, 5/6 on tap including Clachnaharry Village Ale. Local fave for pub food. Friendly, let's just say... harmonious.

1379
8/R17
The Shore Inn Portsoy Down at the harbour good atmosphere (and ales). Food all day in summer, weekends only in winter. A central plank and seat at the Traditional Boats fest (49/EVENTS). May be quiet other times, but a great pub. For sale at TGP so changes may follow.

1380
7/H16
The Old Inn Gairloch Southern approach on A832 near golf course, an 'old inn' across an old bridge; a goodly selection of malts. Some real ales in the cellar. Tourists and locals mix in season, live music some nights. Tasteful Solas Studio Gallery adjacent (2273/ART). Rooms above make this an all-round good reason to stop in Gairloch (1185/ROADSIDE INNS).

The Masonic Arms Gatehouse of Fleet 858/SOUTHWEST RESTAURANTS;
The Steam Packet Isle of Whithorn 1369/BLOODY GOOD PUBS.
The 2 pubs in the South West that look after their ale (and their drinkers).

The Best Gastropubs

Gastropubs in Edinburgh & Glasgow are listed in their own sections.

1381
10/L27
✓ ✓ **The Sorn Inn** www.sorninn.com · 01290 551305 · **Sorn** Main street of village, 8km east of Mauchline 25 km Ayr. Pub with rooms and big reputation for food. Restaurants and tables in bar. Family-run (the Grants with chef Craig Grant). Gastropub of the Year 2005 and Michelin Bib Gourmand. Everything just so and made here, including the ice cream. Lunch & LO 9pm (8pm in bar). All day Sat/Sun.

1382
10/M24
✓ ✓ **The Inn At Kippen** www.theinnatkippen.co.uk · 01786 871010 · **Kippen** This place put Kippen on the foodie map. Great value and excellent special menu for kids. When you add the deli (1541/DELIS) and the Cross Keys (see below), Kippen is suddenly the village pub destination of central Scotland. The Inn is often fully booked. 4 rooms (report: 870/CENTRAL HOTELS). 7 days, lunch & LO 9pm.

1383
10/R26
✓ ✓ **Black Bull** www.blackbull-lauder.com · 01578 722208 · **Lauder** Main street of ribbon town on the A68 between Edinburgh and the Borders, but near enough the city to be a destination meal. 8 individual rooms above, diverse rooms below. Some great Modern British cooking with excellent wine list. 7 days. LO 9pm.

1384
6/J15
✓ ✓ **The Summer Isles Hotel Bar** www.summerisleshotel.co.uk · 01854 622282 · **Achiltibuie** The adjacent bar of this longest romantic hotel on the foreshore facing the isles and the sunset (1025/HIGHLAND HOTELS). All the superior qualities of their famous (Michelin) food operation available at less than half the price in the cosy bistro-like bar although for sale at TGP so standard may change. Great seafood and vegetarian. Apr-Oct, lunch & LO 8.30pm.

1385
10/R23
✓ ✓ **The Grange Inn** 01334 472670 · **St Andrews** 4km out of town off Anstruther/Crail road A917. Perennially popular. Mike and Lena Singer have built on long reputation of this almost Englishy pub with cosy rooms and comfort food with flair. Lunch (not Sat) till LO 1.30pm & dinner (not Sun evening or Mon) LO 8.30pm. Must book weekends.

1386
10/S21
✓ ✓ **The Creel Inn** 01569 750254 · **Catterline near Stonehaven** 2km from main A92 Arbroath-Stonehaven road 8km south Stonehaven (signed) perching above the bay from where the lobsters come. And lots of other seafood. Good wine and huge speciality beer selection. Cove itself has a kind of haunting beauty. Catterline is Joan Eardley (the notable artist) territory. Now it's famous for this pub. 7 days lunch & LO 9pm.

1387
10/S26
✓ **The Wheatsheaf** www.wheatsheaf-swinton.co.uk · 01890 860257 · **Swinton** A hotel pub in an undistinguished village about halfway between Kelso and Berwick (18km) on the B6461. In deepest, flattest Berwickshire, owners Chris and Jan Winson serve up the best pub grub you've had since England. 12 rooms adjacent and in cottages. An all-round good hostelry. Lunch & 6-9.30pm.

1388
9/L26
✓ **Fox and Hounds** www.foxandhoundshouston.co.uk · **Houston** On B790 village main street in Renfrewshire, 30km west of Glasgow by M8 junction 29 (A726), then cross back under motorway on B790. Village pub home to Houston brewery with great ales, excellent pub food and dining room upstairs

for family meals and suppers. Folk come from miles around. Sunday roasts. Fine for kids. Menu from 12noon-10pm (Sun 9pm). Restaurant: 01505 612448. Bar till 12midnight.

1389
10/M24

✓ **The Cross Keys www.kippencrosskeys.co.uk · 01786 870293 · Kippen** Here forever in this quiet backwater town off the A811 15km west of Stirling. With new owners '07 who want to keep it solid and the same, but make it better. We think they may succeed. Bar meals by coal fire, à la carte and family restaurants. An old-style pub food stop, for a'body. LO 9pm.

1390
9/L27

✓ **Wheatsheaf Inn www.wheatsymington.co.uk · 01563 830307 · Symington near Ayr** 2km A77. Pleasant village off the unpleasant A77 with this busy coaching inn opposite church. Folk come from miles around to eat (book at weekends) honest-to-goodness pub fare in various rooms (roast beef every Sunday). Menu on boards. Beer garden. LO 9.30pm.

1391
7/N19

✓ **Old Bridge Inn www.oldbridgeinn.co.uk/aviemore · Aviemore** Off Coylumbridge road at south end of Aviemore as you come in from A9 or Kincraig. 100m main street but sits in hollow. An old inn like it says with basic à la carte and more interesting blackboard specials. Three cask ales on tap. Kids' menu that is not just pizza and chips; ski-bums welcome. Lunch & 6-9pm. In summer, tables over road by the river. Hostel adjacent (1232/HOSTELS). LO 9.30pm.

1392
8/S20

✓ **Lairhillock www.lairhillock.co.uk · 01569 730001 · near Netherley, Stonehaven** In new hands at TGP but known forever for great (7 days lunch and dinner) more informal and downright friendly. Fine for kids. Superb cheese selection, notable malts and ales. Can approach from South Deeside road, but simplest direction for strangers is: 15km south of Aberdeen by main A92 towards Stonehaven, then signed Durris, go 5km to country crossroads. **The Crynoch Restaurant** is adjacent (1098/ABERDEEN RESTAURANTS).

1393
9/H26

✓ **Kilberry Inn near Tarbert, Argyll · 01880 770223** On the single-track B8024 that follows the coast of the Knapdale peninsula between Lochgilphead and Tarbert, this is out on its own. Fortunately Clare Johnson is a great cook (predominantly seafood) and the bar has a lovely ambience. So make the journey (1726/SCENIC ROUTES) for lunch or dinner. LO 9pm. Closed Mon. Mar-Dec.

1394
6/K14

✓ **Kylesku Hotel www.kyleskuhotel.co.uk · 01971 502231 · Kylesku** Off A894 between Scourie and Lochinver in Sutherland. A hotel and pub with a great quayside location on Loch Glencoul where boats leave for trips to see the 'highest waterfall in Europe' (1688/WATERFALLS, 1072/INEXPENSIVE HIGHLAND RESTAURANTS). Friendly atmosphere with local fish, seafood (especially with legs: the prawn thing!) and yummy desserts. 12noon-9pm.

1395
10/R24

✓ **Ship Inn www.ship-elie.com · Elie** Pub on the bay at Elie, the perfect toon in the picturesque East Neuk of Fife (1644/COASTAL VILLAGES). In summer a huge food operation: bar, back room, next door and upstairs (latter has good view; must book weekends). Same menu throughout and blackboard specials. Real popular place especially in summer when terrace overlooking the beach goes like Bondi (and service can lapse). LO 9pm. Also has 5 rooms adjacent in summer (01333 330246).

1396
10/Q23

✓ **The Ship Inn Broughty Ferry** Excellent seafront (Tay estuary – last time we saw dolphins outside and the pub can supply binoculars) snug pub with food upstairs and down (best tables at window upstairs). Famous for clootie dumpling. 7 days, lunch and 5-9pm (1135/DUNDEE RESTAURANTS).

1397
9/J26
✓ **Smiddy Bar at the Kingarth Hotel** www.kingarthhotel.com · 01700 831662 · **Isle of Bute** 13 km Rothesay 24km after Mount Stuart (1911/COUNTRY HOUSES). Good, friendly old inn probably serving the best food on the island. Blackboard menu. The atmosphere is just right. Open all year. Food LO 8pm.

1398
10/M25
✓ **Old Mill** www.killearnontheweb.co.uk · 01360 550068 · **Main Street, Killearn** More than one notable inn in this village (874/CENTRAL HOTELS) but this is cosy, friendly and all an old pub should be (old here is from 1774). Pub and restaurant. Log fires, nice for kids. Garden. 7 days 12noon-9pm.

1399
9/K27
Apple Inn 01292 318819 · **Troon** Small, unpretentious and somewhat unatmospheric pub on Irvine road out of Troon. Great eclectic menu with staples and some flair. Lunch & LO 9.30pm (10pm weekends).

1400
9/L27
Cochrane Inn 01563 570122 · **Gatehead** Part of the Costley hotel empire (835/HOTELS IN AYRSHIRE). A trim and cosy ivy-covered, very inn-like inn – most agreeable. On A759 Troon to Kilmarnock and 2km A71 Kilmarnock-Irvine road. A bugger to get to (locals know how), but excellent gourmet pub with huge local reputation – must book weekends. Lunch & LO 9pm.

1401
10/Q24
Hunting Lodge Hotel 01337 857226 · **Falkland** Main street of much visited town in central Fife, opposite the fabulous Palace (1851/CASTLES). All day menu of mainly stalwarts like 80/- ale steak pie and macaroni cheese. Also next door **The Covenanter Hotel** has an Italian restaurant, **Luigino** (01337 857224), which does a passable wood-oven pizza, pasta, etc. Both open 7 days. LO 8-9.30pm depending on the day.

1402
10/M24
Lion & Unicorn www.lion-unicorn.co.uk · 01786 850204 · **Thornhill** On A873 off A84 road between the M9 and Callander and near Lake of Menteith in the Trossachs. On main road through nondescript village. They come from miles around for pub grub and sizzling steaks. Cosy dining areas and garden. Changing menu, not fancy. 7 days. LO 9pm.

1403
7/H16
Badachro Inn 01445 741255 · **Badachro near Gairloch** South of Gairloch off A832, then B8056 to Redpoint. A spectacular road and fantastic setting for this waterside pub. Great beer and wine list with lots by the glass and great home-made pub grub. Probably tickworthy but le patron comes with a bit of attitude that some visitors could do without (not of course, regular Jamiroquai, who lives nearby). 7 days 12noon-3pm, 6-9pm.

1404
10/R26
Goblin Ha' Hotel www.goblinha.com · 01620 810244 · **Gifford** Twee village in East Lothian heartland; one of 2 hotels (917/LOTHIANS HOTELS). This, the one with the great name, serves a decent pub lunch and supper (6-9pm; 9.30pm on Fri and Sat) in lounge and more basic version in the pub. Conservatory and 'Biergarten'; kids' play area. Recent chain takeover with more pasta/pizza and less panache.

1405
10/L24
The Byre 01877 376292 · **Brig o' Turk** Off A821 at Callander end of the village adjacent Dundarroch Hotel and Loch Achray. Country inn in deepest Trossachs. Less gastro, more basic pub grub in cosy rooms with outside deck in summer. Can walk from here to Duke's Pass (1723/SCENIC ROUTES).

1406 1 **The Crown** 01776 810261 · **Portpatrick** Hugely popular pub on harbour with
1/J30 tables outside in summer. Light, airy conservatory at back serving freshly caught
fish. 12 rooms above. Locals and Irish who sail over for lunch (sic). LO 10pm.

1407 **The Auld Cross Keys Inn** 01450 870305 · **Denholm near Hawick** Not a lot
10/R28 to recommend in Hawick, so this village pub with rooms is worth the 8km journey
on the A698 Jedburgh road. On the Green, with pub and dining lounges through
the back. Blackboard menu, heaps of choice. Curries on Mon/Tue. Real fire and
candles. Sun carvery. Food LO 8pm. 3 rooms if you want to stay.

Moulin Inn Pitlochry Report: 1273/ROADSIDE INNS.
Old Clubhouse Gullane Report: 925/LOTHIANS HOTELS.
Old Inn Gairloch AA Pub of the Year 2003. Report: 1262/ROADSIDE INNS.
The Masonic Gatehouse of Fleet Report: 858/SOUTHWEST RESTAURANTS.
The Ship Inn Gatehouse of Fleet Report: 851/SOUTHWEST HOTELS.

The Best Vegetarian Restaurants

Not surprisingly, perhaps, there are few completely vegetarian restaurants in Scotland. But there are lots in Edinburgh (see p. 52–53) and some in Glasgow (see p. 114).

1408
9/H24
£15 OR LESS

✓ **Kilmartin House Café** 01546 510278 · **Kilmartin** Attached to early-peoples' museum (2321/MUSEUMS) in Kilmartin Glen and on main road north of Lochgilphead. Organic garden produce including tisanes for the revitalising that the great range of home-made lunches (and dinners) don't fix. Not 100% vegetarian but as near as dammit. 7 days, hot food till 3pm, cakes till 5pm and dinner Thu-Sat in summer.

1409
10/R28

✓ **Damascus Drum** 07707 856123 · **Hawick** One of the notable cafés of the Borders (909/BORDER RESTAURANTS), Chris Ryan's bookshop and haven of civilisation is not strictly vegetarian but is mostly, and it gets a tick a) coz it's quirky and good and b) for sticking it out in this least favourite of towns where men and rugby and meat still rule. Coffee/cake, hot dish of the day, quiches and borek (sic). Great atmosphere. Mon-Sat 9am-5pm.

1410
8/P17
£15 OR LESS

✓ **Blue Angel at Findhorn Community** **Findhorn** You will go a long way in the North to find real vegetarian food, so it may be worth the detour from the main A96 Inverness–Elgin road, to Findhorn and the famous community (1325/RETREATS) where there is a great deli (1532/DELIS) and this pleasant caff by the 'Hall' and The Bakehouse (see below). 7 days till 5pm and evenings if event in the hall. (Hot food till 3pm.)

1411
8/P17
£15-22

✓ **The Bakehouse** 01309 691826 · **Findhorn** Same neck of the woods as Blue Angel (above) and run by same people who have the deli at the Findhorn Community. Not strictly vegetarian but lots of vegetarian choice and everything is ethical and 'slow'. 7 days 10am-9pm (till 6pm Sun/Mon).

1412
9/J26
£15 OR LESS

✓ **Musicker** 01700 502287 · **High Street, Rothesay** Opposite castle. Great pastries, paninis and soups, range of coffee (soya milk if you want). Nice books, newspapers, bluesy – jazz CDs for sale. Friendly, relaxed. All this info supplied by Leslie Hills who is very often right and not only about her affection for Bute! Tue-Sat 10am-5pm.

1413
7/G18
£15 OR LESS

✓ **An Tuireann** www.antuireann.org.uk · **Portree, Skye** Off Uig (then Struan) road (at the Co-op). Excellent gallery cafe and restaurant with contemporary menu; salads, hot meals, snacks. Some bacon (and wild boar) creeps in, but mostly vegetarian. 10am-4.30pm. Tue-Sat (& Mon in Jul & Aug). Changing exhibitions.

1414
7/H16
£15-22

The Mountain Restaurant 01445 712316 · **Gairloch** Vegetarian-friendly restaurant with conservatory and tables outside with mountain view. Bookshop and adjacent Nature Shop with every kind of spiritual whatsits you may want. We've had complaints about the price of tea and scones – but look at the size of them! Self-serve food all day. All seems kinda American and very welcome this far north. Mar-Nov till 6pm (later Jul/Aug).

The Best Vegetarian-Friendly Places

HIGHLANDS
The Ceilidh Place 01854 612103 · Ullapool 1037/INEXPENSIVE HIGHLAND HOTELS.
Café Number One 01463 226200 · Inverness 1158/INVERNESS.
Three Chimneys 01470 511258 · Skye 2398/SKYE RESTAURANTS.
Café Arriba 01478 611830 · Skye 2404/SKYE RESTAURANTS.
The Seafood Restaurant Kyle of Lochalsh & Plockton 1068/1069/INEXPENSIVE HIGHLAND RESTAURANTS.
Riverside Bistro 01571 844356 · Lochinver 1077/INEXPENSIVE HIGHLAND RESTAURANTS.
Plockton Hotel 01599 544274 1260/ROADSIDE INNS.
Old Pines 01397 712324 · near Spean Bridge 1046/LESS EXPENSIVE HIGHLAND HOTELS.
Plockton Inn 01599 544222 · Plockton 1048/LESS EXPENSIVE HIGHLAND HOTELS.
Plockton Shores 01599 544263 · Plockton 1066/LESS EXPENSIVE HIGHLAND RESTAURANTS.
Summer Isles Hotel Bar 01854 622282 · Achiltibuie 1384/GASTROPUBS.
Coul House 01997 421487 · Contin 1031/HIGHLAND HOTELS.

NORTH EAST
The Foyer 01224 582277 · Aberdeen 1097/ABERDEEN RESTAURANTS.
Beautiful Mountain 01224 645353 · Aberdeen 1105/ABERDEEN RESTAURANTS.
Milton Restaurant 01330 844566 · Crathes 1000/NORTHEAST HOTELS.

ARGYLL
Argyll Hotel 01681 700334 · Iona 1254/SEASIDE INNS.
St Columba Hotel 01681 700304 · Iona 2428/MULL.
Inver Cottage 01369 860537 826/ARGYLL RESTAURANTS.
The Green Welly Stop 01838 400271 · Tyndrum 1472/BEST TEAROOMS.
An Lochan 01700 811239 · Tighnabruaigh 815/ARGYLL HOTELS.
Julie's Coffee House 01631 565952 · Oban 831/OBAN.

FIFE & LOTHIANS
Pillars of Hercules 01337 857749 · near Falkland 1483/BEST TEAROOMS.
Ostler's Close 01334 655574 · Cupar 942/FIFE RESTAURANTS.
The Vine Leaf 01334 477497 · St Andrews 949/ST ANDREWS.
Old Clubhouse 01620 842008 · Gullane 925/LOTHIANS RESTAURANTS.
Livingston's 01506 846565 · Linlithgow 919/LOTHIAN RESTAURANTS.

CENTRAL
Deans @ Let's Eat 01738 643377 · Perth 970/PERTHSHIRE RESTAURANTS.
Monachyle Mhor 01877 384622 · near Balquhidder 1276/GET-AWAY HOTELS.
The Old Armoury 01796 474281 · Pitlochry 978/PERTHSHIRE RESTAURANTS.
Indulge 01764 660033 · Auchterarder 1478/TEAROOMS.

SOUTH & SOUTH WEST
Marmions 01896 822245 · Melrose 899/BORDERS RESTAURANTS.
Philipburn 01750 20747 · Selkirk 893/BORDERS HOTELS.
The Masonic 01557 81433 · Gatehouse of Fleet 858/SOUTHWEST RESTAURANTS.

ORKNEY
Woodwick House 01856 751330 · Evie B&B, seals, music and woodland. 2429/ORKNEY.

The Best Seafood Restaurants

For seafood restaurants in Edinburgh, see p. 51; for Glasgow, see p. 113.

1415
10/R24
£22-32

✓✓ **The Cellar 01333 310378 · Anstruther** For many years now the best seafood restaurant in Scotland (and long may that continue Mr Jukes!). Behind Fisheries Museum in busy East Neuk of Fife town. Fish and shellfish from only the best waters, one meat option. Cosy French-bistro atmosphere. 941/FIFE RESTAURANTS.

1416
6/P12
£22-32

✓✓ **The Captain's Galley www.captainsgalley.co.uk · 01847 894999 · Scrabster** The place to eat on the North Coast. A reputation built on total integrity. All local produce (from 50 ml radius). No tuna here, just what they catch (conservation ethos in menu). Though menu relatively short (4 choices), it's come straight off a boat. Nice room, nice guy (Jim Cowie): even the fish would approve. Home-made bread, ice cream, everything. Opening hours vary.

1417
10/S20
£22-32

✓✓ **The Tolbooth 01569 762287 · Stonehaven** On corner of harbour, long one of the best restaurants in the area in a great setting – oldest building in town. Upstairs bistro with owner Robert Cleaver who also has the Art Deco restaurant in town (999/NORTHEAST RESTAURANTS) very on the case here. Reliably fresh and simple. Great lobster. With Silver Darling (1109/ABERDEEN RESTAURANTS) not what it was, The Tollbooth floats to the top for seafood in the North East. Was AA Restaurant of the Year '06. Wed-Sun lunch & dinner, LO 9pm.

1418
10/R23
£22-32

✓✓ **The Seafood Restaurant www.theseafoodrestaurant.com · 01334 479475 · St Andrews** When it opened a few years back it effortlessly became the top spot in town. Landmark position (overlooking Old Course) and building – glass-walled pavilion. Chef/proprietor Craig Millar is brilliant with (especially) white fish and the little things that make it zing. Great wines, rich puds but mainly fish pure and simple. 7 days lunch & dinner LO 10pm.

1419
10/R24
£22-32

✓✓ **The Seafood Restaurant www.theseafoodrestaurant.com · 01333 730327 · St Monans, Fife** West end of East Neuk Village. As St Andrews (above), Butler family offer simple title and no fuss in menu either. Conservatory and terrace overlooks sea, waves lap, gulls mew etc. Bar menu lunch & dinner LO 10pm Closed Mon/Tue in winter.

1420
9/K27
£22-32

✓✓ **MacCallum's of Troon Oyster Bar 01292 319339 · Troon** Right down at the quayside, so through Troon at main crossroads, past Fishmarket then go the extra mile. 3km from centre. Red brick building with discreet sign, so eyes peeled. Lovely fish, great atmosphere, unpretentious and worth the trip even from Glasgow. Tue-Sat lunch & LO 9.30pm. Sun lunch only. Adjacent fish 'n' chip shop is one of the best in the land.

1421
9/H23

✓ **The Seafood Temple 01631 566000 · Oban** Top spot perhaps of the 3 great seafood restaurants in Oban (see below) '07/08 – well, it's new and it's now and it is fabulous. Report: 828/ARGYLL RESTAURANTS.

1422
9/H23
£22-32

✓ **The Waterfront www.waterfrontoban.co.uk · 01631 563110 · Oban** On the waterfront at the station and upstairs from unimposing entrance a light, airy room above the bar which nevertheless is serving some of the best seafood around in an authentic setting. Blackboard specials change daily. The fish leap upstairs and onto your plate. Somewhere in Oban to linger on the way to the ferry. Open all year. Lunch & LO 9pm.

1423
8/T19
£22-32

✓**Silver Darling** www.silverdarling.co.uk · 01224 576229 · **Aberdeen**
Down by harbour. For many years one of the best restaurants in the city and
the North East; certainly, a stunning location. 1109/ABERDEEN RESTAURANTS.

1424
7/F17
£22-32

✓**Lochbay Seafood** www.lochbay-seafood-restaurant.co.uk ·
01470 592235 · **Skye** 12km north Dunvegan; A850 to Portree, B886
Waternish peninsula coastal route. A scenic Skye drive leads you to the door of
this small cottage at end of the village row. Overlooks water where your scallops,
prawns and oysters are surfaced. Main dishes served unfussily with puds like
clootie dumpling. Simply very good – you'll need to book. Apr-Oct; lunch & LO
8.30ish. Tue-Sat (open Mon dinner Jun-Aug).

1425
9/K23
£15-22

✓**Loch Fyne Seafood & Smokery** 01499 600264 On A83 the Loch
Lomond to Inveraray road, 20km Inveraray/11km Rest and Be Thankful.
Landmark roadside restaurant and all-round seafood experience on the way out
west. Though now a huge UK chain this is the original (it's not actually in the
chain but a separate entity after management buy-out). People come from afar for
the oysters and the smokery fare, especially the kippers. Spacious and with many
banquettes though somewhat refectory-ish! House white (other whites and
whisky) well chosen. Same menu all day; LO 8.30pm (later in summer). Shop sells
every conceivable packaging of salmon and other Scots produce; shop 8pm.

1426
8/S17
£15 OR LESS

✓**The Harbour Restaurant & Café** 01261 851690 · **Gardenstown near
Banff** Tiny caff right on the harbour in one of many enchanting Moray Coast
villages (1637/COASTAL VILLAGES), this the only caff. Handful of tables in and out.
Simple fish preps and home baking. Charl and Fiona Pretorius, though mainly
Fiona. Mar-Jan, lunch & 6-9pm.

1427
9/K26
£15-22

✓**Fins** 01475 568989 · **Fairlie near Largs** On main A78 south of Fairlie a
seafood bistro, smokery (Fencebay), shop and craft/cookshop (2251/CRAFT-
SHOPS). Roadside fish farm bistro and all-round day-out experience. Best place to
eat for miles in either direction. Chefs Jane and Paul use exemplary restraint and
the wine list is similarly to the point. Nice conservatory with geraniums. Lunch &
dinner LO 8.30/9pm. Closed Mon.

1428
9/L26
£22-32

✓**Creelers** www.creelers.co.uk · 01770 302810 · **Brodick, Arran** Just outside Brodick on road north to castle in uninspiring plastic gift plaza though
the cheese shop is nice (1559/CHEESES). Excellent seafood bistro – great food, fun
staff though as always on islands they come and go. Phone ahead, to be sure.
Easter-Oct. Closed Mon.

1429 1
1/J30
£22-32

Campbell's www.campbellsrestaurant.co.uk · 01776 810314 · **Portpatrick**
Friendly, harbourside restaurant in immensely popular Portpatrick. Some meat
dishes, but mainly seafood. Their own boat brings back crab and lobster. 7 days
lunch & LO 10pm. Closed Jan-Mar & Mon.

1430
10/P23
£22-32/
£15-22

Keracher's www.kerachers-restaurant.co.uk · 01738 449777 · **Corner of
South & Scott Streets, Perth** Keracher's are major fish wholesalers and supply
most of the best hotel dining rooms in Perthshire, so they know their fish and
seafood stuff. Bright upstairs room. Menu not totally fishy, but they know their turf
as well as the surf, so a very good bet. Lunch Tue-Sat, dinner Mon-Sat LO 10pm.

1431 **Crannog at the Waterfront** www.oceanandoak.co.uk · 01397 705589 ·
9/K21 **Fort William** Long established best meal in town. Nice bright contemporary
£22-32 setting, not only great seafood but a real sense of place in this rainy town. 7 days, lunch & LO 9pm (later weekends).

1432 **Ee-Usk** www.eeusk.com · 01631 565666 · **Oban** New build on the north pier
9/H23 by the indefatigable Macleod's (adjacent an Italian restaurant in a similar building
£22-32 which they also run – The Piazza). A full-on seafront caff with urban-bistro feel, great views and fish from that sea. Good wee wine list. 7 days lunch & LO 9.30pm.

1433 **Seafood Café** 01971 502251 · **Tarbet near Scourie** Charming recently rebuilt
6/K13 conservatory restaurant on cove where boats leave for Handa Island bird reserve
£15-22 (1807/BIRDS). Julian catches your seafood from his boat and Jackie cooks it; they have the Rick Stein seal of approval. Cheesecake for dessert. Located at end of unclassified road off the A894 between Laxford Bridge and Scourie; best phone to check openings. Apr-Sep: Mon-Sat 12-8pm. Sun Jul/Aug. Licensed.

1434 **Kishorn Seafood Bar** www.kishornseafoodbar.co.uk · 01520 733240 On
7/H18 A896 at Kishorn on road between Lochcarron (Inverness) and Sheildaig near the
£22-32 road over the hill to Applecross (1712/ROUTES). Fresh local seafood in a roadside diner: Kishorn oysters, Applecross crab; lobsters in a tank out back. Light, bright and a real find in the middle of beautiful nowhere courtesy of the enthusiastic Viv Rollo. Apr-Oct daily 10am-5pm (9pm Jul/Aug). Sun 12noon-5pm.

1435 **The Pierhouse** www.pierhousehotel.co.uk · 01631 730302 · **Port Appin** At
9/K27 the end of the minor road and 3km from the A828 Oban-Fort William road in Port
£15-22 Appin village right by the tiny 'pier' where the passenger ferry leaves for Lismore. Locally caught seafood (Lismore oysters, Mallaig flatfish, hand-dived shellfish) is handed over fresh to the door by boat. Lively atmosphere, wine and wonderful view. Report: 1264/INNS.

1436 **The Seafood Cabin** 01880 760207 · **Skipness** Adjacent Skipness Castle,
9/J26 signed from Claonaig where the CalMac ferry from Lochranza arrives. Cabin,
£15 OR LESS outdoor seating and indoor options in perfect spot for their fresh and local seafood snacks and cakes. Mussels come further (Loch Etive). Smoked stuff from Creelers in Arran. Jun-Sep 11-6pm. Closed Sat.

✓ **Applecross Inn** 01520 744262 The inn at the end of the road with excellent fresh seafood and classic fish 'n' chips. 1285/GET-AWAY HOTELS.

The Best Fish & Chip Shops

1437
1/B1
✓ ✓ **L'Alba D'Oro** **Henderson Row, Edinburgh** Near corner with Dundas St. Large selection of deep-fried goodies, including many vegetarian savouries. Inexpensive proper pasta, real pizzas and superb, surprising Italian wine to go in adjacent takeaway **Anima**, a stools-at-the-window diner (328/TAKEAWAYS). This is still the chip shop of the future. Open until 12midnight. Report: 205/EDINBURGH PIZZA.

1438
9/K27
✓ ✓ **The Wee Hurrie** 01292 319340 · **Troon** Immediately famed and fabulous when it opened '06, the Wee Hurrie is part and parcel of MacCallum's Oyster & Fish Restaurant. See 1420/SEAFOOD RESTAURANTS for directions because it's a fair walk from the town centre. Fresh daily fish displayed and to select. All fried up as you wait. Tue-Sun 12noon-8pm (9pm Fri/Sat).

1439
1/D1
✓ **The Rapido** **77 Broughton Street, Edinburgh** Legendary chippie. Popular with late-nighters stumbling back down the hill to the New Town, including the flotsam of the 'Pink Triangle'. 1.30am (3.30am Fri/Sat).

1440
1/E1
✓ **The Deep Sea** **Leith Walk, Edinburgh** Opposite Playhouse. Open late and often has queues (which are quickly dispatched). The haddock has to be 'of a certain size'. Traditional menu. Still one of the best fish suppers with which to feed your hangover. 2am-ish (3am Fri/Sat).

1441
10/Q23
✓ **Deep Sea** **81 Nethergate, Dundee** At bottom end of Perth Rd; very central. The Sterpaio family have been serving the Dundonians excellent fish 'n' chips since 1939; great range of fish in groundnut (the most expensive) oil. Café with aproned waitress service is a classic. so very traditional, so very tasty. Mon-Sat, 11.30am-6.40pm (7pm carry-out).

1442
WE
✓ **Philadelphia** **445 Great Western Road, Glasgow** Adjacent Big Blue (586/PIZZA) and La Parmigiana (543/BEST RESTAURANTS), owned by same family. Since 1930, a Glasgow fixture and fresher fryer than most. 7 days 12noon-12midnight (Fri/Sat 3am).

1443
10/S20
✓ **The Bay** **Stonehaven** On the prom towards the open-air pool (2198/SWIMMING POOLS), a new, very happening chip shop in a town not short (see Sandy's below). The real fresh fish.

1444
9/J26
✓ **West End** **1 Gallowgate, Rothesay** Winner of awards (though it's time to get their former glories off the windows) and possibly a must-do if you're on Bute, despite their ticket system. Only haddock, but wide range of other fries and fresh pizza. We can't make head nor tail of their hours, but they're mostly open! Closed 2-4pm.

1445
7/N19
✓ **Harkai's** **Aviemore** On main road through town at south end as you come in from A9. Been here since 1965 but I missed it until spending a bit of time here with the Outsider Festival (48/EVENTS) in '07. Big local reputation and unlikely location for a chipper that takes itself seriously. 7 days LO 8.30pm (9pm Jul/Aug).

1446
10/T26
✓ **Giacopazzi's** **Eyemouth** Harbour by the fish market (or what's left of it). A caff and takeaway with the catch on its doorstep. Dispensing excellent fish and chips and their award-winning ice cream quietly here in the far-flung south-east corner of Scotland since 1900. 7 days 11am-9pm. Upstairs to **Oblo's Bistro** (01890 752527). Sun-Thu 10am-midnight, Fri & Sat 10am-1am.

1447 **Seaforth Chippy** **Ullapool** Adjacent ferry terminal. Part of Seaforth Hotel with
6/K15 upstairs bistro but best to stick to fish and chips and walk the harbour. Some
question in Ullapool whether it's the Seaforth or the one round the corner but I'll
stick with this. Chips often pale but fish don't get any fresher. 7 days till 9.30pm.

1448 1 **Balmoral** **Balmoral Road, Dumfries** Seems as old and essential as the Bard
1/N29 himself. Using groundnut oil, it's the best chip in the south. Out the Annan road
heading east, 1km from centre. LO 10.30pm (9.30pm Sun/Mon).

1449 **Fish & Chip Van** **www.silverswift.co.uk/van.htm** · **Tobermory** Parked on
9/G22 Fisherman's Pier by the clock, this van has almost achieved the status of a destination restaurant. Always a queue. Fresh and al fresco. All year. 12noon-9pm.

1450 **Sandy's** **Market Square, Stonehaven** The established Stoney chipper, and
10/S20 always busy despite interlopers (it saw off the Bervie chipper but word is, it won't
see off the Bay). Daily, LO 10pm, 9pm Sun. Big haddock like the old days.

SOME GOOD CHIP SHOPS THAT WOULD BE BETTER
WITHOUT THE LARD
1451 ✓✓ **Valente's** **01592 651991** · **73 Overton Road, Kirkcaldy** Ask directions
10/Q24 to this superb chippy in east of town (not downtown version); worth the
detour and the queue when you get there. Phone if lost. Lard used but vegetable
oil on request. Till 11pm. Branch at 73 Henry Rd (01592 203600). Closed Wed.

1452 ✓ **The New Dolphin** **Chapel Street, Aberdeen** Despite the pre-eminence
8/T19 of the Ashvale in Aberdeen, many would rather swear by this small, always
busy place just off Union St. They both swear by lard. Till 1am; 3am weekends.

1453 ✓ **The Ashvale** **www.theashvale.co.uk** · **Aberdeen, Elgin, Inverurie,**
8/P17 **Ellon, Brechin** Original restaurant (1985) at 46 Great Western Rd near Union
St; 2 other city branches. Restaurant/takeaway complex à la Harry Ramsden (they
stick to dripping but vegetable oil supplied on request). Various sizes of haddock,
sole, plaice. Home-made stovies, etc, all served fresh so you may wait. Hours vary.

1454 ✓ **Peppo's** **53 Ladybridge Street, Arbroath** By the harbour where those fish
10/R22 come in. Fresh as that and chips in dripping. Peppo here since 1951; John and
Frank Orsi carry on a great family tradition feeding the hordes. 7 days 4pm-8pm (a
teatime thing). **Marco's** further along opens earlier and later; uses vegetable oil.

1455 ✓ **The Anstruther Fish Bar** **www.anstrutherfishbar.co.uk** · **Anstruther**
10/R24 On the front in Fife seaside town (1644/COASTAL VILLAGES). Often listed as the
best fish 'n' chips in Scotland/UK/Universe and the continuous queue suggests
they may be right but possibly trading on past reputation. Many locals prefer **The
Pittenweem Fish & Chip Bar**. Tiny door in the wall in Main St next to clock
tower in next town along. So we say, go west! Lard used. Eating-in at Anstruther is
cramped (cardboard trays etc) so takeaway best. 7 days 11.30am-10.30pm.

1456 **Nories** **88 George Street, Oban** Here for over 50 years so what can you tell
9/H23 them – well stop using 'orrible animal fat for a start. Nevertheless, a classic fryer
by the sea, larding up the Obanites and the tourists for generations.

1457 **The North Berwick Fry** **11 Quality Street, North Berwick** Adjacent tourist
10/R25 information centre. Here forever, also in seaside town so you take your poke (now
a foam-plastic box) to the front (or to the gardens opposite). Big reputation,
always busy. 7 days 11.30am-12midnight. New shop in '08.

Great Cafés

For cafés in Edinburgh, see p. 63, Glasgow, p. 117.

1458 ✓✓ **The Castle Restaurant** Inverness On road that winds up to the
7/M18 castle from the main street, near the tourist information centre and the
hostels. No pandering to tourists here, but this great caff has been serving chips
with everything for 40 years though these (crinkle cuts) are not their strong point.
Pork chops, prawn cocktail, perfect fried eggs. They work damned hard. In
Inverness or anywhere nearby, there is no better deal than this! (But see below.)
9am-8.25pm (sic). Closed Sun.

1459 ✓✓ **Girvans** 2 Stephens Brae, Inverness Behind Marks & Spencer at end
7/M17 of pedestrian street. A different proposition to the Castle (above), more
up-market, more perhaps a restaurant, but the atmosphere is of a good old-
fashioned caff serving everything from omelettes to full-blown comforting meals.
Great all-day breakfast on Sun. Tempting cream-laden cakes. Always busy but no
need to book. 7 days 9am-9pm (Sun from 10am).

1460 ✓✓ **The Real Food Café** www.therealfoodcafe.com · Tyndrum
9/K23 Created from a Little Chef on the main A82 just before the junction
Oban/Fort William and what a difference. Excellent food for the road, conscientiously prepared, seriously sourced, the antitheses of frozen, fast and couldn't-
care-less. Fish 'n' chips, burgers, breakfasts, pies – all home-made. A new pit stop
on the way northwest. Some may say it's just a glorified chip shop but it has been
glorified by others apart from me. 7 days 12noon-10pm.

1461 ✓ **The Tea Store** www.theteastore.co.uk · Argyll Street, Ullapool In the
6/K15 street parallel to and one up from the waterfront. Excellent, unpretentious
café serving all-day fry-ups and other snacks. Great home baking including
strawberry tarts in season. Best in Ullapool (or Lewis where you might be heading).
All year. 8.30am-4.30pm. Sun 9am-3pm. (Winter hours vary.)

1462 ✓ **Allan Water Café** www.bridgeofallan.com · Henderson Street,
10/N24 Bridge Of Allan The main street, beside the eponymous bridge. Real whiff
of nostalgia along with the fish 'n' chips and the ice cream, which are the best
around. Worth coming over from Stirling (8km) for a takeaway or a seat in the
comforting woody caff – 'and a reminisce of the life before the mall and the burg-
ering of your high street'. Well, that's what I said before – now they've gone and
gotten a steel/glass mall-like extension. It's still about the chips and ice cream!
7 days, 8am-9pm.

1463 ✓ **The Ritz Café** www.millport.org.uk · Millport See Millport, see the Ritz.
9/K26 Since 1906 and now in its fourth generation, the classic café on the Clyde.
Once overshadowed by Nardini's and a short ferry journey away (from Largs, continuous; then 6km), it should be an essential part of any visit to this part of the
coast, and Millport is not entirely without charm. Toasties, rolls, the famous 'hot
peas'. Exellent ice cream (especially with melted marshmallow). Something of
'things past'. 7 days, 10am-9pm in season. The Ritz for sale at TGP but this is a
national treasure and it would not do to change it much. Other hours vary.

1464 ✓ **The Hub** www.thehubintheforest.co.uk · near Innerleithen · 01721
10/Q27 721736 At entranceway 'the trail head' to Glentress Forest Park on A72 5km
from Peebles. Glentress is mountain bike mecca so this US-style caff in a shack
serves shorts-and-lycra-clad allsorts with big appetites. Frys and baking and cheap

nosh for energy. Breakfast from Forsyth's the butchers (plus vegetarian). Outdoor terrace. Cool spot. 7 days till 6pm (7pm Sat/Sun) & till 10pm Wed (night biking!).

1465
10/M24
✓ **Ben Ledi Café www.benledicafe.co.uk · Callander** Main street near square. Legendary café taken over by the ambitious and industrious Lewis family of Monachyle Mhor (868/CENTRAL HOTELS). Unprepossessing frontage but here, Dick Lewis adds a fresh-fish counter and general panache but doesn't tamper with the basic product: the fish tea with fresh Scrabster-landed fish and great chips. 7 days till 9pm. The takeaway next door is open later.

1466
10/R18
Brydons 01877 376267 · 16 High Street, Hawick Cool, family-run and friendly caff in Hawick main street serving breakfast through to tea. Has the real caff atmosphere. Hot food like mince 'n' tatties, macaroni cheese. This was the food I was brought up on and I went to that damned high school. Surprising collection of teapots. 8am-4.30pm. Closed Sun.

1467
9/K27
The Melbourne 72 Hamilton Street, Saltcoats A tatty but authentic 1950s leftover with good coffee, good panini, breakfasts, filled rolls etc. Juke box nearly as cool as the lassies behind the counter! Used as a film location (*Late Night Shopping*). Damned fine! Daily until 5pm.

The Best Tearooms & Coffee Shops

For Edinburgh, see p. 61–62; for Glasgow, p. 115–16.

1468
10/S27
✓✓ **The Terrace Floors Castle, Kelso** Top tearoom inside and out an old outbuilding that forms one side of the estate walled garden (2295/GARDEN CENTRES) some distance from the castle (1918/COUNTRY HOUSES). Superb, home-made, unpretentious and nothing-French food: hot dishes, home-cured ham, salads and baking. Shop with deli stuff. And the terrace: bliss. 7 days 12noon-5pm. Open all year.

1469
2/F4
✓✓ **Café Gandolfi www.cafegandolfi.com · Glasgow** Glasgow's definitive tearoom, long-standing and a formula that has not been bettered – hence mentioned again on this page. Also in Glasgow the more recent and decidedly boho **Tchai-Ovna**. No chintz nor cream teas here, just good tchai and chat. Reports: 644/651/GLASGOW TEAROOMS.

1470
10/P24
✓✓ **The Powmill Milkbar near Kinross** On the A977 Kinross (on the M90, junction 6) to Kincardine Bridge road, a real milk bar and a real slice of Scottish craic and cake. Apple pie and moist fly cemeteries – an essential stop on any Sunday run (but open every day). The paper plates do little justice to the confections they bear, but they are part of the deal, so don't complain! Hot meals and salads. Good place to take kids. 7 days, 9am-5pm (6pm summer, 4pm winter). Report: 2075/GLEN & RIVER WALKS.

1471 1
1/M29
✓✓ **Kitty's Tearoom New Galloway** Main street of town in the forest. Absolutely splendid. Sylvia Brown's steady hand in the kitchen, great cakes, good tea, and conversations between local ladies. Great salads. High tea 4-6pm very popular including 'a roast'. All this but you must take cake. It's an Alan Bennett world. 11am-7pm, Easter-Oct. Tue-Sun.

1472
9/K23
✓✓ **The Green Welly Stop www.thegreenwellystop.co.uk · Tyndrum** I've said it before but I'll say it again: this ain't no ordinary motorway

service caff. On A82, a strategically placed pit stop on the drive to Oban or Fort William (just before the road divides), with a Scottish produce shop and the gas station (open later). Self-service comfort food to break the journey. Much home-made, very Scottish and a whole lot better than you'd expect. Shop stuffed with everything you don't and do need (including this book). 7 days, 8.30am-5.30pm (5pm in winter).

1473
8/R20
✓ ✓ **The Black-Faced Sheep** 01339 887311 · **Aboyne** Near main Royal Deeside road through Aboyne (A93) and Mark Ronson's excellent coffee shop/gift shop is well-loved by locals (and regulars from all over) but is thankfully missed by the bus parties hurtling towards Balmoral. Home-made breads and cakes, light specials; good coffee (real capp and espresso from Elektra machine). Love affair with Italy about to bear fruit as well: own label wines and olive oil (on way at TGP). 10am-5pm, Sun from 11am.

1474
8/S20
✓ ✓ **The Falls of Freugh** www.fallsoffeugh.com · 01330 822123 · **Banchory** Over bridge south from town, the B974 for Fettercairn (signed), a restaurant-cum-tearoom by a local beauty spot, the Tumbling Falls. Ann Taylor's labour of love with à la carte menu, specials and great bakes. A model of how it should be done, here on the Deeside teaside where there are more than a few places to choose from (see above and below). All year. 7 days till 4.30pm.

1475
8/R20
✓ ✓ **Raemoir Garden Centre** **Banchory** On A980 off main A93, the Deeside road through town, about 3km. You have to beat a path through the garden (centre) to the tearoom, though it's a good 'un (2299/GARDEN CENTRES). The caff is superb with excellent home baking and a full hot-meal menu and expansion plans at TGP. Great quality stuff, the way it used to be. Then shop! 7 days till 5pm (Sun 4.30pm). Centre till 5.30pm.

1476
9/G22
✓ ✓ **Glengorm Farm Coffee Shop** 01688 302321 · **near Tobermory** First right on Tobermory-Dervaig road. Organic food served in well refurbished stable block. Soups, cakes, venison burgers among other hot meals and delicious salads from their famous garden (they supply other restaurants in Mull). All you need after a walk in the grounds of this great estate (2428/MULL HOTELS) and great ceramics adjacent (2244/SHOPPING). Oh... and the *best* cappuccino on Mull. Open all year LO 4.30pm.

1477
10/R25
✓ ✓ **Falko** **Gullane** Main street of genteel East Lothian village (though too much house building seems likely to lower the dulcet tone) on corner. A bakery/coffee shop (though the bakery is actually in Edinburgh) that calls itself a konditerai because those gorgeous cakes and breads are German, Austrian and Swiss and they change with the seasons (stollen comes in October). Master baker and proprietor Falko has his fingers in a very sweet pie. 8am-5.30pm, Sun from 11am. Closed Mon.

1478
10/N23
✓ **Indulge** 01764 660033 · **Auchterarder** Aptly named, deliciously caked tearoom/restaurant at the bottom end of long main street. Eclectic, innovative hot-meal menu and irresistible desserts and teatime goodies to wash down with the Darjeeling. It's a winner. 9.30am-4.30pm. Closed Sun.

1479
9/L28
✓ **Tudor Restaurant** **8 Beresford Terrace, Ayr** Near Odeon and Burns Monument Sq. High tea from 3.15pm, breakfast all day. Roomy, well-used, full of life. Bakery counter at front (fab cream donuts and bacon butties as they're supposed to be) and locals from bairns to OAPs in the body of the kirk. 10am-9pm Mon-Sat, 12noon-8pm Sun.

1480
10/S22

✓ **The Watermill** www.aberfeldywatermill.com · 01887 822896 ·
Mill Street, Aberfeldy Off Main Street direction Kenmore near the Birks
(2096/WOODLAND WALKS). Very civilised gallery, bookshop and downstairs caff on
riverside in conserved mill. They love books (including mine apparently). Home
baking and snacks. 9.30am-4.30pm (Sun from 12noon). Times may change.

1481
7/M20

✓ **Laggan Coffeeshop** www.potterybunkhouse.co.uk · near Laggan On
A889 from Dalwhinnie on A9 that leads to A86, the road west to Spean
Bridge and Kyle. Lovely Linda's road sign points you to this former pottery, craft
shop and bunkhouse (1234/HOSTELS). Great home baking, especially carrot cake,
lemon drizzle and Queen Mary's Tart (a Claire Macdonald recipe). Near great spot
for forest walks and river swimming (1756/PICNICS). Easter-Oct 7 days till 5.30pm.

1482
8/R18

✓ **The Tearoom at Clatt** near Alford & Inverurie In the village hall in the
hamlet of Clatt where local ladies display great home-made Scottish baking –
like a weekly sale of work. Take A96 north of Inverurie, then B9002 follow sign for
Auchleven, then Clatt. Great countryside. Weekends May-Sep 1pm-5pm. One of
the great tea and scone experiences in the world (I hope you see what I mean).

1483
10/Q24

✓ **The Pillars Of Hercules** www.pillars.co.uk · 01337 857749 · near
Falkland Tearoom on organic farm on A912 road 2km from village towards
Strathmiglo and the motorway. Excellent, homely place and fare and all PC.
Home-made cakes, soup etc. See also 1549/FARM SHOPS. 7 days 10am-5pm (shop
till 6pm).

1484
9/L24

✓ **The Coach House** www.lochlomondtrading.com · Luss, Loch Lomond
Long after the soap *Take The High Road* which was set here ended, this village
still throngs with visitors. Gary and Rowena Grove's much (self) publicised success
story also goes like the proverbial fair, though flamboyant Gary has moved on. Not
all home made but they'd need very big ovens for the required mountains of
mountainous scones. The cream is lashed. Nice loos, some outside seating. 7 days
10am-5pm.

1485
9/J22

✓ **Castle Stalker View** www.castlestalkerview.co.uk · Portnacroish
near Port Appin On main A828 Oban-Fort William about half-way. Modern-
build café/gift shop with contemporary snack menu and home cooking. Nice
people so a popular local rendezvous as well as you and me just passing through.
The main thing is the extraordinary view (1750/VIEWS). Mar-Oct 9.30am-5.30pm,
winter Wed-Sun 10am-4pm.

1486
10/R26

✓ **Flat Cat Gallery Coffee Shop** www.flatgallery.co.uk · 2 Market
Street, Lauder Opposite Eagle Hotel. Speeding through Lauder (note speed
camera at Edinburgh end) you might miss this cool coffee spot and serious gallery.
Always interesting work and ethnic things. Home baking, natch. 7 days till 5pm.

1487
9/H26

✓ **The Lighthouse** 01770 850240 · Pirnmill, Arran On road west looking on
to Mull of Kintyre. Perfect pit-stop for home-cooking looking over bay. Full
menu available in curiously contemporary decor. 7 days 10am-9pm Jan-Dec.

1488
10/L23

✓ **Library Tearoom** Balquhidder Centre of village opposite church
(1971/GRAVEYARDS) where many walks start includes great view (1744/VIEWS)
and near long walk to Brig o' Turk (2073/GLEN WALKS). Excellent bakes: carrot cake,
cheese scones, soup and BLT. Only a few tables. Apr-Oct, Thu-Sun 10am-4.30pm.

1489
10/Q24

✓ **Kind Kyttock's Kitchen Falkland** Folk come to Falkland (1851/CASTLES; 2043/HILL WALKS) for many reasons, not least for afternoon tea. Several choices, this the longest established and most highly regarded. Omelettes, toasties, baked potatoes, baking. Good service. A visit to Falkland wouldn't be the same without it! 10.30am-5.30pm. Closed Mon.

1490
7/H18

The Flower Tunnel www.applecross.uk.com/flower_tunnel · Applecross In campsite (1306/CAMPING WITH KIDS) as you arrive in Applecross after amazing journey (1712/SCENIC ROUTES). Coffee-shop in greenhouse full of plants and outdoor seating. Famous pizzas, though bakery closed '05. Apr-Oct. 7 days, supper only high season.

1491
7/H16

Bridge Cottage Poolewe In village and near Inverewe Gardens (1586/ GARDENS), cottage right enough with crafts/pictures up stairs and parlour teashop down. Salads, big cakes; local produce. 7 days till 4.30pm (winter hours vary). Closed Nov.

1492
9/J23

Robin's Nest Main Street, Taynuilt Off the A85 (leading to Bonawe 2329/MUSEUMS and Glen Etive Cruises). Tiny home-baking caff with unusual soups and snacks as well as the good WRI cake. Sarah Muir (aged 12) reminds me that I really should mention the gigantic scones with home-made jam and cream. Oh yes! Easter-Oct 7 days 10am-5pm, Thu-Sun in winter.

1493
9/H23

The Quaich Café Kilmelford On the road south from Oban to Campbeltown. Part of the local village stores, a neat little caff full of home-baked goodies – free range/organic, nice bread and pies. 10.30-4.30pm. Closed Wed & Sun.

1494
9/H25

Crinan Coffee Shop www.crinanhotel.com · Crinan Run by the hotel people (812/BEST HOTELS ARGYLL) up the road – I guess they opened this because Crinan had to have a good coffee shop. Now it does. Fascinating village for yachties and anyone with time to while, this place overlooks the busy canal basin where boats are always going through. Good cakes. Easter-Oct 9am-5.30pm.

1495
10/R27

Papa Joe's Melrose Next to the abbey. Oddly named twiddly twee tearoom in genteel town where cakes really have to be home made and the tea is proper too. Hot snacks. 7 days 9am-4.30pm.

1496
10/Q27

Silver Spoon Innerleithen Road, Peebles At end of main street adjacent Green Tree hotel. Mumsy, definitely not funky tearoom, but with good attitude to baking (and mums). Perfectly Peebles! 7 days. 9am-4.30pm (Sun 11am-4pm. Yes, on tearoom Sun they close early! Love it!).

1497
8/N17

Logie Steading near Forres South of town towards Grantown (A940) – 10km. Or from Carrbridge via B9007. See 2089/WOODLAND WALKS (**Randolph's Leap**). In a lovely spot near the River Findhorn, a courtyard of fine things (2249/ SHOPPING) and a superior tearoom – home bakes and snacks; hot food till 3pm. 7 days 10.30am-5pm (winter hours may vary).

1498
6/J16

Maggie's Tearoom Dundonnell On A832 in Wester Ross, the road to Inverewe Gardens and Gairloch. Roadside cottage with great view. Home-made hot dishes, salads and bakes. Season only. Closed Sun.

1499
9/J26

The Waterfront www.thewaterfrontbistro.co.uk · 01700 505166 · East Princes Street, Rothesay On the front (turn left off the ferry). Small, hard-working caff/restaurant with local reputation and big portions. They say 'real food for real money', ie no credit or debit cards. Newish so still fixing opening but closed Mon/Tue.

1500 1
1/N30
Garden Room Teashop Rockcliffe On main road in/out of this seaside cul de sac. Best on sunny days when you can sit in the garden. Snacks and cakes (though not all home-made). 10.30am-5.30pm. Closed Mon/Tue.

1501 1
1/L30
Reading Glasses Wigtown Few good eating places in Wigtown Booktown but this tiny caff at the back of yet another bookshop is a rest and respite from all that browsing. 3-wifie operation with named, locally sourced ingredients, soup with Wigwam bread (1518/BAKERIES) and home-made cakes. Can be as packed as a bookshelf. 7 days Easter-Oct. 10am-5pm.

1502
9/H21
The Ariundle Centre www.ariundle.co.uk · Strontian At beginning of walk in Ariundle Woods (2093/WOODLAND WALKS) in wonderful Ardnamurchan. Bungalow tearoom with knits and nick nacks. Hot dishes, home bakes. Lovely home-made candlelit dinners 6.30-8.30pm. All year.

1503
9/H24
Crafty Kitchen Ardfern Down the Ardfern B8002 road (4km) from A816 Oban-Lochgilphead road, the yachty seafaring nice manna port of the Craignish peninsula. A book and crafty shop right enough and a kitchen out back from which great home-made cakes and special hot dishes emerge along with superior burgers and fries. Tue-Sun 10am-5pm. Weekends only Nov/Dec. Closed Jan-Mar.

1504
8/S20
Horsemill Restaurant 01330 844525 · Crathes Castle, near Banchory Adjacent magnificent Crathes (1922/COUNTRY HOUSES; 1587/GARDENS) so lots of reasons to go off the Deeside road (A93) and up the drive. More tearoom than restaurant but some hot dishes eg haggis tart with red-onion marmalade and excellent home baking mmm... meringues. Open all year lunch/afternoon tea till 5pm.

1505
7/M17
The Pantry Cromarty In great wee town in Black Isle 45km northeast of Inverness (1639/COASTAL VILLAGES) on corner of Church St. Good home baking and a decent cup of coffee. Easter-end Oct. 10.30am-4pm. Closed Fri.

1506
10/M24
Dun Whinny's Callander Off main street at Glasgow road, a welcoming wee (but not twee) tearoom; not run by wifies. Banoffee pie kind of thing and clootie dumpling. There's a few naff caffs in Callander. This one still OK (2008) in my book. 7 days till 5pm.

✓✓ **Gloagburn Farm & Coffee Shop Tibbermore near Perth** 1547/FARM SHOPS.
✓ **The Corn Kist Milton Haugh near Arbroath** 1545/FARM SHOPS.

The Best Scotch Bakers

1507
10/Q23
✓✓ **Fisher & Donaldson** www.fisheranddonaldson.com · **Dundee, St Andrews & Cupar** Main or original branch in Cupar and a new kind of factory outlet and 3 in Dundee plus 2 in St Andrews. Superior contemporary bakers along traditional lines (born 1919) – surprising (and a pity) that they haven't gone further, although they do supply selected outlets (eg Jenners in Edinburgh with pastries and the most excellent Dr Floyd's bread which is as good as anything you could make yourself). Sample also their yum yums, Danish pastries, other breads. Main square, Cupar; Church St, St Andrews; Whitehall St, 300 Perth Rd and Lochee, Dundee, which is very well served with decent bakers (see below). Dundee Whitehall and Cupar have good tearooms (1158/DUNDEE).

1508
2/B1
✓ **Bradford's** 245 **Sauchiehall Street, Glasgow** Also suburban branches in selected areas, ie they have not over-expanded; for a bakery chain, some lines seem almost home made. Certainly better than all the industrial 'home' bakers around. Individual fruit pies, for example, are uniquely yummy, and the all-important Scotch pie pastry is exemplary. Report: 657/GLASGOW CAFFS.

1509
10/M27
✓ **Alexander Taylor's** 01357 521260 · **Strathaven** Specialising in huge array of savoury breads: sunflower, Bavarian, sourdough, black bun and, at Christmas, stollen. Also make all their shortbreads and oatcakes. Good and wholesome! Mon-Sat 7.30am-5.30pm (Sat from 8.30am!).

1510
6/J14
✓ **Riverside Bistro** www.piesbypost.co.uk · **Lochinver** On way into town from Ullapool etc, not a baker's as such but rightly famous for their brilliant pies from takeaway counter. Huge variety of savoury and fruit from traditional to exotic. And irresistible puds. Sustenance for the hills or just indulge. 7 days.

1511
10/M24
✓ **Scotch Oven Callander** West end of main street in busy touristy town. Here forever but recently taken on by the irrepressible Lewis family of Monachyle Mhor (1276/GETAWAY HOTELS) so presumably those rolls, cakes, the biggest, possibly the best, tattie scones and sublime doughnuts all will be thrust into the 21st century; your picnic on the Braes will be better for it. Also featuring what may be the perfect Scotch pie pastry. Adjacent café awaits their magic touch at TGP. 7 days 7am-5pm (Sun from 9am).

1512
10/Q23
Goodfellow & Steven Dundee, Perth & Fife The other bakers in the Fife/Dundee belt (not a patch on Fisher & Donaldson; but hey). G&S have several branches in Dundee, Perth and Fife. Good Scotch baking with the kind of cakes your mum used to have for a treat.

1513
7/M17
Cromarty Bakery Bank Street, Cromarty One of the many reasons to visit this picturesque seaside town. Abundance of speciality cakes, organic bread, rolls and pies, baked daily on premises. Also tea, coffee, hot savouries and takeaway. Mon, Tue, Thu, Fri 8.30am-5.30pm; Wed/Sat till 4 pm.

1514
10/N22
Breadalbane Bakery & Tearoom Aberfeldy Main street opposite Gulf gas station approaching from east. Real old-style bakers and tearoom where the afternoon drops slow. Scottish staples and some one-offs: Holyrood tart, whisky cake. Takeaway including home-made stovies. 7am-4pm. Closed Sun.

1515
9/H21
The Bakehouse Acharacle, Ardnamurchan Helen Macgillvray's roadside bakery unprepossessing, tiny inside but great bakes including bread, pastries and

especially savouries. Top pork pie in Scotland. Stock up for picnics at Singing Sands (2123/COASTAL WALKS) or Castle Tioram shore (1871/RUINS). All year. Closed Sun.

1516
10/Q22
McLaren's Forfar Town centre next to Queens Hotel and in Kirriemuir. The best in town to sample the famous Forfar bridie, a meaty shortcrust pastie hugely underestimated as a national delicacy. They're so much better than the gross and grossly overblown Cornish pasty but have never progressed beyond this part of Perthshire. As it happens, one of the best examples is the home-made bridie that can be found in the café at Glamis (1855/CASTLES). **Saddler's** in North St, Forfar do them too.

1517
10/R28
Harrows Home Bakery 19 Howegate, Hawick In an attempt perhaps to find anything much to recommend in the benighted cradle of my adolescence, I stumble on this perfect throwback to hard work and hard-bitten carbohydrates. The Harrows family baking away for ever in this backstreet of a backwater town: bread, great rolls, pies and all kind of yesteryear cakes. The biggest 'French fancies' you'll ever stuff in your gob. A wee gem. 5.30am (sic)-4pm Mon-Sat & Sun morning for 'the rolls'.

1518
11/L30
Wigwam Bakery Creetown Recently arisen like their gorgeous bread in this wee cree town on the Solway coast. Supplies discerning diners in the region including **Reading Glasses** in Wigtown (1501/TEAROOMS). Patchy info coz we haven't been, but we hear tell. Go find.

The Best Ice Cream

1519
10/Q25
✓✓ **Luca's www.s-luca.co.uk · 32 High Street, Musselburgh & Edinburgh** Queues out the door in the middle of a Sunday afternoon in February are testament to the enduring popularity of this almost legendary ice-cream parlour (see PIONEERS, p. 24). 3 classic flavours (vanilla, choc and strawberry), 3 arrivistes (mint and cookies, yuck!) and now a plethora of sorbets. Pure ingredients attract folk from Edinburgh (14km) though there is now a branch in town at 16 Morningside Rd, a more designery version (301/CAFÉS). In café through the back, still basic after recent refurbishment, sundry snacks; and you might have to wait. In Edinburgh café upstairs more pizza/pasta and smart sandwiches. Mon-Sat 9am-10pmSun 10.30am-10pm. Edinburgh hours: 7 days 9am (10.30 Sun)-10pm. Luca's (wholesale) spreading everywhere at TGP.

1520
9/L28
✓✓ **Mancini's, The Royal Café www.mancinisicecream.co.uk · 11 New Road, Ayr** On the road to Prestwick. Ice cream that's taken seriously, entered for competitions and usually wins. Best UK Vanilla 2001 and '03. Family biz for aeons. Now amazingly in its fourth generation. Massive number of flavours at their disposal, always new ones. Home-made ice-cream cakes. Café recently refurbished and newer caff in **Prestwick** on the esplanade. Their sorbets taste better than the fruit they're made from. They were first with ice-cream toasties and diabetic ice cream. These Mancinis are surely the kings and princes of ice cream. 7 days till 10.30pm.

1521
11/M30
✓ **Cream O' Galloway www.creamogalloway.co.uk · 01557 814040 · Rainton near Gatehouse Of Fleet** A75 take Sandgreen exit 2km, then left at sign for Carrick. Originally a dairy farm producing cheese, now you can watch them making the creamy concoctions which you find all over. Nature trail, absolutely fab kids adventure play area (1788/KIDS) and decent organic-type café. All very eco. All year 10am-6pm.

1522
10/R23
✓ **Janetta's** **31 South Street, St Andrews** Family firm since 1908. There are two Janetta's, but the one to adore is top end South St. Once only vanilla, Americans at the Open asked for other flavours. Now there are 52 (2 vanillas), and numerous awards. Also frozen yogs. Janetta's is another good reason for being a student at St Andrews. Good café adjacent, family fare, outside tables. LO 5pm & takeaway. 7 days till 5pm, 9pm in summer.

1523
10/Q27
✓ **Caldwell's** **High Street, Innerleithen** On the High St in this ribbon of a town between Peebles and Gala they've been making ice cream since 1911. Purists may bemoan the fact that they've exploded into flavours in the 21st century, but their vanilla is still best. The shop still sells everything from Blue Nun to stuffed rabbits. Mon-Fri till 8.30pm, Sat/Sun 7.30pm.

1524
10/Q22
Visocchi's **Broughty Ferry, Kirriemuir** Originally from St Andrews; ice-cream makers for 75 years and still with the café they opened in Kirriemuir in 1930. On the main drag of the Angus town (1676/GLENS), it's the local caff (very basic menu, no chips but now has Costa coffee). Broughty Ferry (Dundee's seaside suburb) more middle-class, with a contemporary menu; home-made pasta as well as the peach melba. 7 days (1139/DUNDEE EAT & DRINK).

1525
10/N24
The Allan Water Café www.bridgeofallan.com · **Bridge Of Allan** In early editions of this book this was an old-fashioned café in an old-fashioned town, near the eponymous bridge in the main street (since 1902). Fabulously good fish 'n' chips and ice cream. Now it's taken over the whole block and has a new-fashioned metal extension. And the ice cream has many new flavours. It's progress; it's because we can't get enough ice cream. 7 days, 8am-8pm.

1526
11/P27
Cones & Candies **Main Street, Biggar** There's always been a thing about ice cream in Biggar. Let's not go into the local history. This is where you get Taylor's, the perfect vanilla. Nuff said. 7 days till 5.30pm (6pm Sat).

1527
10/L25
Colpi's **Milngavie, Glasgow** In Milngavie centre (pronounced 'Mull-guy') and there since 1928. Many consider this to be Glasgow's finest. Vanilla at the cone counter, other flavours to take home. Till 9pm, 7 days.

1528
11/P30
Drummuir Farm www.drummuirfarm.co.uk · **Collin near Dumfries** 5km off A75 (Carlisle/Annan) road east of Dumfries on B724 (near Clarencefield). A real farm producing real ice cream – still does supersmooth original and honeycomb, seasonal specials; on a fine day, sit out and chill. Indoor and outdoor play areas. Easter-Sep daily to 5.30pm; Oct-Dec & Mar Sat-Sun until 5pm; Jan/Feb closed.

The Really Good Delis

For Edinburgh and Glasgow delis, see p. 68 and p. 121.

1529
7/L18
✓✓ **The Corner on the Square** www.corneronthesquare.co.uk · 01463 783000 · **1 High Street, Beauly** On said corner of the square on right heading west. Fabulous find hereabouts mainly because of its sit-in coffee-shop fare including great baking, quiches, scones, soups etc. Cheeses and Cromarty bakes (1513/BAKERIES). Lunch 12noon-3pm, shop and snacks 9am-5.30pm (Thu till 10pm).

1530
10/R23
✓✓ **I.J. Mellis** www.ijmellischeesemonger.com · **St Andrews** Started out as the cheese guy, now more of a very select deli for food that's good and 'slow'. Coffees, hams, sausages, olives and seasonal stuff like apples and mushrooms (branches vary), so smells mingle. Irresistible! Branches also in Edinburgh (340/EDINBURGH DELIS) and Glasgow (690/GLASGOW DELIS). 7 days though times vary. See also 1556/CHEESES.

✓✓ **Gloagburn Farm & Coffee Shop** **Tibbermore near Perth** Excellent sit-in coffee shop/restaurant but also deli with selected local/organic produce. Report: 1543/FARM SHOPS.

✓✓ **The Pillars of Hercules** 01337 857749 · **near Falkland** Organic grocers with tearoom (1483/TEAROOMS) and outstanding farm shop. Report: 1549/FARM SHOPS.

1531
10/N24
✓ **Clive Ramsay** www.cliveramsay.com · **Main Street, Bridge Of Allan** Here for years, and growing but the new café/restaurant adjacent has fallen into other hands. Deli great for fruit/veg, cheese, olives, seeds and well-chosen usuals including own-brand. The deli has always been better than the adjacent caff – it's now spread to Brucefields, a kinda golf course nearby. 7 days 7am-7pm.

1532
8/P17
✓ **Phoenix Findhorn Community** www.phoenixshop.co.uk · **Findhorn** Serving the new age township and eco village of the Findhorn Community and therefore pursuing a conscientious approach, this has become an exemplary and very high-quality deli, worth the detour from the A96 Inverness-Elgin road. Packed and carefully selected shelves; as much for pleasurable eating as for healthy. Same folk have the excellent **Bakehouse** café in Findhorn itself. Superb ethical eats. 1065/LESS EXPENSIVE HIGHLAND RESTAURANTS. Till 6pm (weekends 5pm).

1533
10/N23
✓ **2 Damned Fine Delis in Crieff: McNees** **Main Street** Near the town clock. Deli/bakers/chocolatiers. More like an old-fashioned grocer. Great home-baking and ready-made meals, home-roasted meats. We could all do with a place like this. Here 17 years. 9am-6pm (Sun 9.30am-4pm).
J.L. Gill **West end, near right turn to Crianlarich** And the real McCoy, here 70 years. Unpredictable choice of provisions: honey, tinned tuna, 10 kinds of oatcakes, lotsa whisky – a real old-style, still the best-style gem. 9am-5.30pm. Closed Sun.

1534
8/Q18
✓ **Spey Larder** www.speylarder.com · **Main Street, Aberlour** In deepest Speyside. Beautiful old shop (1864) spacious and full of great, often local produce (honeys, bread, game in winter, Speyside chanterelles and of course whisky). All year. Closed Sun. 9am-5.30pm.

1535 1
1/L13
Ravenstone Deli 01988 500329 · **Whithorn** Main street up from Whithorn Story Visitor Centre. Hardworking, essential deli, bakery, butcher, pizzeria and coffee shop. Good cheese and olive selection, local produce, some organics, excellent daily bread (baked on premises). Home-cured bacon, home-made sausages and meat locally sourced. Pizzas prêt-a-porter from deli counter. An all-round good thing! 8am-5pm (Sun 9am-3pm). Closed Tue/Wed & possibly winter months.

1536
10/R23
Butler & Co 10 Church Street, St Andrews Excellent deli by the people who have the seafood restaurants here and in St Monans (1418/1419/SEAFOOD RESTAURANTS). Good range of Scottish and other cheeses. Till 5.30pm.

1537
8/P17
Gordon & MacPhail South Street, Elgin Purveyors of fine wines, cheeses, meats, Mediterranean goodies, unusual breads and other epicurean delights to the good burghers of Elgin for nigh on a century. Traditional shopkeeping, in the style of the 'family grocer'. G & M are widely known as bottlers of lesser-known high-quality malts ('Connoisseurs' range) – on sale here as well as every other whisky you've ever heard of and many you ain't. Some rare real ales by the bottle too. Mon-Sat 9am-5.15pm.

1538
10/N22
Dows 01887 829616 · **Main Street, Aberfeldy** Grantully direction near square. People who had the estimable Lurgan Farm shop now in town with traiteur range of ready-to-go meals and selected packet things. Till 5pm. Closed Sun.

1539
10/P23
Provender Brown 01738 587300 · **23 George Street, Perth** As we might expect, a decent deli in the town/city where several good restaurants reside, there's a big farmers' market (first in Scotland) and many folk aren't short of a bob or two. P&B are good for olives, vacuum-packed products and especially cheese. 9am-5.30pm. Closed Sun.

1540
9/K25
Mearns T. McCaskie Wemyss Bay Directly opposite the famed Wemyss Bay railway station and the ferry to Rothesay. Here for a while but overlooked in previous editions. Mainly a butcher of repute: home-cured bacon, sausages, pies; now cheeses, selected wines and other delights. Picnic anyone? 8am-5.30pm (5pm Sat). Closed Sun.

1541
10/M24
Berits & Brown 01786 870077 · **Kippen** The original of emerging deli 'franchise' (there's another in Glasgow at TGP). Not hugely original or special, but nice enough. Café with bespoke sandwiches from counter, soup etc. Adds to Kippen's 'foodie village' credentials. 10am-5pm (6pm Fri/Sat).

1542
10/R28
Quintus' Delicatessan 01450 378678 · **Drumlanrig Square, Hawick** Up the Howegate. Now, I must declare I haven't even been in this deli in the depths of Hawick, but I'm in a generous mood towards my old teenage stamping ground and 'they say' Quintus is a good sort and a foodie sort too. He makes stuff and freezes meals and the wine list is 'interesting'. God knows if he gets any customers. Mon-Sat 10am-5pm. Fri 10am-3pm.

The Really Good Farm Shops

1543
10/P23
✓✓ **Gloagburn Farm & Coffee Shop** Tibbermore Off A85 Perth-Methven and Crieff road from A9 and ring road at Huntingtower, signed Tibbermore (Tibbermore also signed off A9 from Stirling just before Perth). Through village, second farm on right: a family (the Nivens') farm shop on the verandah – excellent fresh produce and inside a deli and café where food (hot dishes, cakes etc) is exemplary. Vacuum-packed meats, frozen meals, fruit 'n' veg. A destination place only 15 minutes from Perth. Open all year 9am-5pm (4pm winter). 7 days.

1544
11/N30
✓✓ **Loch Arthur Creamery & Farm Shop** Beeswing near Dumfries Run by Camphill Trust, this is the genuine article tucked away in a work-ing dairy farm with a strong organic agenda. Great baking, famous organic veg and cheeses and the UK's best granola. Tiny shop but all here is a winner. From Bees-wing take New Abbey road 1km. Mon-Fri 9am-5.30pm, Sat 10am-3pm. Closed Sun.

1545
10/R22
✓✓ **Milton Haugh Farm Shop** 01241 860579 · Carmyllie Off A92 Dundee-Arbroath road at Carnoustie, follow Forfar road, then signs. Far-away farm on B961 (though only 30 minutes from Dundee) that's enormously popular: easy to see why. Great range of fruit and veg, meats and selected deli fare with own-label meals, jams, etc. 5 kinds of excellent oatcakes. Here 4 years, one of the first new wave of farm shops, now also in Dobbies Garden Centre down the road. Excellent 'Corn Kist' Coffee Shop with home-made cakes, soups and specials, so from far and wide you come. 9am-5pm (Sun from 10am). Café 10am-4pm.

1546
8/T19
✓ **The Store** 01358 788083 · Westfield, Foveran near Udny Station Off A90 this beautiful farm shop is a foodlovers' haven and the base for their Aberdeen Angus (well-hung and tender) operation which also supplies their shop in Edinburgh (288/DELIS). Range of vacuum-packed other meats, cooked meals and all the stuff including fruit and veg to have with them. 7 days 10am-5pm.

1547
10/P25
✓ **West Craigie Farm** 0131 319 1048 · near South Queensferry Take the South Queensferry exit from dual carriageway north from Edinburgh, A90 to Forth Road Bridge. Farm is signed 2km. Nowhere on this page demonstrates the growth, potential and appeal of farm shops more than this. A short time ago it was a farm on the edge of town where you could PYO or buy fruit (and fudge I seem to remember) from a back door of the byre. Now you enter a lofty emporium packed with farm/deli goodies and sit on a terrace taking tea and cake overlooking rows and fields of fruit like vineyards in France. The city shimmers in the distance and you so want to hang on to your green belt. It's a soft-fruit smash! All year 9-6pm.

1548
10/R25
✓ **Fenton Barns Farm Shop** 01620 850294 · near North Berwick Leave A1 for Dirleton, Mhairi and Roy's country emporium and caff is between Drem and Dirleton on the Fenton Barns 'estate', an old airfield complex. They also look after the Fruitmarket Gallery Café in Edinburgh (288/TEAROOMS) and manage the huge operation of feeding and refreshing the audiences at the Edinburgh Book festival so efficiently along with selectivity and credibility evident in all they do. Organic meats, free-range eggs, home-made pies, soups, terrines, selected, mainly local fruit and veg, and Roy's great coffee. 7 days 10am-5pm.

1549
10/Q24
✓ **The Pillars of Hercules** www.pillars.co.uk · 01337 857749 · near Falkland On A912 2km from town towards Strathmiglo and motorway. Organic grocers with tearoom (1483/TEAROOMS) on farm/nursery where you can PYO herbs and flowers. Always fruit/veg and great selection of dry goods that's a long way from Sainsbury's and here long before the organic boom. 7 days 10-6pm.

1550 **Cairnie Fruit Farm (and Maze)** 01334 655610 · near **Cupar** A truly
10/Q23 a(maze)ing conversion of a fruit farm into a major family attraction (1786/KIDS), demonstrating if nothing else the inexorable rise of the strawberry. Here this and other berries can be picked, purchased and eaten in all manner of cakes with other farm produce and snack food. Main thing though is the kids' area outside. Apr-Oct 10am-5pm. Closed Mon in Sep. Farm is 4km north of Cupar on minor road past the hospital or 3km from main A92, signed near Kilmany.

1551 **The Storehouse** 01349 830038 · near **Evanton** Roadside 'farm shop' and
7/M17 diner on A9 north of Inverness and Tore roundabout. Not huge on farm-produce front and lots of trinketry, but some meats; good Scottish cheese selection. Self-service restaurant goes like a fair with all things irresistible but not very good for you. Often queues. Lashings of cream. 7 days 9am-6pm, Sun 10am-5pm.

1552 **Allanhill** 01334 477998 · near **St Andrews** 6km out of town off Anstruther/
10/R23 Crail road A917 past The Grange (1358/GASTROPUBS). Simple farm shop and café with tables out in the field and kids' playground. Great views to St Andrews Bay. Known mainly for excellent soft fruits (I had the *best* strawberries and raspberries here Aug '07), but with other selected foodstuff; and plants. Only open 100 days: May-Sep.

1553 **Ardross Farm** 01333 330415 · near **Elie** Between St Monance and Elie on the
10/R24 A917 Fife coastal route. East Neuk farm shop known mainly for its own meat but with long list of seasonal dug vegetables, fruit pies, other carefully selected farm-grown produce. The Pollock family have been here over a century; now they've become UKTV 'Food Heroes'. 7 days 9am-5.30pm, Sun 9am-4pm.

1554 **Knowes Farm Shop Farm** 01620 860010 · near **East Linton** Close to A1 on
10/R25 A198 to North Berwick just before Tyninghame. Converted farm cottage into integrity food store. Organic veg and herbs, duck and quail eggs, home-made pâtés and pavlova. All year 9.30am-5pm (10am-4.30pm in winter). They supply other farm shops, restaurants etc with their excellent home-grown veg.

1555 **Muddy Boots** 07843 630762 · **Balmalcolm** On A914 from A92 south of
10/Q24 Cupar, a farm shop with kitchen and crafts and some integrity over their produce. Their home-grown fruit and veg is high quality and they're keen to educate and inspire kids into good country practice. All year 7 days 9am-6pm (10am-5pm Sun).

Scottish Cheeses

Mull or Tobermory Cheddar www.isleofmullcheese.co.uk From Sgrob-Ruadh Farm (pronounced 'Skibrua'; see below). Comes in big 50lb cheeses and 1lb truckles. Good, strong cheddar, one of the very best in the UK.

Dunsyre Blue/Lanark Blue Made by Humphrey Errington at Carnwath. Next to Stilton, **Dunsyre** (made from the unpasteurised milk of Ayrshire cows) is the best blue in the UK. It is soft, rather like Dolcelatte. **Lanark**, the original, is Scotland's Roquefort and made from ewes' milk. Both can vary but are excellent. Go on, live dangerously – unpasteurise your life.

Locharthur Cheese www.locharthur.org.uk Anything from this South West creamery is worth a nibble: the cheddar, **Criffel** (mild), **Kebbuck** (shaped like a dinosaur's tooth, semi-soft). Widely available but have their own shop (see below).

Bonnet Hard goat's milk cheese from Anne Dorwood's farm at Stewarton in Ayrshire. Also a very good cheddar (and sheep's-milk cheddar).

Wester Lawrenceton Farm Cheeses Forres Pam Rodway's excellent organic cheeses: **Carola, Califer** (goat's milk) and the hard-to-get **Sweetmilk Cheddar**. On sale Findhorn shop and Gordon & MacPhail (1537/DELIS).

Craigmyle Cheeses Torphins, Royal Deeside Lovely **Wummle** (wee or muckle), **Learney, Morvern, Babbity Blue** and the delicate **Clachnaben**. New, enterprising, already award-winning.

Highland Fine Cheeses From the Stone family in Tain. 6 cheeses including **Crowdie** (traditional curd cheese), **Caboc** and **Strathdon Blue** (award winner).

Cairnsmore A hard, tangy, cheddary cheese from Sorbie in Wigtownshire surprisingly made from ewes' milk, smoked or unsmoked.

... AND WHERE TO FIND THEM

The delis on pp. 68, 121 and 265–66 will have good selections (especially Valvona's and Delizique).

1556
10/M26
10/Q25
10/R23
✓ ✓ **I.J. Mellis** www.ijmellischeesemonger.com · **Edinburgh, Glasgow & St Andrews** 30a Victoria St, far end of Morningside Rd and Baker's Pl, Stockbridge (Edinburgh), 492 Great Western Rd (Glasgow), 149 South St (St Andrews). A real cheesemonger. Smell and taste before you buy. Cheeses from all over the UK in prime condition. Daily and seasonal specials. (340/EDINBURGH DELIS, 690/GLASGOW DELIS, 1530/DELIS)

1557
2/XA1
2/A1
✓ **Herbie** www.herbieofedinburgh.co.uk · **66 Raeburn Place, William Street & North West Circus Place, Edinburgh** Excellent selection – everything here is the right stuff. Great bread, bagels etc from independent baker, home-made houmous and with Scottish cheeses, it's practically impossible here to find a Brie or a blue in less than perfect condition. William St (West End) is the takeaway of choice hereabouts.

1558
9/G22
✓ **Sgrob-Ruadh Farm Tobermory** Head out on road to Dervaig, take turning for Glengorm (great coffee shop; 1476/TEAROOMS) and watch for sign and track to farm. Past big green house where they live and follow path to distant doorway into the cheese factory. Honesty box when nobody working.

1559
9/J27
Island Cheeses Arran 5km Brodick, road to castle and Corrie. Excellent selection of their own (the well-known cheddars but many others especially crowdie with garlic and hand-rolled cream cheeses) and others. See them being made. 7 days. 9.30am-5.30pm. Sun 10am-4.30pm.

1560
7/H18
West Highland Dairy www.westhighlanddairy.co.uk · **01599 577203** · **Achmore near Plockton** Mr and Mrs Biss still running their great farm dairy shop selling their own cheeses (goats' and cows' milk), yoghurt, ice cream and cheesecake. Mar-Dec. Signed from village. If you're making the trip specially, phone first to check they're open (usually 10am-5pm).

1561
10/Q27
Riley's 01721 72920257 · **High Street, Peebles** There used to be several foodie outposts in Peebles. At TGP they were reduced to this. An ok deli, good for fish and especially cheeses from Scotland and elsewhere.

Loch Arthur Creamery Beeswing Off A75, A711 road to New Abbey. Excellent for their cheeses and other very good things. 1544/FARM SHOPS.
House Of Bruar near Blair Atholl Roadside emporium. 2252/SHOPPING.
Falls of Shin Visitor Centre near Lairg Harrods of the North. 2254/SHOPPING.
Peter MacLennan 28 High Street, Fort William.
Scottish Speciality Food North Ballachulish By Leven Hotel.
The Kitchen Garden Oban 831/OBAN.
Jenners Department Store Princes Street, Edinburgh Top floor.
Corner on the Square Main Street, Beauly 1529/DELIS.

Whisky: The Best Distillery Tours

The process is basically the same in every distillery, but some are more atmospheric and some have more interesting tours, like these below. www.scotchwhisky.net is a great site on all things whisky.

1562
9/F25

✓ ✓ **The Islay Malts www.islaywhiskysociety.com** Plenty to choose from including, in the north, **Caol Ila** (by appointment 01496 302760), the wholly independent **Bruichladdich** (3 tours daily Mon-Fri, twice daily on Sat, 01496 850221). In the south near Port Ellen, 3 of the world's great malts are in a row on a mystic coast. The distilleries here look like distilleries ought to. **Lagavulin** (01496 302400) and **Laphroaig** (01496 302418) offer fascinating tours where your guide will lay on the anecdotes as well as the process and you get a feel for the life and history as well as the product of these world-famous places. At Laphroaig you can join their 'Friend' scheme (free) and own a piece of their hallowed ground. Tours Jun-Aug only 10.15am and 2.15pm. Lagavulin tours Mon-Fri by appointment, Laphroaig same. **Ardbeg** is perhaps the most visitor-oriented and has a really good café (2426/ISLAY RESTAURANTS) where if you blunder in at mid morning and ask for toast, they make you some toast (01496 302244). All these distilleries are in settings that entirely justify the romantic hyperbole of their advertising. Worth seeing from the outside as well as the floor. **Bowmore** (01496 810441) has professional, more commercial, 1-hour tours twice a day (including video show and the usual dram) and perhaps the most convenient.

1563
8/Q17

Strathisla 01542 783044 · **Keith** The oldest working distillery in the Highlands, literally on the strath of the Isla River and methinks the most evocative atmosphere of all the Speyside distilleries. Tastefully reconstructed, this is a very classy halt for the malt. Used as the 'heart' of Chivas Regal, the malt not commonly available is still a fine dram. You wait for a tour group to gather; there's a dram at the beginning and the end. Mar-Oct 10am-4pm (Sun from 12.30pm).

1564
7/F18

Talisker Carbost, Isle of Skye From Sligachan-Dunvegan road (A863) take B8009 for Carbost and Glen Brittle along the south side of Loch Harport for 5km. Skye's only distillery; since 1830 they've been making this classic after-dinner malt from barley and the burn that runs off the Hawkhill behind. A dram before the informative 40-minute tour. Good visitor centre. Apr-Oct 9.30am-5pm (2-5pm winter by appointment only, 01478 614308). Great gifts nearby (2257/CRAFT SHOPS). Nice pub for grub, accommodation and music nearby: the Old Inn (2046/SKYE).

1565
10/Q25

Glenkinchie 01875 342004 · **Pencaitland near Edinburgh** Only 25km from city centre (via A68 and A6093 before Pathhead), signposted and so very popular. Founded in 1837 in a pastoral place 3km from village, with its own bowling green; a country trip and a whisky tour. State-of-the-art visitor centre. Summer daily till 5pm except Jul/Aug last tours at 6pm. Closed 4pm and weekends in winter.

1566
10/N21
Edradour www.edradour.co.uk · **01796 472095** · **near Pitlochry** Claims to be the smallest distillery in Scotland, producing single malts for blends since 1825 and limited quantities of the Edradour (since 1986) as well as the House of Lords' own brand. Guided tour of charming cottage complex every 20 minutes. 4km from Pitlochry off Kirkmichael road, A924; signed after Moulin village. Complex opening hours though open all year, 7 days.

1567
3/Q10
Highland Park www.highlandpark.co.uk · **01856 874619** · **Kirkwall, Orkney** 2km from town on main A961 road south to South Ronaldsay. The whisky is great (the 18 Years Old won The Best Spirit in the World '05) and the award-winning tour one of the best. The most northerly whisky in a class and a bottle of its own. You walk through the floor maltings and you can touch the warm barley and fair smell the peat. Good combination of the industrial and the traditional. Tours every half hour. Open all year Mon-Fri 10am-5pm. Weekends only in winter.

THE BEST OF THE SPEYSIDE WHISKY TRAIL
Well signposted but bewildering number of tours, though not at every distillery. Many are in featureless industrial complexes but these (with Strathisla above) are the best:

1568
8/P18
The Glenlivet www.theglenlivet.com · **01340 821720** · **Minmore** Starting as an illicit dram celebrated as far south as Edinburgh, George Smith licensed the brand in 1824 and founded this distillery in 1858, registering the already mighty name so that anyone else had to use a prefix. After various successions and mergers, independence was lost in 1978 when Seagrams took over. Now owned by Pernod Ricard. The famous Josie's Well, from which the water springs, is underground and not shown, but small parties and a walk-through which is not on a gantry make the tour as satisfying and as popular, especially with Americans, as the product. Excellent reception centre with bar/restaurant and shop. Apr-Oct 10am-4pm. Sun 12-4pm.

1569
8/Q18
Glenfiddich www.glenfiddich.com · **01340 820373** · **Dufftown** Outside town on the A941 to Craigellachie by the ruins of Balvenie Castle. Well-oiled tourist operation and the only distillery where you can see the whisky bottled on the premises; indeed, the whole process from barley to bar. Also the only major distillery that's free (including dram). Also now runs an artists in residence scheme with changing shows over the summer in gallery adjacent car park (01340 821565) for details. All year 9.30am-4.30pm not weekends in winter. On the same road you can see a whisky-related industry/craft that hasn't changed in decades. **Speyside Cooperage** is 1km from Craigellachie. You watch those poor guys from the gantry (no chance to slack). All year Mon-Fri 9.30am-4.30pm. (Good coffee shop.)

1570
8/Q17
Glen Grant **01340 832118** · **Rothes** In Rothes on the A941 Elgin to Perth road. Not the most picturesque but a distillery tour with an added attraction, viz. the gardens and orchard reconstructed around the shallow bowl of the glen of the burn that runs through the distillery: there's a delightful Dram Pavilion. The French own this one too: reflect as you sit in the library and listen to the founder before you leave. Apr-Oct 10am-5pm, from 12pm on Sun. Last tour 4pm.

1571
8/P18
Cardhu (or Cardow) **01340 872555** · **Carron** Off B9102 from Craigellachie to Grantown through deepest Speyside, a small if charming distillery with its own community, a millpond, picnic tables, etc. Owned by United Distillers, Cardhu is the 'heart of Johnnie Walker' (which, amazingly, has another 30 malts in it). Jul-Sep daily 10am-5pm Mon-Sat, 12-4pm Sun. Otherwise open at least weekdays – phone for details.

1572
8/P17
Benromach www.benromach.com · 01309 675968 · **near Forres** Smallest working distillery so no bus tours or big tourist operation. Human beings with time for a chat. Rescued by Gordon & MacPhail (1512/DELIS) and reopened 1999. 'Malt Whisky Centre' is a good introduction: you may need no other tour even if you've never heard of the brand. Apr-Sep 9.30am-5pm (Sun in Jun-Aug only 12noon-4pm). Winter 10am-4pm.

1573
8/P17
Dallas Dhu 01309 676548 · **near Forres** Not really near the Spey (3km south of Forres on B9010) and no longer a working distillery (ceased 1983), but instant history provided by Historic Scotland and you don't have to go round on a tour. The wax workers are a bit spooky; the product itself is more life-like. Apr-Sep 9.30am-6.30pm, restricted hours in winter.

1574
2/C4
Scotch Whisky Heritage Centre www.whisky-heritage.co.uk · 0131 220 0441 · **Edinburgh** On Castlehill on last stretch to castle (you cannot miss it). Not a distillery of course, but a visitor attraction to celebrate all things a tourist can take in about Scotland's main export. Shop has huge range. 7 days 10am-5pm (extended hours in summer).

1575
10/N23
Promotional Tours: Glenturret near Crieff **& Aberfeldy** A recent and not entirely welcome trend has been to makeover distilleries into interactive ads for certain brands of blends. The quaint old Glenturret distillery by Crieff is now the Famous Grouse Experience (daily all year 08450 451800) while Aberfeldy distillery is now Dewar's World of Whisky (all year, call for times 01887 822010) though it also includes Aberfeldy (the whisky, not the town or the band). The branding density is tiresome but the production tours are super-professional.

Whisky: The Best Malts Selections

EDINBURGH

✓ ✓ **Scotch Malt Whisky Society** www.smws.com · **The Vaults, 87 Giles Street, Leith & 28 Queen Street** Your search will end here. More a club (with membership); visitors must be signed in.

✓ **Royal Mile Whiskies** www.royalmilewhiskies.com · **379 High Street** *Whisky Magazine* Retailer of the Year. Also in London.

Bennet's www.bennets.co.uk · **8 Leven Street** By King's Theatre.

Kay's Bar 39 Jamaica Street

The Bow Bar www.bowbar.com · **80 West Bow**

Cadenhead's www.wmcadenhead.com · **172 Canongate** The shop with the lot.

Canny Man's 237 Morningside Road

The Malt Shovel 11 Cockburn Street 100 whiskies and all.

Blue Blazer Corner Spittal & Bread Streets 372/REAL ALE PUBS.

GLASGOW

 The Pot Still www.thepotstill.co.uk · **154 Hope Street** 450 different bottles of single malt. And proud of it.

The Bon Accord www.thebonaccord.freeserve.co.uk · **153 North Street** 712/REAL ALE.

The Lismore **206 Dumbarton Road** 704/UNIQUE PUBS.

Ubiquitous Chip www.ubiquitouschip.co.uk · **Ashton Lane** Restaurant, bistro and great bar on the corner.

Ben Nevis www.geocities.com/bennevisbar · **Argyle Street** Far west end of the street. 705/UNIQUE PUBS.

REST OF SCOTLAND

1576
9/F26

 **Lochside Hotel** www.lochsidehotel.co.uk · **Bowmore, Islay** More Islay malts than you ever imagined in friendly local near the Bowmore Distillery.

✓ ✓ **Torridon near Kinlochewe** Classic Highland hotel and 300 malts shelf by shelf. And the mountains! 1278/GET-AWAY HOTELS.

✓ ✓ **Clachaig Inn Glencoe** Over 100 malts to go with the range of ales and the range of thirsty hillwalkers. 1360/BLOODY GOOD PUBS.

✓ ✓ **The Drover's Inn Inverarnan** Same as above, with around 75 to choose from and the right atmosphere to drink them in. 13573/BLOODY GOOD PUBS.

✓ ✓ **The Oystercatcher Portmahomack** Gordon Robertson's exceptional malt (and wine collection) in quality restaurant in far-flung village. 1087/HIGHLAND RESTAURANTS.

✓ ✓ **Forss House near Thurso** Hotel bar on North Coast. Often a wee wind outside. Warm up with one of the 300 well-presented malts. 1027/HIGHLAND.

1577
8/P19

✓ ✓ **Minmore House Glenlivet** Beautiful, comfy country-house hotel right next to the distillery (1006/SPEYSIDE).

✓ **The Quaich Bar at The Craigellachie Hotel** Whiskies arranged around cosy bar of this essential Speyside hotel and the river below. 1007/SPEYSIDE.

✓ **Knockinaam Lodge Portpatrick** Comfortable country-house hotel; especially good Lowland selection including the (extinct) local Bladnoch. 848/SOUTH WEST HOTELS.

✓ **The Piano Bar at the Glenmoriston Hotel Inverness** Easy-to-decipher malt list in superior, stylish surroundings. 1019/HIGHLAND HOTELS.

✓ **The Anderson Fortrose** Amazing collection of malts (and beers) in town hotel bar. 1055/LESS EXPENSIVE HIGHLANDS.

1578
9/J23

✓ **Ardanaiseig Hotel www.ardanaiseig.com · Loch Awe** A dram's a must after dinner in the bar overlooking the loch where the bats come in.

✓ **Glenmoriston Arms Hotel Invermoriston** On A82 between Inverness and Fort Augustus. Growing collection of malts in lovely roadside inn with new owners. 1274/ROADSIDE INNS.

✓ **Dunain Park Hotel Inverness** After dinner in one of the best places to eat hereabouts, there's a serious malts list to mull over. 1023/HIGHLAND HOTELS.

✓ **Hotel Eilean Iarmain Skye** Also known as the Isleornsay Hotel (2375/ ISLAND HOTELS); not the biggest range but one of the best places to drink (it).

Kinloch House Hotel near Blairgowrie 1207/COUNTRY-HOUSE HOTELS.

1579
8/P17

Gordon & MacPhail Elgin The whisky provisioner and bottlers of the Connoisseurs brand you see in other shops and bars all over. From these humble beginnings over 100 years ago, they now supply their exclusive and rarity range to the world. Mon-Sat till 5.15pm (5pm Wed). Closed Sun. 1537/DELIS.

1580
8/Q18

The Whisky Shop www.whiskyshopdufftown.co.uk · Dufftown The whisky shop in the main street (by the clock tower) at the heart of whisky country. Within a few miles of numerous distilleries and their sales operations, this place stocks all the product (including many halfs). 10am-5pm Mon-Sat, 2-4pm Sun.

1581
9/H25

Loch Fyne Whiskies www.lfw.co.uk · Inveraray Beyond the church on the A83 a shop with 400 malts to choose from in various sizes and disguises; and whisky ware.

Fox & Hounds Houston 1388/GASTROPUBS.

Taychreggan Hotel Bar West Ferry, Dundee 1144/DUNDEE RESTAURANTS.

1582
9/H23

Oban Inn Oban Good mix of customers, whisky and ale.

Fisherman's Tavern Broughty Ferry 1129/DUNDEE EAT & DRINK.

1583
7/L19

Lock Inn Fort Augustus Canalside setting, good food and plenty whisky.

1584
7/F18

Sligachan Hotel www.sligachan.co.uk · 01478 650204 · Skye On A87 (A850) 11km south of Portree. 71 malts in Seamus' huge cabin bar. Good ale selection; Apr/Sep festivals.

Pittodrie House Hotel Pitcaple In the snug. 988/NORTHEAST HOTELS.

The Lairhillock near Stonehaven Public bar. 1392/GASTROPUBS.

Section 7

Outdoor Places

The Best Gardens

☞ signifies notable tearoom. FREE/ ADMISSION *indicates entry fee due - or not.* NTS *indicates a garden under the care of the National Trust for Scotland.*

1585
9/K25
ADMISSION
☞

✓✓ The Younger Botanic Garden www.rbge.org.uk · Benmore 12km Dunoon on the A815 to Strachur. An 'outstation' of the Royal Botanic in Edinburgh, gifted to the nation by Harry Younger in 1928, but the first plantations dating from 1820. Walks clearly marked through formal gardens, woody grounds and the 'pinetum' where the air is often so sweet and spicy it can seem like the elixir of life. Redwood avenue, terraced hill sides, views; a garden of different moods and fine proportions. Good walk, 'Puck's Glen', nearby (2091/WOODLAND WALKS). Café. Apr-Sep 10am-6pm (5pm Oct-Mar).

1586
7/H16
ADMISSION
☞

✓✓ Inverewe www.nts.org.uk · Poolewe On A832, 80km south of Ullapool. The world-famous gardens on a promontory of Loch Ewe. Begun in 1862, Osgood Mackenzie made it his life's work in 1883 and it continues with large crowds coming to admire his efforts. Helped by the ameliorating effect of the Gulf Stream, the 'wild' garden became the model for many others. The guided tours (1.30pm Mon-Fri Apr-Sep) are probably the best way to get the most out of this extensive garden. Gardens all year till dusk - go in the evening when it's quiet! Shop, visitor centre till 5pm.

1587
8/S20
NTS
ADMISSION
☞

✓✓ Crathes www.nts.org.uk · near Banchory 25km west of Aberdeen and just off A93 on Royal Deeside. One of the most interesting tower houses (1922/COUNTRY HOUSES) surrounded by mind-blowing topiary and walled gardens of inspired design and tranquil atmosphere. Keen gardeners will be in their scented heaven. The Golden Garden (after Gertrude Jekyll) works particularly well and there's a wild garden beyond the old wall that many people miss. All in all, a very *House and Garden* experience though in summer it's stuffed with people as well as plants. Grounds open all year 9am-sunset.

1588
10/P26

✓✓ Little Sparta www.littlesparta.org · 01899 810252 · near Dunsyre Near Biggar southwest of Edinburgh off A702 (5km), go through village then signed. House in bare hill country the home of conceptual artist and national treasure, Ian Hamilton Finlay who died 2006. Gardens lovingly created over years, full of thought-provoking art/sculpture/perspectives. Unlike anywhere else. A privilege to visit. Jun-Sep, Fri & Sun 2-5pm only.

1589
10/N23
ADMISSION

✓✓ Drummond Castle Gardens www.drummondcastlegardens.co.uk · Muthill Near Crieff; signed from A822, 2km from Muthill then up a long avenue, the most exquisite formal gardens viewed first from the terrace by the house. A boxwood parterre of a vast St Andrew's Cross in yellow and red (especially antirrhinums and roses), the Drummond colours, with extraordinary sundial centrepiece; 5 gardeners keep every leaf in place. 7 days Easter and May-Oct 1-5pm (last admission). House not open to public.

1590
11/K31
ADMISSION
☞

✓✓ Logan Botanical Gardens www.rbge.org.uk · near Sandhead 16km south of Stranraer by A77/A716 and 2km on from Sandhead. Remarkable outstation of the Edinburgh Botanics amongst sheltering woodland in the mild South West. Compact and full of pleasant southern surprises. Less crowded than other 'exotic' gardens. Their 'soundwands' giving commentary on demand make it all very interesting. Coffee shop decent. The Gunnera Bog is quite extraterrestrial. Mar-Oct; 7 days, 10am-5pm (6pm Apr-Sep).

1591
9/J24
NTS
✓ ✓ **Crarae www.nts.org.uk · Inverary** 16km southeast on A83 to Lochgilphead. Famed and fabulous. Recently taken over by NTS so difficulties in staying open resolved. The wooded banks of Loch Fyne with gushing burn are as lush as the jungles of Borneo. All year 10am till dusk. Visitor centre till 5pm.

1592
6/N15
✓ ✓ **Dunrobin Castle Gardens Golspie** On A9 1km north of town. The Versailles-inspired gardens that sit below the opulent Highland chateau of the Dukes of Sutherland (1867/CASTLES). Terraced, parterred and immaculate, they stretch to the sea. 30 gardeners once tended them, now there are 4 but little has changed since they impressed a more exclusive clientele. Apr-Oct 10.30am-last admission 4pm (5pm Jun-Sep).

1593
11/K30
✓ **Glenwhan near Glen Luce, near Solway Coast** Signed from A75 and close to more famous **Castle Kennedy** (also very much worth a visit), this the more edifying labour of love. Up through beechy (and in May) bluebell woods and through backyards to horticultural haven teased from bracken and gorse moorland in 1979. Open moorland still beckons at the top of the network of trails through a carefully planted botanical wonder. Many seats, some sculpture. Easter-Sep 10am-5pm.

1594
11/M30
🗅
✓ **Threave near Castle Douglas** 64 acres of magnificent Victorian landscaping in incomparable setting overlooking Galloway coastline. Gardeners shouldn't miss the walled kitchen garden. Horticulturally inspiring; and daunting. Open Feb-Dec 10am-dusk.

1595
10/P27
ADMISSION
✓ **Dawyck www.rgbe.org.uk · Stobo** On B712 Moffat road off A72 Biggar/ Peebles road, 2km from Stobo. Another outstation of the Edinburgh Botanics; a 'recent' acquisition, though tree planting here goes back 300 years. Sloping grounds around the gurgling Scrape burn which trickles into the Tweed. Land-scaped woody pathways for meditative walks. Famous for shrubs, blue Himalayan poppies and 'the azalea terrace'. Great walk on Drovers road, 2km off Stobo Rd before entrance. Tiny tearoom being developed at TGP. Mar-Oct 10am-5pm.

1596
9/J23
HONESTY BOX
✓ **Angus' Garden www.barguillean.co.uk · Taynuilt** 7km from village (which is 12km from Oban on the A85) along the Glen Lonan road. Take first right after Barguillen Garden Centre. A garden laid out by the family who own the centre in memory of their son Angus, a soldier, who was killed in Cyprus. On the slopes around a small loch brimful of lilies and ducks. Informal mix of tended and uncultivated (though wild prevails), a more poignant remembrance is hard to imagine as you while an hour away in this peaceful place. Open all year.

1597
1/XF4
ADMISSION
✓ **Dr Neil's (Secret) Garden Edinburgh** Till now at least a few people know about this superb, almost private garden on the shores of Duddingston Loch. At the end of the road through Holyrood Park, just past Duddingston church, enter through the manse gates. Turn right. At end of the manse lawn, in the cor-ner a gate leads to an extraordinary terraced garden bordering the loch. With wild Arthur's Seat above, you'd swear you were in Argyll. The labour of love of one Claudia Poitier and many volunteers, this is an enchanting corner of the city. 7 days dawn-dusk. The skating minister (Raeburn) was here.

1598
9/H24
NTS
✓ **Arduaine Garden www.arduaine-garden.org.uk · near Kilmelford** 28km south of Oban on A816, one of Argyll's undiscovered arcadias gifted to the NTS and brought to wider attention. Creation of the microclimate in which the

rich, diverse vegetation has flourished, influenced by Osgood Mackenzie of Inverewe and its restoration a testimony to 20 years' hard labour by the Wright brothers. Enter/park by Loch Melfort hotel, gate 100m. Until dusk.

1599
9/G26
ADMISSION

✓ **Achamore Gardens www.gigha.org.uk · Isle of Gigha** 1km from ferry. Walk or cycle (bike hire at post office at top of ferry road); an easy day trip. The 'big house' (which does great B&B) on the island set in 65 acres. Lush tropical plants mingle with early-flourishing rhodies (Feb-March): all due to the mild climate and the devotion of only 2 gardeners. 2 marked walks (40 minutes/2 hours) start from the walled garden (green route takes in the sea view of Islay and Jura). Density and variety of shrubs, pond plants and trees revealed as you meander in this enchanting spot. Leaflet guides at entrance. Open all year dawn to dusk. 2366/MAGICAL ISLANDS.

1600
8/S20

✓ **Drum Castle Rose Garden www.nts.org.uk · near Banchory** 1km from A93, the Deeside road. In the grounds of Drum Castle (the Irvine ancestral home – though nothing remotely to do with my family) a superb walled garden paying homage to the rose and encapsulating 4 centuries of its horticulture. 4 areas (17th-20th centuries). Fabulous, Jul/Aug especially. Open 10am-6pm.

1601
9/J26
ADMISSION

Ascog Hall Fernery www.ascoghallfernery.co.uk · Rothesay Outside town on road to Mount Stuart (1852/CO HOUSES), worth stopping at this small garden and very small Victorian Fern House. Green and lush and dripping! Easter-Oct, 10am-5pm. Closed Mon/Tue. (And don't miss Rothesay's Victorian men's loos (women can visit); they are not small.)

1602
10/R27
ADMISSION
NTS

Priorwood www.nts.org.uk · Melrose Next to Melrose Abbey, a tranquil secret garden behind high walls which specialises in growing flowers and plants for drying. Picking, drying and arranging is continuously in progress. Samples for sale. Run by enthusiasts on behalf of the NTS, they're always willing to talk stamens with you. Also includes an historical apple orchard with trees through the ages. Sadly the heavenly jelly is no longer on sale (damn 'Health 'n' Safety'). Mon-Sat 10am-5pm; Sun 1.30-5pm. Closed 4pm winter. Dried flower shop.

1603
10/Q27
ADMISSION

Kailzie Gardens www.kailziegardens.com · Peebles On B7062 Traquair road. Informal woodland gardens just out of town; not extensive but eminently strollable. Old-fashioned roses and wilder bits. Some poor birds in cages and the odd peacock. Courtyard teashop. Kids' corner. Fishing pond popular. Apr-Oct 11am-5.30pm (restricted access in winter).

1604
10/R27
ADMISSION

Monteviot House Garden & Woodside Nursery near Ancrum & Jedburgh Off A68 at Ancrum, the B6400 to Nisbet (3km), first there's Woodside on left (the Victorian walled garden for the house – now separate) and the terraced to the river (Teviot), mainly formal gardens of the house (the home of the Tory Nicholas Soames, now Lord Lothian). Very pleasant to amble. Woodside has organic demonstrations section and is mainly a garden centre. House: 2 weeks in Jul 1-5pm. Gardens: Apr-Oct 12noon-5pm. Nursery: Mar-Oct 9.30am-5.30pm.

1605
8/S18
ADMISSION
NTS
☕

Pitmedden Garden www.nts.org.uk · near Ellon 35km north of Aberdeen and 10km west of main A92. Formal French gardens recreated in 1950s on site of Sir Alex Seaton's 17th-century ones. The 4 great parterres, 3 based on designs for gardens at Holyrood Palace, are best viewed from the terrace. Charming farmhouse 'museum' seems transplanted. For lovers of symmetry and an orderly universe only (but there is a woodland walk with wildlife garden area). May-Sep 10am-5.30pm.

1606 **Pittodrie House** www.macdonaldhotels.co.uk · near Inverurie An
8/R19 exceptional walled garden in the grounds of Pittodrie House Hotel at Chapel of
Garioch in Aberdeenshire (988/NORTHEAST HOTELS). Different gardens compart-
mentalised by hedges. 500m from house and largely unvisited by most of the
guests, this secret and sheltered haven is both a kitchen garden and a place for
meditations and reflections (and possibly wedding photos).

1607 **Ardkinglas Woodland** www.ardkinglass.com · Cairndow Off the A83 Loch
9/K24 Lomond to Inveraray road. Through village to signed car park and these mature
ADMISSION woodlands in the grounds of Ardkinglas House on the southern bank near the
head of Loch Fyne. Fine pines include the 'tallest tree in Britain'. Magical at dawn
or dusk. 2km Loch Fyne Seafood (1425/SEAFOOD RESTAURANTS) where there is also
a tree-shop garden centre especially for trees and shrubs (2301/GARDEN CENTRES).

1608 **Jura House Walled Garden** www.jurahouseandgardens.co.uk · Ardfin,
9/G26 **Jura** Around 8km from the ferry on the only road. Park opposite and follow track
ADMISSION into woods. Walled garden only part of walk that takes you to coast and ultimately
(though steep) to the beach and the 'Misty Pools'. Beautiful in rain (frequent) or
shine! Open all year 9am-5pm.

1609 **Attadale Gardens** www.attadale.com · Strathcarron On A890 from Kyle of
7/J18 Lochalsh and A87 just south of Strathcarron. Lovely West Highland house and
ADMISSION gardens near Loch Carron. Exotic specials, water gardens, sculpture, great rhodies
May/Jun. Nursery and kitchen garden. New fern garden and Japanese garden '07.
Good restaurant nearby (1075/HIGHLAND RESTAURANTS). Apr-Oct 10am-5pm.
Closed Sun.

1610 **The Hydroponicum** www.thehydroponicum.com · 01854 622202 ·
6/J15 **Achiltibuie** The 'Garden of the Future': a long-established indoor water world
ADMISSION where a huge variety of plants thrive without soil in their various microclimates.
Apr-Sep (and weekends in Oct). Tours: hourly. Limited hours in Oct. Growing kits
to buy (strawberries at Christmas?). Lovely 'Lily Pond' café round a pool using produce grown here. Great salads! Café and exhibition 11am-4pm.

1611 **Ard-Daraich Hill Garden** www.arddaraich.co.uk · 01855 841348 · Ardgour
9/J21 3 km south Ardgour at Corran Ferry (8/JOURNEYS) on A861 to Strontian. Private,
labour of love 'hill' and wild garden which you are at liberty to wander in.
Specialising in rhodies, shrubs, trees. Nursery/small garden centre. Open all year,
7 days.

1612 **The Hidden Gardens** www.thehiddengardens.org.uk · Glasgow This
2/XA5 garden oasis in the asphalt jungle of Glasgow's South Side opened in the disused
wasteland behind The Tramway performance and studio space in 2003. A project
of environmental theatre group nva working with landscape architects City Design
Co-operative, this is a very modern approach to an age-old challenge – how to
make and keep a sanctuary in the city! It works so far. Open 10am-8pm (winter
hours vary). Closed Mon.

Royal Botanic Garden Edinburgh 427/OTHER ATTRACTIONS.

Botanic Garden & Kibble Palace Glasgow 744/OTHER ATTRACTIONS.

The Best Country Parks

1613 ✓✓ **Drumlanrig Castle** www.drumlanrig.com · 01848 330248 ·
11/N29 **Thornhill** On A76, 7km north of Thornhill in the west Borders in whose romance and history it's steeped, much more than merely a country park; spend a good day, both inside the castle and in the grounds. Apart from *that* art collection (Rembrandt, Holbein, alas no longer the Leonardo) and the Craft Courtyard (2266/ CRAFT SHOPS), the delights include: a stunning tearoom, woodland and riverside walks, an adventure playground, the 'Working Forge' and bike hire for explorations along the Nith etc. Open Mar-Sep 11am-5pm. (House: May-22 Aug 12noon-4pm.)

1614 ✓ **Muirshiel** www.clydemuirsheil.co.uk · near **Lochwinnoch** Via Largs
9/L26 (A760) or Glasgow (M8, junction 29 A737 then A760 5km south of Johnstone). North from village on Kilmacolm road for 3km then signed. Muirshiel is name given to wider area, but park proper begins 6km on road along the Calder valley. Despite proximity of conurbation, this is a wild and enchanting place for walking, picnics etc. Trails marked to waterfall and summit views. Extensive events programme. Go look for hen harriers. See also 761/GLASGOW WALKS. Escape!

1615 **John Muir Country Park** www.eastlothian.gov.uk · near **Dunbar** Named
10/R25 after the 19th-century conservationist who founded America's National Parks (and
ECO the Sierra Club) and who was born in Dunbar. This swathe of coastline to the west of the town (known locally as Tyninghame) is an important estuarine nature reserve but is good for family walks and beachcombing. Can enter via B6370 off A198 to North Berwick or by 'cliff-top' trail from Dunbar or from car park on road into Dunbar from west at West Barns (1840/WILDLIFE).

1616 **Strathclyde Park** www.northlan.gov.uk · near **Hamilton & Motherwell**
10/M26 15km southeast of Glasgow. Take M8/A725 interchange or M74 junction 5 or 6. Scotland's most popular country park, especially for water sports. From canoeing to parascending; you can hire the gear (2212/WATER SPORTS). Also: excavated Roman bath house, playgrounds, sports pitches and some pleasant walks. Nearby Baron's Haugh and Dalzell Country Park more notable for their nature trails and gardens. 'Scotland's Theme Park' and the horrid Alona Hotel remind us what country parks should not be about. (1927MONUMENTS.)

1617 **Finlaystone Estate** www.finlaystone.co.uk · **Langbank near Greenock** A8
9/L25 to Greenock, Houston direction at Langbank, then signed. Grand mansion home
⌂ to Chief of Clan Macmillan set in formal gardens in wooded estate. Lots of facilities ('Celtic' tearoom, craft shop etc), leafy walks, walled garden. Rare magic. Oct-Mar weekends only, Apr-Sep daily until 5pm.

1618 **Almondell** www.westlothian.gov.uk · near **East Calder** 12km from
10/P26 Edinburgh city bypass. Well managed park in River Almond valley set amidst area of redundant industry. If you've just spent light years trying to exit from Livingston's notorious road system, you'll need this green oasis with its walks in woods, meadows and along cinder tracks. Picnic sites, visitor centre with refreshments, kids' areas. From Edinburgh take A71 from bypass (Kilmarnock road), then B7015 (Camps) for 7km. Park on right just into East Calder. Walk ahead to woods.

1619 **Hirsel Country Park** www.hirselcountrypark.co.uk · **Coldstream** On A697,
10/S27 north edge town (direction Kelso). 3000 acres the grounds of Hirsel House (not open public). 2-4km walks through farmland and woods including lovely languid lake. Museum, tearoom and nice pottery shop (Abbey Ceramics).

1620   **Muiravonside Country Park** near Linlithgow 4km southwest of Linlithgow
10/N25   on B825. Also signed from junction 4 of M9 Edinburgh/Stirling. Former farm
estate now run by the local authority with 170 acres of woodland walks, parkland,
picnic sites and a visitor centre for school parties or anyone else with an interest in
birds, bees and badgers. Ranger service does guided walks Apr-Sep. Great place to
walk off that lunch at the not-too-distant Champany Inn (272/BURGERS).

1621   **Eglinton** near Irvine By main A78 Largs/Ayr road signed from Irvine/Kilwinning
9/K27   intersection. Spacious lungful of Ayrshire. Visitor centre with interpretation of absolutely everything. Park always open, visitor centre Easter-Oct. Network of walks.

✓ ✓ **Culzean Castle Park** Superb and hugely popular. 1850/CASTLES.

✓ **Haddo House** Aberdeenshire Beautiful grounds. 1910/COUNTRY HOUSES.

Mugdock Country Park near Milngavie Marvellous park close to Glasgow.
5 car parks around the vast site. 757/CITY WALKS.
Tentsmuir near Tayport Estuarine; John Muir, on Tay. 1843/WILDLIFE.
Kelburne Country Centre Largs 1782/KIDS.

■■■■■■■■ # The Best Town Parks

1622   ✓ ✓ **Princes Street Gardens** Edinburgh South side of Princes St. The
1/C3   greenery that launched a thousand postcards, now under threat from a
thousand events. This former loch, drained when the New Town was built, is divided by the Mound. The eastern half has pitch and putt, Winter Wonderland and
the Scott Monument (460/BEST VIEWS), the western has its much-photographed
fountain, open-air café, space for locals and tourists to sprawl on the grass when
sunny, and the Ross Bandstand – heart of Edinburgh's Hogmanay (77/BEST EVENTS)
and the International Festival's fireworks concert (62/EVENTS). Louts with lager,
senior citizens on benches, dazed tourists: all our lives are here. Till dusk.

1623   ✓ ✓ **Hazelhead Park** Aberdeen Via Queens Rd, 3km centre. Extraor-
8/T19   dinary park where the Aberdonians' mysterious gardening skills are
magnificently in evidence. Many facilities including a maze, pets' corner, wonderful tacky tearoom and there are lawns, memorials and botanical splendours
aplenty especially azalea garden in spring and roses in summer. Great sculpture.

1624   ✓ **Duthie Park** Aberdeen Riverside Dr along River Dee from the bridge
8/T19   carrying main A92 Stonehaven road. The other large well-kept park with duck
pond, bandstand, hugely impressive summer rose gardens, carved sculptures and
the famous 'David Welch' Winter Garden of subtropical palms/ferns etc; under
restoration (9.30am-7.30pm summer, winter at dusk).

1625   ✓ **Pittencrieff Park** Dunfermline The extensive park alongside the Abbey
10/P25   and Palace ruins gifted to the town in 1903 by Carnegie. Open areas,
glasshouses, pavilion (more a function room) but most notably a deep verdant
glen criss-crossed with pathways. Great kids' play area. Lush, full of birds, good
after rain. May play a part in the new Carnegie Festival '08.

1626   ✓ **Macrosty Park** www.perthshire.co.uk · Crieff On your left as you leave
10/N23   Crieff for Comrie and Crianlarich; for parking ask locally. A perfect green place
on sloping ground to the River Earn (good level walk – Lady Mary's Walk) with tearooms, kids' area, mature trees and superb bandstand. A really fine old park.

1627
10/Q24
Beveridge Park Kirkcaldy Also in Fife, another big municipal park with a duck and boat pond, wide-open spaces and many amusements (e.g. bowling, tennis, putting, plootering). Ravenscraig a coastal park on the main road east to Dysart is an excellent place to walk. Great prospect of town and Firth, coves and skerries.

1628
10/R28
Wilton Lodge Park Hawick Hawick not overfull of visitor attractions, but it does have a nice park with facilities and diversions enough for everyone e.g. the civic gallery, rugby pitches (they quite like rugby in Hawick), a large kids' playground, a seasonal café and lots of riverside walks by the Teviot. Lots of my school friends lost their virginity in the shed here. All-round open-air recreation centre. South end of town by A7. PS: the shed is no longer here.

1629
11/P28
Station Park www.visitmoffat.co.uk · Moffat On your right as you enter the town from the M74. Well-proportioned people's park; boating pond (with giant swans) main feature. Annan water alongside offers nice walking. Notable also for the monument to Air Chief Marshall Hugh Dowding, Commander in Chief during the Battle of Britain. 'Never... was so much owed so many to so few'.

1630
9/L27
Dean Castle Park www.deancastle.com · Kilmarnock A77 south first turnoff for Kilmarnock then signed; from Ayr A77 north, 3rd turnoff. Surprising green and woody oasis in suburban Kilmarnock; lawns and woods around restored castle and courtyard. Riding centre. Burns Rose Garden.

1631
11/M30
Garries Park Gatehouse of Fleet Notable for its tiny perfect garden which you enter under an arch from the main street of this South West village. A wee gem especially for its large flowers. Leads to bigger public space, but pause in the garden and smell those roses. Then go to the Ship (851/southwest hotels).

1632
2/XC5
Rouken Glen & Linn Park Glasgow · 0141 638 7411 Both on south side of river. Rouken Glen via Pollokshaws/Kilmarnock road to Eastwood Toll then right. Good place to park is second left, Davieland Rd beside pond. Across park from here (or beside main Rouken Glen road) is main visitor area with info centre, garden centre, a Chinese restaurant, kids' play area and woodland walks. Linn Park via Aikenhead and Carmunnock road. After King's Park on left, take right to Simshill Rd and park at golf course beyond houses. A long route there, but worth it; this is one of the undiscovered Elysiums of a city which boasts 60 parks. Activities, wildlife walks, kids' nature trails, horse-riding (0141 637 3096) and Alexander 'Greek' Thomson's Holmwood House; open Easter-Oct 12noon-5pm (NTS).

1633
10/Q23
Camperdown Park www.camperdownpark.com · Dundee Calling itself a country park, Camperdown is the main recreational breathing space for the city and hosts a plethora of distractions (a golf course, a wildlife complex, mansion house etc). Situated beyond Kingsway, the ring-route; go via Coupar Angus turnoff. Best walks across the A923 in Templeton Woods. **Balgray Park** also excellent.

1634
8/P17
Grant Park Forres Frequent winner of the Bonny Bloom competitions (but not recently, so spruce up, Forres!) with its balance of ornamental gardens, open parkland and woody hill side, this is a carefully tended rose. Good municipal facilities like pitch and putt, playground. Cricket in summer and topping topiary. Through woods on Cluny Hill, a tower affords great views of the Moray and Cromarty Firths.

1635
10/N25
Callander Park Falkirk Park on edge of town centre, signed from all over. Overlooked by high-rise blocks and near busy road system, this is nevertheless a beautiful green space with a big hoose (heritage museum), woods and lawns. Comes alive in May as venue for Big in Falkirk (42/events).

The Most Interesting Coastal Villages

1636 ✓ **Plockton www.plockton.com · near Kyle of Lochalsh** A Highland gem
7/H18   of a place 8km over the hill from Kyle, clustered around inlets of a wooded
bay on Loch Carron. Cottage gardens down to the bay and palm trees! Some great
walks over headlands. Plockton Inn probably best bet for reasonable stay and eats
(1048/LESS EXPENSIVE HIGHLAND HOTELS). Plockton Hotel (1260/ROADSIDE INNS, pub
grub) and the new excellent Plockton Shores (1066/LESS EXPENSIVE HIGHLAND RES-
TAURANTS). It's not hard to feel connected with this village (and so many people do).

1637 ✓ **Moray Coast Fishing Villages** From Speybay (where the Spey slips into
            the sea) along to Fraserburgh, some of Scotland's best coastal scenery and
many interesting villages in cliff/cove and beach settings. Especially notable are
Portsoy with 17th-century harbour – and see 39/EVENTS and 346/PUBS;
Sandend with its own popular beach and a fabulous one nearby (1609/BEACHES);
Pennan made famous by the film *Local Hero* (the hotel/pub for sale at TGP;
01346 561201) and its recent mudslide; **Gardenstown** (has a great café/restau-
rant at the harbour 1426/SEAFOOD) with a walk along the water's edge to **Crovie**
(pronounced 'Crivee') the epitome of a coast-clinging community; and **Cullen**,
which is more of a town and has a great beach. (993/NORTHEAST HOTELS.)

1638 ✓ **Stromness Orkney Mainland** 24km from Kirkwall and a different kettle of
3/Q10   fish. Hugging the shore and with narrow streets and wynds, it has a unique
atmosphere, both maritime and European. Some of the most singular shops you'll
see anywhere and the Orkney folk going about their business. Park near harbour
and walk down the cobbled main street if you don't want to scrape your paintwork
(2469/ORKNEY; 2344/GALLERIES).

1639 ✓ **Cromarty near Inverness** At end of road across Black Isle from Inverness
7/M17   (45km northeast), does take longer than you think (well, 30 minutes). Village
with dreamy times-gone-by atmosphere, without being twee. Lots of kids running
about and a pink strand of beach. Delights to discover include: the east kirk, plain
and aesthetic with countryside through the windows behind the altar; Hugh (the
geologist) Miller's cottage/Courthouse museum (2323/BEST HISTORY & HERITAGE);
The Pantry (1505/TEAROOMS); Cromarty Bakery (1513/BEST SCOTCH BAKERS); the
perfect, wee restaurant Sutor Creek (1067/INEXPENSIVE HIGHLANDS); the shore and
cliff walk (2126/COASTAL WALKS); the Pirates' Cemetery and of course the dolphins
(1829/DOLPHINS).

1640 **Culross near Dunfermline** By A994 from Dunfermline or junction 1 of M90
10/N25 just over Forth Road Bridge (15km). Old centre conserved and being restored by
NTS. Mainly residential and not awash with craft and coffee shops. More historical
than merely quaint; a community of careful custodians lives in the white and
yellow red-pantiled houses. Footsteps echo in the cobbled wynds. Palace and
Town House open Easter-Oct 10am-6pm, weekends only Oct. Interesting back
gardens and lovely church at top of hill (1851/CHURCHES). Pamphlet by Rights of
Way Society available locally, is useful.

1641 **Tobermory Mull** Not so much a village or setting for a kids' TV show (the
9/G22 brilliant *Balamory*), rather the main town of Mull, set around a hill on superb
Tobermory Bay. Ferry port for Ardnamurchan, but main Oban ferry is 35km away at
Craignure. Usually a bustling harbour front with quieter streets behind; a
quintessential island atmosphere. Some good inexpensive hotels (and quayside
hostel) well situated to explore the whole island. 2428/MULL; 2393/ISLAND HOTELS;
1241/BEST HOSTELS.

1642 **Port Charlotte** **Islay** A township on the 'Rhinns of Islay', the western
9/F26 peninsula. By A846 from the pts, Askaig and Ellen via Bridgend. Rows of white-
washed, well-kept cottages along and back from shoreline. On road in, there's an
island museum and a coffee/bookshop. Also a 'town' beach and one between Port
Charlotte and Bruichladdich (and especially the one with the war memorial
nearby). Quiet and charming, not merely quaint. 2426/ISLAY; 2389/ISLAND HOTELS;
1845/WILDLIFE CENTRES

1643 **Rockcliffe** **near Dumfries** 25km south on Solway Coast road, A710. On the
11/N30 'Scottish Riviera', the rocky part of the coast around to Kippford (2120/COASTAL
WALKS). A good rock-scrambling foreshore though not so clean, and a village with
few houses and Baron's Craig hotel; set back with great views (27 moderately
expensive rooms) but a somewhat gloomy presence. Tearoom in village (1500/
TEAROOMS).

1644 **East Neuk Villages** **www.eastneukwide.co.uk** The quintessential quaint
10/R24 wee fishing villages along the bit of Fife that forms the mouth of the Firth of Forth,
Crail, Anstruther, Pittenweem, St Monans and **Elie** all have different
characters and attractions especially Crail and Pittenweem harbours, Anstruther as
main centre and home of Fisheries Museum (see also 1455/FISH & CHIPS; 1810/
BIRDS) and perfect Elie (2233/WINDSURFING; 934/936/FIFE HOTELS; 1395/GASTROP-
UBS; 2143/GREAT GOLF). Or see St Andrews. Cycling good, traffic in summer not.

1645 **Aberdour** **www.aberdour.org.uk** Between Dunfermline and Kirkcaldy and
10/P25 near Forth Road Bridge (10km east from junction 1 of M90) or, better still, go by
train from Edinburgh (frequent service: Dundee or Kirkcaldy); delightful station.
Walks round harbour and to headland, Silver Sands beach 1km (456/EDINBURGH
BEACHES), castle ruins. 1950/CHURCHES; 937/FIFE HOTELS.

1646 **Diabeg** **Wester Ross** On north shore of Loch Torridon at the end of the
7/H17 unclassified road from Torridon on one of Scotland's most inaccessible peninsulas.
Diabeg is simply beautiful (though pity about those fish cages). Fantastic road
there and then walk! PS: there's no pub, though a local wifie may do you tea and
buns in season – ask!

1647 **Isle of Whithorn** **www.isleofwhithorn.com** Strange faraway village at end of
11/L31 the road, 35km south Newton Stewart, 6km Whithorn (1901/PREHISTORIC SITES).
Mystical harbour where low tide does mean low, saintly shoreline, a sea angler's
pub, the Steam Packet – very good pub grub (1369/BLOODY GOOD PUBS). Great
deli/pizzeria – Ravenstones 1535/DELIS. Ninian's chapel round the headland not so
uplifting but en route you'll see the *Solway Harvester* memorial by the white building. Everybody visiting Whithorn seems to walk this way.

1648 **Corrie** **www.arran.uk.com** · **Arran** Last but not least, the bonniest bit of Arran
9/J27 (apart from Kildonan and the glens, etc), best reached by bike from Brodick (01770
302244 or 302868). Many walks from here including Goat Fell but nice just to sit
or potter on the foreshore. Hotel has never lived up to expectations but the village
shop is fab. I'd like a memorial bench on that shoreline.

Fantastic Beaches & Bays

1649
6/L12
✓ ✓ **Pete's Beach near Durness** The One of many great beaches on the North Coast (see below) that I've called my own. The hill above it is called 'Ceannabeinne'; you find it 7km east of Durness. Coming from Tongue it's just after where Loch Eriboll comes out to the sea and the road hits the coast again (there's a layby opposite). It's a small perfect cove flanked by walls of coral-pink rock and shallow turquoise sea. Splendid from above (land rises to a bluff with a huge boulder) and from below. There's a bench – come sit by me then leave your footprints in the sand.

1650
9/F24
✓ ✓ **Kiloran Beach Colonsay** 9km from quay and hotel, past Colonsay House: parking and access on hill side. Often described as the finest beach in the Hebrides, it does not disappoint though it has changed character in recent years (a shallower sandbar traps tidal run-off). Craggy cliffs on one side, negotiable rocks on the other and, in between, tiers of grassy dunes. Do go to the end! The island of Colonsay was once bought as a picnic spot. This beach was probably the reason why.

1651
✓ ✓ **Moray Coast www.moray.gov.uk** Many great beaches along coast from Spey Bay to Fraserburgh, notably **Cullen** and **Lossiemouth** (town beaches) and **New Aberdour** (1km from New Aberdour village on B9031, 15km west of Fraserburgh) and **Rosehearty** (8km west of Fraserburgh) both quieter places for walks and picnics. One of the best-kept secrets is the beach at **Sunnyside** where you walk past the incredible ruins of Findlater Castle on the cliff top (how did they build it? A place, on its grassed-over roof, for a picnic) and down to a cove which on my sunny day was simply perfect. Take a left going into Sandend 16km west of Banff, follow road for 2km, turn right, park in the farmyard. Walk from here past dovecote, 1km to cliff. Also signed from A98. See also 2124/COASTAL WALKS.

1652
9/G28
✓ ✓ **Macrihanish** At the bottom of the Kintyre peninsula 10km from Campbeltown. Walk north from Machrihanish village or golf course, or from the car park on the main A83 to Tayinloan and Tarbert at point where it hits/leaves the coast. A joyously long strand (8km) of unspoiled orange-pink sand backed by dunes and facing the 'steepe Atlantic Stream' all the way to Newfoundland (2150/GOLF IN GREAT PLACES).

1653
6/K12
✓ ✓ **Sandwood Bay Kinlochbervie** This mile-long sandy strand with its old 'Stack', is legendary, but therein lies the problem since now too many people know about it and you may have to share in its glorious isolation. Inaccessibility is its saving grace, a 7km walk from the sign off the road at Balchrick (near the cattle grid), 6km from Kinlochbervie or cut a third of the distance in a 4-wheel drive; allow 3hrs return plus time there. More venturesome is the walk from the north and Cape Wrath (2118/COASTAL WALKS). Managed by John Muir Trust. Go easy and go in summer! Also

1654
6/K13
✓ **Oldshoremore** The beach you pass on the road to Balchrick, only 3km from Kinlochbervie. It's easy to reach and a beautiful spot: the water is clear and perfect for swimming, and there are rocky walks and quiet places. **Polin**, 500m north, is a cove you might have to yourself. (1299/CAMPING)

1655
9/F26
✓ **Saligo, Machir Bay & The Big Strand www.islayinfo.com · Islay** The first two are bays on NW of island via A847 road to Port Charlotte, then B8018 past Loch Gorm. Wide beaches; remains of war fortifications in deep dunes,

Machir perhaps best for beach bums. They say 'no swimming' so paddle with extreme prejudice. The Big Strand on Laggan Bay: along Bowmore-Port Ellen road take Oa turnoff, follow Kintra signs. There's camping and great walks in either direction, 8km of glorious sand and dunes (contains the Machrie Golf Course). An airy amble under a wide sky. (2149/GOLF IN GREAT PLACES; 2116/COASTAL WALKS.)

1656
9/J25
✓ **Ostal Beach/Kilbride Bay Millhouse near Tighnabruaich** 3km from Millhouse on B8000 signed Ardlamont (not Portvadie, the ferry), a track to right before white house (often with a chain across to restrict access). Park and walk 1.5km, turning right after lochan. You arrive on a perfect white sandy crescent known locally as Ostal and, apart from the odd swatch of sewage, in certain conditions, a mystical secret place to swim and picnic. The north coast of Arran is like a Greek island in the bay.

1657
5/D18
✓ **South Uist www.southuist.com** Deserted but for birds, an almost unbroken strand of beach running for miles down the west coast; the machair at its best early summer. Take any road off the spinal A865; usually less than 2km. Good spot to try is turnoff at Tobha Mor; real blackhouses and a chapel on the way to the sea.

1658
5/E15
✓ **Scarista Beach South Harris** On main road south of Tarbert (15km) to Rodel. The beach is so beautiful that people have been married there. Hotel over the road is worth staying just for this, but is also a great retreat – also 2 excellent self-catering cottages 2391/ISLAND HOTELS. Golf course on links (2157/GOLF IN GREAT PLACES). Fab in early evening. The sun also rises.

1659
10/R22
✓ **Lunan Bay near Montrose** 5km from main A92 road to Aberdeen and 5km of deep red crescent beach under a wide northern sky. But 'n' Ben, Auchmithie, is an excellent place to start or finish (975/PERTHSHIRE EATS) and good approach (from south), although Gordon's restaurant at Inverkeilor is closer (973/PERTHSHIRE EATS). Best viewpoint from Boddin Farm 3km south Montrose and 3km from A92 signed 'Usan'. Often deserted.

1660
6/J14
✓ **The Secret Beach near Achmelvich** Can approach from Archmelvich car park going north – it's the next proper bay round – or from Lochinver-Stoer/ Drumbeg road: less walk, layby on right 3km after Archmelvich turnoff, 250m beyond sign for 'Cathair Estate'. Park on right (going north) and walk towards sea on left following stream (a sign points to 'Mill'). Well-defined path. Called **Alltan na Bradhan**, it's the site of an old mill (grinding wheels still there), perfect for camping and the best sea for swimming in the area. A tiny patch of sand to call your own.

1661
9/G25
Lowlandman's Bay www.theisleofjura.co.uk · Jura Not strictly a beach (there is a sandy strand before the headland) but a rocky foreshore with ethereal atmosphere; great light and space. Only seals break the spell. Go right at 3-arch bridge to first group of houses (Knockdrome), through yard on left and right around cottages to track to Ardmenish. After deer fences, bay is visible on your right, 1km walk away.

1662
5/C20
Vatersay Outer Hebrides The tiny island joined by a causeway to Barra. Twin crescent beaches on either side of the isthmus, one shallow and sheltered visible from Castlebay, the other an ocean beach with rollers. Dunes/machair; safe swimming. There's a helluva hill between Barra and Vatersay if you're cycling.

1663   **Seal Bay** www.isleofbarra.com · **Barra** 5km Castlebay on west coast, 2km
5/C20 after Isle of Barra Hotel through gate across machair where road right is signed
Taobh a Deas Allathasdal. A flat, rocky Hebridean shore and skerries where seals
flop into the water and eye you with intense curiosity. The better-beach beach is
next to the hotel.

1664   **West Sands St Andrews** As a town beach, this is hard to beat; it dominates
10/R23 the view to west. Wide swathe not too unclean and sea swimmable. Golf courses
behind. Consistently gets 'the blue flag', but beach buffs may prefer **Kinshaldy**
(1844/WILDLIFE) or **Kingsbarns** (10km south on Crail road), or **Elie** (28km south)
where there is a great beach walk taking in the Cammo Estate (with its gardens)
and skirting the great Kingsbarns Golf Course.

1665   **North Coast** To the west of Thurso, along the North Coast, are some of Britain's
6 most unspoiled and unsung beaches. No beach bums, no Beach Boys. There are
so many great little coves, you can have one to yourself even on a hot day, but
those to mention are: **Strathy** and **Armadale** (35km west Thurso), **Farr** and
Torrisdale (48km) and **Coldbackie** (65km). My favourite is elevated to the top
of this category. 1649/BEACHES.

1666   **Sands of Morar near Mallaig** 70km west of Fort William and 6km from
7/H20 Mallaig by newly improved road, these easily accessible beaches may seem over-
populated on summer days and the south stretch nearest to Arisaig may have one
too many caravan parks, but they go on for miles and there's enough space for
everybody. The sand's supposed to be silver but in fact it's a very pleasing pink.
Lots of rocky bits for exploration. One of the best beachy bits (the bay before the
estuary) is 'Camusdarrach', signed from the main road (where *Local Hero* was
filmed), further from road, is quieter and a very good swathe of sand. Traigh, the
golf course makes good use of the dunes (2166/GOOD GOLF).

1667   **The Bay at the Back of the Ocean Iona** Easy 2km walk from frequent ferry
9/F23 from Fionnphort, south of Mull (2360/MAGICAL ISLANDS) or hire a bike from the
store on your left as you walk into the village (01681 700357). Paved road most of
way. John Smith, who is buried beside the abbey, once told me that this was one
of his favourite places. There are 2 great inexpensive hotels on Iona, The Argyll
(1280/GET-AWAY HOTELS) and St Columba (2428/BEST OF MULL).

1668   **Dornoch (& Embo Beaches)** The wide and extensive sandy beach of this
6/N16 pleasant town at the mouth of the Dornoch Firth famous also for its golf links.
4km north, Embo Sands starts with ghastly caravan city, but walk north towards
Golspie. Embo is twinned with Kaunakakai, Hawaii!

1669   **Port of Ness Isle of Lewis** Also signed Port Nis, this is the beach at the end of
5/G12 the Hebrides in the far north of Lewis. Just keep driving. There are some
interesting stops on the way (2280/ART, 2309/2310/MUSEUMS) – until you get to
this tiny bay and harbour down the hill at the end of the road. Anthony Barber's
Harbour View Gallery full of his own work (which you find in many other galleries
and even postcards) is worth a visit (10am-5pm, closed Sun).

1670   **2 Beaches in the far South West Killantringan Bay near Portpatrick** Off
11/J30 A77 before PP signed 'Dunskey Gardens' in summer, follow road signed
Killantringan Lighthouse (dirt track). Park 1km before lighthouse. Beautiful bay for
exploration. **Sandhead Beach** A716 south of Stranraer. Shallow, safe waters of
Luce Bay. Perfect for families (in their damned caravans).

The Great Glens

1671   ✓ ✓ ✓ **Glen Affric** www.glenaffric.org   Beyond Cannich at end of Glen
7/K18   Urquhart A831, 20km from Drumnadrochit on Loch Ness. A
dramatic gorge that strikes westwards into the wild heart of Scotland. Superb for
rambles (2072/GLEN & RIVER WALKS), expeditions, Munro-bagging (further in
beyond Loch Affric) and even just tootling through in the car. Shaped by the Hydro
Board, Loch Benevean also adds to the drama. One of the best places in Scotland
to understand the beauty of Scots Pine. Cycling good (bike hire in Cannich 01456
415251 and at the campsite) as is the detour to Tomich and Plodda Falls (1683/
WATERFALLS). Stop at Dog Falls (1760/PICNICS) but do go to the end of the glen.

1672   ✓ ✓ ✓ **Glen Lyon** www.glenlyon.org · **near Aberfeldy**   One of
10/M22   Scotland's crucial places historically and geographically, much
favoured by fishers/walkers/Munro-baggers. Wordsworth, Tennyson, Gladstone
and Baden Powell all sang its praises. Site of ground-breaking theatre 'The Path' in
2000. The Lyon is a classic Highland river tumbling through corries, gorges and
riverine meadows. Several Munros are within its watershed and rise gloriously on
either side. Road all the way to the loch side (30km). Eagles soar over the remoter
tops at the head of the glen. The Post Office coffee shop does a roaring trade.

1673   ✓ ✓ **Glen Nevis** www.glen-nevis.co.uk · **Fort William**   Used by many a
9/K21   film director and easy to see why. Ben Nevis is only part of magnificent
scenery. Many walks and convenient facilities (1689/WATERFALLS; 2068/SERIOUS
WALKS). West Highland Way emerges here. Visitor centre; cross river to climb Ben
Nevis. Good caff in season (1083/FORT WILLIAM). This woody dramatic glen is a
national treasure.

1674   ✓ ✓ **Glen Etive**   Off from more exalted Glencoe and the A82 at Kingshouse,
9/K22   as anyone you meet there will tell you, this truly is a glen of glens. Treat
with great respect while you make it your own. (1297/CAMPING, 1753/POOLS)

1675   **Strathcarron** www.strathcarron.com · **near Bonar Bridge**   You drive up the
6/L15   north bank of this Highland river from the bridge outside Ardgay (pronounced
'Ordguy') which is 3km over the bridge from Bonar Bridge. Road goes 15km to
Croick and its remarkable church (1956/CHURCHES). The river gurgles and gushes
along its rocky course to the Dornoch Firth and there are innumerable places to
picnic, swim and stroll further up. Quite heavenly on a warm day.

1676   **The Angus Glens** www.angusglens.co.uk   **Glen Clova**, **Glen Prosen** and
10/Q21   **Glen Isla**. All via Kirriemuir. Isla to the west is a woody, approachable glen with a
deep gorge, on B954 near Alyth (1693/WATERFALLS) and the cosy Glenisla Hotel
(1265/INNS). Others via B955, to Dykehead then road bifurcates. Both glens stab
into the heart of the Grampians. 'Minister's Walk' goes between them from behind
the kirk at Prosen village over the hill to B955 before Clova village (7km). Glen
Clova is a walkers' paradise especially from Glendoll 24km from Dykehead; limit of
road. Viewpoint. 'Jock's Road' to Braemar and the Capel Mounth to Ballater (both
24km). Good hotel at Clova (965/PERTHSHIRE HOTELS) with famous 'Loops of
Brandy' walk (2 hours, 2-B-2); stark and beautiful. Also 'green' hostel deep in Glen
Prosen (1249/HOSTELS).

1677   **Glendaruel** www.glendaruel.com · **Cowal Peninsula**   On the A886 between
9/J25   Colintraive and Strachur. Humble but perfectly formed glen of River Ruel, from
2-B-2   Clachan in south (a kirk and an inn) through deciduous meadowland to more

rugged grandeur 10km north. Easy walking and cycling. West road best. Kilmodan carved stones signed. Inver Cottage on Loch Fyne a great coffee/food stop (826/ARGYLL RESTAURANTS).

1678 **Glen Lonan** **near Taynuilt** Between Taynuilt on A85 and A816 south of Oban.
9/J23 Another quiet wee glen, but all the right elements for walking, picnics, cycling and
2-B-2 fishing or just a run in the car. Varying scenery, a bubbling burn (the River Lonan), some standing stones and not many folk. Angus' Garden at the Taynuilt end should not be missed (1596/GARDENS). No marked walks; now get lost!

1679 **Glen Trool** **near Newton Stewart** 26km north by A714 via Bargrennan which
11/L29 is on the Southern Upland Way (1997/LONG WALKS). A gentle wooded glen within the vast Galloway Forest Park (one of the most charming, accessible parts) visitor centre 5km from Bargrennan. Pick up a walk brochure. Many options. (1998/MARY, CHARLIE & BOB) Start of the Merrick climb (2033/HILLS).

1680 **The Sma' Glen** **near Crieff** Off the A85 to Perth, the A822 to Amulree and
10/N23 Aberfeldy. Sma' meaning small, this is the valley of the River Almond where the Mealls (lumpish, shapeless hills) fall steeply down to the road. Where the road turns away from the river, the long distance path to Loch Tay begins (28km). Sma' Glen, 8km, has good picnic spots, but they get busy and midgy in summer.

1681 **Strathfarrar** www.glenaffric.org · **near Beauly or Drumnadrochit** Rare
7/L18 unspoiled glen accessed from A831 leaving Drumnadrochit on Loch Ness via Cannich (30km) or south from Beauly (15km). Signed at Struy. Arrive at gate-keeper's house. Access restricted to 25 cars per day (Closed Tue and till 1.30pm on Wed). For access Mar-Oct, phone 01463 761260; there may be a curfew. 22km to head of glen past lochs. Good climbing, walking, fishing. The real peace and quiet!

The Most Spectacular Waterfalls

One aspect of Scotland that really is improved by rain. All the walks to these falls are graded 1-A-1 unless otherwise stated (see p. 12 for walk codes).

1682 ✓✓ **Falls of Glomach** 25km south of Kyle of Lochalsh off A87 near Shiel
7/J18 Bridge, past Kintail Centre at Morvich then 2km further up Glen Croe to
2-C-3 bridge. Walk starts other side; there are other ways, (eg from the SY Hostel in Glen Affric), but this is most straightforward. Allow 5/7 hours for the pilgrimage to one of Britain's highest falls. Path is steep but well trod. Glomach means gloomy and you might feel so, peering into the ravine; from precipice to pool, it's 200m. But to pay tribute, go down carefully to ledge. Vertigo factor and sense of achievement both fairly high. (1243/HOSTELS.) Consult *Where to Walk in Kintail, Glenelg & Lochalsh*, sold locally for the Kintail Mountain Rescue Team. Ranger service 0844 493 2231.

1683 ✓✓ **Plodda Falls** www.glenaffric.org · **near Tomich near**
7/K18 **Drumnadrochit** A831 from Loch Ness to Cannich (20km), then 7km to Tomich, a further 5km up mainly woodland track to car park. 200m walk down through woods of Scots Pine and ancient Douglas Fir to one of the most enchanting woodland sites in Britain and the Victorian iron bridge over the brink of the 150m fall into the churning river below. The dawn chorus here must be amazing. Freezes into winter wonderland (ice climbers from Inverness take advantage). Good hotel in village (1057/INEXPENSIVE HIGHLANDS HOTELS).

1684
10/N21
⌨

✓ **Falls Of Bruar** near Blair Atholl Close to the main A9 Perth-Inverness road, 12km north of Blair Atholl near House of Bruar shopping experience. (2252/SCOTTISH SHOPPING). Consequently, the short walk to lower falls is very consumer-led but less crowded than you might expect. The lichen-covered walls of the gorge below the upper falls (1km) are less ogled and more dramatic. Circular path is well marked but steep and rocky in places. Tempting to swim on hot days (1765/SWIMMING HOLES).

1685
9/J27
1-B-1

✓ **Glenashdale Falls** Arran 5km walk from bridge on main road at Whiting Bay. Signed up the burn side, but uphill and further on than you think, so allow 2 hours (return). Series of falls in a rocky gorge in the woods with paths so you get right down to the brim and the pools. Swim here, swim in heaven!

1686
9/G22

Eas Fors Mull On the Dervaig to Fionnphort road 3km from Ulva Ferry; a series of cataracts tumbling down on either side of the road. Easily accessible from small car park on left going south (otherwise unmarked). There's a path down the side to the brink where the river plunges into the sea. On a warm day swimming in the sea below the fall is a rare exhilaration.

1687
7/G17
2-C-2

Lealt Falls Skye Impressive torrent of wild mountain water about 20km north of Portree on the A855. Look for sign: 'River Lealt'. There's a car park on a bend on right (going north). You can walk to grassy ledges and look over or go down to the beach.

Kilt Rock, a viewpoint much favoured by bus parties, is a few km further (you look over and along the cliffs). Also...

Eas Mor Glen Brittle near end of road. 24km from Sligachan. A mountain water-fall with the wild Cuillins behind and views to the sea. Approach as part of a serious scramble or merely a 30-minute Cuillin sampler. Start at the Memorial Hut, cross the road, bear right, cross burn and then follow path uphill.

1688
6/L14
2-C-3

Eas A' Chual Aluinn Kylesku 'Britain's highest waterfall' near the head of Glencoul, is not easy to reach. Kylesku is between Scourie and Lochinver off the main A894, 20km south of Scourie. There are 2-hour cruises at 11am/3pm May-Sep (and 2pm Fri) outside hotel (1072/INEXPENSIVE HIGHLAND RESTAURANTS). Falls are a rather distant prospect, but you may be able to alight and get next boat. Baby seals an added attraction Jun-Aug. (Another boat trip from the same quay goes to **Kerracher Gardens** www.kerracher.co.uk, a lochside labour of love that's worth seeing – boats 1pm every day in summer or phone (01971 502345). There's also a track to the top of the falls from 5km north of the Skiag Bridge on the main road (4 hours return), but you will need to take directions locally. The water freefalls for 200m, which is 4 times further than Niagara (take pinch of salt here). There is a spectacular pulpit view down the cliff, 100m to right.

1689
9/K21
3-A-3

Steall Falls www.glen-nevis.co.uk · Glen Nevis, Fort William Take Glen Nevis road at the roundabout outside town centre and drive 'to end' (16km) through glen. Start from the second and final car park, following path marked Corrour, uphill through the woody gorge with River Ness thrashing below. Glen eventually and dramatically opens out and there are great views of the long veils of the Falls. Precarious 3-wire bridge for which you will also need nerves of steel. Always fun to see the macho types bottle out of doing it! Me also (you can cross further down).

1690
7/K16

Corrieshalloch Gorge/Falls of Measach Junction of A832 and A835, 20km south of Ullapool; possible to walk down into the gorge from both roads. Most dramatic approach is from the car park on the A832 Gairloch road. Staircase to swing bridge from whence to consider how such a wee burn could make such a deep gash. Very impressive. A must-stop on the way to/from Ullapool.

1691 **The Grey Mare's Tail between Moffat & Selkirk** On the wildly scenic A708.
10/P28 About halfway, a car park and signs for waterfall. 8km from Tibby Shiels Inn (refreshments! 1366/BLOODY GOOD PUBS). The lower track takes 10/15 minutes to a viewing place still 500m from falls; the higher, on the other side of the Tail burn, threads between the austere hills and up to Loch Skene from which the falls over-flow (45/60 minutes). Mountain goats.

1692 **The Falls of Clyde www.swt.org.uk · New Lanark** Dramatic falls in a long
10/N27 gorge of the Clyde. New Lanark, the conservation village of Robert Owen the social reformer, is signed from Lanark. It's hard to avoid the 'award-winning' tourist bazaar, but the riverbank has... a more natural appeal. The path to the Power Station is about 1km, but the route doesn't get interesting till after it, a 1km climb to the first fall (Cora Linn) and another 1km to the next (Bonnington Linn). Swimming above or below them is not advised (but it's great). Certainly don't swim on an 'open day', when they close the station and divert all the water back down the river in a mighty surge; submerged rocks are another hazard (details from visitor centre: 01555 665262). There is a great Italian restaurant in Lanark and one of the mills is now a hotel. The strange uniformity of New Lanark is better when the other tourists have gone home.

1693 **Reekie Linn Alyth** 8km north of town on back roads to Kirriemuir on B951
10/Q22 between Bridge of Craigisla and Bridge of Lintrathen. A picnic site and car park on bend of road leads by 200m to the wooded gorge of Glen Isla with precipitous viewpoints of defile where Isla is squeezed and falls in tiers for 100ft. Can walk further along the glen. Lochside restaurant nearby (971/PERTHSHIRE EATS) but Peel Farm Shop/Tearoom, which is widely signposted, is disappointing.

1694 **Falls of Acharn near Kenmore** 5km along south side of Loch Tay on an
10/M22 unclassified road. Walk from just after the bridge going west in township of Acharn; falls are signed. Steepish start then 1km up side of gorge; waterfalls on other side. Can be circular route.

1695 **Falls of Rogie www.ullapool.co.uk · near Strathpeffer** Car park on A835
7/L17 Inverness-Ullapool road, 5km Contin/10km Strathpeffer. Accessibility makes short walk (250m) quite popular to these hurtling falls on the Blackwater River. Bridge (built by the Territorial Army) and salmon ladder (they leap in summer). Woodland trails 1-3km marked, include a circular route to Contin (2103/WOODLAND WALKS).

1696 **Foyers Loch Ness** On southern route from Fort Augustus to Inverness, the
7/L19 B862 (1722/SCENIC ROUTES) at the village of Foyers (35km from Inverness). Park next to shops and cross road, go through fence and down steep track to viewing places (slither-proof shoes advised). River Foyers falls 150m into foaming gorge below and then into Loch Ness throwing clouds of spray into the trees (you may get drenched).

1697 **Falls Of Shin www.fallsofshin.co.uk · near Lairg** 6km east of town on
6/M15 signed road, car park and falls nearby are easily accessible. Not quite up to the
⌂ splendours of others on this page, but an excellent place to see salmon battling upstream (best Jun-Aug). Visitor centre with extensive shop; the café/restaurant is excellent (1081/INEXPENSIVE RESTAURANTS) and there's an adventure playground and other reasons to hang around.

The Lochs We Love

1698 ✓ ✓ **Loch Maree** A832 between Kinlochewe and Gairloch. Dotted with
7/J16 islands covered in Scots pine hiding some of the best examples of Viking
graves and apparently a money tree in their midst. Easily viewed from the road
which follows its length for 15km. Beinn Eighe rises behind you and the
omniscient presence of Slioch is opposite. Aultroy Vistor Centre (5km Kinlochewe),
fine walks from car park further on, good accommodation near lochside (1051/
INEXPENSIVE HIGHLAND HOTELS).

1699 ✓ ✓ **Loch An Eilean** 4km Inverdruie off the Coylumbridge road from
7/N19 Aviemore. Car park and tiny visitor centre. An enchanted loch in the
heart of the Rothiemurchus Forest (2092/WOODLAND WALKS for directions). There's
a good visitor centre. You can walk right round the loch (5km, allow 1.5 hours).
This is classic Highland scenery, a calendar landscape of magnificent Scots pine. A
circuit of the loch was a central part of 'Britain's Most Beautiful Run' which was
part of The Outsider Festival '07 (48/EVENTS).

1700 ✓ **Loch Arkaig** 25km Fort William. An enigmatic loch long renowned for its
7/J20 fishing. From the A82 beyond Spean Bridge (at the Commando Monument)
cross the Caledonian Canal, then on by single track road through the Clune Forest
and the 'Dark Mile' past the 'Witches' Pool' (a cauldron of dark water below
cataracts), to the loch. Bonnie Prince Charlie came this way before and after
Culloden; one of his refuge caves is marked on a trail.

1701 **Loch Lubhair near Crianlarich** The loch you pass (on the right) on the A85 to
9/L23 Crianlarich (4km), in Glen Dochart, the upper reaches of the Tay water system.
Small, perfect, with bare hills surrounding and fringed with pines and woody islets.
Beautiful scenery that most people just hurtle past heading for Oban or Fort
William.

1702 **Loch Achray near Brig o' Turk** The small loch at the centre of the Trossachs
10/L24 between **Loch Katrine** (on which the *SS Sir Walter Scott* makes 4/5 sailings a day
– some stop at end of loch: 01877 376316) and **Loch Venachar**. The A821 from
Callander skirts both Venachar and Achray. Many picnic spots and a new fishing
centre and Harbour Café on the main road by Loch Venachar. Ben Venue and Ben
An rise above: great walks (2026/HILLS) and views. A one-way forest road goes
round the other side of Loch Achray through Achray Forest (enter and leave from
the Duke's Pass road between Aberfoyle and Brig o' Turk). Details of trails from
forest visitor centre 3km north Aberfoyle. Bike hire at Loch Katrine/Callander/
Aberfoyle – it's the best way to see these lochs.

1703 **Glen Finglas Reservoir Brig o' Turk** And while we're on the subject of lochs
10/L24 in the Trossachs (see above) here's a hidden gem. Although it's man-made it's a
real beauty, surrounded by soft green hills and the odd burn bubbling in. Approach
'through' Brig o' Turk houses (past the caff) and park 2km up road or from new car
park 2km before Brig o' Turk from Callander. Walk to right (not 'the Dam' road
although this an interesting 1km diversion on the way back). 5 km walk to head of
loch or possible to make the loop round it and back to dam (no path, lots of
scrambling, boots only) or go further to Balquhidder – a walk across the heart of
Scotland (2073/GLEN WALKS).

1704 **Loch Muick near Ballater** At head of road off B976, the South Dee road at
10/Q20 Ballater. 14km up Glen Muick (pronounced 'Mick') to car park, visitor centre and
1km to loch side. Lochnagar rises above (2056/MUNROS) and walk also begins here

for Capel Mounth and Glen Clova (1676/GLENS). 3-hour walk around loch and any number of ambles. The lodge where Vic met John is at the furthest point (well, it would be). Open aspect with grazing deer and not too much forestry. (Ranger's office 01339 742556).

1705 **Loch Eriboll North Coast** 90km west of Thurso. The long sea loch that indents
6/L13 into the North Coast for 15km and which you drive right round on the main A838. Deepest natural anchorage in the UK, exhibiting every aspect of loch side scenery including, alas, fish cages. Ben Hope stands near the head of the loch and there is a perfect beach (my own private Idaho) on the coast (1649/BEACHES). Walks from Hope. There's a good guesthouse on the shore.

1706 **Loch Trool near Newton Stewart** The small, celebrated loch in a bowl of the
11/L29 Galloway Hills reached via Bargrennan 14km north via A714 and 8km to end of road. Woodland visitor centre/café on the way. Get Galloway Forest Park Brochure. Good walks but best viewed from Bruce's Stone (1998/MARY, CHARLIE & BOB) and the slopes of Merrick (2033/HILLS). An idyllic place.

1707 **Loch Morar near Mallaig** 70km west of Fort William by the A850 (a wildly
7/H20 scenic and much improved route). Morar village is 6km from Mallaig and a single track road leads away from the coast to the loch (only 500m but out of sight) then along it for 5km to Bracora. It's the prettiest part with wooded islets, small beaches, loch side meadows and bobbing boats. The road stops at a turning place but a track continues from Bracorina to Tarbet and it's possible to connect with a post boat and sail back to Mallaig on Loch Nevis though this will take some organising(check tourist information centre). Boat hire on the loch itself from Ewen Macdonald (01687 462520). Loch Morar, joined to the coast by the shortest river in Britain, also has the deepest water. There is a spookiness about it and just possibly a monster called Morag.

1708 **Loch Tummel near Pitlochry** West from Pitlochry on B8019 to Rannoch (and
10/N22 the end of the road), Loch Tummel comes into view, as it did for Queen Victoria, scintillating beneath you, and on a clear day with Schiehallion beyond (1743/VIEWS). This north side has good walks (2100/WOODLAND WALKS), but the south road from Faskally just outside Pitlochry is the one to take to get down to the lochside to picnic etc.

1709 **Loch Lundavra near Fort William** Here's a secret loch in the hills, but not far
9/K21 from the well-trodden tracks through the glens and the sunny streets of Fort William. Go up Lundavra Rd from roundabout at west end of main street, out of town, over cattle grid and on (to end of road) 8km. You should have it to yourself; good picnic spots and great view of Ben Nevis. West Highland Way comes this way (2060/LONG WALKS).

Loch Lomond The biggest, maybe not the bonniest (1/BIG ATTRACTIONS) with major visitor centre and retail experience, **Lomond Shores**, at south end near Balloch.

Loch Ness The longest; you haven't heard the last of it (3/BIG ATTRACTIONS).

The Scenic Routes

1710
9/J21
NTS
✓ ✓ ✓ **Glencoe** www.glencoe-nts.org.uk The A82 from Crianlarich to Ballachulish is a fine drive, but from the extraterrestrial Loch Ba onwards, there can be few roads anywhere that have direct contact with such imposing scenery. After Kingshouse and Buachaille Etive Mor on the left, the mountains and ridges rising on either side of Glencoe proper invoke the correct usage of the word 'awesome'. The new visitor centre, more discreet than the former near Glencoe village, sets the topographical and historical scene. (1360/BLOODY GOOD PUBS; 2067/SERIOUS WALKS; 1984/BATTLEGROUNDS; 2011/SPOOKY PLACES; 1243/HOSTELS.)

1711 7/H19
✓ ✓ **Shiel Bridge-Glenelg** The switchback road that climbs from the A87 (Fort William 96km) at Shiel Bridge over the 'hill' and down to the coast opposite the Sleat Peninsula in Skye (short ferry to Kylerhea). As you climb you're almost as high as the surrounding summits and there's the classic view across Loch Duich to the 5 Sisters of Kintail. Coming back you think you're going straight into the loch! It's really worth driving to Glenelg (1904/PREHISTORIC SITES, 1298/CAMPING, 1253/INNS) and beyond to Arnisdale and ethereal Loch Hourn (16km).

1712
7/H18
✓ ✓ **Applecross** www.applecross.uk.com · 120km from Inverness. From Tornapress near Lochcarron for 18km. Leaving the A896 seems like leaving civilisation; the winding ribbon heads into monstrous mountains and the high plateau at the top is another planet. It's not for the faint hearted and Applecross is a relief to see with its campsite/coffee shop and a faraway inn: the legendary Applecross Inn (1258/GET-AWAY HOTELS). Also see 1064/HIGHLAND RESTAURANTS, 1490/COFFEE SHOPS, 1301/1306/CAMPING. This hair-raising road rises 2000 feet in 6 miles. See how they built it at the Applecross Heritage Centre (2315/HERITAGE).

1713
7/J17
✓ ✓ **Glen Torridon** The A896 between Torridon, Diabeg and Kinlochewe. Starting in delightful Diabeg (1602/COASTAL VILLAGES) allows views of staggering Ben Alligin, but either side of Loch Torridon is impressive. Excellent hotel (1278/GET-AWAY HOTELS). Between Kinlochewe and Torridon there's Liatach and Beinn Elghe (1731/VIEWS). Much to climb, much to merely amaze.

1714
9/J26
✓ ✓ **Rothesay-Tighnabruaich** A886/A8003. The most celebrated part of this route is the latter, the A8003 down the side of Loch Riddon to Tighnabruaich along the hill sides which give the breathtaking views of Bute and the Kyles (can be a lot of vegetation in summer – there is one good layby/viewpoint) but the whole way, with its diverse aspects of lochside, riverine and rocky scenery, is supernatural. Includes short crossing between Rhubodach and Colintraive. Great hotel/restaurant at Tighnabruaich (815/ARGYLL HOTELS).

1715
5/E16
✓ **The Golden Road South Harris** The main road in Harris follows the west coast, notable for bays and beaches (1658/BEACHES). This is the other one, winding round a series of coves and inlets with offshore skerries and a treeless rocky hinterland – classic Hebridean landscape, especially Finsbay. Good caff in the middle (2427/HEBRIDES). Tweed is woven in this area; you can visit the crofts but it seems impolite to leave without buying some (2291/TWEED).

1716
6/J14
✓ **Lochinver-Drumbeg-Kylestrome** The coast road north from Lochinver (35km) is marvellous; essential Assynt. Actually best travelled north-south so that you leave the splendid vista of Eddrachilles Bay and pass through lochan, moor and even woodland, touching the coast again by sandy beaches (at Stoer a

road leads 7km to the lighthouse and the walk to the Old Man of Stoer, 2119/COASTAL WALKS) past the wonderful Secret Beach (1669/BEACHES) and approach Lochinver (possible detour to Auchmelvich and beaches) with one of the classic long views of Suilven. Get your pies in Lochinver (1077/HIGHLAND LESS EXPENSIVE).

1717 **Lochinver-Achiltibuie** And south from Lochinver Achiltibuie is 40km from
6/J14 Ullapool; so this is the route from the north; 28km of winding road/unwinding Highland scenery; through glens, mountains and silver sea. Known locally as the 'wee mad road' (it is maddening if you're in a hurry). Passes Achin's Bookshop (2261/SHOPPING), the path to Kirkaig Falls and the mighty Suilven.

1718 **Sleat Peninsula Skye** The unclassified road off the A851 (main Sleat road)
7/G19 especially coming from south, i.e. take road at Ostaig near Gaelic College (great place to stay nearby: 2386/SKYE); it meets coast after 9km. Affords rare views of the Cuillins from a craggy coast. Returning to 'main' road south of Isleornsay, pop into the great hotel pub there (2375/ISLAND HOTELS).

1719 **Leaderfoot-Clintmains** near St Boswells The B6356 between the A68 (look
10/R27 out for Leaderfoot viaduct and signs for Dryburgh) and the B6404 Kelso-St Boswells road. This small road, busy in summer, links Scott's View and Dryburgh Abbey (1978/ABBEYS; find by following Abbey signs) and Smailholm Tower, and passes through classic Border/Tweedside scenery. Don't miss Irvine's View if you want to see the best of the Borders (1739/VIEWS). Nice guesthouse (886/BORDER HOTELS).

1720 **Braemar-Linn Of Dee** 12km of renowned Highland river scenery along the
10/P20 upper valley of the (Royal) Dee. The Linn (rapids) is at the end of the road and the mighty Dee is squeezed until it is no more than 1m wide, but there are river walks and the start of the great Glen Tilt walk to Blair Atholl (2070/SERIOUS WALKS). Deer abound.

1721 **Ballater-Tomintoul** The ski road to the Lecht (2171/SKIING), the A939 which
8/Q20 leaves the Royal Deeside road (A93) west of Ballater before it gets really royal. A ribbon of road in the bare Grampians, past the sentinel ruin Corgarff (open to view, 250m walk) and the valley of the trickling Don. Road proceeds seriously uphill and main viewpoints are south of the Lecht. There is just nobody for miles. Walks in Glenlivet estates south of Tomintoul.

1722 **Fort Augustus-Dores** near Inverness The B862 often single-track road that
7/L19 follows and latterly skirts Loch Ness. Quieter and more interesting than the main west bank A82. Starts in rugged country and follows the straight road built by Wade to tame the Highlands. Reaches the lochside at Foyers (1696/WATERFALLS) and goes all the way to Dores (15km from Inverness) where the dance music gathering, RockNess, is held in Jun (48/EVENTS). Paths to the shore of the loch. Fabulous untrodden woodlands near Errogie (marked) and the spooky graveyard adjacent Boleskin House where Aleister Crowley did his dark magic and Jimmy Page of Led Zeppelin may have done his. 35km total; worth taking slowly.

1723 **The Duke's Pass, Aberfoyle-Brig o' Turk** Of the many roads through the
10/L24 Trossachs, this one is spectacular though gets busy; numerous possibilities for stopping, exploration and great views. Good viewpoint 4km from Loch Achray Hotel, above road and lay-by. One-way forest road goes round Loch Achray. Good hill walking starts (2026/2027/2028/FAVOURITE HILLS) and Loch Katrine Ferry (2km) 4/5 times a day Apr-Oct (01877 376316). Bike hire at Loch Katrine, Aberfoyle and Callander.

1724   **Glenfinnan-Mallaig** The A830, aka the Road to the Isles. Through some of the
9/J20   most impressive and romantic landscapes in the Highlands, splendid in any
weather (it does rain rather a lot) to the coast at the Sands of Morar
(1666/BEACHES). This is deepest Bonnie Prince Charlie country (1997/MARY, CHARLIE
& BOB) and demonstrates what a misty eye he had for magnificent settings. A full-
throttle bikers' dream. The road is shadowed for much of the way by the West
Highland Railway, which is an even better way to enjoy the scenery (11/FAVOURITE
JOURNEYS). Road recently improved, especially the Arisaig-Mallaig section.

1725   **Lochailort-Acharacle** Off from the A830 above at Lochailort and turning south
9/H21   on the A861, the coastal section of this great scenery is superb especially in the
setting sun, or in May when the rhodies are out. Glen Uig Inn is rough and ready!
This is the road to the Castle Tioram shoreline, which should not be missed
(1871/RUINS), and glorious Ardnamurchan.

1726   **Knapdale: Lochgilphead-Tarbert** B8024 off the main A83 follows the coast
9/H25   for most of its route. Views to Jura are immense (and on a clear day, Ireland). Not
much happens here but in the middle in exactly the right place is a superb inn
(1255/ROADSIDE INNS, 1393/GASTROPUBS). Take it easy on this very Scottish 35km
of single track.

1727   **Amulree-Kenmore** Unclassified single-track and very narrow road from the
10/N22   hill-country hamlet of Amulree to cosy Kenmore signed Glen Quaich. Past Loch
Freuchie, a steep climb takes you to a plateau ringed by magnificent (far)
mountains to Loch Tay. Steep descent to Loch Tay and Kenmore. Don't forget to
close the gates.

1728   **Muthill-Comrie** Pure Perthshire. A route which takes you through some of the
10/N23   best scenery in central Scotland and ends up (best this way round) in Comrie with
teashops and other pleasures (1761/PICNICS). Leave Muthill by Crieff road turning
left (2km) into Drummond Castle grounds up a glorious avenue of beech trees
(gate open 2-5pm). Visit garden (1547/GARDENS); continue through estate. At gate,
go right, following signs for Strowan. Very quiet road; we have it to ourselves. First
junction, go left following signs (4km). At T-junction, go left to Comrie (7km). Best
have a map, but if not, who cares? It's all bonny!

1729   **The Heads Of Ayr** The coast road south from Ayr to Culzean (1850/CASTLES)
9/K28   and Turnberry (8325/AYRSHIRE HOTELS) includes these headlands, great views of
Ailsa Craig and Arran and some horrible caravan parks. The Electric Brae south of
Dunure village is famously worth stopping on (your car runs the opposite way to
the slope). Culzean grounds are gorgeous.

The Classic Views

For views of and around Edinburgh and Glasgow see p. 85 and p. 132–33. No views from hill or mountain tops are included here.

1730
7/G17
✓ ✓ ✓ **The Quirang** Skye Best approach is from Uig direction taking the right-hand unclassified road off the hairpin of the A855 above and 2km from town signed 'Staffin via Quirang' (more usual approach from Staffin side is less of a revelation). View (and walk) from car park, the massive rock formations of a towering, contorted ridge. Solidified lava heaved and eroded into fantastic pinnacles. Fine views also across Staffin Bay to Wester Ross. (2419/ISLAND WALKS.)

1731
7/J16
✓ ✓ ✓ The views of **An Teallach** and **Liathach** An Teallach, that great favourite of Scottish hill walkers (40km south of Ullapool by the A835/A832), is best viewed from the side of Little Loch Broom or the A832 just before you get to Dundonald.
The classic view of the other great Torridon mountains (**Beinn Eighe**, pronounced 'Ben A', and **Liathach** together, 100km south by road from Ullapool) in Glen Torridon (1713/ SCENIC ROUTES) 4km from Kinlochewe. This viewpoint is not marked but it's on the track around Loch Clair which is reached from the entrance to the Coulin estate off the A896, Glen Torridon road (be aware of stalking). Park outside gate; no cars allowed, 1km walk to lochside. These mountains have to be seen to be believed.

1732
7/G18
2-B-2
✓ ✓ From **Raasay** **www.raasay.com** There are several fabulous views looking over to Skye from Raasay, the small island reached by ferry from Sconser (2358/ MAGICAL ISLANDS). The panorama from Dun Caan, the hill in the centre of the island (444m) is of Munro proportions, producing an elation incommensurate with the small effort required to get there. Start from the road to the 'North End' or ask at the Activity Centre in the big house: the café (and bar).

1733
6/J15
✓ ✓ **The Summer Isles** **www.summer-isles.com** · **Achiltibuie** The Summer Isles are a scattering of islands seen from the coast of Achiltibuie (and the lounge of the Summer Isles Hotel 981/HIGHLANDS HOTELS) and visited by boat from Ullapool. But the best place to see them, and the stunning perspective of this western shore, is on the road to Altandhu, possibly to the pub there. Best approach is: on way to Achiltibuie, turn right through Polbain, past Polbain Stores, on and through Allandhu, past turning for Reiff and Blairbuie, then 500m ascending inland. There's a bench and a new path (sign for 'Viewpoint') 50m to little plateau with many cairns and this one of the ethereal views of Scotland. On this same road 500m round the corner, the distant mountains of Assynt all in a row: 2 gobsmacking perspectives in 5 minutes.

1734
9/K24
✓ ✓ **The Rest and Be Thankful** On A83 Loch Lomond-Inveraray road where it's met by the B828 from Lochgoilhead. In summer the rest may be from driving stress and you may not be thankful for the camera-toting masses, but this was always one of the most accessible, rewarding viewpoints in the land. Surprisingly, none of the encompassing hills are Munros but they are nonetheless dramatic. Only a few carpets of conifer to smother the grandeur of the crags as you look down the valley.

1735
8/P17
✓ **Califer** near Forres 7km from Forres on A96 to Elgin, turn right signed for 'Pluscarden', follow this road for 5km back towards Forres. You are unaware how high above the coastal plain you are and the layby is discreetly located. When

you walk across a small park with young memorial trees you are rewarded with a truly remarkable sight – down across Findhorn Bay and the wide vista of the Moray Firth to the Black Isle and Ben Wyvis. There is often fantastic light on this coast.

1736
7/G19
✓**Elgol Skye** End of the road, the B8083, 22km from Broadford. The classic view of the Cuillins from across Loch Scavaig and of Soay and Rum. Cruises (Apr-Oct) in the *Bella Jane* (0800 731 3089) or *The Misty Isle* (Apr-Oct, not Sun 01471 866288) to the famous corrie of Loch Coruisk, painted by Turner, romanticised by Walter Scott. A journey you'll remember.

1737
9/G21
Camas Nan Geall Ardnamurchan 12km Salen on B8007. 4km from Ardnamurchan's Natural History Centre (1805/KIDS) 65km Fort William. Coming especially from the Kilchoan direction, a magnificent bay appears below you, where the road first meets the sea. Almost symmetrical with high cliffs and a perfect field (still cultivated) in the bowl fringed by a shingle beach. Car park viewpoint and there is a path down. Amazing Ardnamurchan!

1738
7/K20
Glengarry www.glengarry.net 3km after Tomdoun turnoff on A87, Invergarry-Kyle of Lochalsh road. Layby with viewfinder. An uncluttered vista up and down loch and glen with not a house in sight (pity about the salmon cages). Distant peaks of Knoydart are identified, but not Loch Quoich nestling spookily and full of fish in the wilderness at the head of the glen. Gaelic mouthfuls of mountains on the orientation board. Bonnie Prince Charlie passed this way.

1739
7/R27
Scott's View St Boswells Off A68 at Leaderfoot Bridge near St Boswells, signed Gattonside. 'The View', old Walter's favourite (the horses still stopped there long after he'd gone), is 4km along the road (Dryburgh Abbey 3km further; 1978/ABBEYS). Magnificent sweep of his beloved Border country, but only in one direction. If you cross the road and go through the kissing gate at the end of the new layby and head to the left, you reach a track that heads uphill; but when you see the aerials, head south away from them and you reach...

1740
10/R27
Irvine's View St Boswells The full panorama from the Cheviots to the Lammermuirs. This the finest view in southern Scotland. It's only a furlong further than Scott's View, above – across rough pasture (mind the livestock). On a rise, you may see the spiky standing stone which since my last visit has fallen over. Ominous as that may be, this is where I'd like my bench (Borders Council!). The telecoms masts are ghastly but then I'm never without my moby either. Turn your back on them and gaze across the beautiful Borders to another country... you know, England.

1741
10/R27
Peniel Heugh near Ancrum While we're on the subject of great views in the Borders, you may look no further than this – the sentinel Borders symbol. Report: 1928/BEST MONUMENTS.

1742
10/Q23
The Law Dundee Few cities have such a single good viewpoint. To north of the centre, it reveals the panoramic perspective of the city on the estuary of the silvery Tay. Best to walk from town; the one-way system is a nightmare, though there are signposts.

1743
10/N22
Queen's View Loch Tummel near Pitlochry 8km on B8019 to Kinloch Rannoch. Car park and 100m walk to rocky knoll where pioneers of tourism Queen Victoria and Prince Albert were 'transported into ecstasies' by view of Loch Tummel and Schiehallion (1708/LOCHS; 2100/WOODLAND WALKS). Their view was

flooded by a hydro scheme after World War II; more recently it spawned a whole view-driven visitor experience (costing a quid to park). It all... makes you wonder.

1744
10/L23
The Rallying Place of the Maclarens Balquhidder Short climb from behind the church (1971/GRAVEYARDS) along the track 150m then signed Creag an Turc, steep at first. Superb view down Loch Voil, the Balquhidder Braes and the real Rob Roy Country and great caff with home baking on your descent (1488/ COFFEE SHOPS).

1745
11/Q29
The Malcolm Memorial Langholm 3km from Langholm and signed from main A7, a single-track road leads to a path to this obelisk raised to celebrate the military and masonic achievements of one John Malcolm. The eulogy is fulsome especially compared with that for Hugh MacDiarmid on the cairn by the stunning sculpture at the start of the path (1937/MEMORIALS). Views from the obelisk, however, are among the finest in the south, encompassing a vista from the Lakeland Fells and the Solway Firth to the wild Border hills. Path 1km.

1746
9/L25
Duncryne Hill Gartocharn Gartocharn is between Balloch and Drymen on the A811, and this view, was recommended by writer and outdoorsman Tom Weir as 'the finest viewpoint of any small hill in Scotland'. Turn up Duncryne road at the east end of village and park 1km on left by a small wood (a sign reads 'Woods reserved for Teddy bears'). The hill is only 470ft high and 'easy', but the view of Loch Lomond and the Kilpatrick Hills is superb.

1747
10/N27
1-A-2
Blackhill Lesmahagow 28km south of Glasgow. Another marvellous outlook, but in the opposite direction from above. Take junction 10/11 on M74, then off the B7078 signed Lanark, take the B7018. 4km along past Clarkston Farm, head uphill for 1km and park by Water Board mound. Walk uphill through fields to right for about 1km. Unprepossessing hill which unexpectedly reveals a vast vista of most of East Central Scotland (and most of the uphill is in the car).

1748
6/M13
Tongue From the causeway across the kyle, or better, follow the minor road to Talmine on the west side, look south to Ben Loyal or north to the small islands off the coast.

1749
10/N25
Cairnpapple Hill near Linlithgow Volcanic geology, neolithic henge, east Scottish agriculture, the Forth plain, the Bridges, Grangemouth industrial complex and telecoms masts: not all pretty, but the whole of Scotland at a glance. For directions see 1896/PREHISTORIC SITES.

1750
9/J22
Castle Stalker View Portnacroish Near Port Appin on main A828 Oban-Fort William road. On right going south, the view has been commandeered by a café (1485/TEASHOPS) which ain't bad (closed in evenings) but viewpoint can be accessed at all times 50m away from car park. Always impressive, in certain lights the vista of Port Appin, the castle in the fore and Loch Linnhe, is stupendous.

1751
10/R28
Carter Bar English Border near Jedburgh On the A68 Edinburgh-Newcastle road, the last and first view in Scotland just happens to be superb. The Border hill country spread out before you for many long miles. The tear in my eye is not because of the wind, but because this is the landscape of my youth and where I spent my lightsome days.

Summer Picnics & Great Swimming Holes

Care should be taken when swimming in rivers; don't take them for granted. Kids should be watched. Most of these places are traditional local swimming and picnic spots where people have swum for years, but rivers continuously change their course and their nature. Wearing sandals or old sports shoes is a good idea.

1752
7/G19
✓ ✓ **The Fairy Pools Glen Brittle, Skye** On that rare hot day, this is one of the best places on Skye to head for; swimming in deep pools with the massif of the Cuillins around you. One pool has a stone bridge you can swim under. Head off A863 Dunvegan road from Sligachan Hotel then B8009 and Glenbrittle road. 7km down just as road begins to parallel the glen itself, you'll see a river coming off the hills. Park in lay-by on right. 1km walk, follow this up. Lady Clair Macdonald recommends also, the pools at Torrin near Elgol.

1753
9/K22
✓ ✓ **The Pools in Glen Etive** Glen Etive is a wild, enchanted place where people have been camping for years to walk and climb in the Glencoe area. There are many grassy landings at the river side as well as these perfect pools for bathing. The first is about 5km from the main Glencoe road, the A82 at Kingshouse, but just follow the river and find your own. Take midge cream for evening wear. Lots.

1754
7/N19
✓ ✓ **Feshiebridge** At the bridge itself on the B970 between Kingussie and Inverdruie near Aviemore. 4km from Kincraig. Great walks here into Glen Feshie and in nearby woodland, but under bridge a perfect spot for Highland swimming. Go down to left from south. Rocky ledges, clear water. One of the best but cold even in high summer. Further pools nearby, up river.

1755
10/P22
✓ ✓ **Rumbling Bridge & The Braan Walk near Dunkeld** Excellent stretch of cascading river with pools, rocky banks and ledges. Just off A9 heading north opposite first turning for Dunkeld, the A822 for Aberfeldy, Amulree (signed Crieff/Crianlarich). Car park on right after 4km. Connects with forest paths (the Braan Walk) to the Hermitage (2097/WOODLAND WALKS) – 2km. Fab picnic and swimming spot though take great care. This is the nearest Highland-type river to Edinburgh (about 1 hour).

1756
7/M20
✓ ✓ **Strathmashie** www.strathmashie.co.uk · **near Newtonmore** On A86 Newtonmore-Dalwhinnie (on A9) to Fort William road 7km from Laggan, watch for Forest sign. Car parks on either side of the road; the Druim an Aird car park has finder boards. Great swimming spot, but often campers. Viewpoints, waterfall, pines. If people are here don't despair – there are great forest walks and follow the river; there are many other great pools. Great café with home baking 5km towards A9 (1481/TEAROOMS).

1757
9/K23
✓ ✓ **Rob Roy's Bathtub The Fallach Falls near Inverarnan** A82 north of Ardlui and 3 km past The Drover's Inn (1357/BLOODY GOOD PUBS). Sign on the right (Picnic Area) going north. Park, then follow the path. Some pools on the rocky river course but 500m from car park you reach the main falls and below a perfect round natural pool 30m across. There's an overhanging rock face on one side and smooth slabs at the edge of the falls. Natural suntrap in summer, but the water is 'Baltic' at all times.

1758　✓**Neidpath Peebles** 2km from town on A72, Biggar road; sign for castle.
10/Q27　Park by Hay Lodge Park or possibly the lay-by past the castle track
(sometimes by the castle itself). Idyllic setting of a broad meander of the Tweed,
with medieval Neidpath Castle, a sentinel above. Two 'pools' (3m deep in average
summer) linked by shallow rapids which the adventurous chute down on their
backs. Usually a rope-swing at upper pool. TAKE CARE. Also see (2081/GLEN &
RIVER WALKS). Castle open May-Sep, Wed-Sun.

1759　✓**Randolph's Leap near Forres** Spectacular gorge on the mythical
8/N17　Findhorn which carves out some craggy scenery on its way to a gentle coast.
This no-longer secret glade and fabulous swimming hole are behind a wall on a
bend of the B9007 (see 2089/WOODLAND WALKS for directions) south of Forres and
Nairn and near Logie Steading, a courtyard of good things (a board there maps out
walks). There's now a gate and a board. One Randolph or Alistair as the new tale
tells, may have leapt here; we just bathe and picnic under the trees.

1760　**Dog Falls Glen Affric** Half-way along Glen Affric road from Cannich before you
7/K18　come to the loch, a well-marked picnic spot and great place to swim in the peaty
waters surrounded by the Caledonian Forest (with trails). Birds well sussed to picnic
potential – your car covered in tits and cheeky chaffinches – Hitchcock or what?
(2072/GLEN & RIVER WALKS). Falls (rapids really) to the left.

1761　**Near Comrie www.comrie.org.uk** 2 great pools of different character near
10/M23　the neat little town in deepest Perthshire. **The Linn**, the town pool: go over
humpback bridge from main A85 west to Lochearnhead, signed The Ross. Take left
fork then after 2km there's a parking place on left. River's relatively wide, very
pleasant spot. For more adventurous, **Glenartney**, known locally as 'the cliffs': go
over bridge, the Braco road then signed Glenartney, past Cultybraggan training
camp (no longer in use), and then MoD range on left just before the end-of-road
sign (200m after boarded-up cottage on right, 5km from Comrie). Park and walk
down to river in glen. What with the twin perils of the Army and the Comrie
Angling Club, you might feel you have no right to be here, but you do and this
stretch of river is marvellous. Respect the farmland. Follow road further for more
great picnic spots. Comrie has great pub/hotel bistro (954/PERTHSHIRE HOTELS).

1762　**Greeto Falls Gogo Glen, Largs** Well known locally so ask to find Flatt Rd. At
9/K26　top there's a car park and you follow the beautiful Gogo Glen path, past
Cockmalone Cottage. Superb views of the Clyde. 3 pools to choose from in the
Gogo Burn near the bridge.

1763　**North Sannox Burn Arran** Park at the North Sannox Bridge on the A841 (road
9/J27　from Lochranza to Sannox Bay) and follow the track west to the deer fence and
tree line (1km). Just past there you will find a great pool with small waterfall,
dragonflies and perhaps even an eagle or two wheeling above.

1764　**Swimmers' Quarry Easdale** Cross to Easdale on the wee boat (5-minute con-
9/H23　tinuous service); see 2312/HISTORY for details. Do visit the museum but go beyond
scattered houses following paths to slate quarries full of seawater since 1881 with
clear water like an enormous boutique hotel swimming pool. The L-shaped one
with its little bench is easiest, the water blue like the Med.

1765　**Falls of Bruar near Blair Atholl** Just off A9, 12km north of Blair Atholl. 250m
10/N21　walk from **House of Bruar** car park and shopping experience (2252/SHOPPING) to
lower fall (1684/WATERFALLS) where there is an accessible large deep pool by the

bridge. Cold, fresh mountain water in a woody gorge. The proximity of the 'retail experience' can make it all the more... naturally exhilarating.

1766 **The Scout Pool & The Bracklinn Falls** **Callander** The latter are a Callander
10/M24 must-see, easy-to-find (signposted from south end of Main St, up hill to golf course then next car park up – from there it's a 15-minute walk). The Scout Pool is a traditional swimming hole on same river so a summer thing only. Follow road further 5km from Bracklinn car park till road goes on through iron gate. Park on right. Downhill 150m cross wooden bridge then follow river path to right 250m. Access to huge pool dammed by giant boulders, made less easy by storms 2005, but a beautiful secret spot in the woods.

1767 **The Otter's Pool** **New Galloway Forest** A clearing in the forest reached by a
11/L30 track, 'The Raider's Road', running from 8km north of Laurieston on the A762, for 16km to Clatteringshaws Loch. The track, which is only open Apr-Oct, has a toll of £2 and gets busy. It follows the Water of Dee and halfway down the road – the Otter's Pool. A bronze otter used to mark the spot (it got nicked) and it's a place mainly for kids and paddling; but when the dam runs off it can be deep enough to swim. Road closes dusk. (2101/WOODLAND WALKS.)

1768 **Ancrum** **www.ancrum.com** A secret place on the quiet Ale Water (out of vil-
10/R27 lage towards Lilliesleaf, 3km out 250m from farm sign to Hopton – a recessed gate on the right before a bend and a rough track that locals know). A meadow, a Border burn, a surprisingly deep pool to swim. Go to left of rough vegetation in defile, going downhill follow fence on your right. Cross further gate at bottom (only 100m from road). Arcadia awaits!

1769 **Towford** **near Hounam & Jedburgh** Another Borders burn with a surprising
10/S28 pool. This one legendary but hard to find. Deep in the Cheviots, nobody else for miles. It's where I went as a kid. Only the very intrepid tourist ventures here. Ask a local.

1770 **Paradise** **Sheriffmuir near Dunblane** A pool at the foot of an unexpected
10/N24 leafy gorge on the moor between the Ochils and Strathallan. Here the Wharry Burn is known locally as 'Paradise', and for good reason. Take road from 'behind' Dunblane or Bridge of Allan to the Sheriffmuir Inn; head downhill (back) towards Bridge of Allan and park 1km after the hump back bridge. Head for the pylon nearest the river and you'll find the pool. It can be midgy and it can be perfect.

1771 **Potarch Bridge & Cambus o' May** **On The Dee** 2 places on the 'Royal' Dee,
8/Q20 the first by the reconstructed Victorian bridge (and near the hotel) 3km east of Kincardine O'Neill. Cambus another stretch of river east of Ballater (6km). Locals swim, picnic on rocks, etc, and there are forest walks on the other side of road. The brave jump off the bridge at Cambus (and in wetsuits) – best just to watch. Great tearoom nearby – The Black Faced Sheep in Aboyne (1473/TEAROOMS).

1772 **Invermoriston** **www.invermoriston.org** On main Loch Ness road A82
7/L19 between Inverness and Fort Augustus, this is the best bit. River Moriston tumbles under an ancient bridge. Perfectly Highland. Ledges for picnics, invigorating pools, ozone-friendly. Nice beech woods. Follow signs 'Columba's Well', go under the bridge to the 'wee house'. Tavern/bistro nearby (1274/INNS).

1773 **Dulsie Bridge** **near Nairn** 16km south of Nairn on the A939 to Grantown, this
8/N18 locally revered beauty spot is fabulous for summer swimming. The ancient arched

bridge spans the rocky gorge of the Findhorn (again see Randolph's Leap, above) and there are ledges and even sandy beaches for picnics and from which to launch yourself or paddle into the peaty waters.

1774 **Portsoy Pool** **Portsoy, Moray Coast** A natural swimming pool carved from
8/R17 rock and sluiced by the sea. Managed by local swimming club in Jul/Aug; with tea-room. All a bit weather-dependent but wonderful when warm. Go to cliff trail beyond the furthest houses.

1775 **The Trinkie** **Wick** On south edge of town, follow cliff walk up from harbour or
6/Q13 car through housing estate. 2km. Not a river spot of course, but a pool sluiced and filled by the sea within a natural formation of rocks. A bracing stroll, never mind immersion.

Strathcarron near Bonar Bridge Pick your spot (1675/GLENS).

Good Places To Take Kids

CENTRAL

1776 ✓ ✓ ✓ **Edinburgh Zoo** www.edinburghzoo.org.uk · 0131 334 9171 ·
1/XA4 **Corstorphine Road, Edinburgh** 4km west of Princes St. A large
ECO and long-established zoo which is always evolving and where the natural world from the poles to the plains of Africa is ranged around Corstorphine Hill. Enough huge/exotic/ghastly creatures and friendly, amusing ones to fill an overstimulated day. The penguins do their famous parade at 2.15pm. More familiar creatures hang out at the 'farm'. The koalas are cool as... Café and shop stocked with PC toys and souvenirs. Open all year 7 days. Apr-Sep 9am-6pm, Nov-Feb 9am-4.30pm, Oct & Mar 9am-5pm.

✓ ✓ **Our Dynamic Earth** 0131 550 7800 · **Holyrood Road, Edinburgh**
Edinburgh's major kids' attraction. Report 422/MAIN ATTRACTIONS.

✓ ✓ **Museum of Childhood** 0131 529 414242 · **High Street, Edinburgh**
An Aladdin's cave of toys for all ages. 431/OTHER ATTRACTIONS.

1777 ✓ **Edinburgh Butterfly Farm & Insect World** 0131 663 4932 · near
10/Q25 **Dalkeith** · www.edinburgh-butterfly-world.co.uk On A7, signed Eskbank/Galashiels from ring road (1km). Part of a garden centre complex. Beauty and the beasties in a creepy crawly world: the butterflies are delightful but kids will be far more impressed with the scorpions, locusts and other assorted uglies on show. Red-kneed tarantula not for the faint hearted. 7 days, 9.30am-5.30pm (10am-5pm in winter).

✓ **Glasgow Science Centre** www.glasgowsciencecentre.org ·
0141 420 5000 One of Glasgow's most flash attractions. State-of-the-art interactive, landmark tower and Imax. Report: 740/MAIN ATTRACTIONS.

1778 **Gorgie City Farm** www.gorgiecityfarm.org.uk · 0131 337 4202 · **57 Gorgie**
1 **Road, Edinburgh** A working farm on busy road in the heart of the city. Friendly domestic animals, garden and café. All year 9.30m-4.30pm (4pm in winter). Free.

1779 **Yellowcraigs near Dirleton** Beautiful beach 35km east of Edinburgh via A1,
10/R25 the A198, though Dirleton village then right, for 2km. Expanding car park to cope
with increasing popularity of lovely, scenic beach and dunes (455/EDINBURGH
BEACHES). Recent 'Treasure Island' play pond in the woods is great for kids. Activity
and sea air!

1780 **The Edinburgh Dungeon** www.thedungeons.com · 0131 240 1000 ·
1/D2 **31 Market Street, Edinburgh** Multimillion très contrived experience takes you
through a ghoulish history of Scottish nasties. Hammy of course, but kids will love
the monorail. Times vary.

1781 **Auchingarrich Wildlife Centre** www.auchingarrich.co.uk · **near Comrie**
10/M23 4km from main street turning off at bridge then signed. Sympathetic corralling in
ECO picturesque Perthshire Hills. Excellent for kids. Huge playbarn. Daily hatchings and
lots of baby fluffy things, some of which you can hold. Don't ask what happens to
them when they grow up! Good place to start sex education. Heaps of lovable animals; meerkats especially wonderful. All year 10am-dusk. Coffee shop till 5pm.

1782 **Kelburn Country Centre** www.kelburncountrycentre.com · **Largs** 2km
9/K26 south of Largs on A78. Riding school, gardens, woodland walks up the Kel Burn
and a central visitor/consumer section with shops/exhibits/cafés. Wooden stock-
ade for clambering kids; indoor playbarn with quite scary slides. Falconry displays
(those long-suffering owls). 'The Plaisance' indeed a pleasant place. Stock up on
ice cream at Nardini's caff near the Cumbrae ferry. New 'attraction' 07/08: the
Griffith Art Project whereby the venerable towerhouse/castle is disneyfied by some
'artist' from far away. 7 days 10am-6pm. Apr-Oct. Grounds only in winter 11-dusk.

✓ ✓ **Falkirk Wheel Falkirk** 4/MAIN ATTRACTIONS.

FIFE & DUNDEE
1783 ✓ **Deep Sea World** www.deepseaworld.com · 01383 411880 · **North**
10/P25 **Queensferry** The aquarium in a quarry which may be reaching its swim-by
date. Park 'n' ride system and buses from Edinburgh, or better still by *Maid of the
Forth* from South Queensferry (9/FAVOURITE JOURNEYS). Habitats are viewed from a
conveyor belt where you can stare at the fish and diverse divers teeming around
and above you. Maximum hard sell to this all-weather attraction 'the shark
capital', but kids like it even when they've been queueing for aeons. Cute seals and
sharp sharks! Cafe is fairly awful, but nice views. Open all year 7 days 10am-5pm;
weekends till 6pm (last entry 1 hour before).

1784 ✓ **Sensation** www.sensation.org.uk · 01382 228800 · **Dundee**
10/Q23 Greenmarket across roundabout from Discovery Point and adjacent DCA
(2337/GALLERIES). Purpose-built indoor kids info-tainment attraction. With basis in
Dundee's 'Discover Yourself' and 'Scientific Centre of Excellence' claims, this is an
innovative and very interactive games room with a message. We all learn
something. 7 days 10am-closing varies. Average visit time 2-3 hours.

☕ ✓ **Verdant Works** 01382 225282 · **West Henderson's Wynd, Dundee**
Near Westport. Heritage museum that recreates workings of a jute mill.
Sounds dull, but brilliant for kids and grown-ups. Report: 2308/MUSEUMS.

1785 ✓ **Craigton Park** 01334 473666 · **St Andrews** 3km southwest of St
10/R23 Andrews on the Pitscottie road (enter via Dukes Golf Course). An oasis of fun:
bouncy castles, trampolines, putting, crazy golf, boating lake, a train through the

grounds, adventure playgrounds and glasshouses. A perfect day's amusement especially for nippers. Easter-Sep 10.30am-5.30pm. Entrance charge covers all attractions.

1786
10/Q23
✓ **Cairnie Fruit Farm & Maze** 01334 655610 · near **Cupar** Leave town by minor road from main street heading towards then past the hospital; it is signed (4km), or from main A92; signed near Kilmany (3km). A fruit and farm shop/café (1550/FARM SHOPS), but huge popularity due to kids' play area using farm materials (bales etc) to amuse kids and get them countrified. The maze in the maize field is major. Then there's strawberries for tea! Apr-Oct 10am-5pm (closed Mon in Sep).

1787
10/Q23
Camperdown Park www.camperdownpark.com · **Dundee** The large park just off the ring-road system (the Kingsway and via A923 to Coupar Angus) with a wildlife centre and a nearby play complex. Animal-handling at weekends. 'Over 80 species' bears, bats and wolves! Open all year, but centre 10am-4.30pm, earlier in winter (1633/TOWN PARKS).

SOUTH & SOUTH WEST

1788
11/M31
ECO
✓ ✓ **Cream o' Galloway** www.creamogalloway.co.uk · **Rainton** There is something inherently good about a visitor attraction that is based on the incontrovertible fact that human beings love ice cream. Especially when it's presented with a 'pure and simple' message, an organic café, a herb garden and a fab adventure playground in the woods, part of 5km of child-friendly nature trails. Let's hear it for cows! All year 10am-6pm. Report: 1521/ICE CREAM.

1789
9/L27
✓ **Kidz Play** www.kidz-play.co.uk · 01292 475215 · **Prestwick** Off main street at Station Road, past station to beach and to right. Big shed soft play area for kids. Everything the little blighters will like in the throwing-themselves-around department. Shriek city. Sun-Thu 9.30am-7pm. Fri-Sat 9.30am-7.30pm.

1790
10/L27
✓ **Loudoun Castle** www.loudouncastle.co.uk · near **Galston** Theme park with big ambitions south of Glasgow. Off A71 Kilmarnock-Edinburgh road or from Glasgow via M77, then A719. Behind the ruins of the said Loudoun Castle (burned out in 1941), a fairground which includes the 'largest carousel in Europe' and things called The Rat and Loggers' Leap, has been transplanted in the old walled garden. 'Farm' area and birds-of-prey demos. Nice setting. open Easter-Sep.

1791
10/M25
Palacerigg Country Park www.northlan.gov.uk · 01236 720047 · **Cumbernauld** 6km east of Cumbernauld. 740 acres of parkland; ranger service, nature trails, picnic area and kids farm. 18-hole golf course and putting green. Exhibition area with changing exhibits about forestry, conservation etc. Open all year 7 days; daylight hours. Visitor centre and tearoom.

✓ ✓ **Drumlanrig Castle** near **Dumfries** 1613/COUNTRY PARKS.

NORTH EAST

1792
8/R17
✓ **Macduff Marine Aquarium** www.macduff-aquarium.org.uk On the seafront east of the harbour, a family attraction for this Moray Firth port. It's under-rated, perhaps because neighbouring Banff gets more attention from tourists, but Duff House (2342/GALLERIES) gets fewer visitors than this user- and child-friendly sea-life centre. All fish seem curiously happy with their lot and content to educate and entertain. Open all year 10am-5pm (last admission 4.15pm).

1793
8/S20 ✓ **Storybook Glen www.storybookglenaberdeen.co.uk · near Aberdeen**
Fibreglass fantasy land in verdant glen 16km south of Aberdeen via B9077,
the South Deeside road, a nice drive. Characters from every fairy tale and nursery
story dotted around 20-acre park. Their fixed manic stares give them a spooky
resemblance to people you know. Older kids may find it tame: no guns, no big
technology but nice for little 'uns. Indoor play area. 7 days, 10am-6pm (5pm in
winter), weather permitting. There are also wonderful gardens.

1794
8/T19 ✓ **Satrosphere www.satrosphere.net · Aberdeen** Near beach (off Beach
Boulevard, near Patio Hotel), Scotland's 'original interactive science centre'.
Hands on, it is! Granny will learn as much as she can take in. All year 7 days 10am-
5pm.

1795
8/T18 **Aden www.aberdeenshire.gov.uk · Mintlaw** (Pronounced 'Ah-den'). Country
park just beyond Mintlaw on A950 16km from Peterhead. Former grounds of
mansion with walks and organised activities and events. Farm buildings converted
into Heritage Centre (kids free), café etc. Adventure playground. All year.

HIGHLANDS & ISLANDS

1796
7/N19 ✓ **The Cairngorm Reindeer Herd 01479 861228 · Glenmore near**
ECO   **Aviemore · www.reindeer-company.demon.co.uk** At Glenmore Forest
Park 12km Aviemore along Coylumbridge Rd, 100m behind Glenmore visitor centre. Stop at Centre (shop, exhibition) to buy tickets and follow the guide in your
vehicle up the mountain. From here, 20-minute walk. Real reindeer aplenty in
authentic free-ranging habitat (when they come down off the cloudy hillside in
winter with snow all around). They've come a long way from Sweden (in 1952). 1
hour 30 minute trip. They are so... small. 11am all year plus 2.30pm in summer.
Wear appropriate footwear and phone if weather looks threatening.

1797
7/N19 ✓ **Leault Farm www.leaultfarm.co.uk · near Kincraig** On the main A9,
but easier to find by looking for sign 1km south of Kincraig on the B9152.
Working farm with daily sheepdog trials demonstrating an extraordinary facility
with dogs and sheep (and ducks). A great spectacle and totally authentic in this
setting. Usually 4pm (possibly other times, check tourist information centre).
Closed Sat.

1798
7/N19 ✓ **Landmark Centre www.landmark-centre.co.uk · 01479 841614 ·**
Carrbridge A purpose-built tourist centre with audiovisual displays and a
great deal of shopping. Great for kids messing about in the woods on slides, in a
'maze' etc, in a large adventure playground, Microworld or (especially squealy) the
Wildwater Coaster. The Tower may be too much for Granny but there are fine forest views. Open all year 7 days till 6pm (5pm in winter, 7pm mid Jul-mid Aug).

1799
7/N19 **The Highland Wildlife Park www.highlandwildlifepark.org · 01540**
ECO   **651270 · Kincraig** On B9152 between Aviemore and Kingussie. Large drive-
through 'reserve' run by Royal Zoological Society with wandering herds of deer,
bison etc and pens of other animals. 'Habitats', but mostly cages. Cute little,
vicious little wildcats! Must be time to bring back bears, let the wolves go free and
liven up the caravan parks. Open 10am-6pm (Jul/Aug 7pm, winter 4pm).

1800
9/F26 **Islay Wildlife Information & Field Centre www.islay.co.uk · 01496**
ECO   **850288 · Port Charlotte** Fascinating wildlife centre, activities and day trips.
(1845/WILDLIFE; 2426/ISLAY). Excellent for getting kids interested in wildlife. Then
go find it! Apr-Oct 10am-3pm. Closed Sat (Jul/Aug 7 days 10am-5pm).

1801
9/H22
ECO

Wings Over Mull www.wingsovermull.com · 01680 812594 · **near Craignure, Mull** Off main road south of Duart (1857/CASTLES). Whatever you think about falconry, this is a wonderful place for kids and wide-eyed adults to see these elusive birds of prey up close and over 20 other species including all the native owls (over 40 birds in total). Regular flying displays and birds on perches – they squawk and cheep and mainly sleep; happy enough I suppose and at least 'conserved'. They're very emphatic about their preservation/rehabilitation work. Meanwhile swallows soar above. Apr-Oct 7 days.

1802
9/H22

Mull Railway & Torosay Castle 01680 812494 · **Mull** See it as the Balamory Express? Well: this is a long-established chugalong train from the ferry at Craignure to Torosay Gardens and Castle. 20-minute journey. Lovely way to get there and lovely when you do (1858/CASTLES). A must, really! Apr-Oct.

1803
9/H23
ECO

The Scottish Sealife Sanctuary www.sealsanctuary.co.uk · 01631 720386 · **Oban** 16km north on the A828. On the shore of Loch Creran, one of the oldest UK waterworlds still the best (another unrelated in **St Andrews**). Environmentally conscientious, they 'rescue' seals and house numerous aquatic life. Various aquaria, all kinds of fish going round, multi-level viewing otter enclosure and the seal thing. Feeding times posted – a theatrical experience. Café/shop/adventure playground. Open summer, 10am-6pm. Call for winter hours.

1804
9/H23

Rare Breeds Farm www.obanrarebreeds.com · **Oban** 4km from town via Argyll Sq, then south (A816), bearing left at church, past golf course – suddenly you're in wild hill country. Weird and wonderful collection of animals in hill side pens and runs and a touchy-feely barn, who seem all the more peculiar because they're versions of familiar ones. Leaving the caging questions aside, it's a funny farm for kids and the creatures seem keen enough for the attention and crumbs from the tearoom table. 7 days Apr-Oct.

1805
9/G21
ECO

Natural History Centre www.ardnamurchannaturalhistorycentre.co.uk · 01972 500209 · **Ardnamurchan** A861 Strontian, B8007 Glenmore 14km. Photographer Michael McGregor's award-winning interactive exhibition (under different owners). Kids will enjoy, adults may be impressed. A walk-through of wildlife including live pine martens (if you're lucky) and CCTV of more cautious creatures. Tearoom. Mon-Sat 10.30am-5.30pm, Sun 12noon-5.30pm.

1806
7/M20

Highland Folk Museum www.highlandfolk.com · 01540 661307 · **Kingussie & Newtonmore** Final word in this section to Calum (6½) and Katie (2) who'll be a bit older now but who loved this place (they visited the latter). 'Brilliant play park, old school'. Katie liked the chickens and the waterwheel. They spent 5 hours there among the 250 years of rural life. These 2 sites are separate. Hours changing but 7 days Apr-Oct.

The Best Places To See Birds

See p. 314–15 for Wildlife Reserves, many of which are good for bird-watching.

1807
6/K13

✔✔ **Handa Island** www.swt.org.uk · **near Scourie** Take the boat from Tarbet Pier 6km off A894 5km north of Scourie and land on a beautiful island run by the Scottish Wildlife Trust as a nature reserve. Boats (Apr-early Sep though fewer birds after Aug) are continuous depending on demand (01971 502347). Crossing 30 minutes. Small reception hut and 2.5km walk over island to cliffs which rise 350m and are layered in colonies from fulmars to shags. Allow 3 to 4 hours. Though you must take care not to disturb the birds, you'll be eye to eye with seals and bill to bill with razorbills. Eat at the seafood café on the cove when you return (1433/SEAFOOD RESTAURANTS). Mon-Sat only (some Suns in summer). Last return 5pm.

1808
11/P30
ADMISSION
ECO

✔✔ **Caerlaverock** www.wwt.org.uk · **near Dumfries** 17km south on B725 near Bankend, signed from road. The WWT Caerlaverock Wetlands Centre (01387 770200) is an excellent place to see whooper swans, barnacle geese and more (countless hides, observatories, viewing towers). Has Fair Trade café as well as farmhouse-style accommodation for up to 14. More than just birds too: natterjack toads, badgers so not just for twitchers. Eastpark Farm, Caerlaverock. Centre open daily all year 10am-5pm.

1809
9/F22

✔✔ **Lunga & The Treshnish Islands** www.hebrideantrust.org · **off Mull** Sail from Iona or Fionnphort or Ulva ferry on Mull to these uninhabited islands on a 5/6-hour excursion which probably takes in Staffa and Fingal's Cave. Best months are May-Jul when birds are breeding. Talk of pufflings not making it because their parents can't find sand eels seems premature here. Some trips allow 3 hours on Lunga. Razorbills, guillemots and a carpet of puffins oblivious to your presence. This will be a memorable day. Boat trips (Ulva Ferry 08000 858786; or 01681 700338 from Fionnphort) or ring Tobermory tourist information centre (01688 302182) who will advise of other boatmen. All trips dependent on sea conditions.

1810
10/R24

✔✔ **Isle of May** www.nlb.org.uk · **Firth of Forth** Island at mouth of Forth off Crail/ Anstruther reached by daily boat trip from Anstruther Harbour (01333 310054), May-Oct 9am-2.30pm depending on tides. Boats hold 40-50; trip 45 minutes; allows 3 hours ashore. Can reserve (the day before) but no credit cards. Island (including isthmus to Rona) 1.5km x 0.5km. Info centre and resident wardens. See guillemots, razorbills and kittiwakes on cliffs and shags, terns and thousands of puffins. Most populations increasing. This place is strange as well as beautiful. The puffins in early summer are, as always, engaging.

1811
10/P22
ECO

✔✔ **Loch of the Lowes Dunkeld** 4km northeast Dunkeld on A923 to Blairgowrie. Superbly managed (Scottish Wildlife Trust) site with double-floored hide (always open) and new hide (same hours as visitor centre) and permanent binoculars. Main attractions are the captivating ospreys (from early Apr-Aug). Nest 100m over loch and clearly visible. Their revival (now over 260 pairs in UK) is well documented, including diary of movements, breeding history etc. Also the near-at-hand endless fascination of watching wild birds including woodpeckers, and red squirrels feeding outside the picture window is a real treat. Last time I saw all of the above and 2 jays. What a treat!

1812   ✓ **The Scottish Ornithologists Club House** www.the-soc.org.uk ·
10/Q25   **near Aberlady** On the A198 on the left going into Aberlady from Edinburgh
ECO   side, opposite Gosford Estate (not well signed at TGP). Not a birdwatching site per se (though between the Lagoon and the Seabirds Centre, below and near Aberlady Reserve 2km), but an archive and library and resource centre for all things related to and for lovers of Scottish birds. Beautiful, light modern building looks across bay to reserve. Art exhibitions and much to browse. Friendly staff. Soc are publishing the definitive book *Birds of Scotland* early '08. Open 10am-4pm (12-6pm weekends in summer). Go in October, late afternoon, when the geese come in.

1813   ✓ **The Lagoon Musselburgh** On east edge of town behind the racecourse
10/Q25   (follow road round, take turn-off signed Race Course Parking), at the estuarine mouth of the River Esk. Waders, sea birds, ducks aplenty and often interesting migrants on the mudflats and wide littoral. The 'lagoon' itself is a man-made pond behind with hide and attracts big populations (both birds and binocs). This is the nearest diverse-species area to Edinburgh (15km) and in recent years has become one of the most significant migrant stopovers in the UK.

1814   ✓ **Fowlsheugh** www.rspb.org.uk · **near Stonehaven** 8km south of
10/S21   Stonehaven and signed from A92 with path from Crawton. Sea-bird city on 2km of red sandstone cliffs up to 200' high; take great care. 80,000 pairs of 6 species especially guillemots, kittiwakes, razorbills and also fulmar, shag, puffins. Possible to view the birds without disturbing them and see the 'layers' they occupy on the cliff face. Best seen May-Jul.

1815   ✓ **Loch Garten** www.lochgarten.co.uk · **Boat of Garten** 3km village off
8/N19   B970 into Abernethy Forest. Famous for the ospreys and signed from all
ECO   round. Best Apr-Jun. 2 car parks: the first has nature trails through Scots pine woods and around loch; other has visitor centre with the main hide 250m away: TV screens, binoculars, other wild-bird viewing and informed chat. One pair of birds did wonders for local tourism. Och, but they are magnificent.

1816   ✓ **Loch Gruinart, Loch Indaal Islay** RSPB reserve. Take A847 at Bridgend
9/F25   then B8017 turning north and right for Gruinart. The mudflats and fields at
ECO   the head of the loch provide winter grazing for huge flocks of Barnacle and Greenland geese. They arrive, as do flocks of fellow bird-watchers, in late Oct. Hides and good vantage points near road. The Rhinns and the Oa in the south sustain a huge variety of bird life.

1817   ✓ **Marwick Head** www.rspb.org.uk · **Orkney Mainland** 40km northwest
3/P10   of Kirkwall, via Finstown and Dounby; take left at Birsay after Loch of Isbister cross the B9056 and park at Cumlaquoy. Spectacular sea bird breeding colony on 100m cliffs and nearby at the Loons Reserve, wet meadowland, 8 species of duck and many waders. Orkney sites include the Noup cliffs on Westray, North Hill on Papa Westray and Copinsay, 3km east of the mainland. The remoter, the merrier.

1818   **Isle of Mull** www.isle.of.mull.com Sea eagles. Since the reintroduction of
9/H22   these magnificent eagles, there is now a hide with CCTV viewing. By appt only. Site changes every year. Contact Forest Enterprise (01631 566155) or ask at the tourist information centre.

1819   **Orkney Puffins** 'Wildabout' tour's dusk puffin patrol (01856 851011). Or go solo
3/Q10   at Costa Head, Brough of Birsay and Westray; check Kirkwall tourist information centre for latest.

1820   **The Bass Rock** www.nlb.org.uk · 01620 892838 · **off North Berwick**
10/R25   'Temple of gannets'. A guano-encrusted massif sticking out of the Forth and where Davie Balfour was imprisoned in RLS's *Catriona* (aka *Kidnapped II*). Weather-dependent boat trips available May-Sep courtesy of Fred Marr and the *Sula II*, from North Berwick harbour (also to nearby Fidra). See daily board of sailings at the harbour. Also possible to visit in small groups via the Seabirds Centre (see below). Phone for details. (01620 892838 or 890202).

1821   **Scottish Seabirds Centre** www.seabird.org · 01620 890202 · **North**
10/R25   **Berwick** Award-winning, interactive visitor attraction near Harbour overlooking
   ECO   Bass Rock and Fidra. Video and other state-of-the-art technology makes you feel as if the birds are next to you. Viewing deck for dramatic perspective of gannets diving (140kmph!) Excellent teashop (seafood especially). 10am-6pm (4pm winter/5.30pm weekends).

1822   **Montrose Basin Wildlife Centre** www.swt.org.uk · 01674 676336 1.5km
10/S22   south of Montrose on the A92 to Arbroath. Very accessible Scottish Wildlife Trust centre overlooks the estuarine basin that hosts various residents and migrants. Good for twitchers and kids. And autumn geese. Apr-Oct daily 10.30am-5pm. Call for winter hours.

1823   **Forsinard Nature Reserve** www.caithness.org · 01641 571225 By road,
6/N13   44km from Helmsdale on the A897, or the train stops on route to Wick/Thurso. RSPB (proposed World Heritage Site) reserve, acquired in '95 following public appeal. 17, 500 acres of the 'Flow Country' and the birds that go with it: divers, plovers, merlins and hen harriers (CCTV pics). Guided walks avail. Reserve open all year; visitor centre Apr-Oct daily 9am-6pm.

1824   **Loch of Kinnordy** www.rspb.org.uk · Kirriemuir 4km west of town on B951,
10/Q22   an easily accessible site with 3 hides overlook loch and wetland area managed by RSPB. Geese in late autumn, gulls aplenty; always tickworthy. You may see the vanishing ruglet butterfly.

1825   **Piperdam Golf & Country Park** www.piperdam.com · 01382 581374 ·
10/Q23   **Fowlis by Dundee** This expensive housing development overlooking loch also attracts the upwardly mobile osprey. Good viewing centre. Other upmarket residents include short-eared owls and reed buntings. All enjoy our suburbias.

1826   **Strathbeg** www.rspb.org.uk · **near Fraserburgh** 12km south off main
8/T17   Fraserburgh-Peterhead road, the A952 and signed 'Nature Reserve' at Crimond. Wide, shallow loch very close to coastline, a 'magnet for migrating wildfowl' and from the (unmanned) reception centre at loch side it's possible to get a very good view of them. Marsh/fen, dune and meadow habitats. In winter 30,000 geese/widgeon/mallard/swans and occasional rarities like cranes and egrets. Binoculars in centre and other hides (Towerpool hide is 1km walk).

1827   **Troupe Head between Macduff and Rosehearty, Moray Firth** Near the
8/S17   cliff-clinging villages of Crovie and ill-fated Pennan. Fantastic airy walk from the former (2125/COASTAL WALKS). Puffins, kittiwakes, the whole shebang; and dolphins.

Where To See Dolphins, Whales, Porpoises & Seals

✔ ✔ *The coast around the North of Scotland offers some of the best places in Europe from which to see whales and dolphins and, more ubiquitously, seals. You don't have to go on boat trips, though of course you get closer, the boatman will know where to find them and the trip itself can be exhilarating. Good operators are listed below. Dolphins are most active on a rising tide especially May-Sep.*

MORAY & CROMARTY FIRTHS (near Inverness)

The best area in Scotland. The population of bottlenose dolphins in this area well exceeds 100 and they can be seen all year (though mostly Jun-Sep).

1828 **The Dolphins & Seals of the Moray Firth Centre** 01463 731866 or 01343
7/M18 820339 Just north of the Kessock Bridge on the A9 and adjacent the tourist information centre (01463 731701). Underwater microphones pick up the chatterings of dolphins and porpoises and there's always somebody there to explain. They keep an up-to-date list of recent sightings and all cruises available. Summer only Mon-Sat 9.30am-4.30pm.

1829 **Cromarty** Any vantage around the town is good especially South Sutor for
7/M17 coastal walk and an old lighthouse cottage has been converted into a research station run by Aberdeen Uni. **Chanonry Point, Fortrose**, east end of point beyond lighthouse is the *best* place to see dolphins from land in Britain. Occasional sightings can also be seen at **Balintore**, opposite Seaboard Memorial Hall; **Tarbert Ness** beyond **Portmahomack**, end of path through reserve further out along the Moray Firth possible at **Burghead**, **Lossiemouth** and **Buckie**, **Spey Bay** and **Portknockie**.
Also check the Dolphin Space Programme, an accreditation scheme for boat operators: www.dolphinspace.org

NORTH WEST

On the West Coast, especially near Gairloch the following places may offer sightings of orcas, dolphins and minke whales mainly in summer.

1830 **Rubha Reidh near Gairloch** 20km north by unclassified road beyond Melvaig.
7/H16 Near the Carn Dearg Youth Hostel west of Lonemore where road turns inland is good spot.

1831 **Greenstone Point north of Laide** On the A832 near Inverewe Gardens and
6/J16 Gruinard Bay. Harbour porpoises here Apr-Dec and minke whales May-Oct.

1832 **Red Point of Gairloch** By unclassified road via Badachro. High ground looking
7/H16 over North Minch and south to Loch Torridon. Harbour porpoises often along this coast.

1833 **Rubha Hunish Skye** The far northwest finger of Skye. Walk from Duntulm
7/F18 Castle or Flodigarry. Dolphins and mink whales in autumn.

OTHER PLACES

1834 **Mousa Sound Shetland** 20km south of Lerwick (1892/PREHISTORIC SITES).
4/V4

1835
9/G21
Ardnamurchan **The Point** The most westerly point (and lighthouse) on this wildly beautiful peninsula. Go to end of road or park near Sanna Beach and walk round. Sanna Beach worth going to just to walk the strand. Visitor centre; tearoom.

1836
5/E14
Stornoway **Isle of Lewis** Heading out of town for Eye Peninsula, at Holm near Sandwick south of A866 or from Bayble Bay (all within walking distance).

The Best Sealife Cruises

Eco Ventures www.ecoventures.co.uk · 01381 600323 · **Cromarty** Intimate and informative tours, but pricey. 2 trips per day all year. Booking essential.

Moray Firth Cruises www.inverness-dolphin-cruises.co.uk · 01463 717900 · **Inverness** 4 trips per day Mar-Oct.

Gemini Explorer Buckie · 07747 626280 More Moray Firth cruising in former lifeboat. Good facilities.

Gairloch Marine Wildlife Centre & Cruises 01445 712636 · **Gairloch** Well-established and eco-credible operator in interesting West Coast area.

Summer Isles Cruises www.summer-isles-cruises.co.uk · 01854 622200 Seals and seabirds abound round these beautiful islands. 2 trips per day plus all-day special.

Hebridean Wildlife Cruises 01680 814260 · **Oban** 3 cruise vessels out of Oban for big range of island destinations including St Kilda. Food and accommodation. Maximum 12.

Wildlife Cruises www.jogferry.co.uk · 01955 611353 · **John o' Groats** Puffins, seabirds, seals. 2.30pm daily Jun-Sep. Large panoramic boat. Also all-day trips to Orkney from John o' Groats and Inverness.
Sea.Fari Adventures www.seafari.co.uk Based in **Edinburgh** · 0131 331 4857, **Oban** · 01852 300003 & **Skye** · 01471 833316 Sealife adventure boating specialists. Range of eco-tours and trips in fast, inflatable boats. Sailing out of **Easdale, Isle of Seil** 25km south Oban.

ON THE ISLANDS
Sea-Life Surveys www.sealifesurveys.com · **Tobermory, Mull** · 01688 400223 Various packages from relaxed half-hour trip to the more intense 8-hour. Small groups on comfortable boat and high-speed boats. Good percentage of porpoise, dolphin and whale sightings.

Turus Mara www.turusmara.com · 08000 858786 · **Mull** Daytrips from Ulva Ferry. Various itineraries taking in bird colonies of Treshnish Isles, Staffa and Iona. Dolphins, whales, puffins and seals.

Whale Watching 01688 302916 · **Dervaig, Mull** 12-passenger MV *Flamer* leaves daily from Croig 5km Dervaig. Full day at sea.

Shetland Wildlife & The Company of Whales 01950 422483 · **Shetland** · www.shetlandwildlife.co.uk From day trips to 7-day wildlife holidays. Sealife, birds, whales and otters.

Bressaboats Shetland · **01595 693434** Award-winning wildlife adventure cruises.

Island Cruising www.island-cruising.com · **01851 672381** · **Lewis** Wildlife, birdwatching and diving cruises around the Western Isles and St Kilda.

Seatrek www.seatrek.co.uk · **01851 672464** · **Uig, Lewis** 2.5 hour excursions from 3 western berths destinations. A purist experience.

Islay Marine Charters **01496 850436** · **Islay** Trips on Sound of Islay, round Jura, Colonsay. Fishing and whale watching.

There are two glass-bottom boat companies offering trips in **Skye**.
Family's Pride II www.glassbottomboat.co.uk · **0800 7832175** operate from Broadford Pier and concentrate on the reefs round the local islands.
Seaprobe Atlantis **0800 9804846** based on the mainland at Kyle (over the bridge), stays around Kyle of Lochalsh (conservation) area. Sit underwater in the 'gallery' so better viewing advantage.

WILDLIFE TOURS

Island Encounter Wildlife Safaris www.mullwildlife.co.uk · **01680 300441** · **Mull** All-day tour with local expert. Possible sightings of otters, eagles, seals and falcons. Numerous pick-up points including ferry terminals.

Isle of Mull Wildlife Expeditions www.torrbuan.com · **01688 500121** · **Mull** Long-established personal day-long trips (collected from ferry). Nice.

Wildabout www.wildaboutorkney.com · **01856 851011** · **Orkney** Various trips with experienced guides. Wildlife plus history and folklore. Interactive.

Out & About Tours **01851 612288** · **Lewis** Former countryside ranger leads groups of all sizes on guided walks and day trips of Lewis and Harris. Experience the landscape, culture and wildlife of the islands.

Calum's Seal Trips www.calums-sealtrips.com · **01599 544306** · **Plockton** Wildlife watching doesn't get tamer than this (or the animals) but nice for the kids and the coast around Plockton is stunning. You may see an otter! Check locally for departures.

Otters can be seen all over the northwest Highlands in sheltered inlets, especially early morning and late evening and on an ebb tide. Skye is one of best places in Europe to see them. Go with:
International Otter Survival Fund www.otter.org · **01471 822487** · **Broadford** They organise courses and trips for all wildlife and might point you in the right direction.

Otter Haven www.forestry.gov.uk · **Kylerhea** Basically a viewing hide with CCTV, binoculars and a knowledgeable warden (not always there). Seabirds and seals too and a forest walk. 500m walk along a track from car park signposted on road out of Kylerhea (and from the ferry from Glenelg – 7/JOURNEYS).

Great Wildlife Reserves

These wildlife reserves are not merely bird-watching places. Most of them are easy to get to from major centres; none requires permits.

1837
10/S25
✓✓ **St Abb's Head** www.nlb.org.uk · **near Berwick** 22km North Berwick, 9km north Eyemouth and 10km east of main A1. Spectacular cliff scenery (2121/COASTAL WALKS), a huge sea bird colony, rich marine life and varied flora. Good view from top of stacks, geos and cliff face full of serried ranks of guillemot, kittiwake, razorbill etc. Hanging gardens of grasses and campion. Behind cliffs, grassland rolls down to the Mire Loch and its varied habitat of bird, insect, butterfly life and vegetation. The coffee shop at the car park does a mean scone-stock for the walk!

1838
8/T19
ECO
✓✓ **Sands of Forvie & the Ythan Estuary** www.jncc.gov.uk · **Newburgh** 25km north Aberdeen. Cross bridge outside Newburgh on A975 to Cruden Bay and park. Path follows Ythan estuary, bears north and enters the largest undisturbed dune system in the UK. Dunes in every aspect of formation. Collieston, a 17/18th-century fishing village, is 5km away. These habitats support the largest population of eiders in UK (especially Jun) and huge numbers of terns. It's easy to get lost here, so get lost!

1839
7/J17
ECO
✓ **Beinn Eighe** Bounded by the A832 and A896 west of Kinlochewe, this first National Nature Reserve in Britain includes a remaining fragments of old Caledonian pinewood on the south shore of Loch Maree and rises to the rugged tops with their spectacular views and varied geology. Excellent wood and mountain trails. Best approach via Glen Torridon (1713/SCENIC ROUTES). Start from roadside car park (on A832 beyond Loch Clair). 3km nearer the village on this road is a visitor centre.

1840
10/R25
ECO
John Muir Country Park www.eastlothian.gov.uk · **Dunbar** Vast park between Dunbar and North Berwick named after the Dunbar-born father of the conservation movement. Includes estuary of the Tyne (park also known as Tyninghame), cliffs, sand spits and woodland. Many bird species. crabs, lichens, sea and marsh plants. Enter at east extremity of Dunbar at Belhaven, off the B6370 from A1; or off A198 to North Berwick 3km from A1. Or better, walk from Dunbar by 'cliff top trail' (2km).

1841
9/L26
RSPB
Lochwinnoch www.lochwinnoch.info 30km southwest of Glasgow via M8 junction 28A then A737 past Johnstone onto A760. Also from Largs 20km via A760. Reserve just outside village on lochside and comprises wetland and woodland habitats. A serious 'nature centre' incorporating an observation tower. Hides and marked trails; and a birds-spotted board. Shop and coffee shop. Events programme. Good for kids. Visitor centre open daily 10am-5pm.

1842
7/M20
Insh Marshes www.rspb.org.uk · **Kingussie** 4km from town along B970 (past Ruthven Barracks, 1884/RUINS), 2500 acres of Spey floodplain run by RSPB. Trail (3km) marked out through meadow and wetland and a note of species to look out for (including 6 types of orchid, 7 'red list' birds and half the UK population of goldeneye). Also 2 hides (250m and 450m) high above marshes, vantage points to see waterfowl, birds of prey, otters and deer. Declared a National Nature Reserve in 2003.

1843
10/R23
Tentsmuir www.forestry.gov.uk · **between Newport & Leuchars** North tip of Fife at the mouth of the Tay, reached from Tayport or Leuchars via the B945. Follow signs for Kinshaldy Beach taking road that winds for 4km over flat then

forested land. Park (car park closes 9pm in summer) and cross dunes to broad strand. Walks in both direction: west back to Tayport, east to Leuchars. Also 4km circular walk of beach and forest. Hide 2km away at Ice House Pond. Seals often watch from waves and bask in summer. Lots of butterflies. Waders aplenty and, to the east, one of UK's most significant populations of eider. Most wildfowl offshore. (Ranger: 01334 473047.)

1844 **Vane Farm www.rspb.org.uk · Loch Leven** RSPB reserve on south shore of
10/P24 Loch Leven, beside and bisected by B9097 off junction 5 of M90. Easily reached
☕ and very busy visitor centre with observation lounge and education/orientation
ECO facilities. Hide nearer loch side reached by tunnel under road. Nature Trail on hill
behind through heath and birchwood (2km circular). Good place to introduce kids
to nature watching. (Events: 01577 862355.)

1845 **Islay Wildlife Information & Field Centre www.islay.co.uk · Port**
9/F26 **Charlotte** Jam-packed info centre that's very 'hands-on' and interactive. Up-to-
ECO date displays of geology, natural history (rocks, skeletons, sealife tanks). Recent
sightings of wildlife, flora and fauna lists, video room, reference library. Kids' area
and activity days. Great for kids. Apr-Oct 10am-3pm. Closed Sat (Jul/Aug 10am-
5pm 7 days).

1846 **Balranald www.rspb.org.uk · North Uist** West coast of North Uist reached by
5/C17 the road from Lochmaddy, then the Bayhead turnoff at Clachan Stores (10km
north). This most western, most faraway reach is one of the last redoubts of the
disappearing corncrake. Catch its calling while you can.

Section 8
Historical Places

The Best Castles

NTS: *Under the care of the National Trust for Scotland. Hours vary. Admission.*
HS: *Historic Scotland. Standard hours are: Apr-end Sep, Mon-Sat 9.30am-6.30pm;*
Sun 2-6.30pm. Oct-Mar Mon-Sat 9.30am-4.30pm; Sun 2-4.30pm. Admission.

1847
10/N24
HS

✓ ✓ ✓ **Stirling Castle** www.historic-scotland.gov.uk · 01786 450000
Dominating the town and the plain, this like Edinburgh Castle is
worth the hype and the history. And like Edinburgh, it's a timeless attraction that
can withstand waves of tourism as it survived the centuries of warfare for which it
was built. Despite this primary function, it does seem a very civilised billet, with
peaceful gardens and rampart walks from which the views are excellent (especially
the aerial view of the Royal Gardens, 'the cup and saucer' as they're known
locally). Includes the Renaissance Palace of James V and the Great Hall of James IV
restored to full magnificence. Some rock legends also play here in summer (Wet
Wet Wet in 2005). The caff has always been a bit of a letdown in these historical
circumstances (but it has improved of late).

1848
1/B4
HS

✓ ✓ ✓ **Edinburgh Castle** www.historic-scotland.gov.uk City centre.
Impressive from any angle and all the more so from inside. Despite
the tides of tourists and time, it still enthrals. Superb perspectives of the city and
of Scottish history. Stone of Destiny & the Crown Jewels are the Big Attractions.
Café and restaurant (superb views) with efficient, but uninspiring catering operation; open only castle hours and to castle visitors. Report: 414/MAIN ATTRACTIONS.

1849
8/N17
NTS

✓ ✓ **Brodie Castle** www.nts.org.uk · 0844 493 2100 · near Nairn
6-7km west of Forres off main A96. More a (Z-plan) tower house than a
castle, dating from 1567. In this century and like Cawdor nearby, the subject of
family feuding – now resolved and under the calming influence of the NTS, its
guides discreetly passing over such unpleasantness. With a minimum of historical
hocum, this 16/17th-century, but mainly Victorian, country house is furnished
from rugs to moulded ceilings in the most excellent taste. Every picture (very few
gloomies) bears examination. The nursery and nanny's room, the guest rooms,
indeed all the rooms, are eminently habitable. I could live in the library. Tearoom
and informal walks in grounds. An avenue leads to a lake; in spring the daffodils
are famous. Hours complicated but usually 10.30am-4.30pm (last tour). Closed
Fri/Sat. Grounds open all year till sunset.

1850
9/K28
NTS

✓ ✓ **Culzean Castle** www.culzeanexperience.org · Maybole 24km
south of Ayr on A719. Impossible to convey here the scale and the scope
of the house and the country park. Allow some hours especially for the grounds.
Castle is more like a country house and you examine from the other side of a rope.
From the 12th century, but rebuilt by Robert Adam in 1775, a time of soaring
ambition, its grandeur is almost out of place in this exposed cliff-top position. It
was designed for entertaining, and the oval staircase is magnificent. Wartime
associations (especially with President Eisenhower) plus the enduring fascination
of the aristocracy. 560 acres of grounds including cliff-top walk, formal gardens,
walled garden, Swan Pond (a must) and Happy Valley. Harmonious home farm is
visitor centre with exhibits and shop etc. Caff could be better. Open Apr-Oct 11am-
5.30pm. Many special 'events'. Culzean is pronounced 'Cullane'. And you can stay
(834/AYRSHIRE HOTELS).

1851
10/Q24
NTS

✓ ✓ **Falkland Palace** www.historic-scotland.gov.uk · Falkland Middle
of farming Fife, 15km from M90 junction 8. Not a castle at all, but the
hunting palace of the Stewart dynasty. Despite its recreational rather than political

role, it's one of the landmark buildings in Scottish history and in the 16th century was the finest Renaissance building in Britain. They all came here for archery, falconry and hunting boar and deer on the Lomonds; and for Royal Tennis which is displayed and explained. Still occupied by the Crichton-Stewarts, the house is dark and rich and redolent of those days of 'dancin and deray at Falkland on the Grene'. Mar-Oct 10am-5pm. Sun 1-5pm. Plant shop and events programme. Great walks from village (2043/HILL WALKS). (2078/GLEN WALKS).

1852
6/Q12
ECO
ADMISSION

✓ ✓ **Castle of Mey** **www.castleofmey.org.uk** · **01847 851473** · **near Thurso** Actually near John o' Groats (off A836), castles don't get further-flung than this. Stunted trees, frequent wind and a wild coast but the Queen Mother famously fell in love with this dilapidated house in 1952, filled it with things she found and was given and turned it into one of the most human and endearing of the Royal (if not all aristocratic) residences. Guides in every room tell the story and if you didn't love her already, you will when you leave. Charles and Camilla still visit. May-Jul, mid Aug-Sep but check first. Closed Fri.

1853
7/N17
ADMISSION

✓ **Cawdor Castle** **www.cawdorcastle.com** · **Cawdor near Nairn & Inverness** The mighty Cawdor of Macbeth fame. Most of the family clear off for the summer and leave their romantic yet habitable and yes... stylish castle, sylvan grounds and gurgling Cawdor Burn to you. Pictures from Claude to Craigie Aitcheson, a modern kitchen as fascinating as the enormous one of yore. Even the 'tartan passage' is nicely done. The burn is the colour of tea. An easy drive (25km) to Brodie (above) means you can see 2 of Scotland's most appealing castles in one day. Gardens are gorgeous. May-early Oct, 7 days, 10am-5pm (last admission), 9-hole golf.

1854
10/N21
ADMISSION

✓ **Blair Castle** **www.blair-castle.co.uk** · **01796 481207** · **Blair Atholl** Impressive from the A9, the castle and the landscape of the Dukes of Atholl (present duke not present); 10km north of Pitlochry. Hugely popular; almost a holiday camp atmosphere. Numbered rooms chock-full of 'collections': costumes, toys, plates, weapons, stag skulls, walking sticks – so many things! Upstairs, the more usual stuffed apartments including the Jacobite bits. Walk in the policies (includes 'Hercules Garden' with tranquil ponds). Mar-Oct 9.30am-4.30pm (last admission) daily.

1855
10/Q22
ADMISSION

✓ **Glamis** **www.glamis-castle.co.uk** · **Forfar** 8km from Forfar via A94 or off main A929, Dundee-Aberdeen road (turnoff 10km north of Dundee, a picturesque approach). Fairy-tale castle in majestic setting. Seat of the Strathmore family (Queen Mum spent her childhood here) for 600 years; every room an example of the interior of a certain period. Guided tours (continuous/50 minutes' duration). Restaurant/gallery shop haven for tourists (and for an excellent bridie 1516/BAKERS). Easter-mid Oct, 10.30am. Last admission 4.45pm. Italian Gardens and nature trail well worth 500m walk.

1856
9/J27
NTS

✓ **Brodick Castle** **www.nts.org.uk** · **Arran** 4km from town (bike hire 01770 302244). Impressive, well-maintained castle, exotic formal gardens and extensive grounds. Goat Fell in the background and the sea through the trees. Dating from 13th century and until the 1950s the home of the Dukes of Hamilton. An over-antlered hall leads to liveable rooms with portraits and heirlooms, an atmosphere of long-ago afternoons. Tangible sense of relief in the kitchens now all the entertaining is over. Robert the Bruce's cell is not so convincing. Easter-Oct daily until 4pm (last admission). Marvellous grounds open all year.

1857
9/H23
☕
ADMISSION

✓ **Duart Castle** www.duartcastle.com · **Mull** 13th-century ancestral seat of the Clan Maclean and home to Sir Lachlan and Lady Maclean. Quite a few modifications over the centuries as methods of defence grew in sophistication but with walls as thick as a truck and the sheer isolation of the place it must have made any prospect of attack seem doomed from the outset. Now a happier, homlier place, the only attacking that gets done these days is on scones in the superior tearoom. Apr Sun-Thu 11am-4pm. May-Oct 10.30am-5.30pm. Event programme (mainly) Jul/Aug.

1858
9/H23
ADMISSION

Torosay Castle www.torosay.com · **Mull** 3km from Craignure and the ferry. A Victorian *arriviste* in this strategic corner where Duart Castle has ruled for centuries. Not many apartments open but who could blame them – this is a family home, endearing and eccentric especially their more recent history (like Dad's Loch Ness Monster fixation). The heirlooms are valuable because they have been cherished and there's a human proportion to the house and its contents which is rare in such places. The gardens, attributed to Lorimer, are fabulous, especially the Italianate Statue Walk, and are open all year. The Mull Light Railway from Craignure is one way to go (1802/KIDS), woodland walk another. Tearoom. Mar-Oct 10.30am-5pm. Gardens all year 9am-7pm.

1859
7/F18
ADMISSION

Dunvegan Castle www.dunvegancastle.com · **Skye** 3km Dunvegan village. Romantic history and setting, though more baronial than castellate, the result of mid-19th-century restoration that incorporated the disparate parts. Necessary crowd management leads you through a series of rooms where the Fairy Flag, displayed above a table of exquisite marquetry, has pride of place. Lovely gardens down to the loch; boats leave the jetty 'to see the seals'. Busy café and gift shop at gate side car park. Open Mar-Oct 10am-5.30pm, winter 11am-4pm.

1860
7/J18
ADMISSION

Eilean Donan www.eileandonancastle.com · **Dornie** On A87, 13km before Kyle of Lochalsh. A calendar favourite, often depicted illuminated; and once, with the balloon hovering above, an abiding image from a BBC promo. Inside it's a very decent slice of history for the price. The Banqueting Hall with its Pipers' Gallery must make for splendid dinner parties for the Macraes. Much military regalia amongst the bric-a-brac, but also the impressive Raasay Punchbowl partaken of by Johnson and Boswell. Mystical views from ramparts as well as the human story below the stairs. Apr-Nov, 10am-5.30pm; Mar & Nov 10am-3.30pm & open till 9pm Jul/Aug.

1861
10/N22
ADMISSION

Castle Menzies Weem www.menzies.org · **near Aberfeldy** In Tay valley with spectacular ridge behind (**Walks In The Weem Forest**, part of the Tummel Valley Forest Park; separate car park). On B846, 7km west of Aberfeldy, through Weem. The 16th-century stronghold of the Menzies (pronounced 'Mingiss'), one of Scotland's oldest clans. Sparsely furnished with odd clan memorabilia, the house nevertheless conveys more of a sense of Jacobite times than many more brimful of bric-a-brac. Bonnie Prince Charlie stopped here on the way to Culloden. Open farmland situation, so manured rather than manicured grounds. Apr-Oct 10.30am-5pm, Sun 2-5pm.

1862
10/P23

Scone Palace www.scone-palace.co.uk · **near Perth** On A93 road to Blairgowrie and Braemar. A 'great house', the home to the Earl of Mansfield and gorgeous grounds. Famous for the 'Stone of Scone' (aka The Stone of Destiny) on which the Kings of Scots were crowned, and the Queen Vic bedroom. Maze and pinetum. Many contented animals greet you and a plethora of peacocks. Apr-Oct 7 days 9.30am-5pm (last admission). Fri only in winter 10am-4pm.

1863
10/R24
NTS

Kellie Castle www.nts.org.uk · **near Pittenweem Fife** Major castle in Fife. Dating from 14th century and restored by Robert Lorimer, his influence evidenced by magnificent plaster ceilings and furniture. Notable mural by Phoebe Anna Traquair. The gardens, nursery and kitchen recall all the old Victorian virtues. The old-fashioned roses still bloom for us. Apr-Oct 1-5pm. Grounds open all year.

1864
8/R19
NTS

Craigievar www.nts.org.uk · **near Banchory** 15km north of main A93 Aberdeen-Braemar road between Banchory and Aboyne. A classic tower house, perfect like a porcelain miniature. Random windows, turrets, balustrades. Set amongst sloping lawns and tall trees. Limited access to halt deterioration (only 8 people at a time) means you are spared the shuffling hordes, but don't go unless you are respecter of NTS conventions. Conservation is a serious business here. Mar-Jun, Fri-Tue only 12noon-5.30pm (last admission 4.45pm). Jul/Aug daily.

1865
8/S20
NTS

Drum Castle (the Irvine Ancestral Home) www.drum-castle.org · **near Banchory** Please forgive this, one of the longest entries in the book! 1km off main A93 Aberdeen-Braemar road between Banchory and Peterculter and 20km from Aberdeen centre. For 24 generations this has been the seat of the Irvines. Our lot! Gifted to one William De Irwin by Robert the Bruce, it combines the original keep (the oldest intact tower house in Scotland), a Jacobean mansion and Victorian expansionism. I have 3 times signed the book in the Irvine Room and wandered through the accumulated history hopeful of identifying with something. Hugh Irvine, the family 'artist' whose extravagant self-portrait as the Angel Gabriel raised eyebrows in 1810, seems more interesting than most of my soldiering forebears. Give me a window seat in that library! Grounds have a peaceful and exceptional walled rose garden (Apr-Sep 10am-6pm; 1600/GARDENS). House: Easter-Oct 12.30-5.30pm (from 11am Jul-Aug). Closed Tue/Fri in off-peak months. Tower can be climbed for great views.

1866
8/Q20
ADMISSION

Balmoral **near Ballater** On main A93 between Ballater and Braemar. Limited access to the house (ie only the ballroom – public functions are held here when they're in residence and new corporate thrust '05) so grounds (open Apr-Jul) with Albert's wonderful trees are more rewarding. For royalty rooters only, and if you like Landseers ...Crathie Church along the main road has a good rose window, an altar of Iona marble. John Brown is somewhere in the old graveyard down track from visitor centre, the memorial on the hill is worth a climb for a poignant moment and the view of the policies. The Crathie services have never been quite the same Sunday attraction since Di and Fergie on a prince's arm. Daily 10am-5pm, Last admission 4.30pm. Easter-Jul.

1867
6/N15
ADMISSION

Dunrobin Castle **Golspie** The largest house in the Highlands, the home of the Dukes of Sutherland who once owned more land than anyone else in the British Empire. It's the first Duke who occupies an accursed place in Scots history for his inhumane replacement, in these vast tracts, of people with sheep. His statue stands on Ben Bhraggie above the town (1933/MONUMENTS). Living the life of English grandees, the Sutherlands transformed the castle into a *château* and filled it with their obscene wealth. Once there were 100 servants for a house party of 20 and it had 30 gardeners. Now it's all just history. The gardens are still fabulous (1592/GARDENS). The castle and separate museum are open Apr-mid Oct, usually 10.30am-4pm. Check for times (01408 633177).

Crathes **near Banchory** 1587/GARDENS; 1922/COUNTRY HOUSES.
Fyvie **Aberdeenshire** 1921/COUNTRY HOUSES.

The Most Interesting Ruins

HS: *Under the care of Historic Scotland. Standard hours are: Apr-end Sep 7 days 9.30am-5.30pm. Oct-Mar Mon-Sat 9.30am-4.30pm. Some variations with individual properties; call 0131 668 8831 to check. All HS properties carry admission. 'Friends of Historic Scotland' membership: 0131 668 8600 or any of the manned sites (annual charge but then free admission). www.historic-scotland.gov.uk*

1868
10/N25
HS

✓ ✓ ✓ **Linlithgow Palace www.historic-scotland.gov.uk** Impressive from the M9 and the south approach to this the most agreeable of West Lothian towns, but don't confuse the magnificent Renaissance edifice with St Michael's Church next door, topped with its controversial crown and spear spire. From the Great Hall, built for James I, King of Scots, with its huge adjacent kitchens, and the North Range with loch views, you get a real impression of the lavish lifestyle of the court. Not as busy as some HS attractions on this page but it is fabulous. King's Fountain restoration has added to the Palace appeal.

1869
10/P30
HS

✓ ✓ **Caerlaverock www.wwt.org.uk · near Dumfries** 17km south by B725. Follow signs for Wetlands Reserve (1808/BIRDS), but go past road end. Fairy-tale fortress within double moat and manicured lawns, the daunting frontage being the apex of an uncommon triangular shape. Since 1270, the bastion of the Maxwells, the Wardens of the West Marches. Destroyed by Bruce, besieged in 1640; now with siege engine and AV voiced by Time Team's Tony Robinson. The whole castle experience.

1870
10/S20

✓ **Dunnottar Castle www.dunnottarcastle.co.uk · near Stonehaven** 3km south of Stonehaven on the coast road just off the A92. Like Slains further north, the ruins are impressively and precariously perched on a cliff top. Historical links with Wallace, Mary, Queen of Scots (the odd night) and even Oliver Cromwell, whose Roundheads besieged it in 1650. Mel Gibson's *Hamlet* was filmed here (bet you don't remember the film) and the Crown Jewels of Scotland were once held here. 400m walk from car park. Can walk along cliff top from Stonehaven (2km). Mar-Oct 9am-6pm, Sun 2-5pm. Nov-Mar weekdays only 9am-dusk.

1871
9/H21

✓ **Castle Tioram www.tioram.org · near Acharacle** Romantic ruin where you don't need the saga to sense the place, and maybe the mystery is better than the history. 5km from A861 just north of Acharacle signed 'Dorlin'. Beautiful drive, 5km then park by Dorlin Cottage. Serenely beautiful shoreline then walk across a short causeway. Future of this ruin still under review at TGP. Pronounced 'Cheerum'. Musical beach at nearby Kentra Bay (2123/COASTAL WALKS).

1872
8/P17
HS

✓ **Elgin Cathedral www.historic-scotland.gov.uk · Elgin** Follow signs in town centre. Set in a meadow by the river, a tranquil corner of this busy market town, the scattered ruins and surrounding graveyard of what was once Scotland's finest cathedral. The nasty Wolf of Badenoch burned it down in 1390, but there are some 13th century and medieval renewals. The octagonal chapter-house is especially revered, but this is an impressive and evocative slice of history. HS have made great job of recent restorations. Now tower can be climbed. Around the corner, there's now a biblical garden planted with species mentioned in the Bible. (May-Sep, 10am-7.30pm daily).

1873
8/Q19
HS

✓ **Kildrummy Castle** www.historic-scotland.gov.uk · near **Alford** 15km southwest of Alford on A97 near the hotel (1319/SCOTTISH HOTELS) and across the gorge from its famous gardens. Most complete 13th-century castle in Scotland, an HQ for the Jacobite uprising of 1715 and an evocative and very Highland site. Here the invitation in the old HS advertising to 'bring your imagination' is truly valid. Apr-Sep 9.30am-5.30pm. Now head for the gardens (500m).

1874
5/C20
HS

✓ **Kisimull Castle Isle of Barra** · 01871 810313 The medieval fortress, home of the MacNeils that sits on a rocky outcrop in the bay 200m offshore. Originally built in the 11th century, it was burnt in the 18th and restored by the 45th chief, an American architect, but was unfinished when he died in 1970. An essential pilgrimage for all MacNeils, it is fascinating and atmospheric for the rest of us, a grim exterior belying an unusual internal layout – a courtyard that seems unchanged and rooms betwixt renovation and decay. Open every day in season and has a gift shop. You phone or flip board when you want to visit and they come in the boat. Phone for winter hours or enquire at adjacent tourist information centre.

1875
10/R21
HS

Edzell Castle www.historic-scotland.gov.uk · **Edzell** 3km village off main street, signed. Pleasing red sandstone ruin in bucolic setting – birds twitter, rabbits run. Notable walled parterre garden created by Sir David Lindsay way back in 1604. The wall niches are nice. Lotsa lobelias! Mary Queen of Scots was here (she so got around). Gate on the road is closed at night.

1876
10/M26
HS

Bothwell Castle www.historic-scotland.gov.uk · **Uddingston, Glasgow** 15km east of city via M74, Uddingston turnoff into main street and follow signs. Hugely impressive 13th-century ruin, the home of the Black Douglas, overlooking Clyde (with fine walks). Remarkable considering proximity to city that there is hardly any 21st-century intrusion except yourself. Pay to go inside or just sit and watch the Clyde go by.

1877
7/M17
HS

Fort George www.historic-scotland.gov.uk · near **Inverness** On promontory of Moray Firth 18km northeast via A96 by village of Ardersier. A vast site and 'one of the most outstanding artillery fortifications in Europe'. Planned after Culloden as a base for George II's army and completed 1769, it has remained unaltered ever since and allows a very complete picture. May provoke palpitations in the Nationalist heart, but it's heaven for militarists and altogether impressive (don't miss the museum). It's hardly a ruin of course, and is still occupied by the Army.

1878
9/H23

Dunollie Castle Oban Just outside town via Corran Esplanade towards Ganavan. Best to walk to or park on Esplanade and then walk 1km. (Only small layby and broken gate on main road below castle.) Bit of a scramble up and a slither down (and the run itself is not 'safe'), but views are superb. More atmospheric than Dunstaffnage and not commercialised. You can climb one flight up, but the ruin is only a remnant of the great stronghold of the Lorn Kings that it was. The Macdougals, who took it over in the 12th century, still live in the house below.

1879
9/H25

Tarbert Castle www.tarbert-castle.co.uk · **Tarbert, Argyll** Strategically and dramatically overlooking the sheltered harbour of this epitome of a West Highland port. Unsafe to clamber over, it's for the timeless view rather than an evocation of tangible history that it's worth finding the way up. Steps up from Harbour Rd.

1880
9/J23

Kilchurn Castle www.kilchurncastle.com · **Loch Awe** The romantic ruin at the head of Loch Awe, visited either by a short walk (1km) from car park off the main A85 5km east of Lochawe village (between the Stronmilchan turnoff and the Inveraray road). Pleasant spot for loch reflections. There may be a boat running from the Loch Awe pierhead – details vague at TGP.

1881
10/R23
St Andrews Cathedral www.standrewscathedral.com · **St Andrews** The ruins of the largest church in Scotland before the Reformation, a place of great influence and pilgrimage. St Rule's Tower and the jagged fragment of the huge West Front in their striking position at the convergence of the main streets and overlooking the sea, are remnants of its great glory. 7 days 9.30am-6.30pm (winter 4pm). Suns 2-4.30pm.

1882
10/Q26
HS
Crichton Castle www.historic-scotland.gov.uk · **near Pathhead** 6km west of A68 at Pathhead (28km south of Edinburgh) or via A7 turning east, 3km south of Gorebridge. Massive Border keep dominating the Tyne valley in pristine country-side. Open Apr-Sep. Nearby is the 15th-century collegiate church. Summer Sun only, 2-5pm. They record Radio 3 religious music here. 500m walk from Crichton village. Good picnic spots below by the river though may be overgrown in summer.

1883
10/R25
HS
Tantallon Castle www.historic-scotland.gov.uk · **North Berwick** 5km east of town by coast road; 500m to dramatic cliff top setting with views to Bass Rock. Dates from 1350 with massive 'curtain wall' to see it through stormy weather and stormy history. The Red Douglases and their friends kept the world at bay. Wonderful beach nearby (453/BEACHES). Closed Thu/Fri in winter.

1884
7/M20
HS
Ruthven Barracks www.historic-scotland.gov.uk · **Kingussie** 2km along B970 and visible from A9 especially at night when it's illuminated, these former barracks built by the English Redcoats as part of the campaign to tame the Highlands after the first Jacobite rising in 1715, were actually destroyed by the Jacobites in 1746 after Culloden. It was here that Bonnie Prince Charlie sent his final order, 'Let every man seek his own safety', signalling the absolute end of the doomed cause. Life for the soldiers is well described and visualised. Open all year.

1885
7/L18
HS
Urquhart Castle www.historic-scotland.gov.uk · **Drumnadrochit, Loch Ness** 28km south of Inverness on A82. The classic Highland fortress on a promontory overlooking Loch Ness visited every year by bus loads and boat loads of tourists. Photo opportunities galore amongst the well-kept lawns and extensive ruins of the once formidable stronghold of the Picts and their scions, finally abandoned in the 18th century. Visitor facilities almost cope with demand.

1886
10/M24
HS
Doune Castle www.historic-scotland.gov.uk · **Doune** Follow signs from centre of village which is just off A84 Callander-Dunblane road. Overlooking the River Teith, the well-preserved ruin of a late 14th-century courtyard castle with a great hall and another draughty room where Mary, Queen of Scots once slept. Nice walk to the meadow begins on track to left of castle.

1887
8/T18
Slains Castle www.peterhead.org.uk · **near Cruden Bay** 32km north of Aberdeen off the A975 Meikle Partens car park then 1km perched on the cliffs (1.5km village). Obviously because of its location, but also because there's no reception centre/postcard shop or proper signposts, this is a ruin that talks. Your imagination, like Bram Stoker's (who was inspired after staying here, to write Dracula), can be cast to the winds. The seat of the Earls of Errol, it has been gradually disintegrating since the roof was removed in 1925. Once, it had the finest dining room in Scotland. The waves crash below, as always. Be careful!

The Best Prehistoric Sites

HS: *Historic Scotland. Standard hours: Apr-end Sep Mon-Sat 9.30am-6.30pm; Sun 2-6.30pm. Oct-Mar Mon-Sat 9.30am-4.30pm; Sun 2-4.30pm.*

1888
3/P10
HS
ADMISSION

✔ ✔ ✔ **Skara Brae www.historic-scotland.gov.uk · Orkney Mainland** 32km Kirkwall by A965/B9655 via Finstown and Dounby. Can be a windy walk to this remarkable shoreline site, the subterranean remains of a compact village 5,000 years old. It was engulfed by a sandstorm 600 years later and lay perfectly preserved until uncovered by another storm in 1850. Now it permits one of the most evocative glimpses of truly ancient times in the UK.

1889
3/Q10
HS
FREE

✔ ✔ **The Standing Stones of Stenness www.historic-scotland.gov.uk · Orkney Mainland** Together with the Ring of Brodgar and the great chambered tomb of Maes Howe, all within walking distance of the A965, 18km from Kirkwall, this is as impressive a ceremonial site as you'll find anywhere. From same period as Skara Brae. The individual stones and the scale of the Ring are very imposing and deeply mysterious. The burial cairn is the finest megalithic tomb in the UK. Seen together, they will stimulate even the most jaded sense of wonder.

1890
5/F14
HS
ADMISSION
☞

✔ ✔ **The Callanish Stones www.historic-scotland.gov.uk · Isle of Lewis** 24km from Stornoway. Take Tarbert road and go right at Leurbost. The best preserved and most unusual combination of standing stones in a ring around a tomb, with radiating arms in cross shape. Predating Stonehenge, they were unearthed from the peat in the mid 19th century and have become the major historical attraction of the Hebrides. Other configurations nearby. At dawn there's nobody else there (except camping New Agers). Visitor centre out of sight is a good one with a nice caff. Closed Sun. Free.

1891
7/N17
HS
FREE

✔ **The Clava Cairns www.historic-scotland.gov.uk · near Culloden, near Inverness** Here long before the most infamous battle in Scottish and other histories; another special atmosphere. Not so well signed but continue along the B9006 towards Cawdor Castle, that other great historical landmark (1853/CASTLES), taking a right at the Culloden Moor Inn and follow signs for Clava Lodge (holiday homes), picking up HS sign to right. Chambered cairns in a grove of trees. They're really just piles of stones, but the death rattle echo from 5,000 years ago is perceptible to all especially when no one else is there. Remoteness probably inhibits New Age attentions and allows more private meditations in this extraterrestrial spot.

1892
4/V5
HS
ADMISSION

✔ **The Mousa Broch www.historic-scotland.gov.uk · Shetland** On small island of Mousa, off Shetland mainland 20km south of Lerwick, visible from main A970; but to see it properly, take boat (01950 431367). Isolated in its island fastness, this is the best-preserved broch in Scotland. Walls are 13m high (originally 15m) and galleries run up the middle, in one case to the top. Solid as a rock, this example of a uniquely Scottish phenomenon would once have been a very des res. Also:
Jarlshof in the far south next to Sumburgh airport has remnants and ruins from Neolithic to Viking times – 18th century, with especially impressive 'wheelhouses'.

1893
10/M22
ADMISSION

✔ **Crannog Centre www.crannog.co.uk · Kenmore near Aberfeldy** On south Loch Tay road 1km Kenmore. Superb reconstruction of Iron Age dwelling (there are several under the loch). Credible and worthwhile archaeological project, great for kids: conveys history well. Displays in progress and human story told by pleasant costumed humans. Open Apr-Oct 10am-5.30pm, winter hours vary.

1894
9/H24
HS

✓ **Kilmartin Glen** www.historic-scotland.gov.uk · **near Lochgilphead,**
Templewood 2km south of Kilmartin and 1km (signed) from A816 and
across road from car park, 2 distinct stone circles from a long period of history
between 3000-1200 BC. Story and speculations described on boards. Pastoral
countryside and wide skies. There are apparently 150 other sites in the vicinity, and
an excellent museum/café (2321/MUSEUMS). Site of major environmental theatre
production in '07.

1895
3/Q10
ADMISSION

Tomb of the Eagles www.tomboftheeagles.co.uk · **Orkney Mainland**
33km south of Kirkwall at the foot of South Ronaldsay; signed from Burwick. A
'recent' discovery, the excavation of this cliff cave is on private land. You call in at
the visitor centre first and they'll tell you the whole story. Then there's a 2km walk.
Allow time; ethereal stuff. Open all year, Apr-Oct 9.30am-5.30pm, Nov-Mar 10am-
noon.

1896
10/N25
HS
ADMISSION

Cairnpapple Hill near Linlithgow, West Lothian Approach from the
'Beecraigs' road off west end of Linlithgow main street. Go past the Beecraigs
turnoff and continue for 3km. Cairnpapple is signed. Astonishing Neolithic henge
and later burial site on windy hill with views from Highlands to Pentlands.
Atmosphere even more strange by the very 21st-century communications mast
next door. Cute visitor centre! Summer only 9.30am-5.30pm but can be accessed
any time.

1897
11/L30

Cairnholy www.cairnholy.co.uk · **between Newton Stewart & Gatehouse
of Fleet** 2km off main A75. Signed from road. A mini Callanish of standing stones
around a burial cairn on very human scale and in a serene setting with another site
(with chambered tomb) 150m up the farm track. Excellent view – sit and contemplate what went on 4000-6000 years ago. There will be nobody else around.

1898
10/R21

The Brown and White Caterthuns Kirkton of Menmuir, near Brechin &
Edzell 5km uphill from war memorial at Menmuir, then signed 1km: a steep pull.
Layby with obvious path to both on either side of the road. White easiest (500m
uphill). These iron-age hill top settlements give tremendous sense of scale and
space and afford an impressive panorama of the Highland line. Colours refer to the
heather-covered turf and stone of one and the massive collapsed ramparts of the
White. Sit here for a while and picture the Pict.

1899
6/Q13

The Grey Cairns of Canster near Wick 20km south of Wick, a very straight
road (signed for Cairns) heads west from the A9 for 8km. The cairns are instantly
identifiable near the road and impressively complete. The 'horned cairn' is the best
in the UK. In 2500 BC these stone-piled structures were used for the disposal of
the dead. You can crawl inside them if you're agile (or at night, brave). Nearby, also
signed from A9 is:

1900
6/Q13

Hill o' Many Stanes www.stonepages.com · **near Wick** Aptly named place
with extraordinary number of small standing stones; 200 in 22 rows. If fan shape
was complete, there would be 600. Their very purposeful layout is enigmatic and
strange.

1901
11/L31

The Whithorn Story Whithorn Excavation site (though not active), medieval
priory, shrine of St Ninian, visitor centre and café. More than enough to keep the
whole family occupied – enthusiastic staff. Christianity? Look where it got us. This
is where it started. (Also 1647/COASTAL VILLAGES.) Easter-Oct 10.30am-5pm daily.

1902
11/N30
The Motte of Ur near **Dalbeattie** Off B794 north of Dalbeattie and 6km from main A75 Castle Douglas to Dumfries road. Most extensive bailey earthwork castle in Scotland dating from 12th century. No walls or excavation visible but a great sense of scale and place. Go through village of Haugh and on for 2km south of. Looking down to right at farm buildings the minor road crosses a ford; park here, cross footbridge and head to right – the hillock is above the ford.

1903
10/M25
Bar Hill near **Kirkintilloch** A fine example of the low ruins of a Roman fort on the Antonine Wall which ran across Scotland for 200 years early AD. Great place for an out-of-town walk (767/GLASGOW VIEWS).

1904
7/H19
HS
The Brochs www.historic-scotland.gov.uk · **Glenelg** 110km from Fort William. Glenelg is 14km from the A87 at Shiel Bridge (1711/SCENIC ROUTES). 5km from Glenelg village in beautiful Glen Beag. The 2 brochs, Dun Trodden and Dun Telve, are the best preserved examples on the mainland of these mysterious 1st-century homesteads. Easy here to distinguish the twin stone walls that kept out the cold and the more disagreeable neighbours. The Wagon Café next door open in summer for tea and cake.

1905
5/D17
Barpa Lanyass North Uist 8km south of Lochmaddy, visible from main A867 road, like a hat on the hill (200m away). A 'squashed' beehive burial cairn dating from 1000 BC, the tomb of a chieftain. It's largely intact and the small and nimble can explore inside, crawling through the short entrance tunnel and down through the years.

1906
8/P17
Sueno's Stone Forres Signposted from Grant Park (1634/TOWN PARKS). More late Dark Age than prehistoric, a 9th- or 10th-century carved stone, 6m high in its own glass case. Pictish, magnificent; arguments still over what it shows.

1907
8/S18
Aberdeenshire Prehistoric Trail: East Aquhorthies Stone Circle near **Inverurie** Signed from B993 from Inverurie to Monymusk. A circle of pinkish stones with 2 grey sentinels flanking a huge recumbent stone set in the rolling countryside of the Don Valley. Bennachie over there, then as now! (2040/HILLS) For precise directions inquire at Archaeolink (below).

1908
8/S18
Loanhead Of Daviot Stone Circle near **Inverurie** Head for the village of Daviot on B9001 from Inverurie; or Loanhead, signed off A920 road between Oldmeldrum and Insch. The site is 500m from top of village. Impressive and spooky circle of 11 stones and one recumbent from 4000/5000 BC. Unusual second circle adjacent encloses a cremation cemetery from 1500 BC. Remains of 32 people were found here. Obviously, an important place. God knows what they were up to.

1909
8/R18
ADMISSION
Archaeolink www.archaeolink.co.uk · **near Insch, Aberdeenshire** Geographically between the 2 sites above and within an area of many prehistoric remnants, a more recent interpretative centre. Impressively modern approach to history both from exterior and within, where interactive and audiovisual displays bring the food hunter-gatherer past into the culture hunter-gatherer present. Up the hill, 3 adaptable staff members alternate as Iron/Bronze/Stone Age natives or visiting Romans. Easter-Nov 10am-5pm. Winter 11am-4pm.

Great Country Houses

NTS: *Under the care of the National Trust for Scotland. Hours vary.*
HS: *Under the care of Historic Scotland. Standard hours are: Apr-end Sep Mon-Sat 9.30am-6.30pm; Sun 2-6.30pm. Oct-Mar Mon-Sat 9.30am-4.30pm; Sun 2-4.30pm. All charge admission.* ☕ *signifies* **notable** *café.*

1910
8/S18
NTS
☕

✓✓ **Haddo House** www.nts.org.uk · 01651 851440 · **Tarves, by Ellon** Designed by William Adam for the Earl of Aberdeen, the Palladian-style mansion well known for its musical evenings. Not so much a house, more a leisure land in the best possible taste, with country park to wander, a pleasant café, estate shop and gentle education. Grand, full of things, but the basements are the place to ponder. The window by Burne-Jones in the chapel is glorious. Excellent programme of events, both NTS and Haddo House Trust. House Fri-Mon 11am-5pm, daily in Jul/Aug. Closed Dec-Apr. Gardens all year till sunset.

1911
9/J26
☕

✓✓ **Mount Stuart** www.mountstuart.com · 01700 503877 · **Bute** Unique Victorian Gothic house; echoes 3rd Marquis of Bute's passion for mythology, astronomy, astrology and religion. Amazing splendour and scale yet atmosphere intimate and romantic. Beautiful Italian antiques, notable paintings and fascinating attention to detail with surprising humorous touches. Equally grand gardens with fabulous walks and sea views. Stylish visitor centre: straight out of *Wallpaper* magazine with restaurant/coffee shop and notable, well-curated gallery space. May-Sep 11am-5pm. Grounds 10am-6pm. Allow time here.

1912
10/S26

✓✓ **Manderston** www.manderston.co.uk · **Duns** Off A6105, 2km down Duns-Berwick road. Described as the swan-song of the Great Classical House, one of the finest examples of Edwardian opulence in UK. *The* Edwardian CH of TV fame. All the more fascinating because the family still live there. Below stairs as fascinating as up; sublime gardens (don't miss the woodland garden on other side of the lake, or the marble dairy). Open May-end Sep, Thu/Sun 2-5pm.

1913
10/Q27

✓✓ **Traquair** www.traquair.co.uk · 01896 830323 · **Innerleithen** 2km from A72 Peebles-Gala road. Archetypal romantic Border retreat steeped in Jacobite history (ask about the Bear gates). Human proportions, liveability and lots of atmosphere. An enchanting house, a maze (20th century) and tranquil duck pond in the garden. Traquair ale still brewed. 1745 cottage tearoom, pottery and candlemaking. Apr-Oct House 12-5pm (10.30am-5.30pm Jun-Aug; Oct 11am-4pm, Nov weekends only). Crafty, folky fair in Aug and other events. Woodland walks.

1914
10/Q25
NTS

✓✓ **Newhailes** www.nts.org.uk · 0131 653 5599 · **Musselburgh** Well signed from Portobello end of Musselburgh (3km). NTS flagship project 'stabilising' the microcosm of 18th-century history encapsulated here and uniquely intact. Great rococo interiors, very liveable, especially library. A rural sanctuary near the city and unlikely outdoor pop venue '05. May-Sep, Thu-Mon, 12-5pm. Tours last 1 hour 15 minutes.

1915
10/M28
HS

✓✓ **Dumfries House** near Cumnock One of the finest Palladian mansions in the country saved for the nation '07 by a consortium led by the Prince of Wales (and £5M from the Scottish Government), purchasing it from the Marquis of Bute. The 750 acres and 18th-century apartments with their price-less Chippendale furniture and pristine artefacts are to open to the public in '08.

1916
10/T26

✓ **Paxton** www.paxtonhouse.co.uk · 01289 386291 · **near Berwick** Off B6461 road to Swinton and Kelso about 6km from A1. Country park and Adam mansion with Chippendales, Trotters and a picture gallery which is an outstation of the National Gallery. They've made a very good job of the wallpapering. 80 acres woodland to walk. Good adventure playground. Restored Victorian boathouse and salmon fishing museum on the River Tweed. Red-squirrel hide. Ambitious summer music programme in Jul augurs great things for Paxton. Tours (1 hour) every 45 minutes, Apr-Oct 11am-5pm. Garden 10am-sunset.

1917 **Gosford House** 01875 870201 · **near Aberlady East Lothian** On A198
10/Q25 between Longniddry and Aberlady, the Gosford estate is behind a high wall and strangely stunted vegetation. Imposing house with centre block by Robert Adam and the wing you visit by William Young who did Glasgow City Chambers. The Marble Hall houses the remarkable collections of the unbroken line of the Earls of Wemyss. Priceless art, informally displayed. Superb grounds available with a 'permit' (£5 annually or by the day). Mid Jun-mid Aug, Fri-Sun 2-5pm.

1918 **Floors Castle** www.floorscastle.com · 01573 223333 · **Kelso** More vast
10/S27 mansion than old castle, the ancestral home of the Duke of Roxburghe, overlooks
◻ with imposing grandeur the town and the Tweed. 18th-century with later additions. You're led round lofty public rooms past family collections of fine furniture, tapestries and porcelain. Priceless; spectacularly impractical. Good garden centre (2295/GARDEN CENTRES) and excellent tearoom, The Terrace (1468/TEAROOMS); café also on courtyard by the house. Easter & May-Oct 11am-4.30pm.

1919 **Mellerstain** www.mellerstain.com · 01573 410225 · **near Gordon/Kelso**
10/R27 Home of the Earl of Haddington, signed from A6089 (Kelso-Gordon) or A6105 (Earlston-Greenlaw). One of Scotland's great Georgian houses, begun by William Adam in 1725, completed by Robert. Outstanding decorative interiors (the ceilings are *sans pareil*) especially the library and spectacular exterior 1761. Easter weekend plus May-Sep 12.30-5pm (not Tue or Sat) & Oct (Sun only). Café/shop and beautiful gardens 11.30am-5.30pm.

1920 **Thirlestane** www.thirlestanecastle.co.uk · 01578 722430 · **Lauder** 2km off
10/R26 A68. A castellate/baronial seat of the Earls and Duke of Lauderdale and family home of the Maitlands; it must take some upkeeping. Extraordinary staterooms, especially plaster work; once again the ceilings must be seen to be believed. In contrast, the nurseries (with toy collection), kitchens and laundry are more approachable. Complex opening times.

1921 **Fyvie** www.nts.org.uk · **Aberdeenshire** 40km northwest of Aberdeen, an
8/S18 important stop on the 'Castle Trail' which links the great houses of Aberdeenshire.
NTS Before opulence fatigue sets in, see this pleasant baronial pile first (13 rooms on
◻ show). It was lived-in until the 1980s so feels less remote than most. Fantastic roofscape and ceilings. The *best* tearoom. Tree-lined acres; loch side walks. Jul/Aug 11am-5pm. Other months vary.

1922 8/S20 **Crathes** www.nts.org.uk · **near Banchory** 25km west of Aberdeen on A93. In
NTS superb gardens (1587/GARDENS) a 'fairy-tale castle': a tower house which is actu-
◻ ally interesting to visit. Up and down spiral staircases and into small but liveable rooms. The notable painted ceilings and the Long Gallery at the top are all worth lingering over. 350 years of the Burnett family are ingrained in this oak. Apr-Oct 10am-5.30pm. Big event programme; from orienteering to concerts and craft fairs. Grounds open all year 9.30am-dusk. Top tearoom (1000/NORTHEAST RESTAURANTS).

Abbotsford **near Melrose** Home of Walter Scott (2007/LITERARY PLACES).

Great Monuments, Memorials & Follies

These sites are open at all times and free unless otherwise stated.

1923
9/F27
1-A-2

✓✓ **The American Monument** www.islayinfo.com · **Islay** On the southwest peninsula of the island, known as the Oa (pronounced 'Oh'), 13km from Port Ellen. A monument to commemorate the shipwrecks nearby of 2 American ships, the *Tuscania* and the *Ontranto*; both sank in 1918 at the end of the war. The obelisk overlooks this sea – which is often beset by storms – from a spectacular headland, the sort of disquieting place where you could imagine looking round and finding the person you're with has disappeared. Take road from Port Ellen past Maltings marked Mull of Oa 12km, through gate and left at broken sign. Park and walk 1.5km steadily uphill to monument. Bird life good in Oa area.

1924
10/N24

✓ **Wallace Monument** www.nationalwallacemonument.com · 01786 472140 · **Stirling** Visible for miles and with great views, though not as dramatic as Stirling Castle. Approach from A91 or Bridge of Allan road. 150m walk from car park (or minibus) and 246 steps up. Victorian gothic spire marking the place where Scotland's great patriot swooped down upon the English at the Battle of Stirling Bridge. Mel Gibson's *Braveheart* increased visitors though his face on the Wallace statue is thanks too far. In the 'Hall of Heroes' the heroines section requires a feminist leap of the imagination. The famous sword is very big. Cliff top walk through Abbey Craig woods is worth detour. Monument open daily all year, hours vary.

1925
7/F17
ADMISSION

The Grave of Flora Macdonald **Skye** Kilmuir on A855, Uig-Staffin road, 40km north of Portree. A 10ft-high Celtic cross supported against the wind, high on the ridge overlooking the Uists from whence she came. Long after the legendary journey, her funeral in 1790 attracted the biggest crowd since Culloden. The present memorial replaced the original, which was chipped away by souvenir hunters. Dubious though the whole business may have been, she still helped to shape the folklore of the Highlands.

1926
10/M26

Carfin Grotto www.carfin.org.uk · 01698 268941 · **Motherwell** Between Motherwell and the M8, take the B road into Carfin and it's by Newarthill Rd. Gardens and pathways with shrines, pavilion, chapel and memorials. Latest statues: St Peregrine (patron saint of cancer sufferers) and Pope John Paul II. A major Catholic centre and never less than thought-provoking as the rest of us go station to station. Carfin Pilgrimage Centre adjacent open daily, 10am-5pm all year. Grotto open at all times.

1927
10/M26

Hamilton Mausoleum www.sorbie.net · **Low Park near Strathclyde Park** Off (and visible from) M74 at junction 5/6, 15km from Glasgow (1616/COUNTRY PARKS). Huge, over-the-top/over-the-tomb (though removed 1921) stone memorial to the 10th Duke of Hamilton. Guided tours Wed/Sat/Sun 3pm in summer, 2pm in winter. Eerie and chilling and with remarkable acoustics – the 'longest echo in Europe'. Give it a shout or take your violin. Info and tickets from Hamilton Museum (01698 328232).

1928
10/R27

Peniel Heugh **near Ancrum/Jedburgh** (pronounced 'Pinal-hue'.) An obelisk visible for miles and on a rise which offers some of the most exhilarating views of the Borders. Also known as the Waterloo Monument, it was built on the Marquis of Lothian's estate to commemorate the battle. It's said that the woodland on the surrounding slopes represents the positions of Wellington's troops. From A68 opposite Ancrum turnoff, on B6400, go 1km past Monteviot Gardens up steep, unmarked road to left (cycle sign) for 150m; sign says 'Vehicles Prohibited, etc'. Park, walk up through woods.

1929 **The Hopetoun Monument** **Athelstaneford near Haddington** The needle
10/R25 atop a rare rise in East Lothian (Byres Hill) and a great vantage point from which to view the county from the Forth to the Lammermuirs and Edinburgh over there. Off A6737 Haddington to Aberlady road on B1343 to Athelstaneford. Car park and short climb. Tower usually open and viewfinder boards at top but take a torch; it's a dark climb. Good gentle 'ridge' walk east from here.

1930 **The Tower at the House of the Binns** **near Linlithgow** Off A904 west
10/N25 from the tolls at the Forth Road Bridge on the road to join the M9. This is the perfect chess-piece castle or tower that sits so proudly on the horizon with its saltire blowing behind the NTS-managed House of the Binns. The house, home of the Dalyell family since 1612 (including Our Tam who asked the famous West Lothian question) ain't so interesting but the view of the Forth from the tower, which was built for a bet and cost £29 10 shillings, is splendid. Park by the house and walk 250m. Open all year till 7pm/dusk.

1931 **The Pineapple** **01628 825925 · Airth** From Airth north of Grangemouth, take
10/N25 A905 to Stirling and after 1km the B9124 for Cowie. It sits on the edge of a walled garden at the end of the drive. 45ft high, it was built in 1761 as a garden retreat by an unknown architect and remained 'undiscovered' until 1963. How exotic the fruit must have seemed in the 18th century, never mind this extraordinary folly. Grounds open all year. Oddly enough, you can stay here (2 bedrooms, Landmark Trust). The gardens are kept by NTS (National Trust for Scotland).

1932 **John Lennon Memorial** **www.lennon.net · Durness** In a garden created in
6/L12 2002 (a BBC *Beechgrove Garden* project) amazing in itself surviving these harsh, very northern conditions, an inscribed slate memorial to JL who for many years as a child came here with his aunt for the hols. 'There are places I'll remember all my life' from *Rubber Soul*. Who'd have thought that song (*In My Life*) was about here? And who'd have thought his brief visits would have engendered a whole John Lennon Festival which took place for the first time in late Sep '07. (Its future to be considered.)

1933 **The Monument on Ben Bhraggie** **Golspie** Atop the hill (pronounced
6/N15 'Brachee') that dominates the town, the domineering statue and plinth (over 35m) of the dreaded first Duke of Sutherland; there's a campaign group that would like to see it demolished, but it survives yet. Climb from town fountain on marked path. The hill racers go up in minutes but allow 2 hours return. His private view along the North East Coast is superb (1867/CASTLES; 2313/MUSEUMS).

1934 **McCaig's Tower or Folly** **www.follytowers.com · Oban** Oban's great land-
9/H23 mark built in 1897 by McCaig, a local banker, to give 'work to the unemployed' and as a memorial to his family. It's like a temple or coliseum and time has mellowed whatever incongruous effect it may have had originally. The views of the town and the bay are magnificent and it's easy to get up from several points in town centre. (831/OBAN)

1935 **The Victoria Memorial to Albert** **Balmoral** Atop the fir-covered hill behind
8/Q20 the house, she raised a monument whose distinctive pyramid shape can be seen peeping over the crest from all over the estate. Desolated by his death, the

'broken-hearted' widow had this memorial built in 1862 and spent so much time here, she became a recluse and the Empire trembled. Path begins at shop on way to Lochnagar distillery, 45 minutes up. Forget Balmoral (1866/CASTLES), all the longing and love for Scotland can be felt here, the great estate laid out below.

1936
8/S18
The Prop of Ythsie near Aberdeen 35km northwest of city near Ellon to west of A92, or pass on the 'Castle Trail' since this monument commemorates one George Gordon of Haddo House nearby, who was prime minister 1852-55 (the good-looking guy in the first portrait you come to in the house). Tower visible from all of rolling Aberdeenshire around and there are reciprocal views should you take the easy but unclear route up. On B999 Aberdeen-Tarves road (Haddo-Pitmeddon on the Castle Trail) and 2km from entrance to house. Take road for the Ythsie (pronounced 'icy') farms, car park 100m. Stone circle nearby.

1937
11/Q29
The Monument To Hugh MacDiarmid Langholm Brilliant piece of modern sculpture by Jake Harvey rapidly rusting on the hill above Langholm 3km from A7 at beginning of path to the Malcolm obelisk from where there are great views (1745/VIEWS). MacDiarmid, our national poet, was born in Langholm in 1872 and, though they never liked him much after he left, the monument was commissioned and a cairn beside it raised in 1992. The bare hills surround you.

1938
6/J14
Memorial to Norman MacCaig near Lochinver Follow directions for the remarkable Achin's bookshop (2261/SHOPPING) which is at the start of the great walk to Suilven (2021/HILLS). Simple memorial of Torridon sandstone to Scotland's great poet who wrote so much about this landscape he loved: Assynt. Recent tree removal leaves site a bit forlorn but some words writ here to guide us on the way.

1939
11/L29
Murray Monument near New Galloway Above A712 road to Newton Stewart about halfway between. A fairly austere needle of granite to commemorate a 'shepherd boy', one Alexander Murray, who rose to become a professor of Oriental Languages at Edinburgh University in the early 19th century. A 10-minute walk up for fine views of Galloway Hills; pleasant waterfall nearby. Just as he, barefoot …

1940
10/R27
HS
Smailholm Tower www.historic-scotland.gov.uk · near Kelso & St Boswells The classic Border tower which inspired Walter Scott; plenty of history and romance and a very nice place to stop, picnic whatever. Good views from its crags. Near main road B6404 or off smaller B6937 – well signposted. Open Apr-Sep 9.30am-6.30pm. But fine to visit at any time (1719/SCENIC ROUTES).

Scott Monument Edinburgh 460/EDINBURGH VIEWS.

The Most Interesting Churches

*All 'generally open' unless otherwise stated; those marked * have public services.*

1941
10/Q26
✓ ✓ ✓ ***Rosslyn Chapel** www.rosslynchapel.org.uk · **Roslin** 12km south of Edinburgh city centre. Take A702, then A703 from ring-route road, marked Penicuik. Roslin village 1km from main road and chapel 500m from village crossroads above Roslin Glen. Here since the 15th century but firmly on the world map in recent times because of the *Da Vinci Code*. Grail seekers have been coming forever but now so many, it's guided tours only in summer. No doubting the atmosphere in this temple to the Templars and all holy meaningful stuff in a *Foucault's Pendulum* sense. But a special place. In restoration till 2010. Episcopalian. Mon-Sat 10am-5pm, 12noon-4.45pm Sun. Walk in the glen (441/WALKS OUTSIDE THE CITY). Coffee shop.

1942
9/J23
✓ ✓ ***St Conan's Kirk Loch Awe** A85 33km east of Oban. Perched amongst trees on the side of Loch Awe, this small but spacious church seems to incorporate every ecclesiastical architectural style. Its building was a labour of love for one Walter Campbell who was perhaps striving for beauty rather than consistency. Though modern (begun by him in 1881 and finished by his sister and a board of trustees in 1930), the result is a place of ethereal light and atmosphere, enhanced by and befitting the inherent spirituality of the setting. There's a spooky carved effigy of Robert the Bruce, a cosy cloister and the most amazing flying buttresses. A place to wander and reflect.

1943
3/R12
✓ ✓ **The Italian Chapel** www.visitorkney.com · **Orkney Mainland** 8km south of Kirkwall at Lamb Holm and the first causeway on the way to St Margaret's Hope. In 1943, Italian PoWs brought to work on the Churchill Barriers transformed a Nissen hut, using the most meagre materials, into this remarkable ornate chapel. The meticulous *trompe l'œil* and wrought-iron work are a touching affirmation of faith. At the other end of the architectural scale, **St Magnus Cathedral** in Kirkwall is a great edifice, but also filled with spirituality.

1944
2/XC1
ADMISSION
✓ ✓ **Queen's Cross Church** www.crmsociety.com · **70 Garscube Road, Glasgow** Set where Garscube Rd becomes Maryhill Rd at Springbank St. C.R. Mackintosh's only church. Fascinating and unpredictable in every part of its design. Some elements reminiscent of Glasgow School of Art (built in the same year 1897) and others, like the tower, evoke medieval architecture. Bold and innovative, now restored and functioning as the headquarters of The Mackintosh Society. Mon-Fri 10am-5pm, Sun 2pm-5pm. (Not Sun in winter.) Closed Sat. No services. (794/MACKINTOSH.)

1945
11/N28
✓ ***Durisdeer Parish Church** www.churchesinscotland.co.uk · **near Abington & Thornhill** Off A702 Abington-Thornhill road and near Drumlanrig (1613/COUNTRY PARKS). If I lived near this delightful village in the hills, I'd go to church more often. It's exquisite and the history of Scotland is in the stones. The Queensberry marbles (1709) are displayed in the north transept (enter behind church) and there's a cradle roll and a list of ministers from the 14th century. The plaque to the two brothers who died at Gallipoli is especially touching. Covenanter tales are writ on the gravestones.

1946
9/K26
✓ ***Cathedral Of The Isles Millport, the Isle Of Cumbrae** Frequent ferry service from Largs is met by bus for 6km journey to Millport. Lane from main street by Newton pub, 250m then through gate. The smallest 'cathedral' in

Europe, one of Butterfield's great works (other is Keble College in Oxford). Here, small is outstandingly beautiful and absolutely quiet. (1331/RETREATS; 1463/CAFÉS.)

1947
5/E16
St Clements Rodel, South Harris Tarbert 40km. Classic island kirk in Hebridean landscape. Go by the Golden Road (1715/SCENIC ROUTES). Simple cruciform structure with tower, which the adventurous can climb. Probably influenced by Iona. Now an empty but atmospheric shell, with blackened effigies and important monumental sculpture. Goats in the churchyard graze amongst the headstones of all the young Harris lads lost at sea in the Great War. There are other fallen angels on the outside of the tower.

1948
5/D19
*St Michael's Chapel Eriskay, near South Uist/Barra That rare example of an ordinary modern church without history or grand architecture, which has charm and serenity and imbues the sense of well-being that a religious centre should. The focal point of a relatively devout Catholic community who obviously care about it. Alabaster angels abound. Overlooking the Sound of Barra. A real delight whatever your religion.

1949
10/Q23
*St Athernase www.leuchars.org.uk · Leuchars The parish church on a corner of what is essentially an Air Force base spans centuries of warfare and architecture. The Norman bell tower is remarkable.

1950
10/P25
*St Fillan's Church Aberdour Behind ruined castle (HS) in this pleasant seaside village (1645/COASTAL VILLAGES), a more agreeable old kirk would be hard to find. Restored from a 12th-century ruin in 1926, the warm stonework and stained glass create a very soothing atmosphere (church open at most times, but if closed the graveyard is very fine). Services 10.30am Sun & 6.30pm first Sun of the month.

1951
10/N25
HS
*Culross Abbey Church www.historic-scotland.gov.uk Top of Forth-side village full of interesting buildings and windy streets (1640/COASTAL VILLAGES). Worth hike up hill (signed 'Abbey', ruins are adjacent) for views and this well-loved and looked-after church. Great stained glass (see Sandy's window), and often full of flowers.

1952
10/M25
HS
*Dunblane Cathedral www.dunblanecathedral.org.uk A huge nave of a church built around a Norman tower (from David I) on the Allan Water and restored 1892. The wondrously bright stained glass is mostly 20th century. The poisoned sisters buried under the altar helped change the course of Scottish history.

1953
8/T19
*St Machar's Cathedral www.stmachar.com · Aberdeen The Chanonry in 'Old Aberdeen' off St Machar's Drive about 2km from centre. Best seen as part of a walk round the old 'village within the city' occupied mainly by the university's old and modern buildings. Cathedral's fine granite nave and twin-spired West Front date from 15th century, on site of 6th-century Celtic church. Noted for heraldic ceiling and 19/20th-century stained glass. Seaton Park adjacent has pleasant Donside walks and there's the old Brig o' Balgownie. Church open daily 9am-5pm.

1954
10/Q25
*The East Lothian Churches At Aberlady, Whitekirk, Athelstaneford & Garvald 4 charming churches in bucolic settings; quiet corners to explore and reflect. Easy to find. All have interesting local histories and in the case of Athelstaneford, a national resonance: a 'vision' in the sky near here inspired the flag of Scotland, the saltire. The spooky Doocot Heritage Centre behind the church explains. Aberlady is my favourite, Garvald in days-gone-by a village with nice pub.

1955 **Abercorn Church** near South Queensferry Off A904. 4 km west of round-
10/P25 about at Forth Bridge Toll, just after village of Newton, Abercorn is signed. 11th-
century kirk nestling among ancient yews in a sleepy hamlet, untouched since
Covenanter days. St Ninian said to have preached to the Picts here and though
hard to believe, Abercorn was once on a par with York and Lindisfarne in religious
importance. Church always open. Walk in woods from corner stile or the Hopetoun
Estate.

1956 **Croick Church** near www.croickchurch.com · **Bonar Bridge** 16km west of
6/L15 Ardgay, which is just over the river from Bonar Bridge and through the splendid
glen of Strathcarron (1675/GLENS). This humble and charming church is chiefly
remembered for its place in the history of the Highland clearances. In May 1845,
90 folk took shelter in the graveyard around the church after they had been
cleared from their homes in nearby Glencalvie. Not allowed even in the kirk, their
plight did not go unnoticed and was reported in *The Times*. The harrowing account
is there to read, and the messages they scratched on the windows. Sheep graze all
around.

1957 ***Thomas Coates Memorial Church** www.fenet.net · **Paisley** Built by
10/L26 Coates (of thread fame), an imposing edifice, one of the grandest Baptist churches
in Europe. A monument to God, prosperity and the Industrial Revolution. Opening
hours Fri 2-4pm only. Check tourist information centre (0141 889 0711). Service on
Sun at 11am.

1958 ***The Lamp Of The Lothians St Mary's Collegiate** Haddington ·
10/R25 www.rosslyntemplars.org.uk Follow signs from east main street. At the risk of
sounding profane or at least trite, this is a church that's really got its act together,
both now and throughout ecclesiastical history. It's beautiful and in a fine setting
on the River Tyne, with good stained glass and interesting crypts and corners. But
it's obviously very much at the centre of the community, a lamp as it were, in the
Lothians. Guided tours, brass rubbings (Sat). Concert season in summer. Coffee
shop and gift shop. Don't miss Lady Kitty's garden nearby, including the secret
medicinal garden, a quiet spot to contemplate (if not sort out) your condition. Daily
11am-4pm (2pm-4.30pm Sun). There's a daily service at noon.

1959 ***Dunkeld Cathedral** www.dunkeldcathedral.org.uk In town centre by lane
10/P22 to the banks of the Tay at its most silvery. Medieval splendour amongst lofty trees.
Notable for 13th-century choir and 15th-century nave and tower. Parish church
open for edifying services and other spiritual purposes. Lovely summer recitals.

1960 **Ruthwell Church Ruthwell** 10 miles southeast of Dumfries, B724 near
11/P30 Clarencefield. Collect keys from Mrs Coulthard, Kirkyett House (bungalow where
you turn off the main road); she's the fount of all knowledge concerning this
important building. Unique 18ft Runic Cross within Church, dating from 7th century. Carvings depict Biblical scenes with monk's inscription of 'The Holy Rood'
poem. Fascinating history of its creation, preservation during the religious troubles
of 1640, and subsequent restoration in 1823 by the community. Buy the guidebook
from Mrs C (01387 870249). And some postcards!

1961 **St Mary & St Finnan Church** www.churchesinscotland.co.uk ·
9/J20 **Glenfinnan** On main A830 Fort William-Mallaig road (the Road to the Isles,
1724/SCENIC ROUTES), a beautiful (though inside a bit crumbly) Catholic church in a
spectacular setting. Queen Vic said she never saw a lovelier or more romantic spot.
Late 19th century. Open daily for quiet meditations.

1962
9/H25
HS

Keills Chapel www.historic-scotland.gov.uk · **South of Crinan** The chapel at the end of nowhere. From Lochgilphead, drive towards Crinan, but before you get there, turn south down the B8025 and follow it past lovely little Tayvallich for nearly 20km to the end. Park at the farm then walk the last 200m. You are 7km across the Sound from Jura, at the edge of Knapdale. Early-13th-century chapel houses some remarkable cross slabs, a 7th century cross and ghosts.

St Giles Cathedral Edinburgh 432/OTHER ATTRACTIONS.
Glasgow Cathedral/University Chapel Glasgow 738/742/MAIN ATTRACTIONS.

The Most Interesting Graveyards

1963
2/XF2

✓ ✓ **Glasgow Necropolis** www.glasgowcathedral.org.uk The vast burial ground at the crest of the ridge, running down to the river, that was the focus of the original settlement of Glasgow. Everything began at the foot of this hill and, ultimately, ended at the top where many of the city's most famous (and infamous) sons and daughters are interred within the reach of the long shadow of John Knox's obelisk. Generally open (official times), but best if you can get the full spooky experience to yourself. Check with tourist information centre (0141 287 3961). See 738/MAIN ATTRACTIONS.

1964
1

✓ **Edinburgh Canongate** On left of Royal Mile going down to Palace. Adam Smith and the tragic poet Robert Fergusson revered by Rabbie Burns (who raised the memorial stone in 1787 over his pauper's grave) are buried here in the heart of Auld Reekie. Tourists can easily miss this one. **Greyfriars** A place of ancient mystery, famous for the wee dog who guarded his master's grave for 14 years, for the plundering of graves in the early 18th century for the Anatomy School and for the graves of Allan Ramsay (prominent poet and burgher), James Hutton (the father of geology), William McGonagall (the 'world's worst poet') and sundry serious Highlanders. Annals of a great city are written on these stones. **Warriston** Warriston Rd by B&Q or end of cul-de-sac at Warriston Cres (Canonmills), up bank and along railway line. Overgrown, peaceful, steeped in atmosphere. Gothic horrorland (some of those cruising guys may like that sort of thing). **Dean Cemetery** is an Edinburgh secret and my New Town circle won't let me speak of it.

1965
9/G25

✓ **Isle of Jura** www.theisleofjura.co.uk Killchianaig graveyard in the north. Follow road as far as it goes to Inverlussa, graveyard is on right, just before hamlet. Mairi Ribeach apparently lived until she was 128. In the south at Keils (2km from road north out of Craighouse, bearing left past Keils houses and through the deer fence), her father is buried and he was 180! Both sites are beautiful, isolated and redolent of island history, with much to reflect on, not least the mysterious longevity of the inhabitants and that soon we may all live this long.

1966
7/L18

✓ **Chisholm Graveyard** near Beauly Last resting place of the Chisholms and 3 of the largest Celtic crosses you'll see anywhere, in a secret and atmospheric woodland setting. 15km west of Beauly on A831 to Struy after Aigas dam and 5km after golf course on right-hand side; 1km before Cnoc Hotel opposite Erchless Estate and through a white iron gate on right. Walk 150m on mossy path. Sublime!

1967 **Campbeltown Cemetery** Odd, but one of the nicest things about this end-of-
9/H28 the-line town is the cemetery. It's at the end of a row of fascinating posh houses,
the original merchant and mariner owners of which will be interred in the leafy
plots next door. Still very much in use after centuries of commerce and seafaring
disasters, it has crept up the terraces of a steep and lush overhanging bank. The
white cross and row of WW2 headstones are particularly affecting.

1968 **Kirkoswald Kirkyard near Maybole & Girvan** On main road through village
9/K28 between Ayr and Girvan. The graveyard around the ruined Kirk and famous as the
burial place of the characters in Burns' most famous poem, *Tam o' Shanter*. A must
for Burns fans and famous-grave seekers with Souter Johnnie and Kirkton Jean
buried here.

1969 **Humbie Churchyard Humbie, East Lothian** 25km southeast of Edinburgh via
10/Q26 A68 (turnoff at Fala). This is as reassuring a place to be buried as you could wish
for; if you're set on cremation, come here and think of earth. Deep in the woods
with the burn besides; after hours the sprites and the spirits must have a hell of a
time.

1970 **Ancrum Churchyard near Jedburgh** The quintessential country churchyard;
10/R27 away from the village (2km along B6400), by a lazy river (the Ale Water) crossed to
a farm by a humpback bridge and a chapel in ruins. Elegiac and deeply peaceful
(1768/PICNICS).

1971 **Balquhidder Churchyard** Chiefly notable as the last resting place of one Rob
10/L23 Roy Macgregor who was buried in 1734 after causing a heap of trouble hereabouts
and raised to immortality by Sir Walter Scott and Michael Caton-Jones. Despite
well-trodden path, setting is poignant. For best reflections head along Loch Voil to
Inverlochlarig. Beautiful Sunday evening concerts in kirk Jul/Aug. (check with local
tourist information centres). Nice walk from back corner to the 'Waterfall' and then
to Rallying Place (1744/VIEWS). Great long walk to Brig o' Turk (2073/GLEN WALKS).
Tearoom in **Old Library** in village is cosy and couthie, with very good cakes
(1488/TEAROOMS).

1972 **Logie Old Kirk near Stirling** A crumbling chapel and an ancient graveyard at
10/N24 the foot of the Ochils. The wall is round to keep out the demons, a burn gurgles
beside and there are some fine and very old stones going back to the 16th century.
Take road for Wallace Monument off A91, 2km from Stirling, then first right. The
old kirk is·beyond the new. Continuing on this steep narrow road (then right and
the T-junction) takes you onto the Ochils (2045/HILL WALKS).

1973 **Tout-Na-Qual Dunbeath** An enchanting cemetery 5km from Dunbeath, Neil
6/P14 Gunn's birthplace, and found by walking up the 'Strath' he describes in his book
Highland River (2005/LITERARY PLACES). With a white wall around it, this graveyard,
which before the clearances once served a valley community of 400 souls, can be
seen for miles. Ask at Heritage Centre for route.

The Great Abbeys

NTS: *Under the care of the National Trust for Scotland. Hours vary.*
HS: *Under the care of Historic Scotland. Standard hours are: Apr-end Sep Mon-Sat 9.30am-6.30pm; Sun 2-6.30pm. Oct-Mar Mon-Sat 9.30am-4.30pm; Sun 2-4.30pm.*

1974
9/F23
HS

✓ ✓ **Iona Abbey** www.historic-scotland.gov.uk This hugely significant place of pilgrimage for new age and old age pilgrims and tourists alike is reached from Fionnphort, southwest Mull, by frequent Calmac Ferry (a 5-minute crossing). Walk 1km. Here in 563 AD St Columba began his mission for a Celtic Church that changed the face of Europe. Cloisters, graveyard of Scottish kings and, marked by a modest stone, the inscription already faded by the weather, the grave of John Smith, the patron saint of New Labour. Ethereal, clear light through the unstained windows may illuminate your contemplations. Great sense of being part of a universal church and community. Regular services. Good shop (2262/SHOPPING). Residential courses and retreats (MacLeod Centre adjacent, 01681 700404) include a 'Christmas house party' (2360/MAGICAL ISLANDS).

1975
8/P17

✓ ✓ **Pluscarden Abbey** www.pluscardenabbey.org · **between Forres & Elgin** The oldest abbey monastic community still working in the UK (1324/RETREATS) in one of the most spiritual of places. Founded by Alexander II in 1230 and being restored since 1948. Benedictine services (starting with Vigil and Lauds at 4.45am through Prime-Terce-Sext-None-Vespers at 5.30pm and Compline at 8pm) open to the public. The ancient honey-coloured walls, brilliant stained glass, monks' Gregorian chant: the whole effect is a truly uplifting experience. The bell rings down the valley. Services aside, open to visitors 9am-5pm.

1976
10/L26

✓ ✓ **Paisley Abbey** www.paisleyabbey.org.uk · **0141 889 7654** In the town centre. An abbey founded in 1163, razed (by the English) in 1307 and with successive deteriorations and renovations ever since. Major restoration in the 1920s brought it to present-day cathedral-like magnificence. Exceptional stained glass (the recent window complementing the formidable Strachan East Window), an impressive choir and an edifying sense of space. Sunday Services (11am, 12.15pm, 6.30pm) are superb, especially full-dress communion and there are open days; phone for dates. Otherwise Abbey open all year Mon-Sat 10am-3.30pm. Café/shop.

1977
10/R28
HS

✓ ✓ **Jedburgh Abbey** www.historic-scotland.gov.uk The classic abbey ruin; conveys the most complete impression of the Border abbeys built under the patronage of David I in the 12th century. Its tower and remarkable Catherine window are still intact. Excavations have unearthed example of a 12th-century comb. It's now displayed in the excellent visitor centre which brilliantly illustrates the full story of the abbey's amazing history. Best view from across the Jed in the 'Glebe'. May-Sep 9.30am-5.30pm, Oct-Mar until 4.30pm.

1978
10/R27
HS

✓ **Dryburgh Abbey** www.historic-scotland.gov.uk · **near St Boswells** One of the most evocative of ruins, an aesthetic attraction since the late 18th century. Sustained innumerable attacks from the English since its inauguration by Premonstratensian Canons in 1150. Celebrated by Sir Walter Scott, buried here in 1832 (with his biographer Lockhart at his feet), its setting, amongst huge cedar trees on the banks of the Tweed is one of pure historical romance. 4km A68. (1739/VIEWS.) Apr-Sep 9.30am-5.30pm, Oct-Mar till 4.30pm, Sun 2-4.30pm.

1979   **Sweetheart New Abbey near Dumfries**   12km south by A710. The endearing
11/N30   and enduring warm red sandstone abbey in the shadow of Criffel, so named
HS   because Devorguilla de Balliol, devoted to her husband (he of the Oxford college),
founded the abbey for Cistercian monks and kept his heart in a casket which is
buried with her here. No roof, but the tower is intact. OK tearoom (but 'orrible gift
shop) adjacent: you can sit and gaze at the ruins while eating your apple crumble.

1980   **Melrose Abbey**   www.historic-scotland.gov.uk   Another romantic setting, the
10/R27   abbey seems to give an atmosphere to the whole town. Once again built by David I
HS   (what a guy!) for Cistercian monks from Rievaulx from 1136. It once sustained a
huge community, as evinced by the widespread excavations. There's a museum of
abbey, church and Roman relics; soon to include Robert the Bruce's heart, recently
excavated in the gardens. Nice Tweed walks can start here. Same hours as Jed.

1981   **Arbroath Abbey**   www.historic-scotland.gov.uk   25km north of Dundee.
10/R22   Founded in 1178 and endowed on an unparalleled scale, this is an important place
HS   in Scots history. It's where the Declaration was signed in 1320 to appeal to the
Pope to release the Scots from the yoke of the English (you can buy facsimiles of
the yellow parchment; the original is in the Scottish Records Office in Edinburgh –
oh, and tea towels). It was to Arbroath that the Stone of Destiny (on which
Scottish kings were traditionally crowned) was returned after being 'stolen' from
Westminster Abbey in the 1950s and is now at Edinburgh Castle. Great
interpretation centre before you tour the ruins.

∎ The Great Battlegrounds

NTS: *Under the care of the National Trust for Scotland. Hours vary.*

1982   **Culloden**   www.nts.org.uk · **Inverness**   Signed from A9 and A96 into Inverness
7/M18   and about 8km from town. The new visitor centre, opened in '07, gives more
NTS   prominence, accuracy and scale to the battle (2km walk round site). Positions of
the clans and the troops marked out across the moor; flags enable you to get a
real sense of scale. If you go in spring you see how wet and miserable the Moor
can be (the battle took place on 16 April 1746). No matter how many other folk are
there wandering down the lines, a visit to this most infamous of battlefields can
still leave a pain in the heart. Centre 9am-6pm (winter 11am-4pm). Ground open
at all times for more personal Cullodens.

1983   **Battle Of The Braes**   Skye   10km Portree. Take main A850 road south for 3km
7/F18   then left, marked 'Braes' for 7km. Monument is on a rise on right. The last battle
fought on British soil and a significant place in Scots history. When the clearances,
uninterrupted by any organised opposition, were virtually complete and vast tracts
of Scotland had been depopulated for sheep, the Skye crofters finally stood up in
1882 to the Government troops and said enough is enough. A cairn has been
erected near the spot where they fought on behalf of 'all the crofters of Gaeldom',
a battle which led eventually to the Crofters Act which has guaranteed their rights
ever since. At the end of this road at Peinchorran, there are fine views of Raasay
(which was devastated by clearances) and Glamaig, the conical Cuillin, across Loch
Sligachan.

1984   **Glencoe**   Not much of a battle, of course, but one of the most infamous
9/J21   massacres in British history. Much has been written (John Prebble's *Glencoe* and
others) and the new visitor centre provides audiovisual scenario. There's the
Macdonald monument near Glencoe village and the walk to the more evocative

Signal Rock where the bonfire was lit, now a happy woodland trail in this doom-laden landscape. Many great walks. See 2011/SPOOKY PLACES, 1360/PUBS.

1985
3/Q11
Scapa Flow www.scapaflow.co.uk · Orkney Mainland & Hoy Scapa Flow, surrounded by various of the southern Orkney islands, is one of the most sheltered anchorages in Europe. Hence the huge presence in Orkney of ships and personnel during both wars. The Germans scuttled 54 of their warships here in 1919 and many still lie in the bay. The *Royal Oak* was torpedoed in 1939 with the loss of 833 men. Much still remains of the war years (especially if you're a diver, 2145/DIVING): the rusting hulks, the shore fortifications, the Churchill Barriers and the ghosts of a long-gone army at Scapa and Lyness on Hoy. Excellent 'tour' on MV *Guide* with remote controlled camera exploring 3 wrecks (01856 811360).

1986
10/R27
Lilliard's Edge near St Boswells On main A68, look for Lilliard's Edge Caravan Park 5km south of St Boswells; park and walk back towards St Boswells to the brim of the hill (about 500m), then cross rough ground on right along ridge, following tree-line hedge. Marvellous view attests to strategic location. 200m along, a cairn marks the grave of Lilliard who, in 1545, joined the Battle of Ancrum Moor against the English 'loons' under the Earl of Angus. 'And when her legs were cuttit off, she fought upon her stumps'. An ancient poem etched on the stone records her legendary... feet.

1987
10/N21
Killiecrankie near Pitlochry The first battle of the Jacobite Risings where, in Jul 1689, the Highlanders lost their leader Viscount (aka Bonnie) Dundee, but won the battle, using the narrow Pass of Killiecrankie. One escaping soldier made a famous leap. Well-depicted scenario in visitor centre; short walk to 'The Leap'. Battle viewpoint and cairn is further along road to Blair Atholl, turning right and doubling back near the Garry Guesthouse and on, almost to A9 underpass (3km from visitor centre). You get the lie of the land from here. Many good walks.

1988
10/N24
NTS
Bannockburn www.nts.org.uk · near Stirling 4km town centre via Glasgow road (it's well signposted) or junction 9 of M9 (3km), behind a sad hotel and car-rental centre. Some visitors might be perplexed as to why 24 Jun 1314 was such a big deal for the Scots and, apart from the 50m walk to the flag-pole and the huge statue, there's not a lot doing. But the 'Heritage Centre' does bring the scale of it to life, the horror and the glory. The battlefield itself is thought to lie around the orange building of the High School some distance away, and the best place to see the famous wee burn is from below the magnificent Telford Bridge. Ask at centre (5km by road). NTS arrange mega re-enactments in mid Sep.

Mary, Charlie & Bob

HS: *Under the care of Historic Scotland. Standard hours are: Apr-end Sep Mon-Sat 9.30am-6.30pm; Sun 2-6.30pm. Oct-Mar Mon-Sat 9.30am-4.30pm; Sun 2-4.30pm.*

MARY, QUEEN OF SCOTS (1542–87)
Linlithgow Palace Where she was born. 1868/RUINS.
Holyrood Palace Edinburgh And lived. 417/MAIN ATTRACTIONS.

1989
10/M24
HS
Inchmahome Priory www.historic-scotland.gov.uk · Port of Menteith The priory ruins on the island in Scotland's only lake, where the infant queen spent her early years cared for by Augustinian monks. Short boat journey from quay near lake hotel. Signal the ferryman by turning the board to the island, much as she did. Apr-Oct. 7 days. Last trip 4.30pm.

1990
10/R28
Mary, Queen of Scots' House Jedburgh In gardens via Smiths Wynd off main street. Historians quibble but this long-standing museum claims to be 'the' house where she fell ill in 1566 but still made it over to visit the injured Bothwell at Hermitage Castle 50km away. Tower house in good condition; displays and well-told saga. Mar-Nov 10am-4.30pm, Sun 11am-4.30pm. Winter hours vary slightly.

1991
10/P24
HS
Loch Leven Castle www.historic-scotland.gov.uk · near Kinross Well-signed! The ultimate in romantic penitentiaries; on the island in the middle of the loch, clearly visible from the M90. Not much left of the ruin to fill out the fantasy, but this is where Mary spent 10 months in 1568 before her famous escape and her final attempt to get back the throne. Sailings Apr-Sep, 9.30am-5.30pm (last out 4.30pm) from pier at the National Game Angling Academy (Pier Bar/café serves as you wait) in small launch from Kirkgate Park. 7-minute trip, return as you like.

1992
11/M31
HS
Dundrennan Abbey www.historic-scotland.gov.uk · near Auchencairn Mary got around and there are innumerable places where she spent the night. This was where she spent her last one on Scottish soil, leaving next day from Port Mary (nothing to see there but a beach, 2km along the road skirting the sinister MoD range; the pier's long gone and... well, there's no plaque). The Cistercian abbey (established 1142) which harboured her on her last night is now a tranquil ruin.

'In my end is my beginning,' she said, facing her execution 19 years later.

1993
10/R25
Her 'death mask' is displayed at **Lennoxlove House near Haddington ·** **www.lennoxlove.com**; it does seem small for someone who was supposedly 6 feet tall! Lennoxlove on road to Gifford. Apr-Oct, Wed/Thu/Sun 2-4.30pm.

1994
8/S20
Blair Museum near Peterculter Scotland's 'Catholic treasury' in college at Blairs on South Deeside road. Massive and austere pile closed 1986 with its chapel a repository for religious artefacts, history of the seminary and the 'official' memorial portrait of the recently dead queen – the start of the legend. Apr-Sep, Sat/Sun till 5pm. A lock of Bonnie Prince Charlie's hair is also here (but no T-shirts).

BONNIE PRINCE CHARLIE (1720–88)
1995
5/D19
Prince Charlie's Bay or Strand Eriskay The uncelebrated, unmarked and quietly beautiful beach where Charlie first landed in Scotland to begin the Jacobite Rebellion. Nothing much has changed and this crescent of sand with soft machair and a turquoise sea is still a secret place. 1km from township heading south adjacent pier for Barra ferry. 2368/MAGICAL ISLANDS.

1996   **Loch Nan Uamh, The Prince's Cairn** near Arisaig 7km from Lochailort on
7/H20   A830 (1680/SCENIC ROUTES), 48km Fort William. Signed from the road (100m
layby), a path leads down to the left. This is the 'traditional' spot (pronounced
'Loch Na Nuan') where Charlie embarked for France in Sep 1746, having lost the
battle and the cause. The rocky headland also overlooks the bay and skerries
where he'd landed in Jul the year before to begin the campaign. This place was the
beginning and the end and it has all the romance necessary to be utterly
convincing. Is that a French ship out there in the mist?

1997   **Glenfinnan** www.glenfinnan.org Here he raised his standard to rally the clans
9/J20   to the Jacobite cause. For a while on that day in Aug 1745 it looked as if few were
coming. Then pipes were heard and 600 Camerons came marching from the valley
(where the viaduct now spans). That must have been one helluva moment. It's
thought that he actually stood on the higher ground but there is a powerful sense
of place and history here. The visitor centre has an excellent map of Charlie's path
through Scotland – somehow he touched all the most alluring places! Climb the
tower (NTS) and see the monument from Loch Shiel (1724/ROUTES). Nice church
1km (1961/CHURCHES) and a great hotel with bar (1321/VERY SCOTTISH HOTELS).

Culloden near Inverness 1982/BATTLEGROUNDS.

ROBERT THE BRUCE (1274-1329)

1998   **Bruce's Stone** Glen Trool near Newton Stewart 26km north by A714 via
11/L29   Bargrennan (8km to head of glen) on the Southern Upland Way (2061/LONG WALKS). The
fair Glen Trool is a celebrated spot in Galloway Forest Park (1679/GLENS). The
stone is signed (200m walk) and marks the area where Bruce's guerrilla band
rained boulders onto the pursuing English in 1307 after routing the main army at
Solway Moss. Good walking, including Merrick which starts here (2033/HILLS).

1999   **Bannockburn** near Stirling The climactic battle in 1314, when Bruce decisively
10/N24   whipped the English and secured the kingdom (though Scotland was not
recognised as independent until 1328). The scale of the skirmish can be visualised
at the heritage centre but not so readily 'in the field'. 1988/BATTLEGROUNDS.

2000   **Arbroath Abbey** www.historic-scotland.gov.uk Not much of the Bruce trail
10/R22   here, but this is where the famous Declaration was signed that was the attempt of
HS   the Scots nobility united behind him to gain international recognition of the
independence they had won on the battlefield. What it says is stirring stuff; the
original is in Edinburgh. Great interpretation centre.

2001   **Dunfermline Abbey Church** www.historic-scotland.gov.uk Here, some
10/P25   tangible evidence: his tomb. Buried in 1329, his remains were discovered wrapped
HS   in gold cloth when the site was being cleared for the new church in 1818. Many of
the other great kings, the Alexanders I and III, were not so readily identifiable
(Bruce's ribcage had been cut to remove his heart). With great national emotion he
was reinterred under the pulpit. The church (as opposed to the ruins and Norman
nave adjacent) is open Easter-Oct, winter for services. Great café in Abbot House
through graveyard (2311/MUSEUMS). Look up and see Robert carved on the skyline.

2002   **Melrose Abbey** www.historic-scotland.gov.uk On his deathbed Bruce asked
10/R27   that his heart be buried here after it was taken to the Crusades to aid the Army in
HS   their battles. A likely lead casket thought to contain it was excavated from the
chapter house and it did date from the period. It was reburied here and is marked
with a stone. Let's believe in this!

The Important Literary Places

2003
9/L28
Robert Burns (1759-96) www.robertburns.org · Alloway, Ayr & Dumfries
A well-marked heritage trail through his life and haunts in Ayrshire and Dumfriesshire. His howff at Dumfries is very atmospheric. Best is at **Alloway**. The Auld Brig o' Doon and the Auld Kirk, where Tam o' Shanter saw the witches, dance are evocative, and the Monument and surrounding gardens are lovely. 1km up the road, the cottage, his birthplace, has little atmosphere (now NTS at last, improvements afoot). The Tam o' Shanter Experience visitor centre gets mobbed but is not recommended.
Ayr The Auld Kirk off main street by river; graveyard with diagram of where his friends are buried; open at all times. **Dumfries** House where he spent his last years and mausoleum 250m away at back of a kirkyard stuffed with extravagant masonry. 10km north of Dumfries on A76 at **Ellisland Farm** (home 1788-91) is the most interesting of all the sites. The farmhouse with genuine memorabilia, eg his mirror, fishing-rod, a poem scratched on glass, original manuscripts. There's his favourite walk by the river where he composed *Tam o' Shanter* and a strong atmosphere about the place. Open 7 days summer, closed Sun/Mon in winter. **Brow Well near Ruthwell** on the B725 20km south of Dumfries and near Caerlaverock (1808/BIRDS), is a quiet place, a well with curative properties where he went in the latter stages of his illness. Not many folk go to this one.

Burns and a' That Festival in May: once great, then a lapse. Now being rethought. Report: 41/EVENTS.

2004
10/S21
Lewis Grassic Gibbon (1901-35) www.grassicgibbon.com · Arbuthnott near Stonehaven Although James Leslie Mitchell left the area in 1917, this is where he was born and spent his formative years. Visitor Centre (01561 361668; Apr-Oct 7 days 10am-4.30pm) at the end of the village (via B967, 16km south of Stonehaven off main A92) has details of his life and can point you in the direction of the places he writes about in his trilogy, *A Scots Quair*. The first part, *Sunset Song*, is generally considered to be one of the great Scots novels and this area, the **Howe of the Mearns**, is the place he so effectively evokes. Arbuthnott is reminiscent of 'Kinraddie' and the churchyard 1km away on the other side of road still has the atmosphere of that time of innocence before the war which pervades the book. New, big film of *Sunset Song* on the way at TGP. His ashes are here in a grave in a corner; the inscription: 'the kindness of friends/the warmth of toil/the peace of rest'. From 1928 to when he died 7 years later at the age of only 34, he wrote an incredible 17 books.

2005
6/P14
Neil Gunn (1891-1973) www.neilgunn.org.uk · Dunbeath near Wick Scotland's foremost writer on Highland life, only recently receiving the recognition he deserves, was brought up in this North East fishing village and based 3 of his greatest yarns here, particularly *Highland River*, which must stand in any literature as a brilliant evocation of place. The **Strath** in which it is set is below the house (a nondescript terraced house next to the Stores) and makes for a great walk (2080/ GLEN & RIVER WALKS). There's a commemorative statue by the harbour, not quite the harbour you imagine from the books. The excellent heritage centre depicts the Strath on its floor and has a leaflet for you to follow. Gunn also lived for many years near **Dingwall** and there is a memorial on the back road to Strathpeffer and a wonderful view in a place he often walked (on A834, 4km from Dingwall).

2006
10/P27
James Hogg (1770-1835) St Mary's Loch, Ettrick 'The Ettrick Shepherd' who wrote one of the great works of Scottish literature, *Confessions of a Justified Sinner*, was born, lived and died in the valleys of the **Yarrow** and the **Ettrick**, some of

the most starkly beautiful landscapes in Scotland. **St Mary's Loch** on the A708, 28km west of Selkirk: there's a commemorative statue looking over the loch and the adjacent and supernatural seeming Loch of the Lowes. On the strip of land between is **Tibbie Shiels** pub (and hotel), once a gathering place for the writer and his friends (e.g. Sir Walter Scott) and still a notable hostelry (1366/PUBS). Across the valley divide (11km on foot, part of the Southern Upland Way (2061/LONG WALKS), or 25km by road past the Gordon Inn, Yarrow (1275/ROADSIDE INNS) is the remote village of **Ettrick**, another monument and his grave (and Tibbie Shiels') in the churchyard. His countryside is stark and beautiful. The James Hogg exhibition is at Bowhill House Visitor Centre (01750 22204).

2007 **Sir Walter Scott (1771-1832)** Abbotsford, Melrose No other place in
10/R27 Scotland (and few anywhere) contains so much of a writer's life and work. This was the house he rebuilt from the farmhouse he moved to in 1812 in the countryside he did so much to popularise. The house, until recently lived in by his descendants, is run by trustees. The library and study are pretty much as he left them, with 9,000 rare books, antiquarian even in his day. Pleasant grounds and topiary and a walk by the Tweed which the house overlooks. His grave is at **Dryburgh Abbey** (1978/ABBEYS). House open daily 9.30am-5pm; Sun 2-5pm (in winter 10am).

2008 **Robert Louis Stevenson (1850-94)** Edinburgh Though Stevenson travelled
2 widely – lived in France, emigrated to America and died and was buried in Samoa – he spent the first 30 years of his short life in Edinburgh. He was born and brought up in the New Town, living at **17 Heriot Row** from 1857-80 in a fashionable town house which is still lived in (not open to the public). Most of his youth was spent in this newly built and expanding part of the city in an area bounded then by parkland and farms. Both the **Botanics** (401/OTHER ATTRACTIONS) and **Warriston Cemetery** (1964/GRAVEYARDS) are part of the landscape of his childhood. However, his fondest recollections were of the **Pentland Hills** and, virtually unchanged as they are, it's here that one is following most poignantly in his footsteps. The 'cottage' at **Swanston** (a delightful village with some remarkable thatched cottages reached via the city bypass/Colinton turnoff or from Oxgangs Rd and a bridge over the bypass; the village nestles in a grove of trees below the hills and is a good place to walk from), the ruins of **Glencorse Church** (ruins even then and where he later asked that a prayer be said for him) and **Colinton Manse** can all be seen, but not visited. Edinburgh has no dedicated Stevenson Museum, but **The Writers' Museum** at Makars' Court has exhibits (& of many other writers). The **Hawes Inn** in South Queensferry where he wrote *Kidnapped* has had its history obliterated by a brewery makeover.

2009 **J.K. Rowling (we don't give a lady's birthdate)** www.jkrowling.com ·
2 **Edinburgh & elsewhere** Scotland's most successful writer ever as the creator of Harry Potter, rich beyond her wildest dreams, was once (and famously) an impecunious single mother scribbling away in Edinburgh coffee shops. The most-mentioned is opposite the Festival Theatre and is now a Chinese restaurant (upstairs), but not listed. The **Elephant House** (295/EDINBURGH COFFEE SHOPS) was another and gives you the idea. Harry Potter country as interpreted by Hollywood can be found at **Glenfinnan** (1997/MARY, CHARLIE & BOB) and **Glencoe** especially around the **Clachaig Inn** (1272/INNS). JKR lives near Aberfeldy – you might see her in another coffee shop, the one at the **House of Menzies** (2250/BEST SCOTTISH SHOPPING), though she no longer scribbles publicly.

2010 **Irvine Welsh (b.1958)** www.irvinewelsh.net · Edinburgh Literary
2 immortality awaits confirmation. Tours (*that* toilet etc) likely any day. **Robbie's Bar** might suffice (365/EDINBURGH 'UNSPOILT' PUBS); you will hear the voices.

The Really Spooky Places

2011 **Hidden or Lost Valley Glencoe** The secret glen where the ill-fated
9/J21 Macdonalds hid the cattle they'd stolen from the Lowlands and which became
2-B-2 (with politics and power struggles) their undoing. A narrow wooded cleft takes you
between the imposing and gnarled '3 Sisters' Hills and over the threshold (God
knows how the cattle got there) and into the huge bowl of Coire Gabhail. The place
envelops you in its tragic history, more redolent perhaps than any of the massacre
sites. Park on the A82 5km from the visitor centre 300m west of 2 white buildings
on either side of the road (always cars parked here). Follow clear path down to and
across the River Coe. Ascend keeping burn to left; 1.5km further up, it's best to
ford it. Allow 3 hours. (1984/BATTLEGROUNDS.)

2012 **Under Edinburgh Old Town www.edinburgholdtown.org.uk** · Mary King's
1/D4 Close, a medieval street under the Royal Mile closed in 1753 (**The Real Mary
King's Close** 08702 430160); and the Vaults under South Bridge – built in the 18th
century and sealed up around the time of the Napoleonic Wars (**Mercat Tours**
0131 557 6464). History underfoot for unsuspecting tourists and locals alike.
Glimpses of a rather smelly subterranean life way back then. It's dark during the
day, and you wouldn't want to get locked in.

2013 **The Yesnaby Stacks www.visitorkney.com** · **Orkney Mainland** A cliff top
3/P10 viewpoint that's so wild, so dramatic and, if you walk near the edge, so precarious
that its supernaturalism verges on the uneasy. Shells of lookout posts from the war
echo the melancholy spirit of the place. ('The bloody town's a bloody cuss/No
bloody trains, no bloody bus/And no one cares for bloody us/In bloody Orkney' –
first lines of a poem written then, a soldier's lament.) Near Skara Brae, it's about
30km from Kirkwall and way out west.

2014 **The Fairy Glen Skye** A place so strange, it's hard to believe that it's merely a
7/F17 geological phenomenon. Entering Uig on the A855 (becomes A87) from Portree,
there's a turret on the left (Macrae's Folly). Take road on right marked Balnaknock
for 2km and you enter an area of extraordinary conical hills which, in certain conditions of light and weather, seems to entirely justify its legendary provenance.
Your mood may determine whether you believe they were good or bad fairies, but
there's supposed to be an incredible 365 of these grassy hillocks, some 35m high –
well, how else could they be there?

2015 **Clava Cairns near Culloden, Inverness** Near Culloden (1982/BATTLEGROUNDS)
7/M18 these curious chambered cairns in a grove of trees near a river in the middle of
21st-century nowhere. This spot can be a seriously Blair Witch experience (1891/
PREHISTORIC SITES for details).

2016 **The Clootie Well www.blackisle.org** · **between Tore on the A9 & Avoch**
7/M17 Spooky, spooky place on the road towards Avoch and Cromarty 4km from the
roundabout at Tore north of Inverness. Easily missed, though now a marked car
park on the right side of the road going east. What you see is hundreds of rags
(actually pieces of clothing) hanging on the branches of trees around the spout of
an ancient well. They go way back up the hill behind and have probably been here
for decades. Don't wish you were here. This has what you'd call strange vibrations.

2017 **Burn O' Vat www.visitdeeside.org.uk** · **near Ballater** This impressive and
8/Q20 rather spooky glacial curiosity on Royal Deeside is a popular spot and well worth
the short walk. 8km from Ballater towards Aberdeen on main A93, take B9119 for
Huntly for 2km to the car park at the Muir of Dinnet nature reserve – driving

through forests of strange spindly birch. Some scrambling to reach the huge 'pot' from which the burn flows to Loch Kinord. Forest walks, busy on fine weekends, but very odd when you find it deserted.

2018
11/N29
Crichope Linn near Thornhill A supernatural sliver of glen inhabited by water spirits of various temperaments (and midges). Take road for Cample on A76 Dumfries to Kilmarnock road just south of Thornhill; at village (2km) there's a wooden sign so take left for 2km. Discreet sign and gate in bank on right is easy to miss, but quarry for parking 100m further on, on left, is more obvious. Take care – can be very wet and very slippy. Gorge is a 10-minute schlep from the gate. We saw red squirrels!

2019
9/L24
Sallochy Wood Loch Lomond B837, north of Balmaha, road to Rowardennan. Look for Sallochy Wood car park on the left. Cross back over the road, away from Loch Lomond, and follow the trail signs, up the hill. After the large cedar tree, the path takes you into the woods. Slippery going (on the exposed tree roots) then an unexpected clearing in middle of dense undergrowth. This is the ruined hamlet of Wester Sallochy. Surrounded by gloomy conifers, the roofless buildings still stand, awaiting the return of their long-dead tenants. Not a place to visit at night, but some do, and they leave their mark...

2020
8/S17
Hell's Lum Cave near Gardenstown, Moray Firth Coast A reader, Pauline Hetherington, writes, 'East of Gardenstown is Cullykhan Bay where you can park up and walk. On the approach to the mouth of the cave, you hear dreadful deep moaning sounds, like a sea monster.' With the swishing sea and the squawking gulls, this does sound like an eerie, isolated and unsettling spot. Don't blame me!

The Necropolis Glasgow 1963/GRAVEYARDS.
Hamilton Mausoleum Strathclyde Park 1927/MONUMENTS.
Loanhead of Daviot near Oldmeldrum 1908/PREHISTORIC SITES.

Section 9

Strolls, Walks & Hikes

Favourite Hills

Popular and notable hills in the various regions of Scotland but not including Munros or difficult climbs. Always best to remember that the weather can change very quickly. Take an OS map on higher tops. See p. 12 for walk codes.

2021
6/K14
2-C-3

✓ ✓ **Suilven Lochinver** From close or far away, this is one of Scotland's most awe-inspiring mountains. The 'sugar loaf' can seem almost insurmountable, but in good weather it's not so difficult. Route from Inverkirkaig 5km south of Lochinver on road to Achiltibuie, turns up track by Achin's Bookshop (2261/SCOTTISH SHOPPING) on the path for the Kirkaig Falls; once at the loch, you head for the Bealach, the central waistline through an unexpected dyke and follow track to the top. The slightly quicker route from the north (Glencanisp) following a stalkers' track that eventually leads to Elphin, also heads for the central breach in the mountain's defences. Either way it's a long walk in; 8km before the climb. Allow 8 hours return. At the top, the most enjoyable 100m in the land and below – amazing Assynt. 731m. Take OS map.

2022
6/J15
2-B-3

✓ ✓ **Stac Pollaidh/Polly near Ullapool** This hill described variously as 'perfect', 'preposterous' and 'great fun'; it certainly has character and, rising out of the Sutherland moors on the road to Achiltibuie off the A835 north from Ullapool, demands to be climbed. Route everyone takes is from the car park by Loch Lurgainn 8km from main road. Head for the central ridge which for many folk is enough; the path to the pinnacles is exposed and can be off-putting. Best half day hill climb in the North. 613m. Allow 3-4 hours return.

2023
6/J14

✓ ✓ **Quinag near Lochinver** Like Stac Polly (above), this Corbett has amazing presence and seems more formidable than it actually is. Park off the A894 to Kylesku. An up-and-down route can take in 6 or 7 tops in your 5-hour expedition (or curtail). Once again, awesome Assynt!

2024
9/J27
2-B-2

✓ **Goat Fell Arran** Starting from the car park at Cladach before Brodick Castle grounds 3km from town, or from Corrie further up the coast (12km). A worn path, a steady climb, rarely much of a scramble but a rewarding afternoon's exertion. Some scree and some view! 874m. Usually not a circular route. Allow 4 hours.

2025
9/K24
2-B-3

✓ **The Cobbler (aka Ben Arthur) Arrochar** Perennial favourite of the Glasgow hillwalker and, for sheer exhilaration, the most popular of 'the Arrochar Alps'. A motorway path ascends from the A83 on the other side of Loch Long from Arrochar (park in laybys near Succoth road end; there are always loads of cars) and takes 2.5-3 hours to traverse the up 'n' down route to the top. Just short of a Munro at 881m, it has 3 tops of which the north peak is the simplest scramble (central and south peaks for climbers). Where the way is not marked; consult.

• •

SIX MAGNIFICENT HILLS IN THE TROSSACHS

2026
10/L24
2-B-3

✓ **Ben Venue & Ben A'An** 2 celebrated tops in the Highland microcosm of the Trossachs around Loch Achray, 15km west of Callander; strenuous but not difficult and with superb views. Ben Venue (727m) is the more serious; allow 4-5 hours return. Start from Kinlochard side at Ledard or more usually from the Loch Katrine corner before Loch Achray Hotel. It's waymarked from new car park. Ben A'an (pronounced 'An') (415m) starts with a steep climb from the main A821 along from the Tigh Mor mansions (just before the corner). Scramble at top. Allow 2 to 3 hours.

2027
10/M23
2-B-3
Benn Shian Strathyre Another Trossachs favourite and not taxing. From village main road (the A74 to Lochearnhead), cross bridge opposite Monro Inn, turn left after 200m then path to right at 50m a steep start through woods. Overlooking village and views to Crianlarich and Ben Vorlich (see below). 600m. 1.5 hours.

2028
10/L24
1-B-1
Doon Hill The Faerie Knowe, Aberfoyle Legendary hillock in Aberfoyle, only 1 hour up and back, so a gentle elevation into faerie land. The tree at the top is the home of the 'People of Quietness' and there was once a local minister who had the temerity to tell their secrets (in 1692). Go round it 7 times and your wish will be granted, go round it backwards at your peril (well, you wouldn't, would you?). From main street take Manse Rd adjacent garden centre. 1km past cemetery and manse – then signed.

2029
10/M23
2-B-3
Ben Vorlich The big hill itself is also approached from the south Lochearn road; from Ardvorlich House 5km from A84. Enter 'East Gate' and follow signs for open hillside of Glen Vorlich. Track splits after 1.5km, take right then southeast side to come to north ridge of mountain. Allow 5 hours return.

2030
10/M24
2-B-3
Ben Ledi near Callander Another Corbett looking higher than it is with the Trossachs spread before you as you climb. West from town on A84 through Pass of Leny. First left over bridge to car park. Well trod path, ridge at top. Return via Stank Glen then follow river. Allow 4 hours.

• •

2031
10/H24
2-B-2
✓ **Dunadd Kilmartin north of Lochgilphead** 8km north on A816. Less of a hill, more of a lump, but it's where they crowned the kings of Dalriada for half a millennium. Stand on top when the Atlantic rain is sheeting in and ... you get wet like even the kings did. Kilmartin House Museum nearby for info and great food (2321/HISTORY, 1408/VEGETARIAN RESTAURANTS).

2032
11/N30
2-A-2
Criffel New Abbey near Dumfries 12km south by A710 to New Abbey, which Criffel dominates. It's only 569m, but seems higher. Exceptional views from top as far as English lakes and across to Borders. Granite lump with brilliant outcrops of quartzite. The annual race gets up and back to the Abbey Arms in under an hour; you can take it easier. Start 3km south of village, turnoff A710 100m from one of the curious painted bus shelters signed for Ardwell Mains Farm. Park before the farm buildings and get on up.

2033
11/L29
2-B-3
Merrick near Newton Stewart Go from bonnie Glen Trool via Bargrennan 14km north on the A714. Bruce's Stone is there at the start (1998/MARY, CHARLIE & BOB). The highest peak in Southern Scotland (843m), it's a strenuous though straightforward climb in glorious scenery. 4 hours.

2034
10/R25
BOTH 1-A-1
North Berwick Law The conical volcanic hill, a beacon in the East Lothian landscape. **Traprain Law** nearby, is higher, easy even if celebrated by rock climbers, but has major prehistoric significance as a hill fort citadel of the Goddodin and a definite aura. NBL is easy and rewarding – leave town by Law Rd, path marked beyond houses. Car park and picnic site. Views 'to the Cairngorms' (!) and along the Forth. Famous whalebone at the top.

2035
10/R28
2-A-2
Ruberslaw Denholm near Hawick This smooth hummock above the Teviot valley affords views of 7 counties, including Northumberland. Millennium plaque on top. At 424m, it's a gentle climb taking about 1 hour from the usual start at Denholm Hill Farm (private land, be aware of livestock). Leave Denholm at corner of Green by post office and go past war memorial. Take left after 2km to farm.

2036
10/N27
2-A-2
Tinto Hill near Biggar & Lanark A favourite climb in South/Central Scotland with easy access to start from A73 near Symington, 10km south of Lanark. Park 100m behind Tinto Hills farm shop. Good track, though it has its ups and downs before you get there. Braw views. 707m. Allow 3 hours.

2037
10/L25
2-A-2
Dumgoyne near Blanefield Close to Glasgow and almost a mountain, so a popular non-strenuous hike. Huge presence, sits above A81 and Glengoyne Distillery (open to public). Approach from Strathblane War Memorial via Campsie Dene road. 7km track, allow 3-4 hours (or take the steep way up from the distillery). Refresh/replenish in Killearn (874/CENTRAL HOTELS, 1398/PUB FOOD). Take care on outcrops.

2038 9/L24
2-A-2
Conic Hill Balmaha, Loch Lomond An easier climb than the Ben up the road and a good place to view it from, Conic, on the Highland fault line, is one of the first Highland hills you reach from Glasgow. Stunning views also of Loch Lomond from its 358m peak. Ascend through woodland from the corner of Balmaha car park. Watch for buzzards and your footing on the final crumbly bits. Access all year with new Access Code. Easy walks also on the nearby island, Inchcailloch (2094/WOODLAND WALKS). 1.5 hours up.

2039
10/P23
1-A-1
Kinnoull Hill www.forestry.gov.uk · Perth Various starts from town (the path from beyond Branklyn Garden on the Dundee Rd is less frequented) to the wooded ridge above the Tay with its tower and incredible views to south from the precipitous cliffs. Surprisingly extensive area of hill side common and it's not difficult to get lost. The leaflet/map from Perth tourist information centre helps. Local lurv spot after dark.

2040
8/R19
2-B-2
Bennachie near Aberdeen The pilgrimage hill, an easy 528m often busy at weekends but never a let-down. Various trails take in 'the Taps'. Traditional route from Rowan Tree near Chapel of Garioch (pronounced 'Geery') signed Pittodrie off A96 near Pitcaple. Also from Essons car park on road from Chapel-Monymusk, which is steeper. Or from other side the Lord's Throat road, a longer, more forested approach from banks of the Don. All car parks have trail-finders. From the fortified top you see what Aberdeenshire is about. 2 hours. Bennachie's soulmate, **Tap o' Noth**, is 20km west. Easy approach via Rhynie on A97 (then 3km).

2041
5/C20
Heaval Barra The mini-Matterhorn that rises above Castlebay is an easy and rewarding climb. At 1250ft, it's steep in places but never over-taxing. You see the road to Mingulay. Start up hill through Castlebay, park behind the new-build house, find path via Our Lady of the Sea. 1.5 hours return.

Hill Walks

The following ranges of hills offer walks in various directions and more than one summit. They are all accessible and fairly easy. See p. 12 for walk codes.

2042 **Walks On Skye www.skyewalk.co.uk** Obviously many serious walks in and
MAP 5 around the Cuillins (2057/MUNROS, 2065/SERIOUS WALKS), but almost infinite variety of others. Can do no better than read a great book, *50 Best Routes on Skye and Raasay* by Ralph Storer (available locally), which describes and grades many of the must-dos.

2043 **Lomond Hills** **Fife near Falkland** The conservation village lies below a promi-
10/P24 nent ridge easily reached from the main street especially via Back Wynd (off which
3-10KM there's a car park). More usual approach to both East and West Lomond, the main
CIRC tops, is from Craigmead car park 3km from village towards Leslie trail-finder board.
XBIKES The celebrated Lomonds (aka the Paps of Fife), aren't that high (West is 522m), but
2-A-2 they can see and be seen for miles. Also start from radio masts 3km up road from A912 east of Falkland.

An easy rewarding single climb is **Bishop Hill**. Start 100m from the church in Scotlandwell. A steep path veers left and then there are several ways up. Allow 2 hours. Great view of Loch Leven, Fife and a good swathe of Central Scotland. Gliders glide over from the old airstrip below.

2044 **The Eildons** **Melrose** The 3 much-loved hills or paps visible from most of the
10/R27 Central Borders and easily climbed from the town of Melrose which nestles at their
3KM foot. Leave main sq by road to station (the Dingleton road), after 100m a path
CIRC begins between 2 pebble-dash houses on the left. You climb the smaller first, then
XBIKES the highest central one (422m). You can make a circular route of it by returning to
1-A-2 the golf course. Allow 1.5 hours.

2045 **The Ochils** **www.friendsoftheochils.org.uk** Usual approach from the 'hillfoot
10/N24 towns' at the foot of the glens that cut into their south-facing slopes, along the
2-40KM A91 Stirling-St Andrews road. Alva, Tillicoultry and Dollar all have impressive glen
SOME CIRC walks easily found from the main streets where tracks are marked (2074/GLEN &
XBIKES RIVER WALKS). Good start near Stirling from the Sheriffmuir road uphill from Bridge
1/2-B-2 of Allan about 3km, look for pylons and a lay-by on the right (a reservoir just visible on the left). There are usually other cars here. A stile leads to the hills which stretch away to the east for 40km and afford great views for little effort. Highest point is Ben Cleugh, 721m. Swimming place nearby is paradise (1770/PICNICS).

2046 **The Lammermuirs** **www.lammermuirhills.com** The hills southeast of
10/R26 Edinburgh that divide the rich farmlands of East Lothian and the valley of the
5-155KM Tweed in the Borders. Mostly a high wide moor land but there's wooded gentle hill
SOME CIRC country in the watersheds of the southern rivers and spectacular coastal scenery
MTBIKES between Cockburnspath and St Abbs Head. (1837/WILDLIFE; 2121/COASTAL WALKS.)
1/2-B-2 The eastern part of the Southern Upland Way follows the Lammermuirs to the coast (2061/LONG WALKS). Many moorland walks begin at the car park at the head of Whiteadder Reservoir (A1 to Haddington, B6369 towards Humbie, then east on B6355 through Gifford), a mysterious loch in the bowl of the hills. Excellent walks also centre on Abbey St Bathans to the south – head off A1 at Cockburnspath. Through village to Toot Corner (signed 1km) and off to left, follow path above valley of Whiteadder to Edinshall Broch (2km). Further on, along river (1km), is a swing bridge and a fine place to swim. Circular walks possible; ask in village. Woodhall

Dene a great woody Lammermuir (foothill) option. And the Yester estate near Gifford became more accessible in '07 (447/EDINBURGH WOODLAND WALKS).

2047
10/S27
The Cheviots www.cheviot-hills.co.uk Not strictly in Scotland, but they straddle the border and Border history. There are many fine walks starting from Kirk Yetholm (including the Pennine Way which stretches 400km south to the Peak district and St Cuthbert's Way; 2064/LONG WALKS) including an 8km circular route of typical Cheviot foothill terrain. See *Walking in the Scottish Borders* available from all Border tourist information centres (one of many excellent guides). Most forays start at Wooler 20km from Coldstream and the border. Cheviot itself (2,676ft) a boggy plateau, Hedgehope via the Harthope Burn more fun. Or look for Towford (1769/RIVER PICNICS).

The Campsie Fells near Glasgow 758/WALKS OUTSIDE GLASGOW.
The Pentland Hills near Edinburgh 439/WALKS OUTSIDE EDINBURGH.

Some Great Starter Munros

✔ ✔ *There are almost 300 hills in Scotland over 3000ft as tabled by Sir Hugh Munro in 1891. Those selected here have been chosen for their relative ease of access both to the bottom and thence to the top. All offer rewarding climbs. None should be attempted without proper clothing (especially boots) and sustenance. You may also need an OS map. Never underestimate how quickly weather conditions can change in the Scottish mountains.*

2048
9/L24
Ben Lomond Rowardennan, Loch Lomond Many folk's first Munro, given proximity to Glasgow (soul and city). It's not too taxing a climb and has rewarding views (in good weather). 2 main ascents: 'tourist route' is easier, from toilet block at Rowardennan car park (end of road from Drymen), well-trodden all the way; or 500m up past Youth Hostel, a path follows burn – the 'Ptarmigan Route'. Steeper, but quieter. Circular walk possible. 974m. 3 hours up.

2049
10/M22
Schiehallion near Kinloch Rannoch 'Fairy Hill of the Caledonians' and a bit of a must. New path c/o John Muir Trust over east flank. Start Braes of Foss car park 10k from KR. 10km walk, ascent 750m. 6 hours. 1083m.

2050
10/M21
Carn Aosda Glenshee One of the most accessible starting from Glenshee ski car park follow ski tow up. Ascent only 270m of 917m. So you can bag a Munro in an hour. Easier still, take chairlift to Cairnwell, take in peak behind and then Carn Aosda – hey, you're doing three Munros in a morning. The Grampian Highlands unfold.

2051
7/M20
Meall Chuaich Dalwhinnie Starting from verge of the A9 south of Cuaich ascent only 623m, total walk 14km. Follow aqueduct to power station then Loch Cuaich. An easily bagged 951m.

2052
7/J16
An Teallach Torridon Sea-level start from Dundonnell on the A832 south of Ullapool. One of the most awesome Scots peaks but not the ordeal it looks. Path well trod; great scrambling opportunities for the nimble. Peering over the pinnacle of Lord Berkeley's Seat into the void is a jaw-drop. Take a day. Nice coffee shop called Maggie's near start/finish (1498/TEAROOMS). 1,062m.

2053 **Beinn Alligin Torridon** The other great Torridon trek. Consult re start at
7/J17 Torridon visitor centre on Torridon-Diabeg road. Car park by bridge on road to
Inveralligin and Diabeg, walk through woods over moor by river. Steepish pull up
onto the Horns of Alligin. You can cover 2 Munros in a circular route that takes you
across the top of the world. 985m.

2054 **Ben More Mull** The 'cool, high ben' sits in isolated splendour, the only Munro,
9/G23 bar the Cuillins, not on the mainland. Sea-level start from layby on the coast road
B8073 that skirts the southern coast of Loch Na Keal at Dhiseig House, then a
fairly clear path through the bleak landscape. Tricky near the top but there are
fabulous views across the islands. 966m.

2055 **Ben Wyvis near Garve** Standing apart from its northern neighbours, you can
7/L17 feel the presence of this mountain from a long way off. North of main A835 road
Inverness-Ullapool and very accessible from it, park 6km north of Garve (48km
from Inverness) and follow marked path by stream and through the shattered
remnants of what was once a forest (replanting in progress). Leave the dereliction
behind; the summit approach is by a soft, mossy ridge. Magnificent 1,046m.

2056 **Lochnagar near Ballater** Described as a fine, complex mountain, its nobility
10/Q20 and mystique apparent from afar, not least Balmoral Castle. Approach via Glen
Muick (pronounced 'Mick') road from Ballater to car park at Loch Muick
(1704/LOCHS). Path to mountain well signed and well trodden. 18km return, allow
6-8 hours. Steep at top; the loch supernatural. Apparently on a clear day you can
see the Forth Bridge. 1,155m.

2057 **Bla Bheinn Skye** The magnificent massif, isolated from the other Cuillins, has a
7/G19 sea-level start and seems higher than it is. The *Munro Guide* describes it as
'exceptionally accessible'. It has an eerie jagged beauty and – though some
scrambling is involved and it helps to have a head for exposed situations – there
are no serious dangers. Take B8083 from Broadford to Elgol through Torrin, park
1km south of the head of Loch Slapin, walking west at Allt na Dunaiche along
north bank of stream. Bla Bheinn (pronounced 'Blahven') is an enormously
rewarding climb. Rapid descent for scree runners, but allow 8 hours. 928m.

2058 **Ben Lawers between Killin & Aberfeldy** The massif of 7 summits including 6
10/M22 Munros that dominate the north side of Loch Tay are linked by a twisting ridge
12km long that only once falls below 800m. If you're very fit, it's possible to do the
lot in a day starting from the north or Glen Lyon side. Have an easier day of it
knocking off Beinn Ghlas then Ben Lawers from the visitor centre 5km off the
A827. 4/5 hours.

2059 **Meall Nan Tarmachan** The part of the ridge west of Lawers (above), which
10/M22 takes in a Munro and several tops, is not arduous and is immensely impressive.
Start 1km further on from NTS visitor centre down 100m track and through gate.

Long Walks

✓ ✓ *These walks require preparation, route maps, very good boots etc. But don't carry too much. Sections are always possible. See p. 12 for walk codes.*

2060
2
2-B-3

The West Highland Way www.west-highland-way.co.uk The 150km walk which starts at Milngavie 12km outside Glasgow and goes via some of Scotland's most celebrated scenery to emerge in Glen Nevis before the Ben. The route goes like this: Mugdock Moor-Drymen-Loch Lomond-Rowardennan-Inversnaid-Inverarnan-Crianlarich-Tyndrum-Bridge of Orchy-Rannoch Moor-Kingshouse Hotel-Glencoe-The Devil's Staircase-Kinlochleven. The latter part from Bridge of Orchy is the most dramatic. **The Bridge of Orchy Hotel** (01838 400208; 1267/ ROADSIDE INNS – not cheap!) and **Kingshouse** (01855 851259) are both historic staging posts, as is the **Drover's Inn, Inverarnan** (876/CENTRAL HOTELS). It's a good idea to book accommodation (allowing time for muscle fatigue) and don't carry too much. Info leaflet/pack from shops or **Ranger Service** (01389 722600).
START Officially at Milngavie (pronounced 'Mull-guy') Railway Station (regular service from Glasgow Central, also buses from Buchanan St Bus Station), but actually from Milngavie shopping precinct 500m away. However, the countryside is close. Start from other end on Glen Nevis road from roundabout on A82 north from Fort William. The Way is well marked, but you must have a route map.

2061
11/J30
2-B-3

The Southern Upland Way www.dumgal.gov.uk/southernuplandway 350km walk from Portpatrick south of Stranraer across the Rhinns of Galloway, much moorland, the Galloway Forest Park, the wild heartland of Southern Scotland, then through James Hogg country (2006/LITERARY PLACES) to the gentler east Borders and the sea at Pease Bay (official end, Cockburnspath). Route is Portpatrick-Stranraer-New Luce-Dalry-Sanquhar-Wanlockhead-Beattock-St Mary's Loch-Melrose-Lauder-Abbey St Bathans. The first and latter sections are the most obviously picturesque but highlights include Loch Trool, the Lowther Hills, St Mary's Loch, River Tweed. Usually walked west to east, the Southern Upland Way is a formidable undertaking... Info from **Ranger Service** (01835 830281).
START Portpatrick by the harbour and up along the cliffs past the lighthouse. or Cockburnspath. Map is on side of shop at the Cross.

2062
8/Q17
1-A-3

The Speyside Way A long distance route which generally follows the valley of the River Spey from Buckie on the Moray Firth coast to Aviemore in the foothills of the Cairngorms and thence to Newtonmore, with side spurs to Dufftown up Glen Fiddich (7km) and to Tomintoul over the hill between the River Avon (pronounced 'A'rn') and the River Livet (24km). The main stem of the route largely follows they valley bottom, criss-crossing the Spey several times – a distance of around 100km, and is less strenuous than Southern Upland or West Highland Ways. The Tomintoul spur has more hill-walking character and rises to a great viewpoint at 600m. Throughout walk you are in whisky country with opportunities to visit Cardhu, Glenlivet and other distilleries nearby (1571/1568/WHISKY). Info from **Ranger Service** (01340 881266).
START Usual start is from coast end. Spey Bay is 8km north of Fochabers; the first marker is by the banks of shingle at the river mouth.

2063 7/K18
2-C-3

Glen Affric www.glenaffric.org In enchanting Glen Affric and Loch Affric beyond (2072/GLEN & RIVER WALKS; 1671/GLENS; 1760/PICNICS), some serious walking begins on the 32km Kintail trail. Done either west-east starting at the Morvich Outdoor Centre 2km from A87 near Shiel Bridge, or east-west starting at the Affric Lodge 15km west of Cannich. Route can include one of the approaches to the Falls of Glomach (1682/WATERFALLS).

2064 St Cuthbert's Way www.st-cuthberts-way.co.uk From Melrose in Scottish
10/R27 Borders (where St Cuthbert started his ministry) to Lindisfarne on Holy Island off
2-A-3 Northumberland (where he died) via St Boswells-Kirk Yetholm-Wooler. 100km but
many sections easy. Bowden–Maxton and a stroll by the Tweed especially fine.
Check local tourist information centres. Leaflets/maps available.

Serious Walks

✓ ✓ *None of these should be attempted without OS maps, proper equipment and
preparation. Hill or ridge walking experience may be essential.*

2065 **7/G19** **The Cuillins** www.isleofskye.com · Skye Much scrambling and, if you want it,
3-C-3 serious climbing over these famously unforgiving peaks. The Red ones are easier
and many walks start at the Sligachan Hotel on the main Portree-Broadford road.
Every Jul there's a hill race up Glamaig; the conical one which overlooks the hotel.
Most of the Black Cuillins including the highest, Sgurr Alasdair (993m), and Sgurr
Dearg, 'the Inaccessible Pinnacle' (978m), can be attacked from the campsite or
the youth hostel in Glen Brittle. Good guides are *Introductory Scrambles from Glen
Brittle* by Charles Rhodes, or *50 Best Routes in Skye and Raasay* by Ralph Storer both
available locally, but you will need something. Take extreme care! (2/BIG ATTRAC-
TIONS; 1247/1248/HOSTELS; 1687/WATERFALLS; 2057/MUNROS; 1752/PICNICS.)

2066 **9/J21** **Aonach Eagach** Glencoe One of several possible major expeditions in the
3-C-3 Glencoe area and one of the world's classic ridge walks. Not for the faint-hearted
or the ill-prepared. It's the ridge on your right for almost the whole length of the
glen from Altnafeadh to the road to the Clachaig Inn (rewarding refreshment). Start
from the main road. Car park opposite the one for the Hidden Valley (2011/SPOOKY
PLACES). Stiff pull up then the switchback path across. There is no turning back.
Scary pinnacles two-thirds over, then one more Munro and the knee-trembling,
scree-running descent. On your way, you'll have come close to heaven, seen
Lochaber in its immense glory and reconnoitred some fairly exposed edges and
pinnacles. Go with somebody good as I once did. (1710/SCENIC ROUTES;
1360/BLOODY GOOD PUBS; 1243/HOSTELS; 1984/BATTLEGROUNDS.)

2067 **9/J21** **Buachaille Etive Mor** Glencoe In same area as above and another of the UK's
3-C-3 best high-level hauls. Not as difficult or precarious as the Eagach and long loved by
climbers and walkers, with stunning views from its several false summits to the
actual top with its severe drops. Start on main Glencoe road. 5km past King's
House Hotel. Well-worn path. Allow 6/7 hours return.

2068 **9/K21** **Ben Nevis** Start on Glen Nevis road, 5km Fort William town centre (by bridge
2-B-3 opposite youth hostel or from visitor centre) or signed from A82 after Glen Nevis
roundabout. Both lead to start at Achintee Farm and the Ben Nevis Inn (handy
afterwards; 1083/FORT WILLIAM). This is the main or tourist route which continues
to the top (many consider the tourist route to be very dull, but it is the safest).
Allow the best part of a day (and I do mean the best – the weather can turn quickly
here). For the more interesting arete route, consult locally. Many people are killed
every year, even experienced climbers. It is the biggest, though not the best; you
can see 100 Munros on a clear day (ie about once a year). You climb it because...
well, because you have to. 1344m.

2069 7/J19   **The Five Sisters of Kintail & The Cluanie Ridge** Both generally started
       3-C-3   from A87 along from Cluanie Inn (1364/BLOODY GOOD PUBS) and they will keep you
                right; usually walked east to west. Sisters is an uncomplicated but inspiring ridge
                walk, taking in 3 Munros and 2 tops. It's a hard pull up and you descend to a point
                8km further up the road (so arrange transport). Many side spurs to vantage-points
                and wild views. The Cluanie or south ridge is a classic which covers 7 Munros.
                Starts at inn; 2 ways off back onto A876. Both can be walked in a single day
                (Cluanie allow 9 hours). (1245/HOSTELS.)

                From the Kintail Centre at Morvich off A87 near Shiel Bridge another long distance
                walk starts to Glen Affric (2063/LONG WALKS).

2070 7/N19   **Glen More Forest Park** www.forestry.gov.uk from Coylumbridge and Loch
                Morlich; 32km. (2) joins (3) beyond Loch Morlich and both go through the
                Rothiemurchus Forest (2092/WOODLAND WALKS) and the famous **Lairig Ghru**, the
                ancient right of way through the Cairngorms which passes between Ben Macdui
                and Braeriach. Ascent is over 700m and going can be rough. This is one of the
                great Scottish trails. At end of Jun, the Lairig Ghru Race completes this course
                east-west in 3.5 hours, but generally this is a full-day trip. The famous shelter,
                Corrour Bothy between 'Devil's Point' and Carn A Mhaim, can be a halfway house.
                Near Linn of Dee, routes (1) and (2/3) converge and pass through the ancient
                Caledonian Forest of Mar. Going east-west is less gruelling and there's Aviemore to
                look forward to!

                Glen Affric Or rather beyond Glen Affric and Loch Affric (2072/GLEN WALKS;
                1671/GLENS), the serious walking begins (2063/LONG WALKS).

Glen & River Walks

See also Great Glens, p. 288. Walk codes are on p. 12.

2071
10/N21
UP TO 17KM
CIRC
XBIKES
1-B-2

✓**Glen Tilt Blair Atholl** A walk of variable length in this classic Highland glen, easily accessible from the old Blair Rd off main Blair Atholl road near Bridge of Tilt Hotel, car park by the (very) old bridge. Trail leaflet from park office and local tourist information centres. Fine walking and unspoiled scenery begins only a short distance into the deeply wooded gorge of the River Tilt, but to cover the circular route you have to walk to 'Gilbert's Bridge' (9km return) or the longer trail to Gow's Bridge (17km return). Begin here also the great route into the Cairngorms leading to the Linn of Dee and Braemar, joining the track from Speyside which starts at Feshiebridge or Glenmore Forest (2070/SERIOUS WALKS).

2072
7/K18
5/8 KM
CIRC
BIKES
1-B-2

✓**Glen Affric www.glenaffric.org · Cannich, near Drumnadrochit** Easy short walks are marked and hugely rewarding in this magnificent glen well known as the first stretch in the great east-west route to Kintail (2004/SERIOUS WALKS) and the Falls of Glomach (1682/WATERFALLS). Starting point of this track into the wilds is at the end of the road at Loch Affric; there are many short and circular trails indicated here. Car park is beyond metal road 2km along forest track towards Affric Lodge (cars not allowed to lodge itself). Track closed in stalking season. Easier walks in famous Affric forest from car park at Dog Falls. 7km from Cannich (1760/PICNICS). Waterfalls and spooky tame birds. Good idea to hire bikes at Drumnadrochit or Cannich (01456 415251). Don't miss Glen Affric (1671/GLENS).

2073
10/L23
18KM · XCIRC
XBIKES
2-B-2

✓**Balquhidder to Brig o' Turk** Easy amble through the heart of Scotland via Glenfinglas (1703/LOCHS) with handy pubs (1405/GASTROPUBS) and tearooms (1488/TEAROOMS) at either end. Not circular so best to arrange transport. Usually walked starting at Rob Roy graveyard (1971/GRAVEYARDS), then Ballimore and past Ben Vane to the reservoir and Brig o' Turk.

2074
10/N24
3KM + TOPS
CIRC
XBIKES
1-A-2

✓**Dollar Glen Dollar** The classic fairy glen in Central Scotland, positively hoaching with water spirits, reeking of ozone and euphoric after rain. Erosion has taken its toll and the path no longer goes deep into the gorge. 20km by A91 from Stirling or 18km from M90 at Kinross junction 6. Start at side of the museum or golf club, or further up road (signed Castle Campbell) where there are 2 car parks, the top one 5 minutes from castle. The castle at head of glen is open 7 days till 6pm (Oct-Mar till 4pm) and has boggling views. There's a circular walk back or take off for the Ochil Tops, the hills surrounding the glen. There are also first-class walks (the hill trail is more rewarding than the 'Mill Trail') up the glens of the other hillfoot towns, Alva and Tillicoultry which also lead to the hills (2045/HILL WALKS).

2075
10/N24
3KM
CIRC
XBIKES
1-A-1

✓**Rumbling Bridge near Dollar** Formed by another burn off the Ochils, an easier short walk in a glen with something of the chasmic experience and added delight of the unique double bridge (built 1713). At the end of one of the walkways under the bridge you are looking into a Scottish jungle landscape as the Romantics imagined. Near Powmill on A977 from Kinross (junction 6, M90) then 2km. Up the road is **The Powmill Milkbar** serving excellent home-made food for 40 years. It's 5km west on the A977. Open 7 days till 5pm (6pm weekends) (1470/TEAROOMS). Go after your walk!

2076
10/Q21

✓**Glen Clova www.clova.com** Most dramatic of the Angus glens. Most walks from end at Acharn especially west to Glen Doll and the Loops of (Loch) Brandy walk. Enquire at Glen Clova Hotel (1282/GET-AWAY HOTELS) and repair there afterwards (great walkers pub). Easy, rewarding walks! Check hotel for details.

2077
10/R23
1-A-1

✔ **The Lade Braes** St Andrews Unlike most walks here, this cuts through the town itself following the Kinness Burn. But you are removed from all that! Start at Westport just after the garage on Bridge St or opposite 139 South St. Trailboard and signs. Through Coldshaugh Park (sidespur to Botanics on opposite bank) and the leafy glen and green sward at the edge of this beautiful town. Ends in a duck pond. You pass the back gardens of some very comfortable lives.

2078
10/Q24
3KM
CIRC
XBIKES
1-A-2

Falkland Fife If you're in Falkland for the Palace (1851/CASTLES) or the tearoom (1489/TEAROOMS), add this amble up an enchanting glen to your day. Go through village then signed Cricket Club for Falkland Estate and School (an activity centre) – car park just inside gate (with map) – and gardens are behind it. Glen and refurbished path up the macadam road are obvious. Gushing burn, waterfalls – you can even walk behind one! Good café/restaurant in village.

2079
6/N15
6KM
CIRC
XBIKES
1-B-1

The Big Burn Walk Golspie A non-taxing, perfect glen walk through lush diverse woodland. 3 different entrances including car park marked from A9 near Dunrobin Castle gates but most complete starts beyond Sutherland Arms and Sutherland Stone at the end of the village. Go past derelict mill and under aqueduct following river. A supernature trail unfolds with ancient tangled trees, meadows, waterfalls, cliffs and much wildlife. 3km to falls, return via route to castle woods for best all-round intoxication.

2080
6/P14
XCIRC
XBIKES
1-B-1

The Strath at Dunbeath www.dunbeath-heritage.org.uk The glen or strath so eloquently evoked in Neil Gunn's *Highland River* (2005/LITERARY PLACES), a book which is as much about the geography as the history of his childhood. A path follows the river for many miles. A leaflet from the Dunbeath Heritage Centre points out places on the way as well as map on its entire floor. It's a spate river and in summer becomes a trickle; hard to imagine Gunn's salmon odyssey. It's only 500m to the broch, but it's worth going into the hinterland where it becomes quite mystical (1973/GRAVEYARDS).

2081
10/Q27
5/12KM
CIRC
XBIKES
1-A-1

Tweedside Peebles The river side trail that follows the River Tweed from town (Hay Lodge Park) past Neidpath Castle (1758/PICNICS) and on through classic Border wooded countryside crossing river either 2.5km out (5km round trip), at Manor Bridge 6km out (Lyne Footbridge, 12km). Pick up *Walking in the Scottish Borders* and other Tweedside trail guides at local tourist information centres.

Other good Tweedside walks between Dryburgh Abbey and Bemersyde House grounds and at Newton St Boswells by the golf course.

2082
10/L27
3/5KM · CIRC
XBIKES
1-A-1

Failford Gorge near Mauchline Woody gorge of the River Ayr. Start from bridge at Ayr end of village on B743 Ayr-Mauchline road (4km Mauchline). Easy, marked trail. Pub in village great for ale (they brew their own 'Windie Goat'!) and local craic but better for food is the Sorn Inn east of Mauchline (1381/GASTROPUBS). This is a very pleasant, bucolic part of Ayrshire.

2083
10/M23
3/5KM
CIRC
XBIKES
1-A-1

Glen Lednock near Comrie You can walk from Comrie or take car further up to monument or drive further into glen to reservoir (9km) for more open walks. From town take right off main A85 (to Lochearnhead) at Deil's Cauldron restaurant. Walk and Deil's Cauldron (waterfall and gorge) are signed after 250m. Walk takes less than 1hr and emerges on road near Lord Melville's monument (climb for great views back towards Crieff, about 25 minutes). Other walks up slopes to left after you emerge from the tree-lined gorge road. There's also the start of a hike up Ben Chonzie, 6km up glen at Coishavachan. This is one of the easiest Munros (931m), with a good path and great views, especially to the northwest.

2084
8/R17
Bridge of Alvah Banff Details: 2102/WOODLAND WALKS, mentioned here because the best bit is by the river and the bridge itself. The single span crossing was built in 1772 and stands high above the river in a sheer-sided gorge. The river below is deep and slow. In the right light it's almost Amazonian. Walk takes 1.5 hours from Duff House. There's a picture of Alvah upstairs in the collection.

2085
10/R21
2KM · XCIRC
XBIKES
1-A-1
The Gannochy Bridge & The Rocks Of Solitude near Edzell 2km north of village on B966 to Fettercairn. There's a lay-by after bridge and a wooden door on left (you're in the grounds of the Burn House). Through it is another world and a path above the rocky gorge of the River North Esk (1km). Huge stone ledges over dark pools. You don't have to be alone (well maybe you do).

2086
10KM
CIRC
BIKES
1-A-1
9/J23
Near Taynuilt A walk (recommended by readers) combining education with recreation. Start behind Bonawe Ironworks (2329/HISTORY) and go along the river side to a suspension bridge and thence to Inverawe Smokehouse (open to the public; café). Walk back less interesting but all very nice. Best not to park in Bonawe car park (for HS visitors, and it closes at 6pm).

2087
11/L30
Glen Trool near Newton Stewart A simple non-climbing, well marked route round Loch Trool. A circular 8km but with many options. And a caff. 1679/GREAT GLENS.

Woodland Walks

2088
9/G21
✓✓**Ardnamurchan** www.ardnamurchan.com For anyone who loves trees (or hills, great coastal scenery and raw nature), this far-flung - peninsula is a revelation. Approach from south via Corran ferry on A82 south of Fort William or north from Lochailort on A830 Mallaig–Fort William road (1724/SCENIC ROUTES) or from Mull. Many marked and unmarked trails (see Ariundle below) but consult tourist information centre and local literature. To visit Ardnamurchan is to fall in love with Scotland again and again. Woods especially around Loch Sunart. Good family campsite at Resipole (1315/CAMPING) and good food at Lochaline (1063/LESS EXPENSIVE HIGHLAND RESTAURANTS).

2089
8/N17
1-4KM
CIRC
XBIKES
1-A-2
✓**Randolph's Leap** near Forres Spectacular gorge of the plucky little Findhorn lined with beautiful beech woods and a great place to swim or picnic (1759/PICNICS), so listen up. Go either: 10km south of Forres on the A940 for Grantown, then the B9007 for Ferness and Carrbridge. 1km from the sign for Logie Steading (2249/SHOPPING) and 300m from the narrow stone bridge, there's a pull-over place on the bend. The woods are on the other side of the road. Or: take the A939 south from Nairn or north from Grantown and at Ferness take the B9007 for Forres. Approaching from this direction, it's about 6km along the road; the pull-over is on your right. If you come to Logie Steading in this direction you've missed it; don't – you will miss one of the sylvan secrets of the North. Trailboard at site and at Logie Steading (from which it's a 3.5km walk return).

2090
2-8KM
CIRC
XBIKES
2-A-2
9/J24
✓**Lochaweside** Unclassified road on north side of loch between Kilchrenan and Ford, centred on Dalavich. Illustrated brochure available from local hotels around Kilchrenan and Dalavich post office, describes 6 walks in the mixed, mature forest all starting from car parking places on the road. 3 starting from the Barnaline car park are trail-marked and could be followed without brochure. Avich Falls route crosses River Avich after 2km with falls on return route. Inverinan Glen is always nice. The 'timber trail' from The Big Tree/Cruachan car park 2km south of Dalavich takes in the loch, a waterfall and it's easy on the eye and foot (4km). The

track from the car park north of Kilchrenan on the B845 back to Taynuilt isn't on the brochure, may be less travelled and also fine. There's a pub at Kilchrenan.

2091 9/K25
3KM
CIRC
XBIKES
1-A-1

✓**Puck's Glen** www.forestry.gov.uk · **near Dunoon** Close to the gates of the Younger Botanic Garden at Benmore (1585/GARDENS) on the other side of the A815 to Stracher 12km north of Dunoon. A short, exhilarating woodland walk from a convenient car park. Ascend through trees then down into a faery glen, follow the burn back to the road. Some swimming pools.

2092
7/N19
1-A-2

✓**Rothiemurchus Forest near Aviemore** The place to experience the magic and the majesty of the great Caledonian Forest and the beauty of Scots pine. Approach from B970, the road that parallels the A9 from Coylumbridge to Kincraig/Kingussie. 2km from Inverdruie near Coylumbridge follow sign for Loch an Eilean; one of the most perfect lochans in these or any woods. Loch circuit 5km (1699/LOCHS). Good free brochure for all forest activities from tourist information centres. Rotheimurchus is the home of The Outsider Festival (48/EVENTS).

2093
9/H21
5KM
CIRC
MTBIKES
1-A-2

✓**Ariundle Oakwoods Strontian** 35km Fort William via Corran Ferry. Walk guide brochure at Strontian tourist information centre. Many walks around Loch Sunart and Ariundle: rare oak and other native species. You see how very different Scotland's landscape was before the Industrial Revolution used up the wood. Start over town bridge, turning right for Polloch. Go on past Ariundle Centre, with good home-baking café and park (1502/TEAROOMS). 2 walks; well marked.

2094 9/L25
3KM
CIRC
1-A-2

✓**Inchcailloch Island Loch Lomond** The surprisingly large island near and easily accessed from Balmaha is criss-crossed with easy, interesting woodland walks with the loch always there through the trees. Pleasant afternoon option is to row there from Balmaha boathouse (£10 a boat at TGP). Also regular ferry.

2095 7/H18
CIRC
XBIKES
1-A-1

Balmacarra www.nts.org.uk · **Lochalsh Woodland Garden** 5km south Kyle of Lochalsh on A87. A woodland walk around the shore of Loch Alsh, centred on Lochalsh House. Mixed woodland in fairly formal garden setting where you are confined to paths. Views to Skye. A fragrant and verdant amble. Ranger service.

2096
10/N22
3-3KM
CIRC
XBIKES
1-A-2

The Birks o' Aberfeldy Circular walk through oak, beech and the birch (or birk) woods of the title, easily reached and signed from town main street (1km). Steep-sided wooded glen of the Moness Burn with attractive falls especially the higher one spanned by bridge where the 2 marked walks converge. This is where Burns 'spread the lightsome days' in his eponymous poem. Nice tearoom back in town (1480/TEAROOMS).

2097
10/P22
3-2KM
CIRC
XBIKES
1-A-1

The Hermitage Dunkeld www.visitdunkeld.com On A9 2km north of Dunkeld. Popular, easy, accessible walks along glen and gorge of River Braan with pavilion overlooking the Falls and, further on, 'Ossian's Cave'. Also uphill Craig Vinean walks starts here to good viewpoint (2km). Several woody walks around Dunkeld/Birnam – there's a good leaflet from the tourist information centre. 2km along river is **Rumbling Bridge**, a deep gorge, and beyond it great spots for swimming (1755/SWIMMING HOLES).

2098
7/N19

Glenmore Forest Park www.forestry.gov.uk · **near Aviemore** Along from Coylumbridge (and adjacent Rothiemurchus) on road to ski resort, the forest trail area centred on Loch Morlich (sandy beaches, good swimming, water sports). Visitor centre has maps of walk and bike trails and an activity programme.

2099 **Above The Pass of Leny** Callander A walk through mixed forest (beech, oak,
10/M24 birch, pine) with great Trossachs views. Start from main car park on A84 4km
2 OR 4KM north of Callander (the Falls of Leny are on opposite side of road, 100m away) on
CIRC path at back, to the left – path parallels road at first (don't head straight up). Way-
XBIKES marked and boarded where marshy, the path divides after 1km to head further up
1-A-1 to crest (4km return) or back down (2km). Another glorious walk is to the
Bracklinn falls – signed off east end of Callander Main St; start by the golf
course (1km. See also 1766/SUMMER PICNICS.). Also loop to the Craggs (adding
another 2km).

2100 **Loch Tummel Walks** near Pitlochry The mixed woodland north of Loch
10/N22 Tummel reached by the B8019 from Pitlochry to Rannoch. Visitor centre at
2 -15KM Queen's View (1743/VIEWS) and walks in the Allean Forest which take in some
CIRC historical sites (a restored farmstead, standing stones) start nearby (2-4km). There
BIKES are many other walks in area and the Forest Enterprise brochure is worth following
1-B-2 (available from visitor centre and local tourist information centres). (1730/LOCHS.)

2101 **The New Galloway Forest** www.forestry.gov.uk Huge area of forest and hill
11/L30 country with every type of trail including part of Southern Upland Way from
Bargrennan to Dalry (2061/LONG WALKS). Visitor centres at Kirroughtree (5km
Newton Stewart) and Clatteringshaws Loch on the 'Queen's Way' (9km New
Galloway). Glen and Loch Trool are very fine (1679/GLENS); the 'Retreat Oakwood'
near Laurieston has 5km trails. Kitty's in New Galloway has great cakes and tea
(1471/TEAROOMS). There's a river pool on the Raiders' Rd (1767/PICNICS). One could
ramble on... Get the tourist information centre brochure.

2102 8/R17 **Duff House** www.duffhouse.org.uk · Banff Duff House is the major
7KM attraction around here (2342/PUBLIC GALLERIES), but if you've time it would be a
CIRC pity to miss the wooded policies and the meadows and riverscape of the Deveron.
XBIKES To the Bridge of Alvah where you should be bound is about 7km return; 1.5 hours
1-A-2 return. See also 2084/GLEN & RIVER WALKS.

2103 7/L17 **Torrachilty Forest & Rogie Falls** www.forestry.gov.uk · near Contin &
1-4KM **Strathpeffer** Enter by old bridge just outside Contin on main A835 west to
CIRC Ullapool or further along (4km) at Rogie Falls car park. Shame to miss the falls
XBIKES (1695/WATERFALLS), but the woods and gorge are pleasant enough if it's merely a
1-A-2 stroll you need. Ben Wyvis further up the road is the big challenge (2055/MUNROS).

2104 8/L19 **Abernethy Forest** near Boat of Garten 3km from village off B970, but hard
to miss because the famous ospreys are signposted from all over (1815/BIRDS).
Nevertheless this woodland reserve is a tranquil place among native pinewoods
around the loch with dells and trails. Many other birdies twittering around your
picnic. They don't dispose of the midges.

2105 8/Q17 **Fochabers** www.fochabers-heritage.org.uk on main A98 about 3km east of
town are some excellent woody and winding walks around the glen and Whiteash
Hill (2-5km). Further west on the **Moray Coast Culbin Forest** – head for
Cloddymoss or Kentessack off A96 at Brodie Castle 12km east of Nairn. Acres of
Sitka in sandy coastal forest.

Where To Find Scots Pine

Scots pine, with oak and birch etc, formed the great Caledonian Forest which once covered most of Scotland. Native Scots pine is very different from the regimented rows of pine trees we associate with forestry plantations and which now drape much of the countryside. It is more like a deciduous tree with reddish bark and irregular foliage; no two ever look the same. The remnants of the great stands of pine are beautiful to see, mystical and majestic, a joy to walk among and no less worthy of conservation perhaps than a castle or a bird of prey. Here are some places you will find them:

Rothiemurchus Forest 2092/WOODLAND WALKS.

2106 **Glentanar www.glentanar.co.uk · Royal Deeside** Near Ballater, 10-15km
8/Q20 southwest of Aboyne.

2107 8/P18 Around **Braemar** and **Grantown-On-Spey**.
10/P20

2107A Around **Linn of Dee** (1720/SCENIC ROUTES), especially the back road to Mar Lodge
10/P20 (1344/HOUSE PARTIES).

2108 **Strathyre near Callander** South of village on right of main road after Loch
10/M24 Lubnaig.

2109 **Achray Forest www.forestry.gov.uk · near Aberfoyle** Some pine near the
10/L24 Duke's Pass road, the A821 to Loch Katrine, and amongst the mixed woodland in
the 'forest drive' to Loch Achray.

2110 **Blackwood Of Rannoch www.rannoch.net** South of Loch Rannoch, 30km
10/L22 west of Pitlochry via Kinloch Rannoch. Start from Carie, fair walk in. 250-year-old
pines; an important site.

2111 **Rowardennan Loch Lomond** End of the road along east side of loch near Ben
9/L25 Lomond. Easily accessible pines near the loch side, picnic sites etc.

2112 Shores of **Loch Maree, Loch Torridon** and around **Loch Clair, Glen**
7/J17 **Torridon**. Both near the **Beinn Eighe National Nature Reserve** (1780/GREAT
WILDLIFE RESERVES). Visitor Centre on A832 north of Kinlochewe.

2113 **Glen Affric near Drumnadrochit** 1627/GLENS. Biggest remnant of the
7/L18 Caledonian Forest in classic glen. Many strolls and hikes possible. Try Dog Falls (on
main road) for Affric introduction.

Native pinewoods aren't found south of Perthshire, but there are fine plantation examples in southern Scotland at:

2114 **Glentress near Peebles** 7km on A72 to Innerleithen. Mature forest up the burn
10/Q27 side, though surrounded by commercial forest.

2115 **Shambellie Estate near Dumfries** 1km from New Abbey beside A710 at the
11/N29 Shambellie House, 100yds sign. Ancient stands of pine over the wall amongst
other glorious trees; this is like virgin woodland. Planted 1775-80. Magnificent.

Coastal Walks

2116
9/F26
XCIRC
XBIKES
2-B-2
✓ ✓ **Kintra Islay** On Bowmore-Port Ellen road take Oa turnoff: then Kintra signed 7km. Park in old farmyard by campsite (1294/WILD CAMPING). A fabulous beach (1655/BEACHES) runs in opposite direction and a notable golf course behind it (2149/GOLF IN GREAT PLACES). This walk leads along north coast of the Mull of Oa, an area of diverse beauty, sometimes pastoral, sometimes wild, with a wonderful shoreline. Many great picnic spots.

2117
8/T18
✓ ✓ **The Bullers Of Buchan near Peterhead** 8km south of Peterhead on A975 road to/from Cruden Bay. Park and walk 100m to cottages. To the north is the walk to Longhaven Nature Reserve, a continuation of the dramatic cliffs and more sea bird city. The Bullers is at start of walk, a sheer-sided 'hole' 75m deep with an outlet to the sea through a natural arch. Walk round the edge of it, looking down on layers of birds (who might try to dive-bomb you away from their nests); it's a wonder of nature on an awesome coast. Take great care (and a head for heights).

2118
6/K12
✓ ✓ **Cape Wrath & The Cliffs of Clo Mor** www.capewrath.org.uk Britain's most northwesterly point reached by ferry from 1km off the A838 4km south of Durness by Cape Wrath Hotel; a 10-minute crossing then 40-minute minibus ride to Cape. Ferry holds 12 and runs May-Sep (call for times: 01971 511343). At 280m Clo Mor are the highest cliffs in UK; 4km round trip from Cape. MoD range – access may be restricted. In other direction, the 28km to Kinlochbervie is one of Britain's most wild and wonderful coastal walks. Beaches include Sandwood (1653/BEACHES). While in this North West area: **Smoo Cave** 2km east of Durness.

2119
6/J14
1-B-2
✓ **Old Man Of Stoer near Lochinver** The easy, exhilarating walk to the dramatic 70km sandstone sea stack. Start from lighthouse off unclassified road 14km north Lochinver. Park and follow sheep tracks; cliffs are high and steep. 7km round trip; 2/3 hours. Then find the Secret Beach (1660/BEACHES).

2120
11/N30
1-A-2
✓ **Rockcliffe to Kippford** An easy and can be circular stroll along the 'Scottish Riviera' through woodland near the shore (2km) past the 'Mote of Mark' a Dark Age hill fort with views to Rough Island. The better cliff top walk is in the other direction to Castlehillpoint. Good teashop in Rockcliffe (1500/TEAROOMS).

2121
10/S25
5-10KM
CIRC · XBIKES
1-B-2
✓ **St Abbs Head** Some of the most dramatic coastal scenery in Southern Scotland, scary in a wind, rhapsodic on a blue summer's day. Extensive wildlife reserve and trails through coastal hills and vales to cliffs. Cars can go as far as lighthouse, but best to park at visitor centre near farm on St Abbs village road 3km from A1107 to Eyemouth and follow route (1837/WILDLIFE). Very nice caff here.

2122
7/H18
Applecross This far peninsula is marvellous for many reasons including staying alive and eating out (1712/SCENIC ROUTES), but there are fine walks in and around the foreshore of Applecross Bay including river and woodland strolls. All detailed in a 'scenic walks' leaflet available locally.

2123 9/H21
10KM RET
XCIRC
BIKES
1-B-1
Singing Sands Ardnamurchan 2km north of Acharacle, signed for Arevegaig. 3km to Arevegaig and park before wooden bridge (gate may be locked). Cross wooden bridge, following track round side of Kentra Bay. Follow signs for Gorteneorn, and walk through forest track and woodland to beach. As you pound the sands they should 'sing' to you whilst you bathe in the beautiful views of Rum,

Eigg, Muck and Skye (and just possibly the sea). Check at tourist information centre for directions and other walks booklet. 'Beware unexploded mines', it says. Mmm!

2124 8/R17
8KM · XCIRC
XBIKES
1-A-1
East From Cullen Moray Coast This is the same walk mentioned with reference to Sunnyside (1651/BEACHES), a golden beach with a fabulous ruined castle (Findlater) that might be your destination. There's a track east along from harbour. 2 hours return. Superb coastline.

2125 8/S17
Crovie-Troup Head Moray Coast Another Moray Coast classic that takes in the extraordinary cliff-clinging village of Crovie and the bird-stacked cliffs of the headland. Start at car park and viewpoint above Crovie 15km east of Banff off B9031. Park and walk to end of village, then follow path to Troup Head. 5km return.

2126 7/M17
5KM
CIRC
XBIKES
1-A-1
The South Sutor Cromarty The walk, known locally as 'The 100 Steps' though there are a few more than that, from Cromarty village (1639/COASTAL VILLAGES, 1505/TEAROOMS, 1067/HIGHLAND RESTAURANTS) round the tip of the south promontory at the narrow entrance to the Cromarty Firth. East of village; coastal path hugs shoreline then ascends through woodland to headland. Good bench! Go further to top car park and viewpoint panel. Return by road. There may be dolphins!

2127 10/R24
2-B-2
The Chain Walk Elie Unique and adventurous headland scramble at the west end of Elie (and Earlsferry). Go to end of the road then by path skirting golf course towards headland. Hand- and footholds carved into rock with chains to haul yourself up. Emerge by Shell Bay Caravan Park. Watch tide; don't go alone.

2128 9/J26
2-B-2
Cock of Arran Lochranza This round trip starts in the moors but descends to breathtaking coastal trail past some interesting spots (see 2415/FANTASTIC ISLAND WALKS). Great for twitchers, ramblers and fossils (strong boots needed)! Approx 8km (5 hours) from village. Take a picnic.

Section 10

Sports

Scotland's Great Golf Courses

Those listed open to non-members and available to visitors (including women) at most times, unless otherwise stated. Handicap certificates may be required. There's a brilliant official guide, Official Guide to Golf in Scotland, *published by VisitScotland and available from tourist information centres.*

AYRSHIRE

2129
9/K28
✓ ✓ ✓ **Turnberry** www.turnberry.co.uk · **01655 334032** Ailsa (championship) and Arran. Sometimes possible by application. Otherwise you must stay at hotel (832/AYRSHIRE HOTELS.) Superb. Golf academy a great place to learn.

2130
9/K27
✓ ✓ **Royal Old Course** www.royaltroon.co.uk · **01292 311555 · Troon** Very difficult to get on. No wimmen. Staying at Marine Highland Hotel (01292 314444) helps. Easier is **The Portland Course** (also 01292 311555) across the road from Royal. And 802/AYRSHIRE HOTELS for the adjacent Piersland House Hotel.

2131
9/K27
✓ **Glasgow Gailes/Western Gailes** www.glasgowgailes-golf.com · **0141 942 2011/01294 311258** Superb links courses next to one another, 5km south of Irvine off A78.

2131A
9/L27
Old Prestwick www.prestwickgc.co.uk · **01292 671020** Original home of the Open and 'every challenge you'd wish to meet'. Hotels opposite cost less than a round. Unlikely to get on weekends (Sat members only).

EAST LOTHIAN

There is a great booklet available at the local tourist information centre, entitled Golf in East Lothian.

2132
9/R25
✓ ✓ **Gullane No.1** www.gullanegolfclub.com · **01620 842255** One of 3 varied courses surrounding charming village on links and within driving distance (35km) of Edinburgh. Muirfield is nearby, but you need an introduction. Gullane is okay most days except Sat/Sun. (Handicap required for no.1 only – under 24 men, 30 ladies.) No.3 best for beginners. Visitor centre acts as clubhouse for non-members on nos. 2/3. Clubhouse for members/no.1 players only.

2133
9/R25
✓ ✓ **North Berwick East & West** www.northberwick.org.uk · **01620 892726** East (officially the Glen Golf Club) has stunning views. A superb cliff-top course and is not too long. West more taxing (especially the classic 'Redan') used for Open qualifying; a very fine links. Also has 9-hole kids' course (01620 892135).

2134
9/Q25
Musselburgh Links www.musselburgholdlinks.co.uk · **0131 665 5438** The original home of golf (really: golf recorded here in 1672), but this local authority-run 9-hole links is not exactly top turf and is enclosed by Musselburgh Racecourse. Nostalgia still appeals though. **Royal Musselburgh** (01875 810276) nearby compensates. It dates to 1774, fifth-oldest in Scotland. Busy early mornings and Fri-Sun.

NORTH EAST

2135
10/R23
✓ ✓ **Carnoustie** www.carnoustiegolflinks.co.uk · 01241 853789 3 good links courses; even possible (with handicap cert) to get on the championship course (though weekends difficult). Every hole has character. Buddon Links is cheaper and relatively quiet. Combination tickets available. A well-managed and accessible course, increasingly a golfing must. Open held here '07.

2136
8/T19
✓ **Murcar Links** www.murcar.co.uk · 01224 704354 · **Aberdeen** Getting on Royal Aberdeen Course is difficult for most people, but Murcar is a testing alternative, a seaside course 6km north of centre off Peterhead road signed at roundabout after Exhibition Centre. Handicap certificate needed. Other municipal courses include charming 9-hole at Hazelhead (in an excellent 3-course complex).

2137
8/T18
✓ **Cruden Bay** www.crudenbaygolfclub.co.uk · 01779 812285 · near Peterhead On A975 40km north of Aberdeen. Designed by Tom Simpson and ranked in UK top 50, a spectacular links course with the intangible aura of by-gone days. Quirky holes epitomise old-fashioned style. Weekends difficult to get on.

2138
7/N17
✓ **Nairn** www.nairngolfclub.co.uk · 01667 453208 Traditional seaside links course and one of the easiest championship courses to get on. Good clubhouse, friendly folk. Nairn Dunbar on other side of town also has good links. Handicap certificate required.

2139
6/N16
✓ **Royal Dornoch** www.royaldornoch.com · 01862 810219 Sutherland championship course laid out by Tom Morris in 1877. Recently declared 5th-best course in the world outside the US, but not busy or incessantly pounded. No poor holes. Stimulating sequences. Probably the most northerly great golf course in the world – and not impossible to get on. Sister course the **Struie** also a treat.

FIFE

2140
10/R23
✓ ✓ ✓ **St Andrews** www.standrews.org.uk · 01334 466666 The home and Mecca of golf, very much part of the town and probably the largest golf complex in Europe. Old Course most central, celebrated. Application by ballot the day before (handicap cert needed). For Jubilee (1897, upgraded 1989) and Eden (1914, laid out by Harry S. Holt paying homage to the Old with large, sloping greens), apply the day before. New Course (1895, some rate the best) easiest access. Less demanding are the new Strathtyrum and Balgove (upgraded 9-hole for beginners) courses. All 6 courses contiguous and 'in town'; the Dukes Course (part of Old Course Hotel) 3km away is a great alternative to the links. Reservations (and ballot). A whole lot of golf to be had – get your money out! And course number 7 on its way '08.

2141
10/R24
✓ ✓ **Kingsbarns** www.kingsbarns.com · 01334 460860 Between St Andrews and Crail. One of Fife's newest courses but already hailed as one of its best. Beautiful location – a secret coast and Cammo House grounds. Not cheap.

2142
10/Q24
✓ **Ladybank** www.ladybankgolf.co.uk · 01337 830814 Best inland course in Fife; Tom Morris-designed again. Very well kept and organised. Good facilities. Tree-lined and picturesque.

2143
10/R24
Elie 01333 330301 Splendid open links maintained in top condition; can be windswept. The starter has his famous periscope and may be watching you. Adjacent 9-hole course, often busy with kids, is fun (01333 330955).

2144
10/R24
Crail www.crailgolfingsociety.co.uk · **01333 450686** Balcomie Links originally designed by the legendary Tom Morris, or Craighead Links new sweeping course. All holes in sight of sea. Not expensive; easy to get on.

2145
10/Q24
Lundin Links www.lundingolfclub.co.uk · **01333 320202** Challenging seaside course used as Open qualifier. Some devious contourings. There is a separate course for women (01333 320832).

ELSEWHERE

2146
10/N24
✓ ✓ ✓ **Gleneagles** www.gleneagles.com · **0800 704705** Legendary golf the mainstay of resort complex in perfect Perthshire (hotel 01764 662231; report: 1201/COUNTRY-HOUSE HOTELS). 4 courses including PGA centenary which will host Ryder Cup in 2014. No handicap certificates required.

2147
9/L24
✓ ✓ **Loch Lomond Golf Club** www.lochlomond.com · **01436 655555** · **Luss** On A82 1km from conservation village of Luss. Exclusive American-owned club; membership expensive and the list's closed. We can buy a cheaper season ticket to see the annual Scottish Open (Jul; 01436 655559); but no access to plebs to clubhouse. 18 holes of scenic golf by the Loch. This is golfing for gold.

2148
10/S27
✓ ✓ **Roxburghe Hotel Golf Course** www.roxburghe.net · **01573 450333** · **near Kelso** Only championship course in the Borders. Designed by Dave Thomas along banks of River Teviot. Part of the Floors Castle estate. Open to non-residents. Fairways bar/brasserie clubhouse. Report: 884/BORDER HOTELS.

Good Golf Courses In Great Places

All open to women, non-members and inexpert players. See VisitScotland's Official Guide to Golf in Scotland, *available from tourist information centres.*

2149
9/F26
✓ **Machrie** www.machrie.com · **01496 302310** · **Isle of Islay** 7km Port Ellen. Worth going to Islay (BA's airstrip adjacent course or CalMac ferry from Kennacraig near Tarbert) just for the golf. The Machrie (Golf) Hotel is sparse but convenient. Old-fashioned course to be played by feel and instinct. Splendid, sometimes windy isolation with a warm bar and restaurant at the end of it. The notorious 17th, 'Iffrin' (it means Hell), vortex shaped from the dune system of marram and close-cropped grass, is one of many great holes. 18 holes.

2150
9/G28
✓ **Macrihanish** www.machgolf.com · **01586 810213** · **by Campbeltown** Amongst the dunes and links of the glorious 8km stretch of the Machrihanish Beach (1652/BEACHES). The Atlantic provides thunderous applause for your triumphs over a challenging course. 9/18 holes.

2151
11/N30
✓ **Southerness** www.southernessgolfclub.com · **01387 880677** · **Solway Firth** 25km south of Dumfries by A710. A championship course on links on the silt flats of the Firth. Despite its prestige, visitors do get on. Start times available 10-12pm and 2-4pm. There are few courses as good as this at this price (under £50 a round). Under the wide Solway sky, it's pure – southerness. 18 holes.

2152
10/P22
✓ **Rosemount** www.theblairgowriegolfclub.co.uk · **01250 872622** · **Blairgowrie** Off A93, south of Blairgowrie. An excellent, pampered and well-managed course in the middle of green Perthshire, an alternative perhaps to

Gleneagles, being much easier to get on (most days) and rather cheaper (though not at weekends). 18 holes.

2153
8/N19
✓ **Boat of Garten** www.boatgolf.com · 01479 831282 Challenging, picturesque course in town where ospreys have been known to wheel overhead. Has been called the 'Gleneagles of the North'; certainly the best around, though not for novices. 18 holes.

2154
6/M16
✓ **Tain & Brora** 01862 892314 & 01408 621911 2 northern courses that are a delight to play on. Tain designed by Tom Morris in 1890. Brora stunning with good clubhouse and coos on the course. With Royal Dornoch (above), they're a roving-golfer must.

2155
9/H23
Glencruitten www.obangolf.com · 01631 562868 · **Oban** Picturesque course on the edge of town. Head south (A816) from Argyll Sq, bearing left at church. Course is signed. Quite tricky with many blind holes. Can get busy, so phone first. 18 holes.

2156
7/H16
Gairloch www.gairlochgolfclub.com · 01445 712407 Just as you come into town from the south on A832, it looks over the bay and down to a perfect, pink, sandy beach. Small clubhouse with honesty box out of hours. Not the world's most agonising course; in fact, on a clear day with views to Skye, you can forget agonising over anything. 9 holes.

2157
5/E16
Harris Golf Club www.harrisgolf.com · 01859 550226 · **Scarista, Isle of Harris** Phone number is for the captain, but no need to phone – just turn up on the road between Tarbert and Rodel and leave £10 in the box. First tee commands one of the great views in golf and throughout this basic, but testing course, you are looking out to sea over Scarista beach (1658/BEACHES) and bay. Sunset may put you off your swing.

2158
11/M29
New Galloway www.nggc.co.uk · 01644 420737 Local course on south edge of this fine wee toon. Almost all on a slope but affording great views of Loch Ken and the Galloway Forest behind. No bunkers and only 9 short holes, but exhilarating play. Easy on, except Sun. Just turn up.

2159
10/R28
Minto www.mintogolf.co.uk · 01450 870220 · **Denholm** 9km east of Hawick. Spacious parkland in Teviot valley. Best holes 3rd, 12th and 16th.
Vertish Hill 01450 372293 · **Hawick** A more challenging hill course. Both among the best in Borders. 18. Best holes 2nd and 18th. An excellent guide to all the courses in the Borders in available from tourist information centres: *Freedom of the Fairways*.

2160
10/M22
Taymouth Castle www.scotland-golf.co.uk · 01887 830228 · **Kenmore** Spacious green acres around the enigmatic empty hulk of the castle. Well-tended and organised course between A827 to Aberfeldy and the river. Inexpensive, and guests at the Kenmore Hotel (964/PERTHSHIRE HOTELS) get special rate. 18 holes.

2161
10/R26
Gifford www.giffordgolfclub.com · 01620 810591 Dinky inland course on the edge of a dinky village, bypassed by the queue for the big East Lothian courses and a guarded secret among the regulars. Generally ok, but phone starter (above) for available. 9 holes.

2162 **Strathpeffer** www.strathpeppergolf.co.uk · **01997 421219** Very hilly (and we
7/L17 do mean hilly) course full of character and with exhilarating Highland views. Small-
town friendliness. You are playing up there with the gods and some other old
codgers. 18 holes.

2163 **Elgin** www.elgingolfclub.com · **01343 542338** 1km from town on A941 Perth
8/P17 road. Many memorable holes on moorland/parkland course in an area where links
may lure you to the coast (Nairn, Lossiemouth). 18 holes.

2164 **Durness** www.durnessgolfclub.org · **01971 511364** The most northerly golf
6/L12 course on mainland UK, on the wild headland by Balnakeil Bay, looking over to
Faraid Head. The last hole is 'over the sea'. Only open since 1988, it's already got
cult status. 2km west of Durness.

2165 **Rothesay** www.rothesaygolfclub.com · **01700 503554** Sloping course with
9/J26 breathtaking views of Clyde. Visitors welcome. What could be finer than taking the
train from Glasgow to Wemyss Bay for the ferry over (5/FAVOURITE JOURNEYS) and
18 holes. Finish up with fish 'n' chips at the West End (1444/FISH & CHIPS) on the
way home.

2166 **Traigh** www.triaghgolf.co.uk · **01687 450337** · **Arisaig** A830 Fort William-
7/H20 Mallaig road, 2km north Arisaig. Pronounced 'try' - and you may want to. The
islands are set out like stones in the sea around you and there are 9 hilly holes of
fun. Has been called 'the most beautiful 9 holes in the world'.

Best of the Skiing

In a good year the Scottish ski season can extend from Dec (or even Nov) till the 'lambing snow' of late April. And on a good day it can be as exhilarating as anywhere in Europe. A great brochure, Ski-Scotland, with diagrams of runs, is available from www.ski-scotland.com or from tourist information centres.

Here's a summary (distances in kilometres):

	GLENSHEE	CAIRNGORM	NEVIS RANGE	GLENCOE	THE LECHT
DIST/EDIN	130	215	215	165	200
DIST/GLAS	170	235	200	150	160
NR CENTRE	Perth 65	Inverness 45	Fort William 10	Fort William 40	Aberdeen 95
NR TOWN	Braemar 20	Aviemore 15	Fort William 10	Ballachullish 20	Tomintoul 11
NO OF RUNS	38	19	35	19	21
EASY	10	3	7	4	7
INTERMED	13	6	12	6	7
DIFFICULT	13	9	11	7	6
ADVANCED	2	1	5	2	1
UPLIFTS	24	15	11	7	15
CAFÉS	3	2	2 + units	2	1 + 1 unit
GOOD FOR	*Size*	*Size*	*Uplift*	*Fewer crowds*	*Fewer crowds*
	Access from road	*Non-skiing*	*Access*	*Near road*	*Near road*
	Views Glas Maol	*Views*	*Views/Sunsets*	*Views*	*Families*
	2 distinct areas	*Intermediate*	*Ski School*	*Most alpine*	*Beginners*
	Snowboarding	*Snowboarding*	*Café*		

2167   **GLENSHEE**
10/P21

Base Station 01339 741320
School 01250 885216/07904 983007

SKI & SNOWBOARD HIRE
Base Station 01339 741320
Cairnwell Ski School 01250 885216 · Spittal of Glenshee

WHERE TO STAY
£45-60   **Dalmunzie House Hotel** 01250 885224 9km south. Country house. 9-hole golf adjacent. Family-run. 956/PERTHSHIRE HOTELS.
Bridge of Cally Hotel 01250 886231 36km south. 1271/INNS.
£30-38   **Glenisla** 01575 582223 · Kirkton of Glenisla 32km southeast.
£38-45   **Spittal of Glenshee** 01250 885215 8km south. Cheap 'n' cheerful.

WHERE TO EAT
Cargill's Bistro 01250 876735 · Blairgowrie 977/PERTHSHIRE EATS.
Dalmunzie/Bridge Of Cally Hotel/Glenisla As above.

APRÈS-SKI
Blackwater Inn 17km south on main road. A good all-round pub. Occasional live music.

2168 CAIRNGORM
8/N19

Base Station 01479 861261
School 01479 810296

SKI & SNOWBOARD HIRE
Aviemore Ski & Snowboard Hire & School 01479 811917

WHERE TO STAY

£30-38 **Corrour House** www.corrourhousehotel.co.uk · 01479 810220 11km west.
Aviemore Bunkhouse www.aviemore-bunkhouse.com · 01479 811181
1232/HOSTELS.

£45-60 **Hilton Coylumbridge Hotel** www.hilton.co.uk/coylumbridge · 01479
810661 10km west. Nearest and best of modern Aviemore hotels. 2 pools/sauna.
Ski hire. Okay restaurant. Comfort when you need it.

£30-38 **Cairngorm** 01479 810630 · Aviemore Main street of main town. Busy bar.
Rooms not unreasonably priced and lots of them.

£38-45 **The Cross** 01540 661166 · Kingussie 1021/HIGHLANDS HOTELS.

WHERE TO EAT
The Cross 01540 661166 · Kingussie See Where to Stay, above.
The Einich 01479 812334 · Coylumbridge 1073/INEXPENSIVE HIGHLANDS
RESTAURANTS.
The Boathouse 01540 651394 · Kincraig 1074/INEXPENSIVE HIGHLANDS
RESTAURANTS.
The Old Bridge Inn Aviemore Welcoming, good atmosphere. 1391/GASTRO-
PUBS.

APRÈS-SKI
The Winking Owl Aviemore At end of main street. Owl's Nest.

2169 THE NEVIS RANGE/AONACH MOR
9/K21

Base Station 01397 705825
School 01397 705825

SKI & SNOWBOARD HIRE
Base Station 01397 705825
Nevis Sport 01397 704921 · Fort William
Ellis Brigham 01397 706220

WHERE TO EAT & STAY
See 1083/FORT WILLIAM.

APRÈS-SKI
No pub in immediate vicinity. Nearest all-in ski centre is **Nevis Sport** Fort
William · 01397 704921. Bar (side entrance) till midnight. Self-serve café all day
till 5pm (4.30pm Sun). Bookshop and extensive ski/outdoor shop on ground floor.

2170 GLENCOE
9/J21

Base Station 01855 851226
School 01855 851226

SKI & SNOWBOARD HIRE
Base Station 01855 851226

WHERE TO EAT & STAY
See 1083/FORT WILLIAM and also:
Isles of Glencoe Hotel 01855 811602 · **Ballachulish** Modern development
leisure centre including pool. Good touring base. 1211/KIDS.
Clachaig Inn 01855 811 252 · **Glencoe** Famous 'outdoor inn' for walkers,
climbers etc with pub (1360/BLOODY GOOD PUBS), pub food and inexpensive
accommodation.
Kingshouse Hotel www.kingshouse-scotland.co.uk · 01855 851259 The
classic travellers' inn 1km from A82 through glen and near slopes (8km). Pub with
food/whisky. Inexpensive rooms but very basic.

APRÈS-SKI
As above, especially Clachaig Inn and Kingshouse.

2171 THE LECHT
8/Q19

Base Station 019756 51440
School 019756 51412

SKI & SNOWBOARD HIRE
Base Station 019756 51440

WHERE TO STAY
Nearest town (28km south) with big choice of hotels is Ballater. But also:
Glenavon Hotel www.glenavon-hotel.co.uk · 01807 580218 · **Tomintoul**
On the square in Tomintoul, the nearest town. The most ski- and hiking-friendly
place in the zone.
£30-38 **Richmond Arms Hotel** 01807 580777 · **Tomintoul** On sq. Traditional hotel,
log fires. A very good prospect. 24 rooms.

WHERE TO EAT
£38-45 **The Clockhouse** 01807 580378 · **Main Street, Tomintoul** Good reputation.
Green Inn 01339 755701 · **Ballater** Also has rooms. 1022/NORTHEAST
RESTAURANTS.
Station Restaurant 01339 755050 · **Ballater** Converted from old station.
Daytime only.
£45-60 **Gordon Hotel** 01807 580206 · **Tomintoul** The local hotel with the most
aspirational menu.

APRÈS-SKI
£30-38 **Glenavon Hotel** 01807 580218 · **Tomintoul** Good large bar for skiers, walkers
(southern end of Speyside Way is here) and locals.
Allargue Hotel 019756 51410 · **Cockbridge** On road south to Ballater 5km
from slopes and overlooking Corgarff Castle and the trickle of the River Don.
Rooms also.

The Best Sledging Places

If we ever see good snow again, locals will know where the best slopes are. Here's my suggestions for Edinburgh and Glasgow:

EDINBURGH

2172   **The Braid Hills** The connoisseur's choice, you sledge down friendly and not-too-challenging slopes in a crowded L.S. Lowry landscape that you will remember long after the thaw. Off Braid Hills Drive at the golf course. Can walk in via Blackford Glen Rd. **Corstorphine Hill** Gentle broad slope with woodland at top and trails (438/CITY WALKS) and a busy road at the bottom. Approach via Clermiston Rd off Queensferry Rd. **Queen's Park** The lesser slopes that skirt Arthur's Seat, and further in around Hunter's Bog for the more adventurous or less sociable sledger.

GLASGOW

2173   **Kelvingrove Park** At Park Terr side. No long runs but a winter wonderland when the rime's in the trees. **Gartnavel Hospital Grounds** In West End (Hyndland) off Great Western Rd. You can play safe sledging into the playing field, or more adventurously through the woodlands. **Queen's View** On A809 north of Bearsden 20km from centre. A very popular walk (765/BEST VIEWS) is also a great place to sledge. Variable slopes off the main path. The Highlands can be seen on a clear day. **Ruchill Park** In north of city (766/BEST VIEWS) and **Queen's Park** in south.

The Best Cycling

EASY CYCLING

2174   ✓ **The Borders** The Borders with its gentle hills, river tracks and low urbanisa-
10/S27   tion seems to be paving the cycleway both for mountain biking (see below) and for more leisurely and family pursuits. Good linkage and signage and many routes, eg the 4 Abbeys, the Tweed Cycleway, the Borderloop and individual trails. Guides available from tourist information centres for almost all the Border towns. There's ample choice for all abilities and ages.

2175   **Speyside Way Craigellachie-Ballindalloch** The cycling part of the Way
8/Q18   (1998/LONG WALKS), with great views; flat and no cars. Goes past distilleries.
20KM   Circular by return on minor roads.
CAN BE CIRC   **START** Craigellachie by rangers' office.

2176   **Forth & Clyde Canal Glasgow–Falkirk Wheel** East out of the city, urban at
10/M25   first then nice in the Kelvin Valley; Kilsyth Hills to the north. Falkirk Wheel should
55KM   be seen (4/ATTRACTIONS).
  START The Maryhill Locks, Maryhill Rd.

2177   **Glentrool near Newton Stewart** Two routes from visitor centre (1706/LOCHS,
11/L29   1998/MARY, CHARLIE & BOB). Deep in the forest and well signed. Briefly joins public
15KM   road. The 7 Stanes sections can be difficult.
CAN BE CIRC   **START** Glentrool visitor centre off A714. Bike hire at **Kirroughtree** and network of trails listed from here (see below).

2178
12KM/
VARIOUS
CIRC

Edinburgh Trails Edinburgh streets can be a nightmare for cyclists and there's lots of uphill graft. But there is a vast network of cycle and towpaths especially north of the New Town. Another good run is to Balerno from Union Canal towpath in lower Gilmore Place. End at Balerno High School.

2179
10/L24
11KM
CAN BE CIRC

The Trossachs www.lochlomond-trossachs.org · near Aberfoyle & Callander Many low-level lochside trails. Consult tourist information centres. Nice run is Loch Ard Circle from Aberfoyle going west (signed Inversnaid Scenic Route).

2180
8/N19
20KM
CIRC

Loch An Eilean near Aviemore Lots of bike tracks here in the Rothiemurchus Forrest. This one goes past one of Scotland's most beautiful lochs (1699/LOCHS) and you can go further to Loch Insh via Feshiebridge and around Glen Feshie. Probably best to get a route leaflet at visitor centre (loch car park and Coylumbridge). Outsider Festival uses this route (48/EVENTS). **START** signed from B970 at Coylumbridge.

2181
9/K26

Cumbrae Take ferry from Largs to beautiful Cumbrae Island (1463/CAFÉS). Four or five routes around the island. One a stiff pull to a great viewpoint. Others stick to sea level. Consult leaflet from tourist information centre. All roads quiet.

MOUNTAIN BIKING

2182

✓ ✓ **7 Stanes www.7stanes.gov.uk · Borders & South West** Ambitious and hugely popular network of bike trails in south of Scotland, some still under construction. Include **Glentress/the Tweed Valley** (see below), **Newcastleton, Forest of Ae, Dalbeattie, Mabie, Glentrool** (see above), and **Kirroughtree** (see above). Routes at all levels. Many challenges. Good signage and information available from local tourist information centres.

2183
10/Q27

✓ ✓ **Glentress Forest www.thehubintheforest.co.uk · near Peebles** Specially constructed mountain-bike trails. Well signed and well used in this hugely popular national cycling centre. Great café (1464/CAFÉS).Trails for all levels, plenty of flowing descents and drops. **7 Stanes** cross-country route also starts near by at Traquair.

2184
11/M29
25KM
CIRC

Clatteringshaws Near Glentrool (see above). Various routes around Clatteringshaws Loch in the Galloway Forest and Hills. Most are easy, but some serious climbs and descents. Visitor centre has tearoom. Routes under construction as part of 7 Stanes Project.

2185 8/Q20
25KM
CIRC

Glen Tanner www.royal-deeside.org.uk · Deeside Good way to encounter this beautiful glen in the shadow of Mount Keen. Quite difficult in places. Start: Tombae on the B976 opposite junction of A97 and A93.

2186
7
XCIRC

Great Glen, Fort William-Loch Lochy Easy at first on the Caledonian Canal towpath. Later it gets hilly with long climbs. Great views. **START** Neptune's Staircase at Banavie near Fort William.

2187
10
25KM
CIRC

Perthshire & Angus, Glenfernate-Blair Atholl Beautiful Highland trail that takes in forests, lochs and Glen Tilt (2071/GLEN WALKS). Mainly rough track. Follow directions from tourist information centre leaflets. **START** On the A924 14km east of Pitlochrie, 500m east of school.

The Best Leisure Centres

2188
10/P23
✓ **Perth Leisure Pool** www.liveactive.co.uk · 01738 635454 A perfect example of the mega successful water-based leisureland. Large shaped pool with outside section (open also in winter, when it's even more of a novelty); 2 flumes, 'wild water channel', whirlpools etc. 25m 'training' pool for lengths (check times). Outdoor kids' area. Excellent facility. Daily 10am-8.30pm (Fri 10pm).

2189
7/M18
✓ **Aquadome Inverness** www.invernessleisure.com · 01463 667500 Inverness's all-weather attraction. Leisure waters; including 3 flumes, wave machine and toddler area. Huge competition pool for serious swimming and luxurious health suites; massages, hydrotherapy and (ladies) that essential bikini line wax. All in all, a bigger splash. Mon-Fri 7.30am-10pm, Sat-Sun until 5pm.

2190
10/R25
✓ **Dunbar Pool** www.eastlothian.gov.uk · 01368 865456 Model of its kind, overlooking old harbour (where folks used to swim on a summer's day) and castle ruins. Cool, modern design amidst the warm red sandstone. Flumes and wave machine that mimics the sea outside; lengths just possible in between (though it's often very crowded). Phone for opening hours.

2191
9/K27
Magnum Centre 01294 278381 · **Irvine** From Irvine's throughway, follow signs for Harbourside then Magnum. A big shed, unalluring and now looking rather tatty. But a phenomenally successful pleasuredrome providing every diversion from the monotony of my namesake outside: from soothing bowls to frenetic skating, pools (in season), cafés, courses; you name it. Secrete endorphins and other hormones.

2192
10/M26
The Time Capsule 01236 449572 · **Monklands** They say Monklands, but where you are going is downtown Coatbridge about 15km from Glasgow via M8. Leisure (and 25m) pool and (refurbished) ice-rink. Even if you haven't been swimming for years, this is the sort of place you force the flab into the swimsuit. Cafés and view areas. Facilities of the clean-up-your-act variety (eg squash, health suite). 6.30am-9pm.

2193
10/M26
Dollan Aqua Centre www.southlanarkshire.gov.uk · 01355 260000 · **East Kilbride** An excellent family leisure centre. 50m pool, fitness facilities, soft play area and Scotland's first interactive flume (aquatic pin ball machine with you as the ball!) – there had to be a twist. Mon, Wed, Fri 7.30am-10pm; Tue, Thu 8am-10pm; Sat & Sun 8am-5pm.

2194
2/A4
Scotstoun Leisure Centre www.glasgow.gov.uk · 0141 959 4000 · **Glasgow** Clydeside expressway then A814, right at Victoria Park lights, first left after roundabout. Danes Drive. If 'modernity is suburban' this is state of the art. 10-lane pool, sports halls, health suite, dance studio and gym. Outdoor footie and tennis – it's enormous. Mon-Fri 9am-9pm, Sat till 4pm, Sun till 8pm.

2195
10/R23
East Sands Leisure Centre www.fifedirect.org.uk · 01334 476506 · **St Andrews** From South St take road for Crail then follow signs. About 2km from centre. Bright and colourful centre overlooking the East Sands, the less celebrated beach of St Andrews. Mainly a fairly conventional pool with 25m lane area as well as 50m water slide, toddlers' pool etc. Also 2 squash courts, gym with Pulsestar machines, 'remedial suite', bar and café. 7 days. Hours vary.

2196
10/P25
Beacon Leisure Centre www.fifedirect.org.uk · 01592 872211 · **Burntisland** On the front of quietly-getting-on-with-it Fife town near Kirkcaldy. Family fun pool centre with 'landmark' beacon thing and external flume tubes. It

does work. Loadsa kids and 'waves' do come. Latest swimming in area (9.30pm, but check). 7 days Mon-Fri 8am-6pm, Sat/Sun 11am-5pm.

2197 **Beach Leisure Centre** www.aberdeencity.gov.uk · 01224 655401 · Beach
8/T19 Esplanade, Aberdeen Multisports facility with bars and cafés. Leisure Pool isn't much use for swimming (Aberdeen has many others, 2206/swimming pools) but it's fun for kids with flumes etc. Lynx Ice Arena adjacent for skating, curling, ice hockey. Outside is the long long beach and the North Sea. Call for times.

The Best Swimming Pools & Sports Centres

For Edinburgh, see p. 86–87; for Glasgow, p. 134. See also Leisure Centres, p 375–76.

2198 ✓ **Stonehaven Outdoor Pool** www.stonehavenopenairpool.co.uk ·
10/S20 01569 762134 · Stonehaven The 'Friends of Stonehaven Outdoor Pool' won the day (eat your hearts out North Berwick) and saved a great pool that goes from length to strength. Fabulous 1930s Olympic-sized heated salt-water pool (85ft). Midnight swims in midsummer most Wednesdays (is that cool, or what?). Jun-Sep only: 10am-7.30pm (10am-6pm weekends). Heated salt-water heaven.

2199 ✓ **Gourock Bathing Pool** 01475 631561 The only other open-air (proper)
9/K25 pool in Scotland that's still open! On coast road south of town 45km from Glasgow. 1950s-style leisure. Heated (to 88°), so it doesn't need to be a scorcher (brilliant, but choc-a-block when it is). Open May-early Sep weekdays until 8pm.

2200 ✓ **The Waterfront** Greenock · 01475 797979 Easily spotted at the water-
9/K25 front at Customhouse Way: vast building resembling a modernist whale car-cass; a rather groovy one at that. Big leisure pool, proper swim pool, 65m flume, ice rink, gym and more. Undeniably fun. Daily all year. Hours vary, phone to check.

2201 ✓ **Carnegie Centre** www.fife.gov.uk · 01383 314200 · Pilmuir Street,
10/P25 Dunfermline Excellent sports centre with many courses and classes. 2 pools (ozone-treated), 25m, and kids' pool. Lane swimming lunch time and evenings. Authentic Turkish and Aeretone Suite with men's, women's and mixed sessions. Large gym with Pre-cor stations etc. Badminton, squash, aerobic classes. Usually open till 9pm, but check. Keeping Dunfermline fitter then most of us.

2202 ✓ **The Leisuredrome** www.eastdunbarton.gov.uk · 0141 772 6391 ·
2/XF1 Balmuildy Road, Bishopbriggs At the north edge of Glasgow, best reached by car or 1km walk from station; adjacent Forth and Clyde Canal walkway (755/city walks). Large, modern, efficient with 25m pool, multi gym, sauna, games hall, café etc. Mon-Fri 9am-10/10.30pm.

2203 ✓ **Linlithgow Pool** www.westlothianleisure.com · 01506 775440 On
10/N25 edge of pleasant town off Lanark road. Modern, light, airy sports centre with sauna and steam room at the pool side and West Lothian outside the windows. Excellent community facility, well designed and laid out. All towns should enjoy this quality of life. Daily till 9pm, gym 10pm (Sat pool till 7pm, gym 8pm).

2204 ✓ **Lochbroom Leisure Centre** www.highland.gov.uk · 01854 612884 ·
6/K15 Ullapool 2 streets back from waterfront, but central. Games hall and very nice pool, easy to get in and out, tiny sauna. Small-town friendly atmosphere. 7 days till 8pm (Sat/Sun 6pm).

2205
10/R27
Galashiels Pool www.galashiels.bordernet.co.uk · **01896 752154** Award-winning pool in the Central Borders on the edge of parkland with picture windows bringing the outside in. No leisurama nonsense, just a good deck-level pool (25m) (Teviotdale Leisure Centre). Modern pool in Hawick also good. Phone for times.

2206
8/T19
Aberdeen Baths 01224 587920 City well served with swimming pools. 3 in suburbs are not especially easy to find, though Hazlehead (01224 310062) is signed from inner ring road to west of centre. Only open to public from 6pm weekdays, all day weekends. Bon Accord Baths are a fine example of a municipal pool; recently refurbished, they're centrally situated behind the west end of Union St. Annie Lennox learned to swim here. The newer Beach Leisure Centre has just about thought of everything (2197/LEISURE CENTRES). Hours vary.

2207
9/F26
MacTaggart Centre 01496 810767 · **Bowmore, Islay** Eco-friendly pool (heated by adjacent distillery) overlooking bay. Interesting whisky-cask-shaped ceiling and good fitness suite. Laundry facilities. Closed Mon.

The Best Watersports Centres

2208
10/R24
✓ **Elie Watersports** www.eliewatersports.com · **01333 330962/ 07799 481925** · **Elie** Great beach location in totally charming wee town where there's enough going on to occupy non-watersporters. Easy lagoon for first timers and open season for non-experienced users. Wind-surfers, kayaks, water-ski. Also mountain bikes and inflatable 'biscuits'. 936/FIFE HOTELS, 1395/GASTROPUBS, 2143/GREAT GOLF.

2209
9/J22
✓ **Linnhe Marina** www.linnhemarina.co.uk · **01631 730401/ 07721 503981** · **Lettershuna, Port Appin** 32km north of Oban on A828 near Portnacroish. Established, personally run business in a fine sheltered spot for learning and plootering. More manna than sports these days but they almost guarantee to get you windsurfing over to the island in 2 hours. Individual or group instruction. Wayfarers, Luggers and fishing boats. Moorings. Row boats for hire. Castle Stalker and Lismore are just round the corner, seals and porpoises abound; the joy of sailing. May-Sep 9am-6pm.

2210
9/K26
✓ **Scottish National Watersports Centre 01475 530757** · **Cumbrae** · www.nationalcentrecumbrae.org.uk Ferry from Largs (centre near ferry terminal so 5km Millport) then learn all about how to pilot things that float. You need to book – call them, then bob about 'doon the watter'. Great range of courses. 2-bunkroom accommodation available.

2211
10/P25
✓ **Port Edgar** www.peyc.org.uk · **0131 331 3330** · **South Queensferry** At end of village, under and beyond the Forth Road Bridge. Major marina and water sports centre. Berth your boat, hire dinghies (big range). Big tuition programme for kids and adults including canoes. Home to Port Edgar yacht club.

2212
10/M26
✓ **Strathclyde Park** www.northlan.gov.uk · **01698 266155** Major water sports centre 15km southeast of Glasgow and easily reached from Central Scotland via M8 or M74 (junction 5 or 6). 200-acre loch and centre with instruction on sailing, canoeing, windsurfing, rowing, water-skiing. Hire canoes, Lasers and Wayfarers, windsurfers and trimarans. Call booking office for sessions/times.

2213
7/N19
✓ **Loch Insh Watersports** www.lochinsh.com · 01540 651272 · **Kincraig**
On B970, 2km from Kincraig towards Kingussie and the A9. Marvellous loch site launching from gently sloping dinky beach into shallow forgiving waters of Loch Inch. Hire of canoes, dinghies (Toppers, Lasers, Wayfarers, Seafarers, darts) and windsurfers as well as rowing boats; river trips. Archery and mountain biking. An idyllic place to learn. Watch the others and the sunset from the balcony restaurant (1074/INEXPENSIVE HIGHLAND RESTAURANTS). Sports Apr-Oct 9.30am-5.30pm.

2214
7/N19
✓ **Loch Morlich Watersports** www.lochmorlich.com · 01479 861221 · **near Aviemore** By Glenmore Forest Park, part of the plethora of outdoor activities hereabouts (skiing, walking etc). This is the loch you see from Cairngorm and just as picturesque from the woody shore. Surprising coral-pink beach! Canoes/kayaks/rowing boats and dinghies (Wayfarers, Toppers, Optimists) with instruction in everything. Evening hire possible. Coffee shop up top. Good campsite adjacent (1305/CAMPING WITH KIDS).

2215
11/M30
✓ **Galloway Sailing Centre** www.lochken.co.uk · 01644 420626 · **Loch Ken near Castle Douglas** 15km north on A713 to Ayr. Dinghies, windsurfers, canoes, kayaks, tuition. Also the Climbing Tower so you can zip-wire and take the leap of faith! All this by a serene and forgiving loch by the Galloway Forest. Phone for times and courses. Open Mar-Nov.

2216
7/K20
Great Glen Water Park 01809 501381 3km south of Invergarry on A82. On shores of tiny Loch Oich and Loch Lochy in the Great Glen. Wonderful spot, with many other lochs nearby. Day visitors welcome with windsurfers, Wayfarers, kayaks, canoes and also mountain bikes and fishing rods for hire. Mainly, however, a chalet park with all the usual condo/timeshare facilities (you can rent per week).

2217
9/L26
Clyde Muirshiel Regional Park www.clydemuirshiel.co.uk · 01505 842882 · **Castle Semple Centre, Lochwinnoch** 30km southwest of Glasgow M8 junction 29, A737 past Johnstone then A760. Also 20km from Largs via A760. Loch (near village) is 3km x 1km and at the visitor centre you can hire dinghies and canoes etc (also mountain bikes). Bird reserve on opposite bank (1841/WILDLIFE RESERVES). Peaceful place to learn. 10am-5pm.

2218
9/K25
Kip Marina www.kipmarina.co.uk · 01475 521485 · **Inverkip** Major sailing centre on Clyde coast 50km west of Glasgow via M8, A8 and A78 from Greenock heading south for Wemyss Bay. A yacht heaven as well as haven of Grand Prix status. Sails, charters, pub/restaurant, chandlers and myriad boats. Diving equipment and dinghies for hire.

2219
10/P24
Lochore Meadows www.lochore-meadows.co.uk · 01592 583388 · **near Lochgelly** From Dunfermline-Kirkcaldy motorway take Lochgelly turnoff into town and follow signs for Lochore Country Park. Small, safe loch for learning and perfecting. Canoes and dinghies for hire. Equipped for disabled. Park contains 2 good adventure playgrounds for wide age range. 1 Apr-31 Oct.

2220
10/M23
Lochearnhead Watersports www.lochearnhead-water-sports.co.uk · 01567 830330 On A85 near junction with A84 is a water sports centre specialising in anything that's pulled by a boat: skiing, boarding etc. Certainly the loch is wide open and (usually) gently lapping the sport is nice to watch. Café.

2221
7/G18
Raasay Outdoor Centre www.raasayoutdoorcentre.co.uk · 01478 660266 · **near Skye** Excellent activity place! Day visits or holidays. Friendly, personal attention. A special place: you could learn a lot here.

The Best Diving Sites

Scotland's seas are primal soup, full of life and world-class sites as hard-core divers already know. The East Coast can be tricky if the wind is blowing from the north or east, therefore the West Coast is preferable (the further north the better). Thanks to the Gulf Stream it's not cold, even without a dry suit, and once you're down it's like flying through the Botanics (says my friend Tim Maguire). All West Coast sea lochs are good for general wildlife diving. So when you see all those crazies walking into the sea, remember, they may know something that you don't.

2222 WEST COAST

5 **The Outer Hebrides** Excellent with fantastic visibility especially off the west coast of **Harris** where you can plop in virtually anywhere.

✓ ✓ **St Kilda** offers the best diving in the UK, but it's the hardest to get to. On the edge of the Continental Shelf and the whale migration route, it has huge drop-offs and upwellings of life. Book boat and board well in advance. See 2364/MAGICAL ISLANDS.

9/J22 ✓ ✓ **Loch Creran** This long sea loch north of Oban has been designated a Marine Special Area of Conservation for its biogenic reefs (the most important site for 'serpulid reefs' in Europe. Check Puffin Dive Centre (below) for details.

9/H23 ✓ **Oban** Scuba central with lots of sites in the neighbourhood and easy access to the isles. Charter a boat and search for scallops in **The Garvellach** or dive the wrecks in the **Sound Of Mull**. Somewhere off **Tobermory** there is reputedly, one of Scotland's most enigmatic wrecks, a Spanish galleon. Easier to find are dolphins off the coasts of **Islay & Tiree**. See 1828-36/DOLPHINS for other likely spots.

6/J15 **The Summer Isles** From Ullapool. Wrecks, lee shores and unpolluted waters.

2223 EAST COAST

10/S25 ✓ **St Abbs Head** Accessible from the shore (2121/COASTAL WALKS) or by boat from **Eyemouth**, a marine reserve, so leave the lobsters alone. The spectacular Cathedral Rock is encrusted with green and yellow dead men's fingers and in Aug/Sep is a sanctuary for breeding fish (this cathedral is as beautiful as St Giles and is distinctly non-denominational). Nearby shore-based diving at **Dunbar** is shallow, safe and simple.

10/S25 **The Isle of May** Across the Forth; more advanced. Take a boat from Anstruther (1810/BIRDS). Main site is Piccadilly Circus, a central atrium fed by gullies, full of friendly seals.

2224 ORKNEY

3/Q11 ✓ ✓ **Scapa Flow** www.scapaflow.co.uk World-famous underwater burial site where the Germans scuttled their fleet in 1918. Think Guadalcanal, but colder. Although the scrappies have been in, 3 battleships and 4 light cruisers remain among other wrecks. Most lie in 20-40m deep, so not so dark and dangerous but plan carefully. Still majorly eerie!

DIVE OPERATORS (Don't leave home without one.)
Edinburgh Edinburgh Diving Centre · www.edinburghdiving.co.uk · 0131 229 4838 Shop only.
Deep Blue Scuba · 0131 220 3636 5-star PADI dive centre, full range of course and specialities. Equipment hire.
Coldingham Scoutscroft Dive Centre · 01890 771669
Oban Puffin Dive Centre · www.puffin.org.uk · 01631 566088 Full diving services. Includes extensively equipped shop, changing facilities and a burger van café.
Oban Dives · www.obandive.co.uk · 01631 566618 Shop only.
Skye Dive & Sea the Hebrides · www.dive-and-sea-the-hebrides.co.uk · 01470 592219 Charter only.
Mull Seafare Chandlery & Diving · 01688 302277
Ullapool Atlantic Diving Services (Achiltibuie) · 01854 622261 Charter only.
Orkney Diving Cellar Charters · www.divescapaflow.co.uk · 01856 850055
Sunrise Charters · www.sunrisecharters.co.uk · 01856 874425
Scapa Scuba · www.scapascuba.co.uk · 01856 851218
Scapa Flow Charters · 01856 850879

For wide network of very helpful local diving clubs around the country, contact:
Scottish Sub Aqua Club www.scotsac.com · 0141 425 1021

The Best Windsurfing

FOR BEGINNERS & INSTRUCTION (see also Water Sports)

2225
10/M22
Croft-Na-Caber www.croftnacaber.com · 01887 830588 · Kenmore, Loch Tay

2226 9/H23
Linnhe Marina www.linnhemarina.co.uk · 01631 730401 · near Oban

2227
10/P24
Lochmore Meadows www.lochore-meadows.co.uk · 01592 414300 · Lochgelly, Fife No instruction.

2228
9/J25
Tighnabruaich Sailing School www.tssargyll.co.uk · 01700 811717 · Tighnabruaich

2229
9/K26
Scottish National Watersports Centre 01475 530757 · Cumbrae · www.nationalcentrecumbrae.org.uk

2230
10/M26
Strathclyde Park www.northlan.gov.uk · 01698 266155 · near Motherwell & Glasgow Lots to do in this recreational zone of the conurbation. Water may not be so turquoise. 1616/COUNTRY PARKS.

2231
10/Q24
Elie 01333 330962 · East Neuk of Fife Small, friendly windsurfing and water sports operation on the beach (beyond the Ship Inn).

Windsurfing Spots

2232
9/L24
WEST COAST
Macrihanish Wave-sailing, fabulous long beach (1652/BEACHES). Mainly at Air Force base end. Big waves, for the more advanced.

9/K26 **Prestwick/Troon** Town beaches.

9/L27 **Island Of Cumbrae** Millport beach.

9/G28 **Milarrochy Bay Loch Lomond** 8km from Drymen (45km north of Glasgow). Weekend centre run by 7th Wave. Second beach up from Balmaha. Picturesque.

2233 **EAST COAST**
8/T17 **Fraserburgh** Town beach. Also surfing.

10/R22 **Lunan Bay** 12km north of Arbroath. Also surfing.

10/R23 **Carnoustie** Town beach.

10/R23 **St Andrews** West Sands. Also surfing.

10/Q23 **Longniddry/Gullane** 25/35km east of Edinburgh via A1 and A198.

10/R25 **Bellhaven Bay Dunbar** Bounded by John Muir Country Park.

2234 **NORTH COAST**
6/P12 **Thurso** Many beaches near town and further west. See 1665/BEACHES.

FOR ENTHUSIASTS
2235 ✓ **Isle of Tiree** The windsurfing capital of Scotland. 40km west of Mull.
9/E22 Countless clean, gently sloping beaches all round island (and small inland loch) allowing surfing in all wind directions. See 2365/MAGICAL ISLANDS. Accommodation basic or self-catering (Oban tourist information centre 01631 563122). Loganair fly every day except Sun (0845 7733377) and CalMac run ferries from Oban every day (01475 650100).

INFORMATION/ BOARD HIRE
Glasgow Boardwise · www.boardwise.com · 0141 334 5559 · 1146 Argyle Street
Edinburgh Boardwise · 0131 229 5887 · Lady Lawson Street

North Coast Tempest Surf · www.tempest-surf.co.uk · 01847 892500 · Thurso On the harbour.

The Best Surfing Beaches

A surprise for the sceptical: Scotland has some of the best surfing beaches in Europe. Forget the bronzed beach boys and lemon-bleached hair, surfing in Scotland is titanium-lined, rubber and balaclavas, and you get an ice-cream head even encased in the latest technology. The main season is Sep-Dec.

2236 **WEST COAST**
5/F13 ✓✓ **Isle of Lewis** Probably the best of the lot. Go north of Stornoway, north of Barvas, north of just about anywhere. Leave the A857 and your day job behind. Not the most scenic of sites, but the waves have come a long way, further than you have. Derek at Hebridean Surf Holidays (01851 705862) will tell you when and where to go.

2237 ✓ **Isle of Tiree** Exposed to all the Atlantic swells, gorgeous little Tiree ain't just
9/D22   great for windsurfing. Stay at Millhouse, self-catering hostel (01879 220435);
good facilities.

2238 ✓ **Macrihanish** Near Campbeltown at the foot of the Mull of Kintyre. Long
9/G28   strand to choose from (1652/BEACHES). Clan Skates in Glasgow (0141 339
6523) usually has an up-to-date satellite map and a idea of both the west and
(nearest to central belt) Pease Bay (see below).

2239 NORTH COAST

6/P12 ✓ **Thurso** Surf City, well not quite, but it's a good base to find your own waves.
Especially to the east of town at Dunnet Bay – a 5km long beach with excellent reefs at the north end. They say it has to be the best right-hand breaking
wave on the planet! When it ain't breaking, go west to...

6/N12 ✓ **Melvich & Strathy Bay** Near Bettyhill on the North Coast halfway
between Tongue and Thurso on the A836. From here to Cape Wrath the
power and quality of the waves detonating on the shore have justified compar-
isons with Hawaii. And then there's **Brimsness**.

6/Q13 **Wick** On the Thurso road at Ackergill to the south of Sinclair's Bay (1343/HOUSE
PARTIES). Find the ruined castle and taking care, clamber down the gully to the
beach. A monumental reef break, you are working against the backdrop of the
decaying ruin drenched in history, spume and romance.

2240 EAST COAST

8/T17 **Rattray Head** between Peterhead & Fraserburgh 5km off A90. Hostel/B&B
300m from secret 15km beach with cool surf. (B&B 01346 532236.)

8/T20 **Nigg Bay** Just south of Aberdeen (not to be confused with Nigg across from
Cromarty) and off the vast beach at Lunan Bay (1659/BEACHES) between Arbroath
and Montrose. There's 4 spots around **Fraserburgh** ('the broch').

10/S25 ✓ **Pease Bay** South of Dunbar near Cockburnspath on the A1. The nearest
surfie heaven to the capital. The caravan site has parking and toilets. Very
consistent surf here and therefore very popular.

INFORMATION/ BOARD HIRE

Glasgow Boardwise · www.boardwise.com · 0141 334 5559 · 1146 Argyle
Street
Clan Skates · www.clanskates.co.uk · 0141 339 6523 · 45 Hyndland Street
Edinburgh Boardwise · 0131 229 5887 · Lady Lawson Street
Momentum · 0131 229 6665 · Bruntsfield Place

North Coast Tempest Surf · www.tempest-surf.co.uk ·
01847 892500 · Thurso

Southeast Coast St Veda's Surf Centre · www.stvedas.co.uk · 01890
771679 · Coldingham Sands

Section 11

Shopping

Best Scottish Shopping

*☕ signifies **notable** café.*

2241
7/N16
☕
✓ **Anta Factory Shop** www.anta.co.uk · 01862 832477 · **Fearn near Tain** Off B9175 from Tain to the Nigg ferry, 8km through Hill of Fearn, on corner of disused airfield. Shop with adjacent pottery. Anta also in Edinburgh and London – it's a classy brand. Much tartan curtain fabric; many rugs, throws and pots. You can commission furniture to be covered in their material. Pottery tour by arrangement. Shop. All year daily 9.30am-5.30pm (Sun 11am-5pm, phone for winter hours). Pottery Mon-Fri only. The nice café shuts at 4pm.

2242
7/M16
✓ **Tain Pottery** www.tainpottery.co.uk Off the A9 just south of Tain (opposite side of A9 to road signed for Anta at Fearn; see above). Big working pottery, big stuff and often big, perhaps OTT designs but very popular (they do the National Trust for Scotland). Daily in summer, 9am-5.30pm. Closed Sun in winter.

2243
6/J14
✓ **Highland Stoneware** www.highlandstoneware.com · **Lochinver & Mill Street, Ullapool** On road to Baddidarach as you enter Lochinver on A837; and on way north beyond Ullapool centre. A large-scale pottery business including a shop/warehouse and open studios that you can walk round (Lochinver is more *engagé*). Similar to the 'ceramica' places you find in the Med, but not too terracotta – rather, painted and heavy-glazed stoneware in set styles. Many broken plates adorn your arrivals. Great selection, pricey, but you may have luck in the Lochinver discount section. Mail-order service. Open all year.

2244
9/G22
✓ **Starfish Ceramics Tobermory, Isle of Mull** Actually 7km from Tobermory in the steadings of Glengorm Castle (signed off road to Dervaig) – 2428/MULL. Adjacent to great café (1476/BEST TEAROOMS), this is a working studio/pottery with distinctive stripey useful and decorative work – a cut above many of the more conventional pots on these pages. Open Mon-Sat all year.

2245
10/R24
✓ **Crail Pottery** www.crailpottery.com · **Crail** At the foot of Rose Wynd, signposted from main street (best to walk). In a tree-shaded Mediterranean courtyard and upstairs attic is a cornucopia of brilliant, useful, irresistible things. Open 9am-5pm (weekends from 10am). Don't miss the harbour nearby, one of the most romantic neuks in the Neuk. Pity there's nowhere decent in Crail for tea.

2246
10/N21
✓ **MacNaughton's** www.macnaughtonsofpitlochry.com · **Station Road, Pitlochry** On corner of main street, this the best of many. A vast old-fashioned family-owned outfitter with acres of tartan attire – including obligatory tartan pyjamas and dressing gowns! Make their own cloth, and 9m kilts prepared in 6-8 weeks. This really is the real McCoy. 7 days till 5.30pm (4pm Sun).

2247
10/R27
✓ **Harestanes Countryside Centres near Jedburgh** Off A68 at Ancrum the B6400 to Nisbet. Farm steading complex on Montevoit Estate (1604/ GARDENS) with café/exhibition/superior crafts including the excellent **Buy Design** showing furniture, ceramics and glass. Easter-Oct 10am-5pm. Big event programme.

2248
1/E1
✓ **Kinloch Anderson** www.kinlochanderson.com · **Commercial Street, Leith, Edinburgh** A bit of a trek from uptown, but firmly on the tourist trail and rightly so. Experts in Highland dress and all things tartan; they've supplied *everybody*. They design their own tartans, have a good range of men's tweed jackets; even rugs. Mon-Sat 9am-5.30pm (5pm winter).

2249
8/N17
✓ **Logie Steading near Forres** In beautiful countryside 10km south of Forres signed from A940 Forres-Grantown road. Near pleasant woodlands and picnic spot. (Directions: 2089/WOODLAND WALKS.) Better than usual crafty courtyard. A great place to visit and browse. Highland artists and workshops. Second-hand books, farmshop! Tearoom (1497/TEAROOMS). Mar-Dec, 7 days 10.30am-5pm.

2250
10/N22
✓ **House of Menzies www.houseofmenzies.com · by Aberfeldy** Across river from Aberfeldy, adjacent Menzies Castle (1861/CASTLES) on road to Glen Lyon. Mainly art (local and Edinburgh's Wasp Studios) and wine (huge New World collection) here. Coffee shop in beautiful converted steading. Perhaps less art these days and more nick-nacks but we know what we like, don't we? The glen awaits.

2251
9/K26
Octopus Crafts near Fairlie On A78 Largs to Ardrossan road south of Fairlie. Crafts, wines, cookshop, an excellent restaurant (1427/SEAFOOD RESTAURANTS) and a seafood deli. An all-round roadside experience – the sign says Fencebay Seafood & Crafts. Everything hand-made and/or hand-picked; even wines are well chosen. Good pots. Glass and wood. Choice utensils. They also run courses. Closed Mon.

2252
10/N21
House of Bruar www.houseofbruar.com · Pitlochry Courtyard emporia if not euphoria: a shopaholic honey pot on the A9 north of Blair Atholl especially for those who just missed Pitlochry. Self-service restaurant like a canteen in an old folks' home but retail food side well selected (good range of Scottish cheeses, Mackie's ice cream, MacSween's haggis, etc). Outdoor wear with big labels (Musto, Patagonia), golf shop and garden centre, even antiques. They know what you want. This place is always and amazingly teeming with people. Falls nearby for more spiritual sustenance (1684/WATERFALLS). 7 days 9am-5pm.

2253
8/N17
Brodie Country Fare www.brodiecountryfare.com · between Nairn & Forres By main A96 near Brodie Castle (1849/CASTLES). Not a souvenir shoppie in the traditional sense, more a drive-in one-stop shopping experience on the taste by-pass. Deli food, a fairly up-market boutique designer womenswear and every crafty tartanalia of note. The self-serve restaurant gets as busy as a motorway café and you have to walk through everything else to get there. 7 days till 5.30pm.

2254
7/L17
Falls of Shin Visitor Centre www.fallsofshin.co.uk · near Lairg Self-serve café/restaurant in the visitor centre and shop across the road from the Falls of Shin on the Achany Glen road 8km south of Lairg (1697/WATERFALLS). Good basic food in an unlikely emporium of all things Harrods (Mohammed al Fayed's estate is here). They come from all over at Xmas for hampers etc. 9.30am-6pm all year.

2255
8/P18
Mortimer's & Ritchie's High Street, Grantown on Spey 3 and 41-45 High St respectively in respectable Speyside holiday town where fishing gear is in demand (Ritchie's have stopped fishing). Mortimer's more exclusively angling for your custom, but both with a big range of flies. Big-name outdoor clothing in every shade of olive. Ritchie's also have guns if you want to kill something. Closed Sun.

2256
7/F17
Edinbane Pottery www.edinbane-pottery.co.uk · Skye 500m off A850 Portree (22km) to Dunvegan road. Long-established and reputable working pottery where the various processes are often in progress. Earthy pots of all shapes and sizes and for every purpose. Open all year 9am-6pm. 7 days (not weekends winter).

2257
7/F18
Skye Silver www.skyesilver.com · Colbost 10km Dunvegan on B884 to Glendale. Long established and reputable jewellery made and sold in an old Skye schoolhouse in a distant corner; Three Chimneys restaurant nearby (2398/SKYE RESTAURANTS). Well-made, Celtic designs, good gifts. Mar-Oct 7 days, 10am-6pm.

2258 **Kiln Room Pottery & Coffeeshop** **Laggan** On main A889 route to Fort
7/M20 William and Skye from Dalwhinnie. Simple, usable pottery (though pottery itself no
🖵 longer in use) with distinctive warm colouring. Selected knitwear and useful
things. Home-made cakes and scones; 1481/COFFEE SHOPS. 10am-5.30pm, 7 days.
Hostel out back very inexpensive including comfy lounge with great vista and
unique seven-person hot-tub spa (01528 544231).

2259 **Balnakeil** **Durness, Sutherland** From Durness and the A836 road, take
6/L12 Balnakeil and Faraid Head road for 2km west. Founded in the 1960s in what one
imagines was a haze of hash, this craft village is still home to 'downshifters'.
Paintings, pottery, weaving and a bookshop in prefab huts where community
members live and work (the site was an early-warning station). **Cocoa Mountain**
(01971 511233) have a chocolate bar opening in early '08. Bistro and restaurant.
Some businesses seasonal. All open in summer, daily 10am-6 pm (mostly).

2260 **Skye Batiks** www.skyebatiks.com · **Portree** Near tourist information centre.
7/G18 Very original Sri Lanka 'batiks': cotton fabrics of ancient Celtic designs in every
shape and size. Mainly hand-made, majorly colourful; a unique souvenir of Skye.
Island Outdoors adjacent has outdoor 'fashion' and all-important midge helmets.

2261 **Achin's Bookshop** www.scotbooks.freeuk.com · **Lochinver** At Inverkirkaig
6/J14 5km from Lochinver on the 'wee mad road' to Achiltibuie (1717/SCENIC ROUTES).
Unexpected selection of books in the back of beyond providing something to read
when you've climbed everything or are unlikely to acquire the inclination. Outdoor
wear too and great hats. The path to Kirkaig Falls and Suilven begins at the gate
(see 1938/MONUMENTS). Easter-Oct 7 days; 9.30am-6pm (winter Mon-Sat 10am-
5pm). Adjacent café 10am-5pm, summer only.

2262 **Iona Abbey Shop** www.iona.org.uk/abbey · **Iona** Via CalMac ferry from
9/F23 Fionnphort on Mull. Crafts and souvenirs across the way in separate building.
Proceeds support a worthy, committed organisation. Christian literature, tapes etc,
but mostly artefacts from nearby and around Scotland. Celtic crosses much in
evidence, but then this is where they came from! Mar-Oct 9.30am-5pm. Also, on
ᵎ the way to and from the Abbey, **Columba Steadings** has quality design craftwork
of several brands. Restored farm buildings on the road 200m Abbey. Apr-Oct.

2263 **Borgh Pottery Borve** **Lewis** On northwest coast of island a wee way from
5/F13 Stornoway, but no great detour from the road to Callanish where you are probably
going. Alex and Sue Blair's pleasant gallery of hand-thrown pots with different
glazes; domestic and garden wear. Knits. Open all year 9.30pm-6pm. Closed Sun.

2264 **Galloway Lodge Preserves** www.gallowaylodge.co.uk · **Gatehouse of**
11/M30 **Fleet** On main street. Packed with local jams, marmalades, chutneys and pickles.
Scottish pottery by Scotia Ceramics, Highland Stoneware and Dunoon. Good presents and jam for yourself. 10am-5pm Mon-Sat, and Sun afternoons in summer.

2265 **Crafts & Things** **near Glencoe Village** On A82 between Glencoe village and
9/J21 Ballachulish. Eclectic mix of very many crafts and... well, things. Mind, body and
🖵 mountain books (and this one) and reasonably priced knit/outerwear. Good coffee
shop doing salads, sandwiches and cake, with local artist's work on walls. All-
round nice place. All year, daily until 5.30pm.

2266 **Drumlanrig Castle** www.drumlanrig.com · **near Thornhill** A day out of
11/N29 things to do (1613/COUNTRY PARKS) including craft centre in the old stables. Studio-
type shops with tartan, jewellery and 'bodging'! Hire a bike and ride as you decide.

Where To Buy Art

These galleries, outside the dealer and public-gallery concentrations in Edinburgh and Glasgow, cater also for tourists... but they're all a cut above the rest. See also Small Galleries Edinburgh p. 89, and Glasgow p. 136.

2267
8/Q20 ✓ **McEwan Gallery** www.mcewangallery.com · **near Ballater Deeside** A surprising place but for many years this cottage gallery has been dealing in 19th/20th century, mainly Scottish art. They wrote the book! Summer exhibitions, but open all year 11am-5pm (Sun 2-5pm). Winter hours call (01339 755429). 300m up A939 Tomintoul road.

2268
8/Q19 ✓ **The Lost Gallery** www.lostgallery.co.uk · **Middle of Nowhere, Aberdeenshire** Signed from Bellabeg on A944 near Strathon village. 3km up farm road, then another 3km on rough track to a fab studio/gallery in farmhouse in the Cairngorms with varied work by contemporary Scots and the owner Peter Goodfellow. All year 11am-5pm. Closed Tue. (Phone 01975 651287 if you get... lost.)

2269
7/M16 ✓ **Browns Gallery Tain** Off Main St. Surprising repository of great contemporary Scottish art with regular exhibitions by notable artists like John Byrne, Calvin Colvin, Neil Macpherson. They must like this guy. Whole new gallery space '07. It does Tain proud. Mon-Sat 10am-5pm.

2270
7/L18 ✓ **Kilmorack Gallery** www.kilmorackgallery.co.uk · 01463 783230 · **near Beauly** On A831 for Struy and Cannich 5km southwest of town. Pleasant and serious gallery in converted church by the road. Significant exhibitions of mainly Highland artists including the ubiquitous James Hawkins. Some sculpture.

2271
10/N23 **Castle Gallery** www.castlegallery.co.uk · **Inverness** On road up to castle amid many restaurants, another Highland gallery that takes itself quite seriously. Changing exhibitions. Mon-Sat 9am-5pm.

2272
10/N23 **Strathearn Gallery** www.strathearn-gallery.com · **32 West Street, Crieff** (On Main St). Accessible and affordable. The Maguires do know what you like. Fine and applied arts; lots of ceramics. 7 days till 5pm (Thu-Sat in winter).

2273
7/H16 **Solas Gallery** www.solasgallery.co.uk · **Gairloch** Flowerdale Bay by the Old Inn (1380/INNS) as you come into Gairloch from south. Original work – painting, ceramics – by West Highland artists. Nice space. Easter-Oct.

2274
7/H18 **Plockton Gallery** www.painting-in-plockton.co.uk · **Innes Street, Plockton** Opposite Plockton Inn. 2 floors, lot of wall space for summer exhibitions including some significant artists. Summer only 10am-10pm.

2275
7/G19 **Gallery An Talla Dearg Eilean Iarmain, Sleat, Skye** True Gaelic corner of the world. This gallery open in summer adjacent legendary hotel and bar (2375/SKYE). Artists that we tourists like: Laurence Broderick (who does otters) and Pam Carter (who does the business).

2276
5/E16 **Finsbay Gallery** www.witb.co.uk/links/finsbay.htm · **Golden Road, South Harris** Wonderful windy road down east coast of South Harris. This cute gallery showing mainly Hebridean artists. Another gallery (Skoon)/café nearby (2427/HEBRIDES EATS). Mon-Sat 10am-5pm (winter Thu only).

2277 **St Andrews Fine Art** www.st-andrewsfineart.co.uk Crowded walls of
10/R23 Scottish art from 1800-present. Includes some good work from kent
contemporaries. Peploe-Redpath and their chums. Closed Sun.

2278 **Kranenburg & Fowler Fine Arts** www.kranenburg-fowler.com · 01631
9/H23 **562303 · Star Brae & Stevenson Street, Oban** Geoff and Jan source work from
artists that ranges from the polite to the interesting. Small group of regular
exhibitors and others. Mon-Sat 9.30am-5.30pm. Sun when exhibition 12noon-
4pm.

2279 **Whitehouse Gallery St Mary's Street, Kirkcudbright** Self-proclaimed
11/M31 artists' town (Hornel, Jessie M. King and others did live and work here). Supports
local artists. Worth a browse. Tue-Sat, 10am-5pm.

2280 **Morven Gallery** www.morvengallery.com · **Barvas, Isle Of Lewis** Coast
5/F13 road just north of Barabhas 30km from Callanish and those stones. Janice Scott's
excellent farm steading kind of gallery with well-selected work, mainly local.
Painting, tapestry, ceramics and fab original knits. Baking. Apr-Oct 10am-5.30pm.
Closed Sun.

2281 **Scottish Sculpture Workshops** www.ssw.org.uk · 01464 861372 ·
8/Q19 **Lumsden** Main street of ribbon town on A97 near Alford and Huntly. Not a place
to see work for sale (mainly commissions), but work being made. They also look
after the sculpture garden at Alford end of street by the school. Workshops open all
year. Mon-Fri 9am-5pm.

2282 **Stenton Gallery Stenton, East Lothian** Deep in the green undulations of
10/R25 the East Lothian countryside but not far from the A1 on the B6370 from Dunbar
roundabout. 10 years established, surprisingly extensive gallery with eclectic range
of contemporary Scottish artists. 11am-5pm. Closed Thu.

2283 ✓ ✓ **The Glasgow Art Fair** www.glasgowartfair.com · 0141 552 6027
2/D3 The Scottish marketplace for contemporary art. Mainly home-grown but
London galleries with Scottish connections. Held in mid April in pavilions in George
Square.

**The Degree Shows Edinburgh/Glasgow & Duncan of Jordanstone,
Dundee Art Schools** Work from final-year students. Discover the Bellanys,
Howsons, Douglas Gordons and Simon Starlings of the future. 2-week exhibition
after manic first night (mid Jun).

Prints by many contemporary Scottish artists available from:
Glasgow Print Studios www.gpsart.co.uk · **22 King Street, Merchant
City/Tron area**
Edinburgh Printmakers Workshop www.edinburgh-printmakers.co.uk ·
23 Union Street off Leith Walk
Peacock Visual Arts www.peacockvisualarts.co.uk · **21 Castle Street,
Aberdeen**

Where To Buy Good Woollies

2284
1/A4

✓✓ **Belinda Robertson** www.belindarobertson.com · 0131 557 8118 · 13a Dundas Street, Edinburgh Queen of the commissioned cashmere creations; you can only choose from the *prêt-à-porter* collection in her showroom here (or in London). Her team design and process the stock which is made up in Hawick.

2285
3/Q10

✓ **Judith Glue** www.judithglue.com · 01856 874225 · Kirkwall, Orkney Opposite the cathedral. Distinctive hand-made jumpers, the runic designs are a real winner. Also the widespread but individual Highland and Joker stoneware (jewellery and animal clocks very popular), condiments and preserves. The landscape prints of Orkney are by twin sister, Jane. Mon-Sat 9am-6pm, Sun 10am-5.30pm.

2286
7/G19

Ragamuffin www.ragamuffinonline.co.uk · Armadale Pier, Skye On the pier, so one of the first or last things you can do on Skye is rummage through the Ragamuffin store and get a nice knit. Every kind of jumper and some crafts in this Aladdin's cave within a new-build shed; including tweedy things and mad hats. 7 days 9am-6pm.

2288
8/P17

Johnston's Cashmere Centre Elgin Large Mill Shop kind of operation and full-blown visitor attraction near the Cathedral (1872/RUINS). 'The only British mill to transform fibre to garment' (yarns spun at their factory in Elgin and made into garments in the Borders) and though this is more British High St than Bloomingdale's, New York, these mum-'n'-dad-like jumpers will keep you just as warm. Mon-Sat 9am-5.30pm, Sun 11am-5pm. Slight variations in winter.

2289
10/R27

Lochcarron Visitor Centre www.lochcarron.com · Galashiels If you're in Galashiels (or Hawick), which grew up around woollen mills, you might expect to find a good selection of woollens you can't get everywhere else; and bargains. Well, tough! There's no stand-out place, but Loch Carron is a big tourist attraction with mill tours (Open all year 4 times a day), exhibits and an okay mill shop. Vivienne Westwood has been this way and well... Hawick did invent the Y-front.

2290
10/R28

Hawick Cashmere www.hawickcashmere.com · Hawick Factory in Hawick since 1874, with visitor centre beside the river on Duke St. Also shops in Kelso and Edinburgh. 'State-of-the-art colours and designs'. Not only, but mostly cashmere. Mon-Sat 9.30am-5pm; Sun 11am-4pm (in season).

Harris Tweed

2291
5

Tweeds & Knitwear www.harristweedandknitwear.co.uk · 4 Plockropool, Drinishadder Organised operators (they even cater for coach parties) with weaving demonstrations and wool and knitwear for sale as well as tweed. Closed Sun.

Joan McClennan No 1A, Drinishadder Further down the Golden Road (1715/SCENIC ROUTES). I don't know, but I've been told, this is where you find the real golden fleece. Go look for it.

Luskentyre Harris Tweed www.luskentyreharristweed.co.uk · No 6, Luskentyre 2km off west coast on main road south to Scarista and Rodel.

Donald and Maureen Mackay's place is notable for their bright tartan tweed. 9.30am-6pm Closed Sun.

Lewis Loom Centre www.lewisloomcentre.co.uk · **Stornoway** Main street in the north, far from Harris but near the tourists. Cloth and clothes. Weaving demo. Closed Sun.

2292 **Harris Tweed Shop** Tarbert Main street emporium with big range of Harris
9/G25 Tweed products in the place where the tweed originates. Mon-Sat 9am-5.30pm (from 9.30am in winter).

The Best Garden Centres

⌖ signifies notable café. Others may have cafés not recommended.

2293 ✓✓ **Dougal Philip's New Hopetoun Gardens** near South
10/P25 Queensferry · 01506 834433 · www.newhopetoungardens.co.uk
⌖ The mother of all (Scottish) garden centres with 21 different zones and demonstration gardens (including Oriental and Scottish). Everything you could ever grow or put in a Scottish garden. Acres of accessories. Orangery tearoom has verdant views and tasty home-made stuff. All year 10am-5.30pm. Tearoom closes 4.30pm.

2294 ✓✓ **Floors Castle** www.roxburghe.net · **Kelso** 3km outside town off
10/S27 B6397 St Boswells road (garden centre has separate entrance to main
⌖ visitors' gate in town). Set amongst lovely old greenhouses within walled gardens some distance from house, it has a showpiece herbaceous border all round. First-class coffee shop, The Terrace (1468/TEAROOMS) and patio. 'Very good roses'. Lovely kids' lawn. Centre is open all year. 10am-5pm. (1918/COUNTRY HOUSES.)

2295 ✓ **Kinlochlaich House** www.kinlochlaich-house.co.uk · **Appin** On main
9/J22 A28 Oban-Fort William road just north of Port Appin turnoff, the West Highlands' largest nursery/garden centre. Set in a large walled garden filled with plants and veg soaking up the climes of the warm Gulf stream. Donald Hutchison and daughter nurture these acres enabling you to reap what they sow. With a huge array of plants on offer it's like visiting a friend's garden and being able to take home your fave bits. Charming cottages, apartments and a new treehouse for let (01631 730342). 7 days: 9.30am-5.30pm (10.30am Sun). Closed Sun in winter.

2296 ✓ **Inshraich** www.kincraig.com · 01540 651287 · near Kincraig near
7/N19 Aviemore On B970 between Kincraig and Inverdruie (which is on the
⌖ Coylumbridge ski road out of Aviemore), a nursery that puts others in the shade. John and Gunn Borrowman carrying on (& developing) the horticulture of Jack Drake (from 1930s) and John Lawson (1949). Specialising in alpines and bog plants, but with neat beds of all sorts in the grounds (and a wild garden) of the house by the Spey and frames full of perfect specimens, this is a potterer's paradise. Tearoom with squirrel- and bird-viewing gallery. Mar-Oct 7 days 10am-5pm.

2297 ✓ **Dobbies** www.dobbies.com · 01360 620721 · **Milngavie** Formerly
2/A1 Findlay Clark's, the original home of the garden centre chain in Campsie
⌖ countryside north of city, 20km from centre via A81 or A807 (Milngavie or Kirkintilloch roads) or heading for Milngavie (pronounced 'Mull-guy'), turn right on Boclair Rd. Best of many Dobbies, a vast garden complex and all-round visitor

experience. 'Famous' coffee shop (the famous waitresses are local babes and what they turn into), saddlery with everything except horses. Books, clothes and piles of plants; and live pets. Mon-Sat 9am-6pm (till 8pm Thu), Sun 10am-6pm.

2298
10/P23
✓**Glendoick www.glendoick.com · 01738 860205 · Glencarse near Perth** On A85, 10km from Perth, in the fertile Carse of the Tay. A large family-owned garden centre notable especially for rhododendrons and azaleas, a riot of which can be viewed in the nursery behind (May only). Pagoda Garden (they practice what they preach). Very popular coffee shop with superior home baking. 7 days till 5.30pm, 5pm winter.

2299
8/R20
✓**Raemoir Garden Centre www.raemoirgardencentre.co.uk ·** **Banchory** On A980 off main street 3km north of town. A friendly family-run garden centre and excellent coffee shop that keeps the fastidious gardeners here-abouts happy. Great ceramica. And this is Deeside. If it's good enough for them... (1475/TEAROOMS; plans to expand food). 7 days 9am-5.30pm. Tearoom till 5pm.

2300
7/M18
Brin Herb Nursery www.brinherbnursery.co.uk · 01808 521288 · Flichity near Inverness Off A9 south of Daviot, 12km south of Inverness, then 10km southwest to Farr. An old school and playground dedicated to herbs, plants and all the potions and lotions that come from them. Tearoom in the school room. Easter-Oct Mon-Sat 11am-5.30pm (summer only).

2301
9/K24
The Tree Shop Cairndow, Loch Fyne A garden centre specialising in trees and shrubs. Part of the Ardkinglas Estate near (1km) the Woodland Garden (1607/ GARDENS) with UK's tallest tree. The shop on the main A83 Loch Lomond-Inveraray road also does houseplants and all the usual greeneries. Café. 7 days 9.30am-5pm. It's adjacent to the famous Loch Fyne Seafood Shop & Restaurant (1425/SEAFOOD).

2302
8/Q17
Christie's Fochabers On A98 going into town from Buckie side. Huge garden centre and forest nursery, with tearoom/restaurant. An all-round shopping/ recreational experience With some absolutely ghastly trinketry, but their outside plant section still sound. 9am-5pm, 7 days (from 10am Sun).

2303
5/D17
Keske Nurseries 01876 580333 · Clachan, North Uist In the remote heart of wild and watery North Uist on main road to Benbecula south of Lochmaddy and just after Clachan Stores and the turnoff for Bayhead a cottage nursery. Idiosyncratic approach, but certainly the Hebridean choice for trees, shrubs, vege-tation and bedding plants. Go on, make a statement – plant a tree in this treeless tract. Open Apr-Aug 1-5.30pm. Closed Sun.

2304
10/R25
Smeaton Nursery & Gardens 01620 860501 · East Linton 2km from village on North Berwick road (signed Smeaton). Up a drive in an old estate is this walled garden going back to early 19th century. Wide range; good for fruit (and other) trees, herbaceous etc. Nice to wander round, an additional pleasure is the 'Lake Walk' halfway down drive through small gate in woods. 1km stroll round a secret finger lake in magnificent mature woodland (10am-dusk). Mon-Sat 9.30am-4.30pm; Sun 10.30am-4.30pm. Phone for winter hours.

2305
10/M26
The Clyde Valley www.clyde-valley.com The lush valley of the mighty Clyde is garden centre central. Best reached say from Glasgow by M74, junction 7, then A72 for Lanark. Between Larkhall and Lanark there's a profusion to choose from and many have sprouted coffee/craft shops. Pick your own fruit in summer and your own picnic spot to eat it. Sandyholm at Crossford is recommended.

Section 12

Museums, Galleries, Theatre & Music

Best History & Heritage

For Edinburgh Galleries, see p. 77–80; Glasgow Galleries, see p. 127–29.
☕ signifies notable café.

2306
10/R25
☕

✓✓ **National Museum of Flight & The Concorde Experience**
www.nms.ac.uk · 01620 880308 · near Haddington 3km from A1 south of town. In the old complex of hangars and Nissen huts at the side of East Fortune, an airfield dating to World War I (there's a tacky open-air market on Sun) with a large collection of planes from gliders to jets and especially wartime memorabilia respectfully restored and preserved. Inspired and inspiring displays; not just boys' stuff. Marvel at the bravery back then and sense the unremitting passage of time. From East Fortune the airship R34 made its historic Atlantic crossings. More recent Concorde Experience raises the ante. Separate 'Boarding Pass' required. Hugely impressive outside, claustrophobic in (especially queueing to leave). But did David Frost and Joan Collins ever join the Mile-High Club? All year 7 days; 10am-5pm (till 6pm Jul-Aug, 4pm winter weekends only).

2307
10/R24

✓✓ **The Secret Bunker** www.secretbunker.co.uk · 01333 310301 · near Crail & Anstruther The nuclear bunker and regional seat of government in the event of nuclear war: a twilight labyrinth beneath a hill in rural Fife so vast, well documented and complete, it's both fascinating and chilling. Few 'museums' are as authentic or as resonant, even down to the 1950s records in the jukebox in the claustrophobic canteen. Makes you wonder what 300 people would have made of it, incarcerated there, what the Cold War was all about and what secrets they are brewing these days for the wars yet to come. Apr-Oct 10am-5pm.

2308
10/Q23
☕

✓✓ **Verdant Works** www.scottishmuseums.org.uk · 01382 225282 · Dundee West Henderson's Wynd near Westport. Award-winning heritage museum that for once justifies the accolades. The story of jute and the city it made. Immensely effective high-tech and designer presentation of industrial and social history. Excellent for kids. Almost continuous guided tour. Café. 7 days 10am-6pm; winter Wed-Sun till 4.30pm. Every Sun from 11am.

2309
5/E13
☕

✓✓ **The Blackhouse Village** www.gerrannan.com · 01851 643416 · Gearrannan, Lewis At the end of the road (3km) from A858 the west coast of Lewis, an extraordinary reconstruction of several blackhouses, the traditional thatched dwelling of the Hebrides. One is working Black House Museum (set 1955) with café. Another is a hostel and 4 are self-catering accommodation. Great walk starts here with viewpoints. Apr-Sep 9.30am-5.30pm. Closed Sun. Also:

2310
5/F13
HS

✓ **The Blackhouse at Arnol** www.historic-scotland.gov.uk · 01851 710395 · Lewis The A857 Barvas road from Stornoway, left at junction for 7km, then right through township for 2km. A single blackhouse with earth floor, bed boxes and central peat fire (no chimney hole), occupied by the family and their animals. Remarkably, this house was lived in until the 1960s. Smokists may reflect on that peaty fug. Open all year 9.30am-5.30pm (4.30pm in winter, Oct-Feb). Closed Sun.

2311
10/P25
☕

✓ **The Abbot House** www.abbothouse.co.uk · Dunfermline Maygate in town centre 'historic area'. Very fine conversion of ancient house showing the importance of this town as a religious and trading centre from the beginning of this millennium to medieval times. Encapsulates history from Margaret and Bruce to the Beatles. One of the few tourist attractions where 'award-winning' is a reliable indicator of worth. Café and tranquil garden; gate to the graveyard and Abbey. 7 days 10am-5pm. Excellent coffee shop by ladies who can cook and bake.

2312
9/H23
✓ **Easdale Island Folk Museum** www.scottishmuseums.org.uk On Easdale, an island/township reached by a 5-minute (continuous) boat service from Seil 'island' at the end of the B844 (off the A816, 18km south of Oban). Something special about this grassy hamlet of white-washed houses on a rocky outcrop which has a pub, a tearoom and a craft shop, and this museum across the green. The history of the place (a thriving slate industry erased one stormy night in 1881, when the sea drowned the quarry) is brought to life in displays from local contributions. Easter-Sep 11am-5pm.

2313
6/M13
✓ **Strathnaver Museum** www.strathnavermuseum.org.uk · 01641 521418 · **Bettyhill** On North Coast 60km west of Thurso in a converted church which is very much part of the whole appalling saga: a graphic account of the Highland clearances told through the history of this fishing village and the Strath that lies behind it whence its dispossessed population came; 2,500 folk were driven from their homes – it's worth going up the valley (from 2km west along the main A836) to see (especially at Achenlochy) the beautiful land they had to leave in 1812 to make way for sheep. Detailed leaflet of Strath to follow by car and foot. Elizabeth's Café on roadside for sustenance (especially fish 'n' chips). Museum: Apr-Oct Mon-Sat 10am-5pm (closed at lunchtime).

2314
10/M26
✓ **National Museum of Rural Life** www.nms.ac.uk · 0131 247 4377 · **Kittochside by East Kilbride** I have to admit I've never been to this estimable attraction in the southern hinterland of Glasgow though not for want of trying. East Kilbride 'did my head in' so much that I gave up after an hour or two of trying to find a way out. However folk do say… and they have a big worthy programme for kids. It's somewhere in the middle of all those dual carriageways. Call them, should you get lost. 7 days 10am-5pm.

2315
7/H18
✓ **Applecross Heritage Centre** www.applecrossheritage.org.uk Along the strand from the Applecross Inn (1285/GET-AWAY HOTELS) adjacent lovely church built on ancient monastery, a well-designed building and lay-out of the story of this remarkable, end-of-the-world community. New reading room '07 with such comfy chairs! May-Oct 12noon-5pm.

2316
8/T17
✓ **The Museum of Scottish Lighthouses** Fraserburgh · www.lighthousemuseum.org.uk At Kinnaird Head near the harbour. A top attraction, so signed from all over. Purpose-built and very well done. Something which may appear to be of marginal interest made vital. In praise of the prism and the engineering innovation and skill that allowed Britain once to rule the seas (and the world). A great ambition (to light the coastline) spectacularly realised. *At Scotland's Edge* by Keith Allardyce and Evelyn Hood (or its follow-up) is well worth taking home. Great patter from the guides. Apr-Oct 11am-5pm, till 6pm Jul/Aug; winter closes at 4pm.

2317
7/H18
✓ **Bright Water Visitor Centre & Gavin Maxwell House** 01599 530040 · www.eileanban.org · **Eilean Ban off Kyleakin, Skye** You don't have to be a Maxwell fan, *Ring of Bright Water* reader or even an otter-watcher to appreciate the remarkable restoration of this fascinating man's last house on the island now under the Skye Bridge. The island itself is a natural haven and the Stevenson Lighthouse superb. Limited access and approach via the 'Otter Gate' on the bridge. Contact centre and book ahead. Apr-Oct.

2318
2/E4
✓ **Surgeons' Hall Museum** www.rcsed.ac.uk · 0131 527 1649 · **Royal College of Surgeons, 18 Nicolson Street, Edinburgh** 2 small museums left out of the Edinburgh section's attractions, but too good to miss. Displays of

pathological anatomy in classic Playfair Hall in the main street (opposite Festival Theatre); the History of Surgery round the corner at 9 Hill Sq. Includes permanent exhibits, Dental Museum and Sport and Exercise Medicine Museum. Extraordinary, somewhat macabre exhibits in 'the home of medicine' which celebrated its 500th anniversary in '05. Mon-Fri 12noon-4pm (summer 10am-4pm). Donations.

2319 **West Highland Museum** **www.westhighlandmuseum.org.uk** · **Cameron**
9/K21 **Square, Fort William** Off main street in listed building by tourist information centre. Good refurbishment yet retains mood; the setting doesn't overshadow the contents. 7 rooms of Jacobite memorabilia, archaeology, wildlife, clans, tartans, arms, etc all effectively evoke the local history. Great oil paintings line the walls, including a drawn battle plan of Culloden. The anamorphic painting of Charlie isn't so bonny, but a still fascinating snapshot. Closed Sun except Jul/Aug (2-5pm).

2320 **Mary-Ann's Cottage** **www.caithness.org** · **Dunnet** On North Coast off A836
6/P12 from Thurso to John o' Groats, signed at Dunnet; take the road for Dunnet Head. Lived in till 1990 by Mary-Ann Calder, 3 generations of crofters are in these stones. But not nostalgic or heritage heavy, just an old lady's house, the near present and past. Compare to that other old lady's house 10 minutes up the road (Castle of Mey; 1852/CASTLES). Open summer 2.30-4.30pm. Closed Mon.

2321 **Kilmartin House** **www.kilmartin.org** · **01546 510278** · **near Lochgilphead**
9/H24 North of Lochgilphead on the A816. Centre for landscape and archaeology
Ψ interpretation – so much to know of the early peoples and Kilmartin Glen is littered with historic sites. Intelligent, interesting, run by a small independent trust. Excellent organic café (1408/VEGETARIAN RESTAURANTS) and bookshop without usual tat. Some nice Celtic carvings. All year 10am-5pm daily (4pm Nov/Dec). Closed Jan/Feb.

2322 **Pictavia** **www.pictavia.org.uk** · **01356 626241** · **Brechin** South of Brechin on
10/R21 the Forfar road at Brechin Castle. Centre opened summer '99 to give a multimedia interpretation of our Dark Age ancestors. Sparse on detail, high on kid-orientated interactivity. Listen to some music, pluck a harp and argue about the Battle of Dunnichen – was it that important? Gentle parkland beyond, nice for kids. Usual crap shopping. All year 7 days 9.30am-5.30pm. Winter: weekends only.

2323 **Cromarty Courthouse Museum** **www.cromarty-courthouse.org.uk** ·
7/M17 **01381 600418** · **Church Street, Cromarty** Housed in the 18th-century court-house, this award-winning museum uses moving and talking models to bring to life a courtroom scene and famous Cromarty figures to paint the varied history of this quite special little town. Entrance includes multilingual taped tours of the town 7 days. 10am-5pm (winter 12noon-4pm). Jan & Feb – by appointment.

2324 **Summerlee Heritage Park** **www.northlan.gov.uk** · **01236 638460** ·
10/M26 **Heritage Way, Coatbridge** Follow signs from town centre. Here in the Iron Town is this tribute to the industry, ingenuity and graft that powered the Industrial Revolution and made Glasgow great. Anyone with a mechanical bent or an interest in the social history of the working class will like it here; tots and bored teens may not. Tearoom. 7 days, 10am-5pm (Winter 10am-4pm). Reopening Jun '08 after major redevelopment.

2325 **Skye Museum of Island Life** **www.skyemuseum.co.uk** · **Kilmuir** On A855
7/F17 Uig-Staffin road 32km north of Portree. The most authentic of several converted cottages on Skye where the crofter's life is recreated for the enrichment of ours. The small thatched township includes agricultural implements and domestic

artefacts, many illustrating an improbable fascination with the royal family. Flora Macdonald's grave nearby (1925/MONUMENTS). Apr-Oct 9.30am-5pm. Closed Sun.

2326 **Auchendrain** Inveraray 8km west of town on A83. A whole township
9/J24 reconstructed to give a very fair impression of both the historical and spatial relationship between the cottages and their various occupants. Longhouses and byre dwellings; their furniture and their ghosts. 7 days. Apr-Sep 10am-5pm.

2327 **Inveraray Jail** www.inveraryjail.co.uk · Inveraray 'The story of Scottish
9/J24 crime and punishment' (sic) told in 'award-winning' reconstruction of courtroom with cells, where the waxwork miscreants and their taped voices bring local history to life. Guided tours of Peterhead can't be far off. Open all year, 9.30am-6pm (winter 10am-5pm).

2328 **Arctic Penguin aka Maritime Heritage Centre** www.inveraraypier.com ·
9/J24 Inveraray 'One of the world's last iron sailing ships' moored so you can't miss it at the loch side in Inveraray. More to it than would seem from the outside; displays on the history of Clydeside (the *Queens Mary* and *Elizabeth* memorabilia etc), Highland Clearances, the *Vital Spark*. Lots for kids to get a handle (or hands) on. And a 'puffer' for nostalgic trips. 7 days 10am till 6pm; 5pm winter.

2329 **Bonawe Ironworks Museum** www.historic-scotland.gov.uk · Taynuilt At
9/J23 its zenith (late 18th-early 19th century), this ironworks was a brutal, fire-breathing
HS monster, as 'black as the Earl of Hell's waistcoat'. But now, all is calm as the gently sloping grassy sward carries you around from warehouse to foundry and down onto the shores of Loch Etive to the pier, where the finished product was loaded on to ships to be taken away for the purpose of empire-building (with cannon-balls). Apr-Sep daily until 6.30pm.

2330 **Scottish Fisheries Museum** www.scotfishmuseum.org · 01333 310628 ·
10/R24 Anstruther In and around a cobbled courtyard overlooking the old fishing harbour in this busy East Neuk town. Excellent evocation of traditional industry still alive (if not kicking). Impressive collection of models and actual vessels including those moored at adjacent quay. Crail and Pittenweem harbours nearby for the full picture (and fresh crab/lobster). Open all year 10am-5.30pm, Sun 11am-5pm (closed 4.30pm in winter).

2331 **Robert Smail's Printing Works** www.nts.org.uk · 01896 830206 · Main
10/Q27 Street, Innerleithen A traditional printing works till 1986 and still in use.
NTS Fascinating vignettes/ history. Have a go at hand setting, then have a go at a Caldwell's ice cream (1523/ICE CREAM). Apr-Oct, Thu-Mon 12noon-5pm, Sun 1-5pm. Weekends in Oct. (Closed 1-2pm.)

2332 **Myreton Motor Museum** www.aberlady.org/myreton.html · 01875
10/Q25 870288 · Aberlady On Drem road, past Luffness Mains. Ideal 'little' museum in old barn with restored vehicles dating from 1896. Even for the Luddite, engineering seems an aesthetic here. Dr Finlay's Casebook fans, prepare yourselves. 7 days 11am-4pm; winter weekends only 11am-3pm.

2333 **National Museum of Costume** www.nms.ac.uk · New Abbey near
11/N30 Dumfries Another obsession that became a (national) museum. On 2 floors of Shambellie House set among spectacular woodlands. Fab frocks etc from every 'period'. Apr-Oct 10am-5pm.

2334
6/Q13
Wick Heritage Centre www.caithness.org · 01955 605393 · **Bank Row, Wick** On Amazing civic museum run by volunteers. Jam-packed with items about the sea, town and that hard land. Somebody should ensure these people get MBEs or something. Easter-Oct 10am-5pm. Closed Sun.

2335
8/T19
Aberdeen Maritime Museum www.aagm.co.uk · 01224 337700 · **Shiprow, Aberdeen** Aberdeen faces the sea; this place tells you the stories. Films, exhibits, photos and paintings. Decent café. Mon-Sat 10am-5pm, Sun 12-3pm.

2336
10/L25
The Scottish Maritime Museum www.scottishmaritimemuseum.org Spread out over 3 sites, **Irvine** (01294 278283), **Braehead** (0141 886 1013) and **Dumbarton** (01389 763444). Dumbarton has the ship model experiment tank, Braehead (off junction 25A of the M8) has hands-on engines, while Irvine boasts a massive shed (Victorian engine shop) full of the bits that non-engineers never usually see, and the hulk of an old clipper at Irvine harbour. Completely fascinating. Irvine Easter-Oct, Braehead daily all year. Dumbarton all year Mon-Sat. Hours vary.

The Most Interesting Public Galleries

For Edinburgh, see p. 77-80; Glasgow, p. 127-29. ☕: **notable** café.

2337
10/Q23
☕
✓ ✓ **Dundee Contemporary Arts** www.dca.org.uk · 01382 432000 · **Nethergate, Dundee** State of contemporary art gallery (by award-winning architect Richard Murphy) with great café (1132/DUNDEE RESTAURANTS), cinema facilities, etc. which has transformed the cultural face of Dundee. People actually use it. Oft-quoted evidence of this city's changing status.

2338
8/T19
✓ **Aberdeen Art Gallery** www.aagm.co.uk · Schoolhill, Aberdeen Major gallery with temporary exhibits and eclectic permanent collection from Impressionists to Bellany. Large bequest from local granite merchant Alex Macdonald in 1900 contributes fascinating collection of his contemporaries: Bloomsburys, Scottish, Pre-Raphaelites. Excellent watercolour room. An easy and rewarding gallery to visit. 10am-5pm (Sun 2-5pm).

2339
10/P23
✓ **The Fergusson Gallery** www.scottishmuseums.org.uk · **Marshall Place, Tay Street, Perth** In distinctive round tower (a former waterworks). The assembled works on two floors of J.D. Fergusson (1874-1961). Though he spent much of his life in France, he had an influence on Scottish art and was preeminent amongst those now called the Colourists. It's a long way from Perth to Antibes 1913 but these pictures are a draught of the warm south. Mon-Sat 10am-5pm.

2340
10/Q24
✓ **Kirkcaldy Museum & Art Gallery** www.scottishmuseums.org.uk Near railway station, but ask for directions (it's easy to get lost). One of the best galleries in central Scotland. Splendid introduction to the history of 19th/20th-century Scottish art. Lots of Colourists/McTaggart/Glasgow Boys. And Sickert to Redpath. And famously the only public collection in Scotland showing Scotland's best-selling artist: one Jack Vettriano who was a Fife lad. Museum ain't bad. Kirkcaldy doesn't get much good press but this and the parks (1627/PARKS) are worth the journey (plus Valente's – 1451/FISH AND CHIPS). 7 days till 5pm.

2341
11/M31
NTS
✓ **Hornel Gallery** www.nts.org.uk · Kirkcudbright Hornel's house is a fabulous evocation with a collection of his work and atelier as was. 'Even the Queen was amazed'. Beautiful garden stretches to the river. House and garden Mar-Oct 12noon-5pm. Closed Mon/Tue. Open 7 days Jul/Aug. Garden only: Feb.

2342
8/R17
☕

✓ **Duff House** www.duffhouse.org.uk · **Banff** Nice walk and easy to find
from town centre. Important outstation of the National Galleries of Scotland
in meticulously restored Adam house with interesting history and spacious
grounds. Ramsays, Raeburns, portraiture of mixed appeal and an El Greco. Maybe
OTT for some, but major attraction in the area (go further up the Deveron,
2102/WOODLAND WALKS). Nice tearoom.

2343
11/N29

✓ **Sculpture at Glenkiln Reservoir** near **Dumfries** Take A75 to Castle
Douglas and right to Shawshead; into village, right at T-junction, left to
Dunscore, immediate left, signed for reservoir. Follow road along loch side and
park. Not a gallery at all but sculpture scattered in the hills, woods and meadows
around this reservoir in the Galloway Hills 16km southeast of Dumfries. One or two
are obvious, the rest you have to find: Epstein, Moore, Rodin in the great outdoors!

2344
3/Q10

✓ **The Pier Art Centre** www.pierartscentre.com · 01856 850209 ·
Stromness, Orkney Mainland On main street (1638/COASTAL VILLAGES), a
gallery on a small pier which could have come lock, stock and canvases from
Cornwall. Permanent St Ives-style collection of Barbara Hepworth, Ben Nicholson,
Paolozzi and others shown in a *simpatico* environment with the sea outside.
Hugely enhanced by a £4m refurbishment completed in '07. These important
pictures of the early 20th century now complemented by work of recent notable
artists like Sean Scully and Olafur Eliasson. Mon-Sat 10.30am-5pm.

2345
10/L26

Paisley Art Gallery & Museum www.scottishmuseums.org.uk · 0141 889
3151 · **High Street, Paisley** Permanent collection of the world famous Paisley
shawls and history of weaving techniques. Other exhibitions usually have a local
connection and an interactive element. Notable Greek Ionic-style building. 10am-
5pm, Sun 2-5pm. Closed Mon.

2346
9/F22

Calgary Art In Nature **Calgary, Isle of Mull** Contemporary artwork and
sculpture to be 'found' on a trail through the woods adjacent to the wonderful
beach at Calgary Bay on the far west coast of Mull. The project of Matthew Reade
who runs the Calgary Farmhouse Hotel (2393/ISLAND HOTELS), the 1km trail is fun
rather than thought provoking, but it's a great idea, nice for kids in one of the best
of places.

2347
9/L28

Rozelle House www.south-ayrshire.gov.uk · **Ayr** In Rozelle Park, the only art
in these parts. Exhibitions change monthly (including local artists' work). 4 galleries, and additional 5 rooms featuring the Alexander Goudie collection in Rozelle
House; craft shop. Open all year Mon-Sat 10am-5pm, Apr-Oct also Sun 2-5pm.

Great Theatres & Cinemas

For Edinburgh, see p. 89-90; Glasgow, p. 138-39.

2348
10/Q23

✓ **Dundee Rep** www.dundeerep.co.uk · 01382 223530 · **Tay Square,**
Dundee Cornerstone of Dundee's cultural quarter (with DCA 2337/
GALLERIES). Houses Scotland's only rep company. Ambitious programme. Anyone
into contemporary Scottish drama comes here. Good café/restaurant.

2349
7/M18

✓ **Eden Court Theatre** www.eden-court.co.uk · 01463 234234 ·
Inverness An important theatre complex making a vital contribution to the
cultural life of the Highlands. Still undergoing a lengthy major refurbishment at
TGP. Reopening a year later than planned at the end of '07, but will be wonderful.

2350
10/Q27
✓**Bowhill Little Theatre** www.bowhilllittletheatre.org · 01750 22204 ·
Bowhill House near Selkirk Tiny (72-seat) theatre off the courtyard below
Bowhill House. Intermittent mixed programme (must phone), but always delight-
ful, especially with supper afterwards in Courtyard Restaurant (phone to book).

2351
10/Q27
✓**Eastgate** www.eastgatearts.com · 01721 725777 · **Main Street,**
Peebles Beautiful, state-of-the-art wee theatre clamped on to the back of a
church (by eminent architect Richard Murphy) at Galashiels end of main street.
Eclectic programming. Expect everything! Caff and excellent restaurant adjacent.

2352
10/N21
✓**Pitlochry Theatre** www.pitlochry.org.uk · 01796 484626 · **Pitlochry**
Modern rep theatre across the river from main street performing usually 6
plays on different nights of the week. Well-chosen programme of classics and
popular works, the 500-seat theatre is often full. Very mixed Sunday concerts and
foyer fringe events. Coffee bar and restaurant menu. Also: Port-Na-Craig adjacent,
by river and The Old Armoury (982/978/PERTHSHIRE EATS), though both LO
8.30pm-ish.

2353
10/R23
✓**Byre Theatre** www.byretheatre.com · 01334 476288 · **Abbey Street or**
South Street, St Andrews A lottery-funded major reconstruction. Great
auditorium and café-bar. Major social hub for town and gown. Eclectic programme
of theatre, music, comedy. Prince William however has moved on.

2354
10/M25
Cumbernauld Theatre www.cumbernauldtheatre.co.uk · 01236 732887
Near old part of town on a rise overlooking the Stirling dual carriageway. Follow
signs for Cumbernauld House. Bar/café-restaurant and 258-seat theatre (in the
round) with a mixed programme of one-nighters and short runs of mainly Scottish
touring companies. Also concerts, drama workshops and kids' programmes.

2355
10/R27
The Wynd www.thewynd.com · 01896 820028 · **Melrose** 100-seater arts
venue which regularly entertains locals and Edinburgh folk. From classic Ibsen and
musicals to folk, jazz, dance and film. Intimate atmosphere in an intimate town.

2356
9/H28
Campbeltown Picture House www.weepictures.co.uk · 01586 553899 ·
Campbeltown Cinema Paradiso on the Kintyre peninsula. Lovingly preserved Art
Deco shrine to the movies. Opened 1913, closed 1983, but such was the tide of
nostalgic affection that it was refurbished and reopened resplendent in 1989.
Shows mainly first-run films. To see a film here and emerge onto the esplanade of
Campbeltown Loch is to experience the lost magic of a night at the pictures.

2357
10/R23
The New Picture House www.nphcinema.co.uk · 01334 473509 · **North**
Street, St Andrews 'New' means 1931 and, apart from adding other small
screens, it hasn't changed much, as generations of students will remember fondly.
Mainly first-run flicks; Oct-May, a programme of late-night cult/art movies.

✓**Tolbooth** 01786 274000 · **Stirling** See 883/STIRLING.

✓**Lemon Tree** 01224 642230 · **Aberdeen** 1120/ABERDEEN PUBS WITH FOOD.

Section 13

The Islands

The Magical Islands

2358 7/G18 ✓✓ **Raasay** A small car ferry (car useful, but bikes best) from Sconser between Portree and Broadford on Skye takes you to this, the best of places. The distinctive flat top of Dun Caan presides over an island whose history and natural history is Highland Scotland in microcosm. The village with rows of mining-type cottages is 3km from jetty. **The Outdoor Centre** (01478 660266; www.raasay-house.co.uk) in the big hoose (once the home of the notorious Dr No who, like others before him, allowed Raasay to go to wrack and ruin) has courses galore. They'll put you up if they've got room (mostly bunkrooms). The views from the lawn, or the viewpoint above the house, or better still from Dun Caan with the Cuillins on one side and Torridon on the other, are quite brilliant (2412/ISLAND WALKS). Dolphin Café at the House is licensed. The island hotel (15 rooms) has a bar but could do with some TLC. There's a ruined castle, a secret rhododendron-lined loch for swimming, seals, otters and eagles. Much to explore. Go quietly here.
Regular CalMac ferry from Sconser on Skye.

2359 9/G25 ✓✓ **Jura** www.theisleofjura.co.uk Small regular car ferry from Port Askaig on Islay takes you into a different world. Jura is remote, scarcely populated and has an ineffable grandeur indifferent to the demands of tourism. Ideal for wild camping, alternatively the serviceable hotel and pub (2397/ISLAND HOTELS) in the only village (Craighouse) 15km from ferry at Feolin. Walking guides available at hotel and essential especially for the Paps, the hills that maintain such a powerful hold over the island. Easiest climb is from Three Arch Bridge; allow 6 hours. In May they run up all of them and back to the distillery in 3 hours. Jura House's walled garden is a hidden jewel set above the south coastline; myriad wildflowers and Australasian trees with scenic walks to the shore (1608/GARDENS). The Corryvreckan whirlpool (2422/ISLAND WALKS) is another lure, but you may need a 4-wheel drive to get close enough, and its impressiveness depends upon tides. Orwell's house (Barnhill; where he wrote *1984*) is not open, but there are many fascinating side tracks: the wild west coast; around Loch Tarbert; and the long littoral between Craighouse and Lagg. (Also 1661/BEACHES; 1965/GRAVEYARDS.) With one road, no street lamps and over 5000 deer, the sound of silence is everything.
Western Ferries (01496 840681) regular 7 days, 5-minute service from Port Askaig. Gemini Cruises (07776 082256) go from Crinan which is much quicker than Islay from Central Belt (and will go as and when, eg £60 per boatload to Ardlussa).

2360 9/F23 ✓✓ **Iona** Strewn with daytrippers – not so much a pilgrimage, more an invasion – but Iona still enchants (as it did the Colourists), especially if you can get away to the Bay at the Back of the Ocean (1667/BEACHES) or watch the cavalcade from the hill above the Abbey. Or stay: **Argyll Hotel** best (01681 700334; 1280/GET-AWAY HOTELS); **St Columba Hotel** near the Abbey has more room and a lovely garden (01681 700304; 2428/MULL) or B&B. Abbey shop isn't bad (2262/CRAFT SHOPS). Pilgrimage walks on Wed (10am from St John's Cross). Bike hire from Finlay Ross shop (01681 700357) and Seaview Guesthouse at Fionnphort (01681 700235). Everything about Iona is benign; even the sun shines here when it's raining on Mull: indefinably a special place on the planet.
Regular 15-minute CalMac service from Fionnphort till 6pm, earlier in winter (01681 700512).

2361 9/F24 ✓✓ **Colonsay** www.colonsay.org.uk Accessible to daytrippers in summer (on Wed you can do an overnight stay); this island haven of wildlife, flowers and beaches (1650/BEACHES) deserves more than a few hours exploration. 250 metres from the ferry, the refurbished hotel is congenial and convenient (2388/ISLAND HOTELS). Great bar; self-catering units nearby. Some holiday cottages

and many B&Bs (check Colonsay website), but camping discouraged. Bar meals and supper at the hotel and 'Pantry' at the pier. A wild 18-hole golf course and bookshop (sic) adjacent. Semi-botanical gardens adjacent to Colonsay House and fine walks, especially to Oronsay (2416/ISLAND WALKS). Don't miss the house at Shell Beach which sells oysters and honey.
CalMac from Oban (or Islay). Crossing takes just over 2 hours. Times vary.

2362 7/G20 ✓ ✓ **Eigg** www.isleofeigg.org After changing hands, much to-do and cause célèbre, the islanders seized the time and Eigg is (in-fighting apart) theirs; and of course, ours. A wildlife haven for birds and sealife; otters, eagles and seal colonies. Scot Wildlife Trust warden does weekly walks around the island. Refurbished tearoom at pier. Licensed and evening meals. Bicycle hire (01687 482432). 2 croft houses at Cleadale near Laig bay and the Singing Sands beach; contact Sue Kirk (01687 482405). She also offers full board accommodation and caters for vegetarian and other diets. 2000 sheep on island. Great walk to Sgurr an Eigg – an awesome perch on a summer's day.
CalMac (from Mallaig) (01687 462403) or better, from Arisaig. Arisaig Marine (01687 450224) every day except Thu in summer. Phone for other timings. No car ferry; but motorbikes possible. Day trips to Rum and Muck.

2363 7/F20 ✓ ✓ **Rum** www.road-to-the-isles.org.uk The large island in the group south of Skye, off the coast at Mallaig. The CalMac ferry plies between Canna, Eigg, Muck and Rum but not too conveniently and it's not easy to island-hop and make a decent visit (but see below). Rum the most wild and dramatic has an extraordinary time-warp mansion in Kinloch Castle which is mainly a museum (guided tours tie in with boat trips). Hostel rooms (53 beds) contrast to the antique opulence above and below. Rum is run by Scottish Natural Heritage and there are fine trails, climbs, bird-watching spots. 2 simple walks are marked for the 3-hour visitors, but the island reveals its mysteries more slowly. The Doric temple mausoleum to George Bullough, the industrialist whose Highland fantasy the castle was, is a 9km (3 hour) walk across the island to Harris Bay. Sighting the sea eagles may be one of the best things that ever happens to you. Take a picnic.
CalMac ferry from Mallaig via Eigg (2 hours 15 minutes) or Canna at an ungodly hour. Better from Arisaig (Murdo Grant 01687 450224) Tue/Thu all year plus Sat/Sun in summer (3 hours ashore).

2364 5/A15
NTS
✓ ✓ **St Kilda** www.nts.org.uk There's nothing quite like St Kilda – anywhere. By far the most remote and removed of the islands on this page, it is an expedition to get there and one of a physical, cultural and spiritual nature. Now accorded World Heritage status and run by NTS, it occupies a special place in the heart and soul of the Scots. The NTS ranger's office on St Kilda can be reached on 01870 604628. I have never been.
Visit with Northern Light Charters (01631 740595) or check www.kilda.org.uk.

2365 9/E22 ✓ **Isle of Tiree** www.isleoftiree.com It is an isle, not just an island – it's flat, it has lovely sand and grass and the weather's usually better than the mainland. Bit of wind does keep away the midges. Lots of outdoor activities: windsurfing of course (2235/WINDSURFING), but kayaking, birdwatching and other gentle pursuits. **The Scarinish Hotel** (01879 220308) is friendly, so local and increasingly special **Glebe House** (01879 220758) is a manse with nice rooms and a homely ambience. Tiree is different to the islands on this page. But you may long for trees.
Daily flights from Glasgow (0870 850 9850) & CalMac ferries from Oban (daily in summer).

2366 9/G26 ✓ **Gigha www.gigha.org.uk** Romantic small island off Kintyre coast; with classic views of its island neighbours. Easy mainland access (20-minute ferry) contributes to an island atmosphere that lacks any feeling of isolation. Like Eigg, Gigha was bought by the islanders so its fragile economy is even more dependent on your visit. The island currently remains a whole estate; with gardens open at the main house (1599/GARDENS), a tearoom near ferry and a hotel (2396/ISLAND HOTELS) providing comfortable surroundings. Locals are relaxed and friendly; with bike hire (01583 505251), 3 B&Bs including the big house (01583 505400), café-bar at The Boathouse (seasonal) and golf (9 holes). Many trails and tracks; ask locally for leaflet. Double Beach, where the Queen once swam off the royal yacht; two crescents of sand on either side of the north end of the isthmus of Eilean Garbh. *CalMac ferry from Tayinloan on A83, 27km south of Tarbert (Glasgow 165km). One an hour in summer, fewer in winter.*

2367 9/F22 ✓ **Ulva** Off west coast of Mull. A boat leaves Ulva Ferry on the B8073 26km south of Dervaig. Idyllic wee island with 5 well-marked walks including to the curious basalt columns similar to Staffa, or by causeway to the smaller island of Gometra; plan routes at The Boathouse interpretive centre and tearoom (with Ulva oysters and home-cooked food). 'Sheila's (thatched) Cottage' faithfully restored. No accommodation though camping can be arranged (01688 500264). A charming Telford church has services 4 times a year. Ulva is a perfect day away from the rat race of downtown Tobermory!
All-day 5-minute service (not Sat; Sun summer only) till 5pm. Ferryman (01688 500226).

2368 5/D19 ✓ **Eriskay www.w-isles.gov.uk/eriskay** Made famous by the sinking nearby of the SS *Politician* in 1941 and the salvaging of its cargo of whisky, later immortalised by Compton Mackenzie in *Whisky Galore*, this Hebridean gem has all the 'idyllic island' ingredients: perfect beaches (1999/MARY, CHARLIE & BOB), a hill to climb, a pub (called the Politician and telling the story round its walls; it sells decent pub food all day in summer), and a causeway to South Uist. Limited B&B and no hotel, but camping is ok if you're discreet. Eriskay and Barra together – the pure island experience. (Also 1948/CHURCHES and 2427/THE OUTER HEBRIDES). *CalMac erry from Barra (Airdmhor) 40 minutes: 5 a day in summer, winter hours vary.*

2369 5/C20 ✓ **Mingulay** Deserted mystical island near the southern tip of the Outer Hebrides, the subject of one of the definitive island books, *The Road to Mingulay*. Now easily reached in summer by daily trip from Castlebay, Barra with 1.5-hour journey and 3 hours ashore (enquire at tourist information centre or Castlebay Hotel). Last inhabitants left 1912. Ruined village has the poignant air of St Kilda; similar spectacular cliffs on west side with fantastic rock formations, stacks and a huge natural arch – best viewed from boat. Mingulay was bought by NTS in '99. Only birds and sheep live here now.

2370 5/F15 **The Shiants www.shiantisles.net** 3 magical, uninhabited tiny islands off east coast of Harris. Read about them in one of the most detailed accounts (a 'love letter') to any small island ever written: *Sea Room* by Adam Nicolson, the guy who owns them. There's a bothy and it's possible to visit by visiting first his website.

2371 9/H22 **Lismore www.isleoflismore.com** Sail from Oban (car ferry) or better from Port Appin 5km off main A828, the Oban-Fort William road, 32km north of Oban and where there's a seafood bar/restaurant/hotel (1435/SEAFOOD RESTAURANTS), to sit and wait. A road goes down the centre of the island, but there are many hill and coastal walks and even the near end round Port Ramsay feels away from it all. History, natural history and air. Bike hire on island from Mary McDougal (01631

760213) who will deliver to ferry, or Port Appin Bikes on the way into the village. Lismore Centre opened '07 halfway down the island.
CalMac service from Oban, 4 or 5 times a day (not Sun). From Port Appin (32km north of Oban) several per day, 5mins. Last back 8pm; 9.30pm Fri & Sat, but check; 6.20pm winter (01631 562125).

2372 9/F22 **Staffa** For many a must, especially if you're on Mull. The geological phenomenon of Fingal's Cave and Mendelssohn's homage are well known. But it's still impressive. Several boat-trip options, many including the Treshnish Islands. *Trips from Mull (08000 858786). Trips from Iona/Fionnphort (01681 700338 or 01681 700358). Trips from Oban (01631 566809).*

CalMac www.calmac.co.uk · 08705 650000

The Best Skye Hotels

Skye is large and now has so many good places that it merits its own hotel and restaurant sections among the islands. See The Best Skye Restaurants, p. 408 and The Best of Skye, p. 412.

2373 7/F18
6 ROOMS
TEL · TV
£85+
✓ ✓ **The House Over-By at The Three Chimneys** 01470 511258 · www.threechimneys.co.uk At Colbost 7km west of Dunvegan by the B884 to Glendale. When Eddie and Shirley Spear transformed their house over by into the House Over-By, it was the first boutique-style accommodation in the Highlands. Almost 10 years later it's still a model of understated luxury in a wild place. Perhaps less 'contemporary' than was but some tweaking underway at TGP. Adjacent or just over-by from their accolade-laden restaurant (in world's top lists) (2398/SKYE RESTAURANTS). Separate dining room for healthy buffet breakfast. Outside the sheep, the sea and the sky.

2374 7/H19
9 + 5 ROOMS
+ 4 SUITES
TV
NO PETS
£85+
✓ **Kinloch Lodge** www.kinloch-lodge.co.uk · 01471 833333 · **Sleat Peninsula** South of Broadford 5 minutes, new road in Sleat Peninsula, 55km Portree. The ancestral, but not overly imposing home of Lord and Lady Macdonald with newer build house adjacent – adding 5 very well appointed rooms and spacious, country drawing room. Some redecorating ongoing at TGP and upgrading of all bathrooms; a supersuite, the Loft (sic) na Dal (after the loch outside) is on its way '08. Lady Mac is Claire Macdonald of cookery fame, so her many books for sale in 'the shop', cookery courses through the year and her hand in all the wonderful things you eat (all meals in the Lodge itself). A range of Claire Macdonald jams and puds etc is also heading for an upmarket supermarket near you. Here at Kinloch you're in the home of the brand (claire-macdonald.com).
EAT At Lady Claire's table. 2399/SKYE RESTAURANTS.

2375 7/H19
12 ROOMS
+ 4 SUITES
TEL · TV
NO PETS
£60-85
✓ **Eilean Iarmain** www.eileaniarmain.co.uk · 01471 833332 · **Isleornsay, Sleat** 60km south of Portree. Tucked into the bay this Gaelic inn with its great pub and good dining provides famously comfortable base in south of the island. Some may find the non-compromising, traditional-value approach hard to take: hotel still has round-pin plugs, so no appliances, there's no mobile reception and little old tellies that may or may not work. But this place has the indefinable 'it'. It hasn't changed much and it really doesn't have to. Bar is local craic central. 6 rooms in main hotel best value (6 are in house over-by). Also 4 suites over-by – plus. Environs superb.
EAT Especially in the bar.

2376 7/F18
6 ROOMS
TEL · TV
NO PETS
£45-60

✓ **Ullinish Country Lodge** www.theisleofskye.co.uk · 01470 572214 · **near Struan** On west coast 2km from Sligachan-Dunvegan road. Presented as a restaurant with rooms, this has become a new foodie stopover destination in Skye '07. Spectacular location rather than setting, there are views and walks to die for all around. Awards for 'outstanding food' and curiously 'bedroom design'. Head there now while you can still get in (must eat to stay, first night).

2377 7/G18
14 ROOMS
TEL · TV
£45-85

✓ **Skeabost Country House Hotel** www.oxfordhotelsandinns.com · 01470 532202 · **near Portree** 11km west of Portree on the A850, the Dunvegan road. Venerable Skye chateau with fab interior conserved despite recent chequered history of owners. Now safely and efficiently managed by Oxford Hotels with plans to restore some former glory. Conservatory restaurant, original billiard room (and table), loads of public space and sumptuous bedrooms in silk and satin (the rock 'n' roll suites courtesy of previous owner in the 'music biz'). Exquisite grounds including the babbling River Snizort (hotel has salmon rights for 8 miles and own ghillie) and a sweet little 9-hole golf course. The Skeabost is back!

2378 7/G18
19 ROOMS
TEL · TV
£38-60

✓ **Bosville Hotel** 01478 612846 · **Portree** Refurbished rooms and *the* place to eat in this hotel at the top of the brae heading north from centre on Staffin Rd. Chandlery Restaurant and Bistro (see below) and urban comfort levels.

2379 7/G18
7 ROOMS
TEL · TV
£45-60

✓ **Marmalade** www.marmaladehotels.com· 01478 611711 · **Home Farm Road, Portree** Leave from corner of main square up hill away from sea and keep going 1.5km. Unlikely, almost suburban location until you see the view (from gardens and 4 of the 7 rooms). Skye's boutique hotel, remodelled '06. Rooms above busy bar/restaurant popular with locals (they do takeaway pizza). Rooms are nice, not OTT.

2380 7/G19
9 ROOMS
TV · TEL
NO PETS
£45-60

✓ **Toravaig House Hotel** www.skyehotel.co.uk · 01471 833231 · **Sleat** On main road south from Broadford to Armadale. A personally run hotel on the up and up. Small, charming with contemporary refurbished rooms and pleasing Iona Restaurant; this is increasingly a good Skye option in the civilised south. Their yacht, *Solus*, is at your disposal. (Yes, you read that correctly.)

2381 7/G19
16 ROOMS
TEL · TV
£45-60

✓ **Duisdale House** www.duisdale.com · 01471 833202 · **Sleat** Same people who have Toravaig now own this similar though larger hotel up the road towards Broadford. Nice gardens with restaurant terrace. Refurbished rooms will be completed '08. Residents of both have use of the hotel yacht.

2382 7/G18
12 ROOMS
APR-OCT
TEL
£45-60

Viewfield House www.viewfieldhouse.com · 01478 612217 · **Portree** One of the first hotels you come to in Portree on the road from south (driveway opposite gas station); you need look no further. Individual, grand but comfortable, full of antiques and memorabilia, though not at all stuffy; this is also one of the best-value hotels on the island. Log fires, Supper available if you want but you don't have to eat in. This gives your congenial host Hugh Macdonald a break, which is good. Sail that boat into the sunset more often, Hugh.

2383 7/G18
28 ROOMS
TV · TEL
£45-60

Cuillin Hills Hotel www.cuillinhills-hotel-skye.co.uk · 01478 612003 · **Portree** On the edge of Portree (off road north to Staffin) near water's edge. Secluded mansion house hotel with nice conservatory. Decor: a matter of taste (you may like leather-studded sofas and draped 4-posters) but great views from most rooms. Nice walk from garden (2420/ISLAND WALKS).

2384 7/F17
5 ROOMS
ECO · NO TV
NO TEL
£30 OR LESS

The Stein Inn www.steininn.co.uk · 01470 592362 · **Waternish** Off B886, the Waternish road which is 5km Dunvegan on the road to Portree. Distant but very Skye location in village row on the water and near Lochbay (see below). Ancient inn with atmospheric pub (1259/SEASIDE INNS) and 5 nice rooms above. Peat-smoked kippers and porridge for breakfast. An excellent retreat.

2385 7/G17
11 ROOMS
+ 7 COTT
MAR-DEC
TEL · TV
£60-85

Flodigarry www.flodigarry.co.uk · 01470 552203 · **Staffin** 32km north of Portree. A romantic country house overlooking the sea, with Flora Mac's cottage in the grounds. The setting is uniquely special with the Quirang behind (1730/VIEWS) and the silver sea with its sunsets from the terrace. Bistro (open to non-residents), dining room and conservatory. Cottage in grounds have the history (she did live here) and contemporary interiors.

2386 7/H19
80 ROOMS
NO KIDS
NO PETS
£30 OR LESS

Sabhal Mòr Ostaig www.smo.uhi.ac.uk · 01471 888000 · **Sleat** Pronounced 'Sawal More Ostag'. Part of the Gaelic College in Sleat off A851 north of Armadale. Excellent inexpensive rooms in modern build overlooking Sound of Sleat. Penthouse spectacular. Breakfast in bright café. Best deal on the island; you could learn Gaelic.

2387 7/G19
30 ROOMS
TEL · TV
£45-85

Broadford Hotel www.broadfordhotel.co.uk · 01471 822414 · **Broadford** On left heading north out of Broadford. '07 makeover of long-established Skye hotel with lots of money being spent and ongoing at TGP. Expect '08 to find busy, contemporary roadhouse venture with excellent facilities and rooms, casual and, they say, fine dining. Certainly a new landmark.

The Best Island Hotels

This section excludes Skye which has its own hotels listings on p. 404.

This section excludes Skye which has its own hotels listings on p. 404.

2388 9/F24
9 ROOMS
MAR-DEC
£45-60

✓**Colonsay Hotel** www.colonsay.com · 01951 200316 · **Colonsay** Long established but after lapse now fully refurbished and a superb island hotel 100m from the ferry on this island perfectly proportioned for short stays (2361/ISLANDS). The laird (and the wife) and their partners determined to turn this into a contemporary destination hotel. Cool public rooms and buzzy bar (especially Thu quiz nights). Mobiles only work in the garden. Stunning bench 5km. On your bike.

2389 9/F26
10 ROOMS
TEL · TV
£45-60

✓**Port Charlotte Hotel** www.portcharlottehotel.co.uk · 01496 850360 · **Islay** Epitome perhaps of the comfortable, classy island hotel. Modern, discreet approach in this fine whitewashed village (1642/COASTAL VILLAGES), good whisky choice and good, bistro-style food in dining room; great bar meals. Tourists in summer, hardcore twitchers in winter... and us anytime. Hotel supports local and Scottish artists.
EAT Best on Islay. 2407/ISLAND RESTAURANTS.

2390 9/F26
7 ROOMS
+ 2 APTS
TEL · TV
£45-60

✓**Harbour Inn** www.harbour-inn.com · 01496 810330 · **Bowmore, Islay** 2 doors up from the harbour in centre of main town on lovely, quite lively Islay. Rooms contemporary and comfy, lounge with views and notable restaurant. Bar with malts and bar meals (LO 8.30pm). 2 apartments across the street.

2391 5/E16
5 ROOMS
FEB-DEC
£60-85

✓**Scarista House** www.scaristahouse.com · 01859 550238 · **South Harris** 21km Tarbert, 78km Stornoway. On the west coast famous for its beaches and overlooking one of the best (1658/BEACHES). Tim and Patricia Martin's civilised retreat and home from home. Fixed menu meals in dining rooms over

looking sea. No phones (TV in kitchen), but many books. The golf course over the road is exquisite. Check winter opening. Good family hotel as well as couples on romantic break dining in.
EAT Destination Harris. Fixed menu.

2392 9/G22
6 ROOMS
MAR–OCT
TEL · TV
NO PETS
£45–60

✓**Highland Cottage** www.highlandcottage.co.uk · 01688 302030 · **Breadalbane Street, Tobermory** Opposite fire station. Traditional Tobermory street above harbour (from roundabout on road in from Craignure). 6 small but comfy rooms named after islands (all themed, one called Nantucket). Their reputation grows and it's harder to get in but foodies should try hard. Everything here is small but perfectly formed – relaxed atmosphere with accessible, non-poncified fine dining.
EAT The place to eat on Mull. Fine without fuss. 2428/MULL.

2393 9/F22
9 ROOMS
MAR–NOV
£60–85

✓**Calgary Farmhouse** www.calgary.co.uk · 01688 400256 · **Mull** 7kms south of Dervany (30 minutes Tobermory) near beautiful Calgary Beach. Roadside bistro/restaurant (2411/ISLAND RESTAURANTS) with rooms and gallery/coffeeshop. Excellent island hospitality – Matthew's furniture in public rooms and 'Art in Nature' sculpture walking woods at back down to the beach. Bohemia in the bay. Get up early to see the otters (I never have). 2 self-catering suites above gallery. Good Mod Brit cooking.
EAT Food wobbles a little but great informal ambience.

2394 9/J27
7 ROOMS
EASTER–OCT
TEL · TV
NO KIDS
£60–85

✓**Kilmichael** www.kilmichael.com · 01770 302219 · **Brodick, Arran** On main road to Brodick Castle/Corrie, take left at bend by golf course and you're in the country. 3km down track is this haven from Brodick and beyond. Country-house refined, so not great for kids. Rooms in house or garden courtyard – painstaking detail in food and environs.
EAT Best eats on Arran. 2409/ISLAND RESTAURANTS.

2395 5/C20
12 ROOMS
TEL · TV
£38–45

✓**Castlebay Hotel** www.castlebayhotel.co.uk · 01871 810223 · **Barra** Prominent position overlooking bay and ferry dock. You see where you're staying long before you arrive. Old-style holiday hotel at the centre of Barra life with new owners '07 who are upgrading but keeping unique charm. Good restaurant and bar meals (2427/OUTER HEBRIDES). Adjacent bar one of the best bars for craic and car culture in Scotland and with more than a dash of the Irish (1362/BLOODY GOOD PUBS).

2396 9/G26
12 ROOMS
TEL · TV
£45–60

The Gigha Hotel www.gigha.org.uk · 01583 505254 · **Isle of Gigha** A short walk from the ferry on an island perfectly proportioned for a short visit; easy walking and cycling. Residents' lounge peaceful with dreamy views to Kintyre. Menu with local produce, eg Gigha prawns and scallops (in bar or dining room) but ask what's fresh (fish from Campbeltown). Island life without the remoteness. Also self-catering cottages. 2366/ISLANDS.

2397 9/G25
17 ROOMS
£30–38

Jura Hotel www.jurahotel.co.uk · 01496 820243 · **Craighouse** 15km from Islay ferry at Feolin. Serviceable, basic hotel overlooking Small Isles Bay; will oblige with all walking/exploring requirements. Pub is social hub of island. Rooms at front may be small, but have the views.

✓**Argyll Hotel Iona** 01681 700334   1254/SEASIDE INNS.

St Columba Hotel Iona 01681 700304   2428/BEST OF MULL.

The Best Skye Restaurants

2398 7/F18 ✓✓ **The Three Chimneys** www.threechimneys.co.uk · 01470 511258 ·
£32+ **Colbost** 7km west of Dunvegan on B884 to Glendale. Shirley and Eddie
Spear's classic restaurant in a converted cottage on the edge of the best kind of
nowhere. They shop local for everything (Skye supplies have hugely improved) so
best ingredients. All year. Lunch (except Sun and winter months). Dinner LO
9.30pm. Shirley has given up cheffing duties to Michael Smith and a strong kitchen
team (gentle island girls outfront). It's a long road to Colbost (I always hurtle up
late) but by the start of your starter you know why you came. They can recommend some B&Bs when their own rooms are (as usual) full. 2373/ISLAND HOTELS.

2399 7/H19 ✓ **Kinloch Lodge** www.kinloch-lodge.co.uk · 01471 833333 · Sleat
£32+ **Peninsula** In south on Sleat Peninsula, 55km south of Portree signed off the
'main' Sleat road, along a characterful track. Lord and Lady MacDonald's family
home/hotel offers a taste of the high life without hauteur; a setting and setup
especially appreciated by eg Americans, starting with drinks in the dining room
7.30pm for 8. Lady Claire less on the stoves than before (what with her 'luxury
comestibles' brand rolling out round the country) and dinner more discreetly
efficient, less theatrical than days of yore. But this is elegant dining in a lovely
room and it all makes you want to stay for one of her cookery courses. Perfect
cheeses but you simply must leave room for Claire's puds.

2400 7/G18 ✓ **The Chandlery at The Bosville Hotel** 01478 612846 · Portree Fine
£32+/ dining came to Portree with John Kelly winning awards and more importantly,
£15-22 local approval. A la carte and daily menu well thought-out, sourced and presented.
Bistro menu in adjacent space is Portree's good deal/good food (mainly seafood)
option. Chandlery Apr-Oct, Bistro all year. LO 10pm.

2401 7/F17 ✓ **Lochbay Seafood** www.lochbay-seafood-restaurant.co.uk · 01470
£15-22 **592235** 12km north of Dunvegan off A850. Small; simple fresh seafood in
loch-side setting, David and Alison keep it simply divine. Lunch & dinner Tue-Sat
(and Mon dinner Jun-Aug). Report: 1424/SEAFOOD RESTAURANTS.

2402 7/G18 ✓ **Harbour View** 01478 612069 · Bosville Terrace, Portree On road to
Staffin and north Skye with harbour view at least from the door. Local seafood
in intimate bistro dining room. Small and good local reputation. In summer you
put your name down and wait (it's popular). 7 days Easter-Oct lunch and dinner
(not Sun lunch). LO 9.30pm.

2403 7/G19 **Creelers** www.creelers.co.uk · 01471 822281 · Broadford Just off A87 road
from Kyleakin and bridge to Portree as you come into Broadford. Small cabin
seafood restaurant and takeaway round back, but excellent local reputation. 4pm-
10pm (and takeaway till 10pm). Closed Sun/Mon.

2404 7/G18 **Café Arriba** 01478 611830 · Portree Above/over Over the Rainbow on road
down to harbour. A cool caff on Skye with a view of the bay. Some healthy food,
some not. Good bread/Green Mountain coffee/vegetarian. Does the trick. 7 days.
LO 9pm.

2405 7/G18 **Caledonian Café** Wentworth Street, Portree On the main street. Simple,
serviceable caff open long hours in summer for hungry tourists who don't want to
cough up loadsa dosh to eat. Hot specials and usual caff fare. Home baking and
home-made ice cream. 7 days 8.30am-9pm.

2406 7/G18 **Old Inn** 01478 640205 · **Carbost** Off Sligachan-Dunvegan road near Talisker Distillery. I drove a long way for the craic here at the Old Inn and good grub and in summer music most nights. B&B in lodge and bunkhouse adjacent. A friendly old inn.

The Best Restaurants In The Islands

2407 9/F26 ✓ **Port Charlotte Hotel & Harbour Inn** www.portcharlottehotel.co.uk · 01496 850360 & 01496 810330 · **Bowmore, Islay** Both excellent island inns, with dining rooms and bar meals using local produce that are as good as anything comparable on the mainland. Both look over the western sea. Reports: 2389/2390 ISLAND HOTELS.

2408 9/G22 ✓ **The Dining Room @ Highland Cottage** www.highlandcottage.co.uk ·
£22-32 01688 302030 · **Tobermory** Jo Currie's down-to-earth fine dining; destination for foodies, a treat for locals. Impeccably sourced. The food we like done just that wee bit better than you could ever do it yourself.

2409 9/J27 ✓ **Kilmichael Hotel** 01770 302219 · **Arran** 1km from seafront road in
£22-32 Brodick, this is quite the place to go for dinner. Antony Butterworth excels in the kitchen with best of local and national produce. Charming service. Peacocks in the garden enliven the otherwise mellow soundtrack. Report: 2394/ISLAND HOTELS.

2410 5/C20 **Castlebay Hotel** 01871 810223 · **Castlebay** Chef with experience from the US
£22-32 and all over has lifted Castlebay cooking considerably. Informal dining room or bar overlooking castle and bay. Scores mainly when fresh from the bay (lobster, scallops) but comfort-food staples, too.

2411 9/F22 **Calgary Farmhouse & Dovecote Restaurant** 01688 400256 · **Mull** 7km
£15-22 from Dervaig on B8073 near Mull's famous beach. Roadside farm setting with inexpensive light, piney bedrooms and a bistro/wine bar restaurant using local produce. For Mod Brit cuisine. The Carthouse Gallery/coffeeshop in summer. A quiet spot for the most ambient meal on Mull. No frills.

Lochbay Seafood Skye 12km north of Dunvegan 1424/SKYE.
Creelers 01770 302810 · **Arran** Edge of Brodick 2425/ARRAN.
Digby Chick 01851 700026 · **Stornoway** 2427/OUTER HEBRIDES.
Busta House 01806 522506 · **Shetland** 35km north of Lerwick 2430/
SHETLAND.
✓ **Argyll Hotel** 01681 700334 · **Iona** 1254/SEASIDE INNS.

✓ **Scarista House** 01859 550238 · **Harris** 2391/ISLAND HOTELS.

Fantastic Walks In The Islands

For walk codes, see p. 12.

2412 7/G18   **Dun Caan**   **Raasay**   Still one of my favourite island walks – to the flat top of a
10KM · XCIRC   magic hill (1732/VIEWS), the one you see from most of the east coast of Skye. Take
XBIKES   ferry (2358/MAGICAL ISLANDS), ask for route from Inverarish. Go via old iron mine;
2-B-2   looks steep when you get over the ridge, but it's a dawdle. And amazing.

2413 5/E15   **The Lost Glen**   **Harris**   Take B887 west from Tarbert almost to the end (where at
12KM RET   Hushinish there's a good beach, maybe a sunset), but go right before the Big
XCIRC   House (signed Chliostair Power Station). Park here or further in and walk to dam
XBIKES   (3km from road). Take right track round reservoir and left around the upper loch.
2-B-2   Over the brim you arrive in a wide, wild glen; an overhang 2km ahead is said to
have the steepest angle in Europe. Go quietly; if you don't see deer and eagles
here, you're making too much noise on the grass.

2414 9/G23   **Carsaig**   **Mull**   In south of island, 7km from A849 Fionnphort-Craignure road near
15/20KM   Pennyghael. 2 walks start at pier: going left towards Lochbuie for a spectacular
XCIRC   coastal/woodland walk past Adnunan Stack (7km); or right towards the imposing
XBIKES   headland where, under the cliffs, the Nuns' Cave was a shelter for nuns evicted
2-B-2   from Iona during the Reformation. Nearby is a quarry whose stone was used to
build Iona Abbey and much further on (9km Carsaig), at Malcolm's Point, the
extraordinary Carsaig Arches carved by wind and sea.

2415 9/J26   **Cock of Arran**   **Lochranza**   Turn right at church and follow signs. 8/9km circular
11KM   walk into Glen Chalmadale and high into moorland (260m), then drops down to
CIRC   magnificent shoreline. Here eagles catch the updraft and peregrines lose it. Divers
XBIKES   and ducks share the shore with seals. About 1km from where you meet the shore,
look for Giant Centipede fossil trail. Further on at opening of wall pace 350 steps
and turn left up to Ossian's Cave. Path crosses Fairy Dell Burn and eventually
comes out at Lochranza Bay. Allow 5/6 hours and stout boots (good walk descend-
ing from youth hostel).

2416 9/F24   **Colonsay**   2361/MAGICAL ISLANDS. From hotel or the quay, walk to Colonsay House
12 + 6KM   and its lush, overgrown intermingling of native plants and exotics (8km round trip);
XCIRC   or to the priory on Oronsay, the smaller island. 6km to 'the Strand' (you might get
BIKES   a lift with the postman) then cross at low tide, with enough time (at least 2 hours)
1-A-2   to walk to the ruins. Allow longer if you want to climb the easy peak of Ben
Oronsay. Tide tables at hotel. Nice walk also from Kiloran Beach (1650/BEACHES) to
Balnahard Beach – farm track 12km return.

2417 7/F18   **The Trotternish Ridge**   **website.lineone.net/~trotternish/walking.html** ·
30KM   **Skye**   The 30km Highland walk which takes in the Quirang and the Old Man of
XCIRC   Stoer (see below for both) offers many shorter walks without climbing or scram-
XBIKES   bling as well as the whole monty (a 2-day hike).

2418 7/G17   **The Old Man Of Stoer**   **Skye**   The enigmatic basalt finger visible from the
5KM   Portree-Staffin road (A855). Start from car park on left, 12km from Portree. There's
XCIRC   a well-defined path through woodland and then towards the cliffs and a steep
XBIKES   climb up the grassy slope to the pinnacle which towers 165ft tall. Great views over
2-B-2   Raasay to the mainland. Lots of space and rabbits and birds who make the most of
it. It was the location of major environmental art event by notable nva organisation
in summer 2005.

2419 7/G17
6KM
XCIRC
XBIKES
2-B-2
The Quirang Skye See 1730/VIEWS for directions to start point. The strange formations have names (eg the Table, the Needle, the Prison) and it's possible to walk round all of them. Start of the path from the car park is easy. At the first saddle, take the second scree slope to the Table, rather than the first. When you get to the Needle, the path to the right between two giant pinnacles is the easiest of the 3 options. From the top you can see the Hebrides. This place is supernatural; anything could happen. So be careful.

2420 7/F18
3KM
CIRC
XBIKES
1-A-1
Scorrybreac Skye A much simpler prospect than the above and more quietly spectacular but mentioned here because anyone could do it; it's only 3km and it's more or less in Portree. Head for Cuillin Hills Hotel off Staffin Rd out of town (2383/SKYE HOTELS). Shoreline path signed just below hotel. Passes 'Black Rock', where once Bonnie Prince Charlie left for Raasay, and continues round hill. Nice views back to the bright lights of Portree.

2421 3/Q11
20/25KM
CIRC
MT BIKES
2-B-2
Hoy Orkney There are innumerable walks on the scattered Orkney Islands and on Hoy itself; on a good day you can get round the north part of the island and see some of the most dramatic coastal scenery anywhere. A passenger ferry leaves Stromness 2 or 3 times a day and takes 30mins. Make tracks north or south from junction near pier and use free Hoy brochure from tourist information centre so as not to miss the landmarks, the bird sanctuaries and the Old Man himself.

2422 9/H24
6/24KM
XCIRC
XBIKES
2-C-2
Corryvreckan Jura The whirlpool in the Gulf of Corryvreckan is notorious. Between Jura and Scarba; to see it go to far north of Jura. From end of the road at Ardlussa (25km Craighouse, the village), there's a rough track to Lealt then a walk (a local may drive you) of 12km to Kinuachdrach, then a further walk of 3km. Phenomenon best seen at certain states of tide. There are boat trips from Crinan and Oban – consult tourist information centres. Consult hotel (2303/ISLAND HOTELS) and get the walk guide. 2359/MAGICAL ISLANDS.

2423 7/G20
Sgurr An Eigg Unmissable treat if you're on Eigg. Take to the big ridge. Not a hard pull, and extraordinary views and island perspective from the top. 2362/MAGICAL ISLANDS.

The Best of Skye

2424 7/H19 **The Bridge** The hump (which it gave to a lot of locals) is unromantic but convenient and free; from Kyle. **The Ferries** Mallaig-Armadale, 30 minutes. Tarbert (Harris)-Uig, 1 hour 35 minutes (CalMac, as Mallaig). **The Best Way to Skye** Glenelg-Kylerhea www.skyeferry.co.uk (01599 511302) 5-minute sailing. Continuous Easter-Oct . Winter sailings – check tourist information centre.

WHERE TO STAY & EAT
See the separate sections Skye Hotels p.404–06 and Skye Restaurants, p.408–09.

WHAT TO SEE
The Cuillins (2/BIG ATTRACTIONS); **Raasay** (2358/MAGICAL ISLANDS), (2412/ISLAND WALKS); **The Quirang** (1730/VIEWS), (2419/ISLAND WALKS); **Old Man Of Stoer** (2418/ISLAND WALKS); **Dunvegan** (1859/CASTLES); **Eas Mor** (1687/WATERFALLS); **Elgol** (1736/VIEWS); **Skye Batiks** (2260/SHOPPING); **Skye Museum Of Island Life** (2325/MUSEUMS); **Flora Macdonald's Grave** (1925/MONUMENTS); **Skye Silver**, **Edinbane Pottery** and **Carbost Craft** (2257/2256/SHOPPING); **Fairy Pools** (1752/PICNICS).

Tourist Information 01478 612137
CalMac www.calmac.co.uk · 08705 650000

The Best of Arran

2425 9/J29 **Ferry** Ardrossan-Brodick, 55 minutes. 6 per day Mon-Sat, 4 on Sun. Ardrossan-Glasgow, train or road via A77/A71 1.5 hours. Claonaig-Lochranza, 30 minutes. 9 per day (summer only). The best way to see Arran is on a bike.

WHERE TO STAY

7 ROOMS
TEL · TV
NO KIDS/PETS
£45-60

✓ Kilmichael House 01770 302219 · **Brodick** Period mansion 3km from the main road and into the glens. Elegant interior and furnishings in house and courtyard rooms. Very discreet hence no groups or kids. Still *the* place to eat on Arran, but book (2394/ISLAND HOTELS). Also has self-catering cottages.

28 ROOMS
(36 IN SPA)
TEL · TV
NO PETS
£45-60

Auchrannie House www.auchrannie.co.uk · 01770 302234 · **Brodick** Once an old mansion now expanded all over and become a holiday complex. House still best rooms and eats (Garden Restaurant) and even pool. But the 'Spa Resort' like a Holiday Inn Xpress in the country is best for families – in fact perfect for families – quite stylish modern rooms. Another pool and leisure facilities. Upstairs restaurant a bit Heathrow Airport but fits all sizes! Old house enlarged and recently refurbished. Somewhat overshadowed by the travelodge/spa. Burgeoning time-share in grounds.

5 ROOMS
MAR-JAN · TV
NO KIDS/PETS
£38-45

Argentine House www.argentinearran.co.uk · 01770 700662 · **Whiting Bay** Seaside home on the front at Whiting Bay, a guesthouse run by Swiss couple, the inimitable Baumgärtners. Cluttered, rather boho public rooms but contemporary, light bedrooms. Evening meals Tue/Thu. 'Spaghetti Fun' on Fri/Sat. BYOB.

8 ROOMS
APR-OCT TV
£38-45

Burlington www.burlingtonarran.co.uk · 01770 700255 · **Whiting Bay** Adjacent to the Argentine (above). The Lamonts' homely hoose. Pride themselves on their 'slow-food' menu (see below).

7 ROOMS
EASTER-DEC
TEL · TV
KIDS £30-38
Lochranza Hotel 01770 830223 Small hotel with tranquil views across bay and 13th-century castle. In village. Basic accommodation but home-spun hosp, soups, pâtés, scones and more (scones). Beer garden with food all day in season.

S.Y. Hostel www.syha.org.uk · 0870 004 1140 · **Lochranza** 30km from Brodick.

WHERE TO EAT

£22-32
✓ **Kilmichael House** www.kilmichael.com · 01770 302219 · **Brodick** (See Where to Stay, above.) Unquestionably the best food on Arran. 8 choices and starter/main/ pud. 2409/ISLAND RESTAURANTS.

£15-22
The Lighthouse 01770 850240 Maritime blue and pine room – wholesome menu of great home-made food (1487/BEST TEAROOMS). Same proprietors, now specialising in local seafood, lamb and beef. Best place on island for sundowners and cappuccinos. BYOB. Closed Mon. Feb-Nov 9am-8pm.

£22-32
Creelers www.creelers.co.uk · 01770 302810 · **Brodick** Art, seafood and atmosphere (when you find the place open). Phone ahead – hours a tad unpredictable but great seafood, mostly locally sourced – has own smokery. See 1428/SEAFOOD RESTAURANTS.

£15-22
Burlington Hotel www.burlingtonhotel.com · 01770 700255 · **Whiting Bay** Kitchen under the direction of Robin Gray (who also runs an organic produce business) and the likeable Lamonts. The food is 'slow', the vibe is green and organic. Nice for Arran, nice for you! Apr-Oct. Dinner only, daily.

£15-22
The Distillery Restaurant 01770 830264 · **Lochranza** At the Distillery Visitor Centre, Lochranza. Good light menu in light even clinical room with running water accompaniment. Daily 10am-6pm in season.

£15 OR LESS
Brodick Bar www.thebrodickbar.co.uk Best pub food in Brodick? Probably yes. Bar snacks, but turns into more of a bistro (they call it a 'brasserie', but it can feel like a camp canteen in summer) in the evening. Food until 10pm. Off north end of main street by Royal Mail. Bar open till midnight.

£15-22
Corrie Golf Club Tearoom 01770 810606 · **Sannox** Just outside village (Sannox not Corrie) going north. Best cakes and light snacks on island in hut-like golfing situation. 7 days 9am-6pm though may open early evenings for bookings. Closed in winter.

Machrie Golf Course Tearoom 01770 840329 Another food option attached to a golf course on west coast on main A841. Very good local reputation. 7 days in season (Mar-Oct) 10am-5pm & Mon-Wed 6-8pm.

£15-22
Joshua's 01770 700738 · **Whiting Bay** Shoreline location with conservatory and contemporary look. Home-made up-to-a-point burgers/steaks and snacks. Best book evens in summer. 10am-5pm, 6pm-8.30pm. Closed Sun.

WHAT TO SEE

NT
Brodick Castle 5km walk or cycle from Brodick. Impressive museum and gardens. Tearoom. Flagship NTS property (1856/CASTLES).

2-A-2 **Goat Fell** 6km/5hr great hill walk starting from the car park at Cladach near castle and Brodick or sea start at Corrie. Free route leaflet at tourist information centre. 2024/HILLS.

1-B-1 **Glenashdale Falls** 4km, but 2-hour forest walk from Glenashdale Bridge at Whiting Bay. Steady, easy climb, sylvan setting. 1685/WATERFALLS.

Corrie The best village 9km north of Brodick. Go by bike. 1648/COASTAL VILLAGES.

Machrie Moor Standing Stones Off main coast road 7km north of Blackwater Foot. Various assemblies of Stones, all part of an ancient landscape. We lay down there.

Glen Rosa, Glen Sannox Fine glens: Rosa near Brodick, Sannox 11km north.

1-B-2

Tourist Info 01770 303774 **CalMac** 08705 650000 · www.calmac.co.uk

The Best of Islay & Jura

2426 9/G24 **Ferry** Kennacraig-Port Askaig: 2 hours; Kennacraig-Port Ellen: 2 hours 10 minutes. Port Askaig-Feolin, Jura: (01496 840681) 5 minutes, frequent daily.
By Air BA Linkline (08457 733377) from Glasgow to Port Ellen Airport in south of island.

WHERE TO STAY

10 ROOMS
TEL · TV
£45-60
✓**Port Charlotte Hotel** www.portcharlottehotel.co.uk · 01496 850360 · **Port Charlotte** Restored Victorian inn and gardens on seafront of conservation village. Restful place, restful views. Good bistro-style menu, the best around. Eat in bar/conservatory or dining room. Conscientious owners. 2389/ISLAND HOTELS.

7 ROOMS
TEL · TV
£38-45
✓**Harbour Inn** www.harbour-inn.com · 01496 810330 · **Bowmore** Neil and Carol Scott's lovely island restaurant with rooms. An excellent conservatory lounge, Schooner bar for seafood lunch and less formal supper, and stylish dining room with Modern British menu. Bedrooms vary but all mod and con. 2390/ISLAND HOTELS.

5 RMS · TV
NO KIDS/PETS
NO C/CARDS
£38-45
Kilmeny Farm www.kilmeny.co.uk · 01496 840668 · **near Ballygrant** Margaret and Blair Rozga's top-class guesthouse just off the road south of Port Askaig (the ferry). Huge attention to detail, great home-made food, house-party atmosphere and shared tables. Though small.

5 ROOMS
TV · ECO
NO KIDS
NO C/CARDS
£38-45
Glenmachrie www.glenmachrie.com · 01496 302560 · **near Port Ellen** On A846 between Bowmore and Port Ellen adjacent airport. Sister guesthouse of Kilmeny Farm (above). Here it's Rachel's award-winning farmhouse with everything just so (fluffy bathrobes, toiletries supplied, fruit bowl and a sweet on the pillow) and great meals, especially her famously good breakfast (must have the porridge). Farmers with a green sensibility. And see below.

6 ROOMS
TV
Glenegedale House www.glenegedalehouse.co.uk · 01496 300400 · **near Port Ellen** The new venture by Rachel Whyte near Glenmachrie and opposite

NO KIDS/PETS the airport. The more deluxe option. Rachel flits between the two but most likely
NO C/CARDS here. Real 5-star B&B. Haven't been yet but Rachel... well, she recommends it
£45-60 highly!

16 ROOMS **The Machrie** www.machrie.com · 01496 302310 · **Port Ellen** 7km north on
(+15 LODGES) A846. Restaurant and bar meals in clubhouse atmosphere. Restaurant in old byre
TEL · TV and 15 lodges in the grounds. You'll likely be here for the golf – so you might
NO PETS overlook its rather bleak setting. Food, I'm told, is surprisingly good. The great
£38-45 beach (1655/BEACHES) *is* over there.

£38-45 **Lochside Hotel** www.lochsidehotel.co.uk · 01496 810244 · **Bowmore**
Probably best selection of Islay malts in the world; so great bar and bar meals in
lochside, actually seaside setting. Rooms 50-50. Pub food standard.

11 ROOMS **Bridgend Inn** www.bridgend-hotel.com · 01496 810212 · **Bridgend** Middle
TEL · TV of island on road from Port Askaig, 4km Bowmore. Roadside inn with good pub
£45-60 meals and surprising number of rooms. A reasonable stopover.

15 ROOMS **Jura Hotel** www.jurahotel.co.uk · 01496 820243 · **Craighouse** The best
£30-38 hotel on the island – well, the only one! But it does what you want. Situated in
front of the distillery by the bay. Front rooms best (not all en suite). There's craic in
the bar. Report: 2397/ISLAND HOTELS.

Camping, Caravan Site www.kintrafarm.co.uk · 01496 302051 · **Kintra
Farm** Off main road to Port Ellen; take Oa road, follow Kintra signs 7km. Jul-Aug
B&B in farmhouse. Grassy strand, coastal walks.

Islay Youth Hostel www.syha.org.uk · 01496 850385 · **Port Charlotte**

WHERE TO EAT
✓ **Harbour Inn** **Bowmore** and **Port Charlotte Hotel** See Where to Stay.

£15-22 ✓ **Ardbeg Distillery Café** www.islay.co.uk 5km east of Port Ellen on the
whisky road. Great local reputation for food. Beautiful room. Food home-
made as are those Ardbegs. Most vintages and Ardbeg clothes to boot. All year
Mon-Fri (7 days Jun-Aug) 10am-LO 4pm.

£15-22 **Croft Kitchen** 01496 850230 · **Port Charlotte** Serviceable caff in fine village
where Port Charlotte Hotel is the food destination. The cheap, cheerful all year
option (except Jan). 7 days 10.30am-8.30pm. Book in season.

£15-22 **Ballygrant Inn** www.ballygrant-inn.co.uk · 01496 840277 South of Port
Askaig. Basic pub with dining room and 3 rooms upstairs. Like being in their home
– and it is! Food home-made (great soda bread). Over 100 whiskies. Reports vary
but these are good people. Lunch and dinner (can be late) and bar can be very late.
Nice family will welcome yours.

WHAT TO SEE
Islay: The Distilleries especially Ardbeg (good café), Laphroaig and Lagavulin
(classic settings), all by Port Ellen; tours by appointment. Bowmore has regular
glossy tour; Ardbeg, open daily, good cafe (1562/WHISKY); **Museum of Islay,
Wildlife Info & Field Centre** (1845/WILDLIFE): all at Port Charlotte; **American**

Monument (1923/MONUMENTS); **Oa & Loch Gruinart** (1816/BIRDS); **Port Charlotte** (1642/COASTAL VILLAGES); **Kintra** (2116/COASTAL WALKS); **Finlaggan** The romantic, sparse ruin on 'island' in Loch Finlaggan: last home of the Lords of the Isles. Off A846 5km south of Port Askaig, check tourist information centre for opening.

Jura (2357/MAGICAL ISLANDS): **The Paps of Jura**; **Corryvreckan, Barnhill** (2422/ISLAND WALKS); **Killchianaig, Keils** (1965/GRAVEYARDS); **Lowlandman's Bay** (1661/BEACHES); **Jura House Walled Garden**; utterly magical in the right light (1608/GARDENS).

Tourist Info 01496 810254 **CalMac** 08705 650000

The Best of The Outer Hebrides

2427 5/F14 **Ferries** Ullapool-Stornoway, 2 hours 40 minutes (not Sun). Oban/Mallaig-Lochboisdale, South Uist and Castlebay, Barra; up to 6.5 hours. Uig on Skye-Tarbert, Harris (not Sun) or Lochmaddy, North Uist 1 hour 40 minutes. Also Leverburgh, Harris-Otternish, North Uist (not Sun) 1 hour 10 minutes. **By Air** Local (01851 703240) & BA Linkline (08457 733377). BA 3 times daily (2 Sat; not Sun) from Inverness/Glasgow/Edinburgh. BA Otter to Barra/Benbecula from Glasgow (1/2 a day).

WHERE TO STAY

✓ **Scarista House** www.scaristahouse.com · 01859 550238 · **South Harris** 20km south of Tarbert. Cosy haven near famous but often deserted beach; celebrated retreat. Also self-catering accommodation. 2391/ISLAND HOTELS.

£60-85 ✓ **Blue Reef Cottages** www.stay-hebrides.com · 01859 550370 · **South Harris** 1 km from Scarista House (above) and overlooking the same idyllic beach. I don't usually list self-catering cottages in *StB* but these 2 are exceptional. For couples only though the study could be another bedroom at a pinch. Stylish, good facilities, amazing view. Gourmet meals from lady nearby or eat at Scarista House. 7-day stays. 2-day minimum in winter.

7 ROOMS ✓ **Baile-Na-Cille** 01851 672241 · **Timsgarry, West Lewis** Near Uig 60km APR-OCT west of Stornoway. This is about as far away as it gets but guests return again £38-45 and again to the Collins' house by the sea. Hospitable hosts allow you the run of their place – the books, the games room, the tennis court and the most amazing beach. Great value and especially good for families. 1213/HOTELS KIDS.

4 (+2) RMS **Rodel Hotel** www.rodelhotel.co.uk · 01859 520210 · **South Harris** Hotel at APR-DEC the end of the road, the A859, south of Tarbert, south of everywhere. Superb set-TV ting, you are truly away from it all. Recent makeover, so comfy and contemporary £45-60 (2 self-catering). Large front rooms best. Restaurant gets mixed reception.

Castlebay Hotel www.castlebay-hotel.co.uk · 01871 810223 · **Castlebay, Barra** Overlooks ferry terminal in main town. Excellent value. Decent food. Brilliant bar (2395/ISLAND HOTELS; 1362/BLOODY GOOD PUBS).

8 ROOMS	**Tigh Dearg (The Red House) Hotel** www.tighdearghotel.co.uk · **01876**
TEL · TV	**500700 · Lochmaddy, North Uist** Contemporary, new-build hotel with great
£38-45	views from most rooms. 'Leisure Club' includes sauna/steam. Good disabled access.

26 ROOMS	**Royal Hotel** www.royalstornoway.co.uk · **01851 702109 · Stornoway,**
TEL · TV	**Lewis** The most central of the 3 main hotels in town which are all owned by the
£38-45	same family. HS-1 bistro and Boatshed (probably 'best' hotel dining). The **Cabarfeidh** (01851 702604) is the upmarket ie most expensive option – probably the best bedrooms. These hotels are the only places open in Lewis on Sun, although the **Caladh** (pronounced 'Cala') **Inn** and its caff '11', has been made over and seems best value.

6 ROOMS	**Ardhasaig House** www.ardhasaig.co.uk · **01859 502066 · North Harris**
NO PETS	4km north of Tarbert just off A859 Stornoway road. Neither this modern-build
£45-60	house nor its locally well-connected chef/proprietor (her family owns everything hereabouts) are especially comfortable to be with but there are redeeming features. Nice location and convenient. While madame may not have gone to charm school, she did learn to cook (Andrew Fairley's kitchen has been mentioned). And there's a nice conservatory.

24 ROOMS	**Harris Hotel** www.harrishotel.com · **01859 502154 · Tarbert** In the town-
TEL · TV	ship near the ferry terminal so good base for travels in North/South Harris. Variety
NO PETS	of public rooms and diverse range of bedrooms (view/non-view, refurbished/non-
£38-45/	refurbished, standard/superior), some of which are large and very nice. Friendly
£60-85	and well run. Food not a strong point, but adequate. Also bar meals in pub next door.

11 ROOMS	**Pollachar Inn** **01878 700215 · South Uist** South of Lochboisdale near small
TEL · TV	ferry for Eriskay/Barra (2386/ISLANDS), an inn at the end of the known world.
NO PETS	Excellent value, good craic and the view/sunset across the sea to Barra. All rooms
£38-45	refurbished to a nice standard. Great food so far-flung; local produce. LO 8.45pm.

Hostels Simple hostels within hiking distance. 2 in Lewis, 3 in Harris, 1 each in North and South Uist. Altogether an excellent hostelling holiday prospect with 2 exceptional (1238/HOSTELS) and Barra.

WHERE TO EAT

£22-32   **Digby Chick** 01851 700026 · **11 James Street, Stornoway** Contemporary café/restaurant with seafood speciality and good local reputation. Mon-Sat, lunch & LO 8.30pm.

The Thai Café 01851 70181127 · **Church Street, Stornoway** Opposite police station. An unlikely find but probably the best place to eat in this town. *The Scotsman* said this was the best Thai restaurant in Scotland. Mrs Panida Macdonald's restaurant an institution here and you may have to book. Great atmosphere, excellent real Thai cuisine, though you couldn't be further in every respect from Bangkok. Lunch & LO 11pm. Closed Sun.

The Boatshed at The Royal Hotel Stornoway & **'11' at The Caladh Inn** (see above). Best hotel options (and open Sun).

Tigh Mealros 01851 621333 · **Garynahine, Lewis** On A858 22km southwest of Stornoway. 2km south of Callanish. Unpretentious surf 'n' turf. Scallops (dived) a special. BYOB. Great dry-stone stonework in progress at TGP. Open all year. LO 8.30pm.

Coffee Shops: An Lanntair Gallery www.anlanntair.com · **Stornoway & Callanish Visitor Centre** www.calanaisvisitorcentre.co.uk · **Lewis** The latter is especially good. Daytime hours (1890/PREHISTORIC SITES). An Lanntair re-opening at TGP after moving and metamorphosing.

Scarista House www.scaristahouse.com · **Harris** (*see above*). Dinner possible for non-residents. A 20-minutes Tarbert, 45-minutes Stornoway drive for best meal in the Hebrides. Fixed menu. Book.

Skoon Art Café 01859 530268 · **South Harris** On stunning Golden Road (1715/SCENIC ROUTES) 12km south of Tarbert, this café in a gallery. All done well – interesting soups, great home-baking. Open all year Tue-Sat daytime only.

First Fruits Tearoom 01859 502439 · **Tarbert, Harris** Near tourist information centre and ferry to Uig. Home-cooking that hits the spot. Good atmosphere. Wide-ranging menu includes all-day breakfast. 10.30am-4.30pm Open all year.

Orasay Inn www.orasayinn.com · 01870 610298 · **Lochcarnan, South Uist** 3km from main, spinal A885, signed from road. Small hotel apparently in the middle of nowhere, but with a conservatory and bar that's often packed with those that know. Especially good for seafood, from local halibut to razors and 'witches'. Milky seaweed jelly amongst an extraordinary menu. Also 9 inexpensive rooms. Open all year, lunch & LO 9pm.

Stepping Stones 01870 603377 · **Balvanich, Benbecula** 8 km from main A855. Nondescript building in ex- (though still operational) military air base. Serving the forces and the tourists – it aims to please. 7 days, lunch & LO 9pm (winter hours may vary). Menu changes through day.

Tourist Info 01851 703088 **CalMac** www.calmac.co.uk · 08705 650000

The Best of Mull

2428 9/G23 **Ferry** Oban-Craignure, 45 minutes. Main route; 6 a day.
Lochaline-Fishnish, 15 minutes. 9-15 a day.
Kilchoan-Tobermory, 35 minutes. 7 a day (Sun in summer only).
Winter sailings – call tourist information centre.

WHERE TO STAY
✓ **Highland Cottage** www.highlandcottage.co.uk · 01688 302030 · **Breadalbane Street, Tobermory** Opposite fire station a street above the harbour. Like a country house, well... a gorgeous cottage in town. The top spot. Report: 2392/ISLAND HOTELS.

✓ **Tiroran House** 01681 705232 · **Mull** A treat and a retreat way down in the southwest of Mull near Iona. Light, comfy house in glorious gardens with excellent food and flowers. Sea eagles fly over. Report: 1279/GET-AWAY HOTELS.

✓ **Argyll Hotel** www.argyllhoteliona.co.uk · 01681 700334 · **Iona** Near ferry and on seashore overlooking Mull on road to abbey. Laid-back, cosy accommodation, home cooking, good vegetarian. Report: 1254/SEASIDE INNS.

5 ROOMS
£60-85

✓ **Glengorm Castle** www.glengormcastle.co.uk · 01688 302321 · **near Tobermory** Minor road on right going north outside town takes you to this fine castle on a promontory set in an extensive estate which is yours to wander (excellent walks; collect map from estate). Fab views over to Ardnamurchan, little peaks to climb and a natural 'bathing pool'. Luxurious bedrooms in family home – use the library, complementary bar and grand public spaces. Loads of art, lawn and gardens. Excellent self-catering cottages on estate. B&B only. Excellent coffee shop/restaurant over by (1496/COFFEE SHOPS).

Calgary Farmhouse www.calgary.co.uk · 01688 400256 · **Calgary** Near Dervaig on B8073 near Mull's famous beach. Gallery/coffee shop and good bistro/restaurant. Report: 2393/ISLAND HOTELS.

16 ROOMS
TV
£38-45

Tobermory Hotel 01688 302091 On the waterfront. Creature comforts, great outlook in the middle of Balamory bay. 10 rooms to front. Restaurant ok and others nearby. Very much on the dock of the bay, both hotel and restaurant are probably better than they have to be – no faint praise intended.

27 ROOMS
MID MAR-OCT
£38-45

St Columba Hotel www.stcolumba-hotel.co.uk · 01681 700304 · **Iona** Shares some ownership and ideals of the Argyll (see above) and very close on the road and adjacent to the Abbey. Larger, more utilitarian/purpose built than the Argyll, so some uniformity in rooms. Nice views and extensive lawn and market garden. Relaxing and just a little bit religious. Menu has good vegetarian options. Rooms include 9 singles.

4 ROOMS
MAR-NOV
TV
NO KIDS/PETS
£38-45

Ptarmigan House 01688 302863 · **Tobermory** Above the town (ask for golf course, it's adjacent clubhouse) and above all that. Modern, almost purpose-built guesthouse. High-spec rooms with great views and... a swimming pool. Sue and Michael Fink preside in their suburban heaven: this is a golf hotel with a difference – a Fink thing, not a chain thing. Evening meals on request.

S.Y. Hostel In Tobermory main street on bay. Report: 1241/HOSTELS.

Caravan Parks At Fishnish (all facilities, near ferry) Craignure and Fionnphort.

Camping Calgary Beach, Fishnish and at Loch Na Keal shore. All *naturel*.

WHERE TO EAT

£22-32

✓ **Highland Cottage** 01688 302030 As above and 2314/ISLAND RESTAURANTS. Only real fine-dining option. Also the local night out. Small so must book.

£15-22

✓ **Calgary Farmhouse** www.calgary.co.uk · 01688 400256 · **Calgary Dovecote Restaurant**. Local produce in atmospheric wine-bar setting. Mellow people, art/sculpture in the woods outside. (2411/ISLAND RESTAURANTS) For anyone with a boho, arty bent or kids, this is the coolest dining room on the island.

✓ **Glengorm Farm Coffeeshop** Excellent daytime eats outside Tobermory. The best casual daytime dining. Report: 1476/TEAROOMS.

£15-22   ✓ **Café Fish** 01688 301253 · **Tobermory** The white building at the pier at the corner of the bay. Bright upstairs room and terrace on the dock – their boat moored at the quayside supplying some of their excellent fresh produce. Home cooking, sensible wine list, nice puds. (Probably) all year, lunch & 6-9pm.

£15-22   **The Anchorage** 01688 302313 · **Main Street, Tobermory** Opposite pier. Best on the bay. Seafood, rest of the kilo of mussels, steaks, specials, good vegetarian options. Homely and friendly and keen to impress. 7 days, lunch & LO 9pm. Winter hours will vary.

   Mull Pottery www.mull-pottery.com · 01688 302592 · **Tobermory** Fun mezzanine café above working pottery just outside Tobermory on road south to Craignure. Evening meals (best atmosphere) and usual daytime offerings though all home-baking. Locals do recommend. The ubiquitous teuchter music is on sale downstairs. All year. 7 days. LO 9pm.

£15-22   **Meditteranea** www.mullonthemed.com · 01680 300200 · **Salen** In mid-village on main Craignure-Tobermory road. A real Italian restaurant run by Scottish guy and extended Italian family, though Neapolitan bloke in their Sicilian kitchen. So excellent pasta, salads, puds and specials with Italian (and sometimes Asian) twist. All islands should have one of these. Mar-Oct. Dinner only LO 9pm.

£15 OR LESS   **Island Bakery** www.islandbakery.co.uk · 01688 302225 · **Main Street, Tobermory** Bakery-deli with excellent take-away pizza. Home-made pâtés, quiches, salads and old-fashioned baking. Buy your picnic here. 7 days from 8am. LO 7.45pm (weekend only in winter).

£15 OR LESS   **The Chip Van aka The Fisherman's Pier** 01688 302390 · **Tobermory** Tobermory's famous meals-on-wheels underneath the clock tower on the bay. Usual fare but fresh as... and usually a queue. The situation is unquestionably fine. All year, 12noon-9pm. Closed Sun. (1449/FISH 'N' CHIPS)

£15-22   **Javiers** www.javiersrestaurant.co.uk · 01688 302365 · **Tobermory** Far corner of the bay above MacGochan's pub. Argentinian chef, mix-match and Mexican meals. Local reputation and often packed. All year. Lunch & LO 9.30pm.

WHAT TO SEE

Torosay Castle Walk or train (!) from Craignure. Fabulous gardens and fascinating insight into an endearing family's life. Teashop. (1858/CASTLES.) **Duart Castle** 5km Craignure. Seat of Clan Maclean. Impressive from a distance, homely inside. Good view of clan history and from battlements. Teashop. (1857/CASTLES.) **Eas Fors** Waterfall on Dervaig to Fionnphort road. Very accessible series of cataracts tumbling into the sea (1686/WATERFALLS). **The Mishnish** No mission to Mull complete without a night at the Mish (1358/BLOODY GOOD PUBS), MacGochan's over the bay no contest. **Wings Over Mull** (1801/KIDS). **Ulva & Iona** (many references). **The Treshnish Isles** (Ulva Ferry or Fionnphort). Marvellous trips in summer (1809/BIRDS); walks from **Carsaig Pier** (2414/ISLAND WALKS); or up **Ben More** (2054/MUNROS); **Croig** and **Quinish** in north, near **Dervaig** and **Lochbuie** off the A849 at Strathcoil 9km south of Craignure: these are all serene shorelines to explore. **Aros Park** forest walk, from Tobermory, about 7km round trip.

Tourist Info Craignure · 01680 812377 All year. **Tobermory** · 01688 302182 **CalMac** www.calmac.co.uk · 08705 650000

The Best of Orkney

Ferry Northlink (0845 6000449). Stromness: from Aberdeen – Tue, Thu, Sat, Sun, takes 6 hours; from Scrabster – 2/3 per day, takes 1.5 hours.
John o' Groats to Burwick (01955 611353), 40 minutes, up to 4 a day (May-Sep only). Pentland Ferries from Gill (near John o' Groats) to St Margaret's Hope (01856 831226) – 3 a day, takes 1 hour.
By Air BA (0870 850 9850). To Kirkwall: from Aberdeen – 3 daily; from Edinburgh – 2 daily; from Glasgow – 1 daily; from Inverness – 2 daily; from Wick – 1 daily (not weekends).

WHERE TO STAY

8 ROOMS
TEL · TV · ECO
NO PETS
£38-45

Foveran Hotel www.foveranhotel.co.uk · 01856 872389 · **St Ola** A964 Orphir road; 4km from Kirkwall. Scandinavian-style hotel is a friendly informal place serves traditional food using local ingredients; separate vegetarian menu. Great value. Comfortable light rooms refurbished; garden overlooks Scapa Flow.

33 ROOMS
TEL · TV
£45-60

Ayre Hotel www.ayrehotel.co.uk · 01856 873001 · **Kirkwall** Family hotel with the highest grading on the Orkney mainland. Situated on the harbour front, the whole place is well tidy and well established. It's where to stay in Kirkwall.

6 ROOMS
TEL · TV
£45-60

Cleaton House Hotel www.cleatonhouse.co.uk · 01857 677508 · **Westray** Beautifully refurbished former Victorian manse. Panoramic seascapes, relaxed atmosphere and good food.

13 ROOMS
TEL · TV · ECO
£38-45

Merkister Hotel 01856 771366 · **Harray** A fave with fishers and twitchers; handy for archaeological sites and possibly the Orkney hotel 'of choice'. A la carte or table d'hôte in the conservatory overlooking the loch.

42 ROOMS
TEL · TV
£38-45

Stromness Hotel 01856 850298 Orkney's biggest hotel, made over à la mode. Even has lifts. Central and picturesque.

6 ROOMS
£38-45

Woodwick House www.woodwickhouse.co.uk · 01856 751330 · **Evie** Comfy country house and garden, near shore with views of those islets. A great retreat. Home cooking, local produce. Good value.

S.Y. Hostels www.syha.org.uk · 01856 850589 · **Stromness** Excellent location.
Kirkwall · 01856 872243 The largest.
Other hostels at Hoy, North and South Ronaldsay, Birsay, Sanday.

✓ **Peedie Hostel** 01856 875477 · **Ayre Road, Kirkwall** By the sea. Private bedroom, own keys.

ECO ✓ **Bis Geos Hostel** www.bisgeos.co.uk · 01857 677420 · **Westray** Hostel with 2 self-catering cottages. Traditional features and some luxuries.

✓ **The Barn** www.thebarnwestray.co.uk · 01857 677214 · **Westray** Four-star self-catering hostel in renovated stone barn. Great views.

Camping/Caravan Kirkwall · 01856 879900 & **Stromness** · 01856 873535

WHERE TO EAT

3 ROOMS
£22-32

✔ **The Creel Inn & Restaurant** www.thecreelinn.co.uk · 01856 831311 ·
St Margaret's Hope On South Ronaldsay, 20km south of Kirkwall. In a wild area, an accolade-laden restaurant though fairly expensive Orkney-wise. Many sauces over meat or fish; clootie for pud or Orkney cheeses. Popular with islanders. Dinner only. Seal Rescue Centre nearby. Well-appointed 3 rooms.

£22-32
Foveran Hotel 01856 872389 · **St Ola** 4km Kirkwall. See Where to Stay, above.

£22-32
Woodwick House 01856 751330 · **Evie** As above. See Where to Stay, above.

£15-22
The Hamnavoe Restaurant 01856 850606 · **35 Graham Place, Stromness** Off main street. Seafood is their speciality, but they do haggis. Apr-Oct; Tue-Sun 6.30pm-late. Nov-Mar open weekends only.

£15 OR LESS
Julia's Café & Bistro 01856 850904 · **Stromness** Great home baking, blackboard and vegetarian specials. Internet. A favourite with the locals. Gets busy – fill yourself up before the ferry journey! Open all year, 7 days 7.30am-10pm (closed 5-6.30pm). Phone for winter opening hours.

Thevan Brough of Birsay Bere bannocks (a speciality), home-made soups, Orkney cheese from a van in the car park at the Brough. 7 days from 11am.

WHAT TO SEE

Skara Brae 25km west of Kirkwall. Amazingly well-preserved underground labyrinth, a 5,000-year-old village. Report: 1888/PREHISTORIC SITES.

The Old Man of Hoy on Hoy; 30-minute ferry 2 or 3 times a day from Stromness. 3-hour walk along spectacular coast. See 2421/ISLAND WALKS.

Standing Stones of Stenness, The Ring of Brodgar, Maes Howe Around 18km west of Kirkwall on A965. Strong vibrations. Report: 1889/PREHISTORIC SITES.

Yesnaby Sea Stacks 24km west of Kirkwall. A precarious cliff top at the end of the world. Report: 2013/SPOOKY (or spiritual) PLACES.

Italian Chapel 8km south of Kirkwall at first causeway. A special act of faith. Report: 1945/CHURCHES.

Skaill House 01856 841501 · **Skara Brae** 17th-century 'mansion' built on Pictish cemetery. Set up as it was in the 1950s; with Captain Cook's crockery in the dining room looking remarkably unused. Apr-Sep; 7 days 9.30am-6pm (or by appointment). Tearoom and visitor centre and HS link with Skara.

St Magnus Cathedral (1943/CHURCHES); **Stromness** (1638/COASTAL VILLAGES); **The Pier Arts Centre** (2344/INTERESTING GALLERIES); **Tomb of the Eagles** (1895/PREHISTORIC SITES); **Marwick Head** and many of the smaller islands (1817/BIRDS); **Scapa Flow** (1985/BATTLEGROUNDS; 2224/DIVING); **Highland Park Distillery** (1567/WHISKY); **Puffins** (1819/BIRDS).

Craft Trail & Artists' Studio Trail Take in some traditional arts and crafts. Lots of souvenir potential. The tourist information centre has details and maps.

Many walks. Download walking guides: **www.walkorkney.com**
Tourist Info 01856 872856

The Best of Shetland

2430 4 **Ferry** Northlink (0845 6000 449). Aberdeen-Lerwick: Mon, Wed, Fri – departs 7pm, 12 hours. Tue, Thu, Sat, Sun – departs 5pm (via Orkney, arrives 11.45pm), 14 hours.
By air BA Linkline Orkney (08457 733377) & Shetland (01950 460345). To Sumburgh: from Aberdeen (4 a day, 2 Sat, 2 Sun). From Inverness (1 a day). From Glasgow (2 a day, 1 Sat). From Edinburgh (2 a day).

WHERE TO STAY

5 ROOMS
MAR-OCT
TV
£45-60
Burrastow House 01595 809307 · **Walls** 40 minutes from Lerwick. Most guides and locals agree this is the place to stay on Shetland. Peaceful Georgian house with views to Island of Vaila. Wonderful home-made/produced food. Full of character with food (set menu; order day before), service and rooms the best on the island.

13 ROOMS
TEL · TV
ECO
£38-45
Herrislea House Hotel www.herrisleahouse.co.uk · 01595 840208 · **Tingwall** 7km northwest of Lerwick. Refurbished country house in beautiful setting. Incorporating Starboard Tack café-bar, open daily till 11pm. Basic, good home cooking and useful children's play area. Family-run.

22 ROOMS
TEL · TV
£38-45
Busta House Hotel www.bustahouse.com · 01806 522506 Historic country house at Brae just over 30 minutes from Lerwick. Elegant and tranquil. High standards, great malt selection.

32 ROOMS
TEL · TV
£38-45
Sumburgh Hotel www.sumburgh-hotel.shetland.co.uk · 01950 460201 · **Sumburgh** Refurbished manor house in very south of mainland 42 km from Lerwick. Next to airport and Jarlshof excavations. Sea views as far as Fair Isle (50km south). Beaches and birds! Wide and relatively cheap menu.

17 ROOMS
TEL · TV
NO PETS
£45-60
Kveldsro Hotel 01595 692195 · **Lerwick** Pronounced 'Kel-ro'. Probably best proposition in Lerwick; overlooking harbour. Reasonable standard at a price. Locals do eat here.

6 ROOMS
TEL · TV
£38-45
Westings, The Inn On The Hill 01595 840242 · **Whiteness** 12 km from Lerwick. Breathtaking views down Whiteness Voe. Excellent base for exploring. Large selection of real ales and three different menus. Campsite alongside.

Almara B&B 01806 503261 · **Hillswick** We don't usually venture into the world of the B&B in this book but, although we haven't stayed ourselves, couldn't ignore numerous good reports of Mrs Williamson's four-star establishment. Friendly family home with good food and nice vibes.

S.Y. Hostel www.syha.org.uk In Lerwick, Isleburgh House (01595 692114). Beautifully refurbished and very central. Also home of excellent Isleburgh House Café. Open Apr-Sep.

Camping Bods (fisherman's barns). Cheap sleep in wonderful sea-shore settings. **The Sail Loft** at Voe; **Grieve House** at Whalsay; **Wind House Lodge** at Mid Yell; **Voe House** at Walls; **Betty Mouat's Cottage** at Dunrossness; **Johnnie Notions** at Eashaness. Remember to take sleeping mats. Check tourist information centre for details.

Camping/Caravan: Clickimin 01595 741000 · **Lerwick**

Levenwick 01950 422207
The Garths 01957 733227 · Fetla
Westings 01595 840242 · Whiteness

WHERE TO EAT

£22-32   **Burrastow House** Walls & **Busta House Hotel** Brae See Where to Stay, above. The best meal in the islands.

£15-32   **Sumburgh Hotel** Sumburgh See Where to Stay, above. The organically farmed smoked salmon 'possibly the best in the world' according to 'folk'.

£22-32   **Monty's Bistro** 01595 696555 · **Mounthooley Street, Lerwick** Near tourist information centre. Renovated building in light Med décor. Best bet in town. Good service and imaginative menu using Shetland's finest seasonal ingredients. Bistro closed Sun/Mon (open Mon evening in season). Lunch & LO 9pm.

£15-22/ £22-32   **The Maryfield Hotel** 01595 820207 · **Bressay** 5-minute ferry ride from Lerwick to Bressay. Better known for its seafood rather than accommodation, both bar and dining room menus worth a look. LO are for those off the 8pm ferry. Don't miss the return ferry at 10.30pm Mon-Thu & 12.45am, Fri & Sat. Closed Sun evening, Mon lunch.

£15 OR LESS   **Havly** 01595 692100 · **9 Charlotte Street, Lerwick** Norwegian-style café with family-friendly atmosphere. Great home-made soup, baking, waffles. Open Mon-Fri 10am-3pm, Sat 10am-4.45pm.

£15-22   **Da Haaf Restaurant** www.nafc.ac.uk · 01595 880747 · **Scalloway** Part of the North Atlantic Fisheries College, Port Arthur. Basically a canteen but fresh Shetland seafood overlooking the harbour at reasonable prices more than makes up for the plastic trays and fluorescent lights. Lunch & LO 8pm. Closed Sat/Sun.

£15 OR LESS   **The Castle Café & Takeaway (Scalloway Fish & Chip Shop)** New Road By the castle. Can also sit in. Change of management since last edition so may no longer be the 'best on the islands'. Reports please.

£15 OR LESS   **Osla's Café** 01595 696005 · **Commercial Street or Da Street, Lerwick** Just up from Monty's. Best café. Incredibly good value. Cosy and very child-friendly. Art exhibitions on walls. Upstairs La Piazza is a good bet for supper. LO 9.30pm.

£15 OR LESS   **The Peerie Shop Café** www.peerieshopcafe.com · 01595 692817 · **The Esplanade, Lerwick** A local delicacy!

Pub food also recommended at the following:

£15 OR LESS   **The Mid Brae Inn** 01806 522634 · **Brae** 32km north of Lerwick. Lunch and supper till 8.45pm (9.30pm weekends), 7 days. Big portions of the filling pub-grub variety.

WHAT TO SEE
Mousa Broch & Jarlshof See 1892/PREHISTORIC SITES. Also **Clickimin** broch.

Old Scatness 01595 694688 A fascinating, award-winning excavation – site of one of the world's best-preserved Iron Age villages. Ongoing and accessible; climb the tower and witness the unearthing first-hand. Tours, demonstrations and exhibitions. 5 minutes from airport. Open Jul-Aug only.

St Ninian's Isle Bigton 8km north of Sumburgh on West Coast. An island linked by exquisite shell-sand. Hoard of Pictish silver found in 1958 (now in Edinburgh). Beautiful, serene spot.

Scalloway 7km west of Lerwick, a township once the ancient capital of Shetland, dominated by the atmospheric ruins of Scalloway Castle.

Noup Of Noss Isle Of Noss, off Bressay 8km west of Lerwick by frequent ferry and then boat (also direct from Lerwick 01595 692577 or via tourist information centre), May-Sep only. National Nature Reserve with spectacular array of wildlife.

Up Helly Aa www.up-helly-aa.org.uk Festival in Lerwick on the last Tue in Jan. Ritual with hundreds of torchbearers and much fire and firewater. Norse, northern and pagan. A wild time. Permanent exhibition at St Sunniva Street, Lerwick.

Sea Races The Boat Race every midsummer from Norway. Part of the largest North Sea international annual yacht race.

Bonhoga Gallery & Weisdale Mill 01595 830400 Former grain mill housing Shetland's first purpose-built gallery. Café.

Island Trails Historic tours of Lerwick and the islands. Book through tourist information centre (or 01950 422408). Day trips, evening runs or short tours.

Tourist Info 01595 693434

INDEX

The numbers listed against index entries refer to the page number on which the entry appears and not the entry's item number.